PSYCHOLOGICAL SCIENCE AND THE LAW

Psychological Science and the Law

edited by

Neil Brewer
Amy Bradfield Douglass

THE GUILFORD PRESS
New York   London

Library of Congress Cataloging-in-Publication Data

Names: Brewer, Neil (Neil Douglas) editor. | Douglass, Amy Bradfield, editor.
Title: Psychological science and the law / edited by Neil Brewer, Amy
    Bradfield Douglass.
Description: New York : The Guilford Press, [2019] | Includes bibliographical
    references and index.
Identifiers: LCCN 2018060272 | ISBN 9781462538300 (hardback)
Subjects: LCSH: Forensic psychology. | BISAC: PSYCHOLOGY / Forensic
    Psychology. | MEDICAL / Psychiatry / General. | LAW / Criminal Law /
    General. | SOCIAL SCIENCE / Criminology.
Classification: LCC RA1148 .P79 2019 | DDC 614/.15—dc23
LC record available at *https://lccn.loc.gov/2018060272*

About the Editors

Neil Brewer, PhD, is Matthew Flinders Distinguished Emeritus Professor of Psychology at Flinders University, South Australia. He is a Fellow of the Association for Psychological Science and of the Academy of Social Sciences in Australia. His research addresses eyewitness identification and recall, juror judgments, and, recently, interactions between individuals with autism spectrum disorder and the justice system. Dr. Brewer has served as editor of the *Journal of Experimental Psychology: Applied* and as an editorial board member for all the major psychology–law journals.

Amy Bradfield Douglass, PhD, is Professor of Psychology at Bates College. She teaches statistics and upper-level courses on psychology and law and psychology of religion. Her research focuses on how eyewitnesses make decisions, how eyewitness errors can be prevented, how social interactions with lineup administrators affect retrospective witness judgments, and how people perceive and evaluate eyewitnesses. Dr. Douglass is an editorial board member and former associate editor of *Law and Human Behavior.*

Contributors

Neil Brewer, PhD, College of Education, Psychology, and Social Work, Flinders University, Adelaide, South Australia, Australia

Steve Charman, PhD, Department of Psychology, Florida International University, Miami, Florida

Preeti Chauhan, PhD, Department of Psychology, John Jay College of Criminal Justice, New York, New York

Quin M. Chrobak, PhD, Department of Psychology, University of Wisconsin Oshkosh, Oshkosh, Wisconsin

Brian Cutler, PhD, Faculty of Social Science and Humanities, University of Ontario Institute of Technology, Oshawa, Ontario, Canada

Ryan Ditchfield, BSc, Department of Psychology, Iowa State University, Ames, Iowa

Amy Bradfield Douglass, PhD, Department of Psychology, Bates College, Lewiston, Maine

Laura Fallon, MAPS, Department of Psychology, Memorial University of Newfoundland, St. John's, Newfoundland, Canada

Fiona Gabbert, PhD, Department of Psychology, Goldsmiths University of London, London, United Kingdom

Christopher A. Gunderson, MA, Department of Psychology, University of Denver, Denver, Colorado

Lorraine Hope, PhD, Department of Psychology, University of Portsmouth, Portsmouth, Hampshire, United Kingdom

Kate A. Houston, PhD, Department of Social Sciences,
Texas A&M International University, Laredo, Texas

Ira Hyman, PhD, Department of Psychology, Western Washington University,
Bellingham, Washington

Jeffrey Kaplan, MSc, Faculty of Social Science and Humanities,
University of Ontario Institute of Technology, Oshawa, Ontario, Canada

Richard I. Kemp, PhD, School of Psychology, University of New South Wales,
Sydney, Australia

Lauren E. Kois, PhD, Department of Psychology, University of Alabama,
Tuscaloosa, Alabama

Sean M. Lane, PhD, Department of Psychology, Louisiana State University,
Baton Rouge, Louisiana

Thomas D. Lyon, PhD, Gould School of Law, University of Southern California,
Los Angeles, California

Stephanie Madon, PhD, Department of Psychology, Iowa State University,
Ames, Iowa

Stephanie Marion, PhD, Faculty of Social Science and Humanities,
University of Ontario Institute of Technology, Oshawa, Ontario, Canada

Kelly McWilliams, PhD, Department of Psychology, John Jay College
of Criminal Justice, New York, New York

Gregory Mitchell, PhD, JD, School of Law, University of Virginia,
Charlottesville, Virginia

Alexis Mook, BA, Department of Psychology, Florida International University,
Miami, Florida

Curt More, MS, Department of Psychology, Iowa State University, Ames, Iowa

Matthew A. Palmer, PhD, School of Medicine, University of Tasmania,
Hobart, Tasmania, Australia

Liana C. Peter-Hagene, PhD, Department of Psychology,
Southern Illinois University, Carbondale, Illinois

Hannah Phalen, BA, School of Social and Behavioral Sciences,
Arizona State University, Glendale, Arizona

Devon L. L. Polaschek, PhD, School of Psychology, University of Waikato,
Hamilton, New Zealand

Jessica M. Salerno, PhD, School of Social and Behavioral Sciences,
Arizona State University, Glendale, Arizona

James D. Sauer, PhD, School of Medicine, University of Tasmania,
Hobart, Tasmania, Australia

Annabelle Shestak, MS, Department of Psychology,
University of Massachusetts Lowell, Lowell, Massachusetts

Brent Snook, PhD, Department of Psychology, Memorial University of Newfoundland, St. John's, Newfoundland, Canada

Nancy K. Steblay, PhD, Department of Psychology, Augsburg University, Minneapolis, Minnesota

Leanne ten Brinke, PhD, Department of Psychology, University of Denver, Denver, Colorado

Janet I. Warren, DSW, Institute of Law, Psychiatry, and Public Policy, University of Virginia, Charlottesville, Virginia

Gary L. Wells, PhD, Department of Psychology, Iowa State University, Ames, Iowa

David White, PhD, School of Psychology, University of New South Wales, Sydney, Australia

Miko M. Wilford, PhD, Department of Psychology, University of Massachusetts Lowell, Lowell, Massachusetts

Shanna Williams, PhD, Gould School of Law, University of Southern California, Los Angeles, California

Maria S. Zaragoza, PhD, Department of Psychological Sciences, Kent State University, Kent, Ohio

Acknowledgments

Preparation of this volume was helped considerably by Australian Research Council Grant No. ARC-DP150101905 to Neil Brewer and colleagues and National Science Foundation Grant No. SES-1627433 to Amy Bradfield Douglass and Neil Brewer. Any opinions, findings, and conclusions or recommendations expressed in this material are those of the authors and do not necessarily reflect the views of the National Science Foundation.

Contents

Introduction: Psychology and the Criminal Justice System   1
Amy Bradfield Douglass and Neil Brewer

CHAPTER 1. Criminal Profiling   7
Laura Fallon and Brent Snook

CHAPTER 2. Cognitive Bias in Legal Decision Making   30
Steve Charman, Amy Bradfield Douglass, and Alexis Mook

CHAPTER 3. Interrogations and Confessions   54
Stephanie Madon, Curt More, and Ryan Ditchfield

CHAPTER 4. Deception Detection   79
Christopher A. Gunderson and Leanne ten Brinke

CHAPTER 5. Eyewitness Memory   104
Sean M. Lane and Kate A. Houston

CHAPTER 6. Interviewing Witnesses and Victims   130
Lorraine Hope and Fiona Gabbert

CHAPTER 7. Child Witnesses   157
Thomas D. Lyon, Kelly McWilliams, and Shanna Williams

CHAPTER 8. False Memory 182

Maria S. Zaragoza, Ira Hyman, and Quin M. Chrobak

CHAPTER 9. Eyewitness Identification 208

James D. Sauer, Matthew A. Palmer, and Neil Brewer

CHAPTER 10. Identifying People from Images 238

David White and Richard I. Kemp

CHAPTER 11. Plea Bargaining 266

Miko M. Wilford, Annabelle Shestak, and Gary L. Wells

CHAPTER 12. Competence to Stand Trial 293
and Criminal Responsibility

Lauren E. Kois, Preeti Chauhan, and Janet I. Warren

CHAPTER 13. Expert Testimony 318

Stephanie Marion, Jeffrey Kaplan, and Brian Cutler

CHAPTER 14. Jury Decision Making 338

Liana C. Peter-Hagene, Jessica M. Salerno,
and Hannah Phalen

CHAPTER 15. Aggression, Violence, and Psychopathy 367

Devon L. L. Polaschek

CHAPTER 16. Judicial Decision Making 395

Gregory Mitchell

CHAPTER 17. Translating Psychological Science 417
into Policy and Practice

Nancy K. Steblay

Index 445

Introduction
Psychology and the Criminal Justice System

Amy Bradfield Douglass
Neil Brewer

More than 100 years ago, the interface of psychology and law reached popular consciousness with the publication of Hugo Munsterberg's *On the Witness Stand: Essays on Psychology and Crime*. In a book familiar to psycholegal researchers, Munsterberg systematically demonstrated how legal issues could be informed by research in psychology. His perspective on the potential for intersection between the disciplines was quite expansive, with chapter titles including such topics as "Untrue Confessions" and "The Memory of the Witness." In arguing for stronger connections between the fields of psychology and law, Munsterberg observed that psychology was historically "in complete detachment from the problems of practical life" but had "reached a stage at which it seems natural and sound to give attention also to its possible service for the practical needs of life" (Munsterberg, 1908, p. 7).

In the 110 years since Hugo Munsterberg published *On the Witness Stand,* psychology has certainly given "attention" to the practical problems confronting systems of justice around the world. Importantly, the "attention" from psychology predated the relatively recent introduction of DNA technology, which has now exonerated more than 300 wrongfully convicted individuals in the United States alone (*www.innocenceproject.org*). These DNA exonerations buttressed specific long-standing critiques of common procedural elements in criminal trials. For example, the fact that approximately 75% of wrongfully convicted individuals were mistakenly identified by eyewitnesses vindicated researchers who long claimed that police procedures unnecessarily increased the chances of mistaken identifications (e.g., Wells, 1978). Beyond the specific procedural details of eyewitness identifications, the DNA exonerations have prompted renewed attention to other systematic flaws in how justice functions, including how normal human decision making produces biased outcomes and how systems are biased against people of color, poor people, and people without adequate representation.

In applying psychology to the law, researchers have developed both broad and deep connections. The connection is broad insofar as research addresses all areas of the system, including those aspects that occur early in the process of adjudicating offenses, such as cognitive bias in investigations, criminal profiling of offenders, plea-bargaining decisions, and deception detection. The interface of psychology and law also extends to events that occur later in the process of adjudication, such as pretrial assessments of competence and criminal responsibility, expert testimony in criminal trials, and evaluations of future dangerousness for convicted offenders. The application of psychology to law is also broad in other ways: Research examines people who are not psychologists but who interact with the system in a wide array of contexts—from the actual people charged with violating the law (i.e., criminal or civil defendants) to those responsible for investigating alleged crimes (e.g., police detectives, forensic examiners), and those given responsibility for making the ultimate decision about a defendant's fate (i.e., judges, juries).

The connection between the fields of psychology and law is also deep. Consider the vast array of research on eyewitness memory, Munsterberg's ostensible inspiration for *On the Witness Stand*. In 2018, 110 years after Munsterberg encouraged psychologists to turn their attention to eyewitness memory, the field has an impressive record of producing concrete recommendations for law enforcement, from how to structure lineups and photospreads to how to interview children and victims. In learning about eyewitness memory and performance, psychological scientists have also developed useful theoretical models of memory, including models that explain the propensity for human memory to produce inaccurate information. More narrowly, psychologists have developed a deep understanding of how and why eyewitnesses make identification choices (or do not). Perhaps even more impressive, psychologists have found ways to translate science-based recommendations into improved practice, providing a model for the application of other evidence-based improvements to justice systems in the process.

The current volume is a testament to the fact that law is no longer "absurdly neglected" by psychology, as Munsterberg lamented in 1908. Indeed, the breadth and depth of research described in the following chapters is an affirmation of the extent to which psychological principles and methodology are uniquely suited to providing a sophisticated understanding of phenomena relevant to the intersection of psychology with the law. However, as with any scientific endeavor, our understanding of the topics at the interface of psychology and law is not complete. Therefore, in the chapters that follow, authors explain areas of consensus (where available) and areas of uncertainty or disagreement. In addition, they outline specific directions for future research. In asking authors to review extant literature and generate guidance for future research, we hope that each chapter will accomplish three main goals. First, we hope each chapter serves as an overview for upper-level psychology students new to the field. In reading each chapter, students should learn something about the basic methods in the area, any consensus on experimental findings, and challenges confronting researchers in the area. Second, we hope that expert readers with a background in psychological research will find new perspectives to guide their own thinking in the area. To that end, where possible, we have asked authors to describe new research paradigms or, if none exist, the necessary conditions for developing new paradigms in a given research area. Third, we have tried to ensure that chapters are readable for criminal justice system professionals who lack a formal background in psychology—for example, police officers, lawyers, and judges.

Readers familiar with the interface of psychology and law will note the connections between the current volume and *Psychology and Law: An Empirical Perspective,* edited by Neil Brewer and Kipling Williams (2005). Indeed, there are similarities between the two volumes. For example, both volumes are designed to appeal to audiences looking for in-depth coverage of psychological research relevant to the interface of psychology and law. To that end, both volumes avoid the broad-based coverage typical of introductory textbooks in psychology and law. Instead, we invited authors to focus their attention on key findings that form the foundation of relevant research areas. As noted above, we also asked authors to provide information about areas of controversy (where relevant) and describe potential directions for future research. In this way, we hope that each chapter will be understandable to advanced undergraduate audiences but still provide a unique perspective that will engage a seasoned reader of psychology and law literature.

We have also retained our focus on social and cognitive forensic research. This is reflected in the chapter topics that are consistent across the two volumes. These chapters cover fundamental questions in psychology and law that have inspired decades of research designed to address basic principles of memory and decision making and the role of social factors in legal context. These include chapters on important topics such as eyewitness recall (Lane & Houston, Chapter 5), eyewitness identification decisions (Sauer, Palmer, & Brewer, Chapter 9), false memories (Zaragoza, Hyman, & Chrobak, Chapter 8), jury decision making (Peter-Hagene, Salerno, & Phalen, Chapter 14), children as victims and witnesses (Lyon, McWilliams, & Williams, Chapter 7), interviewing victims and witnesses (Hope & Gabbert, Chapter 7), and deception detection (Gunderson & ten Brinke, Chapter 4).

In other important ways, the current volume departs significantly from the 2005 Brewer and Williams text. First, those readers interested in topics in which researchers seem not to have been so active in recent years may be disappointed. For example, topics such as the influence of pretrial publicity and the comprehension of judicial instructions—covered in detail in Brewer and Williams—were not specifically targeted here. For these topics, we believe the Brewer and Williams volume still provides comprehensive treatment of these important issues.

Second, we have enhanced our focus on cognitive and social forensic research by adding chapters on some key topics that were neglected in the Brewer and Williams (2005) volume, including judicial decision making (Mitchell, Chapter 16) and expert testimony (Marion, Kaplan, & Cutler, Chapter 13). Additional new chapters include Chapter 3, on false confessions and interrogations, in which Madon, More, and Ditchfield present a detailed analysis of the (in)famous Reid technique for extracting confessions from criminal suspects (Inbau, Reid, Buckley, & Jayne, 2013). In Chapter 11, Wilford, Shestak, and Wells take on the question of how defendants make decisions about plea bargains, including the potential relevance of theoretical models of decision making in the plea-bargaining context. In Chapter 2, by Charman, Douglass, and Mook, forensic decision errors—increasingly implicated in cases of wrongful conviction—are differentiated in terms of categorical errors (e.g., erroneously judging two fingerprints to be a match) versus continuous errors (e.g., inappropriately weighting evidence in assessments of guilt). The difference in these errors is highly relevant in designing interventions to minimize the risk of forensic errors. Finally, in Chapter 10, White and Kemp provide a compelling analysis of why it is so difficult to recognize faces and how technology may (or may not) enhance our abilities in the future. With the inclusion of these additional important topics, we are optimistic that researchers from many different areas of psychology and law will find much to interest them.

Third, we are conscious of the fact that our coverage of topics is by no means exhaustive. Indeed, in the 2005 Brewer and Williams volume, those students and researchers with clinical interests likely found much less to interest them than did those of cognitive or social psychological persuasions. Therefore, in the current volume we have extended coverage to encompass several key areas of clinical forensic research. For example, we now have an excellent chapter (Chapter 1) on criminal profiling by Fallon and Snook in which the authors present a thorough analysis of whether the practice of profiling constitutes pseudoscience. In Chapter 12, detailing the process whereby defendants are evaluated for competence to stand trial and/or insanity, Kois, Chauhan, and Warren present an accessible review of the basic psychological questions confronting forensic examiners charged with assessing defendants. In addition, they provide a fascinating perspective on cross-cultural differences in assessment of competence and insanity from countries representing a diverse set of justice systems, including

Australia, China, East Timor, Ghana, India, South Africa, and Taiwan. Finally, students and researchers interested in aggression, violence, and psychopathy will find detailed information in Chapter 15 by Polaschek on how these constructs are studied, critiques of existing empirical tools, and how research can be applied to individual cases.

We end the book with a chapter devoted to the tumultuous process of applying psychological research to policy and practice (Steblay, Chapter 17). In addition to providing a useful guide for students and researchers interested in applying their work to the "real world," this chapter reinforces our enhanced attention to clinical topics. In the Brewer and Williams (2005) volume, the final chapter addressed questions of how to translate psychological research into policy and practice in the context of eyewitness identification research. In the current volume, Steblay addresses the same challenge but expands the coverage to include broader questions, including, for example, how to generate recommendations for clinical issues when randomized controlled trials are not viable methods of data collection. Readers with an interest in the translation of all areas of psychological research to "real-world" problems will find a thoughtful perspective on the challenges and rewards of applying psychological science.

Research at the intersection of psychology and law is capable of providing specific, constructive explanations for—and solutions to—problems in the legal context. These problems include the most fundamental questions in the intersection of psychology and law: Is a suspect lying? Will an incarcerated individual be dangerous in the future? Is an eyewitness accurate? How can false memories be implanted? Is a defendant competent to stand trial? How are plea decisions made? How do juries, experts, and forensic examiners make decisions?

Explaining—and then solving—these problems is only possible when a sufficient body of research exists, that is, multiple empirical investigations providing converging support for a specific recommendation. However, as noted in Chapter 17, the mere existence of research in a legal context is not sufficient to produce demonstrable changes in systems of justice. In that chapter, Steblay argues that psychological scientists must also learn how to effectively communicate their research to legal audiences, develop collaborations with practitioners, and harness psychological knowledge about how cognitive errors can "afflict police investigators and triers-of-fact" (p. 422). Only then can psychological science be maximally applied to the range of contexts in which the methods of our field are ideally suited to providing concrete solutions.

Even when psychological scientists have generated a corpus of excellent research, communicated effectively with legal practitioners, and collaborated successfully with relevant experts, there is no guarantee that legal decisions will be informed by existing research, a fact bemoaned by United States Supreme Court Justice Sonia Sotomayor, who wrote in a dissent that "a vast body of scientific literature [in eyewitness identification research] merits barely a parenthetical mention in the majority opinion" (*Perry v. New Hampshire*, 2012, p. 14). Justice Sotomayor's dissenting opinion was written in response to a case in which the defendant was challenging the eyewitness's identification. However, the sentiment would likely apply to many other areas in which psychological research could potentially inform judicial decisions. Consider jury research: A recent analysis indicates that only seven U.S. Supreme Court decisions have included reference to jury research published in *Law and Human Behavior,* the premier outlet for peer-reviewed research on juries (Rose, 2017). That so few empirical investigations have informed Court decisions speaks to the ongoing challenges of applying excellent psychological research to the courts. We hope that this volume will contribute to the development of research in the interface of psychology and law. Ultimately, we hope this research will result in specific improvements to systems of justice around the world.

ACKNOWLEDGMENTS

Preparation of this chapter was supported by National Science Foundation Grant No. SES-1627433 to Amy Bradfield Douglass and Neil Brewer and Australian Research Council Grant No. ARC-DP150101905 to Neil Brewer and colleagues.

REFERENCES

Brewer, N., & Williams, K. D. (Eds.) (2005). *Psychology and law: An empirical perspective*. New York: Guilford Press.

Inbau, F. E., Reid, J., Buckley, J., & Jayne, B. (2013). *Criminal interrogation and confessions* (5th ed.). Burlington, MA: Jones & Bartlett Learning.

Munsterberg, H. (1908). *On the witness stand: Essays on psychology and crime*. New York: Doubleday.

Perry v. New Hampshire, 565 U.S. 228 (2012).

Rose, M. R. (2017). How typical is *Lockhart v. McCree*? Ecological validity concerns in court opinions. In M. B. Kovera (Ed.), *The psychology of juries* (pp. 227–254). Washington, DC: American Psychological Association.

Wells, G. L. (1978). Applied eyewitness-testimony research: System variables and estimator variables. *Journal of Personality and Social Psychology, 36,* 1546–1557.

CHAPTER 1

Criminal Profiling

Laura Fallon
Brent Snook

Bombs are exploding in New York City. Every few months, without warning, and always in a different and unpredictable location, a bomb goes off, terrifying civilians and occasionally causing injuries. The unknown culprit leaves behind letters at the crime scenes, in which it is warned that this is not the end, and that "justice will be served." The public is panicked, resources are dwindling, and the police are feeling as though they have reached a dead end. They employ handwriting experts, fingerprint analysts, and a bomb squad to help with the case, but nothing seems to be working. Feeling lost during this uncertain situation, the chief of police decides to try something new and enlists the help of his friend Dr. James Brussel, a practicing psychiatrist and criminologist. Using the evidence and known details of the case, Dr. Brussel forms a portrait of the characteristics and traits likely held by the culprit. He predicts the offender's demographic, physical, and character traits, diagnoses him with psychological disorders, and even goes as far as to say that upon arrest, the offender would be wearing a buttoned double-breasted suit. Sure enough, when George Metesky is apprehended, most of the details of Dr. Brussel's profile are correct—even down to the suit (Brussel, 1968).

The preceding "Mad Bomber" case was the first—and is probably still the most well known—case in which modern criminal profiling was used to identify a suspect successfully. Such a vivid and widely recounted anecdote about criminal profiling makes it easy to believe that it works—and difficult to believe otherwise. But what about the following example?

In London, a woman is brutally attacked and murdered in broad day-light while walking with her son and their dog. Many potential sus-pects are identified by the police, but one man in particular appears to stand out—Colin Stagg. The police enlist the help of psychologist Paul Britton, who creates a profile of the offender that Stagg is believed to fit quite well. Although there is no physical evidence to link Stagg to the crime scene, an undercover operation is carried out to implicate him, based on the similarities between him and the profile. The operation involves a policewoman who pretends to be romantically interested in Stagg in order to coax out information about the crime. As a result of the operation and the profile, Stagg is arrested for the murder. At trial, the evidence brought forth by Britton's profile is deemed by the judge to be highly speculative, and the undercover operation is criticized for being excessive and deceptive. After 14 months in custody and over 3 million pounds spent by the police agency in order to apprehend him, Stagg is acquitted. Sixteen years after the murder, a man named Robert Napper confesses to the crime and is subsequently convicted (*Regina v. Stagg*, 1994).

The Stagg case is perhaps one of the most well-known cases in which modern criminal profiling contributed to a miscarriage of justice. Such a tarnished and high-profile example of criminal profiling makes it very easy to believe that it does not work—and difficult to believe otherwise.

Although some may be inclined to take a moderate stance and argue that the reality of criminal profiling is probably somewhere between these two aforementioned cases, we argue in this chapter that it is a dubious practice and that its use by law enforcement agencies should be prohibited until there is compelling empirical evidence that it works. We provide a definition and overview of criminal profiling, outline the theoretical foun-dations of the practice, and review pertinent empirical research pertaining to the validity of the practice. We also discuss two controversies in the field of criminal profiling as a way to illustrate how there has been intellectual stagnation with regard to moving the field forward in a meaningful way. Lastly, we apply Carl Sagan's "baloney detection kit" to criminal profiling and conclude that it has many features of a pseudoscientific practice.

WHAT IS CRIMINAL PROFILING?

The Federal Bureau of Investigation (FBI) originally defined criminal pro-filing as a technique for predicting the behavioral and personality charac-teristics of a perpetrator based upon an analysis of the crimes he or she has committed (Douglas, Ressler, Burgess, & Hartman, 1986). More specifi-cally, it is a process in which crime scene information (e.g., location of a body, the type of weapon used, time of day the crime was committed) is used to make predictions about the behavior and underlying traits (e.g., violent tendencies, mental illnesses) of the perpetrator (Chifflet, 2015). The intended use of the subsequent list of perpetrator characteristics (i.e., the profile) is primarily to help the police identify the culprit. Since that original definition, profilers have expanded their claimed skill set to include, for example, helping investigators develop interviewing and interrogation strategies, suggesting lines of inquiry that the investigation may take, and so on (e.g., Dern, Dern, Horn, & Horn, 2009). It is important to note, however, that there is no universally accepted definition of profiling—that is, each individual profiler could potentially propose his or her own operational definition of what profiling entails.

PREVALENCE OF CRIMINAL PROFILING

Since the 1970s, the use of criminal profiling appears to have grown substantially. The available data show that the FBI provided profiling assistance on 192 occasions between 1971 and 1981 (Pinizzotto, 1984). Two years after those data were published, Douglas and Burgess (1986) indicated that FBI profilers had been asked to assist with 600 criminal investigations per year. More recent data showed that criminal profiling was applied by 12 FBI profilers in approximately 1,000 cases per year (Witkin, 1996). Data on the prevalence of criminal profiling use in the United States since the mid-1990s, however, are currently unavailable.

Criminal profiling has seemingly become a common practice in countries other than the United States (e.g., Davis & Bennett, 2006). For instance, in the United Kingdom, it was reported that 29 profilers were responsible for providing 242 instances of profiling advice between 1981 and 1994, with the use of criminal profiling increasing steadily during that period (Copson, 1995). In recent years, law enforcement in the United Kingdom has begun to move away from traditional methods of criminal profiling and toward a newer method termed "behavioral investigative advice," which is used often to assist with criminal investigations (Alison, Goodwill, Almond, Van den Heuvel, & Winter, 2010). As with the United States, the prevalence of profiling in the United Kingdom since the mid-1990s is presently unknown.

In Canada, criminal profiling is referred to as "criminal investigative analysis" and is conducted exclusively by select police officers from three different organizations (i.e., Royal Canadian Mounted Police, Ontario Provincial Police, Quebec Provincial Police; Criminal Investigative Analysis, n.d.). Although there is an active website pertaining to profiling in Canada, no data are available regarding the frequency with which it is requested or used by Canadian police organizations. The use of criminal profiling has been documented in a variety of other countries as well, including Finland,

Germany, The Netherlands, and Sweden (e.g., Åsgard, 1998). Although the prevalence of criminal profiling use globally remains undocumented, it is still being used around the world today.

HOW IS CRIMINAL PROFILING DONE?

Importantly, the process of conducting profiles lacks standardization, and there are very few details available in the published literature on the specific step-by-step process that profilers follow (but see Canter & Fritzon, 1998, for an exception, in which the process involved for those who take a specific type of statistical profiling approach is articulated). The profile compilation process has been described by some researchers as the "what + why = who" equation (Pinizzotto & Finkel, 1990). The "what" refers to the evidence and other materials analyzed by a profiler (e.g., crime scene photos, autopsy reports). That is, the crime scene is analyzed, and information is collected and compiled by the police (e.g., photos, documentation of fibers, maps of the area, weapons used). The "why" part of the equation, then, refers to the offender's motivations for committing the crime and for his or her behaviors at the crime scene. The profiler examines the crime scene information and other investigative information (e.g., witness statements) for what he or she considers to be important details that help generate predictions about the offender's characteristics (e.g., age, gender, ethnicity, home location, extracurricular interests). The "who" refers to the profile that is constructed and, subsequently, the suspect(s) identified through the process of profiling. The profiler shares—via verbal or written format—the resulting predictions with investigators (Douglas et al., 1986). Although the preceding information provides some general insight into the profiling process, detailed knowledge about what most profilers actually do to make their inferences remains unclear.

Profilers have argued that there are numerous ways in which criminal profiling is used. As mentioned, the most common way the practice is used is to help law enforcement identify offenders who commit specific crimes—particularly, serious crimes involving a great deal of uncertainty (e.g., violent and serial crimes; Holmes & Holmes, 2002). Profilers appear to use any information that they are provided to predict when, where, and how the next crime will occur in a serial crime case or to determine the extent to which an apprehended suspect fits the predicted characteristics of the offender (Bartol & Bartol, 2013). The skills of profilers are also sometimes used to advise police interrogators on how best to question a suspect, design strategies for successful undercover operations, assess the seriousness of a threatening or suspicious note, and help prosecutors create courtroom strategies (Homant & Kennedy, 1998). Note, however, that the ability of profilers to engage in these additional tasks requires the profiler to first be capable of making accurate predictions about the offender—the original purpose of criminal profiling.

QUALIFICATIONS OF A CRIMINAL PROFILER

There is contention in terms of the skills, qualities, and level of education that are required in order for one to be recognized as a profiler. One school of thought contends that prerequisites for profiling include having experience with criminal investigations, an understanding of human behavior, logical and objective thinking, and intuition (Hazelwood, Ressler, Depue, & Douglas, 1995). Broadly, Hazelwood et al. (1995) argued that only experienced law enforcement officers trained in behavioral sciences should be considered profilers. Canter and Alison (2000), on the other hand, asserted that law enforcement experience is not a prerequisite to be a successful profiler; they argued that forensic researchers and clinicians could do the job just as well (also see Copson, Badcock, Boon, & Britton, 1997, for an argument in favor of clinical experience as a critical profiling skill). Importantly, there is no agreed-upon skill or ability that is required in order to be a profiler. It seems that to be a profiler in most countries only requires an individual to convince the police that he or she has the ability to help with an investigation (but see Rainbow, 2008, for exceptions).

There is also a lack of consensus globally in terms of how one becomes a profiler. There does not appear to be a single regulatory body, akin to those that exist in other professional fields (e.g., psychology, dentistry, medicine), that monitors and regulates the training and practice of criminal profiling in the vast majority of countries. Thus there does not appear to be an actual professional designation that labels one as a professional profiler. However, some law enforcement agencies (e.g., FBI) have profiling training programs that claim to educate specialized trainees on how to construct and use a profile. Additionally, centers such as the National Center for the Analysis of Violent Crime (NCAVC) in the United States have been tasked with guiding law enforcement agencies on how to use profiling in criminal investigations and to conduct research on the practice (Turvey, 2012). Currently, aspiring profilers can join the International Criminal Investigative Analysis Fellowship, a private organization run by FBI-trained investigators that seeks to both train and accredit profiling professionals (Devery, 2010). Without a doubt, the greatest advancements in regulating the practice of criminal profiling have occurred in the United Kingdom. According to Rainbow (2008), efforts have been undertaken to govern how profiling advice is provided, who can become profilers (now referred to as "behavioral investigative analysts"), when profiling ought to be used, the evidence required to back up claims made, and so on. Despite the apparent advancements in the United Kingdom, Rainbow (2008) acknowledged that there is still much variation in the approaches used by registered profilers. In addition, oversight of profiling activities around the world is largely absent.

TYPES OF CRIMINAL PROFILING

Although the term "criminal profiling" is used to describe the overall process of identifying offender characteristics, there does not appear to be one single method that all profilers use. Profiling methods can be classified in a variety of ways. One popular way of categorizing profiling methods outlines the difference between clinical and statistical profiling. Clinically oriented techniques are unstructured in nature, incorporating aspects of the profilers' intuitions, knowledge, experience with clinical populations, and training in social sciences to generate predictions (e.g., Ressler & Shachtman, 1992). By contrast, statistically oriented predictions are based upon descriptive and inferential statistical models derived from an analysis of characteristics of offenders who have committed similar types of crime (e.g., Canter, 2004). Of course, it is also possible that profilers will use a mixed-methods approach, combining aspects of both the clinical and statistical forms of profiling.

A similar method of categorizing profiling methods uses the labels "inductive" and "deductive" profiling. Inductive profiling uses information on past offenders to predict how likely or unlikely it is for the current offender to possess a particular background characteristic. The offender's crime scene behavior is compared with that of other, similar offenders, and from this the probability that the present offender exhibits a certain characteristic is calculated (Holmes & Holmes, 2002). This method uses information about historical cases to make inferences about the present case and to estimate the likelihood that an offender possesses certain characteristics (Carson, 2011). Deductive profiling uses logical reasoning and analysis of the evidence left at the crime scene to predict characteristics of an offender. In other words, deductive profiling is case-based and uses the information already available about a case to make logical inferences about the likely offender (Alison, West, & Goodwill, 2004). Also see Muller (2000) for an alternate way to classify profiling approaches.

A specific profiling model was developed by the FBI in the 1980s in order to classify offenders (Hazelwood & Douglas, 1980). Called the "organized–disorganized typology," it assumed that offender behavior can be classified into two categories: organized and disorganized. Profilers using this method will assign offenders into one of the two categories based on their crime scene behavior. Broadly, it is assumed that organized offenders plan their crimes and exert a high level of control, whereas disorganized offenders commit their crimes more impulsively and without a great deal of thought. Organized crime scene behaviors are thought to include, for example, planning the crime in advance, leaving minimal evidence behind, and lack of postmortem maiming of the body. Disorganized crimes are characterized by an abundance of evidence, mutilation of the body, and lack of a getaway vehicle, among other attributes.

The main assumption of the organized–disorganized model is that an offender who commits an organized or disorganized crime will exhibit matching behavioral characteristics and traits. For example, if a crime scene contains signs of organized behavior, it is assumed that the offender who committed the crime will likely be highly intelligent, be socially competent, own a home and car, work at a skilled occupation, and live with a partner (all of which are considered "organized" characteristics). The perpetrator of a disorganized crime, on the other hand, would be assumed to have an unskilled occupation, have below-average intelligence, be sexually incompetent, and exhibit a change in behavior after committing the crime (FBI, 1985). Once categorized, these characteristics are used to create a profile of the likely offender. This model has been used regularly by the FBI and beyond and was integrated into their *Crime Classification Manual*, a guide created to assist profilers. The dichotomy has been updated and expanded over the years; one such change is that the model now accounts for offenders who exhibit both types of behavior, referred to as a "mixed" offender (Douglas, Burgess, Burgess, & Ressler, 1992).

THEORETICAL FOUNDATIONS

The primary assumption of criminal profiling, and the central idea on which its success rests, is that the behavior and actions of offenders can predict their demographic characteristics and personalities (Chifflet, 2015). By extension, it is assumed that offender characteristics are stable across situations and that these characteristics cause their behaviors. This major assumption, seemingly held by many proponents of criminal profiling, can be broken down into three smaller assumptions: homology, behavioral consistency, and behavioral differentiation. The homology assumption reasons that when offenders perform similar behaviors at a crime scene, they will possess similar background characteristics as well (e.g., demographics, socioeconomic status, criminal history). In other words, it assumes that offenders who commit crimes in a similar manner will be similar in other ways, making it easier to predict the type of offender who committed a particular crime. Behavioral consistency is the assumption that an individual serial offender will behave in a similar manner in each crime he or she commits. Behavioral differentiation refers to the claim that the behavior of one individual offender differs from that of other offenders.

The field of criminal profiling relies heavily on the assertion that behavior results from a person's internal disposition. These assumptions are in line with classic trait theory in psychology, which states that traits are stable and general. In other words, this means that an individual should behave similarly across different situations, because it is his or her internal traits that govern his or her behavior across all types of contexts (Mischel, 1968). Translating this to the world of criminal profiling, it is assumed that offender characteristics can be predicted based on their crime scene behavior. In line with this, proponents of profiling generally believe that (1) offenders who commit similar crimes will possess similar background characteristics (the homology assumption), (2) repeat offenders will commit their crimes in a similar manner (behavioral consistency), and (3) offenders will differ from one another (behavioral differentiation).

The fact that criminal profiling has a theoretical basis should be promising. The problem, however, is that trait theory has long been debunked in the psychology community. In fact, serious concerns were already being raised about the legitimacy of the trait-based theory of personality during the same time that profiling was gaining traction within the FBI. In general, the literature has shown that reliance on traits as the main predictor of behavior is entirely misguided and that a person's situation plays just as much of a role in behavior determination (Bowers, 1973; Mischel, 1968). Evidence has confirmed this notion in the specific context of predicting criminal behavior (e.g., Bennell & Canter, 2002). For example, a study by Ullman (2007) that found that resistance by the victim—a situational factor—strongly affects an offender's subsequent actions, which goes against what would be expected from trait theory. In terms of offender consistency (across crimes and other aspects of their lives), there is a small amount of evidence to suggest that certain behaviors relate to certain background characteristics, but this evidence is limited to specific subsets of behavior and does not extend to others (e.g., Davies, Wittebrood, & Jackson, 1997). For the most part, the literature has failed to support the assertion that behavior can be predicted by traits alone (e.g., Woodhams & Toye, 2007).

The homology assumption appears to be the most empirically tested of the three assumptions of criminal profiling. In a classic study, Mokros and Alison (2002) correlated the crime scene actions of 100 rapists with their ages, criminal histories, and demographic factors and failed to find support for the assertion that offenders who perform similar behaviors will possess similar characteristics. Doan and Snook (2008) found no support for the homology assumption in their study of arson and robbery cases, with the assumption being violated in over half of their comparisons. Although much concern has been raised about the homology assumption, some recent advancements appear to have been made in terms of linking crime scene behaviors and offender characteristics. For example, a study by Goodwill, Lehmann, Beauregard, and Andrei (2016) demonstrated that links can be made between offender characteristics and crime scene behaviors when the context of the crime is taken into account and data are interpreted using a dynamic decision-making process. Specifically, they analyzed crime scene data by action phases (i.e., the steps of the crime in which different decisions must be made and actions must be taken) by performing a cluster analysis for each phase. The authors found that meaningful clusters formed across action phases that linked certain behaviors and characteristics, a result that provides tentative support for the ability to infer characteristics from behaviors. Also see similar research attempting to validate the assumptions underlying criminal profiling and identifying the links between crime scene behaviors and offender characteristics (e.g., Goodwill, Allen, & Kolarevic, 2014).

There is also evidence to suggest that issues exist with some of the classic typologies purportedly used by profilers. As mentioned previously, one of the most common typologies used by those in the profiling world is the organized–disorganized dichotomy, which is used to categorize offenders' crime scene behavior and personal characteristics based on the degree of organization or lack thereof exhibited while committing the crime (Ressler, Burgess, Douglas, Hartman, & D'Agostino, 1986). To reiterate, it is assumed that offenders who display organized characteristics will commit organized crimes and disorganized offenders will commit disorganized crimes. Despite its popularity with proponents of criminal profiling, however, evaluations of the organized–disorganized typology have suggested that it does not match actual variations in offender behavior and thus does not have much value in terms of the categorization of offenders (e.g., Canter, Alison, Alison, & Wentink, 2004). Similarly, an evaluation of the sexual serial homicide typology, a system used to categorize offenders whose crimes include sexual violence (see Keppel & Walter, 1999), failed to find evidence to support its classification system (Bennell, Bloomfield, Emeno, & Musolino, 2012). The problems in validating profiling typologies, combined with limited evidence to support the consistency of offender behaviors and the effects of situational factors in determining behavior, shed light on the difficulties with trying to construct an accurate profile of an individual offender.

EMPIRICAL FOUNDATIONS

The field of modern profiling began as a nonscientific practice based mostly upon the experience of FBI agents and minimal, poorly conducted research (e.g., interviews with serial offenders without any checks of reliability or replication; Devery, 2010). Even some of the first to conduct research on criminal profiling stated that "the process is an art and not a science" (Hazelwood & Douglas, 1980, p. 22). Since this time, however, there have been a multitude of papers published on the topic (see Dowden, Bennell, & Bloomfield, 2007, for data showing that peer-reviewed articles on profiling have increased since the 1980s). Much of this literature comes to the conclusion that criminal profiling works, or at least has the potential to work, which paints a promising picture for the future of the practice.

However, there are clear deficiencies in terms of concrete evidence supporting the ability of profilers to make accurate predictions beyond what can be achieved by a layperson. Although there have been copious articles published on profiling, most consist of commentaries or speculation about its effectiveness. Moreover, even the few articles that do report empirical data on profiler abilities contain serious methodological flaws that limit the generalizability to the actual practice.

Snook, Eastwood, Gendreau, Goggin, and Cullen (2007) attempted to provide some context regarding the existing literature on criminal profiling and shed some light on the validity of the practice. They first conducted a literature review of 130 criminal profiling articles, looking specifically at the arguments used by the authors and determining whether they were commonsense or empirical. Their analysis showed that commonsense rationales were used more than empirical arguments 58% of the time. Notably, anecdotes were used most often as sources of knowledge in the articles, and self-serving bias (e.g., attributing positive events to profiling itself and negative events to external factors) was the most common analytical process used when evaluating criminal profiling. Other commonsense arguments were used at high rates as well, which is disconcerting when it comes to the validation of criminal profiling as a scientific practice. Additionally, it was discovered that certain author characteristics affected the level of commonsense or empirical arguments; specifically, articles with a clinical focus, written by law enforcement officials, published in the United States before 1990, and with a positive view of profiling and its utility, were more likely to employ commonsense arguments. Given that there are likely many articles in the profiling literature with one or more of these characteristics, this result is troubling.

Much of the empirical literature examining the accuracy of profilers in making predictions employs a similar method: Participants are recruited from various groups (e.g., profilers, science students, psychologists), given crime scene details, and asked to make predictions about the likely offender in the form of a multiple-choice questionnaire (e.g., Pinizzotto & Finkel, 1990). Accuracy is determined by checking responses with an actual description of the offender, and the performance of the profiler group is then compared with the others to assess relative accuracy. The second part of the Snook et al. (2007) study included results of two meta-analyses combining data from several of these studies. One of the main issues noted in the selected studies was that there was a lack of agreement between researchers on who was considered a profiler. Thus the authors conducted two separate analyses to account for the discrepancy. For one analysis, a profiler was defined as anyone who labels him- or herself as a profiler, as well as experienced law enforcement officials. Results showed that this profiler group performed significantly better than the comparison group in predicting some traits (i.e., physical attributes) but significantly worse for others (e.g., cognitive processes). For the second analysis, the profiler group was changed to only include those who self-label as profilers, and in this case, they performed significantly better than the comparison group in predicting all variables. However, the authors noted that due to small sample sizes and imprecision in estimates (i.e., wide confidence intervals), these results must be viewed as highly tentative. Most importantly, they noted that although it appears from these results that profilers performed well relative to the comparison group, their success rate of 66% was nowhere near an expert level. Given that profilers are viewed as experts in their field, Snook and his colleagues asserted that this result is highly concerning, regardless of how much better the profilers did than the nonprofiler groups.

VALIDATING CRIMINAL PROFILING

The preceding discussion ought to make it clear that there is no conclusive evidence to confirm that profilers are expert predictors. What is required to illustrate profiling effectiveness are independent (i.e., researchers not involved in profiling activities) and controlled experiments testing the predictive abilities of large samples of profilers (using any methodology of their choosing); these experiments must then be replicated multiple times to ensure that robust conclusions can be drawn about profilers' abilities (i.e., to avoid a reproducibility crisis in this area). What is also required are evaluations of profilers' predictions on actual cases, preferably where the ground truth has been verified by objective evidence (e.g., DNA). Again, it is imperative that these field experiments be replicated multiple times. As mentioned earlier, there is some research assessing the skills of profilers and their ability to create successful profiles (e.g., Kocsis, 2003); however, this research is not without serious methodological problems and has not resulted in any compelling evidence to support profiling (see the later discussion of concerns with this body of research). The facts that profiles are difficult to access due to confidentiality and secrecy issues in the criminal justice system, that barriers to international evaluation (e.g., language interpretation) exist, and that profilers appear unwilling to participate in research do not preclude high evaluative standards being a necessity before accepting claims of profiler expertise. Systematic scientific evaluations of profilers' performance is a must before any credence can be given to criminal profiling as a legitimate practice. Put differently, the extraordinary claim of profiler expertise requires extraordinary data.

The current lack of evidence to support profiler abilities may also be due to the fact that the act of matching a profile to an offender is subjective in itself, especially because profiles often include vague and ambiguous statements that could be applied to a wide range of people. In a study conducted by Alison, Smith, Eastman, and Rainbow (2003) that examined 21 profiles, it was found that 24% of claims within the profile were ambiguous (e.g., "the offender will have poor heterosexual skills"), 55%

were not verifiable (e.g., thoughts and feelings of the offender), and 70% were not falsifiable. A more recent content analysis of 47 profiles provided by behavioral investigative analysis experts in the United Kingdom revealed that 8% were ambiguous, 30% were unverifiable, and 57% were unfalsifiable (Almond, Alison, & Porter, 2007). Although there has been slight improvement in terms of the content of profiles in the United Kingdom, there still appears to be much room for improving the quality of advice given to investigators. What makes these results even more concerning is that people have the tendency to rate vague statements as being accurate. This is evidenced by a study in which two police officer groups were given the same profile and were asked to match it to different suspects, only one of whom actually matched the profile. The results showed that the two groups found the profile to be equally accurate, even though only one of the groups was matching it to the actual offender (Alison, Smith, & Morgan, 2003). This finding, along with the evidence of ambiguity in profiles, render it nearly impossible to determine the accuracy of profiles in practice. The lack of compelling empirical evidence on profiler predictive abilities is especially concerning given the fact that profilers and those supporting the practice often defend the accuracy of profiling with the assertion that they "have not been wrong yet!" (Chifflet, 2015, p. 244).

It should be blatantly evident that the provision of high-quality data demonstrating the accuracy of profiler predictions is the keystone to this practice. However, some profiling proponents have argued that it is the belief in the utility, or relevance, of a criminal profile to an investigation that is most important. Some of the earliest examples of research in this area examined criminal cases in the real world to see how often criminal profiling contributed to solving them. Pinizzotto (1984) determined that although profiling helped to resolve 46% of FBI cases examined, it was only shown to have helped specifically with identifying a suspect 17% of the time. Some other researchers have taken the approach of surveying those involved with profiling to determine how useful they consider the practice—a technique sometimes referred to as consumer satisfaction surveys (Chifflet, 2015). When detectives were asked for their opinions on the utility of profiling, studies showed mostly positive results, with respondents agreeing that profiling is useful and stating they would use it again (e.g., Trager & Brewster, 2001). The opinions of other professionals, however, are a different story. Seventy percent of surveyed police psychologists stated that, although profiling may be useful in a law enforcement context, they questioned the validity of the practice (Bartol, 1996; also see Torres, Boccaccini, & Miller's [2006] survey results showing that forensic psychologists/psychiatrists are generally skeptical of profiling). Similarly, a majority of surveyed lawyers questioned both the validity and utility of the practice, along with the lack of empirical evidence available to support it (Woskett, Coyle, & Lincoln, 2007).

Although research on the utility of criminal profiling demonstrates that many professionals directly involved in criminal investigations perceive it as being legitimate, these judgments are inherently subjective. It is possible that positive opinions about profiling come from, as argued by Snook, Cullen, Bennell, Taylor, and Gendreau (2008), the way in which information about profiling is delivered and processed. For example, belief in profiling's effectiveness may come from witnessing a case that was solved after the creation of a profile but not necessarily because of the content of the profile. This *post hoc ergo proper hoc* belief (i.e., after this, so because of this) is problematic and only helps to perpetuate the belief that profiling is a valid practice (Snook et al., 2007; also see Charman, Douglass, & Mook, Chapter 2, this volume, for additional research on cognitive biases in legal decision making). If research on satisfaction with criminal profiling continues to report positive results, and law enforcement professionals continue to believe that it works, police agencies will likely continue to use profiles in investigations. Consequently, this will help to support the erroneous argument that, if profiles are continuing to be used by police, then they must be valid (Chifflet, 2015).

PROFILING DEBATES

Since Snook et al.'s (2007) meta-analysis and Snook et al.'s (2008) critique of the practice, it appears that minimal empirical studies testing the accuracy of profiler predictions have been published. Interestingly, however, both of these studies were key components of two debates about profiling that took place during the first decade of the 2000s. A number of researchers in the field were involved in these debates, each with his or her own viewpoints and arguments. Although debates in the scientific literature are generally productive in moving knowledge forward, the lack of new research in this area since these debates indicates that this appears not to have been the case with these exchanges.

The Profiling Skills Debate

The first debate began with an article by Kocsis (2003) that described the results of three previous studies conducted by him and his colleagues, along with some original data, looking at the accuracy of profilers (Kocsis, 2004; Kocsis, Irwin, Hayes, & Nunn, 2000; Kocsis, Hayes, & Irwin, 2002). This research used a variation on the method explained previously (i.e., using a multiple-choice questionnaire to assess the predictive accuracy of profiler and nonprofiler groups). In one of the studies discussed, participants also constructed written profiles. For these studies, participants were recruited from groups that were expected to represent the "key attributes" of a successful profiler outlined by Hazelwood et al. (1995); according to the researchers, these attributes were (1) an understanding of the criminal mind and human behavior, (2) investigative experience, (3) a capacity for objective and logical analysis, and (4) intuition. Respectively, the groups chosen to represent these skills were psychologists, police officers/other investigative specialists, science students, and psychics. Kocsis and colleagues also tested the abilities of practicing profilers. To determine accuracy, responses to the questionnaire were compared with the original profile of the actual offender. The scores for each group were compared to determine the relative accuracy of those possessing each of the four key skills.

Kocsis (2003) drew several conclusions from his research. He first stated that profilers performed better than all other groups in terms of the total number of correct predictions. He then noted that the science students performed second best after the profilers, supporting the notion that logical and objective reasoning are critical for effective profiling. Due to the poor performance of police officers and psychics in this study, he also suggested that the data do not support the importance of investigative experience or intuition in the construction of successful profiles. He concluded by saying that these results could help recruit and train future profilers and that his research is a step in the direction of criminal profiling becoming more scientific.

Several years after the Kocsis (2003) article was published, Bennell, Jones, Taylor, and Snook (2006) published a critique of Kocsis's research program. Their main concern was with the "profiling skills" component of the research. Bennell and colleagues argued that the particular skills the participants were assumed to possess were never tested, operational definitions of the skills were not provided, and the fact that groups may possess more than one of the outlined skills, in differing combinations and levels, was never accounted for in the study's design. In addition, Bennell and colleagues also pointed out that (1) some of the multiple-choice questions (testing accuracy) were open to interpretation by the respondent (e.g., height: short, average, tall, very tall), (2) the "correct" responses for some of the questions were subjective or unverifiable (e.g., offender's motive), (3) the data analyses were biased in the direction of profilers (i.e., they summed results from several comparison groups, some of which performed poorly, rather than conducting groupwise comparisons), and (4) there were concerns regarding both internal and external validity (e.g., differences in time to complete questionnaire, heterogeneity in profiling group, use of a multiple-choice test). In essence, Bennell and colleagues were skeptical of Kocsis's conclusions about the skill set required to be a successful profiler because of the aforementioned methodological flaws in the research and the fact that proper data analysis would have led to much more tentative conclusions about profiler expertise.

Kocsis (2006) replied to the Bennell et al. (2006) critique but failed to provide any new data on the predictive abilities of profilers or research more conclusively linking skills to profiling success to counter the concerns raised about his research. Although debate is often valuable—and in this case the identification of the skills that allow for accurate profiling is a worthwhile venture—this debate did little to further our understanding of the relationship between skills and profiling performance. In fact, the only real advancement in this area was the publication of one study that attempted to determine the role that critical thinking skills play in criminal profiling, while ensuring that participants' skill levels were tested using a validated scale (Bennell, Corey, Taylor, & Ecker, 2008). The authors chose critical thinking because it is related to logical reasoning, the skill that was shown by Kocsis to have the highest positive relationship with profile accuracy. That study found that critical thinking had no relationship with profiling performance in university students.

The Operational Definition Debate

Following the Bennell et al. (2006) critique of the Kocsis research program, Snook and colleagues (2008) published an article detailing the problems with criminal profiling. They first discussed the lack of empirical evidence supporting the effectiveness of profiling, specifically touching on the lack of validity for the popular typologies used by profilers, the flawed nature of the theory underlying the practice of profiling (i.e., trait theory), and the lack of evidence supporting the accuracy of profilers' predictions being superior to those of other individuals. They then proposed several reasons why people might tend to believe in the utility and success of profiling, despite the lack of evidence to support it. They suggested that it may be an interaction between aspects of the message people receive about profiling (e.g., reliance on anecdotes, arguments from authority figures) and the way the mind processes such information (e.g., source monitoring errors, interpreting ambiguous information).

Dern and colleagues (2009) critiqued the work of Snook et al. (2008) and highlighted what they believed were some misconceptions and errors brought forth by those authors. Primarily, they argued that criminal profiling is in fact much more complex than what Snook and colleagues suggested in their article and specifically in their definition of profiling. Moreover, they contested that Snook and colleagues did not have enough experience with policing or profiling to be able to make the conclusions they did. They argued that in Germany, profiling—referred to as "behavioral case analysis"—involves an extremely thorough and rigorous analysis process, using a full team of case analysts who consult empirical data along with case information to draw conclusions. They suggested that these methods are regularly evaluated, subjected to checks of reliability, and continually improved and updated after each case. All the information gathered through the profiling process is used to provide a deeper understanding of the case, with the goal of providing useful information to the investigation.

They also noted that the typologies mentioned by Snook and colleagues only constitute a minor portion of this type of profiling and that profilers are aware of the problems with them. Additionally, Dern and colleagues suggested that profilers are also aware of issues with trait theory and the importance of situational factors and have been for some time. The authors concluded by saying that although empirical testing of criminal profiling would certainly be beneficial, it is not quite as necessary as Snook and colleagues contended in their article.

Snook, Taylor, Gendreau, and Bennell (2009) later rebuked the claims made by Dern et al. (2009). Rather than discuss them here in detail, it is more important to note that the issues raised by Dern point to a broader issue within the profiling field with regard to the evasion of scientific scrutiny by profilers. Assuming that Snook and colleagues failed to capture the essence of what profilers were doing in Germany, and maybe elsewhere, the points raised by Dern and colleagues highlight a fundamental problem in profiling—that is, evaluations of profiling abilities do not appear in the scientific literature; in fact, it took a scathing review of the field to encourage profiling advocates to provide any details of their activities. In our view, there is a shroud of secrecy surrounding the practice that is at odds with a true scientific discipline. Claims of expertise must be associated with data demonstrating effectiveness, and clear operational definitions must be provided to allow for precise testing of abilities. Broadly, this debate points out the need for greater transparency and empirical testing of profiling if profilers want to be regarded as professionals whose discipline is grounded in sound evidence.

Although all parties involved made legitimate arguments throughout the course of these debates, none were ever conclusively resolved. Since the publication of these articles, research on testing the predictive abilities of profilers has been virtually nonexistent. Discussions between researchers, such as the ones highlighted herein, are important when it comes to advancing our knowledge in academic areas, but without any conclusive evidence one way or the other regarding profiler performance, we are no further ahead than we were at the start of the debates—which, to us, is a poor state of affairs.

IS CRIMINAL PROFILING A PSEUDOSCIENCE?

Determining the effectiveness of criminal profiling can be difficult because there has been very little empirical research examining this topic. Unfortunately, the few studies that have shown some minimal support for the predictive accuracy of profilers are relatively low in quality, due to methodological flaws such as small sample sizes and threats to validity. We acknowledge that the aforementioned data suggest that profilers are far from experts, but the lack of evidence supporting profiling does not mean that it does not have any potential. We encourage researchers to continue to try to convince profilers to have their abilities tested, to continue to test the assumptions underlying profiling, and, most importantly, to have any findings replicated by nonpartisan, independent researchers.

Given the disconnection between the lack of compelling evidence supporting criminal profiling and the unfounded optimism held by some practitioners and academics, we could not help but wonder whether it is merely a pseudoscientific practice (akin to other practices such as psychic detection and facilitated communication). Researchers have suggested a number of ways to characterize a field as scientific or pseudoscientific. One well-known way to do this is to use Carl Sagan's "baloney detection kit," a series of features that help people identify fallacious and fraudulent claims (Sagan, 1997). In an attempt to shed more light on the legitimacy of criminal profiling, we took on the task of testing the practice against some of the features of the kit. Some of the more obvious warning signs of profiling that we uncovered through this examination include the following:

1. A tendency to invoke ad hoc hypotheses. In the case of criminal profiling, it appears that there is no single definition that allows independent researchers to test the predictive abilities of profilers. If one of the many definitions of profiling is used to test performance, profilers are able to evade impact from negative results by saying the definition does not apply to their version of profiling (see the Dern et al., 2009, argument, e.g., regarding the narrow and simplistic nature of operational definition).

2. Intellectual stagnation. As far as we can tell, there have not been any major theoretical breakthroughs since the beginning of the practice. It appears to us that the classic trait theory remains the dominant theory (and the effects of the situation still do not seem to be accounted for in this practice), despite a lack of empirical support for the past 40 years.

3. Excessive reliance on anecdotes and testimonial evidence to support the claim that it works. The narrative review conducted by Snook et al. (2007) showed that the majority of arguments regarding the effectiveness of criminal profiling are grounded in commonsense rationales, including vivid stories and testimonials. This state of affairs appears unchanged in the past 10 years; there has yet to be replication or any updating of this review. On a related note, there appears to be very little fact checking within the field to ensure that even vivid anecdotes are actually correct. For example, in the most widely cited case of the Mad Bomber (referenced at the beginning of this chapter), there now appears to be evidence showing that much of the profile was fraudulent, with many of the details contained within it being added after the suspect was apprehended (see Bartol & Bartol, 2013).

4. Evasion of scrutiny of profilers' ability. It is evident in criminal profiling that profilers refuse to have their abilities empirically tested. With the exception of a few profilers who participated in research with Richard

Kocsis (participants whom we know little about), the vast majority of profilers around the world have never had their abilities tested in a public forum. Having said this, Rainbow (2008) offered a glimmer of hope on this front by indicating that evaluations are ongoing of U.K. profilers; however, we have yet to see any data. This is a particularly important point given that other professional groups tend to be interested and willing to help their field progress by engaging in experimental research (e.g., street patrol officers, teachers, social workers).

5. Lack of controlled experimentation to resolve debates. As reviewed earlier, there have been a couple of debates regarding the state of criminal profiling. However the proponents of profiling who objected to skepticism about the field failed to conduct any controlled experiments or provide any quantitative data to help support their arguments.

6. Burden of proof. The general rule in science is that the individuals who are making a claim that something works are the same individuals responsible for providing data demonstrating evidence for this claim. Related to point 5, profilers have been remiss in providing any evidence (let alone extraordinary evidence) of their claimed extraordinary predictive abilities.

7. Absence of connectivity between the field of criminal profiling and other related disciplines. A common practice within many scientific fields is to draw upon knowledge from any field that can provide insight. It appears to us, at least, that the field of criminal profiling has done a very poor job of considering data from different fields that may have provided insights into the conditions in which profiling may succeed or fail (e.g., Paul Meehl's [1954] groundbreaking research comparing clinical vs. statistical predictions).

FINAL THOUGHTS

In sum, we now know that the leading theory underlying criminal profiling has been debunked, that the popular offender classification typologies used lack empirical support, and that there is no compelling evidence to support the ability of profilers to make accurate predictions. In addition, a review of the published literature shows a lack of standardization around the world in all aspects of the profiling practice (e.g., who can be a profiler, credentials required, methodology employed, skills required). It now appears that it is a relatively inactive field of inquiry, and there are many features of profiling suggesting that it is mere pseudoscience. Although many people may find it easy to agree with the claims that criminal profiling is "only another tool in the investigative toolbox" and that investigators have nothing to lose by employing this practice, people should be reminded of the law of unintended consequences—that is, that there may be serious unintended drawbacks from a seemingly innocuous practice. In fact, some researchers have cautioned law enforcement agencies against using criminal profiling in investigations until more empirical evidence is discovered (e.g., Snook et al., 2008); there are some indications that even human rights commissions are worried about the use of profiling (e.g., Bourque, LeBlanc, Utzschneider, & Wright, 2009).

Hardworking and dedicated investigators already have the tough job of solving crimes. Thus it is critical that they use their resources wisely and avoid practices that could, for one, result in legal action against them for using a dubious practice and, equally damaging, could contribute to miscarriages of justice (see Leo, 2008, for concerns about how profiling may be a contributor to police-induced false confessions). Such practices may also be a waste of time and resources, as they could misdirect investigators and cause them to pursue unhelpful leads. It is therefore imperative that law enforcement personnel be given sound advice on practices that they can avail themselves of during an investigation. Our review, based on the best available evidence to date, leads us to conclude that criminal profiling is still, after nearly 40 years, in its infancy. There is no compelling empirical evidence to support the use of profilers in actual police investigations.

REFERENCES

Alison, L. J., Goodwill, A., Almond, L., Van den Heuvel, C., & Winter, J. (2010). Pragmatic solutions to offender profiling and behavioural investigative advice. *Legal and Criminological Psychology, 15*, 115–132.

Alison, L. J., Smith, M. D., Eastman, O., & Rainbow, L. (2003). Toulmin's philosophy of argument and its relevance to offender profiling. *Psychology, Crime and Law, 9*, 173–183.

Alison, L. J., Smith, M. D., & Morgan, K. (2003). Interpreting the accuracy of offender profiles. *Psychology, Crime and Law, 9*, 185–195.

Alison, L., West, A., & Goodwill, A. (2004). The academic and the practitioner: Pragmatists' views of offender profiling. *Psychology, Public Policy, and Law, 10*, 71–101.

Almond, L., Alison, L., & Porter, L. (2007). An evaluation and comparison of claims made in behavioral investigative advice reports compiled by the National Policing Improvements Agency in the United Kingdom. *Journal of Investigative Psychology and Offender Profiling, 4*, 71–83.

Åsgard, U. (1998). Swedish experiences in offender profiling and evaluation of some aspects of a case of murder and abduction in Germany. In Case Analysis Unit (Ed.), *Methods of case analysis: An international symposium* (pp. 125–130). Weisbaden, Germany: Bundeskriminalamt Kriminalistisches Institut.

Bartol, C. R. (1996). Police psychology: Then, now and beyond. *Criminal Justice and Behavior, 23*, 70–89.

Bartol, C. R., & Bartol, A. M. (2013). *Criminal and behavioral profiling*. Thousand Oaks, CA: SAGE.

Bennell, C., Bloomfield, S., Emeno, K., & Musolino, E. (2012). Classifying serial sexual murder/murderers: An attempt to validate Keppel and Walter's (1999) model. *Criminal Justice and Behavior, 40*, 5–25.

Bennell, C., & Canter, D. V. (2002). Linking commercial burglaries by modus operandi: Tests using regression and ROC analysis. *Science and Justice, 42*, 153–164.

Bennell, C., Corey, S., Taylor, A., & Ecker, J. (2008). What skills are required for effective offender profiling? An examination of the relationship between critical thinking ability and profile accuracy. *Psychology, Crime and Law, 14*, 143–157.

Bennell, C., Jones, N. J., Taylor, P. J., & Snook, B. (2006). Validities and abilities in criminal profiling: A critique of the studies conducted by Richard Kocsis and his colleagues. *International Journal of Offender Therapy and Comparative Criminology, 50*, 344–360.

Bourque, J., LeBlanc, S., Utzschneider, A., & Wright, C. (2009). *The effectiveness of profiling from a national security perspective.* Ottawa, Ontario, Canada: Canadian Human Rights Commission.

Bowers, K. (1973). Situationism in psychology: An analysis and a critique. *Psychological Review, 80*, 307–336.

Brussel, J. A. (1968). *Casebook of a crime psychiatrist.* New York: Bernard Geis Associates.

Canter, D. V. (2004). Offender profiling and investigative psychology. *Journal of Investigative Psychology and Offender Profiling, 1*, 1–15.

Canter, D. V., & Alison, L. J. (2000). Profiling property crime. In D. V. Canter & L. J. Alison (Eds.), *Profiling property crime* (pp. 1–30). Aldershot, UK: Ashgate.

Canter, D. V., Alison, L. J., Alison, E., & Wentink, N. (2004). The organized/ disorganized typology of serial murder: Myth or model? *Psychology, Public Policy, and Law, 10*, 293–320.

Canter, D., & Fritzon, K. (1998). Differentiating arsonists: A model of firesetting actions and characteristics. *Legal and Criminological Psychology, 3*, 73–96.

Carson, D. (2011). Investigative psychology and law: Towards collaboration by focusing on evidence and inferential reasoning. *Journal of Investigative Psychology and Offender Profiling, 8*, 74–89.

Chifflet, P. (2015). Questioning the validity of criminal profiling: An evidence-based approach. *Australian and New Zealand Journal of Criminology, 48*, 238–255.

Copson, G. (1995). *Coals to Newcastle?: Part 1: A study of offender profiling.* London: Home Office, Police Research Group.

Copson, G., Badcock, R., Boon, J., & Britton, P. (1997). Articulating a systematic approach to clinical crime profiling. *Criminal Behaviour and Mental Health, 7*, 13–17.

Criminal Investigative Analysis. (n.d.). Retrieved from *www.rcmp-grc.gc.ca/to-ot/ cpcmecccpede/bs-sc/crim-profil-eng.htm.*

Davies, A., Wittebrood, K., & Jackson, J. L. (1997). Predicting the criminal antecedents of a stranger rapist from his offence behaviour. *Science and Justice, 37*, 161–170.

Davis, M. R., & Bennett, D. (2006, October). Criminal investigative analysis in the Australian context. Retrieved from *www.psychology.org.au/publications/ inpsych/context.*

Dern, H., Dern, C., Horn, A., & Horn, U. (2009). The fire behind the smoke: A reply to Snook and colleagues. *Criminal Justice and Behavior, 36*, 1085–1090.

Devery, C. (2010). Criminal profiling and criminal investigation. *Journal of Contemporary Criminal Justice, 26*, 393–407.

Doan, B., & Snook, B. (2008). A failure to find empirical support for the homology assumption in criminal profiling. *Journal of Police and Criminological Psychology, 23*, 61–70.

Douglas, J. E., & Burgess, A. E. (1986). Criminal profiling: A viable investigative tool against violent crime. *FBI Law Enforcement Bulletin, 55*, 9–13.

Douglas, J. E., Burgess, A. W., Burgess, A. G., & Ressler, R. K. (Eds.). (1992). *Crime classification manual: A standard system for investigating and classifying violent crimes.* New York: Simon & Schuster.

Douglas, J. E., Ressler, R. K., Burgess, A. W., & Hartman, C. R. (1986). Criminal profiling from crime scene analysis. *Behavioral Sciences and the Law, 4*, 401–421.

Dowden, C., Bennell, C., & Bloomfield, S. (2007). Advances in offender profiling: A systematic review of the profiling literature published over the past three decades. *Journal of Police and Criminal Psychology, 22*, 44–56.

Federal Bureau of Investigation. (1985). Crime scene and profile characteristics of organized and disorganized murderers. *FBI Law Enforcement Bulletin, 54*, 18–25.

Goodwill, A. M., Allen, J. C., & Kolarevic, D. (2014). Improvement of thematic classification in offender profiling: Classifying Serbian homicides using multiple correspondence, cluster, and discriminant function analyses. *Journal of Investigative Psychology and Offender Profiling, 11*, 221–236.

Goodwill, A. M., Lehmann, R. J. B., Beauregard, E., & Andrei, A. (2016). An action phase approach to offender profiling. *Legal and Criminological Psychology, 21*, 229–250.

Hazelwood, R. R., & Douglas, J. E. (1980). The lust murderer. *FBI Law Enforcement Bulletin, 49*, 18–22.

Hazelwood, R. R., Ressler, R. K., Depue, R. L., & Douglas, J. E. (1995). Criminal investigative analysis: An overview. In A. W. Burgess & R. R. Hazelwood (Eds.), *Practical aspects of rape investigation: A multidisciplinary approach* (pp. 115–126). Boca Raton, FL: CRC Press.

Holmes, R. M., & Holmes, S. T. (2002). *Profiling violent crimes: An investigative tool.* Thousand Oaks, CA: SAGE.

Homant, R. J., & Kennedy, D. B. (1998). Psychological aspects of crime scene profiling. *Criminal Justice and Behavior, 25*, 319–343.

Keppel, R. D., & Walter, R. (1999). Profiling killers: A revised classification model for understanding sexual murder. *International Journal of Offender Therapy and Comparative Criminology, 43*, 417–434.

Kocsis, R. N. (2003). Criminal psychological profiling: Validities and abilities. *International Journal of Offender Therapy and Comparative Criminology, 47*, 126–144.

Kocsis, R. N. (2004). Psychological profiling of serial arson offenses: An assessment of skills and accuracy. *Criminal Justice and Behavior, 31*, 341–361.

Kocsis, R. N. (2006). Validities and abilities in criminal profiling: The dilemma for David Canter's investigative psychology. *International Journal of Offender Therapy and Comparative Criminology, 50*, 458–477.

Kocsis, R. N., Hayes, A. F., & Irwin, H. J. (2002). Investigative experience and accuracy in psychological profiling of a violent crime. *Journal of Interpersonal Crime, 17,* 811–823.

Kocsis, R. N., Irwin, H. J., Hayes, A. F., & Nunn, R. (2000). Expertise in psychological profiling: A comparative assessment. *Journal of Interpersonal Violence, 15,* 311–331.

Leo, R. A. (2008). *Police interrogation and American justice.* Cambridge, MA: Harvard University Press.

Meehl, P. E. (1954). *Clinical versus statistical prediction: A theoretical analysis and a review of the evidence.* Minneapolis: University of Minnesota Press.

Mischel, W. (1968). *Personality and assessment.* New York: Wiley.

Mokros, A., & Alison, L. J. (2002). Is offender profiling possible?: Testing the predicted homology of crime scene actions and background characteristics in a sample of rapists. *Legal and Criminological Psychology, 7,* 25–44.

Muller, D. A. (2000). Criminal profiling: Real science or just wishful thinking? *Homicide Studies, 4,* 234–264.

Pinizzotto, A. J. (1984). Forensic psychology: Criminal personality profiling. *Journal of Police Science and Administration, 12,* 32–39.

Pinizzotto, A. J., & Finkel, N. J. (1990). Criminal personality profiling: An outcome and process study. *Law and Human Behavior, 14,* 215–233.

Rainbow, L. (2008). Taming the beast: The UK approach to the management of behavioral investigative advice. *Journal of Police and Criminal Psychology, 23,* 90–97.

Regina v. Stagg (Colin), unreported, 14 September 1994, Central Criminal Court.

Ressler, R. K., Burgess, A. W., Douglas, J. E., Hartman, C. R., & D'Agostino, R. B. (1986). Sexual killers and their victims: Identifying patterns through crime scene analysis. *Journal of Interpersonal Violence, 1,* 288–308.

Ressler, R. K., & Shachtman, T. (1992). *Whoever fights monsters: My twenty years tracking serial killers for the FBI.* New York: St. Martin's Press.

Sagan, C. (1997). *The demon-haunted world: Science as a candle in the dark.* New York: Random House.

Snook, B., Cullen, R., Bennell, C., Taylor, P. J., & Gendreau, P. (2008). The criminal profiling illusion: What's behind the smoke and mirrors? *Criminal Justice and Behavior, 35,* 1257–1276.

Snook, B., Eastwood, J., Gendreau, P., Goggin, C., & Cullen, R. (2007). Taking stock of criminal profiling: A narrative review and meta-analysis. *Criminal Justice and Behavior, 34,* 437–453.

Snook, B., Taylor, P. J., Gendreau, P., & Bennell, C. (2009). On the need for scientific experimentation in the criminal profiling field: A reply to Dern et al. (2009). *Criminal Justice and Behavior, 10,* 1091–1094.

Torres, A. M., Boccaccini, M. T., & Miller, H. A. (2006). Perceptions of the validity and utility of criminal profiling among forensic psychologists and psychiatrists. *Professional Psychology: Research and Practice, 37,* 51–58.

Trager, J., & Brewster, J. (2001). The effectiveness of psychological profiles. *Journal of Police and Criminal Psychology, 16,* 20–28.

Turvey, B. E. (2012). *Criminal profiling: An introduction to behavioral evidence analysis.* London: Elsevier.

Ullman, S. (2007). A 10-year update of "Review and critique of empirical studies of rape avoidance." *Criminal Justice and Behavior, 34,* 411–429.

Witkin, G. (1996, April 22). How the FBI paints portraits of the nation's most wanted. *U.S. News & World Report, 120*, 32.

Woodhams, J., & Toye, K. (2007). An empirical test of the assumptions of case linkage and offender profiling with serial commercial robberies. *Psychology, Public Policy, and Law, 13*, 59–85.

Woskett, J., Coyle, I. R., & Lincoln, R. (2007). The probity of profiling: Opinions of Australian lawyers on the utility of criminal profiling in court. *Psychiatry, Psychology and Law, 14*, 306–314.

CHAPTER 2

Cognitive Bias
in Legal Decision Making

Steve Charman
Amy Bradfield Douglass
Alexis Mook

Justice systems around the world are fundamentally human endeavors. As such, they rely on human cognitive systems that are subject to bias. Biases in human cognition are interesting from a psychological perspective, but in the world of legal decision making, anything less than a purely objective decision can have profoundly negative ramifications, from the wrongful conviction of innocent people to failure to apprehend guilty people to broadly felt loss of trust in the justice system. The potential for errors in evaluations of forensic evidence has been highlighted by the National Academy of Sciences in its recent report, *Strengthening Forensic Science in the United States: A Path Forward* (National Academy of Sciences, 2009), in which the authors argued that "new doubts about the accuracy of some forensic sciences practices have intensified with the growing number of exonerations resulting from DNA analysis (and the concomitant realization that guilty parties sometimes walk free)" (p. 37).

Many legal decision-making errors result from underlying cognitive biases in the way that people think about, interpret, evaluate, and integrate information. The term "cognitive bias" is quite broad and can refer to an array of psychological phenomena, including hindsight bias, outcome bias, belief perseverance, context biases, anchoring effects, tunnel vision, and more (e.g., see Findley, 2012). For the purposes of this chapter, we are restricting our discussion of cognitive bias to instances in which contextual information inappropriately affects judgments. This type of bias has been approached from a variety of theoretical perspectives and has been labeled using various terms, including "confirmation bias" (e.g., Dror, Kassin, & Kukucka, 2013), "asymmetric skepticism" (e.g., Marksteiner, Ask, Reinhard, & Granhag, 2011), "coherence effects" (e.g., Holyoak & Simon, 1999), "contextual bias" (e.g., Edmond, Tangen, Searston, & Dror, 2015), "observer effects" (Risinger, Saks, Thompson, & Rosenthal, 2002), and "expectancy effects" (Dror et al., 2011). Although these approaches differ somewhat in their specifics, they all share a common underlying theme: that the interpretation of ambiguous information often occurs in a belief-consistent fashion. Therefore, for the purposes of this chapter, we use the term "cognitive bias" to refer to effects of contextual information on (1) the evaluation of evidence and (2) the integration of evidence into an overall assessment regarding a defendant.

Whereas biases of evidence evaluation have received significant attention within a legal decision-making framework (for overviews, see Kassin, Dror, & Kukucka, 2013; Kukucka, 2018; Risinger et al., 2002), biases of evidence integration have received less attention (but see Charman, 2013; Charman, Carbone, Kekessie, & Villalba, 2016). We argue in this chapter, however, that biases of evidence integration are nonetheless important cognitive biases that are driven by similar (but not identical) psychological processes as biases of evidence evaluation. An appreciation of biases of evidence integration expands the scope of cognitive bias to focus on people in the legal system who not only evaluate individual pieces of evidence (e.g., forensic scientists) but who also must *combine* disparate pieces of evidence to reach an overall conclusion about the guilt of a suspect (e.g., detectives, attorneys, jurors). As described later in the chapter, this distinction also suggests different solutions to the problem of cognitive bias, as many of the proposed mechanisms for reducing bias in evidence evaluation will not successfully reduce bias in evidence integration. Accordingly, this chapter is divided into two sections, one for the domain of evidence evaluation and one for the domain of evidence integration.

There are two general points we wish to make about cognitive bias that apply to both evidence evaluation and evidence integration. First, we assume that cognitive bias as discussed here reflects innocent errors rather than malfeasance. Although deliberate fabrication does occur in forensic cases (for one egregious example, see the description of laboratory technician Fred Zain in West Virginia, National Academy of Sciences, 2009), the cognitive bias discussed in this chapter is presumed to be largely inherent in our human cognitive architecture and therefore reflects natural human tendencies. And although motivation to reach a certain conclusion can certainly exacerbate cognitive biases (e.g., Kunda, 1990), these biases can occur even in the absence of explicit motivation. As such, these biases have the potential to affect many different people in the legal system, even absent a vested interest in the outcome of the case.

Second, we argue that a given instance of cognitive bias is not limited to the biased interpretation of a single piece of evidence. Instead, we point out the cumulative nature of cognitive bias: Flawed analyses of evidence influence evaluations of guilt, which, in turn, bias subsequent analyses of new evidence. Cognitive bias, in other words, compounds upon itself, leading to what has been referred to as the "bias snowball effect" (Dror, 2017), "corroboration inflation" (Kassin, 2012), or an "escalation of errors" (Davis & Leo, 2017). In other words, the biased interpretation of one piece of evidence can subsequently bias the interpretation of other pieces of evidence, thus undermining the legal presumption of evidentiary independence (Hasel & Kassin, 2009). Consequently, cognitive bias has significant downstream consequences as it accumulates throughout the legal process. As we discuss, this compounding effect becomes particularly problematic when integrating evidence.

COGNITIVE BIAS IN EVIDENCE EVALUATION

To date, research has focused primarily on how cognitive biases affect the accuracy of the decisions made by forensic examiners (for a review, see Kukucka, 2018). Unfortunately, the narrow focus on forensic examiners may give the erroneous impression that cognitive bias does not affect other parties in the criminal justice system. Moreover, the focus on forensic examiners implies that they are uniquely "biasable" and consequently uniquely responsible for the negative outcomes that result from biased decision making.

In truth, cognitive bias has the potential to affect every step of a criminal investigation or trial. At the earliest stages, a belief in a suspect's guilt might lead a forensic examiner to erroneously interpret evidence (e.g., incorrectly conclude that the suspect's fingerprints match the fingerprints collected from the scene). This conclusion, in turn, might lead a detective to presume a suspect's guilt, thereby biasing his evaluation of other evidence (e.g., a suspect's alibi may be perceived as weaker and a tentative eyewitness identification stronger than they otherwise would have been). Armed with this seemingly incriminating evidence, the now overconfident detective might convince a prosecutor to file charges, in the process inflating her perceptions of the strength of the evidence. The defense attorney reviews the case in its entirety, his biased perceptions of the accumulated evidence distorting his perceptions of a fair plea offer. At trial, a jury's evaluation of the totality of the evidence might become biased by the simple knowledge that the case has made it to trial (e.g., Sommers & Douglass, 2007) or by exposure to pretrial publicity (e.g., Hope, Memon, & McGeorge, 2004).

As demonstrated earlier, the potential for cognitive bias to infiltrate the criminal justice process extends beyond forensic examiners to affect detectives, attorneys, judges, and jurors. Note, however, that the errors resulting from cognitive bias tend to be particularly obvious when made by forensic examiners compared with when made by other people in the legal system for two reasons. First, forensic examiners' judgments are often categorical, making their errors particularly obvious when compared with an objective standard. For instance, many forensic judgments involve the classification of two samples (e.g., fingerprints, tire marks) as coming from the same source, not coming from the same source, or as being inconclusive. This categorical classification means that if a suspect is proven to be innocent, then it is easy to diagnose whether the forensic examiner made a correct or incorrect classification.

However, many of the types of judgments that affect other people in the legal system are not based on classifying two samples as to whether they match or not, making mistakes more difficult to spot. For instance, a detective or a jury may have to decide how much the suspect looks like a witness-generated facial composite of the perpetrator; these judgments of similarity can be biased by their knowledge of other evidence against the suspect (Charman, Gregory, & Carlucci, 2009). But a judgment of similarity is a continuous measure, and because a composite will never exactly resemble a suspect, there is no objective truth as to how similar the two *should* be perceived as being in the absence of external information. Consequently, it is not as immediately obvious that any such judgment was biased. Similar arguments apply to a variety of other judgments that detectives, attorneys, and juries must make, including judgments of the suspect's alibi strength, how much weight to give an informant's testimony, and so forth. The lack of an objective measure of the accuracy of these types of continuous (as opposed to categorical) judgments makes cognitive bias more difficult to detect among detectives, juries, attorneys, judges, and parole board members.

Second, the conclusions of forensic examiners' tests are often explicit, with official reports detailing their conclusions; consequently, if ground truth is later determined (e.g., via DNA testing), the forensic examiners' errors are easy to identify. Contrast this with the previous example of perceptions of similarity between a suspect and a facial composite: No detective ever has to formally document how similar he or she perceives the faces to be. Similarly, no official record may exist regarding the perceived believability of the suspect's alibi or the perceived veracity of an informant, leaving those potential sources of bias unrecognized. Indeed, prosecutors have almost no accountability as to what factors contribute to a plea offer (e.g., Frederick & Stemen, 2012). In contrast, forensic examiners are required to make a record of the outcome of their evidence evaluation. Consequently, the effects of cognitive bias on forensic examiners are simply more visible—but not because they are particularly susceptible to cognitive bias.

Next we review the empirical evidence supporting the effect of cognitive bias on evaluations of ambiguous evidence and on behavior. We end this section with a discussion of moderators of cognitive bias on evaluations of individual pieces of evidence.

Cognitive Bias Affects Evaluations of Ambiguous Evidence

Although often perceived by lay people as purely objective, forensic evidence often involves a significant amount of interpretation when being evaluated. Notably, the evidence itself is often ambiguous (e.g., a latent fingerprint may be smudged, obscuring easy comparisons to the suspect's fingerprint) or the judgment somewhat subjective (e.g., determining whether various characteristics seen on the latent fingerprint match the corresponding characteristics seen on the suspect's fingerprint). This ambiguity and subjectivity can create opportunity for biased evaluations in a direction consistent with the evaluators' expectations, ultimately resulting in judgments that are less than perfectly reliable (e.g., Dror & Rosenthal, 2008; Dror et al., 2011). These expectations can stem from a variety of sources (see Dror, 2017, for a hierarchy of sources of bias) but, once established, can affect the evaluation of evidence. For example, beliefs in a suspect's guilt (compared to no beliefs or beliefs in a suspect's innocence) lead people to be more likely to judge the suspect's handwriting as a match to handwriting left at the scene of a crime (Kukucka & Kassin, 2014), to interpret missing phonemes in audio transcripts as words consistent with the suspect's guilt (Lange, Thomas, Dana, & Dawes, 2011), and to interpret polygraph results as being indicative of the suspect's guilt (Elaad, Ginton, & Ben-Shakhar, 1994). Cognitive bias can also work in the opposite direction: Beliefs of innocence can lead fingerprint experts to judge fingerprint pairs that they had previously judged to be matches as non-matches (Dror & Charlton, 2006; Dror, Charlton, & Péron, 2006). Even DNA mixture interpretation—thought to be a gold standard of forensics—can be biased by extraneous case information (Dror & Hampikian, 2011).

It is not just beliefs regarding the suspect's guilt or innocence that can bias evidence evaluation. Information that implies an appropriate logical conclusion can shape the eventual conclusions that are made. For instance, physical anthropologists examining a skeleton generate conclusions consistent with contextual information regarding age, sex, and ancestry (Nakhaeizadeh, Dror, & Morgan, 2014). Similarly, bloodstain pattern analysts' classification of bloodstain patterns into various types—a task that requires no information other than the bloodstain itself—is influenced by contextual information (Osborne, Taylor, Healey, & Zajac, 2016). Even an evaluator's generic stereotypes about a suspect can produce biased evaluations of evidence. In one experiment, participants read about suspects to a crime who either fit the criminal stereotype for that crime (e.g., a middle-aged white male accused of child molestation) or who did not (e.g., an Asian woman accused of child molestation). After learning case information, including the demographic characteristics of the accused, participants judged whether two fingerprints matched or not. When the white man was accused of child molestation, 51.9% of participants judged the fingerprints to be a match compared with only 27.1% of the time when the Asian woman was accused of the same crime (Smalarz, Madon, Yang, Guyll, & Buck, 2016). Even more broadly, practicing forensic psychologists produce strikingly different recidivism risk scores for sex offenders when they are hired by the defense rather than the prosecution (Murrie, Boccaccini, Guarnera, & Rufino, 2013).

Biased evaluations of single pieces of evidence are clearly problematic. Even more pernicious, these biased evaluations can accumulate over time. For instance, in one of the few studies looking at cognitive bias among experienced law enforcement officers, Charman, Kavetski, and Mueller (2017) presented police officers and detectives with a fictional criminal case (that they were led to believe was an actual case). After presenting them with either eyewitness or DNA evidence that was either incriminating, exonerating, or neutral, police officers were asked to evaluate four pieces of ambiguous evidence: a facial composite of the perpetrator, the suspect's alibi, a handwriting sample, and an informant's testimony. Consistent with research on cognitive bias, the stronger the police officers' initial beliefs in the suspect's guilt were, the more incriminating they interpreted the ambiguous evidence to be. Perhaps even more interestingly, the extent to which those evaluations were biased then predicted how much the participants updated their beliefs in the suspect's guilt. In other words, consistent with the cumulative effects of cognitive bias, police officers' beliefs of guilt led them to evaluate ambiguous evidence as being more incriminating than it actually was, further bolstering their beliefs in the suspect's guilt.

Other studies using criminal investigators have shown that beliefs regarding the suspect's guilt can also affect the perceived reliability of evidence, leading people to become particularly skeptical of evidence that contradicts their belief. For instance, police officers who were encouraged to believe in the guilt of a suspect in a hypothetical case came to view a witness who provided testimony consistent with that belief as being more reliable and more credible and as having had better viewing conditions than a witness who provided testimony inconsistent with that belief—even though the reported witnessing conditions were identical (Ask & Granhag, 2007). A subsequent study showed that this effect was not limited to perceptions of that specific witness in that particular case; police trainees who heard about a witness who provided testimony inconsistent with their belief in the suspect's guilt came to denigrate witness evidence in general, compared with police trainees who heard about a witness who provided testimony consistent with their belief (Ask, Rebelius, & Granhag, 2008).

Cognitive Bias Affects Behavior

Thus far, we have focused on how people's beliefs can affect their interpretation of ambiguous stimuli. But cognitive bias can also be exhibited in another way—by affecting people's behavior. This can result in a self-fulfilling prophecy, in which people's false beliefs lead them to behave in a manner consistent with those beliefs, eliciting the very behavior they expect from others. This is a known problem in forensic interviews involving children, in which "repeated questions and interviews centered on the theme of abuse, conducted by an interviewer who often believes the child was abused, [result in] an allegation [of abuse]" (Bruck & Ceci, 1999, p. 423). In general, interviewers trained to ask guilt-presumptive questions of children regarding another person elicit information consistent with the suggestion when compared with interviewers trained to ask questions that do not presume guilt (Thompson, Clarke-Stewart, & Lepore, 1997).

Further studies demonstrate that this effect occurs even when people are not trained to use suggestive questions and when the interviewees are adults (as opposed to children, who are particularly susceptible to influence; see, e.g., Dent, 1982; Raskin & Yuille, 1989). The effect also occurs with criminal suspects: Kassin, Goldstein, and Savitsky (2003) manipulated mock investigators' assumptions about the likely guilt of a to-be-interviewed suspect. Investigators who believed the suspect was likely to be guilty asked more guilt-presumptive questions compared with those who believed the suspect was likely to be innocent (e.g., "How did you find the key that was hidden behind the VCR?" vs. "Do you know anything about the key that was hidden behind the VCR?"; Kassin et al., 2003, p. 191; see also Colwell, Miller, Lyons, & Miller, 2006). More importantly, this affected suspects' behavior: Suspects who faced a guilt-presumptive interviewer were rated as more defensive when compared with those questioned by an innocence-presumptive interviewer.

One familiar critique of experimental research testing questions of applied relevance is that observed patterns will not replicate in a real-world setting. However, there is substantial evidence that biases in evidence evaluation do occur among actual people in the legal system and in actual real-world cases. Numerous studies have demonstrated cognitive bias among actual forensic examiners, as well as detectives and police, in both lab and field settings (e.g., Ask & Granhag, 2007; Ask, Granhag, & Rebelius, 2011; Charman et al., 2017; Dror & Charlton, 2006; Dror et al., 2006; Dror & Hampikian, 2011; Dror & Rosenthal, 2008). In addition, a recent analysis of DNA exoneration cases has shown that false confessions by innocent people who were erroneously convicted were often accompanied by forensic evidence that erroneously linked the innocent person to the crime and that the confession tended to precede the forensic evidence, suggesting that knowledge of the confession corrupted subsequent evaluations of evidence (Kassin, Bogart, & Kerner, 2012). Finally, ample anecdotal evidence demonstrates the nonindependence of different pieces of evidence: As just one example, Kassin and colleagues (2012) describe the case of John Kogut, in which alibi witnesses withdrew their support when told he (falsely) confessed. This case, among others, provides clear evidence that biases in evidence evaluation are not restricted to artificial laboratory settings.

Limits to Cognitive Bias

There are some moderators of cognitive bias. First, evidence that is unambiguous seems less vulnerable to contextual influence compared with evidence that is ambiguous. In one study, professional forensic examiners made fingerprint match decisions in the context of crime photographs that were either emotional (e.g., injured victims) or unemotional (e.g., stolen objects). When the fingerprint samples were unambiguously matching (or were not), the contextual information was irrelevant to examiners' decisions. However, when it was ambiguous as to whether the samples matched, examiners made significantly more match decisions when the crime scene photos were emotional than when they were unemotional (Dror, Péron, Hind, & Charlton, 2005; see also Dror & Charlton, 2006; Dror et al., 2006; Lange, Thomas, Dana, & Dawes, 2011; Saks, 2009; Stevenage & Bennett, 2017).

Similarly, cognitive bias is also moderated by evidence elasticity—the extent to which a piece of evidence is perceived as allowing for interpretation. Evaluations of DNA evidence, for example, are typically viewed as inelastic because DNA is perceived as a clear-cut, objective source of information that is not subject to interpretation or error. In contrast, evaluations of eyewitness evidence are seen as relatively more elastic because identifications are recognized as being subject to possible error. Consequently, evaluators become particularly skeptical of elastic eyewitness evidence that contradicts their beliefs, but less so of inelastic DNA evidence that contradicts their beliefs (Ask et al., 2008). In practice, this means that beliefs in a suspect's guilt can be appropriately shifted by evidence that is inconsistent with people's beliefs, but generally only if the evidence is inelastic. In one experiment, when confronted with (inelastic) DNA evidence that was inconsistent with guilt (i.e., blood on the suspect was not from the victim), participants appropriately reduced their belief in the suspect's guilt (Ask, Reinhard, Marksteiner, & Granhag, 2011). However, when confronted with (elastic) eyewitness evidence inconsistent with guilt (i.e., the eyewitness did not identify the suspect from a photospread), participants' guilt judgments were unchanged (see also Ask & Alison, 2010; Ask & Granhag, 2007).

There is also evidence that cognitive bias is stronger when people have an initial belief in a suspect's guilt, rather than his or her innocence. For instance, Marksteiner et al. (2011) showed a typical cognitive bias pattern among police trainees: Those led to believe a suspect was guilty rated subsequent evidence as more reliable if it was incriminating rather than exonerating. However, cognitive bias effects failed to materialize among those initially led to believe the suspect was innocent; these people rated subsequent incriminating and exonerating evidence as equally reliable. Similar asymmetric patterns of cognitive bias have been found in other studies as well (e.g., Charman et al., 2016). Although the exact mechanism behind this pattern is not entirely understood, Marksteiner and colleagues (2011) suggest that it may occur because evaluators have a tendency to (1) interpret information in a belief-consistent fashion and (2) want to reach closure in the case. When one has an initial belief of guilt, these motivations work in concert with one another, motivating the evaluator to perceive incriminating evidence as more reliable than exonerating evidence. However, when one has an initial belief of innocence, these motivations are in conflict: The drive toward interpreting evidence in a belief-consistent manner should lead them to evaluate incriminating evidence as being less reliable, but the drive toward reaching closure should lead them to evaluate incriminating evidence as being more reliable. Consequently, these competing forces attenuate standard cognitive bias effects among people who have initial innocence beliefs.

Summary

Research into cognitive bias as it pertains to the evaluation of ambiguous evidence reveals the alarming breadth of the scope of the problem. People in all roles throughout the legal system have been shown to exhibit similar biases, from forensic scientists to police trainees to experienced detectives and police officers to expert witnesses to jurors. Further, the pernicious effects of prior beliefs regarding the suspect's guilt have numerous downstream consequences, biasing the evaluation of evidence (e.g., erroneously categorizing two fingerprints as a match) and the perceived reliability of evidence (e.g., lowering perceived reliability of belief-inconsistent evidence) and leading to behavior changes that elicit the very responses one expects (e.g., asking guilt-presumptive questions that elicit defensiveness, even from innocent suspects). These effects alone have the capacity to pervert justice. But, in fact, we argue that the negative effects of cognitive bias are even broader than this, affecting not only the manner in which single pieces of evidence are evaluated, but also the manner in which multiple pieces of evidence are integrated to reach an ultimate decision regarding the suspect. We now turn to a discussion of these biases of evidence integration.

COGNITIVE BIAS IN EVIDENCE INTEGRATION

Although biases in evidence evaluation, as we have discussed so far, can be exhibited in a variety of ways, they share a common feature: An evaluator's knowledge and/or beliefs created by contextual information can bias the evaluation of a piece of evidence in a belief-consistent manner. But imagine for a moment a legal system in which cognitive bias of the type discussed so far was not an issue: At every step of the way, people in the legal system— police officers, forensic scientists, detectives, attorneys, judges, jurors— are able to correctly ascertain the actual value of each individual piece of evidence, unbiased by context, stereotypes, beliefs, and expectations, and can correctly combine these pieces of evidence into a mathematically correct determination of the likelihood that the suspect was guilty given that evidence. Perhaps we could model this legal system using a Bayesian approach: Given (1) the a priori likelihood that the suspect is guilty and (2) the diagnostic value of each piece of evidence (i.e., the degree to which each piece of evidence incriminates or exonerates the suspect, often referred to as the "likelihood ratio"), Bayesian statistics tell us how confident we can be in the suspect's guilt. For instance, given an a priori likelihood that a suspect is guilty of, say, 40% and two independent pieces of evidence that produce likelihood ratios of 4 and 5[1], respectively, we can calculate the new likelihood that the suspect is guilty as being 93%. That knowledge could then drive all decisions—whether to pursue this suspect or that one, whether to accept a plea deal, whether to convict.

This is, of course, not the legal system we currently have. But thinking about this Bayesian legal system allows us to identify various sources of bias by showing us how actual decision making deviates from this normative standard. For instance, cognitive bias with respect to evidence evaluation occurs when beliefs and contextual information lead to the distortion of the perceived diagnostic value of that evidence. As an example, a forensic scientist who, due to a belief that the suspect is guilty, mistakenly declares with 100% certainty that a smudged latent fingerprint is a match to that of a suspect is overstating the diagnostic value of that piece of evidence; detectives, attorneys, and juries who hear about this determination will therefore naturally overestimate the ultimate likelihood that the suspect is guilty.[2]

A Bayesian world shows us another way in which people's judgments can be biased when determining the likely guilt of a suspect: They may *combine* the various pieces of evidence in a biased fashion, even if the diagnostic value of each individual piece of evidence is correctly determined. This can occur because people are not Bayesians, mathematically deriving probabilities of the various possible outcomes (e.g., guilty or not guilty) on the basis of the diagnostic value of the various pieces of evidence. Instead, people's ultimate conclusions often revolve around, for example, how well they are able to fit the various pieces of evidence into a coherent narrative (Appleby & Kassin, 2016; Pennington & Hastie, 1992). For instance, consider a juror tasked with combining the various pieces of evidence to

---

[1] A likelihood ratio is calculated as the probability of the observed outcome (e.g., a determination that two fingerprints are a match) if the suspect is guilty divided by the probability of the observed outcome if the suspect is innocent. For instance, a likelihood ratio of 4 means that a "match" classification is four times as likely to occur for a guilty person than for an innocent person.

[2] Additionally, if evidence X biases the interpretation of evidence Y in a belief-consistent manner, then evidence X will effectively be counted twice when later determining the suspect's guilt: Once through its direct influence on people's assessments of guilt, and once indirectly via its influence on evidence Y. This not only artificially inflates the perceived diagnostic value of evidence Y, but also undermines the Bayesian assumption of independence of evidence.

reach a verdict. The desire for coherence may lead this juror to base her verdict not strictly on the diagnostic value of the various pieces of evidence, but rather on the extent to which all of the evidence coheres and fits the prosecution's narrative of the crime. A narrative that allows for a coherent assimilation of the evidence may lead that juror to become overly confident in the guilt of the defendant relative to the diagnostic value of that evidence, even if the original diagnostic value of the individual pieces of evidence was appropriately determined. For instance, evidence that fits well into a narrative of premeditated murder (as opposed to a narrative of self-defense) might result in strong beliefs in the suspect's guilt—even though the actual diagnostic value of the individual pieces of evidence leading to that conclusion are correctly ascertained as being only moderately strong. In other words, people's ultimate decisions can be biased even if their assessments of the individual pieces of evidence are not.

This is a bias of *evidence integration* (Charman, 2013). Unlike biases of evidence *evaluation,* which focus specifically on individual pieces of evidence, biases of evidence integration focus more globally on how the final assessment of the suspect's guilt can be biased when combining multiple pieces of individual evidence. We argue that biases of evidence integration, like biases of evidence evaluation, are a form of cognitive bias: When combining evidence, people's knowledge and expectations and initial leanings toward guilt or innocence can lead them to combine evidence in a belief-consistent manner, resulting in erroneous decisions and overconfidence in those final assessments (e.g., Holyoak & Simon, 1999). However, despite a robust body of research examining biases of evidence evaluation, there has been relatively little research examining biases of evidence integration in a forensic context. There are, however, important reasons to focus future research efforts specifically on these biases.

First, biases of evidence integration are relevant at different points in the legal decision-making process than biases of evidence evaluation. For instance, a forensic examiner's job is to evaluate individual pieces of evidence but is *not* to integrate various pieces of evidence to determine the guilt of a suspect. Instead, evidence integration is performed by detectives (when deciding whether to pursue a suspect), prosecutors (when deciding whether to bring charges against a suspect and what level of charges to bring), defense attorneys (when recommending whether defendants accept a plea deal), judges (when deciding how to apply the law to a specific case), jurors (when rendering an ultimate verdict), parole board members (when deciding whether to grant parole), and others. If we lack an understanding of biases in evidence integration, then we overlook numerous potential sources of systematic biases in the legal system. For instance, if attorneys integrate evidence suboptimally, then they may systematically be leading their clients to accept suboptimal plea deals—yet research on how attorneys make plea deal recommendations on the basis of multiple pieces of evidence is scant (for an exception, see Kutateladze, Lawson, & Andiloro, 2015;

for an extensive treatment of plea bargains, see, e.g., Wilford, Shestak, & Wells, Chapter 11, this volume).

Second, a focus on evidence integration reveals novel biases. For instance, mathematically speaking, the order in which evidence is encountered should not affect the final assessment of the suspect's guilt: Whether one encounters fingerprint evidence prior to or following DNA evidence does not change the true likelihood of guilt. Yet some studies have indicated that, contrary to this normative standard, people's ultimate judgments regarding a suspect are more influenced by a piece of evidence if it is presented last rather than first—a bias that can only be uncovered by considering how people integrate evidence (Charman et al., 2016; Dahl, Brimacombe, & Lindsay, 2009; Price & Dahl, 2014).

Third, reducing biases of evidence integration requires different solutions than does reducing biases of evidence evaluation. For instance, one common recommendation to minimize biases of evidence evaluation is to keep the evaluator blind to as much extraneous information as possible, such as other evidence against a suspect or contextual information about the case (e.g., Kassin et al., 2013; Dror et al., 2015). However, this solution does not work for people whose very role is to integrate numerous sources of evidence to assess the guilt of a suspect, including detectives, attorneys, and jurors. To the extent that people show systematic biases of evidence integration, novel solutions are required.

Fourth, studying evidence integration requires a different theoretical framework than does studying evidence evaluation. In general, studies on evidence evaluation have explained their results theoretically using the confirmation bias, in which a belief leads people to evaluate ambiguous information in a belief-consistent manner (Kassin et al., 2013; Nickerson, 1998). This theoretical approach makes sense to the extent that researchers are studying the effect of a belief on the evaluation of a single piece of evidence at a single point in time. But it is rather constrained when studying the more complex process of how multiple pieces of evidence are integrated into an overall assessment that evolves over time. That requires a more sophisticated theoretical approach, one that can handle the integration of numerous, potentially contradictory pieces of information.

Coherence-Based Reasoning

A coherence-based reasoning model provides such a framework (e.g., Holyoak & Simon, 1999; Simon, Krawczyk, Bleicher, & Holyoak, 2008; Simon, Pham, Le, & Holyoak, 2001; Simon, Snow, & Read, 2004).[3] Coherence-

---

[3] An alternative approach, the story model (Pennington & Hastie, 1992, 1993), provides a similar, but not identical, theoretical framework; however, its applicability outside of a jury decision-making context is less clear (see Simon et al., 2004, for a discussion of the differences between the story model and coherence-based reasoning).

based reasoning applies whenever people must derive a conclusion on the basis of the integration of numerous ambiguous, complex, and contradictory inferences. As such, a coherence-based reasoning model is able to provide a theoretical structure for this type of legal decision making. The underlying idea behind this model as it applies to legal decision making is that various propositions (pieces of evidence, beliefs about the suspect, etc.) to be integrated into a final assessment (e.g., a guilty/not guilty verdict) can be represented as a network of nodes that are interconnected via a series of excitatory and inhibitory links that represent positive or negative relationships, respectively, between the nodes. When individuals are making a decision regarding that information (e.g., deciding on the guilt of a suspect), a parallel constraint satisfaction mechanism settles the entire network into a state that maximizes coherence among the elements. Importantly, this coherence-based reasoning model envisions the act of settling the network into a cohesive state as a continually evolving, bidirectional process, as the evaluations of the various pieces of evidence affect the evaluator's emerging beliefs regarding the guilt of the suspect, and the emerging beliefs affect the evaluations of the various pieces of evidence.

For instance, imagine a detective investigating a case who learns about four pieces of evidence regarding a suspect: cell phone records that place the suspect in the vicinity of the crime, an eyewitness identification of the suspect, the suspect's alibi, and a low level of similarity between the suspect and a facial composite of the perpetrator. Because the phone records and the eyewitness identification are both incriminating, they "hang together" and are connected via a positive link; similarly, the alibi and low level of similarity to the composite are both exonerating and are thus connected to each other via a positive link. Finally, the two pieces of incriminating evidence are connected to the two pieces of exonerating evidence via negative links. Thus, as the detective comes to believe in the validity of the phone record evidence, its activation in this cognitive network simultaneously increases the believability of the eyewitness identification and decreases the believability of the alibi and the relevance of the low similarity to the facial composite. Consequently, over time, the network settles into a coherent state, as one subset of mutually reinforcing evidence (in this case, the incriminating evidence) becomes highly activated, suppressing the entire subset of contradictory evidence (in this case, the exonerating evidence). Because confidence in one's final assessment can be thought of as the relative activation of the subset of supportive evidence to the activation of the subset of nonsupportive evidence, this coherence process will tend to result in the detective becoming highly confident in his or her final assessment of the suspect—despite the seemingly contradictory nature of the evidence.

Coherence models undermine assumptions of normative Bayesian reasoning in at least two ways that lead to systematic cognitive biases in the integration of evidence. First, Bayesian reasoning assumes independence between the various pieces of evidence. Certainly, independence between evaluations of evidence is not obtained when knowledge of the outcome of one piece of evidence (e.g., a fingerprint match) biases the evaluation of a subsequent piece of evidence (e.g., a shoe print match), as discussed in the first half of this chapter. Indeed, it is for this reason that researchers have recommended that someone who is evaluating a piece of evidence not be exposed to other pieces of evidence (Dror et al., 2015). But someone who has to integrate evidence must, by definition, be exposed to multiple pieces of evidence; the very fact that the various pieces of evidence are presented within the context of a single case (as opposed to disparate pieces of unrelated evidence) lead the evaluations of that evidence to become correlated with one another, not because of features of the evidence itself, but because of the psychological coherence imposed upon the evaluation of those pieces of evidence (Holyoak & Simon, 1999).

Second, a Bayesian approach assumes that reasoning is unidirectional: The evidence affects the developing conclusion, but the developing conclusion does not affect the evaluation of evidence. A coherence-based approach, in contrast, assumes that reasoning is bidirectional, in which evidence leads to an emerging conclusion and the emerging conclusion feeds back to influence the evaluation of the evidence. Thus, as evidence begins to produce an emerging belief about the suspect's guilt, that belief also then leads supportive evidence to be perceived as stronger and nonsupportive evidence to be perceived as weaker. Indeed, a series of studies have demonstrated this bidirectional effect: Participants who read a series of legal arguments and began to form tentative conclusions about the guilt of a suspect came over time to evaluate those arguments in a manner that was increasingly consistent with the emerging belief (Holyoak & Simon, 1999; Simon et al., 2004). And when participants' verdicts switched following the introduction of additional evidence, the evaluation of the other pieces of evidence also shifted in a belief-consistent manner in order to maintain coherence (Simon et al., 2004). Similarly, mock jurors led to believe in a suspect's guilt came to view the suspect's confession as being more voluntary than did participants led to believe in the suspect's innocence (Greenspan & Scurich, 2016). Other research has also shown that a belief in a suspect's guilt causes changes to the evaluation of evidence, with belief-consistent evidence being perceived as stronger than belief-inconsistent evidence (e.g., Ask & Granhag, 2007; Ask et al., 2008; Marksteiner et al., 2011).

Advantages of a Coherence-Based Theoretical Approach to Cognitive Bias

Note that a coherence-based approach provides a theoretical framework in which to examine not only biases of evidence integration but also biases of evidence evaluation: Extraneous contextual information imposes constraints on the evaluation of subsequently encountered evidence in order to maximize coherence, resulting in confirmation-bias-type effects. But a coherence-based reasoning approach provides a richer theoretical framework in which to interpret these cognitive bias effects, for numerous reasons.

First, in contrast to a confirmation bias approach, in which the belief-consistent biased evaluation occurs at a single point in time, a coherence-based approach underscores the dynamic, continually evolving nature of evidence evaluation. As new evidence is introduced, or is evaluated as being stronger or weaker, it produces cascading coherence effects throughout the cognitive system as evidence is continually reevaluated to maximize coherence among the entire set of propositions. These reevaluations are not necessarily conscious attempts to reevaluate the evidence but seem to occur automatically as new evidence is encountered and processed (Holyoak & Simon, 1999) and occur even in the absence of any explicit motivation to evaluate evidence coherently (e.g., when simply trying to memorize information; Simon et al., 2004). Thus a coherence-based approach emphasizes how the evaluation of evidence can become increasingly and repeatedly biased as other evidence becomes integrated with it.

Second, a coherence-based reasoning approach explains why the evaluation of various pieces of evidence become highly correlated with one another when presented in the context of a single case, but not when presented as independent pieces of evidence in the abstract (Holyoak & Simon, 1999; Greenspan & Scurich, 2016). Because the evaluations of the various pieces of evidence are linked with each other when presented in the context of one case, the evaluation of one type of evidence has direct effects on the evaluation of other types of evidence. A coherence-based approach can also explain the interdependence between seemingly unrelated beliefs: For instance, when participants were led to feel sympathy for a suspect (by telling them her brother had recently been killed by a drunk driver), they tended to become more exculpatory in their evaluation of evidence regarding her supposed academic misconduct (Simon, Stenstrom, & Read, 2015). A computer simulation showed this effect to be consistent with a constraint satisfaction mechanism in which changing one element of the system (i.e., sympathy) resulted in cascading changes to other elements (e.g., evaluation of various pieces of evidence) in order to maximize coherence.

Third, whereas confirmation bias effects of evidence evaluation often come about via exposure to irrelevant contextual information (and, indeed, many of the solutions to this problem rely on keeping evaluators blind as much as possible to such information), coherence-based reasoning demonstrates how biases can arise even in the absence of irrelevant contextual information. As a person learns about different types of evidence, a cognitive network automatically develops, which then constrains the evaluation and integration of subsequent evidence. Furthermore, coherence effects occur before people have settled on a conclusion or have an established belief (e.g., Simon et al., 2001). Consequently, even someone who is a completely blank slate before being exposed to evidence can come to exhibit evidence integration biases as a result of the tendency to enforce coherence on all pieces of evidence. This fact highlights the need for solutions to evidence integration biases above and beyond simply keeping people blind to extraneous information.

Fourth, coherence models are able to account for the very high confidence in verdicts that people often exhibit after being exposed to ambiguous and contradictory information (e.g., Simon & Holyoak, 2002; Simon et al., 2004). If confidence is conceptualized as the difference between the strength of evidence that supports the ultimate conclusion and the strength of evidence against the ultimate conclusion[4], then high confidence following evidence integration will occur as a result of the natural inclination toward coherence, which, due to its constraint satisfaction mechanism, will automatically enhance belief-consistent evidence while simultaneously suppressing belief-inconsistent evidence. This process thus produces a seemingly lopsided preponderance of evidence for one's ultimate decision, despite the often complex and contradictory nature of the evidence, thereby inflating confidence. Not only does the drive toward coherence bias the integration of evidence, then, but it also makes people feel highly confident in their biased integration.

POSSIBLE SOLUTIONS

Given that biases of evidence evaluation and evidence integration are obviously undesirable when making ultimate decisions about the guilt of a suspect, the obvious question is how can we mitigate them? The first step to reducing the problem of cognitive bias in evaluations of individual pieces of evidence is relatively straightforward: Keep evaluators blind, as much as possible, to task-irrelevant contextual information that might bias their judgments (e.g., Kassin et al., 2013; Kukucka, 2018). Forensic examiners, for instance, generally do not need to be exposed to extraneous information such as other evidence against the suspect, his or her prior criminal record, graphic crime scene photos, or other information about the victim and his or her family. To the extent possible, they should generally be kept blind to even basic information about the crime and the suspect's demographic characteristics, because even generic information can trigger stereotypes that influence evidence evaluation (Smalarz et al., 2016).

But even this straightforward recommendation is not without its limitations. Some judgments virtually require the forensic examiner to be exposed to extraneous information. For instance, the determination of whether two voice samples match each other may require the forensic

---

[4]This conceptualization of confidence is similar to the balance-of-evidence hypothesis, which states that confidence in an old or new judgment task is determined by the relative difference in the evidence favoring the judgment and the evidence disfavoring it (e.g., Van Zandt, 2000).

examiner to be exposed to the contents of the discussions that are being analyzed. Nonetheless, at a minimum, information at the examiner's disposal should be limited as much as possible. Managing and limiting the flow of information from the examiner forms the basis of both the linear sequential unmasking technique (Dror et al., 2015) and context management (e.g., Found & Ganas, 2013; Mattijssen, Stoel, & Kerkhoff, 2015), both of which are methods of limiting irrelevant contextual information while still allowing for relevant case information. However, although there have been attempts to formally define "task relevance" (National Commission on Forensic Science, 2015), it has been argued that what constitutes relevant or irrelevant information is not always clear-cut (Langenburg, 2017). Consequently, we recommend that psychologists work closely with forensic examiners to make these determinations.

An alternative method to reduce cognitive bias is to use "evidence lineups." This method involves embedding the suspect's sample (e.g., a fingerprint) among samples from "fillers"—people known to be innocent. The examiner's task is to determine whether the sample from the crime scene matches any of the samples in the lineup and, if so, which one. This can be helpful because even if the examiner believes the suspect to be guilty due to extraneous contextual information, the presence of fillers prevents the examiner from simply declaring the suspect's sample a "match," as it is not known *which* of the samples is from the suspect. An added benefit of evidence lineups is that they allow for a determination of individual error rates for evaluators and general error rates for various forensic techniques (Wells, Wilford, & Smalarz, 2013).[5]

Unfortunately, these recommendations, although suitable to mitigate biases of evidence evaluation, largely fail to remedy biases of evidence integration. For example, take the recommendation to keep examiners blind to task-irrelevant information. Although it is possible to keep a fingerprint examiner blind to, say, the suspect's confession, this strategy is not possible for people whose very role is to integrate multiple pieces of information. Detectives, attorneys, judges, juries, and parole board members *require* a knowledge of multiple pieces of evidence—indeed, it is largely their role to integrate evidence against a suspect in order to reach an ultimate decision. Thus different strategies are required to reduce biases of evidence integration.

---

[5]A critic may be skeptical of the utility of evidence lineups by pointing to the high rates of error observed among eyewitness lineup tasks. However, errors associated with eyewitness lineups are due largely to memory and social influence variables (e.g., see Brewer & Wells, 2011). In contrast, an evidence lineup is not a memory task and, if performed correctly, should not involve social influence; instead, it is a simple matching task and thus not susceptible to most of the same sources of error known to plague eyewitness lineup tasks.

Solutions to cognitive bias as it relates to evidence integration are likely to derive from techniques that disrupt the tendency toward coherence. For instance, having people think of reasons why a claim might be false leads them to be more likely to abandon belief in that claim when it is later discredited (Anderson & Sechler, 1986). Similarly, across multiple domains, having people think about why their judgments might be wrong can reduce overconfidence and increase the accuracy of one's predictions (e.g., Brewer, Keast, & Rishworth, 2002; Hoch, 1985). Most relevant to current purposes, some research has shown that getting people to consider why the opposite side (in a criminal trial) has a better case reduced the drive toward coherence among all of the evidence (Krawczyk, Simon, & Holyoak, 2003, as reported in Simon et al. [2004]). In contrast, instructions to simply not be biased failed to appreciably decrease coherence effects. This suggests that training or instructions that get people to consider alternative interpretations of evidence (or to consider alternative theories of a case) may reduce coherence effects, allowing for a less biased interpretation of evidence. However, this finding has not always replicated (D. Simon, personal communication, 2017), and more research is needed to test its efficacy.

A second strategy to reduce cognitive bias may be to activate specific goals among the people who are integrating evidence. For instance, police trainees who were exposed to claims (ostensibly from other police investigators) that good investigators value the thorough consideration of evidence, as opposed to the efficient processing of information, showed more open-mindedness to potentially important evidence regarding the guilt of a suspect (Ask, Granhag, & Rebelius, 2011). If part of the reason people engage in coherence-based reasoning is a desire to arrive at an ultimate decision quickly, then getting them to delay that decision by activating thoroughness goals may reduce cognitive bias. However, other research has shown that directly instructing people to delay making a decision as they review evidence may not mitigate these biases (Simon et al., 2001), suggesting that the effectiveness of such a manipulation may depend on whether the person is directly instructed to be thorough or whether that goal is simply activated. However, the methodologies of these two studies were quite different, and more research is needed on this possible solution.

A third related potential solution to cognitive bias is to increase the depth of people's cognitive processing while integrating evidence. For instance, Hernandez and Preston (2013) presented mock jurors with details of a criminal case after presenting them with information regarding either the suspect's positive or negative character. Under normal conditions, this character information biased participants, such that they were more likely to find the suspect guilty if presented with the negative, rather than positive, character information, consistent with coherence effects. However, this bias disappeared under conditions that required participants to expend extra cognitive effort while thinking about the case—but only if they had ample time and cognitive resources. This suggests that interventions that increase the cognitive processing ability of detectives, jurors, and others may reduce their tendencies toward coherence, and thus cognitive bias. How exactly to accomplish this in real-world settings is, again, in need of more research.

CONCLUSION

As the preceding pages have outlined, there is a high potential for cognitive bias to produce profoundly unfair outcomes in the administration of justice. The potential for bias exists at all levels of the justice system, from police officers and fingerprint examiners to prosecutors and judges. These biases affect both evaluations of individual pieces of evidence and evaluations that emerge as individual pieces of evidence are integrated into a coherent assessment. We suggest a cognitive coherence framework that may provide useful guidance for researchers interested in understanding and combating cognitive bias in a forensic context. In addition to explaining cognitive bias effects of evidence integration, this framework underscores that solutions to the problem of cognitive bias must extend beyond isolating evaluators from contextual information. Through the application of this framework, we hope that future research on cognitive bias will contribute meaningfully to scientists' efforts to make justice systems more fair, accurate, and efficient.

ACKNOWLEDGMENTS

We thank the Bates College Summer Research Apprenticeship and Paola Herrera for assistance in preparing this chapter. Preparation of this chapter was also supported by National Science Foundation Grant No. SES-1627433 to Amy Bradfield Douglass and Neil Brewer. Any opinions, findings, and conclusions or recommendations expressed in this material are those of the authors and do not necessarily reflect the views of the National Science Foundation.

REFERENCES

Anderson, C. A., & Sechler, E. S. (1986). Effects of explanation and counterexplanation on the development and use of social theories. *Journal of Personality and Social Psychology, 50*, 24–34.

Appleby, S. C., & Kassin, S. M. (2016). When self-report trumps science: Effects of confessions, DNA, and prosecutorial theories on perceptions of guilt. *Psychology, Public Policy, and Law, 22*, 127–140.

Ask, K., & Alison, L. (2010). Investigators' decision making. In P. A. Granhag

(Ed.), *Forensic psychology in context: Nordic and international perspectives* (pp. 35–55). Cullompton, UK: Willan.

Ask, K., & Granhag, P. A. (2007). Motivational bias in criminal investigators' judgments of witness reliability. *Journal of Applied Social Psychology, 37,* 561–591.

Ask, K., Granhag, P. A., & Rebelius, A. (2011). Investigators under influence: How social norms activate goal-directed processing of criminal evidence. *Applied Cognitive Psychology, 25,* 548–553.

Ask, K., Rebelius, A., & Granhag, P. A. (2008). The "elasticity" of criminal evidence: A moderator of investigator bias. *Applied Cognitive Psychology, 22,* 1245–1259.

Ask, K., Reinhard, M. A., Marksteiner, T., & Granhag, P. A. (2011). Elasticity in evaluations of criminal evidence: Exploring the role of cognitive dissonance. *Legal and Criminological Psychology, 16,* 289–306.

Brewer, N., Keast, A., & Rishworth, A. (2002). The confidence–accuracy relationship in eyewitness identification: The effects of reflection and disconfirmation on correlation and calibration. *Journal of Experimental Psychology: Applied, 8,* 46–58.

Brewer, N., & Wells, G. L. (2011). Eyewitness identification. *Current Directions in Psychological Science, 20,* 24–27.

Bruck, M., & Ceci, S. J. (1999). The suggestibility of children's memory. *Annual Review of Psychology, 50,* 419–439.

Charman, S. D. (2013). The forensic confirmation bias: A problem of evidence integration, not just evidence evaluation. *Journal of Applied Research in Memory and Cognition, 2,* 56–58.

Charman, S. D., Carbone, J., Kekessie, S., & Villalba, D. K. (2016). Evidence evaluation and evidence integration in legal decision making: Order of evidence presentation as a moderator of context effects. *Applied Cognitive Psychology, 30,* 214–225.

Charman, S. D., Gregory, A. H., & Carlucci, M. (2009). Exploring the diagnostic utility of facial composites: Beliefs of guilt can bias perceived similarity between composite and suspect. *Journal of Experimental Psychology: Applied, 15,* 76–90.

Charman, S. D., Kavetski, M., & Mueller, D. H. (2017). Cognitive bias in the legal system: Police officers evaluate ambiguous evidence in a belief-consistent manner. *Journal of Applied Research in Memory and Cognition, 6,* 193–202.

Colwell, L. H., Miller, H. A., Lyons, P. M., Jr., & Miller, R. S. (2006). The training of law enforcement officers in detecting deception: A survey of current practices and suggestions for improving accuracy. *Police Quarterly, 9,* 275–290.

Dahl, L. C., Brimacombe, C. A., & Lindsay, D. S. (2009). Investigating investigators: How presentation order influences participant-investigators' interpretations of eyewitness identification and alibi evidence. *Law and Human Behavior, 33,* 368–380.

Davis, D., & Leo, R. A. (2017). A damning cascade of investigative errors: Flaws in homicide investigation in the USA. In F. Brookman, E. R. Macguire, & M. Maguire (Eds.), *The handbook of homicide* (pp. 578–598). West Sussex, UK: Wiley.

Dent, H. R. (1982). The effects of interviewing strategies on the results of interviews with child witness. In A. Trankell (Ed.), *Reconstructing the past* (pp. 279–298). Deventer, the Netherlands: Kluwer.

Dror, I., & Rosenthal, R. (2008). Meta-analytically quantifying the reliability and biasability of forensic experts. *Journal of Forensic Sciences, 53*, 900–903.

Dror, I. E. (2017). Human expert performance in forensic decision making: Seven different sources of bias. *Australian Journal of Forensic Sciences, 49*, 541–547.

Dror, I. E., Champod, C., Langenburg, G., Charlton, D., Hunt, H., & Rosenthal, R. (2011). Cognitive issues in fingerprint analysis: Inter- and intra-expert consistency and the effect of a "target" comparison. *Forensic Science International, 208*, 10–17.

Dror, I. E., & Charlton, D. (2006). Why experts make errors. *Journal of Forensic Identification, 56*, 600–616.

Dror, I. E., Charlton, D., & Péron, A. E. (2006). Contextual information renders experts vulnerable to making erroneous identifications. *Forensic Science International, 156*, 74–78.

Dror, I. E., & Hampikian, G. (2011). Subjectivity and bias in forensic DNA mixture interpretation. *Science and Justice: Journal of the Forensic Science Society, 51*, 204–208.

Dror, I. E., Kassin, S. M., & Kukucka, J. (2013). New application of psychology to law: Improving forensic evidence and expert witness contributions. *Journal of Applied Research in Memory and Cognition, 2*, 78–81.

Dror, I. E., Péron, A. E., Hind, S., & Charlton, D. (2005). When emotions get the better of us: The effect of contextual top-down processing on matching fingerprints. *Applied Cognitive Psychology, 19*, 799–809.

Dror, I. E., Thompson, W. C., Meissner, C. A., Kornfield, I., Krane, D., Saks, M., et al. (2015). Letter to the editor" Context Management Toolbox: A linear sequential unmasking (LSU) approach for minimizing cognitive bias in forensic decision making. *Journal of Forensic Sciences, 60*, 1111—1112.

Edmond, G., Tangen, J. M., Searston, R. A., & Dror, I. E. (2015). Contextual bias and cross-contamination in the forensic sciences: The corrosive implications for investigations, plea bargains, trials and appeals. *Law, Probability and Risk, 14*, 1–25.

Elaad, E., Ginton, A., & Ben-Shakhar, G. (1994). The effects of prior expectations and outcome knowledge on polygraph examiners' decisions. *Journal of Behavioral Decision Making, 7*, 279–292.

Findley, K. A. (2012). Tunnel vision. In B. L. Cutler (Ed.), *Conviction of the innocent: Lessons from psychological research* (pp. 303–323). Washington, DC: American Psychological Association.

Found, B., & Ganas, J. (2013). The management of domain irrelevant context information in forensic handwriting examination casework. *Science and Justice, 53*, 154–158.

Frederick, B., & Stemen, D. (2012).*The anatomy of discretion: An analysis of prosecutorial decision making.* New York: Vera Institute of Justice.

Greenspan, R., & Scurich, N. (2016). The interdependence of perceived confession voluntariness and case evidence. *Law and Human Behavior, 40*, 650–659.

Hasel, L. E., & Kassin, S. M. (2009). On the presumption of evidentiary independence: Can confessions corrupt eyewitness identifications? *Psychological Science, 20*, 122–126.

Hernandez, I., & Preston, J. L. (2013). Disfluency disrupts the confirmation bias. *Journal of Experimental Social Psychology, 49*, 178–182.

Hoch, S. J. (1985). Counterfactual reasoning and accuracy in predicting personal events. *Journal of Experimental Psychology: Learning, Memory, and Cognition, 11*, 719–731.

Holyoak, K. J., & Simon, D. (1999). Bidirectional reasoning in decision making by constraint satisfaction. *Journal of Experimental Psychology: General, 128*, 3–31.

Hope, L., Memon, A., & McGeorge, P. (2004). Understanding pretrial publicity: Predecisional distortion of evidence by mock jurors. *Journal of Experimental Psychology: Applied, 10*, 111–119.

Kassin, S. M. (2012). Why confessions trump innocence. *American Psychologist, 67*, 431–445.

Kassin, S. M., Bogart, D., & Kerner, J. (2012). Confessions that corrupt: Evidence from the DNA exoneration case files. *Psychological Science, 23*, 41–45.

Kassin, S. M., Dror, I. E., & Kukucka, J. (2013). The forensic confirmation bias: Problems, perspectives, and proposed solutions. *Journal of Applied Research in Memory and Cognition, 2*, 42–52.

Kassin, S. M., Goldstein, C. C., & Savitsky, K. (2003). Behavioral confirmation in the interrogation room: On the dangers of presuming guilt. *Law and Human Behavior, 27*, 187–203.

Krawczyk, D. C., Simon, D., & Holyoak, K. J. (2003). *Information processing and the emergence of cognitive coherence in decision making*. Unpublished doctoral dissertation.

Kukucka, J. (2018). Confirmation bias in the forensic sciences: Causes, consequences, and countermeasures. In W. J. Koen & C. M. Bowers (Eds.), *Forensic science reform: The psychology and sociology of wrongful convictions* (pp. 215–245). New York: Elsevier.

Kukucka, J., & Kassin, S. M. (2014). Do confessions taint perceptions of handwriting evidence?: An empirical test of the forensic confirmation bias. *Law and Human Behavior, 38*, 256–270.

Kunda, Z. (1990). The case for motivated reasoning. *Psychological Bulletin, 108*, 480–498.

Kutateladze, B. L., Lawson, V. Z., & Andiloro, N. R. (2015). Does evidence really matter?: An exploratory analysis of the role of evidence in plea bargaining in felony drug cases. *Law and Human Behavior, 39*, 431.

Lange, N. D., Thomas, R. P., Dana, J., & Dawes, R. M. (2011). Contextual biases in the interpretation of auditory evidence. *Law and Human Behavior, 35*, 178–187.

Langenburg, G. (2017). Addressing potential observer effects in forensic science: A perspective from a forensic scientist who uses linear sequential unmasking techniques. *Australian Journal of Forensic Sciences, 49*, 549–563.

Marksteiner, T., Ask, K., Reinhard, M. A., & Granhag, P. A. (2011). Asymmetrical scepticism towards criminal evidence: The role of goal- and belief-consistency. *Applied Cognitive Psychology, 25*, 541–547.

Mattijssen, E. J., Stoel, R. D., & Kerkhoff, W. (2015). Minimizing contextual bias in forensic firearms examinations. In A. Jamieson & A. Moenssens (Eds.), *Wiley encyclopedia of forensic science* (pp. 1–7). New York: Wiley.

Murrie, D. C., Boccaccini, M. T., Guarnera, L. A., & Rufino, K. A. (2013). Are forensic experts biased by the side that retained them? *Psychological Science, 24,* 1889–1897.

Nakhaeizadeh, S., Dror, I. E., & Morgan, R. M. (2014). Cognitive bias in forensic anthropology: Visual assessment of skeletal remains is susceptible to confirmation bias. *Science and Justice, 54,* 208–214.

National Academy of Sciences. (2009). *Strengthening forensic science in the United States: A path forward.* Washington, DC: National Academies Press.

National Commission on Forensic Science. (2015). Ensuring that forensic analysis is based upon task-relevant information. Available at *www.justice.gov/archives/ncfs/file/795286/download.*

Nickerson, R. S. (1998). Confirmation bias: A ubiquitous phenomenon in many guises. *Review of General Psychology, 2,* 175–220.

Osborne, N. K., Taylor, M. C., Healey, M., & Zajac, R. (2016). Bloodstain pattern classification: Accuracy, effect of contextual information and the role of analyst characteristics. *Science and Justice, 56,* 123–128.

Pennington, N., & Hastie, R. (1992). Explaining the evidence: Tests of the Story Model for juror decision making. *Journal of Personality and Social Psychology, 62,* 189–206.

Pennington, N., & Hastie, R. (1993). The story model for juror decision making. In R. Hastie (Ed.), *Inside the juror: The psychology of juror decision making* (pp. 192–221). New York: Cambridge University Press.

Price, H. L., & Dahl, L. C. (2014). Order and strength matter for evaluation of alibi and eyewitness evidence. *Applied Cognitive Psychology, 28,* 143–150.

Raskin, D., & Yuille, J. (1989). Problems in evaluating interviews of children in sexual abuse cases. In S. J. Ceci, M. P. Toglia, & D. F. Ross (Eds.), *Adults' perceptions of children's testimony* (pp. 184–207). New York: Springer-Verlag.

Risinger, D. M., Saks, M. J., Thompson, W. C., & Rosenthal, R. (2002). The Daubert/Kumho implications of observer effects in forensic science: Hidden problems of expectation and suggestion. *California Law Review, 90,* 1–56.

Saks, M. J. (2009). Judging admissibility. *Journal of Corporation Law, 35,* 135–157.

Simon, D., & Holyoak, K. J. (2002). Structural dynamics of cognition: From consistency theories to constraint satisfaction. *Personality and Social Psychology Review, 6,* 283–294.

Simon, D., Krawczyk, D. C., Bleicher, A., & Holyoak, K. J. (2008). The transience of constructed preferences. *Journal of Behavioral Decision Making, 21,* 1–14.

Simon, D., Pham, L. B., Le, Q. A., & Holyoak, K. J. (2001). The emergence of coherence over the course of decision making. *Journal of Experimental Psychology: Learning, Memory, and Cognition, 27,* 1250–1260.

Simon, D., Snow, C. J., & Read, S. J. (2004). The redux of cognitive consistency theories: Evidence judgments by constraint satisfaction. *Journal of Personality and Social Psychology, 86,* 814–837.

Simon, D., Stenstrom, D. M., & Read, S. J. (2015). The coherence effect: Blending cold and hot cognitions. *Journal of Personality and Social Psychology, 109,* 369–394.

Smalarz, L., Madon, S., Yang, Y., Guyll, M., & Buck, S. (2016). The perfect match: Do criminal stereotypes bias forensic evidence analysis? *Law and Human Behavior, 40,* 420–429.

Sommers, S. R., & Douglass, A. B. (2007). Context matters: Alibi strength varies according to evaluator perspective. *Legal and Criminological Psychology, 12,* 41–54.

Stevenage, S. V., & Bennett, A. (2017). A biased opinion: Demonstration of cognitive bias on a fingerprint matching task through knowledge of DNA test results. *Forensic Science International, 276,* 93–106.

Thompson, W. C., Clarke-Stewart, K. A., & Lepore, S. (1997) What did the janitor do?: Suggestive interviewing and the accuracy of children's accounts. *Law and Human Behavior, 21,* 405–426.

Van Zandt T. (2000). ROC curves and confidence judgments in recognition memory. *Journal of Experimental Psychology: Learning, Memory, and Cognition, 26,* 582–600.

Wells, G. L., Wilford, M., & Smalarz, L. (2013). Forensic science testing: The forensic filler-control method for controlling contextual bias, estimating error rates, and calibrating analysts' reports. *Journal of Applied Research in Memory and Cognition, 2,* 53–55.

CHAPTER 3

Interrogations and Confessions

Stephanie Madon
Curt More
Ryan Ditchfield

It is widely believed that innocent people would not jeopardize their self-interests by confessing to a crime they did not commit. Contrary to this belief, however, there have been more than 360 DNA exonerations in the U.S. to date, approximately 28% of which involved a false confession as a contributing factor (Innocence Project, 2019). Wrongful convictions supported by false confessions raise concerns about the protection of civil liberties and the integrity of the criminal justice system. This chapter draws on a long-standing and widely accepted body of literature to present the science behind police-induced false confessions—that is, confessions that are elicited by police via interrogation processes (Kassin & Wrightsman, 1985). This literature is grounded in case studies of proven false confessions, basic research documenting core principles of human behavior, and applied experimental and nonexperimental research relevant to the situational factors and psychological processes that increase the risk that a suspect, though factually innocent, will confess to a crime. The chapter begins with an overview of police interrogation practices in North America, followed by a discussion and review of the confession literature. The chapter concludes with recommendations for reform and directions for future research.

POLICE INTERROGATION

Historical analyses of police interrogation in the U.S. reveal that, from the middle of the 19th through the early 20th centuries, police practices were firmly rooted in third-degree tactics (Leo, 2008). These tactics, which amounted to torture, included severe physical abuse, physical isolation, excessively long detainment and questioning, deprivation of basic human needs, and threats of death. In response to waning tolerance for police brutality, the U.S. Senate created the Wickersham Commission (1931) to investigate the problem (see Dennis & Erdos, 2005, for similar commissions elsewhere). The Commission's ensuing report shone a spotlight on law enforcement's regular use of third-degree tactics to extract confessions and, in doing so, ignited a movement to professionalize policing (Davis & Leo, 2014).

A hallmark of this movement was the introduction of interrogation training manuals that promoted psychological manipulation and coercion as a substitute for third-degree tactics. Although the contemporary scientific literature has rightly criticized these psychologically based tactics for their potential to elicit false confessions, at the time of their introduction they represented a progressive shift in the way that police approached custodial interrogation (Skolnick, 1982). Even so, the manuals did little to change the underlying structure of police interrogation. As Leo (2008) points out, modern-day interrogation practices continue to operate on a presumption of guilt, and the principal goal continues to be the elicitation of a confession.

The Reid Technique

The most popular of the early interrogation training manuals was *Lie Detection and Criminal Interrogation* (Inbau, 1942). This manual, like its modern-day successor, *Criminal Interrogation and Confessions* (Inbau, Reid, Buckley, & Jayne, 2013), claimed to weed out the innocent and extract a confession from the guilty through a systematic process of questioning. The modern-day Reid technique of interviewing and interrogation purportedly achieves these aims through a sequence of three phases (Inbau et al., 2013). In the first phase, *fact analysis,* police identify a suspect and consider the facts of the case (e.g., motive, opportunity). In the second phase, the *behavioral analysis interview,* police conduct a nonaccusatory interview that is designed to build rapport, obtain background information, and, most importantly, ascertain whether a suspect is being truthful or deceptive. In the third phase, the *Reid technique of interrogation,* police conduct a nine-step accusatorial interrogation in order to elicit a confession. As we discuss next, these latter two phases have been the subject of much debate and scientific inquiry.

Behavioral Analysis Interview

The primary purpose of the behavioral analysis interview is to ascertain whether a suspect is being truthful or deceptive. Suspects who are perceived as truthful are presumed innocent, whereas suspects who are perceived as deceptive are presumed guilty (Inbau et al., 2013). John E. Reid and Associates, a company that provides interrogation training seminars, has made bold assertions about the degree to which police can accurately detect deception using this interview technique. The most recent edition of the Reid training manual claims an accuracy rate of 83% for deceptive suspects and 86% for truthful suspects (Inbau et al., 2013). However, this claim is based on a single study that lacked scientific rigor (Horvath, Jayne, & Buckley, 1994): The sample involved only four experts. These experts were all employees of John E. Reid and Associates. And, most troubling of all, because the study used videotapes that were acquired from actual field interviews, truth and deception could not be definitively determined. By contrast, scientifically rigorous deception detection studies, characterized by large, unbiased samples and established ground truth, typically achieve an accuracy rate that only slightly surpasses chance levels (e.g., Bond & DePaulo, 2006; DePaulo et al., 2003).

Some have argued that the literature's tendency to find near chance levels of accuracy reflect limitations of the research rather than limitations of people's deception detection abilities (e.g., Levine, Blair, & Clare, 2014; O'Sullivan & Ekman, 2004; O'Sullivan, Frank, Hurley, & Tiwana, 2009). Although such an argument is provocative, it falls short when one considers the remarkable stability in estimates of people's deception detection abilities across hundreds of studies using highly variable methods (see Bond & DePaulo, 2006, for a review). Moreover, the handful of studies that have found high accuracy rates (e.g., Horvath et al., 1994; Levine et al., 2014; O'Sullivan & Ekman, 2004) had serious methodological weaknesses similar to those described above (e.g., no ground truth, simple lie detection tasks, absence of a control group, and inappropriate sampling techniques; see Vrij, Meissner, & Kassin, 2015).

There are several reasons why people are poor at distinguishing truth from lies. First, police training manuals often teach police to rely on nonverbal and paraverbal cues that are not diagnostic of truth or deception. The behavioral analysis interview, for instance, trains police to infer truthfulness from suspects who occasionally lean forward, but to infer deception from suspects who slouch (Inbau et al., 2013). Relying on invalid cues to deception will frequently result in erroneous judgments of truth and deception.

Second, although valid cues to deception have been scientifically documented, the differences that separate truth tellers from liars are small. For example, a meta-analysis that examined 158 behaviors across 125 studies found that less than one-third of the behaviors studied differentiated truth tellers from liars, on average (DePaulo et al., 2003). The fact that truth tellers and liars act more alike than different makes it difficult to detect valid cues to deception due to the presence of considerable noise.

Finally, inferring truth and deception on the basis of a known group difference will invariably lead to erroneous judgments (Robinson, 1950). To illustrate, the meta-analysis referenced above found that liars exhibited more signs of anxiety than did truth tellers (DePaulo et al., 2003). Because this is a group difference, however, it cannot be interpreted to mean that *all* liars exhibited more signs of anxiety than *all* truth tellers did. No doubt, some liars exhibited fewer signs of anxiety than did some truth tellers. Put differently, appearing anxious does not make one a liar, and assuming it does will result in some anxious, but innocent, suspects being misclassified as guilty. Because the behavioral analysis interview is designed to identify deceptiveness among *individual* suspects, it is susceptible to this kind of error. In fact, the law of probabilities ensures that the behavioral analysis interview will result in the misclassification of innocent suspects even when it relies on valid cues to deception, such as perceived anxiety.

The Reid Technique of Interrogation

The Reid technique of interrogation is an accusatorial process of questioning that is specifically designed to break down suspects' resistance to self-incrimination. According to Inbau et al. (2013), only suspects whose guilt is "definite or reasonably certain" are subjected to this interrogation procedure (p. 201). However, such a claim is duplicitous and misleading because perception is not veridical (Bruner, 1957) and, in the case of the Reid technique, is derived from a highly subjective and scientifically invalid process of deception detection. The inability of the Reid technique to reliably shield innocent suspects from its interrogation tactics raises serious concerns about the credibility of confession evidence.

Indeed, decades of psychological research confirm that the Reid technique of interrogation constitutes a powerful process of psychological manipulation that encourages suspects to act against their own self-interests (Davis & O'Donohue, 2004). Proponents of the Reid technique claim that only the guilty are susceptible to these manipulative processes (Inbau et al., 2013). However, a large body of laboratory and field research coupled with proven false confession cases converge on the conclusion that the Reid technique of interrogation is insufficiently precise in its effects. The technique ensnares innocent suspects and then, through a reliance on social influence tactics, pressures them to confess. These tactics are implemented through an interrogation procedure involving nine steps (Inbau et al., 2013) carried out in isolation to increase suspects' feelings of anxiety, hopelessness, despair, and ultimately their motivation to escape from the situation (Kassin & Gudjonsson, 2004).

To briefly summarize, during the early phases of an interrogation, police use a confrontational approach to questioning. They make strong accusations of guilt, present suspects with real, exaggerated, or fabricated evidence, and refuse to accept suspects' denials. During the later phases of an interrogation, police try to convince suspects that a confession is in their best interests by minimizing their legal and moral culpability. They rationalize suspects' behavior, portray their motives in sympathetic terms, and downplay the seriousness of the alleged crime and its consequences. When police perceive that suspects' resolve to defend their innocence has weakened, they present a forced-choice alternative question that juxtaposes a repulsive and callous interpretation of their motives to one that is face-saving and morally palatable by comparison but, critically, still incriminating (e.g., "What are you, some kind of sex pervert that preys on young children, or was this a one-time thing because you were curious?"). Following an admission, police press the suspect for details to corroborate the confession's credibility and then facilitate conversion of the verbal confession into a written statement. Though one might assume that innocent suspects would be unable to generate convincing confessions, a content analysis of 20 proven false confessions showed them to be highly contextualized (Appleby, Hasel, & Kassin, 2013). The confessions included information about the false confessors' motives, details of the crimes, specifics about the victims, references to eyewitnesses or accomplices, expressions of remorse, and even apologies. These findings show that richly detailed confessions cannot be taken as prima facie evidence of guilt.

LABORATORY ANALOGUES OF POLICE INTERROGATION

Experimental research is critically important to the advancement of science. Recognizing this, researchers have developed a number of experimental paradigms that capture core elements of police interrogation within laboratory settings. These paradigms have been instrumental in elucidating the situational factors and psychological processes that operate to influence suspects' confession decisions. It is only appropriate, therefore, that we call attention to them in this chapter. We focus on four experimental paradigms that stand out as laboratory analogues of police interrogation in criminal settings.

The Mock-Crime Paradigm (Barland & Raskin, 1975)

The mock-crime paradigm experimentally manipulates guilt and innocence by randomly assigning participants to either commit a mock crime (e.g., shoplifting) or a comparable innocent behavior (e.g., browsing among merchandise). All participants expect to be interrogated about their possible involvement in the crime and are usually instructed to deny guilt no matter the circumstances. Sometimes participants are given incentives to convince the interrogator of their innocence. The mock-crime paradigm has been used to examine the effect of guilt status on a variety of suspect-relevant (e.g., Miranda comprehension and waivers) and interrogator-relevant (e.g., detection deception, use of interrogation tactics) outcomes (e.g., Gillard, Rogers, Kelsey, & Robinson, 2014; Kassin, Goldstein, & Savitsky, 2003;

Kassin, Kukucka, Lawson, & DeCarlo, 2014; Rogers, Gillard, Wooley, & Fiduccia, 2011).

A key strength of this paradigm is that it establishes ground truth and involves both guilty and innocent participants. It also allows for the use of interrogation tactics that closely resemble real-world interrogation practices without raising significant ethical concerns. However, its experimental realism and ecological validity are limited because all participants are aware that no crime was committed and the stakes for confessing are low. The paradigm is also not suitable to examining factors that influence suspects' decisions to confess or deny guilt.

The Alt-Key Paradigm (Kassin & Kiechel, 1996)

In the standard Alt-key paradigm, each participant works on a typing task with a confederate who poses as another participant in the study. The task involves the confederate reciting a series of letters to the participant who types them on a computer keyboard. Prior to starting the typing task, an experimenter cautions the participant against hitting the Alt-key on grounds that doing so will cause the computer to crash and data to be lost. About 1 minute into the typing task, the computer malfunctions, and the experimenter, feigning distress, accuses the participant of hitting the Alt-key. In reality, the malfunction is programmed, and all participants are innocent.

The Alt-key paradigm can measure *compliance* by assessing whether participants sign a handwritten confession, *internalization* by determining whether participants actually believe they hit the Alt-key, and *confabulation* by assessing whether participants generate false memories of the event. The procedures can also be modified to examine how police interrogation tactics (e.g., false evidence) and internal states (e.g., doubt) affect these outcomes. Despite these strengths, the Alt-key paradigm cannot examine true confessions. This limitation has important implications because progress toward improving the diagnosticity of police interrogation tactics requires an understanding of the processes that lead both innocent and guilty suspects to confess.

The Cheating Paradigm (Russano, Meissner, Narchet, & Kassin, 2005)

In the typical cheating paradigm, each participant solves logic problems with a confederate who poses as another participant in the study. Prior to beginning the logic problems, an experimenter instructs the pair to work independently on some problems and jointly on others. In the guilty condition, the confederate persuades the participant to share answers on one of the problems the pair had been instructed to solve individually, thereby making the participant guilty of cheating. In the innocent condition, the confederate and participant follow the experimenter's instructions correctly, thereby making the participant innocent of cheating. Shortly after, the experimenter separates the pair, accuses the participant of cheating on one of the individual logic problems, and pressures the participant to sign a written confession.

The cheating paradigm has several notable strengths. It establishes ground truth and includes both guilty and innocent participants. Cheating is also a relatively serious offense in an academic context and represents an intentional act. In addition, the procedures can be modified to examine outcomes other than a confession (e.g., physiological activity, suggestibility, attention, memory, Miranda comprehension and waivers). Because of the paradigm's experimental realism, however, participants do experience a moderate degree of distress (Guyll et al., 2013). To protect participants' welfare, researchers may consider establishing eligibility criteria to limit the participation of vulnerable populations, monitoring participants for signs of distress, and thoroughly debriefing participants about the procedures and the necessity of the deception. Despite the paradigm's potential risks, research has shown that college students reported no enduring, ill effects from participating in the cheating paradigm (Russano et al., 2005).

The Repetitive-Question Paradigm (Madon, Guyll, Scherr, Greathouse, & Wells, 2012)

In the repetitive-question paradigm, all participants are interviewed about 20 criminal and unethical behaviors and instructed to deny or admit to each one. Although both denials and admissions are punished, the timing and nature of the punishment differs. Via random assignment, some participants answer a set of repetitive questions each and every time they deny a behavior, and risk meeting with a police officer in several weeks to discuss their interview responses in more detail if they tend to admit to the behaviors. Other participants answer the repetitive questions for each admission and risk meeting with the police officer if they tend to deny the behaviors. Sometimes, a control condition is included in which admissions and denials are not associated with any consequences. The rate of admissions to the 20 behaviors constitutes the primary dependent variable, though the paradigm can serve to manipulate self-regulatory resources, making other outcomes possible as well (Madon et al., 2017).

The repetitive-question paradigm models the inherent trade-off that characterizes police interrogation—specifically, participants must repeatedly choose to confess in exchange for a short-term gain (avoiding repetitive questions) at the expense of their long-term interests (meeting with a police officer) or choose to deny guilt to protect their long-term interests (avoiding meeting with a police officer) but endure the short-term negative consequences (answering repetitive questions). However, because the paradigm relies on self-report, it cannot establish ground truth with respect to the veracity of participants' interview responses. Nevertheless, due to random assignment, a group difference in the admission rate does indicate that at least one group was deceitful. Therefore, even though the paradigm cannot speak to false confessions per se, it can show how the inherent structure of police interrogation can compromise the diagnostic value of confession evidence.

FALSE CONFESSIONS

Not all innocent suspects crack under the pressure of interrogation, but it is well documented that some do. And it is not just suspects with dispositional vulnerabilities such as youth, cognitive impairment, mental illness, or suggestive personalities, though these suspects are at special risk (e.g., Feld, 2006; Redlich & Drizin, 2007; Redlich & Goodman, 2003; Redlich & Kassin, 2009); it is also suspects who have no risk factors at all (Leo, Costanzo, & Shaked-Schroer, 2009). The susceptibility of all suspects to interrogation pressures can be attributed to the fact that police interrogation relies on well-established principles of human behavior (e.g., reinforcement, punishment, reciprocity, compliance, consistency, social approval, affiliation) that skillfully exploit people's psychological vulnerabilities (Davis & O'Donohue, 2004; Kassin et al., 2010). In this section, therefore, we discuss how coercive interrogation tactics and psychological vulnerabilities put innocent suspects at risk of self-incrimination.

Coercive Interrogation Tactics

Police interrogation tactics are typically categorized as either *minimization tactics* or *maximization tactics* (Kassin & McNall, 1991). Whereas minimization tactics operate to reduce a suspect's apparent culpability, maximization tactics exaggerate the perceived likelihood of conviction and harshness of punishment. Two points relevant to these tactics warrant mention. First, it is useful to conceptualize minimization and maximization tactics as two sides of the same coin: Police may minimize a murder, for instance, by suggesting that it was committed accidentally or in self-defense, or maximize a murder by suggesting that it was intentional or premeditated. Police may offer face-saving excuses and themes that portray a suspect's motives in sympathetic terms (e.g., blaming the victim or suggesting the suspect blacked out), or may characterize the suspect's motives in reprehensible terms (e.g., using disparaging labels such as "sex pervert" or "sicko" or suggesting that the crime was highly deviant).

Second, although it is scientifically useful to categorize specific interrogation tactics into these two categories, in practice, police package minimization and maximization tactics together. This practice is intended to convince suspects that a confession is in their best interest, with minimization tactics emphasizing the favorable consequences associated with

a confession and maximization tactics emphasizing the negative consequences associated with a steadfast denial. The interrogation of Raymond
Wood (Drizin, 2009) provides a good example of how this can play out
in an interrogation. Wood was suspected of killing his girlfriend in a hit-
and-run accident and interrogated by two Maine state police officers. As
revealed by the interrogation transcript (Drizin, 2009), the interrogating
officers repeatedly used minimization and maximization tactics side by
side for maximum effect. Consider these statements made by the officers:

> "If this is an accident, we can rule it as such, OK?" (minimization)
> "But if you're going to play with me, and look like you're hiding some-
> thing, you have no idea how much evidence I have." (maximization)
> "You know what we pulled off that bumper? Some hair, OK? . . . Some
> hair came off that bumper, all right." (maximization)
> "Did you black out at all during that night? . . . Do you think you
> had too much to drink last night, maybe you were blacking out?"
> (minimization)
> "I'm not saying that happened intentionally, that's not what I'm say-
> ing. Accidents happen. . . . Things happen and get out of control.
> Accidents happen. . . . " (minimization)
> "We could just write you off on what we have already, but we are try-
> ing to get it from you." (maximization)
> "We need you to fill in the blanks, OK? . . . Don't let me fill in the
> blanks, Raymond." (maximization)

Minimization and maximization tactics, such as those used by Wood's
interrogators, are designed to obtain self-incriminating statements from
suspects (Kassin et al., 2010). The problem is that these tactics are not sur-
gically precise. Scientific findings and proven false confession cases demonstrate that the tendency for minimization and maximization tactics to
elicit confessions is not restricted to guilty suspects. Innocent suspects are
also vulnerable to their effects. For example, laboratory experiments that
used the cheating and Alt-key paradigms have shown that characterizing
misconduct as a mistake or an accident, describing misconduct as a minor
infraction, presenting false evidence, and bluffing about forthcoming evidence all increased the false confession rate compared with situations in
which neither minimization nor maximization tactics were used (Kassin &
Kiechel, 1996; Klaver, Lee, & Rose, 2008; Narchet, Meissner, & Russano,
2011; Perillo & Kassin, 2011; Russano et al., 2005).
    The tendency for both minimization and maximization tactics to pull
for a confession has been hypothesized to reflect a fundamental principle of
human behavior: People's tendency to read between the lines (Kunda, 1999).
In terms of this principle, it is theorized that minimization tactics pull for
a confession because they imply that a confession will result in leniency,
whereas maximization tactics pull for a confession because they imply that

a failure to confess will result in conviction and harsh punishment (Kassin & McNall, 1991). Several lines of research support this interpretation. First, mock jurors who read an interrogation transcript inferred leniency regardless of whether the interrogator minimized the crime's seriousness or explicitly promised the suspect leniency in exchange for a confession, and they inferred harsh punishment regardless of whether the interrogator maximized the crime's seriousness or explicitly threatened the suspect with harsh punishment for refusing to confess (Kassin & McNall, 1991). Second, research within the field of criminology indicates that people perceive crimes to vary in terms of their seriousness and that a major factor contributing to these perceptions are people's beliefs about a crime's consequences (Stylianou, 2003). Third, research using the repetitive-question and cheating paradigms indicate that suspects confess more often the less serious their misconduct is perceived or appears (Madon, Yang, Smalarz, Guyll, & Scherr, 2013; Russano et al., 2005).

The tendency for suspects to infer leniency from minimization and harsh punishment from maximization is quite troubling considering that judges routinely suppress confessions that were made in response to explicit promises and threats on grounds of coercion, but routinely admit confessions that were made in response to implied promises and implied threats on grounds that trickery and deception do not invalidate a confession's voluntariness (Kassin et al., 2010). In practice, therefore, police need not jeopardize the admissibility of confession evidence by crossing into the illegal territory of explicit promises and threats precisely because they can convey the same meaning by using minimization and maximization tactics.

Psychological Vulnerabilities

A main reason that minimization and maximization tactics are effective at eliciting confessions is that they exploit three psychological vulnerabilities: the phenomenology of innocence, short-sighted thinking, and reduced self-regulatory resources.

The Phenomenology of Innocence

In seeking to understand why the innocent sometimes confess to crimes, Kassin (2005) proposed the idea that innocent suspects are susceptible to a psychological state referred to as the *phenomenology of innocence*. According to this idea, innocent suspects are of the mind-set that their innocence is sufficient to protect them from negative outcomes. They believe, for instance, that their innocence will be apparent to police, judges, and jurors, and that the truth of their innocence will be borne out by the evidence. As we discuss next, innocent suspects, bolstered by this mind-set, make behavioral decisions that increase their risk of self-incrimination and, ultimately, their risk of wrongful conviction (Kassin, 2005).

Consider, for instance, a suspect's decision to waive or invoke Miranda. In *Miranda v. Arizona* (1966), the U.S. Supreme Court ruled that police must advise suspects of their constitutional rights against self-incrimination prior to custodial questioning. Miranda marks a critical juncture in the process of police interrogation because it is the point at which police explicitly notify suspects that their relationship with police is adversarial and that self-incriminating statements made by suspects during subsequent questioning will be used to convict them (Leo, 2008). This advisement should cause suspects to be wary of speaking with police without the benefit of a lawyer present.

Counterintuitively, however, observational-field research indicates that approximately four out of every five suspects waive their Miranda rights (Leo & Thomas, 1998), and experimental research using the mock-crime paradigm has demonstrated that the waiver rate is higher among the innocent than the guilty (Kassin & Norwick, 2004). Although the decision to waive Miranda is multifaceted, the innocent suspects in this mock-crime experiment overwhelmingly cited their factual innocence as a key factor in their decision, reporting, for instance, "I didn't have anything to hide" and "I did nothing wrong" (p. 216). The decision to waive Miranda is risky because it provides police the opportunity to interrogate suspects with an array of coercive and manipulative tactics that are designed to weaken suspects' resistance to self-incrimination (Leo, 2008). Thus, the decision to waive Miranda opens the door to a pressure-filled interrogation that can undermine suspects' resolve to defend their innocence.

The tendency for innocent suspects to make risky decisions because of a fundamental belief in the protective power of their innocence is also evident in their reactions to interrogation. For example, the innocent are less likely than the guilty to have a strategic plan for answering questions and are more forthcoming with police (Hartwig, Granhag, & Strömwall, 2007). Research using the cheating paradigm has shown that innocent participants evidence a weaker stress response to questioning than do guilty participants in terms of their physiological arousal (Guyll et al., 2013). In addition, innocent participants in this study who chose to defend their innocence paid a physiological price for doing so. Compared with guilty and innocent participants who confessed to cheating, innocent participants who refused to confess showed a pattern of physiological responding that is linked to emotional and mental fatigue.

The above findings raise two troubling conclusions. First, innocent suspects may underestimate the peril inherent in their status as suspects, a miscalculation that may encourage them to take risks that increase their chances of a false confession, such as waiving Miranda, being less planful, and being more forthcoming with police. Second, even suspects who engage in the self-protective act of defending their innocence may experience diminished resources that could eventually cause them to confess as a way to escape from the psychological and emotional strain of interrogation (Davis & Leo, 2012; Madon et al., 2013).

Short-Sighted Thinking

Theory and research from diverse areas of psychology indicate that immediate or proximal factors influence behavior more strongly than delayed
or distal ones (Renner, 1964). Drawing on this literature, scholars have
hypothesized that suspects have a tendency to make short-sighted confession decisions whereby they favor short-term gains at the expense of
their long-term interests when deciding whether or not to confess (Follette,
Davis, & Leo, 2007). To put this in context, when suspects are interrogated
by the police, they are simultaneously confronted with both immediate and
future punishment. During an interrogation, suspects are repeatedly punished by interrogators for denials. A suspect may be subjected to relentless
questioning and confrontation. Police may be unwilling to accept a suspect's denials of guilt. A suspect may be presented with false evidence. And,
in an effort to elicit a confession from an "uncooperative" suspect, police
may interrogate the suspect for an extended period of time (Drizin & Leo,
2004). Although suspects can avoid these forms of immediate punishment
by confessing, doing so jeopardizes their long-term interests by increasing
their chances of conviction and punishment. Thus, the inherent structure
of police interrogation pits suspects' short-term goals (e.g., ending the interrogation) against their long-term goals (e.g., avoiding conviction), making
short-sighted thinking a potential liability.

Several experiments have demonstrated that suspects make short-
sighted confession decisions. These experiments, all of which used the
repetitive-question paradigm, found that participants admitted to misconduct to avoid a repetitive set of questions even though they believed that
doing so increased their risk of having to discuss their misconduct with a
police officer in the near future (Madon et al., 2012, 2013; Scherr, Miller,
& Kassin, 2014; Yang, Madon, & Guyll, 2015). This finding, which reflects
the influence of *temporal discounting,* suggests that suspects likely enter
into an interrogation with a tendency to give too much weight to short-term
rewards when making their confession decisions (e.g., ending questioning,
having a cigarette), an effect that is exacerbated by fatigue, lengthy or anticipated lengthy questioning, and the perception that the alleged misconduct
is a relatively minor offense (Madon et al., 2013; Scherr et al., 2014).

The tendency for suspects to be short-sighted may stem from the perceived uncertainty of future punishment. Research has established that
people discount future events because of their inherent uncertainty (Keren
& Roelofsma, 1995). Although this is not necessarily a wrong perception
(proximal events are generally more certain than distal ones), this reasoning can be problematic for suspects. Because punishment for a crime is
always a future event relative to an interrogation, suspects may tend to
underestimate the chances that future punishment will actually come to
pass. Innocent suspects, for example, may hold on to the hope that exculpatory evidence will be uncovered and prove their innocence, or that the real
perpetrator will be found, or that a jury will return a not guilty verdict.

Likewise, guilty suspects may hope to get off on a technicality or expect to present such a strong defense that the jury will find them not guilty.

Alternatively, the immediate consequences that flow from denials and a confession during an interrogation may seem quite certain. Suspects may expect to be interrogated longer if they continue to deny guilt and may see a confession as their only means of escape. This is certainly how many wrongfully convicted suspects described their interrogation experiences (Warden & Drizin, 2009). Experimental research using the repetitive-question paradigm corroborates this reasoning by showing that participants were more willing to admit to misconduct to avoid the set of repetitive questions when the likelihood of having to meet with a police officer in the near future was characterized as uncertain versus certain (Yang et al., 2015). Thus, the inherent uncertainty of future punishment may contribute to a suspect's decision to confess.

Although both guilty and innocent suspects may discount future punishment, short-sighted thinking may be especially pronounced among the innocent. Because innocent suspects believe that their factual innocence will protect them from negative outcomes, they may perceive conviction and punishment as highly improbable. As such, innocent suspects may believe that they can falsely confess to a crime as a way to escape from an interrogation and yet not have to worry about conviction or punishment due to a strong belief that their innocence will prevail. Of course, this is a woefully misguided perception. The conviction rate among proven false confessors who plead not guilty at trial is estimated to be as high as 81% (Drizin & Leo, 2004).

Self-Regulatory Decline

Police interrogation can act as a psychological pressure cooker that impairs suspects' ability to resist interrogative influence. Nevertheless, suspects rarely cave to interrogation pressures right away. Suspects typically have the fortitude to initially defy interrogators' attempts to elicit a confession (Kelly, Miller, & Redlich, 2016). However, resisting interrogation pressures requires self-regulation (Madon et al., 2017). Self-regulation, which is akin to self-control, is the process by which people resist, override, or inhibit behaviors, thoughts, and emotions that interfere with their long-term goals (Muraven, 2012). Importantly, self-regulation requires resources, and these resources can be temporarily depleted. Like a muscle that fatigues with overuse, psychological theory proposes that too much self-regulation can deplete the resources that sustain it (Muraven & Baumeister, 2000). When this happens, people's ability to act in the service of their long-term goals declines.

For example, during an interrogation, suspects' ability to navigate interrogation pressures requires them to repeatedly override the impulse to forsake long-term interests (e.g., avoiding conviction) in favor of short-term gains (e.g., ending an interrogation). Because repeatedly making this kind of decision expends self-regulatory resources, it can result in severe fatigue, cognitive impairment, and emotional distress, ultimately weakening suspects' resistance to interrogative influence (Davis & Leo, 2012; Madon et al., 2017). Three lines of research support the idea that self-regulatory decline increases suspects' vulnerability to interrogative influence.

First, basic research in social psychology finds that self-regulatory decline can reduce people's ability to control their behaviors. People eat more, smoke more, drink more alcohol, spend more money, cheat more often, and become more talkative the more depleted their self-regulatory resources become (Muraven, 2012). Second, correlational-field research indicates that lengthy interrogations are associated with false confessions. Whereas a routine police interrogation typically lasts between 30 minutes and 2 hours (Leo, 1996), among a sample of proven false confessors, 34% were interrogated between 6 and 12 hours, 39% were interrogated between 12 and 24 hours, and the average length of their interrogations was 16 hours—eight times longer than the typical interrogation (Drizin & Leo, 2004). Third, experimental research using the repetitive-question paradigm has demonstrated that self-regulatory decline affects suspects' responses to police interrogation. Participants who repeatedly had to choose whether to confess to avoid answering a set of repetitive questions or to deny guilt to avoid meeting with a police officer in the future evidenced weakened resistance to the effects of suggestive questioning than did participants who never made this choice (Madon et al., 2017). The fact that this occurred without coercion and among a sample of college students who lacked any obvious impairments suggests that the self-regulatory cost associated with prolonged interrogation is not restricted to egregious interrogation tactics or to suspects who have clear dispositional vulnerabilities.

THEORETICAL MODELS OF FALSE CONFESSIONS

Scholars have proposed a number of theoretical models to explain the causal factors and underlying processes that lead suspects to confess when interrogated by the police. As we discuss next, these models reflect prominent theoretical orientations within the broader psychological literature, including cognitive-behavioral, decision-making, and self-regulatory perspectives.

Cognitive-Behavioral Perspective

Models reflecting a cognitive-behavioral perspective broadly emphasize internal and external factors that encourage suspects to confess by virtue of altering their emotions, thoughts, and actions. For example, drawing on the idea that situational factors and internal states jointly determine behavior, Gudjonsson (1989) proposed a *five-factor model of confessions*. This model proposes that a confession decision is determined by its social, emotional, cognitive, situational, and physiological antecedents and consequences. The model defines antecedents as the factors that encourage a confession and defines consequences as the perceived short-term and long-term effects that are elicited by a confession. Generally speaking, a confession is rewarded by its short-term consequences and punished by its long-term consequences. Consider, for example, isolation, a social factor that is hypothesized to influence suspects' confession decisions (Gudjonsson, 2003). As an antecedent, isolation may cause suspects to feel anxious, disoriented, and dependent on police. To cope with these negative internal states, a suspect may confess, a behavior that would likely elicit approval from police (a short-term consequence) but ultimately disapproval from family, friends, and employers (a long-term consequence).

Also modeled on the cognitive-behavioral perspective is Moston, Stephenson, and Williamson's (1992) *interaction-process model*. This model uses a temporally structured framework to explain the factors and causal pathways that affect how suspects and police behave during the initial and subsequent phases of questioning. The model attributes the initial behavior of suspects and police to three preinterview factors: the beliefs and attitudes of police (e.g., beliefs in a suspect's guilt, preferred strategies), background characteristics of the suspect and the case (e.g., age, sex, personality, criminal history, type of crime, crime severity), and contextual factors (e.g., presence of legal counsel, length of custody, strength of the evidence). The model attributes the subsequent behaviors of suspects and police to the way in which they interpret one another's behaviors. For example, the model predicts that the way in which a suspect interprets a police officer's initial strategy of questioning affects how the suspect responds, and the way in which the police officer interprets the suspect's response influences how the officer responds next, and so forth, until the interrogation concludes. Although the model does not elaborate on the processes that underlie this interaction sequence, it does theorize that suspects continuously gauge the relative advantages and disadvantages of a confession compared with a denial and that suspects will ultimately choose the option that has the greatest perceived advantages. In this respect, the model resembles decision-making models, discussed next.

Decision-Making Models

Contemporary decision-making models are premised on the idea that people's subjective, rather than objective, assessments of likely outcomes drive their behavior (Kahneman & Tversky, 1979). Consistent with this premise, several models of confessions conceptualize interrogated suspects as decision makers who decide how to behave according to their subjective assessments of the resulting consequences. Because suspects' subjective assessments may be based on invalid information conveyed by police, these models all propose that suspects are at risk of making irrational decisions, including the irrational decision to confess.

Ofshe and Leo's (1997) *decision model* characterizes police interrogation as a two-step, systematic process of questioning that alters suspects' perceptions of what they have to gain by confessing. According to the model, police first attempt to move suspects from a position of confidence, in which suspects believe they will benefit from denials, to one of despair, in which suspects believe they will certainly be arrested, prosecuted, and convicted. The model proposes that police shift suspects' perceptions in this direction by employing interrogation tactics that lead suspects to believe that they are trapped by the weight of the evidence. Once suspects have accepted the idea that conviction is inevitable, the model proposes that police transition into the second phase of questioning in which they offer suspects incentives to confess. These range from low-end incentives, such as the suggestion that a confession will alleviate suspects' guilt, to high-end incentives that imply leniency or avoidance of the death penalty. These incentives are theorized to persuade suspects that a confession is in their best interests.

Suspects' decision making has also been modeled using the framework of subjective expected utility theory from behavioral economics (Savage, 1954). Expected utility refers to the overall amount of goodness, happiness, or satisfaction one expects to experience as a result of making a particular choice, and it is presumed that individuals make the choice associated with the greatest expected utility. First applied to interrogations by Hilgendorf and Irving's (1981) *decision-making model of confessions,* subjective expected utility models of interrogations propose that suspects consider the possible outcomes that flow from the choices of a denial and a confession and make the choice that produces outcomes with the greatest expected utility. Critically, the expected utility of any particular outcome is influenced not only by the outcome's expected utility (i.e., how "good" or "bad" it is), but also by its probability—that is, the perceived likelihood that the outcome will actually occur.

Building on the concepts presented by Hilgendorf and Irving (1981), the *interrogation decision-making model* proposed by Yang, Guyll, and Madon (2017) rigorously applies subjective expected utility theory to elucidate how an array of factors can sway suspects' decisions via their influences on the perceived utilities and probabilities of expected outcomes. Categories of factors that are predicted to influence suspects' decision making include crime characteristics (e.g., crime severity), suspect variables (e.g., experience with the criminal justice system), and interrogation effects (e.g., interrogation tactics). For example, if interrogators repeatedly interrupt a suspect's claims of innocence, the subjective expected utility of a denial is predicted to decrease because the suspect does not expect to be believed. By contrast, if interrogators lead the suspect to infer that a confession will result in leniency, the subjective expected utility of a confession is predicted to increase because the suspect expects to avoid harsh punishment.

The interrogation decision-making model has several unique features that distinguish it from other interrogation models. First, it incorporates people's tendency to temporally discount future outcomes. Second, it accounts for the dynamic nature of interrogation by highlighting how the parameters that guide suspects' choices (i.e., probability, utility, temporal discount factor) are themselves functions of time. For instance, over the course of an interrogation, a suspect may learn that denials immediately result in negative consequences, information that may alter the suspect's expectations about the outcomes that will follow from subsequent denials and, therefore, the suspect's subsequent decisions. Third, the model underscores the point that as an interrogation becomes unreasonably lengthy, the subjective expected utility of confessing as a means of escape increases. Thus, by including time as a parameter, the model captures how a suspect might steadily shift from denials to a confession via incremental changes in the subjective expected utilities of those choices. Finally, the model offers a taxonomy of factors that operate to influence suspects' decisions. This taxonomy classifies interrogation tactics on the basis of their effect on the expected utility or probability of an outcome associated with a denial or a confession. Overall, the model provides a broad and comprehensive framework that can integrate a host of factors that operate in the complex and dynamic context of an interrogation.

Self-Regulation Perspectives

According to models derived from a self-regulation perspective, suspects become increasingly vulnerable to interrogation pressures as their capacity to exert self-control declines. For example, Davis and Leo's (2012) *interrogation-related acute situational suggestibility model* proposes that suspects' ability to resist interrogation pressures to self-incriminate wanes over the course of questioning through a process of diminishing self-regulatory resources. In particular, the model predicts that mounting interrogation pressures strengthen suspects' urge to escape while simultaneously depleting the pool of resources they need to resist this urge. If an interrogation continues long enough, the model predicts that suspects will reach a point where the urge to escape exceeds their capacity to override it, putting them at risk of self-incrimination. This model provides insight into the way in which police interrogation achieves its primary aim of breaking down suspects' resistance to self-incrimination. However, there is theoretical reason to believe that self-regulatory decline may reflect only part of a larger process.

Drawing on the idea that stress signals threat and supports the mobilization of coping responses, Madon et al. (2017) proposed a biphasic process of resistance. According to the *biphasic model,* police interrogation initially mobilizes suspects to resist interrogative influence in a manner akin to a fight-or-flight response, but subsequently erodes their resistance through a process of self-regulatory decline as they continue to cope with the demands of interrogation. More specifically, the biphasic model predicts that the threat inherent in the confrontational approach to early questioning that is characteristic of a Reid-style interrogation activates an acute stress response that mobilizes suspects to cope with the demands of interrogation, thereby causing their resistance to interrogative influence to spike. As police interrogation progresses through its subsequent phases, however, suspects are put in a position that demands protracted coping. To navigate these demands effectively, suspects must repeatedly override the impulse to obtain a short-term reward (e.g., ending an interrogation) at the expense of their long-term interests (e.g., avoiding conviction). Because repeatedly making this kind of decision expends self-regulatory resources (Muraven & Baumeister, 2000), the model hypothesizes that it gradually weakens suspects' resistance to interrogation pressures.

The biphasic model applies these hypothesized effects to a broad range of responses. For instance, it predicts that mobilization facilitates suspects' ability to combat the effects of fatigue, avoid the effects of suggestive questioning, and resist self-incrimination, to name but a few. By contrast, the model predicts that self-regulatory decline impairs suspects' ability to defend against such effects. Thus, whereas mobilization explains suspects' tendency to initially resist interrogative influence, self-regulatory decline explains why suspects become increasingly vulnerable to interrogation pressures over the course of questioning.

INTERROGATION REFORMS

Police interrogation is designed to obtain incriminating evidence from guilty suspects (Kassin et al., 2010). However, as we have explained throughout this chapter, not all confessions are true. An important step toward protecting the innocent from self-incrimination is to institute recommended reforms.

Training

A key step to minimizing the problem of false confessions is to provide law enforcement with scientifically based training in three areas (Leo et al., 2009). In the area of deception detection, police must be taught that human lie detection is a myth. There is simply no reliable way to infer guilt or innocence from demeanor cues, no matter how confident police might feel in their judgments. In the area of confessions, police must be taught that false confessions are real, occur with regularity, and may contain many details that seem to support their veracity despite their invalidity. The veracity of a confession rests on supportive evidence. In the area of interrogation methods, police must be taught that the standard practice of using minimization and maximization tactics puts *all* innocent suspects (even adults without obvious impairments) at risk of self-incrimination and that false evidence in particular should never be used. False evidence causes innocent suspects to doubt their own memories, to feel trapped by the evidence, and to see a confession as their only viable option under the circumstances (Kassin et al., 2010).

Time Limits

There is growing consensus that interrogations should not exceed 4 hours. Even proponents of the Reid technique concede that a lengthy interrogation is not necessary to extract a true confession (Inbau, Reid, Buckley, & Jayne, 2001). Lengthy interrogations do, however, substantially increase the false confession rate by causing fatigue and emotional distress, increasing suspects' urge to escape, and depleting their self-regulatory resources (Kassin et al., 2010).

Videotaping

Videotaping is critically important to interrogation reform because it is the only way to create an objective record of what transpired during an interrogation. Videotaping has the potential to protect suspects from wrongful conviction by permitting interested parties to assess whether police violated suspects' rights, subjected them to undue psychological coercion and manipulation, or imparted information that only the police and true perpetrator would know. It also protects police from unjust accusations of improper conduct, which may explain why 81% of police favor the practice (Kassin et al., 2007). To be effective, however, videotaping must capture the entire interrogation process, beginning with Miranda (Lassiter, 2010). Videotaping only a confession is ineffective because it fails to document whether the confession was produced by coercive and manipulative tactics. Finally, to minimize biases, the camera's angle must focus equally on the suspect and interrogator or focus on the interrogator (Lassiter, 2010). A disproportionate focus on the suspect causes observers to perceive the suspect's statements as more voluntary, to judge the suspect as more likely to be guilty, and to be more punitive when making sentencing recommendations (Lassiter, 2010).

Safeguards for Vulnerable Populations

Although all innocent suspects are at risk of self-incrimination when subjected to a coercive and manipulative interrogation, dispositional vulnerabilities associated with youth, cognitive impairment, mental illness, and personality increase this risk substantially (e.g., Drizin & Leo, 2004; Feld, 2006; Gudjonsson, Sigurdsson, Bragason, Newton, & Einarsson, 2008; Malloy, Shulman, & Cauffman, 2014). Recommendations to protect vulnerable suspects include providing them with an appropriate advocate (e.g., attorney) during Miranda and police interrogation as well as prohibiting police from using coercive and manipulative interrogation tactics during questioning (Meissner & Lassiter, 2014).

Probable Cause

The potential for a false confession begins when police misclassify an innocent suspect as guilty (Leo et al., 2009). One way to think about false confessions, therefore, is as a base-rate problem: Reduce how often police target innocent suspects, and the rate of police-induced false confessions will decline. Although some misclassification errors are probably inevitable, the frequency with which they occur can be minimized by requiring police to have probable cause prior to conducting an interrogation (e.g., Leo et al., 2009). Such a requirement would require police to interrogate suspects on the basis of case facts, not on a hunch or vague suspicion, thereby reducing how often innocent suspects are wrongly targeted.

FUTURE DIRECTIONS

As we conclude this chapter, we consider three directions for future research that stand to further the field's understanding of police interrogation and confessions. Central among these is placing greater emphasis on the development and application of theory. Although the field's tendency to examine the effects of specific interrogation tactics on suspects' confession decisions has led to important discoveries, greater understanding about the underlying processes responsible for these effects will foster a more unified and interconnected empirical base. Indeed, a theory-based approach has the potential to identify common causal processes underlying whole classes of interrogation tactics that affect the innocent as well as the guilty. Future theoretical developments will have the greatest scope and utility to the degree that they are specific and make clear and testable predictions.

The science of police interrogation and confessions will also benefit from new experimental paradigms, particularly paradigms that blend the unique strengths of those already established. For instance, a new paradigm might construct a situation in which participants truly believe that they are suspected of a criminal act and subject to legal consequences. Although the ethical concerns raised by such a paradigm would have to be worked out, our lab has been thinking along these lines with a new paradigm that we call the *mock-crime gone wrong*. In this developing paradigm, some participants commit a mock-crime, such as vandalism, whereas others engage in a comparable, innocent behavior. Subsequently, the situation transitions from a mock-crime into what appears to be a real crime when the participant is informed that the university will not excuse the criminal act simply because it was performed as part of an experiment. This paradigm is amenable to multiple suspect-relevant outcomes, including Miranda comprehension and waivers, physiological responding, confessions and denials, internalized confessions, and susceptibility to misinformation and false memories, among others.

Finally, the protection of innocent suspects depends heavily on the development and testing of new interrogation approaches. Current recommended reforms are critically important safeguards, but they operate within a framework of police questioning that is accusatorial and guilt-presumptive, which limits their protective effects. Ultimately, there needs to be a shift away from the standard accusatorial approach of questioning suspects toward a more investigative approach that emphasizes rapport-building, the strategic presentation of evidence, and greater dialogue between investigators and suspects (Meissner, Surmon-Böhr, Oleszkiewicz, & Alison, 2017). More research addressing approaches of this kind is needed, especially research that is performed in partnership and collaboration with law enforcement.

REFERENCES

Appleby, S. C., Hasel, L. E., & Kassin, S. M. (2013). Police-induced confessions: An empirical analysis of their content and impact. *Psychology, Crime and Law, 19*, 111–128.

Barland, G. H., & Raskin, D. C. (1975). An evaluation of field techniques in detection of deception. *Psychophysiology, 12*, 321–330.

Bond, C. F., Jr., & DePaulo, B. M. (2006). Accuracy of deception judgments. *Personality and Social Psychology Review, 10*, 214–234.

Bruner, J. S. (1957). Going beyond the information given. In H. E. Gruber, K. R. Hammond, & R. Jessor (Eds.), *Contemporary approaches to cognition* (pp. 41–69). Cambridge, MA: Harvard University Press

Davis, D., & Leo, R. A. (2012). Interrogation-related regulatory decline: Ego depletion, failures of self-regulation, and the decision to confess. *Psychology, Public Policy, and Law, 18*, 673–704.

Davis, D., & Leo, R. A. (2014). The problem of interrogation-induced false confession: Sources of failure in prevention and detection. In S. J. Morewitz & M. L. Goldstein (Eds.), *Handbook of forensic sociology and psychology* (pp. 47–75). New York: Springer.

Davis, D., & O'Donohue, W. (2004). The road to perdition: Extreme influence tactics in the interrogation room. In W. O'Donahue (Ed.), *Handbook of forensic psychology* (pp. 897–996). San Diego, CA: Academic Press.

Dennis, N., & Erdos, G. (2005). *Cultures and crimes: Policing in four nations.* London: Civitas.

DePaulo, B. M., Lindsay, J. J., Malone, B. E., Muhlenbruck, L., Charlton, K., & Cooper, H. (2003). Cues to deception. *Psychological Bulletin, 129,* 74–118.

Drizin, S. A. (2009, March). *Frailties in the criminal justice process.* Paper presented at the National Judicial Institute (Institut National de la Magistrature), Victoria, Canada.

Drizin, S. A., & Leo, R. A. (2004). The problem of false confessions in the post-DNA world. *North Carolina Law Review, 82,* 891–1007.

Feld, B. C. (2006). Police interrogation of juveniles: An empirical study of policy and practice. *Journal of Criminal Law and Criminology, 97,* 219–316.

Follette, W. C., Davis, D., & Leo, R. A. (2007). Mental health status and vulnerability to police interrogation tactics. *Criminal Justice Symposium Issue: Mental Health and the Law, 22,* 42–49.

Gillard, N. D., Rogers, R., Kelsey, K. R., & Robinson, E. V. (2014). An investigation of implied Miranda waivers and Powell wording in a mock-crime study. *Law and Human Behavior, 38,* 501–508.

Gudjonsson, G. H. (1989). Compliance in an interrogative situation: A new scale. *Personality and Individual Differences, 10,* 535–540.

Gudjonsson, G. H. (2003). *The psychology of interrogations and confessions.* Devon, UK: Willan.

Gudjonsson, G. H., Sigurdsson, J. F., Bragason, O. O., Newton, A. K., & Einarsson, E. (2008). Interrogative suggestibility, compliance and false confessions among prisoners and their relationship with attention deficit hyperactivity disorder (ADHD) symptoms. *Psychological Medicine, 38,* 1037–1044.

Guyll, M., Madon, S., Yang, Y., Lannin, D. G., Scherr, K., & Greathouse, S. (2013). Innocence and resisting confession during interrogation: Effects on physiologic activity. *Law and Human Behavior, 37,* 366–375.

Hartwig, M., Granhag, P. A., & Strömwall, L. A. (2007). Guilty and innocent suspects' strategies during police interrogations. *Psychology, Crime and Law, 13,* 213–227.

Hilgendorf, E. L., & Irving, B. (1981). A decision-making model of confessions. In S. M. Lloyd-Bostock (Ed.), *Psychology in legal contexts: Application and limitations* (pp. 67–84). London, UK: Macmillan.

Horvath, F., Jayne, B., & Buckley, J. (1994). Differentiation of truthful and deceptive criminal suspects in behavior analysis interviews. *Journal of Forensic Science, 39,* 793–807.

Inbau, F. E. (1942). *Lie detection and criminal interrogation.* Baltimore: Williams & Wilkins.

Inbau, F. E., Reid, J. E., Buckley, J. P., & Jayne, B. C. (2001). *Criminal interrogation and confessions* (4th ed.). Gaithersburg, MD: Aspen.

Inbau, F. E., Reid, J., Buckley, J., & Jayne, B. (2013). *Criminal interrogation and confessions* (5th ed.). Burlington, MA: Jones & Bartlett Learning.

Innocence Project. (2019). DNA exonerations in the United States. Retrieved January 21, 2019, from *www.innocenceproject.org/dna-exonerations-in-the-united-states.*

Kahneman, D., & Tversky, A. (1979). Prospect theory: An analysis of decision under risk. *Econometrica, 47,* 263–291.

Kassin, S. M. (2005). On the psychology of confessions: Does innocence put innocents at risk? *American Psychologist, 60,* 215–228.

Kassin, S. M., Drizin, S. A., Grisso, T., Gudjonsson, G. H., Leo, R. A., & Redlich, A. D. (2010). Police-induced confessions: Risk factors and recommendations. *Law and Human Behavior, 34*, 3–38.

Kassin, S. M., Goldstein, C. C., & Savitsky, K. (2003). Behavioral confirmation in the interrogation room: On the dangers of presuming guilt. *Law and Human Behavior, 27*, 187–203.

Kassin, S. M., & Gudjonsson, G. H. (2004). The psychology of confessions: A review of the literature and issues. *Psychological Science in the Public Interest, 5*, 33–67.

Kassin, S. M., & Kiechel, K. L. (1996). The social psychology of false confessions: Compliance, internalization, and confabulation. *Psychological Science, 7*, 125–128.

Kassin, S. M., Kukucka, J., Lawson, V. Z., & DeCarlo, J. (2014). Does video recording alter the behavior of police during interrogation?: A mock crime-and-investigation study. *Law and Human Behavior, 38*, 73–83.

Kassin, S. M., Leo, R. A., Meissner, C. A., Richman, K. D., Colwell, L. H., Leach, A. M., & La Fon, D. (2007). Police interviewing and interrogation: A self-report survey of police practices and beliefs. *Law and Human Behavior, 31*, 381–400.

Kassin, S. M., & McNall, K. (1991). Police interrogations and confessions: Communicating promises and threats by pragmatic implication. *Law and Human Behavior, 15*, 233–251.

Kassin, S. M., & Norwick, R. J. (2004). Why people waive their Miranda rights: The power of innocence. *Law and Human Behavior, 28*, 211–221.

Kassin, S. M., & Wrightsman, L. S. (1985). Confession evidence. In S. M. Kassin & L. S. Wrightsman (Eds.), *The psychology of evidence and trial procedure* (pp. 67–94). Beverly Hills, CA: SAGE.

Kelly, C. E., Miller, J. C., & Redlich, A. D. (2016). The dynamic nature of interrogation. *Law and Human Behavior, 40*, 295–309.

Keren, G., & Roelofsma, P. (1995). Immediacy and certainty in intertemporal choice. *Organizational Behavior and Human Decision Processes, 63*, 287–297.

Klaver, J. R., Lee, Z., & Rose, V. G. (2008). Effects of personality, interrogation techniques and plausibility in an experimental false confession paradigm. *Legal and Criminological Psychology, 13*, 71–88.

Kunda, Z. (1999). *Social cognition: Making sense of people.* Cambridge, MA: MIT Press.

Lassiter, G. D. (2010). Psychological science and sound public policy: Video recording of custodial interrogations. *American Psychologist, 65*, 768–779.

Leo, R. A. (1996). Inside the interrogation room. *Journal of Criminal Law and Criminology, 86*, 266–303.

Leo, R. A. (2008). *Police interrogation and American justice.* Cambridge, MA: Harvard University Press.

Leo, R. A., Costanzo, M., & Shaked-Schroer, N. (2009). Psychological and cultural aspects of interrogations and false confessions: Using research to inform legal decision-making. In D. A. Krauss & J. D. Lieberman (Eds.), *Psychological expertise in court: Psychology in the courtroom* (Vol. 2). Surrey, UK: Ashgate.

Leo, R. A., & Thomas, G. C. (1998). *The Miranda debate: Law, justice, and policing.* Boston: Northeastern University Press.

Levine, T. R., Blair, J. P., & Clare, D. D. (2014). Diagnostic utility: Experimental demonstrations and replications of powerful question effects in high-stakes deception detection. *Human Communication Research, 40*, 262–289.

Madon, S., Guyll, M., Scherr, K. C., Greathouse, S., & Wells, G. L. (2012). Temporal discounting: The differential effect of proximal and distal consequences on confession decisions. *Law and Human Behavior, 36*, 13–20.

Madon, S., Guyll, M., Yang, Y., Smalarz, L., Marschall, J., & Lannin, D. G. (2017). A biphasic process of resistance among suspects: The mobilization and decline of self-regulatory resources. *Law and Human Behavior, 41*, 159–172.

Madon, S., Yang, Y., Smalarz, L., Guyll, M., & Scherr, K. C. (2013). How factors present during the immediate interrogation situation produce short-sighted confession decisions. *Law and Human Behavior, 37*, 60–74.

Malloy, L. C., Shulman, E. P., & Cauffman, E. (2014). Interrogations, confessions, and guilty pleas among serious adolescent offenders. *Law and Human Behavior, 38*, 181–193.

Meissner, C. A., & Lassiter, G. D. (2014). Conclusion: What have we learned?: Implications for practice, policy, and future research. In G. D. Lassiter & C. A. Meissner (Eds.), *Police interrogations and false confessions* (pp. 225–229). Washington, DC: American Psychological Association.

Meissner, C. A., Surmon-Böhr, F., Oleszkiewicz, S., & Alison, L. (2017). Developing an evidence-based perspective on interrogation: A review of the U.S. government's high-value detainee interrogation group research program. *Psychology, Public Policy, and Law, 23*, 438–457.

Miranda v. Arizona, 384 U.S. 436 (1966).

Moston, S., Stephenson, G. M., & Williamson, T. M. (1992). The effects of case characteristics on suspect behavior during police questioning. *British Journal of Criminology, 32*, 23–40.

Muraven, M. (2012). Ego depletion: Theory and evidence. In R. M. Ryan (Ed.), *The Oxford handbook of human motivation* (pp. 111–126). New York: Oxford University Press.

Muraven, M., & Baumeister, R. F. (2000). Self-regulation and depletion of limited resources: Does self-control resemble a muscle? *Psychological Bulletin, 126*, 247–259.

Narchet, F. M., Meissner, C. A., & Russano, M. B. (2011). Modeling the influence of investigator bias on the elicitation of true and false confessions. *Law and Human Behavior, 35*, 452–465.

Ofshe, R. J., & Leo, R. A. (1997). The social psychology of police interrogation: The theory and classification of true and false confessions. *Studies in Law Politics and Society, 16*, 189–254.

O'Sullivan, M., & Ekman, P. (2004). The wizards of deception detection. In P. A. Granhag & L. Strömwall (Eds.), *The detection of deception in forensic contexts* (pp. 269–286). Cambridge, UK: Cambridge University Press.

O'Sullivan, M., Frank, M. G., Hurley, C. M., & Tiwana, J. (2009). Police lie detection accuracy: The effect of lie scenario. *Law and Human Behavior, 35*, 530–538.

Perillo, J. T., & Kassin, S. M. (2011). Inside interrogation: The lie, the bluff, and false confessions. *Law and Human Behavior, 35*, 327–337.

Redlich, A. D., & Drizin, S. (2007). Police interrogation of youth. In C. L. Kessler & L. J. Kraus (Eds.), *The mental health needs of young offenders: Forging paths toward reintegration and rehabilitation* (pp. 61–78). New York: Cambridge University Press.

Redlich, A. D., & Goodman, G. S. (2003). Taking responsibility for an act not committed: The influence of age and suggestibility. *Law and Human Behavior, 27*, 141–156.

Redlich, A. D., & Kassin, S. M. (2009). Police interrogation and false confessions: The inherent risk of youth. In B. L. Bottoms, C. J. Najdowski, & G. S. Goodman (Eds.), *Children as victims, witnesses, and offenders: Psychological science and the law* (pp. 275–294). New York: Guilford Press.

Renner, K. E. (1964). Delay of reinforcement: A historical overview. *Psychological Bulletin, 61*, 341–361.

Robinson, W. S. (1950). Ecological correlations and the behavior of individuals. *American Sociological Review, 15*, 351–357.

Rogers, R., Gillard, N. D., Wooley, C. N., & Fiduccia, C. E. (2011). Decrements in Miranda abilities: An investigation of situational effects via a mock-crime paradigm. *Law and Human Behavior, 35*, 392–401.

Russano, M. B., Meissner, C. A., Narchet, F. M., & Kassin, S. M. (2005). Investigating true and false confessions within a novel experimental paradigm. *Psychological Science, 16*, 481–486.

Savage, L. J. (1954). *The foundation of statistics.* New York: Wiley.

Scherr, K. C., Miller, J. C., & Kassin, S. M. (2014). "Midnight confessions": The effect of chronotype asynchrony on admissions of wrongdoing. *Basic and Applied Social Psychology, 36*, 321–328.

Skolnick, J. H. (1982). Deception by police. *Criminal Justice Ethics, 1*, 40–54.

Stylianou, S. (2003). Measuring crime seriousness perceptions: What have we learned and what else do we want to know. *Journal of Criminal Justice, 31*, 37–56.

Vrij, A., Meissner, C. A., & Kassin, S. M. (2015). Problems in expert deception detection and the risk of false confessions: No proof to the contrary in Levine et al. (2014). *Psychology, Crime and Law, 21*, 901–909.

Warden, R., & Drizin, S. A. (Eds.). (2009). *True stories of false confessions.* Evanston, IL: Northwestern University Press.

Wickersham Commission Report. (1931). *Report on lawlessness in law enforcement* (Vol. 11). Washington, DC: U.S. Government Printing Office.

Yang, Y., Guyll, M., & Madon, S. (2017). The interrogation decision-making model: A general theoretical framework for confessions. *Law and Human Behavior, 41*, 80–92.

Yang, Y., Madon, S., & Guyll, M. (2015). Short-sighted confession decisions: The role of uncertain and delayed consequences. *Law and Human Behavior, 39*, 44–52.

CHAPTER 4

Deception Detection

Christopher A. Gunderson
Leanne ten Brinke

Deception—a successful or unsuccessful deliberate attempt, without fore-warning, to create in another a belief that the communicator considers to be untrue—is ubiquitous in social interaction (Vrij, 2008). When people were asked to keep a diary of how often they engaged in deception over the course of a week, they admitted to lying in one out of four social interactions and to more than 30% of all those they interacted with (DePaulo, Kashy, Kirkendol, Wyer, & Epstein, 1996). Lies are present in many forms of social interaction. Research suggests that lies occur in 14% of emails, 27% of face-to-face interactions, and 37% of phone calls (Hancock, 2007). Most often, these are *social lies*, are told to benefit or avoid harm to others, and are not serious (Vrij, 2008). For example, a friend might feign enjoyment at your birthday party, and you might falsely fawn over unwanted birthday gifts. Social lies grease the wheels of social interaction, and, although social norms suggest that lying is necessarily bad, telling the truth under all circumstances can be equally offensive. Generally, social relationships benefit from these types of deceptive but flattering comments, as people enjoy being liked and receiving compliments (e.g., Curtis & Miller, 1986).

Other lies, however, are not so benevolent or trivial. *Serious lies* occur when someone is motivated to achieve some gain or avoid some punishment (Vrij, 2008). These high-stakes, self-serving lies are of concern to researchers and law enforcement alike, as identifying—and misidentifying—these lies can have serious consequences for the pursuit of justice and public safety. For example, Jeffery Dahmer was a notorious serial killer convicted of killing and dismembering 17 people. Accurate deception detection may have led to his apprehension earlier and saved his victims' lives. Police officers were called when one of Dahmer's victims, bloodied 14-year-old Jamie Doxtator, escaped. When police arrived, Dahmer convinced the police that the boy was his homosexual partner and that they were having an argument. The police left. Dahmer was not apprehended until Tracy Edwards, another victim of Dahmer's, escaped and told police that Dahmer was trying to kill him. Among the horrors in Dahmer's apartment was the dead body of Jamie Doxtator (Waxman, 2016). For obvious reasons, then, criminal justice professionals have a vested interest in detecting deception, which brings us to the question: How capable are humans as lie detectors?

DECEPTION DETECTION ACCURACY

Psychologists have sought an answer to this question in research spanning the past 60 years. Unfortunately, findings paint a dismal picture of humans' lie-detection accuracy. In a meta-analysis of 206 studies, including 25,000 lie–truth judgments, Bond and DePaulo (2006) found that overall accuracy in discriminating lies from truths was 54%—a rate attributable to above-chance accuracy in detecting truths (61%) but not lies (47%). Accuracy rates reflect a common bias toward believing others are truthful, even when provided with information about the base rate of deception in a lie-detection task (see Levine, 2014). Further, human judges are poorly calibrated in their judgments; confidence in one's ability to detect deception is unrelated to accuracy. In a meta-analysis of 18 studies, the confidence–accuracy relationship did not differ significantly from zero ($r = .04$; DePaulo, Charlton, Cooper, Lindsay, & Muhlenbruck, 1997).

What's worse is that professional lie catchers (e.g., police officers, detectives, airport security), in particular, tend to overestimate their ability to detect deceit. When compared with laypeople, professional lie catchers are more confident in their veracity judgments but are not more accurate (Meissner & Kassin, 2002). And, among professional lie catchers, experience appears to breed even greater overconfidence. For example, more experienced parole officers are more confident in their ability to detect deception, but they are not more accurate than their less experienced colleagues (Porter, Woodworth, & Birt, 2000). High confidence in one's ability to catch liars can result in tunnel vision and biased decision making (Porter, Juodis, ten Brinke, Klein, & Wilson, 2010) or may reduce investigator efforts to search for corroborating physical evidence (Colwell, Miller, Lyons, & Miller, 2006). Ultimately, investigator overconfidence may contribute to miscarriages of justice, including the wrongful conviction of innocent individuals or the release of a guilty and dangerous perpetrator into society (Porter & ten Brinke, 2009).

PERCEIVED CUES TO DECEPTION

Dismal accuracy rates and persistent overconfidence in detecting deception suggest that laypersons and professionals may be relying on nondiagnostic cues to guide their veracity decisions. Indeed, survey research finds that laypeople and professionals alike associate many of the same stereotypical behaviors with deception. For example, people often report that liars avoid eye contact, touch themselves (e.g., stroking the back of their heads, touching their noses), move their feet and legs, shift their posture, shrug, and speak quickly (Vrij, 2008, p. 115). In fact, a worldwide study of stereotypes about liars found that averting eye gaze was the most common belief about liars across 75 countries (Global Deception Research Team, 2006). Professional lie catchers, too, endorse similar beliefs; a sample of Canadian judges reported relying on story consistency, story length, gaze aversion, and fidgeting to evaluate credibility in the courtroom (Porter & ten Brinke, 2009). A meta-analysis by DePaulo and colleagues (2003), however, found that averting eye gaze and fidgeting were not reliable indicators of deceit, contrary to popular opinion.

Professionals' incorrect beliefs about cues to deception may be reinforced by training techniques that favor folk wisdom over empirically validated findings. For example, the Reid technique is taught to hundreds of thousands of investigators internationally to identify deceptive suspects (Inbau, Reid, Buckley, & Jayne, 2001). The Reid technique consists of three components: factual analysis, the behavioral analysis interview, and interrogation. First, factual analysis involves evaluating each suspect with respect to the facts of the case, thus eliminating improbable suspects. Next, the behavioral analysis interview is a structured interview conducted with a suspect to (1) establish baseline verbal and nonverbal behavior and (2) ask "behavior-provoking" questions to elicit different verbal and nonverbal responses from truthful (vs. deceptive) suspects. As part of the training in the Reid technique, investigators are told that liars will behave and respond differently from truth tellers during the behavioral analysis interview. Namely, liars (vs. truth-tellers) will appear less comfortable, avert their gazes, shift more in their chairs, engage in more grooming behaviors, and seem less helpful to the investigation. And, finally, if a suspect is deemed highly likely to be involved in the issues under investigation, an interrogation takes place.

Despite the popularity of this technique, the scientific community is critical of its advice. For example, Kassin and Fong (1999) tested whether training in the verbal and nonverbal cues endorsed by the Reid technique increases lie detection accuracy compared with no training in the technique. Specifically, one group of participants committed either a mock crime (e.g., vandalism) or a related but innocent act and were subsequently apprehended by a "security officer." Videotaped interrogations were conducted with both the innocent and "guilty" participants, in which all participants denied involvement in the mock crime. Videos were then assessed for deception with Reid technique–trained or untrained observers. Results indicated that those who were trained in the Reid technique were actually *less* accurate than their untrained counterparts, yet they felt more confident and cited more reasons for their decisions.

In a study using a similar paradigm, Vrij, Mann, and Fisher (2006) investigated whether the behavioral analysis interview would result in different verbal and nonverbal responses from liars and truth tellers. Participants either committed mock crimes or did not and were interviewed with the behavioral analysis interview protocol. Results showed that the behavioral analysis interview did not result in the expected behavioral differences that could discriminate liars from truth tellers. In fact, liars' behavior directly opposed predictions of the behavioral analysis interview such that liars behaved like truth tellers, and vice versa. In sum, popular police training about cues to deception—if not grounded in empirical research—can exacerbate inaccuracy and foster overconfidence.

ACTUAL CUES TO DECEPTION

What behaviors *can* reveal a liar? To date, the most comprehensive study of cues to deception was a meta-analysis performed by DePaulo and her colleagues (2003). Included in this meta-analysis were 120 studies that examined the link between 158 verbal and nonverbal cues to deception. Results indicated that although many behaviors were not related or only weakly related to deceit, a few patterns emerged. The meta-analysis found that, in general, liars tend to appear more tense, are less forthright, and tell less compelling stories. Further, these cues were moderated by motivation and the type of lie that occurred. Next, we review behavioral cues that can aid in detecting deceit.

Liars Appear More Tense

DePaulo and colleagues (2003) found that liars were rated as appearing more nervous than truth tellers, based on their verbal and nonverbal behavior. Further, liars were rated as sounding more tense than truth tellers and were more likely to experience an increase in vocal pitch relative to truth tellers. Liars also exhibited greater pupil dilation, potentially indicating tension, concentration, or both. Liars' faces also tend to look less pleasant. These behaviors are consistent with the *arousal* account of deceptive behavior, which suggests that liars will behave differently from truth tellers because they are more nervous about being caught and potentially feel greater guilt than truth tellers (Zuckerman, DePaulo, & Rosenthal, 1981).

Although one might expect that feelings of nervousness would also manifest in more fidgeting behavior, DePaulo et al. (2003) found that liars were not more likely to engage in these small movements than truth tellers. Liars are likely aware that fidgeting is a commonly cited cue to deception and may actively control this behavior in an effort to appear honest (i.e., *attempted control* theory of deceptive behavior; Vrij, 2008). Relatedly, liars may (over) control other movements, too; for example, liars are less likely than truth tellers to engage in the use of illustrators—hand/arm movements that accompany and demonstrate vocal content (DePaulo et al., 2003).

Liars Are Less Forthright

Liars are faced with the difficult task of creating a fictitious account that sounds plausible, avoiding contradicting information known to the receiver, and remaining consistent over time. In contrast, truth tellers can simply recall the incident from memory and recount it. The *cognitive load* theory of deceptive behavior suggests that liars will behave differently from truth tellers because their task is more cognitively demanding than telling the truth. This theory found considerable support in DePaulo et al.'s (2003) meta-analysis; specifically, liars spend less time talking and tend to provide fewer details in their stories than truth tellers. In particular, they are less likely to include spatial ("The glass was in the sink") and temporal ("I went to the living room first, then checked the mail") details, perhaps because these details are harder to invent, remember, and repeat (Vrij, 2008). More recent research has also found that liars (vs. truth tellers) exhibit a *stability bias*: a failure to accurately estimate effects of forgetting on verbal behavior (Harvey, Vrij, Hope, Leal, & Mann, 2017). Across two experiments, it was found that truth tellers reported less detail after a 3-week delay than when interviewed immediately after a target event. Liars, in contrast, failed to account for forgetting and reported a similar amount of detail both immediately and after a delay of the target event. Harvey and colleagues (2017) suggest that the stability bias may occur for liars as a function of (1) false beliefs regarding memory performance over time, (2) cognitive difficultly with accurately estimating the typical rate of forgetting, and/or (3) an unwillingness to leave out details as doing so could lead to suspicion.

More recent research suggests that cognitive demands may also manifest in longer speech latencies, silent pauses, and speech hesitations (Mann, Vrij, & Bull, 2002; Vrij, 2008). In fact, research that we highlight below suggests that manipulating cognitive load may be a particularly effective way to increase cues to deception and improve lie detection during interviewing (Leal, Vrij, Mann, & Fisher, 2010; Leins, Fisher, Vrij, Leal, & Mann, 2011; Vrij, Fisher, Mann, & Leal, 2008; Warmelink, Vrij, Mann, Jundi, & Granhag, 2012).

Liars Tell Less-Compelling Stories

In addition to providing less-detailed accounts, lies tend to make less sense than the truth. Lies are more discrepant, less logical, and less plausible than the truth (DePaulo et al., 2003). Again, these behavioral cues are consistent with the *cognitive load* theory of deceptive behavior in that it is more mentally taxing to create a logical and plausible false story than it is to recall a true event from memory.

Deceptive accounts may also seem less compelling than the truth because liars seem less engaged in the stories they are telling than truth tellers (DePaulo et al., 2003). Liars use fewer hand gestures to illustrate their narratives and may give the impression that they are more uncertain with their words and tone of voice. In general, liars are more likely to appear distant, impersonal, evasive, and unclear relative to truth tellers. More recent research suggests that liars use more tentative words (e.g., *maybe, perhaps*) and may be less likely to use first-person pronouns in their descriptions, potentially to *psychologically distance* themselves from the lies they are telling (ten Brinke & Porter, 2012).

Moderating Factors: Motivation, Lie Type, and Preparation

Behavioral cues to deception described by DePaulo and colleagues (2003) were moderated by the type of lie that was being told and the motivation of the liar. In studies in which there was some incentive to succeed in lying (e.g., monetary reward), cues to deception were more pronounced than when there was no such incentive. Moreover, lies about transgressions (e.g., cheating, stealing) evidenced more prominent cues to deception than lies not about transgressions (e.g., opinions, age). In short, highly motivated liars are more likely to provide clues to their deception, particularly when they are lying about a transgression, a phenomenon termed the "motivational impairment effect" (DePaulo & Kirkendol, 1989).

Not all liars, however, are caught by surprise, and they may therefore prepare answers to expected questions. If a liar has time to prepare, telling a lie may be less difficult than when a lie is spontaneous. Indeed, previous work has shown that spontaneous (vs. planned) lies result in greater cues to deception (e.g., increased response latency; DePaulo et al., 2003; Vrij, 2008). This effect is the basis of novel research advocating the use of unanticipated questions (described below) to increase the presence of cues to deception and increase lie-detection accuracy (Mac Giolla & Granhag, 2015; Vrij, 2015).

In sum, research up until the early 2000s converged on a dismal set of conclusions: (1) lies occur often and (2) are accompanied by subtle, inconsistent behavioral cues. Unsurprisingly, then, (3) laypersons and professionals alike are poor lie detectors, yet (4) people—especially professional lie catchers—are overconfident in their ability to detect deception.

RECENT ADVANCES IN DECEPTION DETECTION RESEARCH

Out of this seemingly infertile ground, however, have grown novel lines of inquiry that are leading to rapid advances in our understanding of human deception detection. Each of these advances is characterized by a departure from the traditional lie-detection paradigm wherein researchers have invited undergraduate students to be videotaped and to provide low-stakes lies and truths in a contrived, laboratory situation. Indeed, DePaulo et al.'s (2003) meta-analytic findings, described above, are primarily based on undergraduate samples (84% of included studies), and most involved laboratory-based scenarios (DePaulo & Morris, 2004). In lie-detection studies, these same videos generally were observed by often-unmotivated undergraduate students who were asked to make an explicit veracity judgment of the speaker: Is this person lying, or telling the truth? For example, in Bond and DePaulo's (2006) meta-analysis of lie-detection accuracy, 88% of samples were undergraduates, and only 39.8% of studies included some form of motivation (e.g., monetary; performance relevance to individual identity). Below, we describe various departures from this paradigm and the insights offered by a recent explosion of creativity in methodologies to study deception detection.

STUDYING HIGH-STAKES, ECOLOGICALLY VALID LIES

Although we have gained some insight into cues to deception from laboratory-based studies (DePaulo et al., 2003), these are limited by both ethical and ecological validity concerns. For example, high-stakes lies, such as lying about cheating on a partner or concealing illegal drugs, cannot be convincingly created in the lab. Even in studies that raise the stakes for participants, such as offering monetary rewards for successfully lying and punishment for being caught, participants are (1) free to leave anytime and (2) do not choose to lie but are instead instructed to do so. Nonetheless, DePaulo and Morris (2004) have suggested that situations that augment one's motivation to succeed in lying—particularly when the consequences of failing are serious—may produce more reliable cues to deception. As previously mentioned, the DePaulo et al. (2003) meta-analysis found, for example, that a strong motivation to lie was a moderating factor that produced more prominent cues to deception. A more recent meta-analysis, however, found that there is no significant difference in the detectability of high-motivation versus low-motivation lies (Hartwig & Bond, 2014). In our view, however, any attempt to motivate liars in the lab may be so constrained by ethical concerns that they are unlikely to approximate real, high-stakes lies. And there are so few studies of real, high-stakes deception that making any conclusions about the effect of motivation on the presence of cues to deception may be premature. Further, the context of high-stakes deception may result not in an increase in cue strength by degrees, as has been shown in previous studies, but in completely distinct cues relative to low-stakes, laboratory paradigms. For example, recent research on high-stakes lies with a strong emotional component suggests that attention to the face may provide strong cues to credibility.

Two recent studies investigated verbal and nonverbal cues in public appeals for help in finding a missing or murdered loved one. In one study, ten Brinke and Porter (2012) investigated speech, body language, and emotional facial expressions in these high-stakes, emotional public appeals. To determine *ground truth* (establishing the actual guilt or innocence of the pleaders with certainty), a pleader was said to be deceptive if overwhelming evidence (e.g., DNA, possession of the murder weapon, security camera footage, leading police to the victim's body) existed to establish that he or she had been involved in the murder of the missing person. Roughly half of the appeals were provided by deceptive murderers who were convicted of killing the missing person, whereas the remaining appeals were provided by innocent and genuinely distressed relatives, desperately seeking the safe return of their child, parent, or spouse. By coding facial expressions frame-by-frame, ten Brinke and Porter (2012) found that failed attempts to simulate sadness and "leakage" of happiness and disgust revealed the deceptive pleaders' covert emotions. Moreover, liars used fewer and more tentative words than truth tellers. In a similar study, Wright Whelan, Wagstaff, and Wheatcroft (2013) coded a different sample of honest and deceptive public appeals for various verbal and nonverbal behaviors. Deceptive appeals contained more equivocal language, gaze aversion, head shaking, and speech errors, whereas honest appeals contained more references to norms of emotion and behavior (e.g., "How could anybody do this," "Any parent knows how I feel") and more verbal expressions of hope of finding the missing relative, positive emotion toward the relative, and expressions of concern and/or pain. These findings contrast with some of the meta-analytic findings of DePaulo et al. (2003) discussed earlier but support the view that real-life, high-stake (vs. laboratory-based, low-stake) situations may result in more prominent cues to deception (DePaulo & Morris, 2004).

These studies have the advantage of high ecological validity and provide valuable insight into the behaviors that may reveal lies of actual consequence. We encourage future research to continue to examine lies that (1) carry high stakes, (2) are emotional in nature, and (3) are told by the choice of the speaker. Researchers be warned, however; the study of real, high-stakes deception rarely allows for the control or manipulation of variables and comes with the added challenge of establishing ground truth (i.e., who, in the sample, is actually lying vs. telling the truth?).

To address ecological validity concerns associated with the traditional lie-detection paradigm while maintaining experimental control, some researchers have moved out of the lab and begun to conduct research in real-life settings. For example, Vrij and colleagues have recruited travelers at an airport to lie or tell the truth about their travel plans. When compared with truth tellers, liars' travel plans were rated as less plausible and included fewer spontaneous corrections and more contradictions, but did not differ in terms of detail (Vrij, Granhag, Mann, & Leal, 2011). A follow-up study used a similar design but examined participants' deliberate eye contact with their interrogators throughout the interviews. Contrary to folk wisdom, liars displayed *more* deliberate eye contact when compared with truth tellers, and liars and truth tellers did not differ in gaze aversion (Mann et al., 2012).

Another line of ecologically valid research has examined the verifiability of details in true and false insurance claims of damage, theft, or loss. By having participants report on a recent experience for which they could have genuinely submitted an insurance claim (e.g., damaging a laptop by dropping it on the floor) or falsify an incident of damage, theft, or loss, Nahari, Leal, Vrij, Warmelink, and Vernham (2014) found that liars were much more likely to report that there were no witnesses to the incident (86%) than truth tellers (54%). Analysis of genuine versus falsified claim statements also revealed that truth tellers provided more verifiable details than liars—details that could be checked by an investigator (Vrij, Nahari, Isitt, & Leal, 2016). Further, informing participants that their statements would be checked by investigators augmented differences between liars and truth tellers; truth tellers provided more verifiable details, whereas liars could not (Harvey, Vrij, Nahari, & Ludwig, 2017).

Other researchers have continued the tradition of mock-crime experimental paradigms but have created elaborate mock-crime "plots" to increase mundane realism and more closely parallel deception about thefts, espionage, or terrorist attacks. Importantly, this research has also included multiple perpetrators—participants who need to work together to achieve an "objective" but who also must maintain consistency in their alibis when questioned separately. For example, Mac Giolla and Granhag (2015) divided participants into groups of three to either plan a neutral task or engage in a mock crime, respectively. Liars additionally planned a cover story—thematically similar to the truth tellers' neutral task—in case they were apprehended. Truth tellers and liars were allowed 20 minutes to plan their activities before they were "intercepted." Participants' interviews were videotaped and consisted of both anticipated questions (e.g., "What did you intend to do?") and unanticipated questions (e.g., "How did you go about planning this?"). Because liars may plan for possible questions to be asked (discussed below), interviewers can exploit this by asking spatial, temporal, or planning-related questions that liars typically do not plan for (Vrij, 2015). Indeed, truth tellers and liars rated the anticipated question equally expected and equally difficult. Moreover, both groups rated the unanticipated question as less expected than the anticipated question. Critically, liars found the unanticipated question to be less expected and more difficult to answer than truth tellers. After the interviews were transcribed and coded, results showed that truth tellers (vs. liars) provided longer, more detailed answers and exhibited greater within-group consistency for both anticipated and unanticipated questions.

Importantly, these studies examined or simulated a real-life setting. In work by ten Brinke and Porter (2012), lies were told by motivated criminals who chose to engage in deception. Further, work by Vrij and colleagues (2011; Vrij et al., 2016) employed paradigms with more mundane realism than typical mock-crime studies. Taken together, these studies represent a departure from traditional deception experiments, in which unmotivated undergraduate participants tell lies about contrived, mundane laboratory situations. Continued efforts to increase the ecological validity of deception research are likely to reveal greater insights into how liars actually behave. Future research in which participants are given the choice to lie versus tell the truth—instead of being randomly assigned to a veracity condition—is likely to be an important step in the evolution of deception research.

ADOPTING STRATEGIC INTERVIEWING STYLES

In addition to revising the types of lies that are being studied, there has been a surge of interest in investigative interviewing styles. It has become increasingly apparent that an investigator can make a liar's task easy or difficult, depending on how questions are asked and when information (e.g., evidence) is revealed to a suspect. For example, the Reid technique (Inbau et al., 2001) suggests that an interviewer reveal all known information or evidence early in an interview (early revelation) to encourage guilty suspects to confess. However, early revelation is problematic, as it (1) has been linked to false confessions, (2) does not typically lead to confession unless the evidence is overwhelming, and (3) may allow a liar to deploy a "lie script"—a narrative that allows him or her to explain away potentially incriminating pieces of evidence that arise during the interview (see Dando, Bull, Ormerod, & Sandham, 2015).

In contrast, another approach to presenting information or evidence to suspects in an active interview is the strategic use of evidence (SUE) technique (see Granhag & Hartwig, 2015). The goal of the SUE technique is to elicit cues of deception by strategically disclosing evidence. In short, SUE suggests that interviewers disclose evidence in a strategic, *gradual* manner, wherein liars will be more likely to make statement–evidence inconsistencies than truth tellers.

The SUE technique starts with the premise that truth tellers and liars use different *counterinterrogation strategies,* or attempts to convince the interviewer of innocence (Granhag & Hartwig, 2015). Liars come into interviews with a plan or strategy, avoid disclosing critical information, or turn to "escape responses" wherein they deny critical information (Hartwig, Granhag, & Luke, 2014). Truth tellers, in contrast, are simply expected to be forthright. This may be influenced by the belief in a *just world,* or that people "deserve what they get" and "get what they deserve" (for a review, see Hafer & Bègue, 2005). Indeed, recent research using a mock-crime paradigm has shown that innocent suspects (81%) were more likely than guilty suspects (36%) to waive their Miranda rights—an indication of their willingness to be forthright and participate in an interview (Kassin & Norwick, 2004). Importantly, when participants were asked afterward why they waived their Miranda rights, most guilty suspects stated that they did so for self-presentation reasons (e.g., "I would've looked suspicious if I didn't talk"), whereas most innocent suspects stated they waived their rights *because* they were innocent (e.g., "I don't have anything to hide"). Perhaps an innocent suspect, due to his or her belief in a just world, expects that he or she should not get punished for something he or she did not do and that an interviewer will see his or her honesty (see illusion of transparency; Kassin & Fong, 1999).

The interviewer can therefore disclose evidence strategically to influence the suspect's perception of how much an interviewer knows. Withholding evidence can lead suspects to believe the interviewer knows relatively little (Hartwig, Granhag, Strömwall, & Vrij, 2005). With this initial perception, when an interviewer reveals known evidence a little bit at a time, a deceptive suspect is more likely to reveal him- or herself in a *statement-evidence inconsistency* or *within-statement inconsistency.* Statement-evidence inconsistency occurs when there is a discrepancy or contradiction between suspects' accounts and the evidence presented by the interviewer, whereas within-statement inconsistency occurs when a suspect's account changes to fit the evidence presented by the interviewer, making it inconsistent with his or her earlier statement.

Over the last 10 years, the SUE technique has been shown to be effective in eliciting cues to deceit. The technique can improve deception detection accuracy in single suspects (e.g., Hartwig et al., 2005) and small groups of suspects (e.g., Granhag, Rangmar, & Strömwall, 2015). A recent meta-analysis of the literature on the SUE technique indicated that guilty (vs. innocent) suspects tend to make contradictory statements. Moreover, this tendency is augmented when guilty suspects are (1) questioned when uninformed about the evidence against them and (2) when the interviewer discloses evidence later in the interview (Hartwig et al., 2014).

Drawing on similar principles as the SUE technique, a new *cognitive approach to lie detection* is gaining considerable empirical traction. This approach is based on the theory that lying is more cognitively taxing than telling the truth because a liar must suppress the truth (Hartwig et al., 2014; Vrij, 2008; Vrij, 2015), monitor and control his or her demeanor in an active attempt to appear honest (DePaulo & Kirkendol, 1989), and monitor the interviewer's reactions to gauge whether he or she is being believed (Buller & Burgoon, 1996). This new approach imposes additional cognitive demands on truth tellers and liars with the expectation that liars, in particular, will not have the additional resources to deal with this demand and will therefore display more behavioral cues to deception (Vrij, 2015). Researchers have explored a variety of methods for increasing cognitive load, which have proven successful in discriminating liars from truth tellers: recounting events in reverse chronological order, maintaining eye contact, and asking unanticipated questions. We describe each in turn.

First, asking interviewees to tell their stories in reverse order increases cues to deceit and lie detection accuracy. Vrij (2015) suggests that telling stories in reverse order is cognitively taxing because "it opposes the natural forward-order coding of sequentially occurring events and disrupts the reconstruction of an event from a schema" (p. 210). In a 2008 study, Vrij and his colleagues instructed half of the liars and half of the truth tellers to tell a "convincing story" in reverse order denying that they had stolen £10, whereas the other half of the participants did not receive this instruction (natural order). Participants in the reverse-order condition engaged in more cues to deception; they provided fewer details and engaged in more speech hesitations relative to truth tellers, whereas these behavioral differences were not apparent in the natural-order condition. Moreover, observers who watched the statements could distinguish between truth tellers and liars better in the reverse-order condition (60%) than in the natural-order condition (42%; Vrij, Mann, et al., 2008).

Instructing interviewees to maintain eye contact throughout can also increase cognitive load. Vrij, Mann, Leal, and Fisher (2010) used a mock-crime paradigm and instructed half of the liars and truth tellers to maintain eye contact, whereas the other half did not receive this instruction. Liars who were asked to maintain eye contact throughout revealed cues to deceit (e.g., fewer details), whereas liars who did not receive instruction about eye contact did not behave differently from truth tellers. Further, observers who watched the statements perceived liars in the eye-contact (vs. control) condition more as lying than they did the truth tellers. In other words, observers could differentiate between truth tellers and liars only for those asked to maintain eye contact throughout.

Finally, cognitive load can be imposed by asking unanticipated questions. If afforded the opportunity, liars will prepare themselves for interviews and will construct answers to anticipated questions (Granhag, Andersson, Strömwall, & Hartwig, 2004). Unsurprisingly, then, planned lies typically contain fewer deception cues than spontaneous lies (DePaulo et al., 2003). To counteract liars' attempts to prepare for an interview, investigators can ask unanticipated questions, which the liar can refuse to answer—leading to suspicion—or be forced to fabricate a plausible answer spontaneously. The rationale, then, is that unanticipated questions should increase cognitive load by forcing a liar to "think on his or her feet" rather than rely on rehearsed, preplanned lies. In contrast, truth tellers should be able to easily recall details of a genuine experience, regardless of whether the question is anticipated or unanticipated.

To empirically test the unanticipated-question technique, participants in one study either lied or told the truth about an upcoming trip (Warmelink et al., 2012). Interviewers asked participants both anticipated (e.g., "What is the purpose of your trip?") and unanticipated questions (e.g., "What part of the trip was easiest to plan?"). Liars (vs. truth tellers) gave significantly less detail to unanticipated questions but significantly more detail to anticipated questions. These results suggest that liars respond to anticipated questions with prepared answers but struggle to answer unanticipated questions.

Asking an unexpected question can also be approached differently: Investigators can ask an unanticipated question in two different formats. Leins and colleagues (2011) had pairs of truth tellers go to a restaurant for lunch, whereas pairs of liars were asked to pretend they had had the same experience. During a subsequent interview, participants were asked to (1) verbally describe and (2) sketch the layout of the restaurant—two formats of the same unanticipated question. Truth tellers' verbal answers overlapped more with the sketches than did liars' answers. A subsequent study that conceptually replicated this finding also found that it was the question format (verbal vs. sketch) that led to inconsistencies: Truth tellers and liars did not differ on consistency when the question format was the same (verbal–verbal, sketch–sketch) across interviews. Instead, liars (vs. truth tellers) were more inconsistent when two different formats of the same question were presented (e.g., verbal–sketch), suggesting that liars are less cognitively flexible than truth tellers (Leins, Fisher, & Vrij, 2012).

As some unanticipated questions (e.g., spatial questions) will be inappropriate for distinguishing between lies and truths about certain topics (e.g., expressed opinions), another technique is needed. Yet another approach to asking unanticipated questions is to use the "devil's-advocate" technique (Leal et al., 2010). Using this technique, interviewees are first asked an opinion-eliciting question ("What are your reasons for supporting the war against terrorism?") that is followed by a question that argues against their view ("Playing devil's advocate, is there anything you can say that opposes the war against terrorism?"). The rationale is that people are likely to generate more reasons that support their (true) opinion than oppose it (see Ajzen, 2001). Thus, a truth teller will answer an opinion-eliciting question with more words and details than a devil's-advocate question, because the opinion-eliciting question is more compatible with their beliefs. In contrast, a liar is expected to answer the devil's-advocate question with more words and details than the opinion-eliciting question, because the devil's-advocate question is more in line with their actual beliefs.

Using this approach, it has been found that liars and truth tellers respond differently: Truth tellers' opinion-eliciting answers were longer than their devil's-advocate answers, whereas liars' opinion-eliciting answers were shorter than their devil's-advocate answers (Leal et al., 2010). Additionally, observers judged truth tellers' opinion-eliciting answers as more immediate, plausible, and emotionally involved than their devil's-advocate answers. In contrast, liars' opinion-eliciting and devil's-advocate answers did not differ on these judgments.

A recent meta-analysis explored whether the cognitive lie-detection approach would be superior to a traditional interview approach (Vrij, Fisher, & Blank, 2017). They found that the cognitive lie-detection approach (truth detection, 67%; lie detection, 67%; overall, 71%) was superior to a traditional interview approach (truth detection, 57%; lie detection, 47%; overall, 56%). When comparing the various techniques described above, the most effective technique for lie detection was imposing load (e.g., telling the story in reverse order, maintaining eye contact), followed by asking unexpected questions (see also Levine, Blair, & Carpenter, 2018; Vrij, Blank, & Fisher, 2018).

In sum, a cognitive approach to interviewing may enhance lie detection by revealing increased cues to deception. This is accomplished by placing increased cognitive load on interviewees, which is expected to overwhelm liars. Depending on the situation, increasing cognitive load by asking interviewees to the tell their stories in reverse order or to maintain eye contact throughout, asking unanticipated questions, or playing devil's advocate may elicit important clues that reveal a liar.

SEEKING MULTIPLE CUES TO DECEPTION

In the classic children's novel *The Adventures of Pinocchio,* Pinocchio is known for having a short nose that remains so if he is truthful but grows longer every time he lies—a reliable cue to deception. Unfortunately, deception detection in real life involves no single reliable cue to deception akin to Pinocchio's nose. Researchers have thus advocated a multiple-cue approach (Vrij, Granhag, & Porter, 2010), and recent work has examined this approach empirically. That is, can greater accuracy in the detectability of lies be garnered from multiple, empirically validated indicators of deception instead of a single cue?

Previously discussed research by Porter and ten Brinke (2012), for example, found that deceptive (vs. genuine) pleaders—in addition to revealing their emotional deception in the form of falsified sadness and leaked happiness—used fewer and more tentative words. Together, these behaviors each explained unique variance in the behavioral profiles of deceptive murderers and genuinely distressed relatives and could classify 90% of pleaders accurately. Findings suggest that cues tapping into cognitive load, emotional falsification, and psychological distancing uniquely contributed to explaining behavioral differences between deceptive (vs. genuine) pleaders and thus supports a multiple-cue approach to deception detection.

More recently, Hartwig and Bond (2014) performed a meta-analysis to assess the detectability of lies from multiple cues. They found that lies can be detected based on multiple cues with an accuracy rate of 67%, which is significantly greater than the accuracy that could be achieved on the basis of a single, best cue (43%). In short, these results suggest that combining multiple cues can increase lie-detection accuracy. Future studies should expand this line of research by exploring interactions between behaviors—that is, behaviors that occur simultaneously or in short duration to each other—to better understand the integrated nature of multiple cues.

AUTOMATING BEHAVIORAL CODING

Behavioral coding is painstaking, time-consuming, and difficult to complete. Although much has been gleaned about deception from quantifying behaviors in this manner (e.g., Nahari et al., 2014; ten Brinke & Porter, 2012), recent technological advances allow more efficient, objective, and in-depth analysis of verbal and nonverbal behaviors. Thus the field has also moved away from human coders and toward coding behavioral cues to deception via computer programs.

One such tool is the Linguistic Inquiry and Word Count (LIWC; Pennebaker, Boyd, Jordan, & Blackburn, 2015), developed to count and classify words into psychologically relevant dimensions. Along with the LIWC, other linguistic-analysis tools have been developed specifically to detect deception in texts and videos. These tools have implemented machine learning of natural language processing (Nunamaker et al., 2012) and automation (Automated Deception Analysis Machine; Derrick, Meservy, Jenkins, Burgoon, & Nunamaker, 2013) to detect deceit. Are these tools effective in detecting deception? In a recent meta-analysis, Hauch, Blandón-Gitlin, Masip, and Sporer (2015) found that computer programs can indeed detect linguistic cues to deceit. Across 44 studies, they found that liars (vs. truth tellers) experienced greater cognitive load as indicated by using fewer words, being less diverse in the words they chose, and telling less complex stories. Also, they expressed more anger (e.g., "worthless," "annoyed"), distanced themselves more from events by using fewer first-person pronouns (e.g., "I," "me," "my," "mine") and more second- and third-person pronouns (e.g., "you," "he," "she"), used fewer sensory–perceptual words expressing acoustic impressions (e.g., "listen," "sound," "speak"), and referred less often to cognitive processes (e.g., "cause," "know," "think").

Other technological advances in measuring physiological reactivity have been applied to covert deception detection in applied settings (e.g., airport security). One such tool is facial thermal imaging, whereby changes in temperature around the eyes are detected with special cameras. These changes are assumed to be the result of stress or arousal, causing the nervous system to trigger instantaneous increases in blood flow to the ocular muscle (Pavlidis, Eberhardt, & Levine, 2002). Although stress and arousal can be caused by a variety of factors, attempts to deceive are among the factors that have been shown to trigger stress (Puri, Olson, Pavlidis, Levine, & Starren, 2005). Indeed, facial imaging has been successfully used as an aid in deception detection, yielding accuracy rates as high as 87.2% (Tsiamyrtzis et al., 2005). In an applied setting, such as airport security, facial thermal imaging may be used to screen potential terrorists out from innocent passengers. However, because passengers may be stressed or aroused for a variety of reasons (e.g., nervous about flying, afraid that they may miss a flight), some researchers warn of high false-positives using this tool (e.g., Vrij, 2008; Warmelink et al., 2011).

A recent study investigated the efficacy of facial thermal imaging in an airport setting (Warmelink et al., 2011). They asked participants to lie or tell the truth about their upcoming trips and were subsequently interviewed. During the interview, liars contradicted themselves more and told less plausible stories relative to truth tellers. It was also found that liars' skin temperature rose significantly, whereas truth tellers' skin temperature remained constant. However, higher accuracy in detecting deceit was achieved with interviews than with facial thermal imaging. And, as a preinterview screening tool, facial imaging did not perform well: Prior to interviews, facial thermal imaging did not distinguish between liars and truth tellers. Despite these limitations, Moffitt, Burns, Jenkins, Burgoon, and Nunamaker (2010) suggest that continued laboratory experiments to validate the technique may lead to the implementation of a rapid, unobtrusive, and real-time screening measure—a tool that is sorely needed in rapid screening environments.

MEASURING NOVEL BEHAVIORS: REACTION TIMES

Another potentially useful tool to aid deception detection is reaction time (RT). RTs have been often used across areas of psychology to assess people's attitudes about socially sensitive issues and to gain insight into processes people are either unwilling or unable to report. Thus RTs may prove valuable in providing clues about concealed information and deception. In this section, we briefly review the Implicit Association Test (IAT) and the Autobiographical Implicit Association Test (aIAT).

The IAT was developed to measure attitudes indirectly and is a commonly used paradigm in social psychological research (Greenwald, McGhee, & Schwartz, 1998). Notably, the IAT can be used to overcome socially desirable response biases in explicit self-report measures of sensitive attitudes or social issues (for a review, see Krumpal, 2013). In the typical paradigm, participants are asked to categorize words according to certain rules on a computer as fast as they can. For example, in a race-attitude IAT, participants are asked to categorize facial images with value-laden words (e.g., *good, bad*) as they appear on the screen by pressing either a right or left computer key. In initial blocks of trials, participants categorize words (e.g., *joy, love, peace, agony, terrible, horrible*) with left and right key presses to the categories good or bad, respectively. Participants then learn to categorize images of black and white faces into black and white categories, respectively. In subsequent blocks, participants press the left key when words or images from either the good or white category are presented and the right key when words or images from either the bad or black category are presented. Then category pairs are reversed such that participants press the left key when words or images from either the good or black category are presented and the right key when words or images from either the bad or white category are presented. The key assumption of the IAT is that faster pairing of words to categories (viz. RTs) indicates a stronger association between the paired concepts. In other words, racist attitudes are revealed when good–white and bad–black RTs are shorter than RTs on good–black and bad–white trials. The IAT has been used to measure a variety of attitudes, preferences, and stereotypes and is predictive of discrimination toward a social group, brand preference, and political preference (see Nosek, Greenwald, & Banaji, 2007).

Sartori, Agosta, Zogmaister, Ferrara, and Castielo (2008) developed the aIAT to determine whether the IAT could be applied to lie detection. As in the IAT, individuals taking an aIAT are asked to classify four types of stimuli using two response keys that each represent two categories. In the aIAT, categories include "true" or "false," and contrasting autobiographical events are called "crime" or "alibi." When RTs during true–crime and false–alibi trials are faster than true–alibi and false–crime trials, respondents may be falsely denying criminal involvement.

Can the aIAT discriminate truth tellers from liars, and if so, with what accuracy? Sartori et al. (2008) performed six experiments with a diverse sample and utilized different paradigms. They found that the aIAT accurately discriminated (88–100%) between participants randomly assigned to a guilty or innocent condition (Experiment 2) and that it could identify which card a participant chose (Experiment 1), which drug a participant previously used (Experiment 3), where a participant was for his or her last holiday (Experiment 4), whether a participant's driver's license was suspended for driving under the influence (DUI; Experiment 5), and—when two murderers were participants—which crime each committed (Experiment 6). Verschuere, Prati, and Houwer (2009) replicated Experiment 2 from Sartori et al. (2008), but with a lower accuracy of classification of truth tellers and liars (67–87%).

The aIAT has not only been used to discriminate truth tellers from liars but to also reveal intentions and motives for lying. Agosta, Castiello, Rigoni, Lionetti, and Satori (2011) asked students where they intended to spend the night (short-term intention) and about their career plans (long-term intention). Accuracy of 100% was obtained for both short- and long-term intentions. Practitioners be warned, however; no research has been published on how the aIAT performs under applied conditions (see

Verschuere, Suchotzki, & Debey, 2015). A recent meta-analysis (Suchotzki, Verschuere, Van Bockstaele, Ben-Shakhar, & Crombez, 2017) of RT deception detection paradigms, including the aIAT, found that liars could be discriminated from truth tellers but that countermeasures exist; participants or suspects may slow down their responses on truth trials to influence their results. Indeed, when they examined countermeasure studies—wherein participants are instructed to try to "beat" the test—the average effect size ($d = 0.13$) of the RT deception effect was small and nonsignificant. Future research should explore the aIAT in an applied setting (e.g., comparing a crime vs. an alibi) and explore solutions to countermeasures.

DETECTING DECEPTION INDIRECTLY

Thus far, our review has focused on affecting the behavior of the lie teller as a means of increasing lie-detection accuracy. However, recent research has also reconsidered the role of the lie detector in attempts to increase accuracy. Deception detection research recently has seen a resurgent interest in indirect approaches, or the notion that lie detection can be improved by focusing on an indirect question about a behavior ("Is this person thinking hard?") or social impression ("Is this person tense?") rather than asking the direct question ("Is this person lying or telling the truth?"; see DePaulo & Morris, 2004). An early study on this topic, Vrij, Edward, and Bull (2001) randomly assigned police officers to a direct or indirect condition and asked them to evaluate videos of truth tellers and liars being interviewed. In the direct condition, officers were asked whether each of the people they saw on the videotape was lying, whereas those in the indirect condition were asked whether the people they saw on the videotape "had to think hard." They found that police officers could distinguish between truths and lies only in the indirect condition.

More recent research suggests that this form of indirect lie detection may exceed direct lie-detection efforts because asking participants whether someone "had to think hard" draws their attention to empirically valid cues of deceit in the videos: an increased latency and a decreased use of illustrators (Street & Richardson, 2015). In two experiments, Street and Richardson (2015) show that the accuracy of truth–lie judgments from indirect measures of deception detection are a result of attending to a single, diagnostic behavior. That is, when the indirect judgment asks the observer to attend to a cue that is indicative of deception, that judgment will be superior to direct judgments of veracity, which are prone to error based on attention to erroneous cues.

This parsimonious explanation, however, fails to explain improved lie-detection accuracy on implicit measures that do not direct attention to single, diagnostic cues. For example, Anderson (1999) asked one partner in a romantic couple to view a series of slides of very attractive and very unattractive people. The other partner, who could not see the slides, asked their partner after each, "Do you think that person is attractive?" and had to judge the veracity of their partner's answers—half of which were lies, and half of which were truths. Partners judging veracity directly also provided indirect judgments: how confident they felt about each judgment, whether they felt they got enough information, and how suspicious they felt. Although direct judgments were only accurate 52% of the time—not significantly different from chance—indirect measures could distinguish truths from lies. Judge partners felt more confident and believed that they had obtained more information when hearing a truth, whereas they felt more suspicious when they had just heard a lie. It seems then, that romantic partners could indirectly detect deception even if they were not asked to attend to a specific, useful behavioral cue to deception. Perhaps the judge partners had unconsciously associated important behaviors of their partner that were *individually* diagnostic. It is therefore important to note that the sample (i.e., romantic couples) used in Anderson (1999) departs from other research reviewed here.

These studies, combined with research suggesting that engaging less rather than more cognitive effort aids lie detection, has led a series of researchers to propose that the lie-detection processes—in some contexts—may be unconscious. For example, Albrechtsen, Meissner, and Susa (2009) found that giving people less information—14 seconds of video versus 3 minutes of video—improved judgments of veracity by up to 15%. A follow-up study further revealed improved judgments of veracity for participants who were cognitively engaged in a concurrent task compared with those who were not (Albrechtsen et al., 2009). Moreover, Reinhard, Greifeneder, and Scharmach (2013) showed that judges' ability to detect deception across five experiments improved after a period of unconscious processing compared with those who were asked to consciously deliberate or make an immediate decision about veracity. Specifically, participants were first shown videos of truthful and deceptive undergraduates under the guise of an "experiment about interpersonal impression formation." Control participants were asked to make veracity judgments following each video, whereas conscious-thought and unconscious-thought participants watched all videos and then performed different tasks for 3 minutes before making veracity judgments. Conscious-thought participants were asked to actively deliberate about who had lied and told the truth, whereas unconscious-thought participants were given a taxing non-word–search puzzle to work on for 3 minutes. Participants in the unconscious-thought condition outperformed conscious-thought and control participants, discriminating liars from truth tellers with above-chance accuracy. These studies suggest that unconscious or intuitive processing enhances deception detection, whereas deliberating about whether someone is lying worsens deception detection.

Building on these findings, ten Brinke, Vohs, and Carney (2016) posited that at an unconscious level, people can and do accurately detect deception. They proposed the *tipping framework of lie detection,* which states that lie detection is revealed in implicit, nonconscious patterns (e.g., indirect judgments) and that this implicit knowledge may be reflected in conscious thought and direct judgments of veracity when the cost of failing to detect deception is higher than the social costs of asserting that someone is a liar. Consider, for example, an immediate assertion of having witnessed a lie. If incorrect, this assertion could be costly to the declarer's reputation. In other situations, acting on a lie could be more detrimental to the declarer's well-being than to his or her reputation and should accordingly incite a threat response. In this framework, there are thus two competing forces at work: (1) the danger of believing and acting on lies and (2) the social harms that can follow from claiming—whether true or false—that someone is a liar. This framework points to three circumstances that aid in deception detection accuracy: (1) when methods of measurement that circumvent controlled, conscious cognition are used; (2) when individual differences or situational factors portend potent risks to lie-detection failure, such as in high-stakes or threatening settings; and (3) when factors diminish concern over the relationship or reputation costs of asserting that someone has lied. Considerable research is necessary to test the predictions set out by the tipping point framework and to understand how lie detectors process and evaluate liars' behavior.

Other authors have been critical of the tipping point framework. For example, Street and Vadillo (2016) argue that the model is unclear as to what would be considered "low" social cost when proclaiming someone a liar. If lie-detection accuracy is expected to increase when the social costs of doing so are low, what is the demarcation line? Further, they argue that a conscious account—as opposed to an unconscious one—could explain the conflict between the social cost of accusing someone of being a liar and the potential risk of being lied to. They recommend that a good model of unconscious lie detection should (1) explain how the unconscious is supposed to boost accuracy and (2) generate quantifiable and falsifiable predictions that (3) build upon an existing evidence base. In short, more research is needed before conclusions can be made about unconscious lie detection.

CONCLUSION

For 60 years, the study of human lie detection has relied upon a simple paradigm—asking undergraduate students to tell low-consequence lies and truths and showing videos of those statements to other students, who are asked to discriminate the liars from the truth tellers. The result of this effort has led to some dismal conclusions: that cues to deception are often subtle and inconsistent and that people are poor lie detectors. Despite these conclusions, recent advances in deception detection research have paved new roads for discovery. Researchers have also begun to move away from contrived laboratory experiments to studies that involve real-life or high-stakes settings. Advances in interview approaches indicate that increasing cognitive load also increases the presence of behavioral cues to deception. Technological advances have aided in deception detection by providing automated behavioral analysis, including linguistic analysis and facial thermal imaging. And a resurgent interest in implicit lie detection suggests that implicit judgments about liars and truth tellers can be more accurate indicators of credibility than explicit judgments. The recent bursts of creativity in the study of lie detection will no doubt lead to further basic and applied insights into human deception and provide novel avenues for improving lie-detection accuracy.

REFERENCES

Agosta, S., Castiello, U., Rigoni, D., Lionetti, S., & Sartori, G. (2011). The detection and the neural correlates of behavioral (prior) intentions. *Journal of Cognitive Neuroscience, 23,* 3888–3902.

Ajzen, I. (2001). Nature and operation of attitudes. *Annual Review of Psychology, 52,* 27–58.

Albrechtsen, J. S., Meissner, C. A., & Susa, K. J. (2009). Can intuition improve deception detection performance? *Journal of Experimental Social Psychology, 45,* 1052–1055.

Anderson, D. E. (1999, January). Cognitive and motivational processes underlying truth bias. *Dissertation Abstracts International, 60,* 3013.

Bond, C. F., & DePaulo, B. M. (2006). Accuracy of deception judgments. *Personality and Social Psychology Review, 10,* 214–234.

Buller, D. B., & Burgoon, J. K. (1996). Interpersonal deception theory. *Communication Theory, 6,* 203–242.

Colwell, L. H., Miller, H. A., Lyons, P. M., & Miller, R. S. (2006). The training of law enforcement officers in detecting deception: A survey of current practices and suggestions for improving accuracy. *Police Quarterly, 9,* 275–290.

Curtis, R. C., & Miller, K. (1986). Believing another likes or dislikes you: Behaviors making the beliefs come true. *Journal of Personality and Social Psychology, 51,* 284–290.

Dando, C. J., Bull, R., Ormerod, T. C., & Sandham, A. L. (2015). Helping to sort the liars from the truth-tellers: The gradual revelation of information during investigative interviews. *Legal and Criminological Psychology, 20,* 114–128.

DePaulo, B. M., Charlton, K., Cooper, H., Lindsay, J., & Muhlenbruck, L. (1997). The accuracy–confidence correlation in the detection of deception. *Personality and Social Psychology Review, 1,* 346–357.

DePaulo, B. M., Kashy, D. A., Kirkendol, S. E., Wyer, M. M., & Epstein, J. A. (1996). Lying in everyday life. *Journal of Personality and Social Psychology, 70,* 979–995.

DePaulo, B. M., & Kirkendol, S. E. (1989). The motivational impairment effect in the communication of deception. In J. C. Yuille (Ed.), *Credibility assessment* (pp. 51–70). New York: Kluwer Academic/Plenum.

DePaulo, B. M., Lindsay, J. J., Malone, B. E., Muhlenbruck, L., Charlton, K., & Cooper, H. (2003). Cues to deception. *Psychological Bulletin, 129*, 74–118.

DePaulo, B. M., & Morris, W. (2004). Discerning lies from truths: Behavioural cues to deception and the indirect pathway of intuition. In P. Granhag & L. Strömwall (Eds.), *The detection of deception in forensic contexts* (pp. 15–40). Cambridge, UK: Cambridge University Press.

Derrick, D. C., Meservy, T. O., Jenkins, J. L., Burgoon, J. K., & Nunamaker, J. F. (2013). Detecting deceptive chat-based communication using typing behavior and message cues. *ACM Transactions on Management Information Systems, 4*, 1–21.

Global Deception Research Team. (2006). A world of lies. *Journal of Cross-Cultural Psychology, 37*, 60–74.

Granhag, P. A., Andersson, L. O., Strömwall, L. A., & Hartwig, M. (2004). Imprisoned knowledge: Criminals' beliefs about deception. *Legal and Criminological Psychology, 9*, 103–119.

Granhag, P. A., & Hartwig, M. (2015). The strategic use of evidence (SUE) technique: A conceptual overview. In P. A. Granhag, A. Vrij, & B. Verschuere (Eds.), *Deception detection: Current challenges and new approaches* (pp. 231–251). Chichester, UK: Wiley-Blackwell.

Granhag, P. A., Rangmar, J., & Strömwall, L. A. (2015). Small cells of suspects: Eliciting cues to deception by strategic interviewing. *Journal of Investigative Psychology and Offender Profiling, 12*, 127–141.

Greenwald, A. G., McGhee, D. E., & Schwartz, J. L. K. (1998). Measuring individual differences in implicit cognition: The implicit association test. *Journal of Personality and Social Psychology, 74*, 1464–1480.

Hafer, C. L., & Bègue, L. (2005). Experimental research on just-world theory: Problems, developments, and future challenges. *Psychological Bulletin, 131*, 128–167.

Hancock, J. T. (2007). Digital deception: When, where, and how people lie online. In A. Joinson, K. McKenna, T. Postmes, & U. Reips (Eds.), *Oxford handbook of Internet psychology* (pp. 287–301). Oxford, UK: Oxford University Press.

Hartwig, M., & Bond, C. F. (2014). Lie detection from multiple cues: A meta-analysis. *Applied Cognitive Psychology, 28*, 661–676.

Hartwig, M., Granhag, P. A., & Luke, T. (2014). Strategic use of evidence during investigative interviews: The state of the science. In D. C. Raskin, C. R. Honts, J. C. Kircher, D. C. Raskin, C. R. Honts, & J. C. Kircher (Eds.), *Credibility assessment: Scientific research and applications* (pp. 1–36). San Diego, CA: Elsevier Academic Press.

Hartwig, M., Granhag, P. A., Strömwall, L. A., & Vrij, A. (2005). Detecting deception via strategic disclosure of evidence. *Law and Human Behavior, 29*, 469–484.

Harvey, A. C., Vrij, A., Hope, L., Leal, S., & Mann, S. (2017). A stability bias effect among deceivers. *Law and Human Behavior, 41*(6), 519–529.

Harvey, A. C., Vrij, A., Nahari, G., & Ludwig, K. (2017). Applying the verifiability approach to insurance claims settings: Exploring the effect of the information protocol. *Legal and Criminological Psychology, 22*, 47–59.

Hauch, V., Blandón-Gitlin, I., Masip, J., & Sporer, S. L. (2015). Are computers effective lie detectors?: A meta-analysis of linguistic cues to deception. *Personality and Social Psychology Review, 19*, 307–342.

Inbau, F., Reid, J., Buckley, J., & Jayne, B. (2001). *Criminal interrogation and confessions* (4th ed.). Gaithersburg, MD: Aspen.

Kassin, S. M., & Fong, C. T. (1999). "I'm innocent!": Effects of training on judgements of truth and deception in the interrogation room. *Law and Human Behavior, 23*, 499–516.

Kassin, S. M., & Norwick, R. J. (2004). Why people waive their Miranda rights: The power of innocence. *Law and Human Behavior, 28*, 211–221.

Krumpal, I. (2013). Determinants of social desirability bias in sensitive surveys: A literature review. *Quality and Quantity: International Journal of Methodology, 47*, 2025–2047.

Leal, S., Vrij, A., Mann, S., & Fisher, R. P. (2010). Detecting true and false opinions: The devil's advocate approach as a lie detection aid. *Acta Psychologica, 134*, 323–329.

Leins, D., Fisher, R. P., & Vrij, A. (2012). Drawing on liars' lack of cognitive flexibility: Detecting deception through varying report modes. *Applied Cognitive Psychology, 26*, 601–607.

Leins, D., Fisher, R. P., Vrij, A., Leal, S., & Mann, S. (2011). Using sketch drawing to induce inconsistency in liars. *Legal and Criminological Psychology, 16*, 253–265.

Levine, T. (2014). Truth-default theory: A theory of human deception and deception detection. *Journal of Language and Social Psychology, 33*, 378–392.

Levine, T. R., Blair, J. P., & Carpenter, C. J. (2018). A critical look at meta-analytic evidence for the cognitive approach to lie detection: A re-examination of Vrij, Fisher, and Blank (2017). *Legal and Criminological Psychology, 23*(1), 7–19.

Mac Giolla, E., & Granhag, P. A. (2015). Detecting false intent amongst small cells of suspects: Single versus repeated interviews. *Journal of Investigative Psychology and Offender Profiling, 12*, 142–157.

Mann, S., Vrij, A., & Bull, R. (2002). Suspects, lies, and videotape: An analysis of authentic high-stake liars. *Law and Human Behavior, 26*, 365–376.

Mann, S., Vrij, A., Leal, S., Granhag, P. A., Warmelink, L., & Forrester, D. (2012). Windows to the soul?: Deliberate eye contact as a cue to deceit. *Journal of Nonverbal Behavior, 36*, 205–215.

Meissner, C. A., & Kassin, S. M. (2002). "He's guilty!": Investigator bias in judgments of truth and deception. *Law and Human Behavior, 26*, 469–480.

Moffitt, K., Burns, M., Jenkins, J., Burgoon, J. K., & Nunamaker, J. F. (2010). Facial thermal imaging as a technique for deception detection. In *Proceedings of the 43rd Hawaii International Conference on System Sciences, Manoa, Hawaii*. Washington, DC: IEEE Computer Society.

Nahari, G., Leal, S., Vrij, A., Warmelink, L., & Vernham, Z. (2014). Did somebody see it?: Applying the verifiability approach to insurance claim interviews. *Journal of Investigative Psychology and Offender Profiling, 11*, 237–243.

Nosek, B. A., Greenwald, A. G., & Banaji, M. R. (2007). The Implicit Association Test at age 7: A methodological and conceptual review. In J. A. Bargh (Ed.), *Automatic processes in social thinking and behavior* (pp. 265–292). New York: Psychology Press.

Nunamaker, J. F., Burgoon, J. K., Twyman, N. W., Proudfoot, J. G., Schuetzler, R., & Giboney, J. S. (2012). Establishing a foundation for automated human credibility screening. Information Systems and Quantitative Analysis Faculty

Proceedings and Presentations, University of Nebraska Omaha. Available at *http://digitalcommons.unomaha.edu/isqafacproc/27*.

Pavlidis, I., Eberhardt, N. L., & Levine, J. A. (2002). Seeing through the face of deception. *Nature, 415*, 35.

Pennebaker, J. W., Boyd, R. L., Jordan, K., & Blackburn, K. (2015). *The development and psychometric properties of LIWC2015*. Austin: University of Texas at Austin.

Porter, S., Juodis, M., ten Brinke, L. M., Klein, R., & Wilson, K. (2010). Evaluation of the effectiveness of a brief deception detection training program. *Journal of Forensic Psychiatry and Psychology, 21*, 66–76.

Porter, S., & ten Brinke, L. M. (2009). Dangerous decisions: A theoretical framework for understanding how judges assess credibility in the courtroom. *Legal and Criminological Psychology, 14*, 119–134.

Porter, S., Woodworth, M., & Birt, A. R. (2000). Truth, lies, and videotape: An investigation of the ability of federal parole officers to detect deception. *Law and Human Behavior, 24*, 643–658.

Puri, C., Olson, L., Pavlidis, I., Levine, J., & Starren, J. (2005). StressCam: Non-contact measurement of users' emotional states through thermal imaging. In *CHI '05 extended abstracts on human factors in computing systems* (pp. 1725–1728). New York: ACM Press.

Reinhard, M. A., Greifeneder, R., & Scharmach, M. (2013). Unconscious processes improve lie detection. *Journal of Personality and Social Psychology, 105*, 721–739.

Sartori, G., Agosta, S., Zogmaister, C., Ferrara, D., & Castielo, C. (2008). How to accurately detect autobiographic events. *Psychological Science, 19*, 772–780.

Street, C. H., & Richardson, D. C. (2015). The focal account: Indirect lie detection need not access unconscious, implicit knowledge. *Journal of Experimental Psychology: Applied, 21*, 342–355.

Street, C. H., & Vadillo, M. A. (2016). Can the unconscious boost lie-detection accuracy? *Current Directions in Psychological Science, 25*, 246–250.

Suchotzki, K., Verschuere, B., Van Bockstaele, B., Ben-Shakhar, G., & Crombez, G. (2017). Lying takes time: A meta-analysis on reaction time measures of deception. *Psychological Bulletin, 143*, 428–453.

ten Brinke, L. M., & Porter, S. (2012). Cry me a river: Identifying the behavioral consequences of extremely high-stakes interpersonal deception. *Law and Human Behavior, 36*, 469–477.

ten Brinke, L. M., Vohs, K. D., & Carney, D. R. (2016). Can ordinary people detect deception after all? *Trends in Cognitive Sciences, 20*, 579–588.

Tsiamyrtzis, P., Dowdall, J., Shastri, D., Pavlidis, I., Frank, M. G., & Eckman, P. (2005). Lie detection: Recovery of the periorbital signal through tandem tracking and noise suppression in thermal facial video. *Proceedings of SPIE: The International Society for Optical Engineering, 5778*, 555–566.

Verschuere, B., Prati, V., & Houwer, J. D. (2009). Cheating the lie detector. *Psychological Science, 20*, 410–413.

Verschuere, B., Suchotzki, K., & Debey, E. (2015). Detecting deception through reaction times. In P. Granhag, A. Vrij, & B. Verschuere (Eds.), *Detecting deception: Current challenges and cognitive approaches* (pp. 269–291). Chichester, UK: Wiley.

Vrij, A. (2008). *Detecting lies and deceit: Pitfalls and opportunities* (2nd ed.). New York: Wiley.

Vrij, A. (2015). A cognitive approach to lie detection. In P. Granhag, A. Vrij, & B. Verschuere (Eds.), *Detecting deception: Current challenges and cognitive approaches* (pp. 203–229). Chichester, UK: Wiley.

Vrij, A., Blank, H., & Fisher, R. P. (2018). A re-analysis that supports our main results: A reply to Levine et al. *Legal and Criminological Psychology, 23*(1), 20–23.

Vrij, A., Edward, K., & Bull, R. (2001). Police officers' ability to detect deceit: The benefit of indirect deception detection measures. *Legal and Criminological Psychology, 6*, 185–196.

Vrij, A., Fisher, R. P., & Blank, H. (2017). A cognitive approach to lie detection: A meta-analysis. *Legal and Criminological Psychology, 22*, 1–21.

Vrij, A., Fisher, R., Mann, S., & Leal, S. (2008). A cognitive load approach to lie detection. *Journal of Investigative Psychology and Offender Profiling, 5*, 39–43.

Vrij, A., Granhag, P. A., Mann, S., & Leal, S. (2011). Lying about flying: The first experiment to detect false intent. *Psychology, Crime and Law, 17*, 611–620.

Vrij, A., Granhag, P. A., & Porter, S. (2010). Pitfalls and opportunities in nonverbal and verbal lie detection. *Psychological Science, 11*, 89–121.

Vrij, A., Mann, S., & Fisher, R. P. (2006). An empirical test of the behaviour analysis interview. *Law and Human Behavior, 30*, 329–345.

Vrij, A., Mann, S. A., Fisher, R. P., Leal, S., Milne, R., & Bull, R. (2008). Increasing cognitive load to facilitate lie detection: The benefit of recalling an event in reverse order. *Law and Human Behavior, 32*, 253–265.

Vrij, A., Mann, S., Leal, S., & Fisher, R. (2010). "Look into my eyes": Can an instruction to maintain eye contact facilitate lie detection? *Psychology, Crime and Law, 16*, 327–348.

Vrij, A., Nahari, G., Isitt, R., & Leal, S. (2016). Using the verifiability lie detection approach in an insurance claim setting. *Journal of Investigative Psychology and Offender Profiling, 13*, 183–197.

Warmelink, L., Vrij, A., Mann, S., Jundi, S., & Granhag, P. A. (2012). The effect of question expectedness and experience on lying about intentions. *Acta Psychologica, 141*, 178–183.

Warmelink, L., Vrij, A., Mann, S., Leal, S., Forrester, D., & Fisher, R. P. (2011). Thermal imaging as a lie detection tool at airports. *Law and Human Behavior, 35*, 40–48.

Waxman, O. B. (2016). How police caught Jeffery Dahmer. Retrieved January 7, 2017, from *http://time.com/4412621/jeffrey-dahmer-cannibal-murderer-25th-anniversary-arrest*.

Wright Whelan, C., Wagstaff, G. F., & Wheatcroft, J. M. (2013). High-stakes lies: Verbal and nonverbal cues to deception in public appeals for help with missing or murdered relatives. *Psychiatry, Psychology and Law, 21*, 523–537.

Zuckerman, M., DePaulo, B. M., & Rosenthal, R. (1981). Verbal and nonverbal communication of deception. In L. Berkowitz (Ed.), *Advances in experimental social psychology* (pp. 1–59). New York: Academic Press.

CHAPTER 5

Eyewitness Memory

Sean M. Lane
Kate A. Houston

Imagine that you are walking your Labrador in a local park one evening. The sun is starting to set, and your mind is already turning to the list of tasks you hope to complete the next day. You hear a noise and notice what looks like a fight breaking out on the path ahead of you. Someone is running toward you, and as the person passes by you realize that this person is clutching an expensive-looking handbag. Ahead of you, a woman is screaming that her purse has been stolen. It all happens in a matter of seconds, and afterward you notice your heart is pounding from the excitement. Later, the police arrive and take your statement, and, perhaps weeks later, you are asked to pick the mugger out of a lineup. Finally, months later, you are asked to testify in a courtroom about what you saw and heard that day. This example describes a somewhat typical eyewitness scenario of a theft or mugging. In such a scenario, there may be multiple witnesses, but few items of biological evidence; therefore, the investigation and (potentially) subsequent trial will rely heavily on these witnesses' memories. But are these memories reliable? Judges and jurors are charged with making this decision at trial, and there is much research evidence that they find witnesses who provide detailed and confident testimony to be particularly convincing. Yet, as amply demonstrated by numerous research studies (see Wells & Olson, 2003, for a review) and DNA exoneration cases (e.g., Scheck, Neufeld, & Dwyer, 2000), eyewitness memory can sometimes be inaccurate and result in the wrongful conviction of innocent suspects.

Now imagine another scenario. You are out to dinner with your partner and some friends, regaling them with stories of your latest vacation. You are describing, with great detail and humor, one night that you went to a small restaurant where the tables were set out very close together, when the inevitable happened: A customer pushed her chair back into the path of a server, causing the server and the food he was carrying to fall to the ground. Luckily, no one was hurt, and everyone had a good laugh about it. On the way home from dinner that evening, your partner turns to you and remarks that the story you told was completely inaccurate. The restaurant you had described was one you visited together years ago, not on your recent vacation, and the incident in which a server got knocked over had in fact happened in a bar, where it was dark and crowded. Therefore, you have made multiple errors in your recall, which, although it made for a good story, was a poor reflection of reality. Luckily, telling your friends a less-than-accurate story of an incident that happened on vacation has no real consequences other than embarrassment.

The same psychological and neurological processes that encode, consolidate, store, and retrieve vacation memories also encode, consolidate, store, and retrieve eyewitness memories. However, the consequences of an error in eyewitness memory can have a direct and lasting impact on the life and liberty of another person. The focus of this chapter is to describe what is known about these processes and how factors commonly associated with eyewitness events can influence them. We began this chapter by providing a prototypical example of an eyewitness event, and we use this example as a framework for discussing the factors that influence initial perception and encoding of the event to initial (e.g., interview) and subsequent (e.g., in the courtroom) retrieval of the event. We conclude by suggesting the need for a deeper interaction between basic and applied eyewitness memory research and by pointing out new areas of potential exploration.

A GENERAL INTRODUCTION TO MEMORY PROCESSES

Key Terms

When we experience events in our lives, we rarely approach remembering them the way we do in a classroom—deliberately trying to commit information to memory. Instead, the "default" approach of our brains is to try to comprehend the nature of ongoing events and to predict the immediate future (i.e., what will happen next; Bar, 2007). In other words, expectations are generated. This is an important point, because it means that memories of prior similar experiences can influence what we focus on during an event and how we interpret the object(s) of our attention. Thus, right from the very beginning of memory creation, there are opportunities for the memories of the different people observing the same event to diverge.

Researchers use a common set of terms for describing the process of how memories are created and remembered. *Encoding* refers to the transformation of an initial experience into a representation (a memory *trace*) in the brain. This trace will generally include information generated by perceptual (e.g., seeing, hearing) and reflective (e.g., thoughts, feelings) processes that are used to comprehend an event, as well as prior knowledge that was activated at the time. The period between encoding and remembering is called *storage*. For several hours, a newly encoded neural representation is relatively fragile and easily disrupted. However, protein synthesis gradually strengthens it, a process called *consolidation* (for a review, see McGaugh, 2000). The process of reactivating a stored representation is called *retrieval,* and it can be attempted intentionally by someone or incidentally triggered. This reactivation is thought to be cue-dependent, meaning that a memory search is triggered by information generated by the person (e.g., "What was I doing yesterday at 1:00 P.M.?") or encountered in the environment (e.g., remembering a previous experience upon seeing a photograph). The likelihood that a cue will reactivate a memory depends on the overlap between the cue information and the information stored in memory (*encoding specificity*; Tulving & Thomson, 1971). The greater the overlap, the more likely it is that a cue will trigger a memory trace—for example, you may see someone wearing a similar jacket to the one the bag thief wore and the memory for the incident is triggered, or you may hear someone shouting in the park and the memories of the theft become activated. The implication of this is that a memory may be retrieved at one point of time but not be remembered at another. Thus the fact that you may not remember the color of the bag thief's jacket or whether the thief spoke to or threatened the victim when initially interviewed does not mean that you will be unable to remember these aspects at a later point in time.

As in the eyewitness domain, general memory researchers investigate the many different ways in which someone remembers an event. Typically, whereas eyewitness memory researchers often use staged crimes and interviews to measure memory performance, generally memory researchers use tests that differ in the specificity of retrieval cues that are available at the time of retrieval. For instance, *recognition* tests involve distinguishing between stimuli (e.g., faces, scenes) that have been encountered before in the experiment (e.g., during a study phase) and those that have not. Participants do so by indicating which faces or scenes are old and which are new (old–new recognition) or choosing which one of a series of items were seen previously (e.g., forced choice). The analogous recognition test in eyewitness situations concerns lineup identifications in which a witness attempts to pick the perpetrator of a crime from other people in the lineup (although lineups typically have a "not present" option). *Recall* tests differ in that they involve generating a response to a cue. In *free recall* tests, these cues are fairly general, such as "Remember all the items you saw during the first phase of the experiment." Typically, these types of tests are more difficult for participants than recognition, as they must provide their own internal search cues to try to retrieve the target information. During interviews, it is common for investigators to provide general prompts (e.g., "Tell me what you remember about the crime") to witnesses to guide a discussion about the witnessed event, making this a type of recall test.

MEMORY AS CONSTRUCTION

Surveys of the public find that people typically believe that memory is a matter of *reproduction* and operates much like a mechanical device such as a video camera (e.g., Simons & Chabris, 2011; for a review, see Lane & Karam-Zanders, 2014). That is, we experience the world, these experiences are represented in the brain, and at some later point in time, they are brought back much as they occurred. Although there is some general truth to this belief (e.g., at least some aspects of experiences are represented in the brain), it is incorrect or incomplete in a number of others. For instance, unlike a video that is played back, the likelihood that a human being remembers an event can be affected by context (e.g., Smith, 1979). Memory researchers instead characterize memory as being *constructive* (e.g., Bartlett, 1932; Neisser, 1967). When people experience an event, prior knowledge influences how that event is perceived (e.g., Kersten, Mamassian, & Yuille, 2004), and the resulting memory trace includes additional reflective activity (e.g., what someone was thinking or feeling). When we attempt to remember our past, we are thought to do so via (re)construction as well. Our retrieved "memories" include not only elements of the representation of the original experience (the memory trace) but information in the retrieval cue, as well as general knowledge that we use to fill in missing information (Neisser, 1967; Tulving, 1983). Thus, instead of the notion that you simply reactivate an existing memory representation of an experience, retrieval is more appropriately characterized as involving pattern completion (e.g., Ochsner, Schacter, & Edwards, 1997). This means, for example, that the memory you recall may be different depending on which cues were used to elicit it (e.g., Loftus & Palmer, 1974). For example, you might recall a crime more completely if you attempted to remember the event in the same place it occurred but would remember less if you were in a different context.

MEMORY THEORIES

A number of basic theories have been proposed to describe memory performance on a wide variety of tasks, including recognition (e.g., Gillund & Shiffrin, 1984; Hintzman, 1988), recall (e.g., Howard & Kahana, 2002), and source monitoring (e.g., Johnson, Hashtroudi, & Lindsay, 1993). For the purposes of this chapter, we briefly describe signal detection theory

(SDT) and dual-process theories of recognition and the source-monitoring framework to provide a general introduction in anticipation of subsequent chapters dealing with memory-related issues.

As noted previously, recognition involves distinguishing between things (e.g., faces, objects) that you have seen before and others that you have not. SDT (e.g., Macmillan & Creelman, 2007; Wickens, 2002) characterizes this recognition decision as being based on the quantity of evidence retrieved from memory in response to the test item (which acts as a cue), as well as the criterion set by the person for saying the item had been previously encountered (i.e., for saying that it is "old" rather than "new"). The evidence of memory is assumed to be continuous in nature, and test items cue different amounts of evidence from memory. SDT represents the evidence involved in this old–new decision in terms of two overlapping distributions—one for "old" items and the other for "new" items. Test items that have been previously encountered (old items) will, on average, retrieve more evidence for their prior presentation than items that have not been encountered before (new items). The degree of overlap between the distributions of these two types of items represents the difficulty of discriminating between them (the distance between the curves is calculated as d'), holding response criterion constant. Curves that are far apart represent relatively easy discrimination judgments, whereas curves with substantial overlap represent very difficult judgments. Where a person places his or her response criterion along the continuum of evidence is called *beta* (although C is typically a more commonly provided measure; Snodgrass & Corwin, 1988). Items with evidence that exceeds the criterion are called "old," whereas those falling below the criterion are "new." Someone can set a high criterion in the sense that more evidence is required to say "old" (a conservative criterion). In this case, the person will say "old" to new items less often (a lower false-alarm rate) but will also say "old" less often to old items (a lower hit rate). Conversely, someone can set a lower criterion for saying "old" (a more liberal criterion). In this case, the person will say "old" to new items more often (a higher false-alarm rate) but will also say "old" more often to old items (a higher hit rate). The criterion someone adopts can vary depending on instructions (e.g., "Please tell me if anyone looks familiar in the lineup" vs. "Please look at the lineup and let me know if you are certain the perpetrator is there") or incentives (e.g., being rewarded for remembering more vs. avoiding errors), among other factors.

SDT not only provides a way to measure performance on recognition tests but is also an example of a *single-process* model of recognition. In such theories, the assumption is that people are able to make their test decisions on the basis of a single type of continuous memory evidence (e.g., *familiarity*; for a discussion, see Wixted & Mickes, 2010). However, these models often differ in terms of other assumptions, such as the type of retrieval process used (for a review of global matching models, see Clark & Gronlund, 1996; for more general models see, e.g., Dougal & Rotello,

2007). In contrast, *dual-process* models of recognition argue that a second process must be taken into account to explain recognition performance (for extensive reviews, see Diana, Reder, Arndt, & Park, 2006; Yonelinas, 2002). Most commonly, such theories assume (1) a *familiarity* process that retrieves relatively undifferentiated trace information and (2) a *recollective* process that involves the retrieval of specific item and contextual information from the original event (e.g., what the purse snatcher looked like or details of the crime setting, such as the place in the park where the crime took place). Some dual-process theories assume that both processes involve continuous sources of evidence (e.g., Diana et al., 2006), and others assume that the recollective process is "all or none" (e.g., Yonelinas, 2002). Whether single- or dual-process theories best characterize the empirical data on recognition is still being debated (see Diana et al., 2006; Yonelinas, 2002; Wixted, 2004, for reviews), but there are models that combine assumptions of both types of theories (see Wixted & Mickes, 2010).

In many situations, it is important to be able to remember the origin of a memory (*source monitoring*). For instance, a witness might need to distinguish whether a "fact" he or she remembers came from the witnessed event or was information learned afterward (e.g., from a police interview or a newspaper article about the crime; e.g., see Zaragoza & Lane, 1994). More mundane examples of source monitoring include remembering which of your two friends told you about an upcoming meeting or whether you took your pill or only thought about doing so. The source-monitoring framework (SMF; Johnson et al., 1993) assumes that such judgments are made by evaluating features that reflect processing that occurred at the time of encoding. Different sources, on average, vary in terms of the amount or type of features that characterize them. For instance, memories of events that you have experienced are more likely to contain perceptual (e.g., shape, color) or contextual (e.g., location, time) detail than events that were only imagined. In contrast, memories of events that were imagined are more likely to contain features consistent with the construction of an image (i.e., cognitive operations) than memories of events that were experienced. Thus features in a retrieved trace can be compared with potential sources to determine the likely source. Of course, such processes do not definitively designate the source of a memory. Various factors, including impaired encoding (e.g., from divided attention; see Lane, 2006), limited time at retrieval to evaluate features (e.g., Zaragoza & Lane, 1998), or extensive overlap between the characteristics of two sources increase the likelihood of source-monitoring errors (see Lindsay, 2008). Within the psychology and law literature, the source-monitoring perspective has had the most influence on our understanding of the misinformation effect—the extent to which people make the source error of misattributing postevent information as having been seen in an eyewitness event (e.g., Loftus, 2005; Zaragoza & Lane, 1994).

PERCEIVING, COMPREHENDING, AND ENCODING

As in our initial scenario, crimes typically occur without warning and thus with the witness failing to pay full attention to the event. Although traditionally studied in separation, there has been a concerted push in the literature to study attention and memory together and to consider them intrinsically linked (e.g., Chun & Turk-Browne, 2008). In short, attention is believed to be a catalyst for working memory capacity, helping to determine which information moves from short-term into long-term memory. Engle and Kane (2007) even propose that the interaction between attention and memory may be the key determinant of proficiency for wide-ranging cognitive abilities. Attention is the mechanism by which resources for processing and encoding information are directed toward a target stimulus. Or, to put it another way, attention selects whether you devote processing resources to the individual who has stolen the bag or the victim of the theft who is screaming. In this way, attention results in limiting our perception, thus which information we encode, and therefore what memories we create (Chun & Turk-Browne, 2008).

Interestingly, laboratory studies provide evidence for the selectivity of attention even under conditions highly optimized for encoding. Chun (2005) created face–scene composites by superimposing faces on top of geographical scenes. As the trials progressed, either the face or the geographical scene would change, with participants directed to either focus on the faces or on scenes only. Participants were in an ideal environment for encoding, with no distractions or other demands on their attention. However, upon a recognition test, participants instructed to focus on the scenes only could not recognize the faces they had been presented with, and those instructed to focus on the faces only could not recognize the scenes they had previously been presented with. Chun (2005) concluded that attention directs resources not only toward intentional memory creation but also away from the creation of incidental memories. Attention, in this way, served as a filter for encoding, and if information was deemed irrelevant to the task at hand, it simply was not encoded.

Divided-attention studies have long shown that when attention is divided during encoding, the completeness and accuracy of memory suffers (e.g., Anderson & Craik, 1974; Craik, Moshe, Ishaik, & Anderson, 2000). One of our inbuilt strategies to help us to cope with multiple demands on our memory involves the use of stereotypes: handy scripts of prototypical events that we can use to "fill in the blanks" of our incomplete memory. Typically, stereotypes and schemas for how we think a crime "should" unfold take over and can influence what information we create memories for (Tuckey & Brewer, 2003). For instance, from our initial scenario, would you remember that the gender of our bag thief was male? In fact, the gender of the perpetrator was not disclosed. However, the stereotype of a young male stealing a handbag is a strong one, and one that we may use to allow our attention resources to be diverted to create memories for other, novel aspects of the event.

STRESS, EMOTION, AND MEMORY FOR COMPLEX EVENTS

An inference could easily be made that the majority of eyewitnesses will experience some degree of stress or emotion during the witnessing of a crime (Wells, Memon, & Penrod, 2006). However, ethical review boards often prevent psychologists from inducing stress akin to that experienced by an eyewitness. Although there are very good reasons for such a restriction on research, not least the potential to cause long-term psychological distress, it does mean that the laboratory scenario is quite far removed from the real-world crime scenario. Due to such ethical restrictions, videotaped crime scenarios or staged live crime events that include low to moderate violence but never personal threat have been utilized in the majority of the extant literature.

One exception to this rule are the studies conducted by Charles Morgan III and colleagues (Morgan et al., 2007; Morgan, et al., 2004), which have investigated the memories of personnel who are completing military training exercises that involve direct personal threat and heightened stress. The participants in Morgan and colleagues' (2004; Morgan et al., 2007) studies were male soldiers who had enrolled in survival school training, which involved both sleep and food deprivation over a period of 48 hours. The soldiers were then subjected to isolation from their colleagues and were interrogated in a well-lit room for 30 minutes at a time. This cycle of events was repeated over the training period, with interrogations separated by approximately 4 hours. Morgan et al. (2004) investigated two interrogation phases: a high-stress and a low-stress interrogation. Simply put, the high-stress interrogation involved physical confrontation by the interrogator toward the soldier, and the low-stress condition did not (Morgan et al., 2004).

Morgan et al. (2004) found that soldiers who had taken part in high-stress interrogations were significantly worse at subsequently identifying any of their interrogators than those who had taken part in the low-stress interrogations, even though the soldiers were exposed to the interrogators for periods of 30 minutes at a time. Morgan et al. (2004) concluded that these data provided strong evidence that eyewitnesses who encounter heightened stress and personal threat while attempting to encode details of the event and/or perpetrator are likely to be highly error prone when asked to subsequently identify the perpetrator. Morgan et al. (2007) extended these results, with more than one-third of the soldiers who had undergone highly stressful interrogations being unable to recognize their interrogators.

A meta-analysis of the effects of high stress on memory provides further support for the theory that stress or negative emotion may have a detrimental impact on eyewitness recall and recognition performance. Deffenbacher, Bornstein, Penrod, and McGorty (2004) analyzed 27 instances of the effects of high stress on recognition memory in the form of face identification tests. Deffenbacher et al. (2004) also analyzed 36 tests of high stress on eyewitness recall performance. They found that heightened stress or negative emotion experienced during encoding impaired both eyewitness recall and recognition memory and, in particular, reduced correct identification rates of perpetrators by participants.

Taken together, the extant research suggests that if we experienced stress when witnessing the bag theft in the park, then that experience is likely to impair both the accuracy of our statement and the accuracy of our identification decision. Although these conclusions are drawn from a literature that has primarily focused on the effects of stress on eyewitness memory, their findings are often applied to the effects of negative emotion on memory. However, the effects of negative emotion on memory may be more complex.

Whereas the early literature on emotion and memory drew conclusions about negative emotion impairing memory holistically, more recent research has instead found that individuals who witness a negative emotional event may have enhanced memory for the gist or core idea of the event but impaired memory for details on the periphery (e.g., Reisberg & Heuer, 2004; Reisberg & Heuer, 2007; Safer, Christianson, Autry, & Österlund, 1998). Enhanced memory for central details plus impaired memory for peripheral details have been termed the central and peripheral effect in the literature (e.g., Reisberg & Heuer, 2004). Although arguments about the existence of a central and peripheral effect began to appear in the early 1990s, the theory that is routinely used to explain such findings is based upon the work of Easterbrook, which was published in 1959. Easterbrook (1959) argued that the detection of an emotional/anxiety-provoking stimulus would result in an individual only encoding information that is central and disregarding peripheral information. Easterbrook (1959) terms this phenomenon "attentional narrowing" because negative emotion appears to cause attention to narrow to the extent that only central details of the scene/event are encoded. In application to the eyewitness scenario, Easterbrook's (1959) theory suggests that an eyewitness who experienced negative emotion during the witnessing of a crime may have a better memory for details that are central. However, the same eyewitness could also have an impaired or even incomplete memory for other details of the crime that were excluded from encoding because they were peripheral. Easterbrook's theory continues to be strongly supported by the majority of the current literature (e.g., Reisberg & Heuer, 2004, 2007; see also Edelstein, Alexander, Goodman, & Newton, 2004). However, the literature is still unclear regarding differences in the experience of, and the cognitive effects of, negative emotions at the individual level.

FORMS OF MEMORY RETRIEVAL
Recall

It's time to provide a statement of what we saw in the park to the police. It follows from those studies previously discussed that if we experienced fear during the bag theft, then we may have failed to pay attention to peripheral aspects of a crime event, such as other potential witnesses. Instead, negative emotions such as fear may cause us to focus on details that are directly in our line of sight, or that are plot relevant, such as the bag thief running toward us, or our Labrador, rather than the victim, and this could result in an incomplete recall of the crime. Thus, one conclusion to draw from this literature is that eyewitness recall may be impaired by negative emotion and stress but only if peripheral details need to be recalled during the police interview. However, it is logical to assume that one detail that is central to both attention and the plot during a crime is likely to be the perpetrator; therefore, such attentional narrowing may be of little forensic/investigative consequence. We investigated this idea by comparing the recall of participants who experienced negative emotion with those who remained neutral (Houston, Clifford, Phillips & Memon, 2013). In line with central–peripheral effect literature, we found that emotional participants provided a more complete description of the perpetrator than neutral participants did. However, neutral participants provided a more complete description of an interaction between the perpetrator and victim than did emotional participants (Houston et al., 2013). Furthermore, emotional participants were less likely to accurately identify the perpetrator from a target-present lineup than the neutral participants were (Houston et al., 2013). These data suggest that the experience of negative emotions directed the participants' attention to focus on the perpetrator but at the expense of being able to remember his actions, which would be forensically relevant, and that negative emotion also impaired their ability to visually recognize the perpetrator in a target-present lineup.

There are many other variables that can affect an eyewitness's ability to recall details of the perpetrator and crime. For example, although the exact parameters are unclear, there is a general rule of thumb that the longer the witness is exposed to the perpetrator, the more he or she will be able to remember (e.g., Wells & Olson, 2003). However, this relationship is not as clear-cut as it may at first appear. Factors such as the time of day (dusk and nighttime vs. daytime; Yarmey, 1986) and visibility (obstructed view due to weather, shrubbery, vehicles, other people vs. unobstructed view; Boyce, Lindsay, & Brimacombe, 2008) can interact with the length of time the witness views the crime to reduce the accuracy and reliability of memory.

Finally, there is the cross-race effect, which is the finding that descriptions and identifications of perpetrators who are of a different race from the witness are more error prone than descriptions and identifications of a same-race perpetrator (see Brigham, Bennett, Meissner, & Mitchell, 2007, for a review). In isolation, any of these factors are sufficient to impair the completeness and accuracy of eyewitness memory. Taken together, these factors call into doubt the ability of the emotional witness to be accurate in his or her statement.

Collaborative Recall

There are multiple witnesses to the bag theft in the park, and while you wait for the police to arrive, you talk to each other about what you've seen and what has just happened. Can these discussions affect what you report to the police? Does the phrase "two heads are better than one" apply when the retrieval of crime-relevant information is at stake? A recent study found that 58% of witnesses surveyed in a police identification suite in the United Kingdom reported discussing details of the crime with a cowitness (Skagerberg & Wright, 2008). Although so-called collaborative recall, typically measured as recall of a single event by two or more individuals, produces more details than individual recall, this increase tends to be because more erroneous details, false details, and false memories have been reported (e.g., Douglass & Bustamante, 2014; Harris, Keil, Sutton, & Barnier, 2010; Yaron-Antar & Nachson, 2006). However, there are important nuances to the finding that two heads may not be better than one in this instance. Factors such as who our collaborators are (strangers, friends, long-term romantic partners), what we are trying to recall (emotional events or word lists), and how our collaboration is being measured all have a role to play.

Collaborative recall tends to be investigated with two different kinds of stimuli: Deese–Roediger–McDermott word lists (hereafter referred to as DRM paradigm) or staged–real-life emotional events. The benefit of DRM paradigms for collaborative memory studies is that memory intrusions/false memories can be easily measured and verified as false (Takahashi, 2007). However, what is gained in measurability in the DRM paradigm studies is lost in ecological validity. DRM paradigm studies tend to either show lower recall of both correct and incorrect details for collaborative groups compared with individual groups (e.g. Basden, Basden, Bryner, & Thomas, 1997; Takahashi, 2007) or produce no differences between groups (e.g., Harris et al., 2010). However, when studies assess memories for traumatic events, such as the assassination of Israel's prime minister in 1995, we find that volume of recall improves in collaborative groups compared with individuals, even though the increase includes incorrect as well as correct details (Yaron-Antar & Nachson, 2006). These findings suggest that collaborative recall may affect memorial processes differently when the memory target is an emotional event compared with a word list.

An area of collaborative recall which has received a lot of attention is whether the collaboration is with a stranger or a family member or close friend. The extant research appears to suggest that incidents of false memories are higher in collaborative groups composed of long-term romantic partners than of strangers (see French, Garry & Mori, 2008; Harris, Keil, Sutton, Barnier, & McIlwain, 2011; Harris et al., 2010). The enhanced error rate for collaborative memories of long-term romantic couples is often attributed to the larger degree of social influence that couples have over one another. In such studies, it is often observed that one member of the couple simply accepts what the other remembers and assimilates the partner's memory into his or her own reporting, without offering an alternative (French et al., 2008; Harris et al., 2010). However, Harris et al. (2010) also found that there are situations in which collaborative recall with couples can be beneficial. When couples engaged in strategies such as interactive cuing and repeating back what the other partner had remembered, collaborative facilitation was evident—couples produced more detailed and accurate memories than individuals (Harris et al., 2010; Harris et al., 2011). These data suggest that there may be strategies to improve the accuracy of collaborative memory, based on the use of cues and repetition of information.

Finally, the nature of the collaborative recall appears to be crucially important and, furthermore, may be a distinctly advantageous strategy for utilizing collaborative recall to high levels of effectiveness for crimes that involve multiple witnesses. In collaborative memory studies, three groups are typically compared: the individual, the collaborative, and the nominal. The nominal group consists of the consolidation of the individual memory reports, with any repetitions removed, to produce a measure of how many details and how many accurate details collaborative groups could provide. To the best of our knowledge, nominal groups outperform collaborative groups and individuals on every test of collaborative memory (Harris et al., 2010; French et al., 2008; Harris et al., 2011; Takahashi, 2007; Yaron-Antar & Nachson, 2006; see also Douglass & Bustamante, 2014). And herein may lie a possible effective strategy for crimes with multiple eyewitnesses. The extant literature reviewed reveals that collaborative remembering tends to lead to the dissemination of misinformation (e.g., Gabbert, Memon, & Allen, 2003), which can then lead to less complete and accurate reports than individual memories (e.g., French et al., 2008; Harris et al., 2011). Therefore, one strategy could be to take the individual recall of all available witnesses and combine them, rather than interviewing such witnesses together. Indeed, such a strategy is recommended by Douglass and Bustamante (2014) as a way of collecting more accurate and detailed statements than witnesses are capable of producing on their own. However, one cannot escape the argument that the majority of witnesses discuss the crime with their cowitnesses (Skagerberg & Wright, 2008) and that collaborative memory in general leads to an inhibition effect, whereby individual retrieval strategies are disrupted by information offered from others in the group (e.g., Yaron-Antar & Nachson, 2006). Therefore, combining individual accounts may only be advantageous if those accounts are collected at the scene of the crime, prior to the witnesses having an opportunity to discuss their memories with anyone other than the interviewing officer.

REMEMBERING CHANGES MEMORY

So far, we have talked about various tests of memory primarily in terms of an end point. For example, we've just discussed factors that influence recall performance. However, memories are, by their very nature, dynamic. The act of retrieval itself can influence a memory, making it more accessible at a later time, or by changing its composition. Understanding how remembering can change memory has relevance for eyewitness testimony, as it is common practice in forensic settings to interview witnesses multiple times (e.g., Kassin et al., 2007). From the laboratory, it has been known for some time that repeated testing allows individuals the opportunity to recall information that was not previously recalled during prior tests (*reminiscence*; for discussion, see Payne, 1987). In some cases, the amount of newly recalled information exceeds the amount of information forgotten from a previous test (*hypermnesia*). Furthermore, retrieving a memory influences the likelihood of retrieving that information at a later time. For example, over the last 15 years, there has been substantial interest in the *testing effect*—the robust finding that memory retention is boosted more substantially by an intervening test than by having another chance to restudy the information (e.g., Bjork & Bjork, 1992; Carpenter & DeLosh, 2006; Roediger & Karpicke, 2006).

However, remembering can sometimes lead to negative effects on memory accuracy. For instance, *consolidation* describes the biological process by which a memory moves from a relatively fragile state to a more stable one over time. Research on *reconsolidation* (e.g., Hupbach, Gomez, Hardt, & Nadel, 2007; for a review, see Schiller & Phelps, 2011) suggests that being reminded of a previous experience may make the original memory more vulnerable to interference and modification. There is also evidence that an initial recall test can sometimes increase the likelihood that a person will incorporate later misinformation into his or her memory of an event (e.g., Chan, Thomas, & Bulevich, 2009; although not always, see, e.g., Lane, Mather, Villa, & Morita, 2001). Finally, there is research suggesting that *how* an event is remembered can have a profound influence on what is subsequently remembered about the original experience (e.g., Lane et al., 2001; Marsh, 2007). For example, a witness may describe the event in a factual manner to police but tell a story about it to friends and family. Such differences matter, because when one tells a story to other people about an experience, there is a tendency to emphasize or exaggerate certain elements of the event over others as a means of making a particular point or telling a "good" story. Research has documented that storytelling following an event is more likely to lead to subsequent memory errors than when the event is recalled factually (reviewed in Marsh, 2007). All of this research suggests that it is important to consider how an interview may influence a witness's future ability to remember information, rather than focusing solely on how to maximize the amount of information gained from a single interview. It also invites a consideration of how witnesses recall and think about witnessed events when they are outside the investigation room, beyond the long-held concern about witnesses' exposure to misinformation from other witnesses (e.g., Loftus, Miller, & Burns, 1978).

METACOGNITION

Metacognition involves knowledge of, and thinking about, cognition (e.g., Flavell, 1979). Researchers in this area typically see metacognition as involving three components: *knowledge* about cognition (e.g., what types of strategies are most effective for remembering), *monitoring processes* (judgments about one's current cognitive state), and *control processes* (regulation of subsequent cognitive processing; see Son & Schwartz, 2002, for a review). For example, when being interviewed about the bag theft in the park, your goal is to remember as much accurate information as possible about the witnessed event. Based on your general knowledge about memory, you might try a specific strategy (e.g., imagining the original scene) to help remember details about the event. Then, once a particular detail comes to mind, you might evaluate your confidence in its accuracy (monitoring), and if this confidence reaches a sufficient level, a description would be reported (control; for a theoretical review, see, e.g., Koriat & Goldsmith, 1996). One important element of this conception is that it distinguishes between memory performance and one's assessment of that performance (e.g., a person's confidence in his or her memory, or his or her appraisal of the attention he or she paid to a particular detail during an event). In many forensic situations, judges and jurors must rely solely on the confidence and detail expressed in a witness's report as an index of accuracy because there is no physical corroborative evidence. This issue highlights the fact that the efficiency of metacognitive processes is key not only to people's ability to evaluate the accuracy of their own memories but also to their evaluation of the memories of others (e.g., sometimes called *social metacognition,* e.g., Frith, 2012; Jost, Kruglanski, & Nelson, 1998).

The basic research literature on metacognition is quite large, and it has influenced work on the role of metacognition in eyewitness situations (Luna, Higham, & Martin-Luengo, 2011; Weber & Brewer, 2008). For the purposes of this chapter, however, we briefly discuss one type of metacognition that is relied upon quite heavily in legal settings—the role of witness confidence as an indicator of memory accuracy. On this particular topic, basic and applied researchers have, at least initially, come to different conclusions about the diagnosticity of expressed confidence and memory accuracy (for reviews, see Brewer & Weber, 2008; Roediger, Wixted, & DeSoto, 2012). Studies looking at standard recognition laboratory tasks finds that high confidence is associated with high accuracy (e.g., Van Zandt, 2000; Wixted & Mickes, 2010). In contrast, and especially in early studies, researchers using eyewitness identification tasks found low correlations between confidence and accuracy (e.g., see literature reviews by Wells & Murray, 1984; Sporer, Penrod, Read, & Cutler, 1995). Thus it is not surprising that many researchers in the latter field concluded that witness confidence is not a good predictor of accuracy (e.g., Kassin, Tubb, Hosch, & Memon, 2001). Subsequent research has generally found a stronger confidence–accuracy relationship when certain factors are controlled (e.g., moderator variables, measurement, and study design; Lindsay, Read & Sharma, 1998; Sporer et al, 1995; Weber & Brewer, 2003). Thus there is general agreement that high confidence can broadly distinguish between accurate and inaccurate eyewitness identification judgments (for a review, see Wixted & Wells, 2017). However, there are important caveats to this conclusion. The diagnosticity of eyewitness confidence is greatest when elicited at the time of identification using a fair lineup but can drop dramatically when confidence is elicited afterward (e.g., after receiving postidentification feedback; Wells & Bradfield, 1998, 1999). Furthermore, high confidence is not an absolute guarantee of accuracy, as some researchers have found substantial error rates (e.g., 20%; Sauer, Brewer, Zweck, & Weber, 2010) even when participants are 100% sure of their identification. Because of this, researchers in the field have sought ways to improve the diagnosticity of confidence judgments, including by changing the way they are elicited (e.g., Sauer, Brewer, & Weber, 2008) or by limiting the time to make identification judgments (e.g., Brewer, Weber, Wootton, & Lindsay, 2012), and this remains a fertile area for future work.

CONCLUSION

Moving Forward: The Intersection of Basic and Applied Research on Memory

The sheer volume of research examining factors that affect eyewitness memory is clearly impressive (e.g., Wells & Olson, 2003; see Lampinen, Neuschatz, & Cling, 2012; Cutler, 2013, for recent reviews), and its products have led to the development of important applications (e.g., National Research Council, 2014; National Institute of Justice Technical Working Group for Eyewitness Evidence, 1999). But has the field developed a deep understanding of the mechanisms underlying eyewitness memory? Some researchers have argued that the answer is "not yet" (Lane & Meissner, 2008; Turtle, Read, Lindsay, & Brimacombe, 2008), because, although the field has successfully catalogued factors that affect eyewitness memory, theoretical development has progressed more slowly (e.g., Brewer & Weber, 2008; Turtle et al., 2008; although there are exceptions, e.g., Loftus et al., 1978; Clark, 2003). Focusing on such theoretical development has, as a positive by-product, the opportunity to develop better applications. The more we know about these underlying processes, the better we will be able to design ways to improve eyewitness accuracy or our ability to evaluate it (e.g., Lane & Meissner, 2008).

In addition, there are a number of important topics (some of which have been discussed here) being studied in basic behavioral and neuroscientific research on perception and memory that have implications for eyewitness memory, although these experiments typically use simpler, less forensically relevant materials than those used in applied research. Applied researchers can be unaware of these developments, because they often publish in different journals and attend different conferences than basic researchers. In contrast, basic researchers often work on fairly circumscribed topics and may not have systematically considered how the variables they study could be influenced in more complex real-world situations. Similarly, they often do not know about the relevant work being conducted by researchers from more applied domains. This dichotomy of "low-road" (ecological) research and "high-road" (basic) research, first articulated by Neisser (1978), generally views the relationship between the fields as primarily in a single direction (i.e., results from the lab are brought to the field, or results from the field should inform laboratory work). A "middle-road" approach has been proposed as a way to get beyond the limitations of this dichotomy (Lane & Meissner, 2008). This approach has three main interrelated elements. The first is that the focus of the field should be on building a more comprehensive theory of eyewitness memory. The second is that there should be greater interaction between basic and applied research (and researchers) and a valuing of work across that spectrum. The third is that embracing a diversity of theoretical approaches and methodologies is a strength rather than a weakness. Such diversity helps overcome the weakness of an overreliance on particular tasks (*methodological fixation*) by allowing a comparison of the results from different methodologies or measures (*converging operations*; e.g., Garner, Hake, & Eriksen, 1956). Apart from the specifics of this middle-road approach, we believe that the field has the potential to make substantial inroads to key questions by opening itself to promising developments in other, related fields.

Promising Areas of Research

If the field of eyewitness memory has not yet developed a deep understanding of underlying mechanisms, which aspects are most in need of exploration? We suspect the answer to this question is likely to vary dramatically depending on the researcher. Nevertheless, we offer a brief list of topics that merit further exploration.

Supporting the Discrimination of True from False Memories

One can argue that there are (at least) two points during the legal process when it might be possible to differentiate between accurate and inaccurate eyewitness memories. The first concerns the ability of witnesses to make such a discrimination when attempting to retrieve memories of the eyewitness event. The second occurs when law enforcement or triers of fact (i.e., judges and jurors) are faced with the task of assessing the reliability of a witness. In the former case, supporting witnesses in their assessment reduces the likelihood that inaccuracy will become part of the case evidence. In the second, supporting the accuracy of the decision-making process has the potential of "catching" false memories such that they do not unduly influence the outcome. From the perspective of the legal system, this is similar to the distinction between "early selection" and "late correction" strategies for reducing errors (Jacoby, Kelley, & McElree, 1999).

ASSISTING THE WITNESS

One key way to avoid memory errors is to make sure that a person's expectations about a memory task (metamnemonic knowledge) reflect the specific features necessary to discriminate between true and false memories (e.g., Lane, Roussel, Villa, & Morita, 2007; Gallo, 2013). A witness who is well calibrated in this regard, for instance, would be able to form more effective retrieval cues (e.g., Jacoby, Shimizu, Daniels, & Rhodes, 2005) or could use better criteria to assess a retrieved memory record (e.g., Johnson et al., 1993). Laboratory manipulations that have been found to increase accuracy include providing pretest warnings (e.g., Starns, Lane, Alonzo, & Roussel, 2007) or using questions to get participants to attend to key features (e.g., criterial recollection task; Gallo, McDonough, & Scimeca, 2010). It may be difficult to directly apply these techniques to applied settings (for discussion, see Lane et al., 2007). Therefore, other viable options, such as training witnesses during a preinterview period about the nature of the memory task they are about to face, may be useful in this regard. Additionally, pairing traditional interview techniques such as the cognitive interview (e.g., Fisher, Geiselman, & Amador, 1989) with measures developed in the laboratory that guide people to carefully consider the phenomenal experience accompanying a recollection— for example, *graded recollection* (Gallo et al., 2010; Palmer, Brewer, McKinnon, & Weber, 2010) or the Memory Characteristics Questionnaire (MCQ; Johnson, Foley, Suengas, & Raye, 1988)—have been shown to be effective.

ASSISTING THE TRIERS OF FACT

There has also been promising research designed to explore ways of increasing our sensitivity to the accuracy of other people's memories. One type of approach involves calling attention to the procedures used to collect eye-witness memories and the conditions at the time of encoding. An example is the I-I-Eye aid (Wise, Fishman, & Safer, 2009; Pawlenko, Safer, Wise, & Holfeld, 2013), and early work suggests it may helpful in discriminating between "strong" and "weak" witnesses. In contrast to focusing on the impact of external factors, a second approach involves focusing the asses-sor on the features present in the eyewitness report itself. For instance, a number of studies have explored the utility of the Judgments of Memory Characteristics Questionnaire (JMCQ; e.g., Clark-Foos, Brewer, & Marsh, 2015). Similar to the work discussed in the previous paragraph, research has found improved ability to discriminate between accurate and inaccu-rate memories when participants are guided to key distinguishing features (Short & Bodner, 2011) or when the use of those features is reinforced (Clark-Foos et al., 2015). Furthermore, some researchers have suggested that subjective judgments about memory reports could be assisted by algo-rithms tuned to weight key features (e.g., spatial and perceptual detail) more heavily (e.g., Short & Bodner, 2011).

Greater Precision and Understanding of Complexity

Although there is great interest in finding a deterministic cue to eyewit-ness accuracy, this is currently an unlikely development, at least in the near future. However, the fact that evidence about eyewitness accuracy is probabilistic in nature should not deter its use in cases (Brewer & Weber, 2008; Newman & Lindsay, 2009). Nevertheless, it is also true that the results of research on eyewitness memory could be more fruitfully applied if we had more precise estimates of the impact of various variables and types of information. Such research would likely require the development of more sophisticated mathematical models of eyewitness memory, as well as the appropriately designed experiments. In addition, the field is begin-ning to consider the possibility of fusing information from various sources about the event to come to a more holistic appraisal of what occurred. For instance, there have been recent demonstrations that it is possible to integrate information from multiple witnesses to help reconstruct events (e.g., Dunn & Kirsner, 2011; Waubert de Puiseau, Aßfalg, Erdfelder, & Bernstein, 2012). As we discuss next, a related important step is to begin to understand how key factors might interact to affect eyewitness memory in actual crimes.

THE INTERACTIVE INFLUENCE OF VARIABLES INFLUENCING EYEWITNESS ACCURACY

For reasons of experimental rigor, researchers typically study the effect of memory variables on eyewitness testimony in isolation. Yet crimes rarely occur with only a single possible variable that may affect the accuracy and reliability of subsequent testimony being present. Because of this, experts are typically unable to offer testimony on how such variables may interact. What if the crime happens at night, takes you by surprise, the perpetrator is unfamiliar, and you discuss the crime with others before the police arrive? Is any one of these variables more powerful than the others? Does a combination of variables in one event reduce the likelihood of accurate testimony even more than the presence of one variable alone? Such questions suggest the importance of studying the effects of variables in laboratory tasks in combination. Furthermore, there is a currently little known about the incidence of various factors in real-life crimes (i.e., the base rate). Field data from law enforcement could reveal, for instance, whether certain variables known to negatively affect the accuracy and reliability of eyewitness memory tend to occur frequently together (e.g., Do crimes involving weapons happen more often at night than during the day? Do most crimes with multiple eyewitnesses happen during the day, rather than at night?). In both domains, more sophisticated analytical techniques would allow researchers to assess the degree of variability accounted for by each variable and detect mediating and moderating effects on the accuracy and completeness of testimony.

FINAL THOUGHTS

The same perceptual and cognitive processes that we use to beguile our friends with stories during dinner also come into play when we are asked to describe what happened in stressful, high-stakes situations such as the bag snatching that began this chapter. Thus these high-stress, high-stakes situations are both like and unlike more mundane everyday occurrences. From a scientific perspective, eyewitness situations provide an important opportunity to explore how perception and cognition work under stressful conditions with high-stakes consequences. From an applied perspective, the prospect of improving the accuracy of eyewitness memory has the potential to change lives. The field has benefitted from both perspectives in its development and, as documented in the chapters that follow, has an exciting future.

REFERENCES

Anderson, C. M. B., & Craik, F. I. M. (1974). The effect of a concurrent task on recall from primary memory. *Journal of Verbal Behavior, 13,* 107–113.

Bar, M. (2007). The proactive brain: Using analogies and associations to generate predictions. *Trends in Cognitive Sciences, 11,* 280–289.

Bartlett, F. C. (1932). *Remembering: An experimental and social study.* Cambridge, UK: Cambridge University Press.

Basden, B. H., Basden, D. R., Bryner, S., & Thomas, R. L., III. (1997). A comparison of group and individual remembering: Does collaboration disrupt retrieval strategies? *Journal of Experimental Psychology: Learning, Memory, and Cognition, 23*, 1176–1189.

Bjork, R. A., & Bjork, E. L. (1992). A new theory of disuse and an old theory of stimulus fluctuation. In A. Healy, S. Kosslyn, & R. Shiffrin (Eds.), *From learning processes to cognitive processes: Essays in honor of William K. Estes* (Vol. 2, pp. 35–67). Hillsdale, NJ: Erlbaum.

Boyce, M. A., Lindsay, D. S., & Brimacombe, C. A. E. (2008). Investigating investigators: Examining the impact of eyewitness identification evidence on student investigators. *Law and Human Behavior, 32*, 439–453.

Brewer, N., & Weber, N. (2008). Eyewitness confidence and latency: Indices of memory processes not just markers of accuracy. *Applied Cognitive Psychology, 22*, 827–840.

Brewer, N., Weber, N., Wootton, D., & Lindsay, D. S. (2012). Identifying the bad guy in a lineup using confidence judgments under deadline pressure. *Psychological Science, 23*, 1208–1214.

Brigham, J. C., Bennett, L. B., Meissner, C. A., & Mitchell, T. L. (2007). The influence of race on eyewitness memory. In R. C. L. Lindsay, D. F. Ross, J. D. Read, & M. P. Toglia (Eds.), *The handbook of eyewitness psychology: Vol. 2. Memory for people* (pp. 257–281). Mahwah, NJ: Erlbaum.

Carpenter, S. K., & DeLosh, E. L. (2006). Impoverished cue support enhances subsequent retention: Support for the elaborative retrieval explanation of the testing effect. *Memory and Cognition, 34*, 268–276.

Chan, J. C. K., Thomas, A. K., & Bulevich, J. B. (2009). Recalling a witnessed event increases eyewitness suggestibility: The reversed testing effect. *Psychological Science, 20*, 66–73.

Chun, M. M. (2005). Attentional modulation of learning-related repetition attenuation effects in human parahippocampal cortex. *Journal of Neuroscience, 25*, 3593–3600.

Chun, M. M., & Turk-Browne, N. B. (2008). Associative learning mechanisms in vision. In S. J. Luck & A. Hollingworth (Eds.), *Visual memory* (pp. 209–245). New York: Oxford University Press.

Clark, S. E. (2003). A memory and decision model for eyewitness identification. *Applied Cognitive Psychology, 17*, 629–654.

Clark, S. E., & Gronlund, S. D. (1996). Global matching models of recognition memory: How the models match the data. *Psychonomic Bulletin and Review, 3*, 37–60.

Clark-Foos, A., Brewer, G., & Marsh, R. L. (2015). Judging the reality of others' memories. *Memory, 23*, 427–436.

Craik, F. I. M., Moshe, N.-B., Ishaik, G., & Anderson, N. D. (2000). Divided attention during encoding and retrieval: Differential control effects? *Journal of Experimental Psychology: Learning, Memory, and Cognition, 26*, 1744–1749.

Cutler, B. L. (2013). *Reform of eyewitness identification procedures.* Washington, DC: American Psychological Association.

Deffenbacher, K. A., Bornstein, B. H., Penrod, S. D., & McGorty, E. K. (2004). A meta-analytic review of the effects of high stress on eyewitness memory. *Law and Human Behavior, 28*, 687–706.

Diana, R. A., Reder, L. M., Arndt, J., & Park, H. (2006). Models of recognition: A review of arguments in favor of a dual-process account. *Psychonomic Bulletin and Review, 13*, 1–21.

Dougal, S., & Rotello, C. M. (2007). "Remembering" emotional words is based on response bias, not recollection. *Psychonomic Bulletin and Review, 14*, 423–429.

Douglass, A. B., & Bustamante, L. (2014). Social influences on eyewitness memory. In T. Perfect & D. Lindsay (Eds.), *The SAGE handbook of applied memory* (pp. 614–632). Thousand Oaks, CA: SAGE.

Dunn, J. C., & Kirsner, K. (2011). The search for HMAS Sydney II: Analysis and integration of survivor reports. *Applied Cognitive Psychology, 25*, 513–527.

Easterbrook, J. A. (1959). The effect of emotion on cue utilisation and the organisation of behavior. *Psychological Review, 66*, 183–201.

Edelstein, R. S., Alexander, K. W., Goodman, G. S., & Newton, J. W. (2004). Emotion and eyewitness memory. In D. Reisberg & P. Hertel (Eds.), *Memory and emotion* (pp. 272–307). New York: Oxford University Press.

Engle, R. W., & Kane, M. J. (2007). Executive attention, working memory capacity, and a two-factor theory of cognitive control. In B. H. Ross (Ed.), *The psychology of learning and motivation: Advances in research and theory* (Vol. 44, pp. 145–199). New York: Elsevier Science.

Fisher, R. P., Geiselman, R. E., & Amador, M. (1989). Field test of the Cognitive Interview: Enhancing the recollection of actual victims and witnesses of crime. *Journal of Applied Psychology, 74*(5), 722.

Flavell, J. H. (1979). Metacognition and cognitive monitoring: A new area of cognitive-developmental inquiry. *American Psychologist, 34*, 906–911.

French, L., Garry, M., & Mori, K. (2008). You say tomato?: Collaborative remembering leads to more false memories for intimate couples than for strangers. *Memory, 16*, 262–273.

Frith, C. D. (2012). The role of metacognition in human social interactions. *Philosophical Transactions of the Royal Society B: Biological Sciences, 367*, 2213–2223.

Gabbert, F., Memon, A., & Allen, K. (2003). Memory conformity: Can eyewitnesses influence each other's memories for an event? *Applied Cognitive Psychology, 17*, 433–453.

Gallo, D. (2013). *Associative illusions of memory: False memory research in DRM and related tasks.* Hove, UK: Psychology Press.

Gallo, D. A., McDonough, I. M., & Scimeca, J. (2010). Dissociating source memory decisions in the prefrontal cortex: fMRI of diagnostic and disqualifying monitoring. *Journal of Cognitive Neuroscience, 22*, 955–969.

Garner, W. R., Hake, H. W., & Eriksen, C. W. (1956). Operationism and the concept of perception. *Psychological Review, 63*, 149–159.

Gillund, G., & Shiffrin, R. M. (1984). A retrieval model for both recognition and recall. *Psychological Review, 91*, 1–67.

Harris, C., Keil, P., Sutton, J., & Barnier, A. (2010). Collaborative remembering: When can remembering with others be beneficial? In W. Christensen, E. Schier, & J. Sutton (Eds.), *ASCS09: Proceedings of the 9th Conference of the Australasian Society for Cognitive Science* (pp. 131–134). Sydney, Australia: Macquarie Centre for Cognitive Science.

Harris, C., Keil, P., Sutton, J., Barnier, A., & McIlwain, D. J. F. (2011). We remember, we forget: Collaborative remembering in older couples. *Discourse Processes, 48,* 267–303.

Hintzman, D. L. (1988). Judgments of frequency and recognition memory in a multiple-trace memory model. *Psychological Review, 95,* 528–551.

Houston, K. A., Clifford, B. R., Phillips, L. H., & Memon, A. (2013). The emotional eyewitness: The effects of emotion on specific aspects of eyewitness recall and recognition performance. *Emotion, 13,* 118–128.

Howard, M. W., & Kahana, M. J. (2002). A distributed representation of temporal context. *Journal of Mathematical Psychology, 46,* 269–299.

Hupbach, A., Gomez, R., Hardt, O., & Nadel, L. (2007). Reconsolidation of episodic memories: A subtle reminder triggers integration of new information. *Learning and Memory, 14,* 47–53.

Jacoby, L. L., Kelley, C. M., & McElree, B. D. (1999). The role of cognitive control: Early selection vs. late correction. In S. Chaiken & Y. Trope (Eds.), *Dual-process theories in social psychology* (pp. 383–400). New York: Guilford Press.

Jacoby, L. L., Shimizu, Y., Daniels, K. A., & Rhodes, M. G. (2005). Modes of cognitive control in recognition and source memory: Depth of retrieval. *Psychonomic Bulletin and Review, 12*(5), 852–857.

Johnson, M. K., Foley, M. A., Suengas, A. G., & Raye, C. L. (1988). Phenomenal characteristics of memories for perceived and imagined autobiographical events. *Journal of Experimental Psychology: General, 117*(4), 371.

Johnson, M. K., Hashtroudi, S., & Lindsay, D. S. (1993). Source monitoring. *Psychological Bulletin, 114,* 3–28.

Jost, J. T., Kruglanski, A. W., & Nelson, T. O. (1998). Social metacognition: An expansionist review. *Personality and Social Psychology Review, 2,* 137–154.

Kassin, S. M., Leo, R. A., Meissner, C. A., Richman, K. D., Colwell, L. H., Leach, A. M., et al. (2007). Police interviewing and interrogation: A self-report survey of police practices and beliefs. *Law and Human Behavior, 31,* 381–400.

Kassin, S. M., Tubb, V. A., Hosch, H. M., & Memon, A. (2001). On the "general acceptance" of eyewitness testimony research: A new survey of the experts. *American Psychologist, 56,* 405–416.

Kersten, D., Mamassian, P., & Yuille, A. (2004). Object perception as Bayesian inference. *Annual Review of Psychology, 55,* 271–304.

Koriat, A., & Goldsmith, M. (1996). Monitoring and control processes in the strategic regulation of memory accuracy. *Psychological Review, 103,* 490–517.

Lampinen, J. M., Neuschatz, J. S., & Cling, A. D. (2012). *The psychology of eyewitness identification.* New York: Psychology Press.

Lane, S. (2006). Dividing attention during a witnessed event increases eyewitness suggestibility. *Applied Cognitive Psychology, 20,* 119–212.

Lane, S. M., & Karam-Zanders, T. (2014). What do people know about memory? In T. J. Perfect & D. S. Lindsay (Eds.), *The SAGE handbook of applied memory* (pp. 348–365). Thousand Oaks, CA: SAGE.

Lane, S. M., Mather, M., Villa, D., & Morita, S. (2001). How events are reviewed matters: Effects of varied focus on eyewitness suggestibility. *Memory and Cognition, 29,* 940–947.

Lane, S. M., & Meissner, C. A. (2008). A "middle road" approach to bridging the basic–applied divide in eyewitness identification research. *Applied Cognitive Psychology, 22,* 779–787.

Lane, S. M., Roussel, C. C., Villa, D., & Morita, S. (2007). Features and feedback: Enhancing metamnemonic knowledge at retrieval reduces source monitoring errors. *Journal of Experimental Psychology: Learning, Memory, and Cognition, 33*, 1131–1142.

Lindsay, D. S. (2008). Source monitoring. In H. L. Roediger, III (Ed.), *Learning and memory: A comprehensive reference: Vol. 2. Cognitive psychology of memory* (pp. 325–348). Oxford, UK: Elsevier.

Lindsay, D. S., Read, J. D., & Sharma, K. (1998). Accuracy and confidence in person identification: The relationship is strong when witnessing conditions vary widely. *Psychological Science, 9*, 215–218.

Loftus, E. F. (2005). Planting misinformation in the human mind: A 30-year investigation of the malleability of memory. *Learning and Memory, 12*, 361–366.

Loftus, E. F., Miller, D. G., & Burns, H. J. (1978). Semantic integration of verbal information into visual memory. *Journal of Experimental Psychology: Human Learning and Memory, 4*, 19–31.

Loftus, E. F., & Palmer, J. C. (1974). Reconstruction of automobile destruction: An example of the interaction between language and memory. *Journal of Verbal Learning and Verbal Behavior, 13*, 585–589.

Luna, K., Higham, P. A., & Martin-Luengo, B. (2011). The regulation of memory accuracy with multiple answers: The plurality option. *Journal of Experimental Psychology: Applied, 17*, 148–158.

Macmillan, N. A., & Creelman, C. D. (2005) *Detection theory: A user's guide.* Mahwah, NJ: Erlbaum.

Marsh, E. J. (2007). Retelling is not the same as recalling: Implications for memory. *Current Directions in Psychological Science, 16*, 16–20.

McGaugh, J. L. (2000). Memory: A century of consolidation. *Science, 287*(5451), 248–251.

Morgan, C. A., III, Hazlett, G., Baranoski, M., Doran, A., Southwick, S., & Loftus, E. F. (2007). Accuracy of eyewitness identification is significantly associated with performance on a standardized test of face recognition. *International Journal of Law and Psychiatry, 30*, 213–223.

Morgan, C. A., III, Hazlett, G., Doran, A., Garrett, S., Hoyt, G., Thomas, P., et al. (2004). Accuracy of eyewitness memory for persons encountered during exposure to highly intense stress. *International Journal of Law and Psychiatry, 27*, 265–279.

National Institute of Justice Technical Working Group for Eyewitness Evidence. (1999). *Eyewitness evidence: A guide for law enforcement.* Washington, DC: U.S. Department of Justice, Office of Justice Programs, National Institute of Justice.

National Research Council. (2014). *Identifying the culprit: Assessing eyewitness identification.* Washington DC: National Academies Press.

Neisser, U. (1967). *Cognitive psychology.* New York: Appleton Century Crofts.

Neisser, U. (1978). Anticipations, images, and introspection. *Cognition, 6*, 169–174.

Newman, E. J., & Lindsay, D. S. (2009). False memories: What the hell are they for? *Applied Cognitive Psychology, 23*, 1105–1121.

Ochsner, K. N., Schacter, D. L., & Edwards, K. (1997). Illusory recall of vocal affect. *Memory, 5*, 433–455.

Palmer, M. A., Brewer, N., McKinnon, A. C., & Weber, N. (2010). Phenomenological reports diagnose accuracy of eyewitness identification decisions. *Acta Psychologica, 133,* 137–145.

Pawlenko, N. B., Safer, M. A., Wise, R. A., & Holfeld, B. (2013). A teaching aid for improving jurors' assessments of eyewitness accuracy. *Applied Cognitive Psychology, 27,* 190–197.

Payne, D. G. (1987). Hypermnesia and reminiscence in recall: A historical and empirical review. *Psychological Bulletin, 101,* 5–27.

Reisberg, D., & Heuer, F. (2004). Memory for emotional events. In D. Reisberg & P. Hertel (Eds.), *Memory and emotion* (pp. 3–41). New York: Oxford University Press.

Reisberg, D., & Heuer, F. (2007). The influence of emotion on memory in forensic settings. In M. P. Toglia, J. D. Read, D. F. Ross, & R. C. L. Lindsay (Eds.), *Handbook of eyewitness psychology: Vol. 1. Memory for events* (pp. 81–116). Mahwah, NJ: Erlbaum.

Roediger, H. L., III, & Karpicke, J. D. (2006). The power of testing memory: Basic research and implications for educational practice. *Perspectives on Psychological Science, 1,* 181–210.

Roediger, H. L., III, Wixted, J. H., & DeSoto, K. A. (2012). The curious complexity between confidence and accuracy in reports from memory. In L. Nadel & W. Sinnott-Armstrong (Eds.), *Memory and law* (pp. 84–118). New York: Oxford University Press.

Safer, M. A., Christianson, S., Autry, M. A., & Österlund, K. (1998). Tunnel memory for traumatic events. *Applied Cognitive Psychology, 12,* 99–117.

Sauer, J., Brewer, N., & Weber, N. (2008). Multiple confidence estimates as indices of eyewitness memory. *Journal of Experimental Psychology: General, 137,* 528–547.

Sauer, J., Brewer, N., Zweck, T., & Weber, N. (2010). The effect of retention interval on the confidence–accuracy relationship for eyewitness identification. *Law and Human Behavior, 34,* 337–347.

Scheck, B., Neufeld, P., & Dwyer, J. (2000). *Actual innocence.* New York: Random House.

Schiller, D., & Phelps, E. A. (2011). Does reconsolidation occur in humans? *Frontiers in Behavioral Neuroscience, 5,* 24.

Short, J. L., & Bodner, G. E. (2011). Differentiating accounts of actual, suggested and fabricated childhood events using the Judgment of Memory Characteristics questionnaire. *Applied Cognitive Psychology, 25,* 775–781.

Simons, D. J., & Chabris, C. F. (2011). What people believe about how memory works: A representative survey of the US population. *PLOS ONE, 6,* e22757.

Skagerberg, E. M., & Wright, D. B. (2008). The prevalence of co-witnesses and co-witness discussions in real eyewitnesses. *Psychology, Crime and Law, 14,* 513–521.

Smith, S. M. (1979). Remembering in and out of context. *Journal of Experimental Psychology: Human Learning and Memory, 5,* 460–471.

Snodgrass, J. G., & Corwin, J. (1988). Pragmatics of measuring recognition memory: Applications to dementia and amnesia. *Journal of Experimental Psychology: General, 117,* 34–50.

Son, L. K., & Schwartz, B. L. (2002). The relation between metacognitive monitoring and control. In T. J. Perfect & B. L. Schwartz (Eds.), *Applied metacognition* (pp. 15–38). New York: Cambridge University Press.

Sporer, S. L., Penrod, S., Read, D., & Cutler, B. (1995). Choosing, confidence, and accuracy: A meta-analysis of the confidence–accuracy relation in eyewitness identification studies. *Psychological Bulletin, 118*, 315–327.

Starns, J. J., Lane, S. M., Alonzo, J. D., & Roussel, C. C. (2007). Metamnemonic control over the discriminability of memory evidence: A signal-detection analysis of warning effects in the associative list paradigm. *Journal of Memory and Language, 56*, 592–607.

Takahashi, M. (2007). Does collaborative remembering reduce false memories? *British Journal of Psychology, 98*, 1–13.

Tuckey, M. R., & Brewer, N. (2003). The influence of schemas, stimulus ambiguity, and interview schedule on eyewitness memory over time. *Journal of Experimental Psychology: Applied, 9*, 101–118.

Tulving, E. (1983). *Elements of episodic memory.* New York: Oxford University Press.

Tulving, E., & Thomson, D. M. (1971). Retrieval processes in recognition memory: Effects of associative context. *Journal of Experimental Psychology, 87*, 116–124.

Turtle, J., Read, J. D., Lindsay, D. S., & Brimacombe, C. A. (2008). Toward a more informative psychological science of eyewitness evidence. *Applied Cognitive Psychology, 22*, 769–778.

Van Zandt, T. (2000). How to fit a response time distribution. *Psychonomic Bulletin and Review, 7*, 424–465.

Waubert de Puiseau, B., Aßfalg, A., Erdfelder, E., & Bernstein, D. M. (2012). Extracting the truth from conflicting eyewitness reports: A formal modeling approach. *Journal of Experimental Psychology: Applied, 18*, 390–403.

Weber, N., & Brewer, N. (2003). The effect of judgment type and confidence scale on confidence–accuracy calibration in face recognition. *Journal of Applied Psychology, 88*, 490–499.

Weber, N., & Brewer, N. (2008). Eyewitness recall: Regulation of grain size and the role of confidence. *Journal of Experimental Psychology: Applied, 14*, 50–60.

Wells, G. L., & Bradfield, A. L. (1998). "Good, you identified the suspect": Feedback to eyewitnesses distorts their reports of the witnessing experience. *Journal of Applied Psychology, 83*, 360–376.

Wells, G. L., & Bradfield, A. L. (1999). Distortions in eyewitnesses' recollections: Can the postidentification-feedback effect be moderated? *Psychological Science, 10*, 138–144.

Wells, G. L., Memon, A., & Penrod, S. D. (2006). Eyewitness evidence: Improving its probative value. *Psychological Science in the Public Interest, 7*, 45–75.

Wells, G. L., & Murray, D. M. (1984). Eyewitness confidence. In G. L. Wells & E. F. Loftus (Eds.), *Eyewitness testimony: Psychological perspectives* (pp. 155–170). Cambridge, UK: Cambridge University Press.

Wells, G. L., & Olson, E. A. (2003). Eyewitness testimony. *Annual Review of Psychology, 54*, 277–295.

Wickens, C. D. (2002). Multiple resources and performance prediction. *Theoretical Issues in Ergonomics Science, 3*, 159–177.

Wise, R. A., Fishman, C. S., & Safer, M. A. (2009). How to analyze the accuracy of eyewitness testimony in a criminal case. *Connecticut Law Review, 42*, 435–513.

Wixted, J. T. (2004). The psychology and neuroscience of forgetting. *Annual Review of Psychology, 55*, 235–269.

Wixted, J. T., & Mickes, L. (2010). A continuous dual-process model of remember/know judgments. *Psychological Review, 117*, 1025–1054.

Wixted, J. T., & Wells, G. L. (2017). The relationship between eyewitness confidence and identification accuracy: A new synthesis. *Psychological Science in the Public Interest, 18*, 10–65.

Yarmey, A. D. (1986). Verbal, visual, and voice identification of a rape suspect under different levels of illumination. *Journal of Applied Psychology, 71*, 363–370.

Yaron-Antar, A., & Nachson, I. (2006). Collaborative remembering of emotional events: The case of Rabin's assassination. *Memory, 14*, 46–56.

Yonelinas, A. P. (2002). The nature of recollection and familiarity: A review of 30 years of research. *Journal of Memory and Language, 46*, 441–517.

Zaragoza, M. S., & Lane, S. M. (1994). Source misattributions and the suggestibility of eyewitness memory. *Journal of Experimental Psychology: Learning, Memory, and Cognition, 20*, 934–945.

Zaragoza, M. S., & Lane, S. M. (1998). Processing resources and eyewitness suggestibility. *Legal and Criminological Psychology, 3*, 305–320.

CHAPTER 6

Interviewing Witnesses and Victims

Lorraine Hope
Fiona Gabbert

Solving crimes and prosecuting perpetrators relies on investigators generating a detailed understanding of what took place during a criminal incident. Information provided by witnesses and victims not only informs understanding in this context but also plays a central role in legal decision making and, ultimately, the delivery of justice (Shepherd & Griffiths, 2013). Effective interviews with witnesses that elicit accurate and detailed information are, therefore, a crucial feature of the investigative process—and the onus is on the interviewer to maximize both the quality and quantity of information obtained. However, eliciting accurate and detailed information about an incident from witnesses is a complex process. For a number of psychological reasons, even cooperative witnesses do not spontaneously report all the information they know. Further, interviewers can inadvertently limit or contaminate witness accounts through the use of misleading or otherwise inadequate questioning techniques. Ultimately, poorly conducted interviews are unlikely to result in reliable evidence and, worse, may contribute to the miscarriage of justice.

The quality of the information obtained in the course of investigative interviews is determined by a number of unrelated factors, some of which are outside the control of the interviewer, but some of which relate directly to the activity of the interviewer. In this chapter, we examine some of the factors likely to affect the detail and accuracy of witness memory before the investigative interview even begins. Next, we consider the psychological factors known to underpin successful interviews with cooperative witnesses and promote effective social dynamics between the interviewer and interviewee. (For interviews with suspect and hostile witnesses, see Madon,

More, & Ditchfield, Chapter 3, and Gunderson & ten Brinke, Chapter 4, this volume, on interrogations and detecting deception, respectively.) These factors include building and maintaining rapport, establishing the role of the interviewer(s) and interviewee, providing retrieval support, and promoting accurate and detailed accounts. Appreciation of these factors from a psychological perspective has informed the development of approaches to eliciting information from witnesses and victims in the course of investigative interviews, such as the Cognitive Interview (CI; Fisher & Geiselman, 1992) and the National Institute of Child Health and Human Development (NICHD) protocol (Sternberg, Lamb, Orbach, Esplin, & Mitchell, 2001). We critically assess these contemporary investigative interviewing techniques and more recent innovations in empirical research on investigative interviewing. We also consider translational issues in the transfer of research-based and theoretically informed interviewing techniques to the field, where various pragmatic factors may hamper successful outcomes. Given that investigative interviewing is a challenging skill to master and demands a sound understanding of memory, communication, and other cognitive, social, and environmental factors that may affect the content and accuracy of witness accounts, we examine issues pertaining to training and retention of investigative interviewing skills.

INVESTIGATIVE INTERVIEWING: CHALLENGES IN THE REAL WORLD

Given that competent forensic investigative interviewing is at the core of excellent investigative practice, it is vital that investigators are equipped to conduct ethically defensible interviews of high quality. However, investigative interviewing is a complex skill to master. Indeed, Powell (2014) sums up this complexity well: "It is not intuitive. It is not easily learned on the job. It is not an art form. Rather, it evolves from scientific enquiry—from the systematic study of human behaviour; the evaluation of new improved methods, laws and systems, against agreed outcomes; and the establishment of mechanisms to transmit new knowledge and promote change in practice and procedure." Further, investigative interviewing is a complex interaction that takes place within a much broader cognitive, social, and environmental context. Before examining the challenges inherent in the interaction between the interviewee and interviewer, it is worth highlighting a number of contextual factors that contribute both to the complexity of the interaction and the difficulty of obtaining detailed and accurate information from cooperative witnesses.

Contextual Factors Affecting Witness Memory

In any investigation, a primary concern for the interview lies in obtaining an accurate and detailed account of the incident from witness memory.

However, human memory is fallible. Not only does information decay over time, but human memory is also vulnerable to distortion and error. To make matters worse, investigative interviews often need to be conducted with witnesses and victims who, due to the nature of the crime, may not have been paying attention or were distracted. This may be because the crime was brief or somehow incidental and the consequences only realized later (e.g., identity fraud, theft, distraction crimes) or because, for a variety of reasons, the witnessing conditions were suboptimal (e.g., chaotic scene, poor lighting, limited viewing conditions). In such instances, the amount of attention afforded to encoding the crime may be compromised, and witnesses may only have weak or partial memory for aspects of the incident (e.g., Hope et al., 2016).

Alternatively, it may be that the witness was under the influence of alcohol or other substances at the time of the incident (Palmer, Flowe, Takarangi, & Humphries, 2013). Although basic research on the effects of alcohol on memory tends to show memory impairment with intoxication (see Mintzer, 2007, for a review), research examining the effects of alcohol intoxication on witness memory has produced somewhat inconsistent findings. In laboratory-based research, intoxicated witnesses have been found to be no less accurate or more vulnerable to suggestion than sober witnesses (Schreiber Compo et al., 2017). However, some field studies have observed impaired recall and increased susceptibility to misinformation (e.g., Van Oorsouw & Merckelbach, 2012), noting that effects were also present after a delay when the participant was sober again (for similar temporary effects of smoking marijuana on witness memory, see Yuille, Tollestrup, Marxsen, Porter, & Herve, 1998).

In other instances, witnesses and victims may have been highly stressed or fearful during encoding of the incident. High levels of stress experienced in naturalistic settings generally impair memory, and these detrimental effects have been well documented (e.g., Hope et al., 2016; Hope, Lewinski, Dixon, Blocksidge, & Gabbert, 2012; Morgan, Southwick, Steffian, Hazlett, & Loftus, 2013). The effect of arousal on memory performance appears to reflect an inverted U-shaped curve with memory for events best when stress levels are moderate (for a review, see Finsterwald & Alberini, 2014). Increased levels of suggestibility have been associated with stress at encoding. In a study involving over 800 soldiers taking part in challenging survival training, Morgan et al. (2013) found that soldiers exposed to misinformation (a photo of a person who was not an interrogator) following a high-stress interrogation were 40% more likely to incorrectly identify this person as their interrogator than those who did not receive the misinformation. Following exposure to misinformation, 27% of soldiers mistakenly reported that their interrogator threatened them with a weapon. Similarly, Hope et al. (2016) found that almost one-fifth of officers in a simulated firearms scenario incorrectly reported that the perpetrator pointed a weapon at them during the scenario.

This is not an exhaustive outline of the contextual factors at encoding that may affect both the quality and quantity of information provided by witnesses in investigative interviews. However, it is important that investigators consider the encoding context in the planning and conduct of interviews with witnesses—not only will this facilitate assessment of the crime scene or incident, but it will also ensure that the interviewer is alert to potentially increased suggestibility. Further, acknowledging any challenges in the encoding context may also assist the witness and reduce any actual or perceived pressure to report details of the incident that he or she either did not encode or can no longer recollect.

Investigative Interviews in Practice

Given the potential complexity of the context in which investigative interviews are often conducted and the demands of the investigative interviewer's task, it is not surprising that observational and empirical research suggest many interviews conducted in practice are of poor quality (Sternberg, Lamb, Davies, & Westcott, 2001). Indeed, there are many well-documented high-profile examples of bad interviewing practice leading to the arrest and, in some cases, conviction of innocent people (e.g., the McMartin case in the United States; the Birmingham Six in the United Kingdom; Oude Pekela in The Netherlands).

Over 30 years ago, Fisher, Geiselman, and Raymond (1987) analyzed a sample of interviews conducted by U.S. police and noted significant deficits in the interviewing approaches observed. Interviewers typically gave witnesses little opportunity to provide a free-recall account of what they had seen but instead interjected with direct or closed questions. Little or no effort was made to implement any techniques that might have improved or supported witness memory retrieval. In addition to interrupting the witness, other inadequate features of the interviews included confusing question sequences (not compatible with the witness's memory for the sequence in which the event occurred), negative question phrasing (e.g., "Didn't you see the man involved?"), judgmental remarks (e.g., "That was a stupid decision you made"), use of jargon or other inappropriate language, pressurized short-form questioning that gave the witnesses little opportunity to respond in any detail (and as a consequence resulted in brief or single-word replies), and failure to follow up on potential leads. Further, there was little uniformity of approach or structure across interviews and interviewers. Similar observations were made by George and Clifford (1992) for a sample of interviews conducted by British police.

More recent work continues to highlight shortcomings in the quality of interview skills (e.g., Lamb, 2016). Failing to establish rapport, interrupting interviewees, asking primarily closed questions, and failing to provide effective retrieval support due to lack of training or understanding of relevant techniques can all—individually and collectively—impair an interviewee's ability to provide an accurate and complete account. For example, using rapid-fire closed questions effectively relegates cooperative witnesses, who may have valuable information to report, to the passive role of question answerers rather than the more active role of information generators/providers. Despite a larger number of questions being asked in such an approach, the overall information elicited in terms of amount of detail is impaired. Further, interviewers taking this approach often ask leading questions that suggest a particular answer or contain information the interviewer is seeking to have confirmed (Fisher, Geiselman, & Raymond, 1987).

Interviews with Cooperative Witnesses

A number of protocols for interviewing cooperative witnesses have been developed in direct response to overcoming the shortcomings and challenges described above, the most prominent of which are the CI (Fisher & Geiselman, 1992) and the NICHD protocol (Sternberg, Lamb, Orbach, et al., 2001). These protocols, evaluated in more detail below, provide a structured yet flexible combination of psychologically informed techniques for interviewers to observe. Broadly speaking, these techniques have been found to significantly increase the amount of information elicited with little cost to accuracy (see Memon, Meissner, & Fraser, 2010, for a review). From a psychological and social communication perspective, a number of core features of these protocols underpin these apparent advantages, including the (1) development of good rapport between the interviewer and the interviewee; (2) management of interviewee expectations about the interview and his or her role in it; (3) use of open-ended questions and instructions to promote both detail and accuracy; (4) use of retrieval support techniques and, if appropriate, flexible reporting formats; and (5) maintenance of an open investigatory mind-set by the interviewer. In the next section, we outline these core features and the underpinning rationales and evidence for their inclusion in ethical and effective investigative interviewing techniques (see also Fisher, 2010; Fisher, Schreiber Compo, Rivard, & Hirn, 2014).

Developing Good Rapport

Rapport between the interviewer and the interviewee has been described as a critical and central feature of effective investigative interviewing, and the importance of building rapport is heavily emphasized in guidance and training manuals (e.g., Achieving Best Evidence [ABE]: Ministry of Justice, 2011; NICHD protocol: Lamb, Orbach, Hershkowitz, Esplin, & Horowitz, 2007). However, rapport is a complex and likely multidimensional concept, and, to date, no shared definition of rapport or consensus about how it might be achieved has been established. For example, researchers and practitioners have variously defined rapport as: "The bond or connection between an investigative interviewer and interviewee" (Vallano, Evans,

Schreiber Compo, & Kieckhaefer, 2015, p. 369); "A working relationship between source and interviewer" (Abbe & Brandon, 2013, p. 216); "A positive mood between interviewer and interviewee" (Ministry of Justice, 2011, p. 70), and, somewhat conflictingly, "The establishment of a relationship, which does not have to be friendly in nature" (U.S. Army Field Manual, 2006, Section 8.3).

Similar discrepancies occur in research methodologies: Diverse approaches have been used to both manipulate and measure rapport. For example, Collins, Lincoln, and Frank (2002) manipulated rapport via voice tone (gentle vs. abrupt), body posture (stiff vs. relaxed), interpersonal behavior (engaged vs. disinterested), and personalization and name usage (present vs. absent). Kieckhaefer, Vallano, and Schreiber Compo (2014) manipulated active listening, name usage, and sharing of personal yet unofficial information. Holmberg and Madsen (2014) manipulated whether interviewers adopted a humanitarian versus a dominant interview style.

The absence of a precise or operational definition leaves the term "rapport" open to interpretation, which has consequences for how it is researched, evaluated, trained, and practiced. However, despite definitional ambiguity, there is overlap in how some characteristics of rapport have been described, such as linguistic and behavioral similarities. These descriptions are underpinned by observational research showing that people (in Western societies at least) adopt particular behaviors (such as relaxed body language, attentiveness, similar communication styles, perceived common ground, use of empathy and mutual respect) when interacting with people they trust and/or when people are motivated to affiliate with others (Abbe & Brandon, 2013). At a more fine-grained level, it has been proposed that rapport comprises (1) mutual attention, as reflected in the degree of involvement between the interviewee and interviewer; (2) positivity, as reflected in the degree of friendliness, warmth, and respect in the interaction, and (3) coordination, as reflected in the extent of behavioral synchrony (Tickle-Degnen & Rosenthal, 1990; see also Abbe & Brandon, 2013; Douglass, Brewer, Semmler, Bustamante, & Hiley, 2013).

Regardless of how rapport is defined, findings from psychological research suggest that developing rapport facilitates communication and information elicitation (Abbe & Brandon, 2013; Alison, Alison, Noone, Elntib, & Christiansen, 2013). Furthermore, interviewers who make an effort to develop rapport with an interviewee elicit significantly more detailed and accurate memory reports from witnesses (Collins et al., 2002), suspects (Alison et al., 2013), and in intelligence gathering contexts (e.g., Soufan & Freedman, 2011). However, across the literature, it remains unclear how the observed rapport advantage occurs. The effects of rapport could be motivational (e.g., the interviewee tries harder) or rapport could assist memory retrieval in other ways (e.g., a positive relationship with the interviewer reduces unnecessary distraction; for further discussion, see Vrij, Hope, & Fisher, 2014).

Setting Ground Rules and Managing Interviewee Expectations

Given the importance of detailed information for investigative leads and subsequent evidence, facilitating witness accounts that are richly detailed and accurate is imperative. Even when good rapport has been established between the interviewer and interviewee, witnesses do not spontaneously report all the information they have. There are several possible reasons for this apparent reluctance. First, it is quite possible that witnesses expect that an interviewer will ask them a number of questions and that their role is simply to answer those questions (and only those questions). This question–answer representation of a police interview is commonplace in popular culture, media, and movies. Witnesses might also make a number of assumptions about what the interviewer knows (or might plausibly know) already and edit their account accordingly, effectively second-guessing the facts of the case.

Second, the social context of an investigation generally accords the interviewer higher or expert status and associated control of the interview. However, as noted by Fisher and Geiselman (1992), it seems obvious that the person with firsthand knowledge of the incident should control the interview. It is, therefore, vital to transfer control of the interview to the witness. The importance of the witness's contribution to the investigation should be emphasized; interviewers should explain that they were not present and do not know what the witness saw. Furthermore, given that there is a difference between remembering information and reporting information, witnesses should be instructed to "report everything" to minimize the risk of potentially important information being withheld.

Third, the investigative interview context is, in terms of interpersonal interaction, highly unusual in that it violates the norms of most ordinary conversations in a number of ways. The reporting of very specific details is unusual in a conversational context; thus witness reports may be somewhat less detailed or complete than necessary to pursue effective investigations (Gabbert, Hope, Carter, Boon, & Fisher, 2015). In particular, witnesses do not report information that they assume to be unimportant. Therefore, informing the interviewees about the type and level of detail they are expected to report and attenuating any tendency to provide a relatively undetailed summary or overview are the first steps toward promoting a detailed account. For example, the threshold of reporting can be influenced by using instructions such as "Your description should contain enough detail to enable me to pick the person out in a crowd" (see Koriat, Goldsmith, & Pansky, 2000, for a review of metacognitive monitoring and control processes in memory).

Fourth, witnesses may guess at or "fill in the gaps" for any missing information that they cannot remember; interviewers should encourage accuracy by warning against this practice. Encouraging the use of "Don't know" or "Not sure" responses may also be beneficial. Encouraging or explicitly "permitting" such responses allows the witness to acknowledge when he or she does not know the answer or cannot recall certain details and should work to attenuate concerns about credibility and pressure to provide information the witness is unsure of (Fisher & Geiselman, 1992). Furthermore, research suggests that "Don't know" responses can be explored in meaningful ways to determine whether the witness genuinely has no recollection of particular information or whether he or she may have access to some information but with low levels of confidence and thus has chosen to withhold it (e.g., Scoboria & Fisico, 2013; Hope et al., 2016).

Finally, witnesses and victims may harbor a variety of beliefs and expectations about the purpose of the interview and how the information they provide might be used. Thus the interviewer needs to make the needs and objectives of the investigation clear in order to elicit a detailed but accurate account.

Questioning to Promote Both Detail and Accuracy

Early observations noted that different question types affect the quality of responses (e.g., Varendonck, 1911). Since then, focusing on the use of police questioning techniques, research has confirmed that investigative interviews featuring relatively more open questions tend to elicit longer, more detailed, and more accurate responses than those featuring a predominance of closed questions (see Oxburgh, Myklebust, & Grant, 2010, for a review of question typologies). Consequently, prominent investigative interview protocols endorse the use of open questions to elicit free narrative reports. Open questions allow for an unlimited free-recall narrative response from an interviewee (e.g., "Tell me in your own words what happened"). Witnesses are encouraged to provide a detailed account of the incident in their own words, at their own pace, without interruption by the interviewer.

Questions inviting narrative responses have a number of benefits. First, they enable the interviewee to engage in a report of the incident without editing or summarizing based on assumptions about the interviewer's knowledge or requirements. Not only is this approach likely to facilitate a higher quality recall of relevant information, but it also reduces the likelihood of the investigation following a particular agenda or bias. Second, generating a free narrative about a target incident is likely to engage the rememberer in a more elaborative and effortful free retrieval and is less distracting than formulating responses to short- or closed-answer questions (see Powell, Fisher, & Wright, 2005). Third, free recall reports of this nature are usually more accurate than responses to short-answer or closed questions, principally because the interviewer is less likely to lead the witness when framing questions in this manner. Open questions can also be used to elicit further information about relevant topic areas that have been identified from the broad narrative response (e.g., "You mentioned X. Tell me more about X"). These more focused, open questions to access breadth and depth of information are commonly referred to as "TED" questions (Tell/Explain/Describe); they continue to give witnesses the flexibility to choose what to report, albeit in response to more focused prompts for information.

Witnesses providing information in response to open questions face competing demands for informativeness (i.e., providing as much information as possible) and accuracy (i.e., providing correct information). These competing demands require effective metacognition (i.e., thinking about one's own report), and research suggests that, in an attempt to balance these demands, individuals regulate the *granularity* (i.e., level of detail reported) of the information they provide (e.g., Weber & Brewer, 2008). Models of strategic memory reporting (Goldsmith, Koriat, & Weinberg-Eliexer, 2002) propose that, when responding to questions, the rememberer first attempts to retrieve a highly detailed, fine-grained response. The likely or probable accuracy of this candidate response is assessed and, if it exceeds a preset criterion for accuracy, the response is provided. If the probable accuracy falls below the criterion, the rememberer attempts to retrieve a less detailed, coarse-grained response. As such, information retrieved by a witness must exceed a criterion level of certainty to be reported. This self-regulation of memory output likely underpins the higher levels of accuracy typically observed for responses to open-ended questions (compared with other question types).

In some cases, open questions targeting breadth and depth of information may fail to elicit the level of detail required to meaningfully progress a particular line of inquiry. In such cases, the use of (nonleading) probing questions to expand on the information provided may be appropriate. Such questions are commonly known as the WH questions (Who–What–Where–When–How). In contrast to open questions (e.g., "Describe the car"), probing questions (e.g., "What color was the car?") typically prompt short, factual responses from an interviewee (e.g., "red"; Oxburgh et al., 2010). These can be useful in gathering investigation-important information and, when used sparingly, can be effective in that they can bypass dependence on individual memory organization and instead provide direct, target-specific, and topic-relevant information. Probing questions may also be useful if interviewees are unresponsive to open-ended questions or are not able to provide a precise and/or coherent account of what happened (Eisen, Qin, Goodman, & Davis, 2002).

When open and WH questions have been exhausted, interviewers may need to ask a closed question (sometimes known as "specific"; Oxburgh et al., 2010). These often elicit "yes/no" clarification responses (e.g., "Did you drive the car?", "Did X say that?"). Generally, however, such questions should only be used sparingly and when the usefulness of open-ended and probing formats has been exhausted. Given limited processing resources, extensive questioning is not only tiring for both interviewers and interviewees but also tends to focus the interviewees' attention on the interviewer (rather than on their memory for the information). Furthermore, the attention of the interviewers becomes focused on the generation of questions rather that listening carefully to the interviewees' responses.

Sometimes confusion occurs both within the investigative interviewing literature and in practice concerning the use of closed questions. In some quarters, the use of closed questions has been criticized as suggestive or leading and thus indicative of poor interviewing technique. However, it is important to draw a distinction between (mis)leading closed questions and nonleading closed questions that allow for cued-recall responses. Leading and misleading questions are those that suggest something to the interviewee that he or she has not revealed him- or herself (e.g., "Was the car black?" suggesting that (1) there was a car and (2) it was black). The suggestive nature of this type of question promotes the notion that the witness is simply required to confirm information that is already known. Extensive research documents the negative effects of leading and misleading questions in investigative interviewing contexts (Sharman & Powell, 2012). Similarly, questions with multiple parts (sometimes known as "multiple questions") and option-posing questions (sometimes known as "forced choice" questions) have been shown to result in less accurate and more suggestible responding (Oxburgh et al., 2010; Shepherd & Griffiths, 2013), particularly in vulnerable victims and witnesses (Maras & Wilcock, 2013).

In sum, given that the aim of an investigative interview is to elicit as much reliable information from a witness as possible in his or her own words, formulating and asking appropriate, nonleading questions is vital. This is best achieved using a hierarchy of appropriate questions (open to probing) followed by closed questions (if necessary). For each topic area, the same question hierarchy (open to probing) should be used to elicit all of the information required for investigatory and/or evidential purposes. Thus probing questions, and even closed questions, can be considered *appropriate* if used after open questions for breadth and depth have been exhausted but *inappropriate* if used at the wrong point in the interview (e.g., before attempts to elicit the information using open-ended approaches).

Unfortunately, although this ideal, structured approach to conducting an investigative interview appears simple, there is a tendency for interviewers to use too many (inappropriate) closed, leading, or multiple questions to elicit information, sometimes in a "rapid-fire" question–answer format (Fisher, Geiselman, & Raymond, 1987). Despite investment in "best practice" interview training in many countries (e.g., *Achieving Best Evidence*: Ministry of Justice, 2011) and the widespread availability of guidelines endorsing the use of open-ended questions, surveys of forensic interviews in the United Kingdom, United States, Canada, Norway, Sweden, Israel, and Finland continue to show deficits in the use of open-ended memory prompts and observe that interviewers frequently revert to a closed interview style (e.g., Lamb, 2016; Sternberg, Lamb, Orbach, et al., 2001; and others).

Providing Retrieval Support

Common to several prominent interview protocols are retrieval support activities designed to maximize the quality and quantity of information retrieved and reported. Some of these are widely used mnemonics that form part of the CI, whereas others reflect more recent innovations in the investigative interviewing literature.

MENTAL REINSTATEMENT OF CONTEXT

The "encoding-specificity principle" outlined by Tulving and Thomson (1973) proposed that a match between the original context (when experiences were encoded) and the recall context facilitates memory. Early support for this principle was observed when divers who learned items underwater recalled those items better when tested under water than on dry land. In an investigative context, there are a variety of reasons why physically reinstating the context is inappropriate (e.g., the context has changed since the incident was encoded; the context no longer exists or, most likely, cannot or should not be recreated). A powerful alternative, mental reinstatement of context, involves the mental revisiting of the encoding context. Interviewees are instructed to think back to the original event and psychologically reexperience mental, physical, emotional, and sensory aspects of that event (e.g., "What could you see? What could you hear? What could you smell? How did you feel?"). Mentally reinstating context in this way typically promotes the recall of additional accurate information and is particularly effective following a long delay (Fisher & Geiselman, 1992).

VARIED AND MULTIPLE RETRIEVALS

Retrieving information from memory increases the activation level of items of information in memory, as well as the associations between items. Thus, not only does an attempt to remember detailed information strengthen memory, but it also increases (1) the likelihood of subsequent retrieval and (2) the retrieval of further information, reflecting the well-documented "testing effect." This effect is thought to occur, at least in part, due to the elaboration and activation of memory traces that can result when retrieval processes are engaged during remembering (Roediger & Butler, 2011). In the investigative interviewing context, attempting to remember an event on multiple occasions using different memory strategies, such as remembering the event in reverse order (from end to beginning), can also result in the recollection of information not initially reported (e.g., Fisher & Geiselman, 1992).

REPORTING MODALITY

Communicating certain types of information may be difficult to do verbally or in a linear narrative. Interviews should therefore explore whether some of the information a witness has to report might be better described or communicated nonverbally. For instance, it may be useful to ask witnesses to generate a sketch of the scene to report important spatial information, including details relating to direction of movement or travel (which may be particularly pertinent for the investigation of road traffic incidents or direction of escape routes). Research also suggests that drawing a sketch may also promote retrieval of relevant details (Dando, Wilcock, Milne, & Henry, 2009). Similarly, using a time line enhances communication of the links between persons and actions in multiperpetrator events and the temporal order of action (Hope, Mullis, & Gabbert, 2013).

SELF-GENERATED CUES

A self-generated cue is defined as any detail salient for the individual, and generated by the individual him- or herself, which is intended to facilitate more complete retrieval of a target memory. The rationale for this mnemonic is based upon Anderson's (1983) spreading activation theory, Tulving and Thomson's (1973) cue-overlap theory, and Nairne's (2002) cue-distinctiveness theory, all of which support the idea that the quality of the overlap between encoded information and retrieval cue predicts the likelihood of successful retrieval. Research suggests that self-generated cues enhance mock witness recall performance relative to other mnemonics, including those generated by the interviewer (Kontogianni, Hope, Vrij, Taylor, & Gabbert, 2018).

THE CI AND THE NICHD PROTOCOL

There are many interview models and protocols currently used by practitioners across the world, with significant variation in the extent to which their formats and effectiveness are supported by scientific evidence, irrespective of the claims made by their proponents. However, two of the most effective, established, and used interview protocols are the CI (Fisher & Geiselman, 1992) and the NICHD protocol (Lamb et al., 2007). These approaches are considered the "gold standard" in that they adhere to the principle of using the best-practice ethical techniques to elicit reliable information from interviewees and have been meaningfully informed by psychological science, particularly with respect to the functioning of human memory. Although the two approaches draw upon very similar key concepts and theoretical underpinnings, there are differences that have affected the development of each. Specifically, the CI was developed largely to enhance the memory of adults who are cooperative witnesses for the purpose of advancing the investigation and providing investigators with accurate leads to pursue (see Memon et al., 2010, for a review). In contrast, the NICHD protocol was developed primarily for use with children (see Lamb, Hershkowitz, Orbach, & Esplin, 2008).

The CI (Fisher & Geiselman, 1992; Fisher, Geiselman, Raymond, Jurkevich, & Warhaftig, 1987) emerged from psychological literature on the nature of episodic memory and memory retrieval processes and incorporates the principles of social dynamics, cognition, and communication (Fisher, 2010). In brief, the CI is based on two principles of memory: (1) a memory trace consists of a network of related information, and (2) there are several possible ways of retrieving an encoded event, so information that cannot be retrieved initially may become accessible using a different retrieval approach. Capitalizing on these theoretical principles, Fisher and Geiselman (1992) developed several techniques to facilitate the accurate retrieval of witnessed episodes (report everything, mentally reinstate context, change temporal order, and change perspective). In a revised version of the CI (the "Enhanced CI"; Fisher, Geiselman, Raymond, Jurkevich, & Warhaftig, 1987), strategies aimed at optimizing both the retrieval process and the social and communication aspects of an investigative interview were incorporated (e.g., rapport building, transferring control of the interview to the witness, focused retrieval, and witness-compatible questioning). As such, the CI is best described as a collection of techniques, only some of which might be used in any given interview (Fisher et al., 2014)

In a meta-analysis including studies published since 1999, Memon et al. (2010) found that, when used appropriately by skilled interviewers who fully understand and engage with the key cognitive and social principles, the CI results in a "large and significant increase in correct details" (p. 357), as well as reducing the use of inappropriate questioning during interviews. The meta-analysis also revealed a smaller but significant increase in the reporting of incorrect details in the CI interview relative to standard or structured interview formats. Memon et al. (2010) suggested that this increase in incorrect details may be due to variation in the version of the CI used and advocated greater emphasis on the use of "I don't know" and "Do not guess" instructions when interviewing. Although heavily reliant on investigator resources, including time and high-quality training, the CI is effective across investigative domains (e.g., crimes, accidents, health-related experiences), interviewees (e.g., children, adults, older adults), and nationalities (e.g., U.S., U.K., Brazil; for a review, see Fisher, 2010; see also Vrij et al., 2014).

In contrast to the CI for interviewing cooperative adults, the NICHD protocol was developed for the purposes of eliciting reliable evidence from child witnesses who, for developmental reasons or due to the nature of crimes against them, might appear to be uncooperative. The NICHD protocol was developed in response to observations that investigative interviewers working with child witnesses and victims demonstrated poor interview practice in that they had difficulty adhering to open questions and frequently used inappropriate techniques such as closed and suggestive questions (Lamb, 2016). Given this context, a range of professionals, including lawyers; developmental, clinical, and forensic psychologists; police officers;

and social workers sought to create a forensic interview protocol that out-lined developmentally appropriate instructions and question types designed to encourage reliance on best-practice techniques. In particular, the goal was for the protocol to be suitable for use by interviewers who do not have a specialized knowledge of memory development or suggestibility research and with varying levels of experience and training.

The NICHD protocol essentially provides structured guidance or a "script" for interviewers to follow that is consistent with best practice. The protocol commences with interviewers explaining what their role and the purpose of the interview are and establishing some "ground rules" (e.g., that the interviewee should only report events that really took place and inform the interviewer if anything is not accurate, clear, or otherwise con-fused). Rapport is considered an important element of the interaction and is developed throughout the early "presubstantive" phase, which includes a "practice narrative" that serves to encourage the child (who may be a victim or witness) to talk in depth, while also informing the interviewer of the child's verbal ability. Instructions and carefully phrased open-ended prompts enable the interviewer to encourage children to provide as much information as possible (see Lamb et al., 2007; *www.nichdprotocol.com*).

The NICHD protocol has been the focus of extensive evaluation and research since its introduction to the field. This body of research consis-tently shows that the quality of interviewing reliably and dramatically improves when interviewers employ the NICHD protocol (Lamb et al., 2007; for a meta-analysis, see Benia, Hauck-Filho, Dillenburg, & Milnitsky Stein, 2015). For example, an analysis of over 40,000 real-world NICHD interviews indicates that the protocol improves the quality of interviews, leading to more open-ended questions and half as many direct, leading, or forced-choice questions when compared with standard or structured inter-views (see Lamb, 2016). Furthermore, analysis of real child sexual abuse case data confirmed that using the NICHD protocol interview resulted in more guilty pleas and, where cases were tried, more guilty verdicts than nonprotocol interviews (Pipe, Orbach, Lamb, & Abbott, & Stewart, 2013).

FROM RESEARCH TO PRACTICE: TRANSLATIONAL ISSUES

Although both CI and NICHD approaches offer investigators a systematic way in which witness information can be effectively elicited, both have encountered some challenges in translation from research to practice. For instance, the CI has been described as a demanding procedure, both for the interviewer (to learn, understand, and administer) and for witnesses (to engage with; Fisher, Geiselman, Raymond, Jurkevich, & Warhaftig, 1987). Survey data from police officers reveal that the CI is perceived as too time-consuming and cumbersome and that some of the individual compo-nents are reported to be ineffective and/or difficult to administer (Dando,

Wilcock, & Milne, 2008; La Rooy, Lamb, & Memon, 2011). A direct and alarming consequence of this general perception of the CI is that interviewers frequently report that they *do not use the technique at all,* despite its being the only evidence-based witness interview procedure currently available and incorporated in investigative interviewing training curricula. It is likely that many failures to engage with the CI reflect a fundamental misunderstanding of the CI and, in particular, of its flexible nature. As pointed out by Fisher et al. (2014), "the skill of conducting an interview is to know which techniques can be implemented, given the specific conditions of the interview, and how best to implement the techniques" (p. 563). As such, the CI cannot be taught as a "check-box" protocol and requires high-quality training to ensure both understanding and successful implementation.

There are also a number of features of research on investigative interviewing that should be taken into account when considering the viability of translation from research to practice. As is common in the vast majority of applied experimental work, much of the initial research conducted in the development of new techniques and tools (and assessment of existing ones) is conducted under what might be described as pristine laboratory conditions. Such experiments typically involve optimal encoding contexts (clear, unimpeded, and expected viewing of a neutral nonarousing event), rigorously controlled application of procedural protocols, and the testing of highly educated young adult samples speaking in their first language. Broadly speaking, this approach is appropriate in order to evaluate the initial performance of new methodologies (relative to established or other different comparison methods) and to provide some indicator as to whether a particular line of research is viable or promising. However, inevitably, these initial testing conditions do not reflect the realities of many witnessing conditions, including important features of the encoding contexts (see earlier section) and features of the witness or victim (e.g., age, distress, vulnerabilities pertaining to disability, mental health, trauma). Although research has begun exploring the efficacy of different interviewing methods for different samples, including samples varying in age (see Wright & Holliday, 2007), with autism spectrum disorder (see Maras & Wilcock, 2013), and with trauma (Krix et al., 2016), further work is needed to examine performance under different "real-world" conditions. Assessments of the "maturity" of research (e.g., replication across different laboratories and contexts), the extent to which methodologies reflect both internal and external validity, and both the viability and reliability of any field-based evaluations are important for those tasked with translating research into practice.

One area that has been particularly neglected in the investigative interviewing literature pertains to the challenges and opportunities present in cross-cultural interviewing contexts. Given the current geopolitical context of war, terrorism, human trafficking, and organized crime, the pursuit of justice increasingly relies on productive interactions between individuals from diverse cultural backgrounds. In this vein, police–civilian interactions are increasingly occurring at a cultural crossroads (Giebels & Taylor, 2009). To date, however, there have only been limited attempts to evaluate the role of culture in the conduct of effective investigative interviewing with victims and witnesses (with the majority of the limited literature available tending to focus on interviews with suspects; e.g., Giebels, Oostinga, Taylor, & Curtis, 2017; Taylor, Larner, Conchie, & Menacere, 2017).

Consideration of culture may, in some cases, be fundamentally important to the conduct of effective investigative interviews. Culture affects the ways that individuals communicate and may be particularly relevant when seeking to establish rapport and promote cooperation in interviewing contexts. The nature of reporting may also vary due to cultural factors. For example, low-context communication, characteristic of Western (individualistic) communication, is factual, direct, and linear (Gudykunst & Ting-Toomey, 1988; Hofstede, 2001). However, communication in high-context (collectivist) cultures tends to be more indirect and context-oriented (i.e., topics may not be addressed directly or aspects of topics may be left unsaid). As such, attempts at direct and rational persuasion with an interviewee from a high-context culture may be problematic, particularly if his or her culture values honor. In such circumstances, the nature of direct questions that typify rational arguments may be perceived as a threat to credibility and therefore to public image and honor (Gelfand et al., 2015). Given that most research in the investigative interviewing domain has not considered the role of culture, it is clear that further work is required to ensure the effective translation of research on investigative interviewing to practice across cultures.

TRAINING AND RETENTION OF INVESTIGATIVE INTERVIEWING SKILLS

Within the investigative interviewing literature, there is remarkably high consistency between researchers about which techniques (and associated skills) are most effective in eliciting full and reliable accounts from witnesses. Identifying successful methods to train people in the use of these techniques and application of the relevant and necessary skills is, therefore, critical. Typically, investigative interviewer courses are short, albeit intensive, lasting for a few days. Although there are often national standards and curricula that courses are expected to meet (e.g., *Achieving Best Evidence*: Ministry of Justice, 2011), the content of individual courses can vary widely, and training resources are often not standardized. Worse, anecdotal accounts suggest that investigative interviewing training is not always delivered by trainers or consultants with requisite knowledge, understanding, skills, or experience. Furthermore, training programs are subject to time and financial constraints, with training, feedback, and ongoing practice and support often unavailable or inappropriate (Powell & Wright, 2008).

The most common way to evaluate the effectiveness of any investigative interview training procedure is by examining the use of desirable question types—for example, whether there is an increase in the proportion of open questions used from pretraining to posttraining performance and a decrease in the proportion of closed questions and leading questions being used (Lamb, 2016). The volume and rate of questions is often also subsumed within this measure. In addition, some evaluations assess the extent to which interviewers competently use more complex skills, such as building rapport, structuring topic areas for questioning, and using mnemonics to facilitate retrieval. Other evaluations measure the extent to which interviewers adhere to an interview protocol such as the CI or the NICHD protocol (Lamb et al., 2007) or to an interview framework such as PEACE[1] (Clarke & Milne, 2001). Trainees' perceptions of the effectiveness of courses or their knowledge of best-practice interviewing are *not* useful indicators of training effectiveness, as research shows there is no significant relationship between these factors and adherence to best-practice guidelines (Wright & Powell, 2007).

Evaluations of investigative interview training largely make for disappointing reading. Despite the provision and implementation of best-practice guidelines and respective interviewer training, field studies frequently show that interviewers around the world fail to execute the task effectively (for a recent review, see Lamb, 2016). For example, Davies, Wilson, Mitchell, and Milsom (1995) evaluated the quality of interviews in the United Kingdom following the implementation of the Memorandum of Good Practice and found the average time spent in free-narrative phase was 1 minute, 44 seconds, compared with 18 minutes, 36 seconds spent using closed questions. Furthermore, 28% of interviewers did not attempt to elicit a narrative response at all. A follow-up evaluation by Davies, Westcott, and Horan (2000) found that, across a sample of investigative interviews conducted between 1991 and 1997, only 2% included open questions (see also Clarke & Milne, 2001). Similarly, Myklebust and Bjorklund (2006) studied 100 Norwegian child-abuse investigators following a two-tier (moderate and advanced) interviewing training program, finding no significant difference in the questioning skills of the investigators at the end of the program. In a more focused evaluation of interview training, Warren et al. (1999) examined the effects of a 10-day course designed to improve the knowledge and skills of experienced child-abuse investigators. Although interviewers demonstrated an improvement in their declarative knowledge about children's abilities and appropriate interview practices, there was no

---

[1]PEACE is a mnemonic for P (Planning and preparation), E (Engage and explain), A (Account), C (Closure), and E (Evaluation, of the interview and the interviewer's performance). For more on the PEACE framework and how it is implemented in U.K. policing, see *www.app.college.police.uk/app-content/investigations/investigative-interviewing/#peace-framework*.

change in subsequent interview practice. Specifically, there was no significant improvement in use of open questions, nor a significant change in the frequency of use of leading questions. The lack of association between an interviewer's *knowledge* of best-practice interviewing and actual interview *practice* has repeatedly been demonstrated by researchers, suggesting that possessing relevant knowledge is necessary but not sufficient for being able to interview effectively. Indeed, it is now considered essential that investigative interview training also incorporate practice and feedback sessions (see Lamb, 2016; St.-Yves et al., 2014).

Demonstrating the importance of the need for both theory and practice components of investigative interview training, Lamb et al. (2002) compared four training regimens: (1) theory only, with no opportunity for practice; (2) theory and practice, in structured modules; (3) theory and practice based on the NICHD protocol and monthly *group* meetings with a supervisor, and (4) theory and practice based on the NICHD protocol, *individual* posttraining written feedback, and monthly group meetings with a supervisor. The latter two conditions outperformed the first two, as demonstrated by an increase in the use of open questions and appropriate use of closed questions. This better interview performance was also found to elicit more information from children in their free-narrative responses. No difference was observed between the latter two conditions, suggesting that group feedback might be as effective as feedback given on an individual basis.

Although effective training incorporating both theory and practice has been found to improve the quality of investigative interviews in the short term, the use of best-practice skills declines quickly. Studies that have measured performance prior to, immediately after, and then well after the completion of a course shows that this skills fade is especially pronounced in the absence of supervision or continued practice in maintaining these skills (for reviews, see Powell, Fisher, & Wright, 2005; St.-Yves et al., 2014).

Given the critical role of reliable witness evidence in the pursuit and delivery of justice, further research and investment is needed to generate an evidence base for best-practice training methods. Finding ways to encourage best-practice behavior, such as the use of structured protocols and aide-memoirs, so that it becomes second nature will help mitigate skills fade. For now, research shows that general best-practice guidelines alone are relatively ineffective in modifying interviewers' behaviors. Instead, investigative interview training must feature both theory and practice sessions. Furthermore, evidence suggests that improvements in interviewing practice occur reliably only when training courses involve multiple modules distributed over time with repeated opportunities for interviewers to consolidate learning and to obtain feedback on the quality of the interviews they do conduct (Lamb, 2016). The use of structured interview protocols (e.g., NICHD protocol) appears to promote significant improvements in investigative interview performance over a longer duration, likely because of the operational guidance and directive support provided.

NEW DEVELOPMENTS IN INVESTIGATIVE INTERVIEWING

Over the past 10 years, a number of supplementary tools and techniques for eliciting information from witnesses and victims have emerged from research. These innovations, largely driven by the identification of gaps in practice or specific investigative needs, typically draw on existing best-practice approaches to investigative interviewing.

For example, the Self-Administered Interview (SAI©; Gabbert, Hope, & Fisher, 2009) was developed to address the serious challenge faced by investigators when an incident occurs for which there are numerous eye-witnesses (e.g., a terrorist attack, a large-scale major incident or accident, serious assault on a train). Any of these witnesses may hold potentially vital information about the incident and descriptions of the perpetrators (i.e., information that will provide critical leads for the investigation and/or compelling evidence in a trial). However, investigators may not have the resources in terms of time, expertise, or personnel to conduct interviews with many witnesses shortly after an incident. The SAI is a generic response tool in that it is suitable for obtaining information about a wide range of different incidents. It takes the form of a standardized protocol of instructions and open-ended questions and nonleading cues that enable witnesses to provide their own statements and is therefore ideal for use when restricted resources mean that a traditional interview is not possible. Empirical testing revealed that the SAI recall tool elicited significantly more information from witnesses with high accuracy rates. Furthermore, the initial completion of an SAI increased the amount of information provided by witnesses in a delayed interview (Hope, Gabbert, Fisher, & Jamieson, 2014). Subsequent research also showed that witnesses who completed an SAI were more resistant to misleading information encountered after an incident (Gabbert, Hope, Fisher, & Jamieson, 2012). Other research has noted an interesting transfer effect, such that reporting about one event using the SAI enhances subsequent reporting about another event (Gawrylowicz, Memon, & Scoboria, 2013). A recent meta-analysis (Pfeil, 2017) reporting the results for 15 empirical studies observed a substantial increase in the reporting of correct details for the SAI, with a large summary effect size ($d = 1.20$), comparable to the benefit found for the CI (see Memon et al., 2010). Analyses also suggested that this increase in reporting of correct details also transfers to a later witness interview ($d = 0.92$). Despite being a relatively new investigative tool for officers tasked with eliciting initial witness accounts, the SAI has been implemented effectively in a growing number of incidents involving multiple witnesses, including murders, shootings, assaults, and other major crime incidents (see Hope, Gabbert, & Fisher, 2011).

Dispensing with the linear verbal narrative common to most interviewing formats discussed so far, the time-line technique is a multimodal format designed to facilitate witness reporting about complex event sequences (Hope et al., 2013; Kontogianni et al., 2018). Drawing on social survey methodologies (e.g., event history calendars) used previously to elicit information about autobiographical events (e.g., Belli, Stafford, & Alwin, 2009), this technique is a self-administered recall and reporting technique designed to optimize an interviewee's ability to recall information within a particular time period in sequence, to identify people involved, and to link those people with their specific actions. Hope et al.'s (2013) participants used a time-line-based reporting format and reported their account of a witnessed event on a "time line" of the relevant time period for the target event. Additional retrieval support was provided through the use of instructions and interactive reporting materials. Mock witnesses who provided their accounts about a multiperpetrator event using a time-line technique provided more (1) person-description details, (2) person-action details, and (3) sequence details than requesting a free report at no cost to accuracy. Testing also included the comparison of component elements of the time-line technique (i.e., instructions, reporting cards, visual time line; Experiment 2), but optimal performance was observed when the full time-line format was used.

Other innovative approaches to eliciting information, drawing on the way in which memory is organized, include the "category clustering recall" mnemonic proposed by Paulo, Albuquerque, and Bull (2016). This mnemonic is based on the general idea that recalling in "category clusters" might be effective because it is compatible with the way in which we use semantic categories to encode, organize, and recall information. The category clustering recall technique involves asking people to organize their recall into information categories (person details, person location details, object details, object location details, action details, conversation details, and sound details). In Paulo et al.'s (2016) study, participants watched a mock robbery video and were interviewed 48-hours later with either (1) an enhanced CI; (2) a revised enhanced CI, with category clustering recall instead of the change order mnemonic; or (3) a revised enhanced CI, with category clustering recall conjunctly used with "eye closure" (see Vredeveldt, Baddeley, & Hitch, 2014) and additional open-ended follow-up questions. Participants interviewed with category clustering recall reported more information without compromising accuracy (although eye closure and follow-up questions were not found to further benefit recall).

Despite a small number of innovations over the past 10 years or so, we agree with Fisher et al. (2014) that research efforts have largely focused on validation of existing methods rather than advancing the field in new theory-driven directions. We echo their call to researchers to turn their focus to the development of novel, flexible, theory-driven approaches for eliciting information in increasingly complex and dynamic investigative contexts. There should also be greater exploration of the wider requirement of ethical, efficient, and effective information elicitation techniques beyond policing contexts. Many of the techniques developed for investigative interviewing could well be adapted or developed in novel ways for a variety of different contexts, such as elicitation of patient histories by medical professionals, investigation of occupational incidents, debriefing of intelligence sources, and reporting by operational staff such as law enforcement personnel and emergency responders.

CONCLUSION

Victims and witnesses deserve to be interviewed in a manner that is ethical, effective, and evidence-based by professionals who have been trained and are expected to conduct high-quality investigative interviews. Significant progress has been made over the past 30 years in generating an evidence base to support appropriate and effective investigative interviews. However, new challenges in witnessing and interviewing contexts—including (1) increased use of and access to social media, which is likely to result in increased sharing (and cross-contamination) of witness accounts, (2) the need for more effective intelligence gathering, (3) the likelihood of cross-cultural interactions and witness reluctance, and (4) increased pressure from governments worldwide to deliver more with fewer resources—present investigators in the police and allied professions with significant difficulties. Researchers need to be alert to these pragmatic challenges and engage in close collaborative work with investigative practitioners to address emerging challenges. More than ever, research on investigative interviewing and other applied topics must be conducted to high methodological standards, including the recruitment of adequate sample sizes to test well-defined, theory-driven hypotheses, inclusion of relevant control groups, and use of appropriate statistical analyses (see Hope, 2016, for further discussion). Ultimately, the apprehension of the guilty, the prevention of future crimes, and the delivery of justice may well rest on an interviewer succeeding in eliciting a detailed, accurate, reliable account from a witness. For this reason, more than any other, there is no room for complacency with respect to either research or practice in investigative interviewing.

ACKNOWLEDGMENT

Lorraine Hope's work in writing this chapter was partially funded by the Centre for Research and Evidence on Security Threats (ESRC Award: ES/N009614/1).

REFERENCES

Abbe, A., & Brandon, S. E. (2013). Building and maintaining rapport in investigative interviews. *Police Practice and Research, 15*, 207–220.
Alison, L. J., Alison, E., Noone, G., Elntib, S., & Christiansen, P. (2013). Why

tough tactics fail and rapport gets results: Observing Rapport-Based Interpersonal Techniques (ORBIT) to generate useful information from terrorists. *Psychology, Public Policy, and Law, 19*, 411–431.

Anderson, J. R. (1983). A spreading activation theory of memory. *Journal of Verbal Learning and Verbal Behavior, 22*, 261–295.

Belli, R. F., Stafford, F. P., & Alwin, D. F. (Eds.). (2009). *Calendar and time diary methods in life course research.* Thousand Oaks, CA: SAGE.

Benia, L. R., Hauck-Filho, N., Dillenburg, M., & Milnitsky Stein, L. (2015). The NICHD investigative interview protocol: A meta-analytic review. *Journal of Child Sexual Abuse, 24*, 259–279.

Clarke, C., & Milne, R. J. (2001). *National evaluation of the PEACE investigative interviewing course* (Report No. PRAS/149). London: Home Office.

Collins, R., Lincoln, R., & Frank, M. G. (2002). The effect of rapport in forensic interviewing. *Psychiatry, Psychology and Law, 9*, 69–78.

Dando, C., Wilcock, R., & Milne, R. (2008). Victims and witnesses of crime: Police officers' perceptions of interviewing practices. *Legal and Criminological Psychology, 13*, 59–70.

Dando, C., Wilcock, R., Milne, R., & Henry, L. (2009). A modified cognitive interview procedure for frontline police investigators. *Applied Cognitive Psychology, 23*, 698–716.

Davies, G. M., Westcott, H. L., & Horan, N. (2000). The impact of questioning style on the content of investigative interviews with suspected child abuse victims, *Psychology, Crime and Law, 6*, 81–97.

Davies, G. M., Wilson, C., Mitchell, R., & Milsom, J . (1995). *Videotaping children's evidence: An evaluation.* London: Home Office.

Douglass, A. B., Brewer, N., Semmler, C., Bustamante, L., & Hiley, A. (2013). The dynamic interaction between eyewitnesses and interviewers: The impact of differences in perspective on memory reports and interviewer behavior. *Law and Human Behavior, 37*, 290–301.

Eisen, M. L., Qin, J., Goodman, G. S., & Davis, S. L. (2002). Memory and suggestibility in maltreated children: Age, stress arousal, dissociation, and psychopathology. *Journal of Experimental Child Psychology, 83*, 167–212.

Finsterwald, C., & Alberini, C. M. (2014). Stress and glucocorticoid receptor-dependent mechanisms in long-term memory: From adaptive responses to psychopathologies. *Neurobiology of Learning and Memory, 112*, 17–29.

Fisher, R. P. (2010). Interviewing cooperative witnesses. *Legal and Criminological Psychology, 15*, 25–38.

Fisher, R. P., & Geiselman, R. E. (1992). *Memory-enhancing techniques for investigative interviewing: The cognitive interview.* Springfield, IL: Charles C Thomas.

Fisher, R. P., Geiselman, R. E., & Raymond, D. S. (1987). Critical analysis of police interview techniques. *Journal of Police Science and Administration, 15*, 177–185.

Fisher, R. P., Geiselman, R. E., Raymond, D. S., Jurkevich, L. M., & Warhaftig, M. L. (1987). Enhancing eyewitness memory: Refining the Cognitive Interview. *Journal of Police Science and Administration, 15*, 291–297.

Fisher, R. P., Schreiber Compo, N., Rivard, J., & Hirn, D. (2014). Interviewing witnesses. In T. Perfect & S. Lindsay (Eds.), *Handbook of applied memory* (pp. 559–578). Los Angeles: SAGE.

Gabbert, F., Hope, L., Carter, E., Boon, R., & Fisher, R. (2015). The role of initial witness accounts within the investigative process. In G. Oxburgh, T. Myklebust, T. Grant, & R. Milne (Eds.), *Communication in investigative and legal contexts: Integrated approaches from forensic psychology, linguistics and law enforcement* (pp. 107–131). Chichester, UK: Wiley-Blackwell.

Gabbert, F., Hope, L., & Fisher, R. P. (2009). Protecting eyewitness evidence: Examining the efficacy of a self-administered interview tool. *Law and Human Behavior, 33*, 298–307.

Gabbert, F., Hope, L., Fisher, R. P., & Jamieson, K. (2012). Protecting against susceptibility to misinformation with the use of a self-administered interview. *Applied Cognitive Psychology, 26*, 568–575.

Gawrylowicz, J., Memon, A., & Scoboria, A. (2013): Equipping witnesses with transferable skills: The Self-Administered Interview©. *Psychology, Crime and Law, 20*, 315–325.

Gelfand, M. J., Severance, L., Lee, T., Bruss, C. B., Lun, J., Abdel-Latif, A. H., et al. (2015). Getting to yes: The linguistic signature of the deal in the U.S. and Egypt. *Journal of Organizational Behavior*. Retrieved from *https://psyc.umd. edu/publication/gelfand-m-j-severance-l-lee-t-bruss-c-b-et-al-2015-getting-yes-linguistic-signature-deal*.

George, R. C., & Clifford, B. R. (1992). Making the most of witnesses. *Policing, 8*, 185–198.

Giebels, E., Oostinga, M. S. D., Taylor, P. J., & Curtis, J. L. (2017). The cultural dimension of uncertainty avoidance impacts police–civilian interaction. *Law and Human Behaviour, 41*, 93–102.

Giebels, E., & Taylor, P. J. (2009). Interaction patterns in crisis negotiations: Persuasive arguments and cultural differences. *Journal of Applied Psychology, 94*, 5–19.

Goldsmith, M., Koriat, A., & Weinberg-Eliexer, A. (2002). Strategic regulation of grain size in memory reporting. *Journal of Experimental Psychology: General, 131*, 73–95.

Gudykunst, W. B., & Ting-Toomey, S. (1988). *Culture and interpersonal communication*. Newbury Park, CA: SAGE.

Hofstede, G. (2001). *Culture's consequences: Comparing values, behaviors, institutions, and organizations across nations*. Thousand Oaks, CA: SAGE.

Holmberg, U., & Madsen, K. (2014). Rapport operationalized as a humanitarian interview in investigative interview settings. *Psychiatry, Psychology and Law, 21*, 591–610.

Hope, L. (2016). Evaluating the effects of stress and fatigue on police officer response and recall: A challenge for research, training, practice and policy. *Journal of Applied Research in Memory and Cognition, 5*, 239–245.

Hope, L., Blocksidge, D., Gabbert, F., Sauer, J. D., Lewinski, W., Mirashi, A., et al. (2016). Memory and the operational witness: Police officer recall of firearms encounters as a function of active response role. *Law and Human Behavior, 40*, 23–35.

Hope, L., Gabbert, F., & Fisher, R. P. (2011). From laboratory to the street: Capturing witness memory using a Self-Administered Interview. *Legal and Criminological Psychology, 16*, 211–226.

Hope, L., Gabbert, F., Fisher, R. P., & Jamieson, K. (2014). Protecting and enhancing eyewitness memory: The impact of an initial recall attempt on performance in an investigative interview. *Applied Cognitive Psychology, 28*, 304–313.

Hope, L., Lewinski, W., Dixon, J., Blocksidge, D., & Gabbert, F. (2012). Witnesses in action: The effect of physical exertion on recall and recognition. *Psychological Science, 23*, 386–390.

Hope, L., Mullis, R., & Gabbert, F. (2013). Who? What? When?: Using a timeline technique to facilitate recall of a complex event. *Journal of Applied Research in Memory and Cognition, 2*, 20–24.

Kieckhaefer, J. M., Vallano, J. P., & Schreiber Compo, N. (2014). Examining the positive effects of rapport building: When and why does rapport building benefit adult eyewitness memory? *Memory, 22*, 1010–1023.

Kontogianni, F., Hope, L., Vrij, A., Taylor, P. J., & Gabbert, F. (2018). The benefits of a self-generated cue mnemonic for timeline interviewing. *Journal of Applied Research in Memory and Cognition, 7*, 454–461.

Koriat, A., Goldsmith, M., & Pansky, A. (2000). Toward a psychology of memory accuracy. *Annual Review of Psychology, 51*, 483–539.

Krix, A. C., Sauerland, M., Raymaekers, L. H. C., Memon, A., Quaedflieg, C. W. E. M., & Smeets, T. (2016). Eyewitness evidence obtained with the Self-Administered Interview© is unaffected by stress. *Applied Cognitive Psychology, 30*, 103–112.

La Rooy, D., Lamb, M. E., & Memon, A. (2011). Forensic interviews with children in Scotland: A survey of interview practices among police. *Journal of Police and Criminal Psychology, 26*, 26–34.

Lamb, M. E. (2016). Difficulties translating research on forensic interview practices to practitioners: Finding water, leading horses, but can we get them to drink? *American Psychologist, 71*, 710–718.

Lamb, M. E., Hershkowitz, I., Orbach, Y., & Esplin, P. W. (2008). *Tell me what happened*. Chichester, UK: Wiley.

Lamb, M. E., Orbach, Y., Hershkowitz, I., Esplin, P. W., & Horowitz, D. (2007). A structured forensic interview protocol improves the quality and informativeness of investigative interviews with children: A review of research using the NICHD investigative interview protocol. *Child Abuse and Neglect, 31*, 1201–1231.

Lamb, M. E., Sternberg, K. J., Orbach, Y., Hershkowitz, I., Horowitz, D., & Esplin, P. W. (2002). The effects of intensive training and ongoing supervision on the quality of investigative interviews with alleged sex abuse victims. *Applied Developmental Science, 6*, 114–125.

Maras, K., & Wilcock, R. (2013). Suggestibility in vulnerable groups. In A. M. Ridley, F. Gabbert, & D. J. La Rooy (Eds.), *Suggestibility in legal contexts: Psychological research and forensic implications* (pp. 149–170). Chichester, UK: Wiley-Blackwell.

Memon, A., Meissner, C. A., & Fraser, J. (2010). The cognitive interview: A meta-analytic review and study space analysis of the past 25 years. *Psychology, Public Policy, and Law, 16*, 340–372.

Ministry of Justice. (2011). Achieving best evidence: Guidance on interviewing victims and witnesses and guidance on using special measures. London:

Ministry of Justice. Retrieved August 1, 2017, from *www.cps.gov.uk/publications/prosecution/victims.html.*

Mintzer, M. Z. (2007). The acute effects of alcohol on memory: A review of laboratory studies in healthy adults. *International Journal on Disability and Human Development, 6,* 397–403.

Morgan, C. A., Southwick, S., Steffian, G., Hazlett, G. A., & Loftus, E. F. (2013). Misinformation can influence memory for recently experienced, highly stressful events. *International Journal of Law and Psychiatry, 36,* 11–17.

Myklebust, T., & Bjorklund, R. (2006). The effect of long term training on police officers' use of open and closed questions in field investigative interviews with children. *Journal of Investigative Psychology and Offender Profiling, 3,* 165–181.

Nairne, J. S. (2002). The myth of the encoding–retrieval match. *Memory, 10,* 389–395.

Oxburgh, G. E., Myklebust, T., & Grant, T. D. (2010). The question of question types in police interviews: A review of the literature from a psychological and linguistic perspective. *International Journal of Speech, Language and the Law, 17,* 45–66.

Palmer, F., Flowe, H. D., Takarangi, M. K., & Humphries, J. E. (2013). Intoxicated witnesses and suspects: An archival analysis of their involvement in criminal case processing. *Law and Human Behavior, 37,* 54–59.

Paulo, R. M., Albuquerque, P. B., & Bull, R. (2016). Improving the enhanced cognitive interview with a new interview strategy: Category clustering recall. *Applied Cognitive Psychology, 30,* 775–784.

Pfeil, K. (2017). *The effectiveness of the Self-Administered Interview: A meta-analytic review and empirical study with older adult witnesses.* Unpublished doctoral thesis, University of Cambridge, Cambridge, UK.

Pipe, M. E., Orbach, Y., Lamb, M. E., Abbott, C. B., & Stewart, H. (2013). Do case outcomes change when investigative interviewing practices change? *Psychology, Public Policy, and Law, 19,* 179–190.

Powell, M. B. (2014). Centre for Investigative Interviewing launched. Retrieved from *www.deakin.edu.au/research/research-news/articles/centre-for-investigative-interviewing-launched.*

Powell, M. B., Fisher, R. P., & Wright, R. (2005). Investigative interviewing. In N. Brewer & K. D. Williams (Eds.), *Psychology and law: An empirical perspective* (pp. 11–42). New York: Guilford Press.

Powell, M. B., & Wright, R. (2008). Investigative interviewers' perceptions of the value of different training tasks on their adherence to open-ended questions with children. *Psychiatry, Psychology and Law, 15,* 272–283.

Roediger, H. L., III, & Butler, A. C. (2011). The critical role of retrieval practice in long-term retention. *Trends in Cognitive Sciences, 15,* 20–27.

Schreiber Compo, N., Carol, R. N., Evans, J. R., Pimentel, P., Nichols-Lopez, K., Holness, H., et al. (2017). Witness memory and alcohol: The effects of state-dependent recall. *Law and Human Behavior, 41,* 202–215.

Scoboria, A., & Fisico, S. (2013). Encouraging and clarifying "don't know" responses enhances interview quality. *Journal of Experimental Psychology: Applied, 19,* 72–82.

Sharman, S. J., & Powell, M. B. (2012). A comparison of adult witnesses' suggestibility across various types of leading questions, *Applied Cognitive Psychology, 26*, 48–53.

Shepherd, E., & Griffiths, A. (2013). *Investigative interviewing: The conversation management approach* (2nd ed.). London: Oxford University Press.

Soufan, A. H., & Freedman, D. (2011). *The black banners: The inside story of 9/11 and the war against al-Qaeda*. New York: Norton.

St.-Yves, M., Griffiths, A., Cyr, M., Gabbert, F., Carmans, M., Sellie, C., et al. (2014). Training in investigative interviewing: Observations and challenges. In M. St.-Yves & A. Griffiths (Eds.), *Investigative interviewing: The essential handbook of best practices* (pp. 245–269). Toronto, Ontario, Canada: Carswell.

Sternberg, K. J., Lamb, M. E., Davies, G. M., & Westcott, H. L. (2001). The memorandum of good practice: Theory versus application. *Child Abuse and Neglect, 25*, 669–681.

Sternberg, K. J., Lamb, M. E., Orbach, Y., Esplin, P. W., & Mitchell, S. (2001). Use of a structured investigative protocol enhances young children's responses to free-recall prompts in the course of forensic interviews. *Journal of Applied Psychology, 86*, 997–1005.

Taylor, P. J., Larner, S., Conchie, S. M., & Menacere, T. (2017). Culture moderates changes in linguistic self-presentation and detail provision when deceiving others. *Royal Society Open Science, 4*, 170128

Tickle-Degnen, L., & Rosenthal, R. (1990). The nature of rapport and its nonverbal correlates. *Psychological Inquiry, 1*, 285–293.

Tulving, E., & Thomson, D. M. (1973). Encoding specificity and retrieval processes in episodic memory. *Psychological Review, 80*, 352–373.

United States Army. (2006). *Field manual 2-22.3: Human Intelligence Collector Operations*. Washington, DC: Author. Retrieved from *http://fas.org/irp/doddir/army/fm2-22-3.pdf*.

Vallano, J. P., Evans, J. R., Schreiber Compo, N., & Kieckhaefer, J. M. (2015). Rapport-building during witness and suspect interviews: A survey of law enforcement. *Applied Cognitive Psychology, 29*, 369–380.

van Oorsouw, K., & Merckelbach, H. (2012). The effect of alcohol on crime-related amnesia: A field study. *Applied Cognitive Psychology, 26*, 82–90.

Varendonck, J. (1911). Les temoignages d'enfants dans un proces retentissant [The testimony of children in a famous trial]. *Archives de Psychologie, 11*, 129–171.

Vredeveldt, A., Baddeley, A. D., & Hitch, G. J. (2014). The effectiveness of eye-closure in repeated interviews. *Legal and Criminological Psychology, 19*, 282–295.

Vrij, A., Hope, L., & Fisher, R. P. (2014). Eliciting reliable information in investigative interviews. *Policy Insights from the Behavioral and Brain Sciences, 1*, 129–136.

Warren, A. R., Woodall, C. E., Thomas, M., Nunno, M., Keeney, J. M., Larson, S. M., et al. (1999). Assessing the effectiveness of a training program for interviewing child witnesses. *Applied Developmental Science, 3*, 128–135.

Weber, N., & Brewer, N. (2008). Eyewitness recall: Regulation of grain size and the role of confidence. *Journal of Experimental Psychology: Applied, 14*, 50–60.

Wright, A. M., & Holliday, R. E. (2007). Enhancing the recall of young, young–old and old–old adults with the cognitive interview and a modified version of the cognitive interview. *Applied Cognitive Psychology, 21,* 19–43.

Wright, R., & Powell, M. (2007). What makes a good investigative interviewer of children?: A comparison of police officers' and experts' perceptions. *Policing: An International Journal of Police Strategies and Management, 30,* 21–31.

Yuille, J. C., Tollestrup, P. A., Marxsen, D., Porter, S., & Herve, H. F. M. (1998). An exploration on the effects of marijuana on eyewitness memory. *International Journal of Law and Psychiatry, 21,* 117–128.

CHAPTER 7

Child Witnesses

Thomas D. Lyon
Kelly McWilliams
Shanna Williams

In this chapter we provide an overview of psychological issues involving children's capacities as witnesses. First, in order to understand the most important questions for researchers, we discuss the kinds of cases in which children are usually involved. Across different courts, one most often sees children describing abuse at the hands of familiar adults. In order to assess children's reports, memory research is obviously important, but of equal importance is research examining children's willingness to disclose wrongdoing. Second, we describe the difficulties children encounter in disclosing abuse, particularly when it is perpetrated by adults close to them. These dynamics lead most children to remain silent and only the most forthright children to disclose. As a result, investigators will typically encounter children unusually willing to disclose but susceptible to pressures to deny and recant.

Third, we suggest a framework for assessing children's allegations in which child-generated and adult-generated information lie on opposite ends of a spectrum. Child-generated information is preferable because it minimizes the likelihood of adult influence. Questions can be placed along the same continuum, with recall questions optimal because the child is responsible for generating more information, whereas recognition questions rely more on information supplied by the interviewer. The primary problem with poorly trained interviewers is that they rely too much on recognition questions. At the same time, the benefits of recall questions are tempered by the need to ask more specific questions both to access children's memory and to minimize reluctance. We emphasize the utility of specific recall questions for information that is otherwise overlooked and the need to follow up recognition questions with recall questions in order to minimize error.

Fourth, we discuss suggestibility and highlight how the most prominent suggestibility studies have examined the effects of telling children that
false events occurred, as opposed to asking them whether they occurred.
We review research demonstrating that recognition questions are not inherently suggestive. Rather, we argue that the primary problem with recognition questions is captured by the phenomenon of formal reticence, whereby
children provide minimally responsive answers to questions based on the
form of the question. Children routinely answer yes/no questions with
unelaborated yes or no answers, and interviews filled with recognition
questions lead to a host of problems, including responses that are underinformative and ambiguous and questions that are linguistically difficult and
fail to capture the child's perspective. Last, we discuss the implications of
our review for interviewing children about other types of events and suggest fruitful areas for future research.

WHEN ARE CHILDREN WITNESSES?

Children may appear as witnesses in many different types of legal proceedings: criminal, dependency, family, and other courts. In criminal cases,
they are most likely testifying to sexual abuse, physical abuse, or witnessing
domestic violence (Goodman, Quas, Bulkley, & Shapiro, 1999). The relative frequencies largely reflect the fact that prosecutors present children as
witnesses only when they feel they must. It is in these types of cases that
the child's testimony is necessary in order to prove the allegations, because
the child is the only eyewitness (other than the perpetrator) to the alleged
crime. Furthermore, because of the difficulties young children encounter
in braving testimony, very few preschoolers make it to the stand in criminal cases, with school-age children and teenagers predominating (Evans &
Lyon, 2012).

Dependency court cases are non-criminal cases in which the state
intervenes on behalf of a child because of alleged maltreatment by a parent or legal custodian. It is likely that one would see the same pattern as
in criminal court, with children's testimony most often needed in sexual
abuse cases. In physical abuse cases, for example, children's testimony is
less essential than in sexual abuse, because there is more likely to be other
evidence of wrongdoing (Rush, Lyon, Ahern, & Quas, 2014). This is also
true in other types of maltreatment, which include exposure to domestic
violence, parental drug use, filthy homes, and so forth.

Family court cases include divorce proceedings and other types of
cases in which children's custody is at issue (e.g., guardianships). Typically,
in these cases the state does not argue that the parents are at fault, but
rather resolves differences between private parties (mother vs. father; parent vs. relatives). The allegations with respect to the children are likely to be
less serious, though they will mirror criminal and dependency court claims.

The common theme across the different types of legal proceedings is that children are most often testifying about alleged victimization at the hand of familiar adults, typically parents or caretakers. Thus their ability to recount events in which they were personally involved is most often at issue, rather than their ability to identify strangers committing crimes against others. Moreover, when children accuse adults close to them of wrongdoing, motivational issues are obviously important. Therefore, it is not just memory failure that can lead to distortion of their reports.

Historically, the most recent wave of research on child witnesses was inspired by widely publicized day-care cases in which preschool children made sometimes bizarre allegations against day-care providers (Ceci & Bruck, 1995). It was natural to focus on false allegations because of the implausibility of the allegations, and because the cases were tried in criminal court, in which it is well accepted that false convictions are much worse than false acquittals. However, in most cases of alleged child abuse, the allegations are more mundane and much more likely to be heard in dependency or family courts rather than criminally prosecuted. It is important to worry about false denials, as well as false allegations.

THE DIFFICULTIES CHILDREN ENCOUNTER IN ACCUSING FAMILIAR ADULTS OF ABUSE

When children make allegations against parents or other familiar people, and there are no obvious pressures on them to allege abuse (such as in hotly contested custody cases), one should not be surprised to see initial denial, inconsistencies, and recantations, particularly if their allegations are met with suspicion from other family members (Lyon & Ahern, 2011). In order to understand the patterns of children's disclosures of abuse, it is relevant to consider observational research examining the dynamics of sexual abuse and sexual abuse disclosure, as well as experimental work examining children's deception abilities and influences on their honesty. This research highlights the ways in which adult pressures on children are not just a potential source of false allegations—a point long emphasized by divorce lawyers—but also a likely explanation for false denials and recantations.

Nationally representative surveys of adults reveal that most respondents who disclose sexual abuse to surveyors do not recall disclosing the abuse to anyone as a child, and only 10% report that their abuse was ever reported to authorities (see reviews in London, Bruck, Wright, & Ceci, 2008; Lyon, 2009). The surveys find that intrafamilial abuse is least likely to be disclosed and that the most common explanations for a failure to disclose refer to embarrassment, shame, and expectations that the disclosure recipient would blame the child or fail to believe the allegation (Lyon, 2009).

The research examining how admitted perpetrators describe their modus operandi also helps to explain nondisclosure and reluctance (see reviews in Leclerc, Proulx, & Beauregard, 2009; Smallbone & Wortley, 2001; Lyon & Ahern, 2011). Perpetrators commonly desensitize the child to sexual touch through progressively more invasive sexual touch and talk, which tests the child's willingness to acquiesce and the likelihood that the child will disclose. If the child discloses at an early stage of the process, the perpetrator can claim that the touch was merely affectionate, accidental, or otherwise nonsexual. Once the abuse has begun, perpetrators typically make an effort to keep the abuse a secret. The perpetrator may overtly threaten the child with harm (Smith & Elstein 1993), but more often the threats concern harms to the perpetrator (whom the child wants to protect; Smallbone & Wortley, 2001) and harms to the family if the abuse is disclosed (Lang & Frenzel, 1988).

Nondisclosure can also be understood from the child's perspective. Among the youngest children, there is a lack of awareness that the abuse is wrong and difficulty in describing sexual behavior (Cederborg, Lamb, & Laurell, 2007). Children are likely to feel complicit in sexual abuse and hence will often experience self-blame (Quas, Goodman, & Jones, 2003). The more manipulative forms of abuse are likely to increase children's perceptions that they are partially responsible for the abuse. If the child fails to resist, she (or he) is more likely to believe that she consented. If she delays in reporting, she is more likely to believe that subsequent acts of abuse were consensual, or at least that her failure to disclose was responsible for their reoccurrence.

Studies examining children who ultimately disclosed their abuse support the contention that fears of negative consequences to the perpetrator, the self, and others close to the child deter immediate disclosure (Goodman-Brown et al., 2003; Hershkowitz, Lanes, & Lamb, 2007; Malloy, Brubacher, & Lamb, 2011). Moreover, delays in disclosing are greater when the perpetrator is close to the child (London et al., 2008), when the perpetrator groomed the child (Hershkowitz, 2006), and when the child anticipated that nonoffending adults would not support the disclosure (Hershkowitz et al., 2007).

Although we have focused on sexual abuse, the most common type of case in which children are called to testify, similar dynamics operate to deter children from disclosing physical abuse and domestic violence (Hershkowitz, 2006; Hershkowitz & Elul, 1999). Furthermore, developmental research helps to explain a general resistance among children to disclosing wrongdoing by adults close to them. Children are more likely to lie for a parent than a stranger (Tye, Amato, Honts, Devitt, & Peters, 1999). By 4 years of age, children recognize this distinction, and by 6 years of age, they endorse this difference as a norm (Lyon, Ahern, Malloy, & Quas, 2010). By 6 years of age, children recognize that parents are less likely to believe their children when they accuse the other parent (rather than a stranger) of wrongdoing, and by 8 years of age, children recognize that parents are less likely to contact authorities when the other parent has harmed the child

(Malloy, Quas, Lyon, & Ahern, 2014). Hence, quite early in life, children learn that when bad things happen in the family, they stay in the family.

The literature thus supports the proposition that sexual abuse is difficult to disclose. Why then do some reviewers claim that sexually abused children are forthright about their abuse (London et al., 2008)? They base their claims on officially substantiated cases of sexual abuse. Because children are not routinely screened for sexual abuse, sexual abuse cases usually come to the attention of the authorities because of a disclosure (Heger, Ticson, Velasquez, & Bernier, 2002). Because other evidence of abuse is typically lacking (e.g., medical evidence, eyewitnesses, or confessions by the perpetrator), sexual abuse cases are substantiated primarily by a disclosure (Haskett, Wayland, Hutcheson, & Tavana, 1995). Hence, if a child does not disclose abuse, he or she is unlikely to be *suspected* of being a victim and unlikely to be *substantiated* as a victim. It is therefore unsurprising that the disclosure rates of substantiated cases of sexual abuse are often close to 100%.

Protocols for interviewing children recognize that most sexual abuse victims are formally questioned only after they have disclosed. For example, the National Institute of Child Health and Human Development (NICHD) protocol begins with the statement "Tell me why you came to speak with me," which elicits disclosures in a majority of children who ultimately disclose abuse (Sternberg, Lamb, Davies, & Westcott, 2001). If the initial question does not produce a disclosure, the protocol then recommends that the interviewer refer obliquely to prior disclosures (e.g., "I heard you talked to a teacher. Tell me what you talked about") before becoming more direct.

At the same time, proponents of the NICHD protocol approach emphasize that a substantial percentage of children for whom there are strong suspicions of abuse (but no prior disclosure) fail to disclose (Hershkowitz, Lamb, & Katz, 2014). Furthermore, because of children's ambivalence about disclosing, one should not be surprised to see inconsistencies in disclosure. Indeed, if a child is under 10 years of age, accuses a parent or parent figure of sexual abuse, and has an unsupportive caretaker (e.g., a mother who says she does not believe that abuse occurred), he or she is more likely than not to recant (Malloy, Lyon, & Quas, 2007).

An important issue for research is to identify effective means of overcoming children's reluctance without increasing the risk of false allegations. Lab research has shown that children are most likely to disclose transgressions that they would otherwise keep secret if, without the interviewer providing details of the suspected event, they are asked to promise to tell the truth, reassured about disclosing negative events, and told that the suspect has already told "everything that happened" (Lyon, 2014). The research also finds that a substantial percentage of children maintain their silence and that recognition questions explicitly asking about wrongdoing elicit additional disclosures while risking false alarms. In the field, researchers have shown that providing additional emotional support can increase disclosure rates among children known to have been abused (through corroborative evidence), at the same time that large percentages of children fail to disclose (Hershkowitz et al., 2014).

A FRAMEWORK FOR ASSESSING CHILD WITNESSES' REPORTS: CHILD-GENERATED VERSUS ADULT-GENERATED INFORMATION

When children do disclose, the key question is whether their disclosures are truthful. A useful framework for thinking about the veracity of child witnesses' reports is to distinguish between child-generated and adult-generated information. Child-generated information is generally preferable: A spontaneous complaint of abuse by a child to an impartial third party is most likely to be true and most likely to be free of external influence. At the other end of the spectrum, adult-generated information is most suspect. The distinction captures the major pressures that have been blamed for both false allegations and false denials—adult influences that either lead children to make false reports (and even form false memories) or lead children to deny or recant true allegations.

Interviews, in which the adult asks questions and the child answers them, are neither entirely adult-generated nor child-generated. Rather, the questions within the interview lie along the continuum. Distinctions between recall and recognition or open-ended and closed-ended questions are based on the extent to which the adult's questions contain information. Interview instructions recommended in interview protocols largely aim at decreasing the adult's influence and increasing the child's reliance on his or her own memory; these instructions include telling the child that it is acceptable to say "I don't know" to indicate when he or she doesn't understand a question, to correct the interviewer, and statements that the adult is ignorant about the child's experiences (American Professional Society on the Abuse of Children [APSAC], 2012).

Obviously, "leading" or "suggestive" questions are on the adult-generated end of the spectrum. However, classifying questions in this way has several difficulties. First, it implies that the primary problem with different types of questions is the extent to which they suggest specific answers to children. As we discuss, the problems with question types go well beyond suggestibility. Second, although there is universal agreement that interviewers should avoid leading or suggestive questions (Bruck & Ceci, 1995), there is disagreement over what kinds of questions are leading or suggestive (Peterson, Dowden, & Tobin, 1999). "Leading" is particularly troublesome, because it is a legal term and is defined primarily by trial judges rather than by researchers (Goodman, Bottoms, Schwartz-Kenney, & Rudy, 1991). "Suggestive" is ill defined; for example, there is disagreement among psychologists over whether yes/no questions are suggestive (Ceci & Friedman, 2000), an issue we take up later in the chapter.

Unfortunately, other terms used to classify question types (including "specific questions" and "direct questions") are also used inconsistently across studies (Peterson & Biggs, 1997; Waterman, Blades, & Spencer, 2001).

Disagreements over the classification of question types makes it difficult both to compare results across studies and to apply the results of research to actual cases. In order for the field to make real progress, terms should be clearly operationalized in order for research to be comparable and replicable. A particularly helpful step is to emphasize classic distinctions made by memory researchers.

Recall versus Recognition

A useful distinction among question types is whether they rely on recall or recognition memory. Recall includes free-recall questions (very general requests for information) and cued-recall questions (more specific requests). Cued-recall questions would include most *wh-* questions (*who, what, where, when, why,* and *how*). Recognition includes yes/no and forced-choice questions. Yes/no questions, of course, are questions that can be answered yes or no. Forced-choice questions are questions that include an "or" and ask the respondent to choose among possible answers (e.g., "Was it inside or outside?"). In the coding scheme used by the developers of the NICHD interviewing protocol, free-recall questions are often called invitations, cued-recall questions are called directives, and recognition questions are called option-posing questions (Lamb, Hershkowitz, Orbach, & Esplin, 2008).

In normal conversations, yes/no questions are ubiquitous (Stivers, 2010). They predominate when parents question their children (Salomo, Lieven, & Tomasello, 2013). Without special training, child interviewers rely on them quite heavily. Schreiber and colleagues (2006) examined child protective service interviews conducted in a western state in the 1990s and found that 60% of the questions could be answered yes or no. Yes/no questions are also the most common sort of question prosecutors ask child witnesses in court. Stolzenberg and Lyon (2014) found that 67% of attorneys' questions could be answered yes or no. With training and feedback, interviewers can learn to reduce their use of yes/no questions and increase their use of recall questions (Lamb et al., 2008).

Interviewers are routinely advised to maximize their use of recall questions because they minimize errors. However, there is more than one kind of error. Recall questions decrease commission errors but increase omission errors (recall is less complete), whereas recognition questions avoid omission errors but increase commission errors (Schneider, 2015). In other words, recall has higher specificity, and recognition has higher sensitivity. The reason is that recall questions provide fewer cues to memory and, in doing so, avoid false cues (which lead to commission errors), but they also provide fewer true cues (thus increasing omissions). This trade-off also exists when the issue is willingness rather than memory. When children are reluctant to disclose a detail, they are more likely to omit it from recall than they are to explicitly deny it when asked recognition questions (Stolzenberg, McWilliams, & Lyon, 2017b).

Recall difficulties are magnified in children; their recall reports are less complete than adults'. This is in part due to the fact that they are less likely to generate cues on their own. Effective self-generation of cues in part relies on general knowledge about the world. Children are less knowledgeable, and their knowledge is less well integrated (so that the associations among different components of knowledge are weaker). Children are also less aware of how memory functions, which leads them to be less likely to generate cues even if it would be helpful to do so (Schneider, 2015).

A series of studies by Ornstein and his colleagues examining children's memory of pediatric examinations suggests that recognition questions can increase the completeness of reports, though the benefits decrease with age. For example, Ornstein, Gordon, and Larus (1992) interviewed 3- and 6-year-olds about a physical examination immediately afterward and again either 1 or 3 weeks later. Children were first asked "Tell me what happened during your checkup" and "Tell me what the doctor did to you." They were then asked increasingly specific yes/no questions regarding aspects of the exam they failed to mention in response to less specific questions. The children's recall reports were often quite sparse, whereas the more specific forms of questions elicited substantially more detail. Specifically, one-fourth to one-third of the 3-year-olds' correct reporting emerged in response to open-ended questions, and about one-half of the 6-year-olds' correct reporting did so. Thus the specific questions more than tripled the number of details the 3-year-olds could recall, and more than doubled the 6-year-olds' production. However, as noted above, recognition questions increase the likelihood of commission errors, and this is magnified in children. This is largely due to their greater tendency to guess and their corresponding failure to give "don't know" responses to recognition questions (Poole & Lindsay 2001; Rudy & Goodman, 1991). Furthermore, although recognition questions avoid omission errors, they can make matters worse. If children are reluctant or forgetful, recognition questions lead them to explicitly deny details that they would otherwise merely omit. If the child subsequently acknowledges the detail, his or her report appears suspicious because of the overt inconsistency.

Because of the risks and benefits of recall and recognition questions, a good approach is to start with recall questions and only move to recognition questions when recall fails and essential details are missing (Lyon, 2014). Furthermore, interviewers should not ask a string of recognition questions, but should use pairing, in which they follow up yes responses to recognition questions with recall questions (Lamb et al., 2008). Pairing can clarify yes responses that would otherwise constitute false positives (Stolzenberg et al., 2017b; e.g., asking "What happened?" if child responds yes to "Did something bad happen?").

Furthermore, the child-interviewing literature has identified questions that are likely to enhance the productivity of children's recall, called general invitations and cued invitations (Lamb et al., 2008). General invitations include the most broadly worded free-recall questions (such as "Tell me everything that happened" and "you said [X], what happened next?"), and cued invitations are recall questions in which a detail mentioned by the child serves as a cue for elaboration (such as "you said [detail]; what happened next?" or "you said [detail]; tell me more about that.") Memory research examining children's recall productivity has typically failed to ask followups to initial requests for free recall (Davis & Bottoms, 2002) or has relied on a relatively small number of nonspecific followups such as "Tell me what else happened" (e.g., Kulkofsky, Wang, & Ceci, 2008). Cued invitations are likely more productive than questions such as "Tell me what else happened" because they specify content, but likely less error-prone because they use the child's words and, unlike *wh-* questions, do not narrow the focus. In Ornstein and colleagues' studies of children's memories for pediatric examinations, more extensive use of recall questions might have reduced the incremental benefits of recognition questions.

What is needed is more research identifying the circumstances in which children's recall can be enhanced so as to obviate the need to ask more specific *wh-* and recognition questions. One experimental study has found that cued invitations enhance recall of a play activity without increasing error (Brown et al., 2013). Similarly, observational research has found that cued invitations produce large amounts of information in field studies examining NICHD protocol interviews of children disclosing abuse (Lamb et al., 2008). However, there is evidence that cued invitations are less effective with highly reluctant children (e.g., children suffering physical abuse at the hands of parents, Hershkowitz & Elul, 1999) and young preschoolers (3- and 4-year-olds; Hershkowitz, Lamb, Orbach, Katz, & Horowitz, 2012). Moreover, researchers are finding that free-recall and cued invitations often fail to elicit certain types of details that are important in abuse investigations, such as conversations between the child and others (Malloy, Brubacher, & Lamb, 2013). We have found that specific recall questions can elicit otherwise overlooked content, including conversations (Stolzenberg & Lyon, 2014; e.g., "What did the man say to you?") and emotional reactions to abuse (Lyon, Scurich, Choi, Handmaker, & Blank, 2012; e.g., "How did you feel?"). Furthermore, with respect to deliberate nondisclosure of information, we have found that although cued invitations have some utility in increasing disclosure (Ahern, Stolzenberg, McWilliams, & Lyon, 2016), large percentages of children maintain secrets in the face of such questioning, necessitating other strategies to overcome reluctance.

Suggestibility

Much of the research relevant to children's reports has focused on suggestive questioning, which concerns how children's memory reports may be distorted by external influences. A classic finding is that children are more suggestible than adults and that preschool children are especially vulnerable (Ceci & Bruck, 1993). There are several reasons for age differences in suggestibility. Suggestibility is greater as memory is weaker; if one has a strong memory for an event, it is easier to reject false suggestions because they conflict with one's memory. Because children's memory is generally weaker (Brainerd, Reyna, Howe, & Kevershan, 1990), this will lead to greater suggestibility. Second, children are less adept at source monitoring (Thierry, Spence, & Memon, 2001). Source monitoring is the process by which one identifies the source of one's beliefs. From a practical standpoint, this leads to confusion between what one knows because of one's experience and what one knows because of what one has been told. These difficulties are particularly profound in preschool children, who initially have limited awareness of the causal connection between perceptual access and knowledge (Gopnik & Graf, 1988). Third, children are deferential to adults' authority and knowledge (Lampinen & Smith, 1995). Note that this interacts with understanding of knowledge acquisition; if children do not understand the need for perceptual access for knowledge acquisition, they may overattribute knowledge to adults because of adults' greater status.

Researchers examining abuse interviews conducted during the high-profile day-care cases documented how young children were repeatedly interviewed with highly suggestive techniques (Bruck & Ceci, 1995; Schreiber et al, 2006). In turn, these cases inspired much of the experimental demonstrations of children's suggestibility. The suggestive techniques include exposing preschool children to adults describing false events (Principe, Kanaya, Ceci, & Singh, 2006), repeated questioning of preschool children with guided visualization of false events (Ceci, Loftus, Leichtman, & Bruck, 1994), parents' repeated narration of stories that embellish experiences with false events (Poole & Lindsay, 2001), and repeated negative stereotyping combined with exposing preschool children to evidence of wrongdoing (Leichtman & Ceci, 1995). Not surprisingly, the largest effects have been achieved by combining the various suggestive techniques (Bruck, Ceci, & Hembrooke, 2002; Leichtman & Ceci, 1995).

What makes the results of these studies particularly remarkable is that children's subsequent recall frequently included the suggested material and that the youngest children often maintained that they had personally experienced the events when asked source-monitoring questions (e.g., Leichtman & Ceci, 1995; Poole & Lindsay, 2001). Most suggestibility research reports children's responses to suggestive questioning without determining whether there were carryover effects, such that subsequent questioning would also elicit errors. When carryover effects occur, children's reports appear to be child-generated when they are in fact adult-generated, such that even a well-trained interviewer would likely elicit false reports from a child.

The research both highlights the suggestibility of children, particularly preschool children, and the types of suggestion that are necessary for false information to be incorporated in children's subsequent reports. The most impressive demonstrations tell children that the events occurred (as opposed to asking them whether they occurred) and help children generate additional false details to embellish their reports. One of the most cited pair of suggestibility studies—the mousetrap study and the bicycle study— illustrates the distinction. In the original mousetrap study, interviewers repeatedly asked children over several weeks whether various events had occurred and, if children assented, asked for details. They told each child that they had spoken to the child's parents about things that had happened, but they added that not all of the events had occurred. Although many preschool children made false reports, the likelihood that they assented did not increase over time (Ceci, Huffman, Smith, & Loftus, 1994). In the bicycle study, interviewers told children that the queried events had in fact occurred and helped them visualize the events. Children's false reports reliably increased over time (Ceci, Loftus, et al., 1994).

The observational research documenting high rates of suggestive influences in the high-profile cases found that typical interviews suffered from more mundane problems, such as the predominance of yes/no questions mentioned previously (Schreiber et al., 2006). Hence, the most important issue in typical cases is whether suggestive influences *prior to the first formal interview* are responsible for the child's report. The child's disclosure history is particularly important; initial disclosures to friends or disinterested adults are more trustworthy, whereas initial disclosures to adults that are adverse to the suspect are obviously subject to question. One can easily imagine cases in which adults malign other adults in front of young children; divorce cases are the obvious problem. At the same time, it is also easy to imagine cases in which children's abuse disclosures are second-guessed. As a result, a fruitful area of research concerns children's abilities to recall what adults have told them, because they may give investigators insight into the pressures they have encountered (Lyon & Stolzenberg, 2014).

Are Yes/No Questions Suggestive?

Even if interviews are not highly suggestive, yes/no questions nevertheless elicit concern. It is often assumed that yes/no questions are inherently suggestive because of the implicit assumption that the correct answer is yes (Ceci & Friedman, 2000). However, there is little evidence that this is true. Among research with varied content, there is no consistent evidence for a yes-bias or no-bias among young children. For example, Peterson and Grant (2001) had 3- and 4-year-old children play with two confederates (they drew pictures and made necklaces), and 1 week later an interviewer asked yes/no questions about the actions, appearances, speech, and emotions of the confederates. The authors systematically varied whether questions with the same content were correctly answered yes or no. Children were more accurate when responding to yes/no questions when the correct answer was yes, suggesting a yes-bias (see also Peterson et al., 1999). On the other hand, when Peterson and Biggs (1997) questioned 2- to 13-year-olds a few days after an emergency room visit using free recall, *wh-* questions, and yes/no questions, 3- to 4-year-olds' yes responses were more accurate than their no responses, suggesting a no-bias. Other research has revealed no systematic biases (Brady, Poole, Warren, & Jones, 1999). Apparent yes-biases can be an artifact of the way in which the questions are generated. For example, if children are only asked about nonoccurring events, their tendency to guess can lead to false affirmation rates of 50%. That is, an unbiased guesser will still answer yes half the time.

A classic finding cited in support of yes-biases is that a large percentage of 3-year-olds answered affirmatively when asked incomprehensible questions (such as "el camino real?"; Fay, 1975). Fritzley and colleagues systematically studied children's responses to incomprehensible questions, and although they found a yes-bias among 2-year-olds, it disappeared among 3-year-olds and actually turned into a no-bias by 4 years of age (Fritzley & Lee, 2003; Fritzley, Lindsay, & Lee, 2013).

When questions are comprehensible, what appears to be a yes-bias may actually be a plausibility bias. Plausibility is defined in terms of the child's knowledge base about the event in question. For example, in some of the aforementioned medical examination studies by Ornstein and colleagues, the children were asked yes/no questions about "absent features" of the exam, which concerned "aspects of routine physical examinations that happened not to be included in particular checkups" (e.g., "Did the doctor check your eyes?") and "extra-event" questions, which inquired about activities that were never included in an examination (e.g., "Did the doctor cut your hair?" "Did the nurse sit on top of you?"). Children were substantially more likely to falsely respond yes to the absent features. Specifically, 3-year-olds incorrectly responded yes as much as 50% of the time to the absent-feature questions, and older children (up to 7 years of age) did so as much as one-third of the time (Ornstein et al., 1992; Ornstein, Baker-Ward, Myers, Principe, & Gordon, 1995). In contrast, when asked the extra-event questions, children's accuracy was "uniformly impressive" and did not deteriorate over the 12-week delay interval (Ornstein et al., 1995, p. 356), a pattern replicated by a study finding very low rates of yes responses to questions about details not relevant to a recently experienced dental examination (Rocha, Marche, & Briere, 2013).

Whatever the source of false yes responses, they tend to exhibit substantial decreases with age. This is revealed in a number of studies that examined suggestive techniques and included yes/no questions without suggestion. Poole and Lindsay (2001) investigated children's memory for an interaction with a science teacher after delays of 3 months and 4 months. In the absence of parental coaching, the 3- to 4-year-olds incorrectly answered yes 21–24% of the time in response to yes/no questions about nonoccurring events, whereas, by age 5, no more than 5% of the children did so. Likewise, when Garven, Wood, Malpass, and Shaw (1998) questioned

3- to 6-year-old children 1 week after a brief classroom visit by "Manny Morales," asking yes/no questions without reinforcement, the 3-year-olds answered 31% of the yes/no questions about fictitious events incorrectly, but no more than 8% of the 5- and 6-year-olds did so.

These findings are comparable to Gail Goodman's studies, in which one also finds evidence of worse performance among the younger preschool children. For example, Goodman and colleagues (1991) questioned children about an inoculation 2 and 4 weeks after it took place. Children 3–4 years old falsely answered yes up to 20% of the time when asked "Did she put anything in your mouth," whereas only 4% of the 5- to 7-year-olds did so. Likewise, 3- to 4-year-olds falsely answered yes about 10% of the time when asked "Did she touch you anywhere other than on your arm or leg," whereas only 4% of the 5- to 7-year-olds did so (see Davis & Bottoms, 2002, for similar results).

If a study excludes 3-year-olds and tests for implausible content, then yes/no questions are less likely to elicit high rates of error. In a study examining the effects of stereotype induction (informing the subject that a target person does bad things), with yes/no questions as a control, Lepore and Sesco (1994) questioned 4- to 6-year-olds about a play session with an adult teaching assistant (TA) immediately afterward and 1 week later, children were nearly 100% accurate when asked three yes/no questions that might lead to suspicions of abuse: "Did the TA take off some of your clothes?", "Did the TA kiss you?", and "Did the TA ever touch other kids at the school?" (The uncertainty over terminology noted above was present here: The authors referred to the yes/no questions as "cued recall.")

A countervailing bias relevant to concerns over false abuse allegations is children's tendency to deny negative or aversive content. When the content is negative, self-incriminating, or unpleasant, no biases are likely: Children learn to "just say no." For instance, when asked yes/no questions, children begin to deny transgressions by 2 years of age, and their tendency to do so quickly increases by 4 years of age (Talwar & Crossman, 2012). Children will also deny others' transgressions (Talwar, Lee, Bala, & Lindsay, 2004) and actions in which they and another are jointly implicated (Lyon, Malloy, Quas, & Talwar, 2008). This tendency to say no has also been observed in the field; children are less likely to disclose abuse when "Tell me why you are here" is rephrased as a yes/no question, "Do you know why you are here?" (Hughes-Scholes & Powell, 2012).

Making Recognition Questions Suggestive

Recognition questions can be made suggestive by changing their form. They are more likely to elicit acquiescence if they are phrased as tag questions (e.g., "Did he touch you" is made more suggestive if changed to "He touched you, didn't he?"). As with other types of suggestion, tag questions have the largest effect on younger children, with the effects disappearing by about 8 years of age (Cassel, Roebers, & Bjorklund, 1996). Yes/no questions can also be made suggestive when paired with other types of suggestion, such as punishing "no" responses (e.g., "You're not doing good") and positively reinforcing "yes" responses (e.g., "You're doing excellent now"; Garven, Wood, & Malpass, 2000).

Forced-choice questions present special problems. As noted above, children will not answer "I don't know" and therefore are guaranteed to make an error if neither answer is correct. Hence, a particularly suggestive question is a forced-choice question embedded within a false presupposition (e.g., "When he hurt you, was he angry or sad?"; Lyon et al., 2008). These sorts of questions are quite common in studies exhibiting the largest suggestibility effects (Leichtman & Ceci, 1995). Note that the questions essentially tell the child that the event occurred and help create additional details that the child him- or herself chooses. In forensic interviews and in trials, forced-choice questions are much less common than yes/no questions (Schreiber et al., 2006 [5% in forensic interviews]; Stolzenberg & Lyon, 2014 [2% in trials]). However, they are quite likely used when certain types of information are sought, such as clothing placement (discussed below).

Beyond Suggestibility: Formal Reticence

If yes/no questions are not inherently suggestive, and if they are helpful in eliciting details that children don't produce in free recall, then one might argue that they play an important role in forensic interviewing. However, there are good reasons for forensic interviewers to avoid yes/no questions (and other recognition questions, including forced-choice questions) whenever possible, even when suggestibility is not a concern. The reasons for these concerns can be understood in light of a response tendency among children that we have termed "formal reticence."

Formal reticence refers to children's tendency to provide answers that are minimally responsive given the form of the question. When asked yes/no questions, younger children tend to provide unelaborated yes and no responses (Stolzenberg & Lyon, 2014). When asked forced-choice questions, younger children tend to simply choose one of the responses (Peterson & Grant, 2001; Rocha et al., 2013). When asked recall questions, younger children will generate more information than in response to recognition questions (the nature of recall questions requires the person answering the question to generate information), but the information they provide tends to be the minimum amount of information required (Klemfuss, Quas, & Lyon, 2014). It seems likely that limited executive functioning, in particular immature inhibition and limited working memory, contributes to formal reticence (Evans, Stolzenberg, Lee, & Lyon, 2014). Elaborative responses require the speaker to withhold an impulsive response and to search, identify, and articulate information while maintaining the question in mind.

Formal reticence leads to some of the problems we noted above with recognition questions. Even if they do not know the answer, children will answer yes/no and forced-choice questions with a yes, no, or a choice, given the easy accessibility of those responses, and the greater demands of generating an "I don't know" response. Children's response tendencies when asked yes/no questions, including endorsing plausible details and rejecting unpleasant content, are consistent with superficial processing of the question rather than an effortful search through memory.

RECOGNITION QUESTIONS LEAD TO UNDERINFORMATIVE RESPONSES

Formal reticence leads to additional problems with recognition questions. Children's brief responses are often underinformative. For example, oftentimes the best answer to a forced-choice question is "neither" or "both," but children's failure to go beyond the form of the question in providing an answer makes such answers rare. For example, a major means of distinguishing between abusive and nonabusive touch concerns the touching with respect to the child's clothing. In both court and in the lab, however, young children will provide unelaborated responses to yes/no and forced-choice questions about clothing placement when placement is intermediate, thus failing to communicate that the clothes are partially on and partially off (Stolzenberg & Lyon, 2017; Stolzenberg, McWilliams, & Lyon, 2017a). For example, asked a question such as "Were your pants on or off?" children will typically answer "on" or "off," and only rarely elaborate with an answer such as "they were partly on." A solution is to ask a *wh-* question ("Where were your clothes?" or "What happened to your clothes?"), which more likely leads to an intermediate response.

Formal reticence increases the dangers of referential ambiguity, an overlooked problem with many questions asked of child witnesses (Lyon, 2013). Referential ambiguity occurs when a statement can have more than one meaning. There are large developmental differences in children's ability to detect referential ambiguity in their own speech and in other's statements (Matthews, Lieven, & Tomasello, 2007). The easy availability of an unelaborated response to a recognition question reduces the likelihood that a child will *detect* a referentially ambiguous question, and the lack of an explanation of an unelaborated response decreases the likelihood that an adult will *recognize* referentially ambiguous answers.

We have identified two areas in which formal reticence leads to referential ambiguity. In order to overcome children's tendency to guess, interviewers and attorneys will often ask children whether they know or remember some information rather than directly ask for the information. Adults hearing such questions (e.g., "Do you remember when it was?") understand that the question implies "If you do remember, then tell me when it was." However, we have shown that children frequently provide unelaborated responses to "Do you know?" and "Do you remember?" questions, and that this tendency is related to age and inhibitory control (Evans et al., 2014).

When a child provides an unelaborated yes to a "Do you remember?" or "Do you know?" question with an embedded recall question, then his or her answer is merely a minor inconvenience, because the adult can easily follow up with the recall question. For example, if a child answered yes to "Do you remember when it was?" then the adult could simply ask "When was it?" But a more serious problem occurs when adults ask "Do you know?" and "Do you remember?" questions with embedded yes/no questions (e.g., "Do you remember if it was dark?"). When children answer these questions with unelaborated yes or no responses, they fail to communicate whether they are answering the explicit question (whether they remember) or the implicit question (whether it was dark).

Date of abuse is legally significant, and attorneys and interviewers often attempt to elicit approximate dates from children by asking them about when abuse occurred with respect to landmarks—dateable and significant events in the child's life, such as birthdays or holidays. However, children provide unelaborated yes/no responses to questions about the proximity of events to their birthday and unelaborated responses to forced-choice questions about whether events were before or after their birthday, thus failing to communicate which birthday they are using as a landmark (McWilliams, Lyon, & Quas, 2019). For example, asked whether a particular court visit is before or after their birthday, children will typically answer either "before" or "after," and virtually never answer "both" or ask for clarification (e.g., "which birthday?").

Formal reticence can lead to different patterns of responses to yes/no and forced-choice questions, making children seem inconsistent. This is illustrated in a recent series of studies we conducted examining children's understanding of "ask" and "tell." These words are important in sexual abuse cases, because they are used to assess whether disclosure recipients asked or told children information and whether suspects asked or told children to perform various acts (Stolzenberg, McWilliams, & Lyon, 2017c). We found evidence that children initially associate "telling" with "saying," so that they believe asking is a *type of telling*. Hence, they will affirm that a question is telling if asked a yes/no question. For example, if asked whether their mothers "told" them what happened with a suspect, they are likely to respond affirmatively even if their mothers only asked. Because of formal reticence, they will not elaborate on their answers by noting that "ask" is a more precise description of their mother's statement. If asked a forced-choice question ("Did your mother ask you or tell you?"), they are more likely to respond with "ask," because they recognize that ask is the more precise word. Because of formal reticence, however, they will not elaborate on their answer by noting that, in their view, their mother *both* asked them and told them.

Formal reticence also describes children's minimally sufficient responses to recall questions (Klemfuss et al., 2014). However, recall questions inherently require more from the child witness, because by definition they require the respondent to generate information. Moreover, researchers have shown that children's reticence in the face of recall questions can be alleviated to some extent by different means of encouraging more elaborate responses. First, there is evidence that narrative practice, in which the interviewer asks the child a series of recall questions designed to encourage the child to provide a narrative report of recent experiences, increases the productivity of the child's subsequent recall in response to questions about the target event, without compromising accuracy (Brown et al., 2013; Lyon et al., 2014). Second, there is support for the use of cued invitations, which, as noted earlier, entail asking the child to "Tell me more about [child-generated content]" in order to elicit elaboration about a subject or to ask "You said [child-generated content]; what happened next?" in order to establish a sequence of events (Brown et al., 2013). Importantly, however, cued invitations need to be tied to specific content; unelaborated requests to "Tell me more" or recall questions such as "What else happened?" are relatively ineffective (Evans, Roberts, Price, & Stefek, 2010), probably due to children's limited working memory (they must recall the information they previously uttered) and their limited understanding of what information is important or interesting to the questioner.

RECOGNITION QUESTIONS MEAN THAT THE INTERVIEWER SAYS MORE THAN THE CHILD

Still more problems with recognition questions become apparent when one reflects upon the implication that children will provide unelaborated responses to recognition questions: The questioner will necessarily do most of the talking.

MISSING THE CHILD'S PERSPECTIVE

In adult–adult conversations, closed-ended questions are productive because respondents elaborate on their responses. For example, if a coworker asks, "Did you have a good trip?," it would be uncooperative to simply answer yes or no. Rather, one interprets the question as, "Tell me about your trip." The elaboration on one's response generates content that in turn enables the questioner to ask further questions. In contrast, a child's yes response to a question such as "Did you have a good trip?" does not generate any information beyond the content conveyed by the question. In order to keep the conversation going, the questioner must generate additional content on his or her own.

If the questioner is generating all the content, then the narrative that emerges reflects the questioner's perspective more than the child's perspective. For example, if one is asking a child about sexual abuse and asking predominantly yes/no questions, then one will ask about aspects of an abusive event with which one is familiar. If something unusual occurred, it is unlikely to be discovered. Moreover, the child's perspective is likely to be overlooked. This will make it more difficult to determine whether the child's report is credible, because the report that emerges will look similar to a report that an adult may have suggested to the child.

DIFFICULT LANGUAGE

Another problem when the interviewer does most of the talking is that this maximizes the likelihood that the child's limited language abilities will undermine the reliability of the child's report. The child may answer yes or no to a question because the child misunderstands some part of the question. Of course, children often misspeak, and therefore their narratives will contain errors as well. However, when a child spontaneously uses a word incorrectly or says something ungrammatical, one is more likely to detect a problem, because the statement will often appear nonsensical and the child can be asked to elaborate.

Of course, one ought to avoid asking children questions that they may not understand. This is easier said than done. Young children often have limited understanding of terms that are ubiquitous in conversation and extremely important in abuse investigations, such as prepositions (e.g., *on, off, in,* and *under*; Stolzenberg et al., 2017b). Interviewers are sometimes offered age guides, but these impose huge working memory requirements on interviewers who should already be attending closely to the wording of their questions and the information provided by the child. Even if one could keep in mind the age at which children tend to understand various words, this provides a poor guide to how any individual child will respond, given variance in children's language development and variance among children in the age at which they first acquire different words.

Another possible solution is to test individual children's understanding of words before using them. For example, interviewers sometimes attempt to test children's understanding of different prepositions by asking them to place various objects in or under other objects, but, in addition to taking up precious time, there is little evidence that children's understanding of prepositions in that context does a good job of predicting their understanding in other contexts (e.g., "under a box" may be perceived differently than "under one's clothing," because one is perceived vertically and the other proximally; Stolzenberg et al., 2017b). Asking a child if he or she knows what a word means is going to exaggerate comprehension, because children will answer yes if the word sounds like a word with which they are familiar (Saywitz, Jaenicke, & Camparo, 1990). Asking a child to define a word is going to understate comprehension, because children understand far more than they can explain (Flavell et al., 1987).

We can attest to the difficulty of developing tasks that accurately assess comprehension. We have spent considerable time developing tasks for assessing children's understanding of the words *truth* and *lie* because of courts' insistence that their understanding be tested (Lyon, 2011). Despite our best efforts, however, our tasks are still insensitive to some understanding: Children who fail our truth/lie understanding tasks are nevertheless more likely to be honest when asked to promise to tell the truth (Lyon et al., 2008).

Yet another possible solution is to instruct the child to signal incomprehension. Interview protocols generally recommend that interviewers give children instructions about the propriety of answering "I don't understand" and "I don't know," and there is some evidence supporting these instructions (Brubacher, Poole, & Dickinson, 2015). However, the instructions cannot work unless children are aware of their incomprehension or their ignorance and unless they bring that awareness to the fore in answering questions. Given the ease with which children can generate answers to recognition questions, and given the likelihood that children will think they can make some sense of most questions, instructions will have limited utility. This is particularly true of younger children, who have limited awareness of when they lack knowledge (Schneider, 2015) or comprehension (Lyons & Ghetti, 2011). The best solution is to minimize the number of recognition questions and maximize the number of recall questions, because the interviewer will say less, the child will say more, and children are more likely to recognize and acknowledge their ignorance when recall questions are asked (Waterman et al., 2001).

CONCLUSION

We have provided an overview of research on child witnesses that emphasizes the importance of recognizing the types of cases in which children are most likely to be involved: accusations of wrongdoing (typically sexual abuse) against familiar adults. These cases raise memory issues, to be sure, but also raise concerns about motivational issues and deliberate distortion of reports, creating risks of both false allegations and false denials attributable to adult pressures. In addition to memory research, it is helpful to consider both field and lab research on the dynamics of disclosure. This research highlights barriers to disclosure, particularly when children are accusing adults close to them. Future research should continue to develop nonsuggestive means of overcoming reluctance, as well as to identify topics that may require more specific questioning in order to elicit details that child victims fail to recall or deliberately omit. Moreover, the importance of addressing adult influences opens up new opportunities for memory research, specifically children's ability to recall conversations.

At the same time that we have emphasized how the typical child witness is asked about his or her interactions with a familiar adult, and thus unlike the eyewitness asked to identify a stranger, much of what we have said applies to concerns about the reliability of child witnesses generally.

Untrained interviewers are likely to rely on recognition rather than recall questions, no matter the topic. In turn, children's formal reticence, which describes their minimal responsiveness, and the numerous problems encountered when interviewers rely on recognition questions are issues for all child interviews. Furthermore, although we have implicitly assumed that the motivational difficulties facing children victimized by familiar adults are unique, an important question is the role that reluctance plays in eyewitness identification of strangers, for children as well as adults. It may be that child victims are not that different after all.

ACKNOWLEDGMENT

Preparation of this chapter was supported by NICHD Grant No. HD087685. Correspondence concerning this chapter should be addressed to Thomas D. Lyon, University of Southern California Gould School of Law, 699 Exposition Blvd., Los Angeles, CA 90089-0071.

REFERENCES

Ahern, E. C., Stolzenberg, S. N., McWilliams, K., & Lyon, T. D. (2016). The effects of secret instructions and yes/no questions on maltreated and non-maltreated children's reports of a minor transgression. *Behavioral Sciences and the Law, 34*, 784–802.

American Professional Society on the Abuse of Children. (2012). *Guidelines for psychosocial evaluation of suspected sexual abuse in young children* (rev. ed.). Chicago: Author.

Brady, M. S., Poole, D. A., Warren, A. R., & Jones, H. R. (1999). Young children's responses to yes–no questions: Patterns and problems. *Applied Developmental Science, 3*, 47–57.

Brainerd, C. J., Reyna, V. F., Howe, M. L., & Kevershan, J. (1990). The last shall be first: How memory strength affects children's retrieval. *Psychological Science, 1*, 247–252.

Brown, D. A., Lamb, M. E., Lewis, C., Pipe, M. E., Orbach, Y., & Wolfman, M. (2013). The NICHD Investigative Interview protocol: An analogue study. *Journal of Experimental Psychology: Applied, 19*, 367–382.

Brubacher, S. P., Poole, D. A., & Dickinson, J. J. (2015). The use of ground rules in investigative interviews with children: A synthesis and call for research. *Developmental Review, 36*, 15–33.

Bruck, M., & Ceci, S. J. (1995). Amicus brief for the case of State of New Jersey v. Michaels presented by Committee of Concerned Social Scientists. *Psychology, Public Policy, and Law, 1*, 272–322.

Bruck, M., Ceci, S. J., & Hembrooke, H. (2002). The nature of children's true and false narratives. *Developmental Review, 22*, 520–554.

Cassel, W. S., Roebers, C. E., & Bjorklund, D. F. (1996). Developmental patterns of eyewitness responses to repeated and increasingly suggestive questions. *Journal of Experimental Child Psychology, 61*, 116–133.

Ceci, S. J., & Bruck, M. (1993). Suggestibility of the child witness: A historical review and synthesis. *Psychological Bulletin, 113*, 403–439.

Ceci, S. J., & Bruck, M. (1995). *Jeopardy in the courtroom: A scientific analysis of children's testimony*. Washington, DC: American Psychological Association.

Ceci, S. J., & Friedman, R. D. (2000). The suggestibility of children: Scientific research and legal implications. *Cornell Law Review, 86*, 34–108.

Ceci, S. J., Huffman, M. L. C., Smith, E., & Loftus, E. F. (1994). Repeatedly thinking about a non-event: Source misattributions among preschoolers. *Consciousness and Cognition, 3*, 388–407.

Ceci, S. J., Loftus, E. F., Leichtman, M. D., & Bruck, M. (1994). The possible role of source misattributions in the creation of false beliefs among preschoolers. *International Journal of Clinical and Experimental Hypnosis, 42*, 304–320.

Cederborg, A. C., Lamb, M. E., & Laurell, O. (2007). Delay of disclosure, minimization and denial when the evidence is unambiguous: A multi-victim case. In M. E. Pipe, M. E. Lamb, Y. Orbach, & A. C. Cederborg (Eds.), *Child sexual abuse: Disclosure, delay and denial*. New York: Taylor & Francis.

Davis, S. L., & Bottoms, B. L. (2002). Effects of social support on children's eyewitness reports: A test of the underlying mechanism. *Law and Human Behavior, 26*, 185–215.

Evans, A. D., & Lyon, T. D. (2012). Assessing children's competency to take the oath in court: The influence of question type on children's accuracy. *Law and Human Behavior, 36*, 195–205.

Evans, A. D., Roberts, K. P., Price. H. L., & Stefek, C. P. (2010). The use of paraphrasing in investigative interviews. *Child Abuse and Neglect, 34*, 585–592.

Evans, A. D., Stolzenberg, S. N., Lee, K., & Lyon, T. D. (2014). Young children's difficulty with indirect speech acts: Implications for questioning child witnesses. *Behavioral Sciences and the Law, 32*, 775–788.

Fay, W. H. (1975). Occurrence of children's echoic responses according to interlocutory question types. *Journal of Speech, Language, and Hearing Research, 18*, 336–345.

Flavell, J. H., Flavell, E. R., & Green, F. L. (1987). Young children's knowledge about the apparent-real and pretend-real distinctions. *Developmental Psychology, 23*, 816–822.

Fritzley, V. H., & Lee, K. (2003). Do young children always say yes to yes–no questions?: A metadevelopmental study of the affirmation bias. *Child Development, 74*, 1297–1313.

Fritzley, V. H., Lindsay, R. C. L., & Lee, K. (2013). Young children's response tendencies toward yes–no questions concerning actions. *Child Development, 84*, 711–725.

Garven, S., Wood, J. M., & Malpass, R. S. (2000). Allegations of wrongdoing: The effects of reinforcement on children's mundane and fantastic claims. *Journal of Applied Psychology, 85*, 38–49.

Garven, S., Wood, J. M., Malpass, R. S., & Shaw, J. S. (1998). More than suggestion: The effect of interviewing techniques from the McMartin preschool case. *Journal of Applied Psychology, 83*, 347–359.

Goodman, G. S., Bottoms, B. L., Schwartz-Kenney, B. M., & Rudy, L. (1991). Children's testimony about a stressful event: Improving children's reports. *Journal of Narrative and Life History, 1*, 69–99.

Goodman, G. S., Quas, J. A., Bulkley, J., & Shapiro, C. (1999). Innovations for child witnesses: A national survey. *Psychology, Public Policy, and Law, 5,* 255–281.

Goodman-Brown, T. B., Edelstein, R. S., Goodman, G. S., Jones, D. P. H., & Gordon, D. S. (2003). Why children tell: A model of children's disclosure of sexual abuse. *Child Abuse and Neglect, 27,* 525–540.

Gopnik, A., & Graf, P. (1988). Knowing how you know: Young children's ability to identify and remember the sources of their beliefs. *Child Development, 59,* 1366–1371.

Haskett, M. E., Wayland, K., Hutcheson, J. S., & Tavana, T. (1995). Substantiation of sexual abuse allegations: Factors involved in the decision-making process. *Journal of Child Sexual Abuse, 4,* 19–47.

Heger, A., Ticson, L., Velasquez, O., & Bernier, R. (2002). Children referred for possible sexual abuse: Medical findings in 2384 children. *Child Abuse and Neglect, 26,* 645–659.

Hershkowitz, I. (2006). Delayed disclosure of alleged child abuse victims in Israel. *American Journal of Orthopsychiatry, 76,* 444–450.

Hershkowitz, I., & Elul, A. (1999). The effects of investigative utterances on Israeli children's reports of physical abuse. *Applied Developmental Science, 3,* 28–33.

Hershkowitz, I., Lamb, M. E., & Katz, C. (2014). Allegation rates in forensic child abuse investigations: Comparing the revised and standard NICHD protocols. *Psychology, Public Policy, and Law, 20,* 336–344.

Hershkowitz, I., Lamb, M. E., Orbach, Y., Katz, C., & Horowitz, D. (2012). The development of communicative and narrative skills among preschoolers: Lessons from forensic interviews about child abuse. *Child Development, 83,* 611–622.

Hershkowitz, I., Lanes, O., & Lamb, M. E. (2007). Exploring the disclosure of child sexual abuse with alleged victims and their parents. *Child Abuse and Neglect, 31,* 111–123.

Hughes-Scholes, C. H., & Powell, M. B. (2012). Techniques used by investigative interviewers to elicit disclosures of abuse from child witnesses: A critique. *Police Practice and Research, 14,* 45–52.

Klemfuss, J. Z., Quas, J. A., & Lyon, T. D. (2014). Attorneys' questions and children's productivity in child sexual abuse criminal trials. *Applied Cognitive Psychology, 28,* 780–788.

Kulkofsky, S., Wang, Q., & Ceci, S. J. (2008). Do better stories make better memories?: Narrative quality and memory accuracy in preschool children. *Applied Cognitive Psychology, 22,* 21–38.

Lamb, M. E., Hershkowitz, I., Orbach, Y., & Esplin, P. N. (2008). *Tell me what happened: Structured investigative interviews of child victims and witnesses.* London: Wiley.

Lampinen, J. M., & Smith, V. L. (1995). The incredible (and sometimes incredulous) child witness: Child eyewitnesses' sensitivity to source credibility cues. *Journal of Applied Psychology, 80,* 621–627.

Lang, R. A., & Frenzel, R. R. (1988). How sex offenders lure children. *Sexual Abuse, 1,* 303–317.

Leclerc, B., Proulx, J., & Beauregard, E. (2009). Examining the modus operandi of sexual offenders against children and its practical implications. *Aggression and Violent Behavior, 14,* 5–12.

Leichtman, M. D., & Ceci, S. J. (1995). The effects of stereotypes and suggestions on preschoolers' reports. *Developmental Psychology, 31*, 568–578.

Lepore, S. J., & Sesco, B. (1994). Distorting children's reports and interpretations of events through suggestion. *Journal of Applied Psychology, 79*, 108–120.

London, K., Bruck, M., Wright, D. B., & Ceci, S. J. (2008). Review of the contemporary literature on how children report sexual abuse to others: Findings, methodological issues, and implications for forensic interviewers. *Memory, 16*, 29–47.

Lyon, T. D. (2009). Abuse disclosure: What adults can tell. In B. L. Bottoms, C. J. Najdowski, & G. S. Goodman (Eds.), *Children as victims, witnesses, and offenders: Psychological science and the law* (pp. 19–35). New York: Guilford Press.

Lyon, T. D. (2011). Assessing the competency of child witnesses: Best practice informed by psychology and law. In M. E. Lamb, D. J. LaRooy, L. C. Malloy, & C. Katz (Eds.), *Children's testimony: A handbook of psychological research and forensic practice* (2nd ed., pp. 69–85). New York: Wiley.

Lyon, T. D. (2013). Child witnesses and imagination: Lying, hypothetical reasoning, and referential ambiguity. In M. Taylor (Ed.), *The Oxford handbook of the development of imagination* (pp. 116–157). New York: Oxford University Press.

Lyon, T. D. (2014). Interviewing children. *Annual Review of Law and Social Science, 10*, 73–89.

Lyon, T. D., & Ahern, E. C. (2011). Young children's emerging ability to make false statements. *Developmental Psychology, 47*, 61–66.

Lyon, T. D., Ahern, E. C., Malloy, L. C., & Quas, J. A. (2010). Children's reasoning about adult transgression secrecy: Effects of adult identity, child age, and maltreatment. *Child Development, 81*, 1714–1728.

Lyon, T. D., Malloy, L. C., Quas, J. A., & Talwar, V. A. (2008). Coaching, truth induction, and young maltreated children's false allegations and false denials. *Child Development, 79*, 914–929.

Lyon, T. D., Scurich, N., Choi, K., Handmaker, S., & Blank, R. (2012). "How did you feel?": Increasing child sexual abuse witnesses' production of evaluative information. *Law and Human Behavior, 36*, 448–457.

Lyon, T. D., & Stolzenberg, S. N. (2014). Children's memory for conversations about sexual abuse: Legal and psychological implications. *Roger Williams Law Review, 19*, 411–450.

Lyon, T. D., Wandrey, L., Ahern, E., Licht, R., Sim, M. P., & Quas, J. A. (2014). Eliciting maltreated and nonmaltreated children's transgression disclosures: Narrative practice rapport building and a putative confession. *Child Development, 85*, 1756–1769.

Lyons, K. E., & Ghetti, S. (2011). The development of uncertainty monitoring in early childhood. *Child Development, 82*, 1778–1787.

Malloy, L. C., Brubacher, S. P., & Lamb, M. E. (2011). Expected consequences of disclosure revealed in investigative interviews with suspected victims of child sexual abuse. *Applied Developmental Science, 15*, 8–19.

Malloy, L. C., Brubacher, S. P., & Lamb, M. E. (2013). "Because she's one who listens": Children discuss disclosure recipients in forensic interviews. *Child Maltreatment, 18*, 245–251.

Malloy, L. C., Lyon, T. D., & Quas, J. A. (2007). Filial dependency and recantation of child sexual abuse allegations. *Journal of the American Academy of Child and Adolescent Psychiatry, 46,* 162–170.

Malloy, L. C., Quas, J. A., Lyon, T. D., & Ahern, E. C. (2014). Disclosing adult wrongdoing: Maltreated and non-maltreated children's expectations and preferences. *Journal of Experimental Child Psychology, 124,* 78–96.

Matthews, D., Lieven, E., & Tomasello, M. (2007). How toddlers and preschoolers learn to uniquely identify referents for others: A training study. *Child Development, 78,* 1744–1759.

McWilliams, K., Lyon, T. D., & Quas, J. A. (2019). Maltreated children's ability to make temporal judgements using a recurring landmark event. *Journal of Interpersonal Violence, 34,* 873–883.

Ornstein, P. A., Baker-Ward, L., Myers, J., Principe, G. F., & Gordon, B. N. (1995). Young children's long-term retention of medical experiences: Implications for testimony. In F. E. Weinert & W. Schneider (Eds.), *Memory performance and competencies: Issues in growth and development* (pp. 349–371). Mahwah, NJ: Erlbaum.

Ornstein, P. A., Gordon, B. N., & Larus, D. M. (1992). Children's memory for a personally experienced event: Implications for testimony. *Applied Cognitive Psychology, 6,* 49–60.

Peterson, C., & Biggs, M. (1997). Interviewing children about trauma: Problems with "specific" questions. *Journal of Traumatic Stress, 10,* 279–290.

Peterson, C., Dowden, C., & Tobin, J. (1999). Interviewing preschoolers: Comparisons of yes/no and wh- questions. *Law and Human Behavior, 23,* 539–555.

Peterson, C., & Grant, M. (2001). Forced choice: Are forensic interviewers asking the right questions? *Canadian Journal of Behavioural Science, 33,* 118–127.

Poole, D. A., & Lindsay, D. S. (2001). Children's eyewitness reports after exposure to misinformation from parents. *Journal of Experimental Psychology: Applied, 7,* 27–50.

Principe, G. F., Kanaya, T., Ceci, S. J., & Singh, M. (2006). Believing is seeing: How rumors can engender false memories in preschoolers. *Psychological Science, 17,* 243–248.

Quas, J. A., Goodman, G. S., & Jones, D. P. H. (2003). Predictors of attributions of self-blame and internalizing behavior problems in sexually abused children. *Journal of Child Psychology and Psychiatry, 44,* 723–736.

Rocha, E. M., Marche, T. A., & Briere, J. L. (2013). The effect of forced-choice questions on children's suggestibility: A comparison of multiple-choice and yes/no questions. *Canadian Journal of Behavioural Science, 45,* 1–11.

Rudy, L., & Goodman, G. S. (1991). Effects of participation on children's reports: Implications for children's testimony. *Developmental Psychology, 27,* 527–538.

Rush, E. B., Lyon, T. D., Ahern, E. C., & Quas, J. A. (2014). Disclosure suspicion bias and abuse disclosure: Comparisons between sexual and physical abuse. *Child Maltreatment, 19,* 113–118.

Salomo, D., Lieven, E., & Tomasello, M. (2013). Children's ability to answer different types of questions. *Journal of Child Language, 40,* 469–491.

Saywitz, K., Jaenicke, C., & Camparo, L. (1990). Children's knowledge of legal terminology. *Law and Human Behavior, 14,* 523–535.

Schneider, W. (2015). *Memory development from early childhood through emerging adulthood.* New York: Springer.

Schreiber, N., Bellah, L. D., Martinez, Y., McLaurin, K. A., Strok, R., Garven, S., et al. (2006). Suggestive interviewing in the McMartin Preschool and Kelly Michaels daycare abuse cases: A case study. *Social Influence, 1*, 16–47.

Smallbone, S. W., & Wortley, R. K. (2001). *Child sexual abuse: Offender characteristics and modus operandi.* Canberra: Australian Institute of Criminology.

Smith, B. E., & Elstein, S. G. (1993). *The prosecution of child sexual abuse cases: Final report.* Washington, DC: National Center for Child Abuse and Neglect.

Sternberg, K. J., Lamb, M. E., Davies, G. A., & Westcott, H. L. (2001). The Memorandum of Good Practice: Theory versus application. *Child Abuse and Neglect, 25*, 669–681.

Stivers, T. (2010). An overview of the question–response system in American English conversation. *Journal of Pragmatics, 42*, 2772–2781.

Stolzenberg, S. N., & Lyon, T. D. (2014). How attorneys question children about the dynamics of sexual abuse and disclosure in criminal trials. *Psychology, Public Policy, and Law, 20*, 19–30.

Stolzenberg, S. N., & Lyon, T. D. (2017). "Where were your clothes?": Eliciting descriptions of clothing placement from children alleging sexual abuse in criminal trials and forensic interviews. *Legal and Criminological Psychology, 22*, 197–212.

Stolzenberg, S. N., McWilliams, K., & Lyon, T. D. (2017a). Spatial language, question type, and young children's ability to describe clothing: Legal and developmental implications. *Law and Human Behavior, 41*, 398–409.

Stolzenberg, S. N., McWilliams, K., & Lyon, T. D. (2017b). The effects of the hypothetical putative confession and negatively valenced yes/no questions on maltreated and nonmaltreated children's disclosure of a minor transgression. *Child Maltreatment, 22*, 167–173.

Stolzenberg, S. N., McWilliams, K., & Lyon, T. D. (2017c). Ask versus tell: Potential confusions when child witnesses are questioned about conversations. *Journal of Experimental Psychology: Applied, 23*, 447–459.

Talwar, V., & Crossman, A. M. (2012). Children's lies and their detection: Implications for child witness testimony. *Developmental Review, 32*, 337–359.

Talwar, V., Lee, K., Bala, N., & Lindsay, R. (2004). Children's lie-telling to conceal a parent's transgression: Legal implications. *Law and Human Behavior, 28*, 411–435.

Thierry, K. L., Spence, M. J., & Memon, A. (2001). Before misinformation is encountered: Source monitoring decreases child witness suggestibility. *Journal of Cognition and Development, 2*, 1–26.

Tye, M. C., Amato, S. L., Honts, C. R., Devitt, M. K., & Peters, D. (1999). The willingness of children to lie and the assessment of credibility in an ecologically relevant laboratory setting. *Applied Developmental Science, 3*, 92–109.

Waterman, A. H., Blades, M., & Spencer, C. (2001). Interviewing children and adults: The effect of question format on the tendency to speculate. *Applied Cognitive Psychology, 15*, 521–531.

CHAPTER 8

False Memory

Maria S. Zaragoza
Ira Hyman
Quin M. Chrobak

The human cognitive system is capable of impressive feats. Synthesizing information over time, drawing inferences, detecting patterns, speculating, abstracting implications, and creating new ideas—going beyond the perceived world and imagining what could be—these are the very cognitive capabilities that underlie some of humanity's most important intellectual achievements and scientific advances. Somewhat paradoxically, the very skills and predilections that contribute to human intelligence can sometimes undermine people's ability to serve as accurate eyewitnesses.

The task of the eyewitness is to report as accurately and completely as possible those events she or he witnessed. However, human memory does not function like a high-fidelity recording device that preserves the precise time and date that each experience was stored. To the contrary, memory is fundamentally constructive. Rather than preserving an exact replica of each experience, memory preserves people's interpretations of their experiences. These interpretations are inherently colored by prior knowledge, expectations, and inferences they draw when attempting to comprehend their experiences. Further undermining people's ability to provide accurate eyewitness testimony is their tendency to integrate and synthesize related experiences, a tendency that renders people highly prone to confusing information from related sources. Witnessed forensic events do not occur in isolation but are embedded in a series of related life experiences and events (e.g., investigative interviews, newspaper and media reports of the witnessed events, conversations with others). These additional experiences have the potential of contaminating the target memory, leading to errors and distortions.

In some cases, people's tendency to confuse related sources of information in memory can result in the creation of genuine false memories—situations in which people remember events as being different than they actually were. In this chapter, we review research and theory on false memories, with an emphasis on false-memory phenomena that are especially relevant to the legal system. Specifically, we focus on situations in which eyewitnesses develop false memories as a consequence of suggestive interviews or other sources of postevent misinformation.

EMPIRICAL EVIDENCE FOR FALSE MEMORIES

False Eyewitness Memories Resulting from Suggestive Interviews

Although concerns about the suggestibility of eyewitness memory have existed since the time of Munsterberg (1908), it was not until the 1970s that researchers began to conduct systematic experimental studies on this topic. Much of this early work was pioneered by Elizabeth Loftus and her colleagues (e.g., Loftus, 1975, 1977, 1979a; Loftus, Miller, & Burns, 1978; Loftus & Palmer, 1974), who developed an experimental paradigm for investigating the effects of postevent misinformation on the accuracy of eyewitness memory reports. In the standard misinformation paradigm, participants first view an eyewitness event and are later exposed to false or misleading information about the events they witnessed (e.g., participants who viewed a traffic accident involving a stop sign were incorrectly told it was a yield sign). In the final phase, participants receive a memory test about the events they witnessed. The consistent finding is that misled participants reliably incorporate these misleading suggestions into their eyewitness reports and do so significantly more often than control participants who were not misled (e.g., Loftus et al., 1978). For example, in Loftus et al. (1978), misled participants given a forced choice were more likely to claim that they remembered a yield sign (the misleading suggestion) than the stop sign (which they originally saw).

The "misinformation effect" documented by Loftus is one of the most robust and reliable findings in cognitive psychology. Demonstrations of the surprising ease with which people adopt misinformation sparked tremendous interest in both the legal and scientific communities because it raised serious concerns about the reliability of eyewitness memory. Since its initial publication, countless studies have replicated and extended these findings. Misinformation effects have been demonstrated in participants of all ages (from preschoolers to older adults), for a variety of different types of events (live events, emotional events, naturally occurring events), types of misinformation (about people, places, and things), methods of delivering the misinformation (narratives, questionnaires, and face-to-face interviews), and all manner of methods for assessing memory for the witnessed event (e.g., free recall, cued recall, and recognition). Investigation of the misinformation effect remains an active research area to this day, almost 40 years later.

But do misinformation effects provide evidence of false memories? In the standard eyewitness suggestibility experiment, there is significant deception. The misinformation is presented to participants as an accurate description of the events they witnessed by an experimenter whom they are likely to view as knowledgeable and credible. As many have noted (see, e.g., Lindsay, 1990; Oeberst & Blank, 2012), this situation is imbued with substantial experimental demand. Participants may feel pressured to report the suggestion, whether or not they believe the suggested information or misremember seeing it in the original event. Hence, to rule out the possibility that participants report misinformation simply because they are playing along, it is necessary to make every effort to eliminate this demand. As a result, in many studies participants are alerted to the possibility that the information provided by the postevent source may not correspond to the events they witnessed.

Although it is a relatively straightforward matter to change the demand characteristics of the experiment, it is somewhat more difficult to discriminate between situations in which a participant-witness has a *false belief* in the suggested information as opposed to a *false memory* of having witnessed the suggested details. Even a high-confidence endorsement of the suggested details may simply reflect a strong false belief that the suggested events transpired rather than a genuine false memory of having witnessed the suggested misinformation. As mentioned above, in cases in which participants have no memory that contradicts the misleading suggestions, they have little reason to distrust the experimenter and may therefore come to believe that the suggested information is true. In an attempt to be helpful, participant-witnesses are likely to report everything they know about the event without regard to whether they specifically recollect witnessing it at the original event or whether they learned it from another source.

One method that investigators have used to address this possibility is to give the witnesses a *source-monitoring test* that forces them to discriminate between possible sources of information in memory. In the typical study, participants are asked to identify the source of the suggested item by choosing among multiple possible sources (e.g., the witnessed event, the postevent questions, both, or neither). Note that source-monitoring test procedures inform participants prior to the test that the postevent narrative/questions contained information that was not in the witnessed event, thus reducing any perceived demand to go along with the suggested information. When misled participants are given a source-monitoring test, rather than a traditional recognition test, their tendency to claim they remember witnessing the suggested items is substantially reduced (Zaragoza & Lane, 1994) and in some cases eliminated (Lindsay & Johnson, 1989; Zaragoza & Koshmider, 1989). Nevertheless, a great deal of evidence supports the conclusion that misled participants will claim to remember witnessing the suggested details, even when given a source-monitoring test (Belli, Lindsay, Gales, & McCarthy, 1994; Lindsay, 1990; Chambers & Zaragoza, 2001; Drivdahl & Zaragoza, 2001; Frost, Ingraham, & Wilson, 2002; Hekkanen & McEvoy, 2002; Lane, Mather, Villa, & Morita, 2001; Mitchell & Zaragoza, 1996; Zaragoza & Lane, 1994; Zaragoza & Mitchell, 1996). Even with stronger warnings, participants persist in claiming that they remember witnessing the suggested items on the source-monitoring test. For example, researchers have told participants that the misleading source contained inaccuracies (Zaragoza & Lane, 1994), that the experimenter was trying to trick them (Chambers & Zaragoza, 2001), and that they should not report *any* information from the postevent source on the test (Lindsay, 1990). Remarkably, these stronger warnings do not always eliminate false reports.

Participants' tendency to claim they remember witnessing the suggested items on the source-monitoring test could reflect either a false belief that the suggested item was part of the event or a genuine false memory of having witnessed the suggested item. To address this possibility, several studies have also assessed the phenomenological experience that accompanies participants' "memory" of witnessing the suggested event (cf., Schooler, Gerhard, & Loftus, 1986). One method that has been used to assess the phenomenological experience of false memories is Tulving's (1985) remember/know procedure. Following recall or recognition of a test item, participants are asked to indicate whether they *remember* seeing it during the original event or whether they just *know* it occurred but cannot actually remember the specific episode (see also Zaragoza & Mitchell, 1996, for a related measure in which participants are asked to distinguish between *remembering* and *believing*). The distinction between *remembering* and *knowing* is carefully explained to participants (see, e.g., Gardiner & Java, 1993; Rajaram, 1993), and it is emphasized that one can be quite confident that something happened without being able to recollect the specific experience. The question of interest is whether misled participants given remember/know instructions would indicate they *remember* witnessing suggested details, and several studies have now shown that they do (e.g., Drivdahl & Zaragoza, 2001; Frost, 2000; Roediger, Jacoby, & McDermott, 1996; Zaragoza & Mitchell, 1996), even when participants are given explicit warnings that they had been misled (Chambers & Zaragoza, 2001). These findings indicate that suggested memories are sometimes experienced in much the same way as memories derived from perceptual experience.

In summary, research on the misinformation effect has demonstrated that people are capable of developing genuine false memories for items and details that they did not witness. In all of these studies, participants are bystanders to the witnessed events, and they develop false memories for isolated items and events that are in most cases not central to the outcome or storyline. Are people susceptible to developing false memories about their own lives and autobiographical experiences? We turn now to research bearing on this question.

False Autobiographical Memories from Childhood

Both anecdotal evidence and investigations of errors in autobiographical memory have demonstrated that people make many errors when remembering personal experiences. Cognitive psychologists became interested in the possible construction of false memories because of the reports of recovered memories generated in therapy and other contexts (Lindsay & Read, 1994; Loftus, 1993). Could people create false memories of childhood experiences, including traumatic experiences?

Experimental research on the creation of false childhood memories generally follows the memory implantation method, an extension of misinformation effect procedures (Hyman, Husband, & Billings, 1995; Loftus & Pickrell, 1995). In this method, researchers typically obtain descriptions of events that actually happened during someone's childhood. Family members provide these event descriptions, and the participant is then asked to recall these events. The crucial feature is that one of the events is false—something the researchers are reasonably sure never happened based on parent verification. In most of the studies, the participant returns for two or three interviews over the course of several days. At each of the repeated interviews, participants are asked to recall this false event and are typically encouraged to recount the fictitious event in detail (e.g., how did the event unfold, who was there, how did they feel). Whereas participants typically start out saying they do not remember the false event, after repeated interviews, some participants start "recovering" memories of the false event.

Using the memory implantation technique, researchers have suggested a great variety of false childhood memories. The false events that people claim to remember include being lost in a mall (Loftus & Pickrell, 1995), spilling punch on the parents of the bride at a wedding reception (Hyman & Billings, 1998; Hyman et al., 1995; Hyman & Pentland, 1996); a car accident, an overnight hospitalization, and a clown at a birthday party (Hyman et al., 1995); a ride in a hot-air balloon (Wade, Garry, Read, & Lindsay, 2002; Garry & Wade, 2005; Hessen-Kayfitz & Scoboria, 2012); pulling a prank on a teacher (Lindsay, Hagen, Read, Wade, & Garry, 2004; Desjardins & Scoboria, 2007); being attacked by an animal and being seriously harmed by another child (Porter, Yuille, & Lehman, 1999); being involved in aggressive acts as the perpetrator or victim (Laney & Takarangi, 2013); and committing a crime (Shaw & Porter, 2015). Clearly, the construction of false memories is a reliable effect. False autobiographical memories have been created in a variety of research labs, by different researchers, for distinct events, and of events with various emotional intensities.

Nonetheless, the creation of false childhood memories remains a controversial area of research. In a recent review of these false childhood memory studies and other investigations of autobiographical memory errors, Brewin and Andrews (2016) raised several concerns. They argued that few people are likely to create full false memories. They were concerned that many participants expressed doubt about their false memories. Furthermore, they argued that some supposedly false memories may reflect true memories that people have recalled in response to the suggestions—a type of source-monitoring problem. Brewin and Andrews (2016) acknowledged that people may create false memories, but they questioned the value of this work for understanding memory recovery in therapy. They concluded that the existing research shows that very few people will create false memories.

One concern with the evaluation that Brewin and Andrews (2016) made is that they focused on trying to determine the percentage of people who will create false childhood memories (Lindsay & Hyman, 2017). The memory implantation research was never focused on trying to determine the number of people who create false memories. Instead, the original work was concerned with documenting that people will create false memories at all. Once that finding was clear, the researchers turned to trying to better understand the nature of false memories (i.e., false memories vs. false beliefs) and trying to understand the conditions that increase or decrease the likelihood of memory creation (Hyman & Kleinknecht, 1999; Scoboria et al., 2017).

Recently, Scoboria et al. (2017) conducted a mega-analysis of memory implantation studies. A mega-analysis differs from a traditional meta-analysis in that, in the former, all of the original data are recoded. In this mega-analysis, the researchers obtained the transcripts from eight different memory implantation studies and coded all of the responses to false suggestions using a single coding scheme involving the same criteria. In coding the over 400 transcripts, Scoboria and colleagues measured several features they deemed important for false memories. First, they noted that participants must clearly accept the suggested event as something that could have or that did happen to them. This indicates that the individual accepts the event as personally plausible. Second, the individuals must elaborate on the suggested event and provide descriptions of their images of the false experience. Crucially, the respondents must not reject the false memory. Some individuals accept an event as plausible, agree that it occurred, provide a coherent narrative account of the event, but then deny remembering the experience they just described. Thus, according to Scoboria et al. (2017), false memory is composed of belief in the event, the critical components of a memory (e.g., elaboration, imagery), and claiming the narrative and image as a personal memory. With this definition, Scoboria and colleagues found that 23% of individuals accepted the false event but did not have a memory—that is, belief without remembering. Another 30.5% provided false memories, with 11.1% classified as robust memories, 10.8% as full memories, and 8.5% as partial false memories.

In summary, there are many methodological challenges associated with studying false autobiographical memories from childhood. In particular, the possibility that "false memories" are actually true memories that participants recovered in response to the suggestion is difficult to rule out with certainty (in spite of the parents' reports). Nevertheless, there is now a significant body of evidence gathered across a large number of laboratories that collectively point to the conclusion that it is indeed possible to "implant" false autobiographical memories from childhood.

Eliciting False Memories from Witnesses: Suggestive Interviews Involving Forced Fabrication

As outlined in the previous sections, there is a wealth of empirical evidence documenting that false memories can be implanted (Loftus, 2005). However, in real-world forensic investigations in which suggestive interviewing is a concern, attempts to lead a witness are not restricted to interviewer suggestions of false information. Rather, in some forensic interviews, the interviewer attempts to *elicit* from the witness testimony about events that the witness did not see, does not remember, or that did not actually take place. In such cases, interviewers may press witnesses to go beyond their actual memory, pressuring them to speculate or even fabricate information about events that never happened. In such highly coercive interview contexts, witnesses may succumb to this pressure in an attempt to satisfy the interviewer and knowingly provide a fabricated account (in a manner akin to forced confessions; see Madon, More, & Ditchfield, Chapter 3, this volume).

Consider, for example, the case of Julius Murphy, who was convicted and sentenced to death in 1998 for capital murder for the death of a stranded motorist. Nearly 20 years later, in 2015, attorneys were able to win a retrial after evidence came to light that the primary evidence against him came from two eyewitnesses who had been threatened by police with charges of murder or conspiracy if they did not provide fabricated testimony that they had witnessed Murphy commit the murder. Does this type of coercive interviewing have negative consequences for the witness's memory? In particular, might people come to develop false memories for fictitious events they had earlier knowingly fabricated under duress? As reviewed below, the empirical evidence shows that the answer is sometimes yes.

To assess whether people might come to develop false memories for forcibly fabricated events, researchers have modified the traditional misinformation paradigm in one important way: In these studies, the interviewer does not *provide* the false or misleading information to participants. Rather, in the forced fabrication paradigm, the interviewer elicits fabricated information from participants by pressing the witness to describe a fictitious object or event that, although plausible, was not part of the original eyewitness event (e.g., participants might be asked to describe where the protagonist was bleeding when he fell, even though there was no blood; Zaragoza, Payment, Ackil, Drivdahl, & Beck, 2001). Because participants are asked questions about items and events that never happened, they must fabricate, or make something up. Importantly, participant-witnesses are not permitted to evade the interviewer's request to provide an answer to the false-event questions. Rather, participants are informed ahead of time that they must respond to all questions, even if they have to guess. Although participants vehemently resist answering these false-event questions, the interviewer "forces" them to comply by repeatedly insisting that they just "give their best guess" until participants eventually acquiesce by providing a relevant fabricated response.

To illustrate the coercive nature of these interviews and participants' resistance to answering these false-event questions, we provide below a portion of an interview with a participant from one of our studies (Chrobak & Zaragoza, 2008). In the example, the participant had earlier witnessed a video clip from a movie involving two brothers at a summer camp. In one of the scenes, a camp counselor named Delaney stands up to make an announcement in the dining hall when he inexplicably loses his balance and falls to the floor, knocking platters of food off the table. This scene was used as the basis for a false-event question wherein participants were pressed to describe a fictitious practical joke that the experimenter claimed had caused Delaney to fall (although the film did not depict a practical joke). The interchange between the experimenter (E) and the participant (P) follows.

E: The next scene takes place in the dining hall. Delaney is asked to stand up and give an announcement. A practical joke is pulled on him that causes him to fall and end up on the ground. What was it?

P: Uhh, I'm not sure what the practical joke was, ehh. . . . I know that he fell, I thought he did it on purpose though.

E: Just give your best guess about the practical joke.

P: Yeah, I really don't, like I thought like he did it on purpose to get everyone's attention. I didn't know there was a practical joke going on.

E: Just give your best guess.

P: Umm, let's see, I really don't remember, like I don't.

E: Well, what did he slip on?

P: A piece of food?

E: Ok what was the practical joke that they pulled?

P: Umm, like what do you mean like?

E: How did it get there?

P: I guess someone put it there.

E: Who might have put it there?

P: Probably, umm, not his little brother but what's that other guy that's causing trouble in the beginning?

E: Ratface?

P: Yeah probably Ratface.

E: And what food did he put there?

P: Uhh maybe a banana? I don't know.

E: And how might he have put it there?

P: Uh, sneaking up there.

E: How did he sneak up there?

P: [laughs] I don't remember. Umm . . .

E: Just give your best guess.

P: Umm he just was, doing it when no one was looking.

This transcript illustrates several characteristic features of forced fabrication interviews. First, in order to comply with the experimenter's demands, participants have to make up, or fabricate, a response to the false-event questions. In this case, the participant had to invent the practical joke, because no practical joke was actually depicted. Second, participants' resistance to answering false-event questions clearly indicates their awareness that they do not know the answer. In the above example, the participant repeatedly states that he does not remember a prank and, in fact, directly questions whether there was a prank at all. Moreover, as is typically the case, the resistance is so strong that it takes several conversational turns before the interviewer is able to elicit any information relevant to the question and a number of additional conversational turns before the interviewer is able to elicit an account from the participant that contains the desired level of detail and specificity.

To assess false-memory development, participants are given delayed tests of memory for the witnessed event. In some cases, this means probing participants for the specific information they had earlier fabricated. For example, 5 days after the interview provided above, the participant returned to the lab and a different experimenter asked him, "When you watched the video, did you see Ratface put a banana on the floor by Delaney when all of the ladies and boys were in the dining hall?" Although this participant correctly rejected the forcibly fabricated event as not witnessed on this initial test, the findings were quite different when he was tested again 8 weeks later. Specifically, 8 weeks after viewing the video event, this participant returned to the lab for a surprise free-recall test and was instructed to recall the events witnessed in the video as completely and accurately as possible—as if providing testimony in a court of law. Aside from this general instruction, participants were not given any additional prompts or cues and were free to provide as much or as little information as they wished (see Chrobak & Zaragoza, 2008; 2013). During this surprise free-recall test, this participant freely provided the following account of the dining hall scene:

"And I think what happens next is they are in the cafeteria and Delaney is um, supposed to get everyone's attention, some reason. But he is um, like I think I think *Ratface pulls a trick on him with a banana peel or something, he slips and he falls and he is, gets in trouble by the chief* and says that's the wrong way to get attention from the crowd."

The very same participant who had correctly and publicly rejected the forced fabrication as false on the 5-day recognition test nevertheless incorporated a detailed version of his fabricated event into the testimony freely provided 2 months later. Indeed, in this study, almost half of the participants who correctly rejected their forced fabrications on a 1-week recognition test freely incorporated their forced fabrications into their testimony 8 weeks later. It is clear that after 8 weeks, this participant could no longer remember that the banana peel prank was an event he had fabricated under duress.

The finding that forced fabrication can result in false eyewitness memories has now been demonstrated in a number of studies involving both children (Ackil & Zaragoza, 1998) and adults (Ackil & Zaragoza, 2011; Chrobak, Rindal, & Zaragoza, 2015; Chrobak & Zaragoza, 2008, 2013; Frost, LaCroix, & Sanborn, 2003; Hanba & Zaragoza, 2007; Pezdek, Sperry, & Owens, 2007; Pezdek, Lam, & Sperry, 2009; Zaragoza et al., 2001). The forced fabrications range from isolated items or details (Frost et al., 2003; Hanba & Zaragoza, 2007; Pezdek et al., 2007; Pezdek et al., 2009; Zaragoza et al., 2001) to fabricated accounts that are broad in scope and extended in time (Chrobak & Zaragoza, 2008, 2013).

Do People Develop Genuine False Memories for Forcibly Fabricated Information?

Of course, the finding that participants report their forced fabrications on a test of the witnessed event does not, in and of itself, provide evidence of false-memory development. Given the social demands of an interview situation, participants might report their forced fabrications even if they are aware that they do not remember witnessing these fabricated events. For example, participants might feel pressure to respond consistently across test sessions. In addition, they may find it unflattering to admit that their responses during the initial interview were mere fabrications. Alternatively, they may assume that they are supposed to report their forced fabrications. Researchers who have studied the effects of forced fabrication on memory have taken care to design studies in such a way that these social demands are eliminated (or at least minimized). In particular, in all studies of the forced fabrication effect reviewed here, the experimenter who tested participants' memory on the delayed tests was different from the one who had carried out the forced fabrication interview, thus minimizing any perceived pressure to respond consistently across test sessions. Importantly, several studies have shown that in spite of the explicit warning that they had been misled, many participants will endorse their forced fabrications on memory tests of the witnessed event (e.g., Ackil & Zaragoza, 1998; Hanba & Zaragoza, 2007; Zaragoza et al., 2001). Although warnings can reduce (Ackil & Zaragoza, 2011) and even eliminate false memories for fabricated events in some cases (Chrobak & Zaragoza, 2008; Chrobak et al., 2015), participants have endorsed their fabrications with a high level of confidence despite the presence of a pretest warning (e.g., Zaragoza et al., 2001). Furthermore, the effects of warnings diminish when participants are tested after long delays of several weeks. Finally, at least one study has reported evidence of participants "remembering" their prior forced fabrications and doing so at a higher rate than control participants (Frost et al., 2003). Collectively, then, the evidence suggests that participants do sometimes develop genuine false memories for their forced fabrications.

MECHANISMS OF FALSE-MEMORY DEVELOPMENT: A THEORETICAL FRAMEWORK

Claiming to remember witnessing an item that was only suggested is an example of a source-misattribution error. Source-misattribution errors occur when a memory derived from one source (e.g., misleading suggestions provided by an experimenter) is misattributed to another source (e.g., the witnessed event). Marcia Johnson and colleagues (see Johnson & Raye, 1981; Johnson, Hashtroudi, & Lindsay, 1993; Lindsay, 2008) have developed a general theoretical framework, the source-monitoring framework (SMF), that provides some insight into how such errors happen (see also Jacoby, Kelley, & Dywan, 1989, for a similar approach).

According to the SMF, memory for source is an *attribution* that is the product of both conscious and nonconscious judgment processes. From this view, information about the source of a memory is not stored directly but is based on an evaluation of the characteristics of the memory representation. The SMF assumes that memory representations are records of the processing that occurred at encoding and thus contain features or characteristics that reflect the conditions under which the memory was acquired. These characteristics include temporal and spatial cues, modality of presentation, emotional reactions, records of reflective processes, visual clarity, semantic information, and a variety of other features potentially encoded during an event. So, for example, if a memory contains a great deal of visual detail, an individual would likely attribute this memory to an event he or she saw. People can, and often do, accurately attribute the source of their memories, because memories from different sources tend to differ on average in the quantity and quality of the characteristics associated with them. Memories of perceived events typically have more vivid perceptual, temporal, and spatial information than memories of imagined events (Johnson, Foley, Suengas, & Raye, 1988). Nevertheless, because there can be overlap in the distributions of the features associated with memories from different sources, errors can occur. For example, imagining words spoken in another person's voice increases people's tendency to confuse what they imagined the person said with what they actually heard the person say. According to the SMF, these errors occur due to increases in the overlap between the characteristics of the two sources of information (Johnson, Foley, & Leach, 1988).

In situations in which eyewitness suggestibility is a concern, the overlap between the witnessed event and postevent interviews is extensive. First, the two episodes are intimately related because they share a common referent—the witnessed event. Note that the common-referent factor is inherent in every eyewitness interview because the postevent interview is always about the witnessed event (Mitchell & Zaragoza, 2001). As a consequence, with the exception of several misleading details in the postevent interview, the content of the original and postevent episodes is nearly identical. Hence, from the perspective of the SMF, it is not surprising that participants sometimes confuse suggested items for items they experienced firsthand.

The SMF also assumes that the accuracy of source-monitoring judgments is heavily influenced by the circumstances at the time of retrieval (i.e., the appropriateness and stringency of the decision-making processes and criteria used). A good illustration of this is Lindsay and Johnson's (1989) finding that a suggestibility effect is more likely to be obtained with a yes/no recognition test than a source-monitoring test. They proposed that yes/no recognition tests may encourage participants to use a familiarity criterion. Because the test list consists primarily of witnessed items interspersed with novel foils, responding on the basis of familiarity will in most cases lead to a correct response. For this reason, participants may slip into a tendency of using high familiarity as the basis for deciding whether or not a test item was seen. Of course, the suggested items are familiar not because they were witnessed but because participants had been exposed to them recently in the context of a postevent narrative. Thus people incorrectly accept the misinformation as a memory they observed. In contrast to the yes/no test, source-monitoring tests direct participants to retrieve and use source-specifying information, thereby enhancing participants' ability to discriminate between memories of the witnessed event and memories of the postevent narrative.

Just as the criteria for deciding whether something was "seen" might change as a function of test demands, the SMF also posits that the criteria by which people judge whether something is a memory might change over time. Specifically, Johnson et al. (1993) posited that the amount of perceptual detail needed to accept a recalled experience as a real memory (and not imagined or suggested) is much greater for a recent event than for events from the distant past (see also Belli & Loftus, 1994). Finally, an important aspect of the SMF is that people can mistake the origin of some items in memory even if memory for the item itself is very good.

In summary, the SMF predicts that false memories for suggested events will be especially likely under circumstances in which the suggested information contains characteristics that are highly similar to those of a witnessed or experienced event. Conversely, the SMF also predicts that false memories for suggested events will be minimized under conditions in which participants can identify the suggested information as "not witnessed." As discussed below, the available research supports these predictions.

FACTORS THAT CATALYZE FALSE-MEMORY CREATION

Imagination and Reflective Elaboration

Imagery clearly plays a critical role in memory. When trying to remember new information, forming mental images of that information facilitates encoding and improves memory (e.g., Bower & Winzenz, 1970; McDaniel & Einstein, 1986). Unfortunately, when the information is false or misleading, forming a mental image may also facilitate the creation of false memories. The reason is that imagination imbues a memory with sensory/perceptual characteristics that render it more similar to an actually perceived event.

In terms of autobiographical memories, imagery influences both acceptance of an event and the construction of full false memories. Garry, Manning, Loftus, and Sherman (1996) asked people to repeatedly imagine childhood events and found that people afterward rated the events as more likely to have happened to them—increasing belief in the event. Using a different methodology, Hyman, Gilstrap, Decker, and Wilkinson (1998) also found that imagining possible autobiographical experiences leads to greater confidence and belief in remembering the event. Imagery also plays a critical role in the creation of false autobiographical memories. Using the memory implantation method, Hyman and Pentland (1996) compared people who were asked to imagine false events and those simply asked to think about the events. Imagery led to a dramatic increase in the creation of false memories. Scoboria et al. (2017) looked at the effect of imagery across multiple studies and conditions. They found that people were more than twice as likely to create false childhood memories in the imagery conditions than in the nonimagery conditions.

Having a mental image of an event is a critical aspect of classifying an event as remembered (Scoboria et al., 2017). When people make judgments of possible events, the ease of imagining the experience may influence their judgment. Because imagery improves memory, imagined false suggestions are more likely to remain available in memory over the course of several days. Thus leading people to construct images of fictitious events may increase the likelihood of both acceptance that the suggested event occurred and false-memory creation.

Other studies have assessed the effects of imagining suggested events more indirectly. Rather than instructing participants to imagine a suggested event, participants were asked questions that encouraged them to mentally elaborate on the sensory and perceptual characteristics of the suggested events (Drivdahl & Zaragoza, 2001), the emotional consequences of the suggested events (Drivdahl, Zaragoza, & Learned, 2009), or the meaning and implications of the suggested event (Zaragoza, Mitchell, Payment, & Drivdahl, 2011). The consistent finding is that reflectively elaborating on the suggested events in ways that render the suggested memory more familiar, clear, vivid, and rich in sensory and emotional detail increases the incidence of false memories and the confidence with which they are held.

Photos

Another manipulation that can encourage imagery and reflective elaboration is the provision of photos. In an early investigation, Wade and colleagues (2002) presented individuals with pictures of childhood events and asked them to recall the experience. In addition to accurate photos, the researchers also created a false picture by incorporating a picture of the individual with a parent into a picture of the basket of a hot-air balloon using image-editing software. Over the course of three interviews, the participants reviewed the photo and imagined the experience. Results indicated that 50% of the participants constructed a false memory of riding in a hot-air balloon.

In a further investigation, Garry and Wade (2005) compared the technique of using a photo that depicts a false event with that of providing participants with a narrative of the event. The photo was not as effective in leading people to construct a false memory as was a narrative without a photo. Hessen-Kayfitz and Scoboria (2012) argued that the more precisely a false photo depicts a suggested false event, the *less likely* people are to construct false memories. Such detailed photos do not match easily with the way in which someone remembers their childhood and the way in which they imagine the event occurring. For this reason, the mismatch between the precise photo and their self-knowledge decreases the effectiveness of the photo in creating a false memory.

In contrast, providing participants with more general photographic information may be especially likely to catalyze the construction of false memories. For example, Lindsay et al. (2004) showed people their class photos from early elementary school. When participants were asked to remember the false event of playing a prank on their teacher, they were more likely to create memories than people who did not see photos (see also Desjardins & Scoboria, 2007). Presumably, providing this general photograph brought to mind schematic knowledge of the individual's childhood that, when combined with the false event, created an especially compelling false memory (Hyman et al., 1995; Hyman & Kleinknecht, 1999).

Confirmatory Interviewer Feedback

In an effort to elicit cooperation from witnesses and set them at ease, it is natural for interviewers to reinforce reluctant or unsure witnesses when they comply with the interviewer's request for information. However, when interviewers reinforce unsure or erroneous testimony, it has the potential of inflating witness confidence in their mistaken testimony and distorting their memories (see Steblay, Wells, & Douglass, 2014, for a recent review of research on confirmatory interviewer feedback and erroneous lineup identifications).

Of particular relevance here is the finding that confirmatory interviewer feedback provided in the context of forced fabrication interviews is a potent catalyst for false-memory creation (Frost et al. 2003; Hanba & Zaragoza, 2007; Zaragoza et al., 2001). For example, in Zaragoza et al. (2001), participants witnessed a video event and underwent a forced fabrication interview in which they were pressed to respond to both true-event and false-event questions. As in the typical forced fabrication study, participants resisted providing fabricated responses, but eventually acquiesced. The novel manipulation was that immediately following their fabricated responses the experimenter provided feedback that was either confirmatory (e.g., "That's right, _____ is the correct answer!") or neutral/noninformative (e.g., "_____, OK", delivered with flat affect). Relative to neutral feedback, confirmatory interviewer feedback led to significant increases in the incidence of false memories and increased confidence in those false memories after 1 week. Confirmatory feedback also increased the likelihood that participants would incorporate their forced fabrications into their freely provided accounts 1 month later (Zaragoza et al., 2001). Importantly, even those participants who could not remember the confirmatory feedback showed increased false-memory rates, thus demonstrating that participants were not simply going along with the feedback. In addition, results indicated that, although overt verbal resistance was associated with reduced false memory when participants received neutral feedback following their fabrications, there was no advantage associated with overt verbal resistance when their fabrications had earlier been reinforced with confirmatory feedback, even when participants had been warned that the interviewer had asked them about events that never actually happened. In a followup study, confirmatory feedback provided during an initial forced fabrication interview led participants to later provide fabricated responses with a speed and confidence that resembled their responses to true-event questions (Hanba & Zaragoza, 2007). Hence, it appears that confirmatory feedback leads participants to suppress, or discount, their uncertainty in their fabricated responses, thereby predisposing the fabricated memory to developing into a false memory.

Limited Processing Resources

When attentional resources are limited, memory for an item's source is more likely to be disrupted than is the familiarity of the memory's contents. Encoding and retrieval of source-relevant information are highly effortful, attention-demanding processes, whereas familiarity is a relatively automatic consequence of exposure to an item (Johnson, Kounios, & Reeder, 1994). Thus, limiting attentional resources can cause a relatively selective impairment of source-specifying information that renders the memory highly susceptible to misattribution (cf., Jacoby, Woloshyn, & Kelley, 1989). Zaragoza and Lane (1998) verified these predictions. In one experiment, participants encountered the misinformation under conditions of either divided or full attention, and in a second experiment participants were either given ample time to make the source judgment or forced to provide source judgments very quickly. The results showed that a scarcity of attentional resources—either when encoding misinformation or when retrieving misinformation—led to impoverished memory for the suggested information's true source, but no impairment in memory for the content of the suggested item. This, in turn, led participants to misremember the suggestion as part of the witnessed event. These results are consistent with the finding that forgetting of source information that occurs over long retention intervals is accompanied by increased suggestibility (see, e.g., Lindsay, 1990; Zaragoza & Mitchell, 1996). In sum, the finding that attentional resources influence suggestibility is highly relevant to assessing and predicting suggestibility in real-world contexts, in which multiple environmental and internal stimuli compete for attentional resources (cf., Chrobak et al., 2015).

When False Memories Serve a Purpose

The likelihood of developing false memories for postevent suggestions is also a function of the explanatory function the suggestion serves (Chrobak & Zaragoza, 2013; Rindal, Chrobak, Zaragoza, & Weihing, 2017). Across several studies, participants were especially likely to develop false memories for postevent suggestions when the misleading suggestions helped to explain a consequential outcome they had witnessed. In Rindal et al. (2017), for example, participants watched a movie clip of two brothers at a summer camp in which the camp counselor is depicted sneaking out at night (although where he went or what he did is not depicted). For some participants, the film clip depicted the counselor getting reprimanded by the director, and for other participants the film did not (the reprimand scene was replaced). All participants were later exposed to the false suggestion that the counselor had toilet-papered the camp director's cabin. Subsequently, the extent to which participants erroneously recollected having witnessed the fictitious toilet-papering incident was a function of the suggestion's explanatory role. That is, relative to participants who had not seen the counselor get reprimanded, participants who did see the reprimand were more likely to develop false memories of the suggested toilet-papering incident, presumably because the suggested event helped to explain why he got in trouble. Participants were also less likely to recollect having witnessed the suggested toilet-papering incident (on measures of subjective experience) when this suggestions' explanatory strength had been reduced by the presence of an alternative explanation that could explain why he got in trouble (when participants learned that drugs had been found in the campers' cabin).

Collectively, the results provide strong evidence that the search for explanatory coherence influences people's tendency to misremember witnessing events that were only suggested to them (see also Chrobak & Zaragoza, 2013, for similar findings with forced fabrication). These findings are of particular relevance to real-world forensic situations. In many cases, the purpose of eyewitness testimony is to provide an explanation for an outcome (e.g., an accident, robbery, or murder) that may not have a well-determined cause. Consequently, witnesses may be especially likely to develop false memories for explanatory suggestions encountered in this context.

MITIGATING FALSE MEMORIES: FACTORS THAT INCREASE THE LIKELIHOOD PEOPLE WILL DISCRIMINATE BETWEEN SUGGESTION AND REALITY

Implausibility of Suggestion

In order to construct a false memory, people must first accept the false suggestion as potentially true. Hence, the false suggestion must be a plausible event (Hyman & Kleinknecht, 1999). The vast majority of misinformation studies (including studies of forced fabrication) have employed misinformation that is highly plausible. However, in the domain of false childhood memories, some studies have manipulated the plausibility of the implanted false memory. Perhaps not surprisingly, people are more likely to construct false memories of plausible events than of less plausible events (Pezdek, Finger, & Hodge, 1997; Pezdek & Hodge, 1999; Scoboria, Mazzoni, Jarry, & Shapero, 2012). But event plausibility does not completely determine the creation of false memories (Scoboria et al., 2012). In part, plausibility is a judgment that people make (Hyman & Kleinknecht, 1999) and these judgements reflect not only the overall likelihood of an event but also whether people believe the event is likely to have happened to them.

Low-Credibility Source

The credibility of the postevent source is also an important variable that influences whether people will accept a suggestion. Whereas participants are easily influenced by misinformation that is provided by a credible source, they will resist effectively a suggestion that is provided by a source that lacks credibility or whom they perceive as having intentions to mislead (Dodd & Bradshaw, 1980; Smith & Ellsworth, 1987; Underwood & Pezdek, 1998). Indeed, even young children are less influenced by suggestion when it is provided by a peer rather than an authoritative adult (Ceci, Ross, & Toglia, 1987; Lampinen & Smith, 1995). A related finding is that the magnitude of the misinformation effect is also influenced by more subtle social cues, such as the perceived power and social attractiveness conveyed by the accent of the person providing the misinformation (Vornik, Sharman, & Garry, 2003).

Maximizing Accuracy and Completeness of Witnessed Memory

Related to the issue of plausibility, people are much less likely to develop false memories for suggested information if they can retrieve information in memory that uniquely identifies the suggestion as "not witnessed." A prime example of this is the finding that misinformation effects are reduced (Tousignant, Hall, & Loftus, 1986) and can even be eliminated (Putnam, Sungkhasettee, & Roediger, 2017) when participants detect a discrepancy between the misleading suggestion and their memory of the witnessed event. Of course, discrepancy detection is contingent on accurate memory for the witnessed detail. Similarly, in extreme cases in which participants are given blatantly contradictory suggestions, they are sometimes not misled at all (Loftus, 1979b).

Discrepancy or change detection is possible when participants are exposed to directly contradictory and mutually exclusive misinformation (e.g., an intersection can have a stop sign or a yield sign, but not both). In many situations involving exposure to misinformation, however, the suggestion serves to supplement the events that were witnessed rather than to directly contradict them (e.g., the suggestion that there was a yield sign at an intersection where no sign existed). Indeed, the vast majority of the studies reviewed in this chapter (i.e., many of the misinformation effect studies, all of the false childhood memory studies, and all forced fabrication studies) used supplemental misinformation. Moreover, in those cases in which participants fail to encode or forget the target details, the contradictory misinformation serves as supplemental information that serves to fill a gap in memory. Unfortunately, it is much more difficult for people to identify suggested misinformation as "not witnessed" when they have no memory to contradict it—they may simply assume that they failed to notice it and accept it as true.

Because discrepancy detection is contingent on accurate memory for the witnessed event, manipulations that enhance the accuracy, completeness, and durability of the witnessed memory should increase resistance to suggestion. One such manipulation that has been shown to reduce suggestibility is to have witnesses recall the witnessed event immediately after viewing it (Gabbert, Hope, Fisher, & Jamieson, 2012; LaPaglia & Chan, 2012; Pansky & Tenenboim, 2011). Immediate recall reinforces and enhances memory for the witnessed event, presumably increasing the likelihood that witnesses will detect that misleading suggestions are discrepant with what they saw. In a related finding, Memon, Zaragoza, Clifford, and Kidd (2010) showed that administering the Cognitive Interview (an investigative tool that produces detailed reports from an eyewitness without reducing accuracy; Fisher & Geiselman, 1992) *before* participants underwent a forced fabrication interview reduced false assents to fabricated items. Importantly, when the Cognitive Interview was administered after the forced fabrication interview, it had no effect on false memory for fabricated events, thus showing that the benefit of the Cognitive Interview resulted from preserving memory for the witnessed event (Memon et al., 2010).

Encouraging Accurate Source Monitoring

As reviewed earlier, many studies have shown that warning participants that they had been misled (after being misled but before taking the final test) has been shown to reduce false memories (see Blank & Launay, 2014, for a comprehensive review). One especially effective type of warning is a procedure called enlightenment (Oeberst & Blank, 2012). Enlightenment goes beyond simply warning participants that they may have been misled by telling them why they were misled. In the enlightenment procedure, participants are completely debriefed before they take the final memory test; that is, they are informed that they are participating in a study regarding the effects of discrepant postevent information on eyewitness memory and that they were exposed to information that directly contradicts what they witnessed. Moreover, participants are directed to retrieve both the original information and the postevent suggestion. Oeberst and Blank (2012) found that in some cases (e.g., when memory for the witnessed event was strong) the enlightenment procedure completely reversed the misinformation effect, even among participants who had already endorsed the misinformation. Although these findings need to be replicated and extended to assess their generality, they highlight the potential for developing interventions that might reverse the effects of misinformation, at least under circumstances in which it is known that a witness has been misled.

Finally, the extent to which participants endorse suggested information as witnessed is also heavily influenced by the circumstances at the time of test. Whereas accurate retrieval of source-specifying information is effortful and demanding of cognitive resources, information about an item's familiarity is accessed relatively automatically. As a consequence, the high familiarity of a suggested item can sometimes be mistaken as evidence that the suggestion came from the witnessed event. As reviewed earlier, studies have shown that these false-memory errors can be minimized (though rarely eliminated) when participants are given source-monitoring tests that direct them to discriminate between the various sources of information in memory (cf., Lindsay & Johnson, 1989; Zaragoza & Lane, 1994). In other words, when participants are informed that the suggestion could have come from several sources and are asked to identify its source, they are much better able to remember that the suggestion was not witnessed than when the test simply asks them to make global judgments about whether or not it was witnessed.

SUMMARY AND EVIDENCE-BASED RECOMMENDATIONS FOR THE LEGAL SYSTEM

Witnesses to forensically relevant events are likely to be interviewed repeatedly and by different people. In addition to interviews with police and other investigators (at the scene or police station), there will be interviews with attorneys during deposition and potentially again at trial. Furthermore, witnesses may describe the event to others and may collaboratively recall with other witnesses. Although interviewers may have no intention to mislead the witness, they may end up doing so as a consequence of their efforts to extract the testimony they need to move an investigation forward. For example, when a witness has difficulty remembering some key piece of information, the interviewer may unwittingly suggest what it was or press the witness to speculate about what it could have been. The research reported here shows that both types of suggestive interviews can result in false eyewitness memories that are held with high confidence.

What can be done to maximize the accuracy and validity of eyewitness memory? Memory will be most accurate when assessed immediately after the witnessed event: Forgetting will be minimized, and there will be little opportunity for the memory to be contaminated by other sources. Hence a first recommendation is to have the witness provide a complete account of the witnessed event, freely and in her or his own words, as soon after the target event as possible. The witness's freely provided account should be recorded verbatim. An added benefit is that an immediate recounting of the witnessed event will help to solidify and preserve the witness's memory, rendering the memory more resistant to forgetting and to suggestive influences she or he may encounter later.

The second set of recommendations involves guidelines for interviewing witnesses. To the extent possible, interviewers should use open-ended questions and avoid the use of specific or potentially leading questions.

Interviewers should never press witnesses to speculate about events they do not remember and should be willing to accept "I don't know" in response to their questions. In addition, they should be careful not to reinforce tentative and unsure responses, as this can inflate confidence in uncertain testimony. When interviewing witnesses, it is important to alert them to the possibility that they may have been exposed to other sources of information about the witnessed event (e.g., media, other witnesses, other interviews, conversations with others) and to remind them that their job is to report only what they remember witnessing firsthand. That is, they should report only those events they specifically remember seeing and refrain from reporting other things they may believe happened. Interviewers can assist witnesses in evaluating the validity and source of their own memories by encouraging them to focus on aspects or dimensions of their memories that can help them distinguish between real and suggested memories (e.g., "Is your memory vivid or blurry?", "Do you remember what you were thinking when you saw that?"; see, e.g., Mather, Henkel & Johnson, 1997, for evidence that examining specific features of memories can improve source accuracy). Ideally, all interviews with a witness should be video recorded; this will discourage interviewers from using overtly leading and coercive interview methods and can provide an opportunity for detecting suggestive interviews after the fact. Although one cannot eliminate exposure to all potential sources of taint, it is possible to minimize them and their influence on eyewitness memory.

REFERENCES

Ackil, J. K., & Zaragoza, M. S. (1998). Memorial consequences of forced confabulation: Age differences in susceptibility to false memories. *Developmental Psychology, 34*, 1358–1372.

Ackil, J. K., & Zaragoza, M. S. (2011). Forced fabrication versus interviewer suggestions: Differences in false memory depend on how memory is assessed. *Applied Cognitive Psychology, 25*, 933–942.

Belli, R. F., Lindsay, D. S., Gales, M. S., & McCarthy, T. T. (1994). Memory impairment and source misattribution in postevent misinformation experiments with short retention intervals. *Memory and Cognition, 22*, 40–54.

Belli, R. F., & Loftus, E. F. (1994). Recovered memories of childhood abuse: A source monitoring perspective. In S. J. Lynn & J. Rhue (Eds.), *Dissociation: Theory, clinical, and research perspectives* (pp. 415–433). New York: Guilford Press.

Blank, H., & Launay, C. (2014). How to protect eyewitness memory against the misinformation effect: A meta-analysis of post-warning studies. *Journal of Applied Research in Memory and Cognition, 3*, 77–88.

Bower, G. H., & Winzenz, D. (1970). Comparison of associative learning strategies. *Psychonomic Science, 20*, 119–120.

Brewin, C. R., & Andrews, B. (2016). Creating memories for false autobiographical events in childhood: A systematic review. *Applied Cognitive Psychology, 31,* 2–23.

Ceci, S. J., Ross, D. F., & Toglia, M. P. (1987). Suggestibility in children's memory: Psycholegal implications. *Journal of Experimental Psychology: General, 116,* 38–49.

Chambers, K. L., & Zaragoza, M. S. (2001). Intended and unintended effects of explicit warnings on eyewitness suggestibility: Evidence from source identification tests. *Memory and Cognition, 29,* 1120–1129.

Chrobak, Q. M., Rindal, E. J., & Zaragoza, M. S. (2015). The impact of multi-faceted questions on eyewitness accuracy following forced fabrication interviews. *Journal of General Psychology, 142,* 150–166.

Chrobak, Q. M., & Zaragoza, M. S. (2008). Inventing stories: Forcing witnesses to fabricate entire fictitious events leads to freely reported false memories. *Psychonomic Bulletin and Review, 15,* 1190–1195.

Chrobak, Q. M., & Zaragoza, M. S. (2013). When forced fabrications become truth: Causal explanations and false memory development. *Journal of Experimental Psychology: General, 142,* 827–844.

Desjardins, T., & Scoboria, A. (2007). "You and your best friend Suzy put Slime in Ms. Smollett's desk": Producing false memories with self-relevant details. *Psychonomic Bulletin and Review, 14,* 1090–1095.

Dodd, D. H., & Bradshaw, J. M. (1980). Leading questions and memory: Pragmatic constraints. *Journal of Verbal Learning and Verbal Behavior, 19,* 695–704.

Drivdahl, S. B., & Zaragoza, M. S. (2001). The role of perceptual elaboration and individual differences in the creation of false memories for suggested events. *Applied Cognitive Psychology, 15,* 265–281.

Drivdahl, S. B., Zaragoza, M. S., & Learned, D. (2009). The role of emotional elaboration in the creation of false memories. *Applied Cognitive Psychology, 23,* 13–35.

Fisher, R. P., & Geiselman, R. E. (1992). *Memory-enhancing techniques for investigative interviewing: The Cognitive Interview.* Springfield, IL: Charles C Thomas.

Frost, P. (2000). The quality of false memory over time: Is misinformation "remembered" or "known"? *Psychonomic Bulletin and Review, 7,* 531–536.

Frost, P., Ingraham, M., & Wilson, B. (2002). Why misinformation is more likely to be recognised over time: A source monitoring account. *Memory, 10,* 179–185.

Frost, P., Lacroix, D., & Sanborn, N. (2003). Increasing false recognition rates with confirmatory feedback: A phenomenological analysis. *American Journal of Psychology, 116,* 515–525.

Gabbert, F., Hope, L., Fisher, R. P., & Jamieson, K. (2012). Protecting against misleading postevent information with a Self-Administered Cognitive Interview. *Applied Cognitive Psychology, 26,* 568–575.

Gardiner, J. M., & Java, R. I. (1993). Recognition memory and awareness: An experiential approach. *European Journal of Cognitive Psychology, 5,* 337–346.

Garry, M., Manning, C. G., Loftus, E. F., & Sherman, S. J. (1996). Imagination inflation: Imagining a childhood event inflates confidence that it occurred. *Psychonomic Bulletin and Review, 3,* 208–214.

Garry, M., & Wade, K. A. (2005). Actually, a picture is worth less than 45 words: Narratives produce more false memories than photographs. *Psychonomic Bulletin and Review, 12,* 359–366.

Hanba, J. M., & Zaragoza, M. S. (2007). Interviewer feedback in repeated interviews involving forced confabulation. *Applied Cognitive Psychology, 21,* 433–455.

Hekkanen, S. T., & McEvoy, C. (2002). False memories and source-monitoring problems: Criterion differences. *Applied Cognitive Psychology, 16,* 73–85.

Hessen-Kayfitz, J., & Scoboria, A. (2012). False memory is in the details: Photographic details predict memory formation. *Applied Cognitive Psychology, 26,* 333–341.

Hyman, I. E., Husband, T. H., & Billings, F. J. (1995). False memories of childhood experiences. *Applied Cognitive Psychology, 9,* 181–197.

Hyman, I. E., & Kleinknecht, E. E. (1999). False childhood memories: Research, theory, and applications. In L. M. Williams & V. L. Banyard (Eds.), *Trauma and memory* (pp. 175–188). Thousand Oaks, CA: SAGE.

Hyman, I. E., Jr., & Billings, F. J. (1998). Individual differences and the creation of false childhood memories. *Memory, 6,* 1–20.

Hyman, I. E., Jr., Gilstrap, L. L., Decker, K., & Wilkinson, C. (1998). Manipulating remember and know judgements of autobiographical memories: An investigation of false memory creation. *Applied Cognitive Psychology, 12,* 371–386.

Hyman, I. E., Jr., & Pentland, J. (1996). The role of mental imagery in the creation of false childhood memories. *Journal of Memory and Language, 35,* 101–117.

Jacoby, L. L., Kelley, C. M., & Dywan, J. (1989). Memory attributions. In H. L. Roediger & F. I. M. Craik (Eds.), *Varieties of memory and consciousness: Essays in honor of Endel Tulving* (pp. 391–422). Hillsdale, NJ: Erlbaum.

Jacoby, L. J., Woloshyn, V., & Kelley, C. (1989). Becoming famous without being recognized: Unconscious influences of memory produced by dividing attention. *Journal of Experimental Psychology, 118,* 115–125.

Johnson, M. K., Foley, M. A., & Leach, K. (1988). The consequences for memory of imagining another person's voice. *Memory and Cognition, 16,* 337–342.

Johnson, M. K., Foley, M. A., Suengas, A. G., & Raye, C. L. (1988). Phenomenal characteristics of memories for perceived and imagined autobiographical events. *Journal of Experimental Psychology: General, 117,* 371–376.

Johnson, M. K., Hashtroudi, S., & Lindsay, D. S. (1993). Source monitoring. *Psychological Bulletin, 114,* 3–28.

Johnson, M. K., Kounios, J., & Reeder, J. A. (1994). Timecourse studies of reality monitoring and recognition. *Journal of Experimental Psychology: Learning, Memory, and Cognition, 20,* 1409–1419.

Johnson, M. K., & Raye, C. L. (1981). Reality monitoring. *Psychological Review, 88,* 67–85.

Lampinen, J. M., & Smith, V. L. (1995). The incredible (and sometimes incredulous) child witness: Child eyewitnesses' sensitivity to source credibility cues. *Journal of Applied Psychology, 80,* 621–627.

Lane, S. M., Mather, M., Villa, D., & Morita, S. K. (2001). How events are reviewed matters: Effects of varied focus on eyewitness suggestibility. *Memory and Cognition, 29,* 940–947.

Laney, C., & Takarangi, M. K. T. (2013). False memories for aggressive acts. *Acta Psychologica, 143*, 227–234.

LaPaglia, J. A., & Chan, J. C. K. (2012). Retrieval does not always enhance suggestibility: Testing can improve witness identification performance. *Law and Human Behavior, 36*, 478–487.

Lindsay, D. S. (1990). Misleading suggestions can impair eyewitnesses' ability to remember event details. *Journal of Experimental Psychology: Learning, Memory, and Cognition, 16*, 1077–1083.

Lindsay, D. S. (2008). Source monitoring. In J. Byrne (Series Ed.) & H. L. Roediger, III (Vol. Ed.), *Learning and memory: A comprehensive reference: Vol. 2. Cognitive psychology of memory* (pp. 325–348). Oxford, UK: Elsevier.

Lindsay, D. S., Hagen, L., Read, J. D., Wade, K. A., & Garry, M. (2004). True photographs and false memories. *Psychological Science, 15*, 149–154.

Lindsay, D. S., & Hyman, I. E., Jr. (2017). Commentary on Brewin and Andrews. *Applied Cognitive Psychology, 31*, 37–39.

Lindsay, D. S., & Johnson, M. K. (1989). The eyewitness suggestibility effect and memory for source. *Memory and Cognition, 17*, 349–358.

Lindsay, D. S., & Read, J. D. (1994). Psychotherapy and memories of childhood sexual abuse: A cognitive perspective. *Applied Cognitive Psychology, 8*, 281–338.

Loftus, E. F. (1975). Leading questions and the eyewitness report. *Cognitive Psychology, 7*, 560–572.

Loftus, E. F. (1977). Shifting human color memory. *Memory and Cognition, 5*, 696–699.

Loftus, E. F. (1979a). The malleability of human memory. *American Scientist, 67*, 312–320.

Loftus, E. F. (1979b). Reactions to blatantly contradictory information. *Memory and Cognition, 7*, 368–374.

Loftus, E. F. (1993). The reality of repressed memories. *American Psychologist, 48*, 518–537.

Loftus, E. F. (2005). Planting misinformation in the human mind: A 30-year investigation of the malleability of memory. *Learning and Memory, 12*, 361–366.

Loftus, E. F., Miller, D. G., & Burns, H. J. (1978). Semantic integration of verbal information into a visual memory. *Journal of Experimental Psychology: Human Learning and Memory, 4*, 19–31.

Loftus, E. F., & Palmer, C. (1974). Reconstruction of automobile destruction: An example of the interaction between language and memory. *Journal of Verbal Learning and Verbal Behavior, 13*, 585–589.

Loftus, E. F., & Pickrell, J. E. (1995). The formation of false memories. *Psychiatric Annals, 25*, 720–725.

Mather, M., Henkel, L. A., & Johnson, M. K. (1997). Evaluating characteristics of false memories: Remember/know judgments and memory characteristics questionnaire compared. *Memory and Cognition, 25*, 826–837.

McDaniel, M. A., & Einstein, G. O. (1986). Bizarre imagery as an effective memory aid: The importance of distinctiveness. *Journal of Experimental Psychology: Learning, Memory, and Cognition, 12*, 54–65.

Memon, A., Zaragoza, M. S., Clifford, B., & Kidd, L. (2010). Inoculation or antidote?: The effects of Cognitive Interview timing on false memory for forcibly fabricated events. *Law and Human Behavior, 34*, 105–117.

Mitchell, K. J., & Zaragoza, M. S. (1996). Repeated exposure to suggestion and false memory: The role of contextual variability. *Journal of Memory and Language, 35*, 246–260.

Mitchell, K. J., & Zaragoza, M. S. (2001). Contextual overlap and eyewitness suggestibility. *Memory and Cognition, 29*, 616–626.

Münsterberg, H. (1908). *On the witness stand.* Garden City, NY: Doubleday.

Oeberst, A., & Blank, H. (2012). Undoing suggestive influence on memory: The reversibility of the eyewitness misinformation effect. *Cognition, 125*, 141–159.

Pansky, A., & Tenenboim, E. (2011). Inoculating against eyewitness suggestibility via interpolated verbatim vs. gist testing. *Memory and Cognition, 39*, 155–170.

Pezdek, K., Finger, K., & Hodge, D. (1997). Planting false childhood memories: The role of event plausibility. *Psychological Science, 8*, 437–441.

Pezdek, K., & Hodge, D. (1999). Planting false childhood memories in children: The role of event plausibility. *Child Development, 70*, 887–895.

Pezdek, K., Lam, S. T., & Sperry, K. (2009). Forced confabulation more strongly influences event memory if suggestions are other-generated than self-generated. *Legal and Criminological Psychology, 14*, 241–252.

Pezdek, K., Sperry, K., & Owens, S. M. (2007). Interviewing witnesses: The effect of forced confabulation on event memory. *Law and Human Behavior, 31*, 463–478.

Porter, S., Yuille, J. C., & Lehman, D. R. (1999). The nature of real, implanted and fabricated memories for emotional childhood events: Implications for the false memory debate. *Law and Human Behavior, 23*, 517–538.

Putnam, A. L., Sungkhasettee, V., & Roediger, H. L. (2017). When misinformation improves memory: The effects of recollecting change. *Psychological Science, 28*, 36–46.

Rajaram, S. (1993). Remembering and knowing: Two means of access to the personal past. *Memory and Cognition, 21*, 89–102.

Rindal, E. J., Chrobak, Q. M., Zaragoza, M. S., & Weihing, C. A. (2017). Mechanisms of eyewitness suggestibility: Tests of the explanatory role hypothesis. *Psychonomic Bulletin and Review, 24*, 1413–1425.

Roediger, H. L., Jacoby, D., & McDermott, K. B. (1996). Misinformation effects in recall: Creating false memories through repeated retrieval. *Journal of Memory and Language, 35*, 300–318.

Schooler, J. W., Gerhard, D., & Loftus, E. F. (1986). Qualities of the unreal. *Journal of Experimental Psychology: Learning, Memory, and Cognition, 12*, 171–181.

Scoboria, A., Mazzoni, G., Jarry, J., & Shapero, D. (2012). Implausibility inhibits but does not eliminate false autobiographical beliefs. *Canadian Journal of Experimental Psychology, 66*, 259–267.

Scoboria, A., Wade, K. A., Lindsay, D. S., Azad, T., Strange, D., Ost, J., et al. (2017). A mega-analysis of memory reports from eight peer-reviewed false memory implantation studies. *Memory, 25*, 146–163.

Shaw, J., & Porter, S. (2015). Constructing rich false memories of committing crime. *Psychological Science, 26*, 291–301.

Smith, V. L., & Ellsworth, P. C. (1987). The social psychology of eyewitness accuracy: Misleading questions and communicator expertise. *Journal of Applied Psychology, 72*, 294–300.

Steblay, N. K., Wells, G. L., & Douglass, A. B. (2014). The eyewitness post identification feedback effect 15 years later: Theoretical and policy implications. *Psychology, Public Policy, and Law, 20*, 1–18.

Tousignant, J. P., Hall, D., & Loftus, E. F. (1986). Discrepancy detection and vulnerability to misleading postevent information. *Memory and Cognition, 14*, 329–338.

Tulving, E. (1985). Memory and consciousness. *Canadian Psychology, 26*, 1–12.

Underwood, J., & Pezdek, K. (1998). Memory suggestibility as an example of the sleeper effect. *Psychonomic Bulletin and Review, 5*, 449–453.

Vornik, L. A., Sharman, S. J., & Garry, M. (2003). The power of the spoken word: Sociolinguistic cues influence the misinformation effect. *Memory, 11*, 101–109.

Wade, K. A., Garry, M., Read, J. D., & Lindsay, D. S. (2002). A picture is worth a thousand lies: Using false photographs to create false childhood memories. *Psychonomic Bulletin and Review, 9*, 597–603.

Zaragoza, M. S., & Koshmider, J. W. (1989). Misled subjects may know more than their performance implies. *Journal of Experimental Psychology: Learning, Memory, and Cognition, 15*, 246–255.

Zaragoza, M. S., & Lane, S. M. (1994). Source misattributions and the suggestibility of eyewitness memory. *Journal of Experimental Psychology: Learning, Memory, and Cognition, 20*, 934–945.

Zaragoza, M. S., & Lane, S. M. (1998). Processing resources and eyewitness suggestibility. *Legal and Criminological Psychology, 3*(Pt. 2), 305–320.

Zaragoza, M. S., & Mitchell, K. J. (1996). Repeated exposure to suggestion and the creation of false memories. *Psychological Science, 7*, 294–300.

Zaragoza, M. S., Mitchell, K. J., Payment, K., & Drivdahl, S. (2011). False memories for suggestions: The impact of conceptual elaboration. *Journal of Memory and Language, 64*, 18–31.

Zaragoza, M. S., Payment, K. E., Ackil, J. K., Drivdahl, S. B., & Beck, M. (2001). Interviewing witnesses: Forced confabulation and confirmatory feedback increase false memories. *Psychological Science, 12*, 473–477.

CHAPTER 9

Eyewitness Identification

James D. Sauer
Matthew A. Palmer
Neil Brewer

After viewing a crime (or other event of interest), an eyewitness will often be presented with some form of identification task (either live or a photo array) and asked whether he or she recognizes someone from the lineup as the person of interest from the initial event. The lineup will generally include a suspect (who may or may not be the culprit) and a number of fillers (individuals known to be innocent). The witness can either identify the suspect, identify a filler, reject the lineup (i.e., decline to identify anyone), or, in some cases, indicate that he or she is unable to make a decision (i.e., respond "don't know"). The witness's response can have important consequences for the ongoing investigation and, more broadly, for attempts to prosecute the guilty. If the witness identifies the suspect, the likelihood of the suspect being prosecuted increases. If the witness rejects the lineup, the police may decide to redirect their investigative efforts to pursue an alternative line of enquiry or look for an alternative witness. Eyewitness identification evidence is both compelling and prone to error (Steblay, Dysart, Fulero, & Lindsay, 2003; Steblay, Dysart, & Wells, 2011). Given the weight placed by triers of fact on identification evidence, it is unsurprising that false identifications (i.e., of innocent suspects) are a leading cause of wrongful conviction in many jurisdictions (see Innocence Project, 2017). Moreover, a witness's failure to identify the culprit if he or she is present in the lineup can undermine investigative and prosecutorial efforts. An awareness of these consequences has motivated a substantial body of research literature aimed at improving our understanding of the causes of identification error and evaluating various imaginative attempts to mitigate these errors.

In this chapter we summarize what we consider are the major findings to emerge from the now considerable literature. In many cases, however, there already exist substantial reviews or meta-analyses, and, consequently, we only review these areas quite briefly, noting the main findings and pointing readers in the direction of major reviews. This applies especially to the consideration of variables that are known to affect identification performance and yet are outside the control of justice system professionals charged with administering lineups. In contrast, we devote more attention to a number of important questions for which, in many cases, we cannot provide conclusive answers based on the current state of the literature. Our objective here is to prompt a critical reconsideration of what is known, what is unknown, and how we might best advance the use of psychological science to benefit practitioners in the criminal justice system.

THINGS WE KNOW ABOUT IDENTIFICATION TEST PERFORMANCE BUT CANNOT CHANGE

The research literature identifies a number of factors important to understanding identification performance, although it is important to bear in mind that many of them (often referred to as estimator variables; Wells, 1978) are outside the control of the justice system. An identification is a recognition memory task. Thus factors at encoding or between the encoding and test phases that affect memory quality tend to show predictable effects on identification accuracy. For example, increased exposure durations and better viewing conditions (e.g., shorter viewing distances) tend to be associated with improved recognition performance (e.g., Lindsay, Semmler, Weber, Brewer, & Lindsay, 2008; Memon, Hope, & Bull, 2003; Palmer, Brewer, Weber, & Nagesh, 2013). Similarly, divided (vs. full) attention at encoding—whether prompted by the presence of a weapon (Steblay, 1992) or some more general mechanism (e.g., Palmer et al., 2013)—is also associated with reduced identification performance. There is also evidence that, consistent with basic memory tasks, stimulus distinctiveness is associated with improved face recognition, though much of this evidence comes from basic face recognition tasks rather than eyewitness identification tasks (e.g., Light, Kayra-Stuart, & Hollander, 1979; Sauer, Brewer, & Weber, 2008; Semmler & Brewer, 2006). There are also general tendencies for people to be better able to identify faces of their own (vs. another) race (the *cross-race effect*; Meissner & Brigham, 2001) and for longer retention intervals between the crime and the identification test to be associated with poorer identification performance (e.g., Palmer et al., 2013; Sauer, Brewer, Zweck, & Weber, 2010). Witness characteristics also show reliable effects on identification performance, with the most striking example being the tendency for child witnesses to be less accurate than adults (Fitzgerald & Price, 2015). The effect of all of these variables is manifested in either a lower chance of a correct identification when the culprit is present in the lineup, a higher likelihood of an erroneous identification decision (i.e., an innocent suspect or filler pick) when the culprit is not present, or both of these outcomes.

These effects are all intuitive and well grounded in memory theory. Moreover, an appreciation of their nature is important from the perspectives of understanding identification decision making and evaluating the likely reliability of identification evidence. But we must add several caveats. First, knowing that identification performance varies in a predictable manner with changes on these variables does not mean that the accuracy of any individual identification test outcome can be "diagnosed." For example, knowing that identification performance deteriorates as the retention interval between crime and identification test lengthens does not allow the conclusion that a particular identification made after a particular interval (e.g., 3 days or 3 months) will be accurate or inaccurate. Or, knowing that child witnesses are more likely to choose from a culprit-absent lineup does not mean that the police suspect must be innocent if a child witness picked the police suspect from the lineup but an adult witness did not. Second, in a number of cases, the generality of these effects across stimulus materials has not been established. Thus it is unclear how dependent these effects are on the idiosyncratic properties of the stimuli and testing protocols for which they have been observed. Third, even in cases in which "main effects" are robust, the literature provides a limited understanding of the boundary conditions for these effects or the extent to which these effects might be moderated by other factors of applied and theoretical relevance. For example, increased exposure duration might attenuate deleterious effects on identification performance related to the distracting presence of a weapon at encoding or a very long retention interval. We explore these caveats in more depth in the section on generalizing findings from the lab environment to applied settings, later in this chapter.

PREDICTING IDENTIFICATION ACCURACY

Given that identification errors are common, researchers have attempted to identify independent markers of identification accuracy. Although a variety of approaches to indexing identification accuracy have been pursued (e.g., phenomenological reports, Dunning & Stern, 1994; Palmer, Brewer, McKinnon, & Weber, 2010; eye movement patterns, Mansour & Flowe, 2010; Mansour, Lindsay, Brewer, & Munhall, 2009), we focus on the two most-studied markers of accuracy: eyewitness confidence and response latency (i.e., the time taken to make the identification response). Below we consider the utility of these factors as markers of accuracy of identification decisions.

Confidence and Accuracy for Eyewitness Identifications

Eyewitness confidence exerts a powerful influence on decision making in legal settings. Police, lawyers, and jurors believe confidence is reliably linked to accuracy (Deffenbacher & Loftus, 1982; Potter & Brewer, 1999). Further, experimental manipulations of witness confidence affect mock jurors' perceptions of witness credibility and defendant guilt (Bradfield & Wells, 2000; Cutler, Penrod, & Dexter, 1990).

More importantly, there is compelling theoretical support for a positive confidence–accuracy relationship. Various theories of confidence processing—emerging from a variety of human judgment and decision-making domains (see Horry & Brewer, 2016, for a review)—hold that confidence and accuracy share an evidential basis related to memory quality and stimulus discriminability. For example, in a recognition memory task (e.g., a lineup), an individual will typically compare a presented test stimulus (e.g., a lineup member) with a memorial image of a previously viewed stimulus (e.g., a culprit). This comparison generates some degree of evidence that the two stimuli match. This evidence forms the primary basis for both the decision and confidence, and this shared evidential basis supports a positive confidence–accuracy relationship. As the quality of the witness's memory and the degree of match between an identified lineup member and the witness's memory of the culprit increase, so do the likely accuracy of and the witness's confidence in that decision.

Despite strong theoretical support for a positive confidence–accuracy relation, meta-analyses of correlational investigations of the confidence–accuracy relationship suggested a moderate relationship at best (reporting average coefficients between 0 and .4; e.g., Sporer, Penrod, Read, & Cutler, 1995). These findings may have motivated the skepticism about the confidence–accuracy relationship among eyewitness researchers (e.g., 73% of surveyed experts being willing to testify that confidence is not a reliable predictor of identification accuracy; Kassin, Tubb, Hosch, & Memon, 2001). However, researchers have subsequently argued that the point-biserial correlation is an inappropriate index of the confidence–accuracy relation (e.g., Juslin, Olsson, & Winman, 1996) and have demonstrated repeatedly (using an alternative method of analysis: *calibration*) that robust confidence–accuracy relations often coexist with typically weak confidence–accuracy correlations (e.g., Brewer & Wells, 2006; Palmer et al., 2013; Sauer et al., 2010). The calibration approach involves plotting the proportion of accurate decisions for each level of confidence. Perfect confidence–accuracy calibration is obtained when 100% of decisions made with 100% confidence are correct, 80% of decisions made with 80% confidence are correct, 50% of decisions made with 50% confidence are correct, and so on. Visual comparison of the obtained and ideal calibration functions (together with associated statistical indices) provides information about the linearity of the relationship and tendencies toward over- or underconfidence (for further detail, see Brewer & Wells, 2006, or Juslin et al., 1996).

The extant literature on confidence–accuracy calibration demonstrates, for choosers (i.e., witnesses who identify a lineup member as the culprit), a generally linear, positive relationship between confidence and accuracy (Brewer & Wells, 2006; Palmer et al., 2013; Sauer et al., 2010; Wixted, Mickes, Dunn, Clark, & Wells, 2016; Wixted & Wells, 2017). As confidence increases, so does the likely accuracy of the identification. Thus confidence can provide useful information about the reliability of an identification. However, the literature provides a number of important caveats to this conclusion. First, this relationship typically displays overconfidence. Although accuracy increases systematically with confidence, mean accuracy at each level of confidence tends to be lower than the level of confidence expressed. Further, overconfidence (1) increases as a function of task difficulty (Palmer et al., 2013; Sauer et al., 2010) and target-absent base rates (i.e., the proportion of occasions in which the culprit is not present; Brewer & Wells, 2006); (2) can be large for child witnesses (Keast, Brewer, & Wells, 2007), and (3) is influenced by participants' metacognitive beliefs about their memory ability (Brewer, Keast, & Rishworth, 2002). Second, and following from the above, very high levels of confidence do not guarantee accuracy (Brewer & Wells, 2009). Third, the linear confidence–accuracy relation observed for choosers does not hold for nonchoosers (i.e., witnesses who reject the lineup). Finally, confirming postidentification feedback can inflate confidence and, in turn, undermine the confidence–accuracy relationship (Semmler, Brewer, & Wells, 2004; Wells & Bradfield, 1998, 1999).

Postidentification feedback can be obtained from a variety of sources (e.g., lineup administrators, cowitnesses) and may be communicated explicitly (e.g., "Good, you identified the suspect") or inferred from nonverbal behavior (e.g., lineup administrators' facial expressions). Thus, to be informative about the reliability of an identification decision, confidence must be assessed immediately following the decision and prior to any witness interaction with lineup administrators or cowitnesses. Moreover, to preserve the informational value of confidence ratings, we would argue that only confidence recorded immediately following the decision should be tendered as evidence in court (Sauer & Brewer, 2015). Although such a recommendation would likely attract considerable opposition from within the legal system, it is critical that such a practice become commonplace if confidence is to inform assessment of identification reliability. Even so, we note that any procedural factors (e.g., biases) that influence confidence but not accuracy may still undermine the confidence–accuracy relation.

Despite robust empirical support for a meaningful relationship between confidence and accuracy, the absence of established protocols for systematically collecting and preserving witness confidence ratings in most criminal justice systems currently represents a significant practical hurdle to the effective use of confidence as an index of identification accuracy (Sauer & Brewer, 2015). However, this problem could easily be remedied via computerized lineup administration incorporating a built-in request for a confidence judgment following the identification decision (Brewer, 2011).

Response Latency and Accuracy for Eyewitness Identifications

As with confidence, there are strong theoretical grounds for predicting a relationship between response latency and accuracy. A strong (vs. weak) memorial representation of the culprit and a lineup member who provides a good (vs. poor) match to this memory should promote recognition (a largely automatic process) and, consequently, faster responding with increased accuracy (e.g., Sporer, 1992, 1993). The extant literature supports these predictions, consistently demonstrating lower response times for accurate (vs. inaccurate) identifications (e.g., Brewer, Caon, Todd, & Weber, 2006; Dunning & Perretta, 2002; Sporer, 1994). However, despite robust evidence for a negative latency–accuracy relationship, two points are worth noting. First, eyewitnesses can operate at any point on the speed–accuracy continuum. Thus individual differences in decision making may muddy the latency–accuracy relationship in applied settings. For example, one witness may have a strong recognition experience and respond quickly and accurately, whereas another may have the same initial recognition experience and settle quickly on her or his preferred candidate but spend additional time interrogating this initial preference before offering a (correct) overt response. Alternatively, a witness may be uncertain but guess quickly and incorrectly. Thus a slow response does not guarantee an error, and a quick response does not guarantee accuracy. Second, and related to the previous point, the absence of a reliable metric indicating when a response is "quick enough" to indicate accuracy severely limits the applied utility of latency as a marker of identification accuracy.

Some early research suggested that specific latency "windows" might reliably diagnose identification accuracy, at least for simultaneous lineups. For example, Smith, Lindsay, and Pryke (2000) reported an accuracy rate of approximately 70% for identifications made in under 16 seconds compared with accuracy rates of approximately 43% for identifications made in 16–30 seconds and approximately 18% for more than 30 seconds. Dunning and Perretta (2002) then reported that, across multiple experiments, identifications made within a 10- to 12-second time boundary showed very high accuracy rates (approximately 87%) compared with identifications made outside this boundary approximately 50%). However, subsequent research seriously challenged the generalizability of these time boundaries and the associated accuracy rates. First, across a number of large-scale experiments using identical encoding and test stimuli, Weber, Brewer, Wells, Semmler, and Keast (2004) demonstrated that the time boundary that best discriminated correct from incorrect identifications varied considerably (from 5 to 29 seconds). Further, the accuracy rates for decisions made within and outside optimum time boundaries were much lower than those reported by Dunning and Perretta (with accuracy rates ranging from approximately 20–79% before the boundary and approximately 11–56% after the boundary). Brewer et al. (2006) also demonstrated that (1) optimum time boundaries could be experimentally manipulated (via manipulations that affect stimulus discriminability) and (2) accuracy rates associated with optimum time boundaries were again lower than those reported by Dunning and Perretta (2002). Finally, Sauer, Brewer, and Wells (2008) were unable to identify a stable latency-based metric for diagnosing the reliability of identifications made from sequential lineups. Thus, despite sound theoretical and empirical support for a negative latency–accuracy relationship, variability in empirically derived optimum time boundaries and the diagnostic value of these boundaries undermines the utility of response latency as an index of accuracy in applied settings. Nonetheless, latency may contribute to evaluations of identification evidence if viewed as an index of memory quality rather than simply identification accuracy.

Confidence and Latency Combined as Indices of Memory Quality

Neither confidence nor latency provide a foolproof method for diagnosing identification accuracy. However, both—especially when considered together—can provide useful information about the quality of a witness's memory, the strength of her or his recognition experience, and, consequently, the informational value of the identification evidence. Various theoretical frameworks propose confidence and latency index memory strength and stimulus discriminability (e.g., Vickers, 1979). Thus, provided the lineup is fair, if a witness identifies the suspect quickly and with high confidence, this likely indicates that the witness's memory for the culprit is strong, that the suspect matches this memory well, and that the identification is more likely to indicate suspect guilt. Consistent with this prediction, in lab settings, studies have demonstrated impressive levels of accuracy for rapid identifications made with high confidence (Brewer & Wells, 2006; Sauerland & Sporer, 2009; Weber et al., 2004).

However, in applied settings, we generally cannot establish ground truth (in the absence of supporting DNA evidence). We must infer likely guilt from the identification evidence rather than assessing the identification against a known state of the world (i.e., suspect guilt or innocence). Thus, when discussing methods for evaluating identification, thinking in terms of these methods' ability to diagnose accuracy potentially fosters an overly simplistic way of conceptualizing identification evidence in these settings. Thus, as per Brewer and Weber (2008), we suggest that the value of considering confidence and latency lies not in their ability to definitively diagnose accuracy but, rather, in their potential to add information about the quality of memorial evidence underlying the identification decision. This point leads to two important considerations when thinking about how identification evidence should be collected and interpreted. First, despite the apparent clarity of an identification as an indication of suspect guilt, we must bear in mind that recognition is not an "all or nothing" process. Memory is fallible, and recognition decisions reflect both the quality of memorial evidence available and the individual's decision criterion. This criterion can vary according to social factors unrelated to memory quality. Thus an identification is not a clear-cut indication of guilt and, consequently, should be interpreted probabilistically and alongside other forms of forensic evidence when assessing the likely guilt of a suspect. An identification is just one piece of evidence against the suspect, and the value of this evidence depends on the quality of the witness's memory (and the quality of procedures used to obtain the identification). As indices of memory quality, confidence and latency can help inform an assessment of the evidentiary value of an identification. Second, an identification decision on its own is less informative than it may appear. Although an identification probably indicates that, of the presented lineup members, the selected person provides the best match to the witness's memory of the culprit, it says nothing about the strength of that match or the extent to which the selected individual was favored over the alternatives (i.e., the witness's ability to discriminate a culprit among fillers). This second point leads to proposed alternative to traditional identification tests, discussed in a later section.

THINGS WE KNOW AND CAN CHANGE ABOUT IDENTIFICATION TEST PERFORMANCE

Presentation of the Lineup

Some aspects of lineup administration are uncontroversial and supported by the vast majority of eyewitness researchers. One example is the use of single-suspect lineups, whereby one lineup member is the police suspect and all other lineup members are known-to-be-innocent fillers. Compared with multiple-suspect lineups, single-suspect lineups reduce the incidence of false identification because they allow incorrect filler identifications to be classified as known errors (Wells & Turtle, 1986; see Wells, Smalarz, & Smith, 2015, for a detailed discussion of *filler siphoning*). In contrast, multiple-suspect lineups—and especially all-suspect lineups (in which all lineup members are suspects)—dramatically increase the chances that an innocent person will be prosecuted.

Double-blind testing—whereby the lineup administrator does not know which lineup member is the police suspect—is another example (for a detailed discussion, see Kovera & Evelo, 2017). Single-blind testing, whereby the administrator but not the witness knows which lineup member is the suspect, leaves open the possibility that the administrator might influence the witness's decision (e.g., "Would you like to take another look at number 4?"). Even with the best intentions, an administrator might convey subtle cues about which lineup member is the suspect (e.g., by waiting longer for the witness to make a decision about the suspect). Double-blind testing reduces the possibility of the administrator influencing the witness's decision. Some have argued that double-blind testing reduces correct identification rates (i.e., by minimizing administrator influence that leads to correct identifications; Clark, 2012). However, others have argued (and we agree) that, given witnesses' propensity for identification error, enhancing the reliability of obtained identifications—by ensuring as much as possible that these identifications indicate recognition rather than administrator influence—is crucial (Wells, Steblay, & Dysart, 2012).

The use of unbiased instructions (also termed *warning* or *admonishing* the witness) refers to reminding the witness prior to viewing the lineup that the person they are looking for may or may not be present. This simple instruction significantly reduces positive identifications from target-absent lineups (Malpass & Devine, 1981; Steblay, 1997). Omitting this instruction (i.e., using biased instructions) likely increases correct identifications when the perpetrator is present in the lineup (Clark, 2012) but at the great cost of an increase in false identifications from culprit-absent lineups (e.g., Wells, Steblay, & Dysart, 2012).

Simultaneous versus Sequential Presentation

Whether to present lineup members all at once (simultaneously) or one at a time (sequentially) has been a topic of great debate among eyewitness researchers. The idea behind sequential presentation was to reduce the scope for witnesses to compare lineup members in terms of relative similarity to the perpetrator (a *relative* judgment strategy) and encourage witnesses to assess the match between lineup members and their memory of the perpetrator (*absolute* judgment strategy), thus leading to better quality identification decisions (Wells, 1984; Lindsay & Wells, 1985).

Much evidence supports this approach. Meta-analyses of numerous experiments show that, compared with simultaneous presentation, sequential presentation reduces correct identifications from target-present lineups but also reduces incorrect picks from target-absent lineups to a greater extent, resulting in an overall increase in identification accuracy (Steblay, Dysart, Fulero, & Lindsay, 2001; Steblay et al., 2011). However, several recent developments have led researchers to question the mechanisms that produce different response patterns for sequential and simultaneous lineups and the advantages of sequential presentation.

One class of developments concerns new approaches to measuring identification accuracy. Most evidence favoring sequential presentation relies on assessment of response patterns for target-present and -absent lineups and the diagnosticity of suspect identifications (which speaks to the practical utility of identification responses for informing police investigations of the suspect in question). More recently, some researchers have used signal-detection analyses to assess differences in response patterns and concluded that these analyses suggest that sequential presentation does not improve witnesses' ability to distinguish perpetrators from innocent lineup fillers but instead prompts witnesses to be more conservative in their propensity to choose from lineups (Clark, 2012; Palmer & Brewer, 2012). In other words, sequential presentation does not enable witnesses to make better identification decisions; it discourages them from making positive identifications.

Other researchers have used receiver operating characteristic (ROC) analyses to compare responses for sequential and simultaneous lineups. This involves calculating, for each level of identification confidence, the cumulative rate of correct identifications from target-present lineups (correct identification rate) and the cumulative rate of false identifications of an innocent suspect from target-absent lineups (false identification rate) for each level of confidence. Better performance is indicated by a higher ratio of correct identifications to false identifications. Plotting the correct identification rate against the false identification rate for each level of confidence produces an ROC curve; the area under this curve gives an index of overall identification performance.

Comparisons of ROC curves for sequential and simultaneous lineup presentation suggest very different conclusions from those drawn earlier: Sequential presentation is not superior to simultaneous presentation, and in some cases may produce worse identification performance than simultaneous presentation (e.g., Mickes, Flowe, & Wixted, 2012). Some researchers have suggested that simultaneous presentation may produce better identification performance because, compared with sequential presentation, it allows witnesses greater scope to consider diagnostic features when making identification decisions (i.e., features that allow the witness to discriminate between lineup members, as opposed to nondiagnostic features that are shared by all lineup members; Wixted & Mickes, 2014).

One potentially important consideration in comparisons of lineup presentation methods is the role of *backloading* in the sequential lineup. Backloading involves adding extra lineup members in order to conceal from the witness the actual number of people in the lineup (e.g., by adding extra photos to a stack of lineup photos). Without backloading, witnesses shift their decision criteria as they move through a sequential lineup, becoming more likely to make a positive identification as they near the end of the lineup (Horry, Palmer, & Brewer, 2012). Backloading is a crucial part of the sequential procedure because it undermines this shift in decision criterion, reducing the likelihood of false identifications from late positions in target-absent sequential lineups (Horry et al., 2012). Although these results show that backloading is important, it has been overlooked in recent comparisons of sequential and simultaneous lineups.

Together, these results paint a somewhat murky picture regarding the superiority of sequential lineup presentation over simultaneous presentation. In our view, however, perhaps the most important point to emerge from the debate about these two procedures is that neither one produces impressive accuracy rates, and neither is likely to prove to be the most effective way of assessing the witness's recognition of the suspect (Brewer & Palmer, 2010; Wells, Memon, & Penrod, 2006).

Novel Approaches to Collecting Identification Evidence

Procedural changes aimed at improving the reliability of identification evidence have generally been conservative. Although research has identified a number of best-practice guidelines for administering lineups that can reduce the risk of a false identification, the nature of the lineup task itself has remained relatively constant: Participants view a series of lineup members and either identify someone as the culprit or reject the lineup as a whole. There have been some variations on this procedure based on the notion of using multiple lineups to better assess witnesses' memory (e.g., Palmer, Brewer, & Weber, 2012; Pryke, Lindsay, Dysart, & Dupuis, 2004; Wells, 1984), but here we consider a departure from this standard practice that suggests a new way of collecting and thinking about identification evidence.

As discussed previously, confidence for recognition memory decisions is thought to index the degree of match between a presented item and an image in memory. With this in mind, researchers have suggested that avoiding explicit categorical identifications and, instead, having witnesses rate their confidence (from 0–100%) that each lineup member is the culprit (referred to as *culprit likelihood ratings*) may provide a number of benefits (Brewer, Weber, Wootton, & Lindsay, 2012; Sauer & Brewer, 2015; Sauer, Brewer, & Weber, 2008, 2012; Sauer, Weber, & Brewer, 2012). First, ratings might provide a more informative index of recognition (i.e., the strength of recognition for the suspect) and discrimination (the extent to which the suspect is favored over the alternative). Second, compared with categorical responses, ratings may more directly assess the construct of interest: the degree of match between individual lineup members and the witness's memory of the culprit. As suggested above, although an identification probably indicates that the selected lineup member is the most plausible of the available options, it says little about how well the selected lineup member matches the witness's memory of the culprit.

Initial tests of this approach provided two encouraging findings. First, research revealed a generally linear, positive relationship between confidence ratings and the likelihood that a face has been previously seen for basic face recognition tasks (Sauer, Weber, & Brewer, 2012). Second, after applying algorithms to determine when a rating or pattern of ratings could be taken as indicating a positive identification, ratings were consistently more diagnostic of recognition than categorical responses in basic face recognition and eyewitness identification tasks (Brewer et al., 2012; Sauer, Brewer, & Weber, 2008, 2012; Sauer, Weber, & Brewer, 2012).

Collapsing culprit likelihood ratings into categorical classifications allows a demonstration of their diagnostic value but also reduces the richness of the recognition information provided. Brewer et al. (2012) presented an additional and more informative perspective. For each set of ratings (i.e., for each lineup viewed), the researchers determined whether (1) there was a single highest, maximum rating value and (2) whether the maximum value indicated the suspect. If the maximum value implicated the suspect (i.e., the suspect was favored over the others), the researchers examined variations in the likely guilt of the suspect as a function of the discrepancy between the maximum and next highest values. This approach produced two notable findings. First, the likely guilt of the suspect increased almost monotonically as a function of the discrepancy between the maximum and next highest confidence ratings. Second, when this discrepancy was large (e.g., $\geq 80\%$), the likely guilt of the suspect was very high (e.g., 80–100%), and, until the discrepancy fell to 30–50%, culprit likelihood ratings were a better predictor of suspect guilt than were categorical identification decisions. Further to demonstrating that patterns of culprit likelihood ratings can offer reliable diagnostic information about suspect guilt for individual witnesses, Brewer et al.'s (2012) findings—specifically, the monotonic positive relationship between the discrepancy measure and the likely guilt of the suspect—suggest that a probabilistic treatment of identification evidence may offer a viable alternative to categorical decisions. Relating to the ideological goal of increasing the informational value of identification evidence, the legal system may benefit from eschewing traditional, categorical responses and, instead, considering what patterns of ratings say about the *likely* guilt of the suspect/defendant.

The boundary conditions for ratings-based identification procedures clearly require further investigation. However, such approaches may address a number of systemic problems with traditional identification practices. First, these approaches may attenuate the nonmemorial influences on criterion placement that contribute to identification error by compromising the extent to which the eventual decision reflects the degree of match between a lineup member, or members, and the witness's memory of the culprit. Second, these approaches provide legal decision makers with a richer source of information upon which to base assessments of likely guilt (i.e., speaking to both strength of recognition and degree of discrimination). Further, when a traditional lineup produces a rejection, it provides no information about the degree of match between the suspect and the witness's memory of the culprit (other than that the degree of match did not exceed the criterion for identification). In contrast, in all cases, ratings-based procedures provide investigators with useful information about (1) the extent to which the suspect matches the witness's memory of the culprit and (2) the similarity of the suspect to the witness's memory relative to other lineup members.

An approach such as this one clearly entails a radical departure from traditional conceptualizations of identification evidence. Lineup tasks would no longer provide a single, categorical outcome that is assumed to somehow resolve the ambiguity around a suspect/defendant's guilt. Instead, triers of fact would need to view a lineup task as providing another source of probabilistic evidence about the possible guilt of the suspect. This may be a difficult notion for police and the courts to accept. However, in response to this concern, two points bear consideration. First, recent research suggests that although mock jurors might need support in interpreting ratings-based identification evidence, they do not dismiss such evidence as uninformative (Sauer, Palmer, & Brewer, 2017). Second, a radical departure from traditional approaches might be more palatable if one bears in mind how often traditional approaches produce erroneous decisions (e.g., Steblay et al., 2011).

Novel Approaches to Improving the Accuracy of Child Eyewitness Identifications

Although experiments testing child eyewitness performance tend to be underpowered, the literature provides compelling evidence of a "choosing problem": Compared with adult participants, children are more likely to falsely identify a suspect from a target-absent lineup (see Fitzgerald & Price, 2015, for a meta-analysis and review). Fitzgerald and Price (2015) summarize a number of mechanisms proposed to explain children's proneness to pick from target-absent lineups. Some explanations revolve around the social demands of the task and children's increased susceptibility to suggestion. These explanations suggest that a lineup is, to some extent, inherently suggestive and that children are prone to pick because they believe an identification is expected of them (e.g., Davies, 1996). Other explanations suggest more cognitive mechanisms, proposing that increased false identification rates for child witnesses might reflect underdeveloped face processing ability (e.g., Davies, Tarrant, & Flin, 1989), an overreliance on relative familiarity as a cue for decision making (compared with the ability to recall to reject; e.g., Gross & Hayne, 1996), or an inability to effectively process larger stimulus sets (e.g., lineups containing six or more individuals; see Price & Fitzgerald, 2016). A third category of explanations suggests that children's tendency to pick from target-absent lineups may reflect developmental differences in response inhibition, with younger children experiencing difficulties inhibiting a positive response (e.g., Davies et al., 1989; Zajac & Karageorge, 2009).

Researchers have conducted trials of a variety of approaches, targeting varied combinations of the mechanisms identified above, to address this choosing problem. For example, Pozzulo and Lindsay's (1999) elimination lineup includes a range of procedural elements designed to reduce children's reliance on the relative familiarity of lineup members when making their decisions and to help children reject the lineup when the culprit is absent. In the fast-elimination version of this procedure, the child first identifies the lineup member who best matches his or her memory of the offender and, if the selected lineup member is the suspect, is then explicitly asked if the selected person is the culprit. The fast-elimination version requires the child to begin by eliminating the lineup members who look least like his or her memory of the culprit. If the final remaining lineup member is the suspect, the child is explicitly asked if that person is the culprit. Either elimination procedure can be combined with modified instructions that emphasize the problem of false identifications and encourage the witness to make an absolute judgment (vs. relying on relative familiarity). Zajac and Karageorge's (2009) "wildcard" technique[1] includes a "tangible rejection option" in the array (e.g., a silhouetted figure or stick drawing) to make the rejection option more salient to child witnesses who may assume they are required to pick from the lineup. This approach also makes the identification and rejection behaviors more similar, because both require the child to actively select an option from the array. Zajac and Karageorge (2009) found that, compared with a standard lineup task, the wildcard procedure increased correct rejections (reducing false identifications) from target-absent lineups without reducing correct identifications from target-present lineups (see also Havard & Memon, 2013). Although earlier approaches reported nonsignificant benefits of similar techniques, these studies showed trends in the expected direction, and the failure to reach statistical significance may reflect their reliance on small sample sizes ($Ns < 20$ per cell; e.g., Beal, Schmitt, & Dekle, 1995; Davies et al., 1989). Finally, Price and Fitzgerald's (2016) face-off procedure attempts to accommodate children's difficulties with (1) making choices from large arrays and (2) resisting the urge to pick when the target is absent by breaking the lineup task into a series of simple judgments comparing two lineup members.

All three of these approaches represent nice examples of theoretically motivated procedural innovation, and all three have shown some promise. However, replication across varied stimulus sets and samples, and further investigations of boundary conditions, will be required before any approach can claim decisive empirical support.

THINGS WE KNOW LITTLE ABOUT

Lineup Composition

Researchers (e.g., Wells & Turtle, 1986) and practitioners (e.g., Technical Working Group for Eyewitness Evidence, 1999) generally agree that, when constructing a lineup, a single suspect should be placed among a number of fillers (i.e., known innocent lineup members) selected so that the suspect

---

[1] Similar approaches have been referred to as the "mystery" option or "Mr. Nobody" option (see also Beal, Schmitt, & Dekle, 1995; Davies et al., 1989; Havard & Memon, 2013).

does not "unduly stand out" as the only plausible candidate for identification. Essentially, the lineup should be "fair." However, intuitive as this proposal is, it is unclear how best to achieve this goal. Here we consider some of the unresolved questions relating to lineup composition and lineup fairness. We identify three broad areas in which the literature falls short of providing clear and compelling guidance. First, how many fillers should be in a lineup? Second, how should these fillers be selected? Third, how generalizable are lab findings to applied settings?

Lineup Size

Given that a lineup should contain one suspect and some fillers, an obvious question is, How many fillers are required? Across jurisdictions, there is considerable variation in requirements (or guidelines) relating to *nominal size* (i.e., the number of people in the lineup). For example, the United Kingdom's VIPER system presents nine-member lineups (i.e., one suspect and eight fillers), whereas in the United States, the National Institute of Justice's Technical Working Group for Eyewitness Evidence (1999) guidelines on eyewitness identification protocol suggest "a minimum of five fillers" for a photo array and four for a live lineup. Canada's Sophonow Inquiry Report recommended including at least nine fillers, and Russia's Criminal Procedure Code suggests a minimum of two fillers. Given this variability, it may be of some comfort that, although empirical investigations of the effects of nominal size are scarce, there is some evidence that nominal size has little effect on correct or false identification rates (Nosworthy & Lindsay, 1990; although very large arrays are likley to reduce false identifications of innocent suspects based on guesses; Levi, 1998). A more important consideration is likely to be the *functional size* of the lineup (i.e., the number of plausible candidates in the lineup). However, despite a general consensus that functional size is important and that low functional size increases the risk of false identification, this issue remains underresearched. Although the literature suggests that a functional size of three or more represents a fair lineup (Brigham, Ready, & Spier, 1990; Nosworthy & Lindsay, 1990), the boundary conditions for this suggestion remain largely untested. For example, we do not know how the effects of functional size are moderated by factors affecting memory quality, lineup presentation, or influences on witness's decision criteria.

Selecting Fillers

We now consider what we know, and do not know, about selecting fillers for a lineup. The overarching and intuitive principle is that selection of fillers should promote lineup fairness. However, fairness is multifaceted. First, the lineup should be fair for the suspect, ensuring that the suspect does not unduly stand out. Thus there must be some degree of physical similarity between the suspect and the fillers. Second, the lineup should be fair for the witness. Luus and Wells (1991) argued that a lineup in which the degree of similarity between the suspect and fillers is too high places an unreasonable demand on a witness's memory and capacity for discrimination. Essentially, then, a fair lineup must offer some protection to innocent suspects while still allowing a witness to recognize and identify a guilty suspect. Two approaches to selecting fillers are commonly discussed in the literature. The match-to-suspect (or similarity) approach involves selecting fillers based on their physical similarity to the suspect. As an alternative, Luus and Wells (1991) proposed the match-to-description approach, arguing that selected fillers should possess all the physical characteristics included in the witness's description of the culprit but may vary on any undescribed features. Theoretically, the match-to-description approach has a number of advantages over the match-to-similarity approach. First, it ensures that fillers possess all the features salient enough to be included in the witness's recalled memory for the perpetrator. In contrast, a match-to-suspect approach may include fillers who do not possess features that were salient to the witness if these features were not also salient to the person constructing the lineup. Second, it allows for some heterogeneity among lineup members to aid the witness's discrimination, whereas a match-to-similarity may place an unreasonable demand on the witness's ability to discriminate. Finally, compared with subjective perceptions of physical similarity, the description provides a more objective and concrete basis for filler selection. These sound theoretical grounds for recommending the match-to-description approach may explain why this approach has received fairly consistent "in principle" support in the literature (e.g., Wells et al., 1998) and has been included in the National Institute of Justice guidelines (1999).

Interestingly, however, empirical support for the match-to-description approach is limited. Although Wells, Rydell, and Seelau (1993) found that the match-to-description approach improved correct identification rates (with no increase in false identification rates), subsequent research revealed nonsignificant differences in identification accuracy rates; in one case, the match-to-description approach increased false identification rates along with gains in correct identifications (see Fitzgerald, Oriet, & Price, 2015, for a review). Although power issues in individual studies and differences in description quality across studies may account for some of the variability in findings, meta-analyses suggest that, overall, filler selection strategy has little effect on the diagnosticity of suspect identifications (Clark & Godfrey, 2009; Clark, Howell, & Davey, 2008).

Moreover, there are potentially important practical limitations to the match-to-description approach. First, it relies heavily on the quality of the witness's initial description, and the limited available research suggests that, especially in the field, witnesses' descriptions omit critical details. For example, according to Lindsay, Martin, and Webber's (1994) data, less than half of real crime witnesses' descriptions included details on age, race, height, build, and hair color or length. Less than 10% of descriptions included details on facial features (e.g., eyes, complexion, or facial hair). Second, witnesses will probably not report all recalled details: Some details, even if distinctive and/or vividly recalled, may be difficult to articulate. Thus the descriptions used as a basis for filler selection may omit important information required or fail to provide sufficient information to construct a fair lineup, and it seems likely that some combination of the match-to-description and match-to-suspect approaches will be required. Indeed, the National Institute of Justice guidelines (1999) suggest that when a description provides an inadequate basis for selecting fillers, selection should be based on ensuring that fillers "resemble the suspect in significant features" (p. 29). However, it is not clear how the significance of any such features should be determined.

Despite these issues with match-to-description lineups, ensuring that, at a minimum, all lineup members match the witness's description of the culprit provides an easy and effective method for preventing the presentation of a severely biased lineup in which only the suspect stands out. Once a pool of fillers is identified that meets that criterion, filler selections can be prioritized according to their similarity to the suspect. Unfortunately, however, we do not yet have any objective guidelines or procedures for similarity-based filler selection that will maximize the probability of a correct identification and minimize the likelihood of a mistaken identification.

Generalizing from the Lab to Applied Settings

Applied research always entails a compromise between experimental control and ecological validity. Design choices that justifiably promote experimental control will often necessitate important caveats on the generalizability of findings to applied settings. Here we consider an important example of this issue relevant to understanding lineup composition effects on identification performance. When constructing lineups in lab environments, researchers typically select lineup fillers from a pool of potential lineup members based on some combination of the potential fillers' match to (1) a description of the target (often obtained from a group of pilot participants) and (2) the target's physical appearance (typically assessed through a blend of rigorous visual inspection and intuition). The target-present lineup is then constructed by placing the target among the selected fillers. Typically, the target-absent lineup keeps the same fillers and replaces the target with a designated innocent suspect selected from the original pool of fillers and generally bearing a relatively high resemblance to the target. This "same fillers" approach allows for greater experimental control when examining the effects of experimental manipulations on correct and false identification rates. However, it differs importantly from the filler selection process in applied settings (see Clark & Tunnicliff, 2001, for a review). In applied settings, investigators often do not know who the actual target is. Thus, in target-absent lineups, fillers are selected based on their match to the *suspect,* not their match to the *target.* Clark and Tunnicliff (2001) compared false identification rates using the match-to-target and match-to-suspect approaches to filler selection for target-absent lineups. Compared with the match-to-suspect approach (common in applied settings), the match-to-target approach (common in lab settings) produced lower false identification rates and a lower conditional probability of innocent-suspect identification (i.e., the likelihood that the innocent suspect was identified given that the witness picked someone from a target-absent lineup). Thus the typical experimental approach to selecting target-absent fillers may underestimate innocent-suspect identification rates in applied settings. Consequently, to the limited extent that the literature does speak to lineup composition effects on identification performance in lab settings, we should exercise caution when generalizing these findings to real-world identification performance.

In sum, although few would argue that lineup composition is an important factor in understanding identification performance—and that biased lineups increase the risk of false identifications—a careful consideration of the literature reveals that we still know relatively little about how best to construct fair lineups for applied settings. Brewer, Weber, and Semmler (2005) noted that the absence of a thorough and systematic body of literature investigating lineup composition effects on responding has prevented a clear understanding of many important underlying issues. Unfortunately, this remains the case.

Influence of Nonmemorial Cues

One potentially important class of variables is nonmemorial factors that influence identification decisions. Ideally, witnesses would make identification decisions based only on the degree of match between their memory of the perpetrator and the members of the lineup (e.g., Brewer et al., 2012; Sauer, Brewer, & Weber, 2008). However, this is not always the case; witnesses often pick someone from a lineup even when the match between their memory and the chosen lineup member does not support such a decision (e.g., Wells, 1993). This can happen, for example, if the witness assumes that the actual perpetrator is in the lineup and that their task is to pick out that person.

In situations in which a witness is motivated to choose someone from a lineup but cannot do so on the basis of a match with his or her memory of the perpetrator, factors unrelated to memory can influence identification decisions. This notion aligns well with various decision-making models (e.g., Gigerenzer & Goldstein, 1996; Kahneman & Frederick, 2002). According to such models, when faced with a decision, people attempt to make a good decision based on directly relevant information. However, if a good decision is unable to be made based on such information, the decision maker might turn to other cues that are perceived as valid indicators that might support a decision. In the present context, an eyewitness should attempt to base his or her identification decision on the degree of match between his or her memory of the perpetrator and members of the lineup. However, if a decision cannot be reached this way, then the witness might consider other, nonmemorial cues. Perhaps the most obvious possibility is that the witness could look for cues from the lineup administrator that could indicate which lineup member is the suspect. However, even in the absence of such cues (e.g., if the lineup is administered via computer), various nonmemorial cues can influence identification decisions.

For example, the witness might look at cues relating to facial expression or body language. If, for example, one lineup member is perceived as less trustworthy, more stereotypically "criminal" in appearance, or more nervous than others, it could provide the basis for choosing that person from the lineup (e.g., Flowe, 2012; Flowe, Klatt, & Colloff, 2014; Weigold & Wentura, 2004; Wilson & Rule, 2015). From an objective viewpoint, such cues are clearly not reliable diagnostic indicators of the identity of the perpetrator. However, if the witness does not dismiss such cues as nonvalid, they can provide a basis for choosing one lineup member over the others.

Identification decisions might also be influenced by nonmemorial cues unrelated to the perceived nature of lineup members, such as variations in the quality of photographs (e.g., does one image appear clearer than others or with a different background?). Alternatively, a witness might consider where in the lineup the suspect is most likely to appear. Systematic position biases occur in many hide-and-seek tasks (e.g., games of "battleships"; students guessing on multiple-choice questions; Bar-Hillel, 2015), and similar biases influence guessing from lineups. Witnesses expect suspects to be more likely to appear in central locations in simultaneous lineups rather than edge locations and in the top row (rather than the bottom) of a photo array arranged as a grid (O'Connell & Synnott, 2009; Palmer, Sauer, & Holt, 2017). Position effects also occur in sequential lineups. Choosing increases as the lineup progresses, and, as a result, the target (or a particularly plausible filler) is increasingly likely to be identified from later positions in the lineup (e.g., Carlson, Gronlund, & Clark, 2008; Clark & Davey, 2005; Horry et al., 2012).

Overall, the effect of nonmemorial cues on identification decisions should be modest, because we assume that most witnesses will try to base their decisions on an assessment of memory match. However, there may be specific circumstances under which such cues have a much larger effect. For example, if a witness feels a strong sense of expectation to pick someone from the lineup (e.g., "We're really keen to nail this guy") and feels that all lineup members are plausible matches for the suspect, the influence of nonmemorial cues that allow one lineup member to be distinguished from the others might be especially strong.

Influence of Memorial Factors

There are likely to be some factors that are not well understood but that likely play an important role in eyewitness identification decisions. Our limited understanding of such factors may reflect a paucity of data on the issue, the fact that the effect is difficult to capture in laboratory studies, or the fact that the effect emerges only under certain conditions.

Context Reinstatement

One example is context reinstatement; that is, reestablishing the context from encoding at the time of a memory test. Context reinstatement has proven to be an effective means of increasing the recall of accurate information from memory (e.g., Godden & Baddeley 1975), and for this reason it is included in the Cognitive Interview protocol (Fisher & Geiselman, 1992). However, its influence on recognition memory tasks is less clear-cut (Smith, Glenberg, & Bjork, 1978; Smith & Vela, 2001). Similarly, effects of context reinstatement on eyewitness identification accuracy have produced varying results. Some studies have shown benefits of reinstatement for identification accuracy and others have not, although the data overall suggest that identification accuracy may benefit from physical context reinstatement (i.e., actually returning to the encoding context) more than mental reinstatement (e.g., Cutler & Penrod, 1988; Cutler, Penrod, & Martens, 1987; Gwyer & Clifford, 1997; Krafka & Penrod, 1985; Sanders, 1984; Smith & Vela, 1992).

Unconscious Transference

Another example is unconscious transference, whereby a witness confuses an innocent person (e.g., a bystander at the scene of a crime) for the perpetrator he or she is trying to recognize (e.g., Loftus, 1976). This can occur if a witness confuses the familiarity of the innocent person with the context of having seen that person commit the crime in question (e.g., Perfect & Harris, 2003) or if the witness fails to notice that the perpetrator and the innocent bystander are not the same person (e.g., Davis, Loftus, Vanous, & Cucciare, 2008; Fitzgerald, Oriet, & Price, 2014). Although unconscious transference effects have been found in some studies, they have not emerged in others. Perhaps most notably, one series of highly realistic field experiments conducted under highly realistic conditions (i.e., numerous perpetrators and bystanders; retention intervals varying up to 2 weeks) failed to produce any evidence of unconscious transference (Read, Tollestrup, Hammersley, McFazden, & Christensen, 1990). This highlights the importance of considering conditions that might facilitate the mechanisms thought to underpin unconscious transference. Even if clear and reliable effects do not emerge across experiments, very strong effects may occur in isolated cases when the requisite conditions align.

The Importance of Considering Interactions between Variables

Throughout this chapter, we have touched on the importance of examining interactions between factors that influence eyewitness identification decisions. We believe this is a crucial issue for future research in this field, because there are many theoretically motivated reasons why the effects of one factor might be expected to vary depending on some other factor. For example, retention interval influences identification performance, but its effects may be moderated by numerous other factors that promote the formation of a strong memory at encoding. These might include the distinctiveness of the perpetrator; that is, shorter retention intervals promote better memory performance, but the benefits of a short delay between encoding and identification tests may be smaller when the perpetrator is especially distinctive in appearance (and, hence, memorable even after a long delay).

Exposure duration might prove a consistent moderator of the effects of other factors known to affect identification accuracy. For example, the presence of a weapon can impair memory for a perpetrator because it draws attention away from the appearance of the perpetrator. However, this effect might diminish with longer exposure duration. That is, if the witness views an armed perpetrator for an extended time, the witness might begin to direct more attention to the perpetrator's appearance, especially if the witness's perception of physical threat diminishes over time. Similarly, cross-race effects (whereby identification accuracy is worse when attempting to identify someone from another race rather than one's own race) might weaken under long exposure duration conditions if exposure is sufficient to facilitate a strong memory for an other-race perpetrator.

The need to study potential interactions between variables that affect eyewitness identification clearly presents a challenge to eyewitness researchers. It also highlights the fact that, although research in this area has progressed enormously over the past few decades, there is still much work to be done.

The Base Rate for Culprit-Present Lineups

Finally, we highlight one generally neglected example of how the full applied implications of much eyewitness identification research can only be appreciated by recognizing the match, or mismatch, between one aspect of the researcher's experimental design and the reality of lineup administration practices in the real world. A common practice in laboratory identification research is to present witnesses with either culprit-present or -absent lineups, with studies often presenting 50% of each. One of the reasons for following this approach is obviously to allow researchers to distinguish whether experimentally manipulated variables are affecting witnesses' tendencies to choose from the lineup or the capacity to make accurate recognition decisions. As Brewer et al. (2005) noted, however, conclusions about precisely how individual variables affect identification performance are likely to vary depending on the base rate of culprit-present lineups. In a similar vein, Brewer and Wells (2006, p. 25) showed how varying the proportion of culprit-present lineups leads to quite different conclusions about the relationship between identification confidence and accuracy and, specifically, about the diagnostic value of confidence for determining accuracy. More recently, Wells, Yang, and Smalarz (2015) conducted the first comprehensive examination of how culprit-present base rates can influence the reliability of identification test evidence under a variety of different experimental manipulations. Of course, as noted by both Brewer et al. (2005) and Wells et al. (2015), culprit-present base rates likely vary markedly depending on idiosyncratic jurisdictional practices (e.g., base rates will probably be lower if police use the lineup as a hypothesis testing instrument rather than as the culmination of an exhaustive investigative process), with such variations having important implications for the information gained from positive identifications, lineup rejections, and filler picks (cf. Wells et al., 2015).

CONCLUSION

Although researchers have developed many improvements to identification procedures, it is vital to remember that implementing these in police settings may not be straightforward. Consider the example of double-blind lineup administration, a procedure supported by strong evidence and endorsed widely by researchers. This procedure requires that the officer investigating the case (with knowledge of which lineup member is the suspect) does not conduct the lineup. Although the benefit of this policy might seem obvious to a researcher, an officer who has invested time and effort into building rapport with a witness may be reluctant to hand over a crucial component of the investigation to another person. The uptake of recommended procedures among investigators can be facilitated via carefully developed training protocols that (1) explain the evidence behind procedures and the benefits of implementing procedures and (2) implement them in minimally disruptive ways. For example, double-blind administration allows prosecutors at trial to rule out undue influence on the witness from the lineup administrator. This could be done with the investigating officer retaining control of all aspects of the investigation and only being absent for the actual presentation of the lineup, which would be administered by another officer or via computer (e.g., Brooks, 2017; Town of Norwood, 2017). In a similar vein, obtaining an immediate postdecision record of the witness's confidence would be very simple to achieve using computerized testing. Steblay (Chapter 17, this volume) provides a detailed discussion of challenges and issues relevant to translating research findings into policy.

ACKNOWLEDGMENT

The preparation of this chapter was supported by funding from Australian Research Council grants no. DP150101905 to Neil Brewer et al. and no. DP140103746 to M. Palmer et al.

REFERENCES

Bar-Hillel, M. (2015). Position effects in choice from simultaneous displays: A conundrum solved. *Perspectives on Psychological Science, 10*, 419–433.

Beal, C. R., Schmitt, K. L., & Dekle, D. J. (1995). Eyewitness identification of children: Effects of absolute judgments, nonverbal response options, and event encoding. *Law and Human Behavior, 19*, 197–216.

Bradfield, A. L., & Wells, G. L. (2000). The perceived validity of eyewitness identification testimony: A test of the five Biggers criteria. *Law and Human Behavior, 24*, 581–594.

Brewer, N. (2011, April). Practical advantages in computerized photo line-ups [Opinion]. Police Journal. Available at *http://journal.pasa.asn.au/apps/uploadedFiles/news/852/Opinion.pdf.*

Brewer, N., Caon, A., Todd, C., & Weber, N. (2006). Eyewitness identification accuracy and response latency. *Law and Human Behavior, 30*, 31–50.

Brewer, N., Keast, A., & Rishworth, A. (2002). The confidence–accuracy relationship in eyewitness identification: The effects of reflection and disconfirmation on correlation and calibration. *Journal of Experimental Psychology: Applied, 8*, 44–56.

Brewer, N., & Palmer, M. A. (2010). Eyewitness identification tests. *Legal and Criminological Psychology, 15*, 77–96.

Brewer, N., & Weber, N. (2008). Eyewitness confidence and latency: Indices of memory processes not just markers of accuracy. *Applied Cognitive Psychology, 22*, 827–840.

Brewer, N., Weber, N., & Semmler, C. (2005). Eyewitness identification. In N. Brewer & K. D. Williams (Eds.), *Psychology and law: An empirical perspective* (pp. 177–221). New York: Guilford Press.

Brewer, N., Weber, N., Wootton, D., & Lindsay, D. S. (2012). Identifying the bad guy in a lineup using confidence judgments under deadline pressure. *Psychological Science, 23*, 1208–1214.

Brewer, N., & Wells, G. L. (2006). The confidence–accuracy relationship in eyewitness identification: Effects of lineup instructions, functional size and target-absent base rates. *Journal of Experimental Psychology: Applied, 12*, 11–30.

Brewer, N., & Wells, G. L. (2009). Obtaining and interpreting eyewitness identification test evidence: The influence of police–witness interactions. In T. Williamson, R. Bull, & T. Valentine (Eds.), *Handbook of psychology of investigative interviewing: Current developments and future directions* (pp. 205–220). Chichester, UK: Wiley-Blackwell.

Brigham, J. C., Ready, D. J., & Spier, S. A. (1990). Standards for evaluating the fairness of photograph lineups. *Basic and Applied Social Psychology, 11*, 149–163.

Brooks, W. G., III. (2017, May 24). *U.S. identification procedures*. Paper presented at Eyewitness Identification Workshop, Boston, MA.

Carlson, C. A., Gronlund, S. D., & Clark, S. E. (2008). Lineup composition, suspect position, and the sequential lineup advantage. *Journal of Experimental Psychology: Applied, 14*, 118–128.

Clark, S. E. (2012). Costs and benefits of eyewitness identification reform: Psychological science and public policy. *Perspectives on Psychological Science, 7*, 238–259.

Clark, S. E., & Davey, S. L. (2005). The target-to-foils shift in simultaneous and sequential lineups. *Law and Human Behavior, 29*, 151–172.

Clark, S. E., & Godfrey, R. D. (2009). Eyewitness identification evidence and innocence risk. *Psychonomic Bulletin and Review, 16*, 22–42.

Clark, S. E., Howell, R., & Davey, S. (2008). Regularities in eyewitness identification. *Law and Human Behavior, 32*, 187–218.

Clark, S. E., & Tunnicliff, J. (2001). Selecting lineup foils in eyewitness identification experiments: Experimental control and real-world simulation. *Law and Human Behavior, 25*, 199–216.

Cutler, B. L., & Penrod, S. D. (1988). Context reinstatement and eyewitness identification. In G. M. Davies & D. M. Thomson (Eds.), *Memory in context: Context in memory* (pp. 231–244). Oxford, UK: Wiley.

Cutler, B. L., Penrod, S. D., & Dexter, H. R. (1990). Juror sensitivity to eyewitness identification evidence. *Law and Human Behavior, 14*, 185–191.

Cutler, B. L., Penrod, S. D., & Martens, T. K. (1987). The reliability of eyewitness identification: The role of system and estimator variables. *Law and Human Behavior, 11*(3), 233–258.

Davies, G. (1996). Children's identification evidence. In S. L. Sporer, R. S. Malpass, & G. Koehnken (Eds.), *Psychological issues in eyewitness identification* (pp. 233–258). Mahwah, NJ: Erlbaum.

Davies, G., Tarrant, A., & Flin, R. (1989). Close encounters of the witness kind: Children's memory for a simulated health inspection. *British Journal of Psychology, 80*, 415–429.

Davis, D., Loftus, E., Vanous, S., & Cucciare, M. (2008). Unconscious transference can be an instance of change blindness. *Applied Cognitive Psychology, 22*, 605–623.

Deffenbacher, K. A., & Loftus, E. F. (1982). Do jurors share a common understanding concerning eyewitness behavior? *Law and Human Behavior, 6*, 15–30.

Dunning, D., & Perretta, S. (2002). Automaticity and eyewitness accuracy: A 10- to 12-second rule for distinguishing accurate from inaccurate positive identifications. *Journal of Applied Psychology, 87*, 951–962.

Dunning, D., & Stern, L. B. (1994). Distinguishing accurate from inaccurate eyewitness identifications via inquiries about decision processes. *Journal of Personality and Social Psychology, 67*, 818–835.

Fisher, R. P., & Geiselman, R. E. (1992). *Memory-enhancing techniques in investigative interviewing: The Cognitive Interview*. Springfield, IL: Charles C Thomas.

Fitzgerald, R. J., Oriet, C., & Price, H. L. (2014). Change blindness and eyewitness identification: Effects on accuracy and confidence. *Legal and Criminological Psychology, 21*, 189–201.

Fitzgerald, R. J., Oriet, C., & Price, H. L. (2015). Suspect filler similarity in eyewitness lineups: A literature review and a novel methodology. *Law and Human Behavior, 39*, 62–74.

Fitzgerald, R. J., & Price, H. L. (2015). Eyewitness identification across the life span: A meta-analysis of age differences. *Psychological Bulletin, 141*, 1228–1265.

Flowe, H. D. (2012). Do characteristics of faces that convey trustworthiness and dominance underlie perceptions of criminality? *PLOS ONE, 7*, e37253.

Flowe, H. D., Klatt, T., & Colloff, M. F. (2014). Selecting fillers on emotional appearance improves lineup identification accuracy. *Law and Human Behavior, 38*, 509–519.

Gigerenzer, G., & Goldstein, D. G. (1996). Reasoning the fast and frugal way: Models of bounded rationality. *Psychological Review, 103*, 650–669.

Godden, D. R., & Baddeley, A. D. (1975). Context-dependent memory in two natural environments: On land and underwater. *British Journal of Psychology, 66*, 325–331.

Gross, J., & Hayne, H. (1996). Eyewitness identification by 5- to 6-year-old children. *Law and Human Behavior, 20*, 359–373.

Gwyer, P., & Clifford, B. R. (1997). The effects of the Cognitive Interview on recall, identification, confidence and the confidence/accuracy relationship. *Applied Cognitive Psychology, 11*, 121–145.

Havard, C., & Memon, A. (2013). The mystery man can help reduce false identification for child witnesses: Evidence from video line-ups. *Applied Cognitive Psychology, 27*, 50–59.

Horry, R., & Brewer, N. (2016). How target-lure similarity shapes confidence judgments in multiple-alternative decision tasks. *Journal of Experimental Psychology: General, 145*, 1615–1634.

Horry, R., Palmer, M., & Brewer, N. (2012). Backloading in the sequential lineup prevents within-lineup criterion shifts that undermine eyewitness identification performance. *Journal of Experimental Psychology: Applied, 18*, 346–360.

Innocence Project. (2017). Innocence Project. Retrieved December 1, 2017, from *www.innocenceproject.org/about/index.php*.

Juslin, P., Olsson, N., & Winman, A. (1996). Calibration and diagnosticity of confidence in eyewitness identification: Comments on what can be inferred from the low confidence–accuracy correlation. *Journal of Experimental Psychology: Learning, Memory, and Cognition, 22*, 1304–1316.

Kahneman, D., & Frederick, S. (2002). Representativeness revisited: Attribute substitution in intuitive judgment. In T. Gilovich, D. Griffin, & D. Kahneman (Eds.), *Heuristics and biases: The psychology of intuitive judgment* (pp. 49–81). New York: Cambridge University Press.

Kassin, S. M., Tubb, V. A., Hosch, H. M., & Memon, A. (2001). On the "general acceptance" of eyewitness testimony research: A new survey of the experts. *American Psychologist, 56*, 405–416.

Keast, A., Brewer, N., & Wells, G. L. (2007). Children's metacognitive judgments in an eyewitness identification task. *Journal of Experimental Child Psychology, 97*, 286–314.

Kovera, M. B., & Evelo, A. J. (2017). The case for double-blind lineup administration. *Psychology, Public Policy, and Law, 23*, 421–437.

Krafka, C., & Penrod, S. (1985). Reinstatement of context in a field experiment on eyewitness identification. *Journal of Personality and Social Psychology, 49,* 58–69.

Levi, A. M. (1998). Protecting innocent defendants, nailing the guilty: A modified sequential lineup. *Applied Cognitive Psychology, 12,* 265–275.

Light, L. L., Kayra-Stuart, F., & Hollander, S. (1979). Recognition memory for typical and unusual faces. *Journal of Experimental Psychology: Human Learning and Memory, 5,* 212–228.

Lindsay, R. C. L., Martin, R., & Webber, L. (1994). Default values in eyewitness descriptions: A problem for the match-to-description lineup foil selection strategy. *Law and Human Behavior, 18,* 527–541.

Lindsay, R. C. L., Semmler, C., Weber, N., Brewer, N., & Lindsay, M. R. (2008). How variations in distance affect eyewitness reports and identification accuracy. *Law and Human Behavior, 32,* 526–535.

Lindsay, R. C. L., & Wells, G. L. (1985). Improving eyewitness identifications from lineups: Simultaneous versus sequential lineup presentation. *Journal of Applied Psychology, 70,* 556–564.

Loftus, E. (1976). Unconscious transference in eyewitness identification. *Law and Psychology Review, 2,* 93–98.

Luus, E. C. A., & Wells, G. L. (1991). Eyewitness identification and the selection of distracters for lineups. *Law and Human Behavior, 15,* 43–57.

Malpass, R. S., & Devine, P. G. (1981). Eyewitness identification: Lineup instructions and the absence of the offender. *Journal of Applied Psychology, 66,* 482–489.

Mansour, J. K., & Flowe, H. D. (2010, Autumn). Eye tracking and eyewitness memory. *Forensic Update, 101.*

Mansour, J. K., Lindsay, R. C. L., Brewer, N., & Munhall, K. G. (2009). Characterizing visual behaviour in a lineup task. *Applied Cognitive Psychology, 23,* 1012–1026.

Meissner, C. A., & Brigham, J. C. (2001). Thirty years of investigating the own-race bias in memory for faces: A meta-analytic review. *Psychology, Public Policy, and Law, 7,* 3–35.

Memon, A., Hope, L., & Bull, R. (2003). Exposure duration: Effects on eyewitness accuracy and confidence. *British Journal of Psychology, 94,* 339–354.

Mickes, L., Flowe, H. D., & Wixted, J. T. (2012). Receiver operating characteristic analysis of eyewitness memory: Comparing the diagnostic accuracy of simultaneous versus sequential lineups. *Journal of Experimental Psychology: Applied, 18*(4), 361–376.

Nosworthy, G. J., & Lindsay, R. C. L. (1990). Does nominal lineup size matter? *Journal of Applied Psychology, 75,* 358–361.

O'Connell, M., & Synnott, J. (2009). A position of influence: Variation in offender identification rates by location in a lineup. *Journal of Investigative Psychology and Offender Profiling, 6,* 139–149.

Palmer, M. A., & Brewer, N. (2012). Sequential lineup presentation promotes less-biased criterion setting but does not improve discriminability. *Law and Human Behavior, 36*(3), 247–255.

Palmer, M. A., Brewer, N., McKinnon, A. C., & Weber, N. (2010). Phenomenological reports diagnose accuracy of eyewitness identification decisions. *Acta Psychologica, 133,* 137–145.

Palmer, M. A., Brewer, N., & Weber, N. (2012). The information gained from witnesses' responses to an initial "blank" lineup. *Law and Human Behavior, 36*, 439–447.

Palmer, M. A., Brewer, N., Weber, N., & Nagesh, A. (2013). The confidence–accuracy relationship for eyewitness identification decisions: Effects of exposure duration, retention interval, and divided attention. *Journal of Experimental Psychology: Applied, 19*, 55–71.

Palmer, M. A., Sauer, J. D., & Holt, G. A. (2017). Undermining position effects in choices from arrays, with implications for police lineups. *Journal of Experimental Psychology: Applied, 23*, 71–84.

Perfect, T. J., & Harris, L. J. (2003). Adult age differences in unconscious transference: Source confusion or identity blending? *Memory and Cognition, 31*, 570–580.

Potter, R., & Brewer, N. (1999). Perceptions of witness behaviour accuracy relationships held by police, lawyers and jurors. *Psychiatry, Psychology and Law, 6*, 97–103.

Pozzulo, J. D., & Lindsay, R. C. L. (1999). Elimination lineups: An improved identification procedure for child eyewitnesses. *Journal of Applied Psychology, 84*, 167–176.

Price, H. L., & Fitzgerald, R. J. (2016). Face-off: A new identification procedure for child eyewitnesses. *Journal of Experimental Psychology: Applied, 22*, 366–380.

Pryke, S., Lindsay, R. C. L., Dysart, J. E., & Dupuis, P. (2004). Multiple independent identification decisions: A method of calibrating eyewitness identifications. *Journal of Applied Psychology, 89*, 73–84.

Read, J. D., Tollestrup, P., Hammersley, R., McFadzen, E., & Christensen, A. (1990). The unconscious transference effect: Are innocent bystanders ever misidentified? *Applied Cognitive Psychology, 4*, 3–31.

Sanders, G. S. (1984). Effects of context cues on eyewitness identification responses. *Journal of Applied Social Psychology, 14*, 386–397.

Sauer, J. D., & Brewer, N. (2015). Confidence and accuracy of eyewitness identification. In T. Valentine & J. P. Davis (Eds.), *Forensic facial identification: Theory and practice of identification from eyewitnesses, composites and CCTV* (pp. 185–208). Chichester, UK: Wiley Blackwell.

Sauer, J. D., Brewer, N., & Weber, N. (2008). Multiple confidence estimates as indices of eyewitness memory. *Journal of Experimental Psychology: General, 137*, 528–547.

Sauer, J. D., Brewer, N., & Weber, N. (2012). Using confidence ratings to identify a target among foils. *Journal of Applied Research in Memory and Cognition, 1*, 80–88.

Sauer, J. D., Brewer, N., & Wells, G. L. (2008). Is there a magical time boundary for diagnosing eyewitness identification accuracy in sequential line-ups? *Legal and Criminological Psychology, 13*, 123–135.

Sauer, J. D., Brewer, N., Zweck, T., & Weber, N. (2010). The effect of retention interval on the confidence–accuracy relationship for eyewitness identification. *Law and Human Behavior, 34*, 337–347.

Sauer, J. D., Palmer, M. A., & Brewer, N. (2017). Mock-juror evaluations of traditional and ratings-based eyewitness identification evidence. *Law and Human Behavior, 41*, 375–384.

Sauer, J. D., Weber, N., & Brewer, N. (2012). Using ecphoric confidence ratings to discriminate seen from unseen faces: The effects of retention interval and distinctiveness. *Psychonomic Bulletin and Review, 19,* 490–498.

Sauerland, M., & Sporer, S. L. (2009). Fast and confident: Postdicting eyewitness identification accuracy in a field study. *Journal of Experimental Psychology: Applied, 15,* 46–62.

Semmler, C., & Brewer, N. (2006). Postidentification feedback effects on face recognition confidence: Evidence for metacognitive influences. *Applied Cognitive Psychology, 20,* 895–916.

Semmler, C., Brewer, N., & Wells, G. L. (2004). Effects of postidentification feedback on eyewitness identification and nonidentification confidence. *Journal of Applied Psychology, 89,* 334–346.

Smith, S. M., Glenberg, A., & Bjork, R. A. (1978). Environmental context and human memory. *Memory and Cognition, 6,* 342–353.

Smith, S. M., Lindsay, R. C. L., & Pryke, S. (2000). Postdictors of eyewitness errors: Can false identifications be diagnosed? *Journal of Applied Psychology, 85,* 542–550.

Smith, S. M., & Vela, E. (1992). Environmental context-dependent eyewitness recognition. *Applied Cognitive Psychology, 6,* 125–139.

Smith, S. M., & Vela, E. (2001). Environmental context-dependent memory: A review and meta-analysis. *Psychonomic Bulletin and Review, 8,* 203–220.

Sporer, S. L. (1992). Post-dicting eyewitness accuracy: Confidence, decision-times and person descriptions of choosers and non-choosers. *European Journal of Social Psychology, 22,* 157–180.

Sporer, S. L. (1993). Eyewitness identification accuracy, confidence, and decision times in simultaneous and sequential lineups. *Journal of Applied Psychology, 78,* 22–33.

Sporer, S. L. (1994). Decision times and eyewitness identification accuracy in simultaneous and sequential lineups. In D. F. Ross, D. J. Read, & M. P. Toglia (Eds.), *Adult eyewitness testimony: Current trends and developments* (pp. 300–327). New York: Cambridge University Press.

Sporer, S. L., Penrod, S. D., Read, D., & Cutler, B. L. (1995). Choosing, confidence, and accuracy: A meta-analysis of the confidence–accuracy relation in eyewitness identification studies. *Psychological Bulletin, 118,* 315–327.

Steblay, N. (1992). A meta-analytic review of the weapon focus effect. *Law and Human Behavior, 16,* 413–424.

Steblay, N. M. (1997). Social influence in eyewitness recall: A meta-analytic review of lineup instruction effects. *Law and Human Behavior, 21,* 283–297.

Steblay, N. M., Dysart, J., Fulero, S., & Lindsay, R. C. L. (2001). Eyewitness accuracy rates in sequential and simultaneous lineup presentations: A meta-analytic comparison. *Law and Human Behavior, 25,* 459–473.

Steblay, N., Dysart, J., Fulero, S., & Lindsay, R. C. L. (2003). Eyewitness accuracy rates in police showups and lineup presentations: A meta-analytic comparison. *Law and Human Behavior, 27,* 523–540.

Steblay, N. K., Dysart, J. E., & Wells, G. L. (2011). Seventy-two tests of the sequential lineup superiority effect: A meta-analysis and policy discussion. *Psychology, Public Policy, and Law, 17,* 99–139.

Technical Working Group for Eyewitness Evidence. (1999). *Eyewitness evidence:*

A guide for law enforcement. Washington DC: U.S. Department of Justice, Office of Justice Programs.

Town of Norwood. (2017). Norwood PD Policy: Eyewitness identification 2017 (Policy and Procedure No. 1.12). Retrieved May 24, 2017, from *www.norwoodma.gov/departments/police/mptc_training_material.php.*

Vickers, D. (1979). *Decision processes in visual perception.* New York: Academic Press.

Weber, N., Brewer, N., Wells, G. L., Semmler, C., & Keast, A. (2004). Eyewitness identification accuracy and response latency: The unruly 10–12-second rule. *Journal of Experimental Psychology: Applied, 10,* 139–147.

Weigold, A., & Wentura, D. (2004). Who's the one in trouble?: Experimental evidence for a "psychic state" bias in lineups. *European Journal of Social Psychology, 34,* 121–133.

Wells, G. L. (1978). Applied eyewitness-testimony research: System variables and estimator variables. *Journal of Personality and Social Psychology, 36,* 1546–1557.

Wells, G. L. (1984). The psychology of lineup identifications. *Journal of Applied Social Psychology, 14,* 89–103.

Wells, G. L. (1993). What do we know about eyewitness identification? *American Psychologist, 48,* 553–571.

Wells, G. L., & Bradfield, A. L. (1998). "Good, you identified the suspect": Feedback to eyewitnesses distorts their reports of the witnessing experience. *Journal of Applied Psychology, 83,* 360–376.

Wells, G. L., & Bradfield, A. L. (1999). Distortions in eyewitnesses' recollections: Can the postidentification-feedback effect be moderated? *Psychological Science, 10,* 138–144.

Wells, G. L., Memon, A., & Penrod, S. D. (2006). Eyewitness evidence: Improving its probative value. *Psychological Science in the Public Interest, 7,* 45–75.

Wells, G. L., Rydell, S. M., & Seelau, E. P. (1993). The selection of distractors for eyewitness lineups. *Journal of Applied Psychology, 78,* 835–844.

Wells, G. L., Smalarz, L., & Smith, A. M. (2015). ROC analysis of lineups does not measure underlying discriminability and has limited value. *Journal of Applied Research in Memory and Cognition, 4,* 313–317.

Wells, G. L., Small, M., Penrod, S., Malpass, R. S., Fulero, S. M., & Brimacombe, C. A. E. (1998). Eyewitness identification procedures: Recommendations for lineups and photospreads. *Law and Human Behavior, 22,* 603–647.

Wells, G. L., Steblay, N. K., & Dysart, J. E. (2012). Eyewitness identification reforms: Are suggestiveness-induced hits and guesses true hits? *Perspectives on Psychological Science, 7,* 264–271.

Wells, G. L., & Turtle, J. W. (1986). Eyewitness identification: The importance of lineup models. *Psychological Bulletin, 99,* 320–329.

Wells, G. L., Yang, Y., & Smalarz, L. (2015). Eyewitness identification: Bayesian information gain, base-rate effect equivalency curves, and reasonable suspicion. *Law and Human Behavior, 39,* 99–122.

Wilson, J. P., & Rule, N. O. (2015). Facial trustworthiness predicts extreme criminal-sentencing outcomes. *Psychological Science, 26,* 1325–1331.

Wixted, J. T., & Mickes, L. (2014). A signal-detection-based diagnostic feature-detection model of eyewitness identification. *Psychological Review, 121,* 262–276.

Wixted, J. T., Mickes, L., Dunn, J. C., Clark, S. E., & Wells, W. (2016). Estimating the reliability of eyewitness identifications from police lineups. *Proceedings of the National Academy of Sciences of the USA, 113*, 304–309.

Wixted, J. T., & Wells, G. L. (2017). The relationship between eyewitness confidence and identification accuracy: A new synthesis. *Psychological Science in the Public Interest, 18*, 10–65.

Zajac, R., & Karageorge, A. (2009). The wildcard: A simple technique for improving children's target-absent lineup performance. *Applied Cognitive Psychology, 23*, 358–368.

CHAPTER 10

Identifying People from Images

David White
Richard I. Kemp

Identifying unfamiliar people from images is critical to crime prevention, criminal investigation, and in court deliberations. Is the applicant who he or she claims to be? Does the suspect match the culprit captured on closed-circuit television (CCTV)? Is the person depicted on this wanted poster someone I know? The criminal justice system relies on the accuracy of these decisions, but is this reliance warranted?

In this chapter we review psychological studies examining the many ways that images are used to identify people in these settings. We start with the task of verifying identity from photo identification cards. Establishing a person's identity is key to crime prevention, criminal investigation, and identity fraud, which can be the precursor to serious and organized crime. Because images on photo IDs—for example, driver's licenses or passports— are typically subject to strict quality control measures, this also represents optimal conditions for matching faces of unfamiliar people. Therefore, studies examining accuracy on this task provide a useful baseline of human accuracy in face identification and for understanding problems that arise when using images for identification in court.

We then turn to the more challenging case of identifying people from CCTV. This is the most common image identification evidence presented in court and is becoming a particularly important research area in light of increased levels of surveillance in modern society. In the final section, we review literature evaluating methods for generating image likenesses of culprits from a witness's memory.

PHOTO IDENTIFICATION

Photo ID remains the most common method for verifying a person's identity. We rely on images of faces to link cardholders to biographical details on their identity documents and, as a result, place substantial trust in the ability of passport officers, police, and security professionals to decide whether or not the unfamiliar face of the cardholder matches the photo on their identity document. But how accurate are these decisions? People often assume that the task is trivial. First, the task does not involve memory; the image is compared with the person standing in front of you. Second, passport images are subject to strict guidelines to ensure that they are high quality, taken in standardized conditions and under good lighting. Third, we routinely recognize people in our daily lives from the briefest glimpse of their faces.

Perhaps for these reasons, people are often surprised to learn that performance on these face identification tasks is highly error prone. In an early study, Kemp, Towell, and Pike (1997) asked supermarket cashiers to verify the identities of participants posing as shoppers by comparing their appearance to photo ID cards. Shoppers presented their photo IDs to cashiers, who then decided whether the photo matched the face of the card bearer. On half of the trials, IDs were "valid," meaning that the photo was an image of the shopper taken in the weeks prior to the experiment. In the other half, "invalid" images of another person were presented. Invalid IDs that were chosen to resemble the shopper were incorrectly accepted by the cashier on over half of the trials, and overall error rate on the task was 35%—not much better accuracy than would be expected by random guessing.

In the late 1990s, a number of lab-based studies replicated Kemp et al.'s (1997) finding by examining face-matching performance under more optimal conditions. For example, in a series of studies by Vicki Bruce, Mike Burton, and colleagues (e.g. Bruce et al., 1999; Henderson, Bruce & Burton, 2001), participants were provided with a target face above an array of 10 images that may or may not contain the target identity. All were high-quality images, taken on the same day, in the same neutral pose, and under very similar lighting conditions. This computer-based task was designed to provide an analogue to police lineups—with the important difference that the task does not involve memory. An example of the face-matching task is shown in Figure 10.1.

Despite these favorable conditions for matching, participants in Bruce et al.'s (1999) experiments made errors in approximately 30% of decisions. Subsequent studies have replicated this poor level of accuracy under a variety of conditions. For example, replacing the target photograph with a live person does not improve accuracy (Megreya & Burton, 2008). Other studies have reduced task demands further by presenting two images side-by-side on a computer monitor and asking participants to decide whether they are of the same person or two different people. This does not redress task difficulty, with error rates in pairwise matching decisions typically around

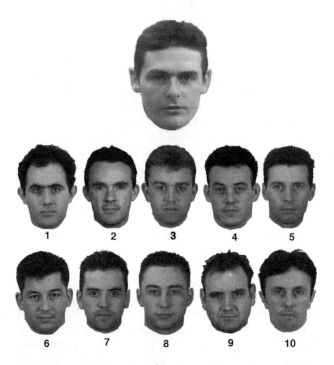

FIGURE 10.1. A typical example of a trial from a one-to-many face-matching study showing the level of similarity between the faces in these studies (Bruce et al., 1999; see also White, Dunn, Schmid, & Kemp, 2015). Participants must decide whether the target person pictured above the array appears in the array and, if so, decide which image matches the target. The correct answer is shown in the "Author Note" at the end of this chapter. From Megreya, White, and Burton (2011). Copyright 2011 by Sage Publications. Reprinted by permission.

20% (Henderson et al., 2001; Megreya & Burton, 2006, 2007; Burton, White, & McNeill, 2010).

Given the reliance that society places on these decisions, face-matching errors in professional roles can carry potentially serious outcomes. But does professional experience protect people from making these errors? Early work by Burton et al. (1999) asked police officers to match images of unfamiliar faces with CCTV footage. Despite being more confident in their identification decisions, police officers were not any more accurate. Although police officers' apparent obliviousness to the difficulty of the task is concerning, face matching was not explicitly part of officers' job descriptions. More recently, however, White, Kemp, Jenkins, Matheson, and Burton (2014) tested the performance of Australian passport officers who are explicitly required to match faces routinely in their daily work. Surprisingly, despite receiving training in face identification, passport officers were no better at face matching than a group of novice university students.

Why Is Unfamiliar Face Matching So Difficult?

Unfamiliar face-matching tasks do not require participants to memorize faces. Images are presented on the screen simultaneously, and participants typically can take as much time as they like before reaching a decision. So the difficulty of this task is not caused by the fallibility of human memory (see Sauer, Palmer, & Brewer, Chapter 9, this volume), but appears to be a perceptual limitation. Despite the best efforts of passport-issuing authorities to optimize the quality of passport photos—ensuring, for example, that subjects are evenly lit, facing the camera, and in a neutral pose—the evidence we have reviewed above clearly shows that people make large numbers of identity verification errors. So, why is this perceptual task so difficult?

At least part of this difficulty can be explained by the intrinsic limitations of photography in capturing facial identity. For now, let's ignore the changes in facial appearance caused by aging, expression, head angle, and lighting and focus only on the optimal conditions for matching in which all of these variables are controlled. Figure 10.2 shows three people all pictured on the same day and under controlled conditions. The top row shows the same individual taken just seconds apart, in precisely the same studio

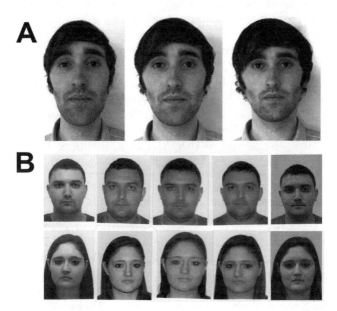

FIGURE 10.2. Top row: Three images of the same individual taken seconds apart, but from different distances (from left to right: 50 cm, 100 cm, 300 cm); from Burton, Schweinberger, Jenkins, and Kaufmann (2015). Bottom rows: Passport-compliant photographs of two people (rows), all taken on the same day but by different passport photo vendors (columns). From Spiteri, Porter, and Kemp (2015).

conditions and with precisely the same camera. Nevertheless, the change in appearance from the leftmost image to the rightmost image is striking and is caused simply by the person placing himself further away from the camera. This simple change in subject-to-camera distance has plainly altered the perceived shape of this person's face (Burton, Schweinberger, Jenkins, & Kaufmann, 2015). In a recent study, Noyes and Jenkins (2017) examined the effect that this change has on accuracy, while controlling for all other variables. This simple change has a substantial impact on the accuracy of face-matching decisions, reducing accuracy on a same- or different-person decision by 10%.

Now consider the bottom two rows of Figure 10.2, which show five passport compliant photographs of two individuals. In each column, images are from a different passport photo vendor in the same local area. Despite these images all being taken on the same day, in neutral pose and conforming to passport image guidelines regarding lighting and head angle, they nevertheless give rise to quite different appearances. This is partly due to the different lens and sensor characteristics of the cameras, which has a rather marked effect on the appearance of skin tone, hair color, and face shape. This example underlines the essential difficulty of identifying people from photographs: No matter how hard one tries, it is very difficult to ensure that the same face appears the same in any two photographs.

Naturally, optimal conditions for matching are rarely encountered outside of the laboratory. So far, we have presented accuracy scores for the most straightforward matching tasks. However, face-matching accuracy is reduced further by a range of viewer- and face-related factors that are encountered in the real world, including aging of the face (Megreya, Sandford, & Burton, 2013); disguise (Noyes & Jenkins, 2016); changes in lighting, pose, and expression (Hancock, Bruce, & Burton, 2000; Jenkins, White, Van Montfort, & Burton, 2011); time pressure (Fysh & Bindemann, 2017); lack of sleep (Beattie, Walsh, McLaren, Biello, & White, 2016) and state anxiety (Attwood, Penton-Voak, Burton, & Munafò, 2013).

Why Do People Assume Unfamiliar Face Matching Is Easy?

Participants are often surprised at the difficulty of matching images of unfamiliar faces and predict it will be a straightforward task. This may explain why people have been relying on photo IDs ever since photography made the practice possible (Bertillon, 1889), and yet it is only relatively recently—in the past 20 years—that scientists have discovered the practice is largely ineffective. Perhaps instead of asking "Why this task is so difficult?", we should instead be asking "Why do people expect it to be easy?" Where does our intuition that photo ID is a reliable method of identity verification stem from?

A recent proposal is that we overgeneralize our expertise in recognizing *familiar* faces to the case of unfamiliar face matching (see Jenkins &

Burton, 2011). We are very good at recognizing faces of people we know, and we experience the effortless recognition of these faces many times each day. Perhaps then, we think images of unfamiliar faces are useful tokens of identity because we recognize *familiar* faces so effortlessly? As can be seen from Figure 10.3, familiarity transforms face-matching tasks from a simple image-to-image comparison (left pair) to a task of recognition (right pair). The image pair on the left shows an item from the Glasgow Face Matching Test (GFMT; Burton et al., 2010). This is a difficult item, and around one-third of people incorrectly answer that they believe the images are of two different people. In the right-hand image pair, there are substantial disparities in age, pose, expression, image quality, makeup, and distance from the camera. However, most people have no difficulty in recognizing this person, and hence deciding that these images are of the same person.

Ritchie and colleagues (2015) have recently provided some empirical support for the hypothesis that people overgeneralize expertise with familiar faces. They asked participants to complete pairwise face-matching decisions such as those presented in Figure 10.3. Participants had to first decide whether the two images were of the same person or of different people. Half of the image pairs were of local U.K. celebrities, and so were familiar to the U.K. participants tested in this study, and half were local Australian celebrities, who were unfamiliar to the U.K. participants. Critically, participants also had to estimate the proportion of German participants—that is, people who were unfamiliar with all the faces in the study—who would get this decision right. Consistent with other work, face-matching accuracy was far better for familiar than for unfamiliar celebrities. More interestingly, perhaps, U.K. participants also predicted that the German participants would perform better on U.K. than on Australian celebrity pairs—the faces with which they themselves were familiar. Given that Germans would be unfamiliar with both sets of celebrities, the intuition of

FIGURE 10.3. Two face-matching decisions: Do these pairs of images show the same person or different people? The image pair on the left is an item from the Glasgow Face Matching Test (GFMT; Burton, White, & McNeill, 2010), and the pair on the right shows a familiar person. Answers are provided in the text. Left image pair reprinted with permission from Springer Nature. Copyright 2010.

U.K. participants would appear to be based on their subjective experience of the task.

This result may go some way to explain why people tend to be overconfident when performing unfamiliar face-matching tasks (see Bruce et al., 1999; Burton, Wilson, Cowan, & Bruce, 1999). Our misplaced reliance on our ability to identify *unfamiliar* faces may stem from intuitions based on our experience with *familiar* faces. Regardless of the cause, overconfidence may help explain why we are not more aware of our inability to match unfamiliar faces. Indeed, this overconfidence may be the biggest problem outlined in this section. Poor performance in unfamiliar face identification tasks is not necessarily a problem *per se*: so long as people are aware of the difficulty of this task, then mitigating action can be taken. The greatest danger arises when people are both confident and wrong, and so it will be important for future research to address why this misplaced confidence arises and how it can be redressed.

FORENSIC FACE IDENTIFICATION

Cameras are everywhere in the modern world. Although not unique in this regard, British people appear to have a particular obsession with recording each other, and it is a belief often held that the United Kingdom is the most closely observed society in the world. One recent estimate suggests that in 2016 there were around 5 million CCTV cameras in the United Kingdom, a nation with a population of about 65 million (British Security Industry Associations, 2015). This estimate includes cameras facing public spaces, such as streets and parks, and also cameras monitoring private places, such as shops, schools, worksites, storerooms, and others. Critically, this estimate does not include the cameras most adults carry with them in their smartphones. As a result of the ubiquity of recording devices, today it is rare for media coverage of any significant news event not to be accompanied by a montage of video clips from public and private fixed cameras and handheld smartphones.

The fact that the world is now so closely monitored affects our lives in many ways, including on the operation of the legal system. It is now routine for offenders to be recorded while committing an offense, and these recordings can be critical to police investigation and may become evidence in cases ranging from vandalism and motoring offenses through to robbery, murder, and terrorist attacks. In such cases, a critical issue is the identity of the culprit depicted in the images. Broadly, there are two distinct processes likely to operate here:

1. Investigators who have no suspect in mind may use the surveillance image of the culprit to search databases of potential suspects. This is the

modern-day equivalent of asking a witness to search through "mugshot" books.

2. Once a suspect has been identified and charged, prosecutors need to present evidence that the offender depicted in the images is the person charged with the offense. In some court cases this becomes the central legal question; both prosecution and defense may accept most of the facts of the case, leaving only the identity of the offender in question.

One-to-Many Searches Using Surveillance Images

In the first of these scenarios, surveillance images are used as a search template in what is called a "one-to-many" search of a database. One surveillance image is compared with each of the images in the database using face recognition software. However, it is important to note that this software does not identify the suspect in a database; rather, it ranks the database in terms of apparent similarity to the search template and returns a "candidate list" of the highest ranked images to a human operator to consider. Well-designed algorithms, trained on appropriate datasets and searching in relatively small databases of good-quality images, will often, but not always, return a ranked list that contains the target in the first or second rank (Grother & Ngan, 2014).

However, this is not inevitably the case. The target may not be present in the database, in which case the highest rank return will be of a very similar-looking person who is not the target. Even if the target is present in the database, he or she may appear far down in the ranking, perhaps due to image quality issues or alterations in appearance resulting from aging or changes to facial paraphernalia, including eyeglasses and hair. The issue of image quality is especially critical when using surveillance images from CCTV to search databases. For operational reasons and to prevent tampering, CCTV cameras are normally positioned several meters off the ground on buildings and poles, leading to a difficult angle of view, and these systems are often designed to cover large areas, resulting in distorted, low-resolution images of the offender. Further data loss may occur if the images are compressed for storage, and many CCTV systems only save one or two images per second (Edmond, Biber, Kemp, & Porter, 2009).

If we add to this the fact that there may be variations in lighting leading to shadows and overexposed areas in an image, that many offenses occur at night, and that offenders often wear head coverings, such as peaked caps and other devices designed to mask the face, then it becomes apparent that surveillance images are commonly of very poor quality, showing low resolution, and partial views of offenders captured from difficult angles of view. Recent benchmarking tests of leading face recognition software shows that these face recognition algorithms are particularly error prone when comparing images captured in these conditions (Phillips, Hill, Swindle, & O'Toole, 2015).

The limitations of using face recognition software to identify suspects was underlined in the search for the perpetrators of the Boston Marathon bombing in April 2013. Police quickly located relatively good-quality surveillance images of two suspects who were nicknamed "white hat" and "black hat." These images, shown in Figure 10.4, were released to the public soon after. *The Washington Post* reported that, in the hours following the bombings, these images were used to search several databases, which, we now know, contained driver's licenses and other images of the bombers (Montgomery, Horwitz, & Fisher, 2013; Klontz & Jain, 2013). However, face recognition software failed to identify the suspects. Instead, the aunt of the two brothers pictured on CCTV recognized them and reported their identities to the FBI.

Although not without limitations, it is clear that one-to-many searches of databases using surveillance images are becoming an important feature of crime investigations. The United States and Australia now have nationwide systems that enable police officers to perform one-to-many searches of citizenship, mug shot, and driver's license databases (Garvie, Bedoya, & Frankle, 2016). Importantly, human adjudication is required to examine the possible matches returned by the computer system. Coincidently, this task is very similar to the Bruce et al. (1999) lineup task that is illustrated in Figure 10.1. Given what we know about human performance in this task,

Probe images from CCTV   Database images
                                (visa applications)

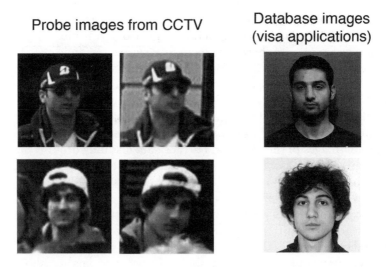

FIGURE 10.4. CCTV images of the "Boston Bombers" released by the FBI (left). We now know these images were used to search image databases containing high-quality images of the brothers (right), but that these searches failed to identify the terrorists, who were ultimately recognized by a relative.

this is a potentially dangerous situation. A recent study by White, Dunn, Schmid, and Kemp (2015) showed that passport officers who use this software in their daily work make errors on one in every two candidate lists they review, despite all images in these tests being high quality and complying with passport standards. Even more concerning is that in 40% of trials, these passport officers selected a person that was not the target as a match.

So, although these systems provide a new weapon in the fight against crime, they also have substantial potential to waste valuable police time following up false leads. More seriously, in searches of databases containing plausible suspects—for example, past offenders—this process poses a significant risk of wrongful convictions in the future. Moreover, the accuracy of face recognition software can be biased toward making errors when searching for ethnic minorities (Phillips, Jiang, Narvekar, Ayyad, & O'Toole, 2011). Combined with the fact that humans are also more likely to make errors when identifying faces from different ethnic groups from their own (see Meissner & Brigham, 2001; Megreya, White, & Burton, 2011), this raises the additional concern that face identification systems will build racial bias into the criminal justice system (Garvie et al., 2016).

Increased use of face recognition software in criminal investigation has not been accompanied by improved understanding of its operational accuracy. Operational accuracy relies on a complex interaction between computer performance, human performance, and properties of the images being searched (see Towler, Kemp, & White, 2017; White, Norell, Phillips, & O'Toole, 2017), and so it will be important for researchers in this area to adopt an interdisciplinary outlook in the future. Such an approach is necessary to provide accurate estimates of system performance and to design ways in which to improve system accuracy (Phillips et al., 2018). Psychological research can play a key role in this emerging field, both in understanding human performance in computer-assisted face identification tasks and in understanding how people perceive, understand, and interact with this technology.

Ultimately, a critical safeguard against false convictions stemming from facial image evidence will be the legal processes that occur at trial. Prosecutors will be required to convince the triers of fact—judges and jurors—beyond a reasonable doubt that the defendant is the person shown in the surveillance images. But how accurately will the courts be able to make this one-to-one matching decision?

One-to-One Matching of Surveillance Images

The way in which courts make use of surveillance images has changed over time and varies between jurisdictions (Edmond et al., 2009, Edmond et al., 2010). Some courts leave it to the jurors to determine whether the defendant is the person depicted, whereas other courts have allowed forensic image analysts to give expert evidence to help them interpret the images.

We now consider the evidence regarding the ability of these two groups to make these identification decisions.

Can Jurors Identify Defendants from Surveillance Images?

The clear conclusion from studies of unfamiliar face matching conducted over the past two decades, which we summarized earlier in the chapter, is that this is a difficult and error-prone task. This difficulty is confounded by the fact that people tend to overestimate their ability to determine whether two images are of the same person (e.g., Burton et al., 1999; Ritchie et al., 2015). In the forensic setting, this makes it likely that jurors will make false-positive errors, incorrectly concluding that a surveillance image is of the defendant, and their judgment may be further influenced by the suggestive context of the courtroom and the fact that no alternative suspects are offered. In almost all cases, jurors have to make a one-to-one matching decision without having seen any alternative candidates.

A few studies have sought to model the situation faced by jurors in such cases. Across three experiments, Davis and Valentine (2009) tested participants' ability to determine whether the culprit seen in a video clip was the defendant who stood in front of them. Experiment 1 employed eight different defendants and video clips showing the culprit both in full face and profile, while occupying at least half of the frame. Even given these unrealistically good video images, performance was far from perfect. Participants incorrectly identified the defendant in 17% of cases in which the video showed someone else (i.e., they made a false-positive error akin to convicting an innocent defendant), and in 22% of cases they failed to identify a "guilty" defendant who appeared in the video. Importantly, accuracy varied across defendants. For example, one defendant was always identified when present in the video (100% hit rate) but was also likely to be falsely identified when innocent (44% false-positive rate). In contrast, another defendant escaped conviction on 36% of occasions and was falsely convicted on just 5% of trials.

Thus, not only are the error rates high overall, but they also vary greatly—probably due in part to the degree of resemblance between the defendant and the individual acting as the similar-looking culprit. Experiment 3 in this series was designed to investigate whether the identification errors seen in Experiment 1 were also the result of limitations in the quality of the surveillance video. In this study, the surveillance footage was replaced with high-quality videos showing the culprit's face in frontal and profile views. Over a quarter (26%) of participants failed to convict a guilty defendant who stood in front of them as they watched a video recorded just a week earlier. Even when the video was only 1 hour old, participants failed to identity the guilty defendant from the video in 17% of cases. More worrying still, participants wrongly identified an innocent defendant in over 40% of cases.

Overall, this evidence suggests that judges and jurors are likely to be prone to making errors, including false-identification errors, when asked to determine whether the defendant is the person seen in a surveillance image. In courts that rely on expert witnesses to help interpret these images, do these experts fare any better?

Can "Experts" Identify Defendants from Surveillance Images?

Courts in several jurisdictions have grappled with the issue of how to deal with identification evidence from surveillance images (Edmond et al., 2009). For example, in Australia, prosecutors initially attempted to use evidence from police officers who claimed to be able to identify the defendant in the images tendered as evidence. This approach was rejected by the courts on the basis that the police officers had no training or expertise that would allow them to make more accurate identification decisions than the jury. In response to these rulings, prosecutors sought out expert witnesses who could analyze the surveillance images, leading to a series of cases in which identification evidence was presented and supported by expert evidence from forensic image analysts or, as the press sometimes termed these individuals, "facial mappers" (Edmond et al., 2009). A similar process has occurred in other countries, leading to the emergence of groups of individuals claiming this specialist identification expertise.

Cases have come to light in which expert evidence has proven to be wrong. The first of these cases involves expert evidence provided in a murder case in the United Kingdom, as reported by barrister Campbell-Tiech (2005). In this case police asked four different facial mapping analysts to compare photographs of the suspect with surveillance images, and all four agreed that there was some support for a match. Sometime later, the investigators decided that they had arrested the wrong person and named a new suspect, whose image was sent to these same four analysts. Of the four, the first two now reached "inconclusive" findings, the third said there was support for the conclusion that the surveillance images did not depict the new suspect, and the fourth concluded that there was "powerful support" for the conclusion that they were the same person. Presumably troubled by the third expert's conclusions, the police asked this person to reconsider the evidence, making it apparent that they believed the new suspect was the person shown on the CCTV. This expert now reported that he could not exclude the possibility that it was the same person. Thus this one piece of surveillance video had been linked to two different suspects with widely varying levels of identification confidence.

The second case of a known ID error is even more bizarre. In 2009 the Australian newspaper *The Sunday Telegraph* published 30-year-old pictures of a seminaked woman who they wrongly claimed was politician Pauline Hanson. Ms. Hanson denied the images were of her, and a few days later, after other facts emerged, the newspaper apologized and retracted the story (Breen, 2009). However, shortly before this retraction, several forensic image analysts were asked their opinion of the images, including two individuals who at the time were regularly giving facial mapping evidence in Australian courts–Professor Maciej Henneberg and Dr. Meiya Sutisno. Whereas Dr. Sutisno concluded that the images were probably not of Ms. Hanson, Professor Henneberg was reported as saying that the photographs were "99.2 percent sure" to be of Ms. Hanson after apparently calculating that there was a 0.8% chance that two people would share such similar features (Leys, 2009). Thus two experienced experts who regularly testify in criminal matters gave diametrically different opinions when asked to compare the high-quality photos to images of Ms. Hanson.

In both these cases, an individual who claims expertise in forensic image analysis and whose evidence has been accepted in court has been shown to have made an identification error. In the Hanson case, this error occurred even though the images under consideration were high quality (we do not have permission to reproduce the images here, but inquisitive readers can easily find them on the Web if so inclined). Of course, errors made by this small sample of "experts" may not be reflective of accuracy in this profession more broadly, and methods used by forensic facial examiners vary from one examiner to the next. Nevertheless, some key approaches used by experts in court have been shown to be unreliable, such as the practice of identification by measuring distances between facial features, known as "facial mapping" (e.g., Kleinberg, Vanezis, & Burton, 2007), and the use of certain digital tools (Strathie, McNeill, & White, 2012; Strathie & McNeill, 2016). This has resulted, in recent years, in the creation of international standards for facial comparison practitioners (Facial Identification Scientific Working Group, 2012).

More recently, psychologists and forensic scientists have begun to conduct systematic tests of expert accuracy in facial image comparison. Initial results from these studies show that experienced facial comparison experts do outperform novices. For example, Norell et al. (2015) compared the performance of a group of 17 forensic facial analysis experts with that of untrained students. Participants compared a high-quality reference photograph captured some months or years earlier to a "questioned image" and indicated their response and confidence, using a 9-point scale similar to that used by many practitioners. The questioned image was of either high, medium, or low quality and was designed to approximate a surveillance image. Overall, the expert made slightly more correct decisions (76% vs. about 72%) and fewer errors (3% vs. about 21%) than the novices. The experts were more likely to make use of the inconclusive midpoint of the scale, and this was especially true when examining lower-quality images. However, it is important to note that the experts made several errors and were only error free when examining the highest quality images showing the same person. When the images were of different people, even the high-quality photographs resulted in some erroneous positive identification decisions by the experts. Given that many of these experts "apply their knowledge in casework for legal authorities," these errors must cause some concern.

Further evidence that expert groups can outperform novices comes from a study that tested the performance of a group of forensic facial examiners attending an international facial biometrics meeting organized by the FBI (White, Phillips, Hahn, Hill, & O'Toole, 2015). This group was compared with university students and a control group who were not facial examiners and who attended the meeting in another professional capacity—for example, because they administered biometric systems or performed managerial roles. All three groups were tested on the same battery of tests of facial perception, including the GFMT (see Figure 10.3) and two other challenging tests designed for this study. Across all tests, the examiners outperformed the control group, who outperformed the student group.

In one of the new tests designed for this study, examiners outperformed both other groups, particularly when given longer to make their decisions (30 seconds vs. 2 seconds). This is clear evidence for superior face matching in an "expert" group, but again it should be noted that experts did make errors. However, this study may not provide an accurate estimate of operational accuracy in forensic facial examiners. First, the methods used in this study did not permit experts unlimited time to reach their decisions. Second, experts were not provided access to digital tools or procedural documents that would usually support their decision making. A more recent study by Phillips and colleagues (2018) addressed these limitations, by allowing forensic examiners to use their normal procedures and providing them with 3 months to complete 20 image comparison decisions. In these conditions, the average accuracy of facial forensic examiners was over 20 percentage points better than a group of untrained students. Nevertheless, while examiners performed very well on average, there was a striking amount of variation in performance across individual examiners. Some examiners performed the task perfectly, achieving 100% correct, while some examiners had an error rate of 40%.

It is also important to note that the images used in these tests were of relatively good quality and were not reflective of surveillance imagery that would typically be analyzed in casework (e.g., all faces were looking straight at the camera, which is very rare in CCTV images). It remains to be seen how professional examiners perform under these conditions. Overall, the current experimental evidence suggests that some groups of forensic image analysts are more accurate than the general population (for a detailed review, see White et al., 2017). However, even with good-quality images that are not representative of typical casework, these experts make identification errors, including false-positive identification errors that could potentially lead to the imprisonment of innocent suspects.

Does Practice Make Perfect?

Why do these expert groups outperform novices? This is a critical question from a legal perspective, because judges, lawyers, and jurors must decide whether claims to expertise by facial comparison analysts are founded on legitimate grounds (see Marion, Kaplan, & Cutler, Chapter 13, this volume).

For example, many experts claim that their expertise rests on their professional experience in this area. One might reasonably expect that the superior abilities of facial forensic examiners is the result of many years of practice at matching unfamiliar faces. Although plausible, current evidence suggests this is not the case. White, Kemp, et al. (2014) examined the performance of a group of passport officers with up to 20 years of experience who, as part of their daily work to validate passport applications, were required to make photo-to-photo and photo-to-person comparisons. In the first test, they were required to decide whether a photograph presented on a computer screen matched the person standing in front of them. The passport officers falsely accepted 14% of the fraudulent applications presented and falsely rejected 6% of valid photographs. In a second test, passport officers completed a photo-to-photo comparison test in which they were required to match recent photographs to images captured 2 years earlier. Participants made errors on about 30% of match trials and about 11% of mismatch trials. Critically, the passport officers were no more accurate than the inexperienced students, and the same result emerged when the two groups were compared on a standardized test of face matching, the GFMT.

Perhaps the most compelling finding was that, across all three tests, there was no association between length of employment experience and accuracy: Some new employees achieved around 95% accuracy on the GFMT, whereas others with 20 years of experience performed little better than chance (see Figure 10.5). This same pattern has been observed in a more recent test of German border control officers. Indeed, Wirth and Carbon (2017) report that performance was actually *worse* in individuals with longer service. Moreover, across both studies, the vast majority of errors were made when falsely accepting two nonmatching photographs as showing the same person—precisely the type of error that security professionals should be aiming to avoid! Apparently, then, performing unfamiliar face tasks repeatedly in daily work is not sufficient to improve performance. This finding has important implications for both recruitment of staff that are required to identify faces and also when assessing expertise in court.

Can Face Identification Be Trained?

If experience alone cannot account for the superior performance of some expert groups, then perhaps the answer lies with the training these individuals have received. Many police and government bodies around the world

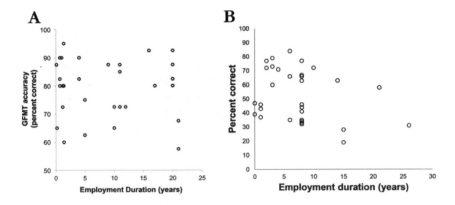

FIGURE 10.5. Relationship between length of service as a passport officer and performance on face-matching tasks (A: White, Kemp, Jenkins, Matheson, & Burton, 2014; B: White, Phillips, Hahn, Hill, & O'Toole, 2015).

have developed training programs for individuals who perform unfamiliar face-matching tasks in their daily work. In a study employing low-quality video clips that are typical of CCTV footage, Lee, Wilkinson, Memon, and Houston (2009) investigated whether individuals with training in forensic facial identification made accurate identification decisions. A small group of 15 graduates with MSc degrees in human identification with varying amounts of experience were compared with a group of untrained participants. However, graduates and untrained groups had similar error rates, making correct identification decisions in only about 67% of cases, and false-positive errors in about 22% of cases. Thus, in around a quarter of cases, these experts wrongly identified the defendant as the person in the surveillance images. Furthermore, experience had little impact; graduates with 3 or more years of professional experience in the field were no more accurate than those with up to 1 year of experience.

More recently, Towler (2017) undertook an analysis of professional facial comparison training programs and identified a number of common components, including training in facial anatomy and forensic photography. To test the impact of training in these domains, the researchers asked students to complete a standardized test of face-matching performance before and after they undertook relevant university-level courses and found no evidence of any improvement following training. This result is consistent with other before-and-after evaluations of workplace training in face identification (Woodhead, Baddeley, & Simmonds, 1979). In addition, laboratory studies show that certain strategies that are taught in these training courses are ineffective (Towler, White, & Kemp, 2014).

However, one other component of these training programs does appear to have merit. Many training programs promote a feature-comparison technique, which encourages practitioners to compare the face feature by feature rather than in a more holistic manner. Interestingly, this approach contrasts with the evidence from studies of familiar face recognition that accurate recognition of familiar faces is supported by holistic rather than feature-based processing (e.g., Carey, De Schonen, & Ellis, 1992).

To test whether this feature-by-feature approach enhanced unfamiliar face matching, Towler, White, and Kemp (2017) asked participants to rate the similarity of each of 11 features (e.g., ears, jawline, eyes, mouth, nose) before deciding whether the faces were of the same or different people. Two experiments showed that this approach enhanced the performance of novice participants, and a third study found that forensic facial image examiners trained to use this technique were, compared with students, more accurate overall. Interestingly, and consistent with the results of a previous study (White, Phillips, et al., 2015), facial examiners were also found to be less impaired by image inversion. Inverted faces are particularly difficult to recognize, and this is thought to reflect the fact that recognition memory for faces is driven by holistic processing (e.g., Carey et al., 1992). The smaller inversion effect shown by experts is therefore suggestive that they are relying less on holistic and more on feature-based processing of the images. This is consistent with the training they receive, and also with the proposal that unfamiliar face-matching tasks are driven by different perceptual processes than familiar face recognition (e.g., Megreya & Burton, 2006).

Super-Recognizers: People with Natural Aptitude for Face Identification

In recent years, awareness of the difficulty of unfamiliar face-matching tasks has extended outside of academia. With increased awareness of the problem, the onus has fallen on researchers to provide solutions that are robust enough to translate into tangible "real-world" gains in accuracy and that can be used to improve the reliability of face identification in security and forensic professions.

One solution that has particular potential is to select individuals who are naturally good at face matching for these roles. The data from many of the studies reviewed in this chapter show striking variation in accuracy from one individual to the next, with some performing at close to chance levels, whereas others are almost always correct. These wide ranges of accuracy have been highlighted in many studies, both in novices (Megreya & Burton, 2007) and professional populations (White, Kemp, et al., 2014; White, Phillips, et al., 2015; Wirth & Carbon, 2017; Phillips et al., 2018). Whereas some individuals perform very poorly (barely above chance), others perform extremely well—at 100% on standardized tests. Figure 10.5 in the previous section illustrates this point. Although it is clear that professional experience does not predict accuracy, it is also clear that some passport officers performed very well in these tests and others performed very poorly.

People with extraordinary ability to recognize faces have been called "super-recognizers,' based on the fact that their accuracy in face recognition tasks significantly exceeds that of typical individuals (Russell, Duchaine, & Nakayama, 2009). Mounting evidence that individual differences in face identification are stable over time (Megreya & Burton, 2007), coupled with evidence showing that these abilities are hereditary (Wilmer et al., 2010; Shakeshaft & Plomin, 2015), has led to the proposal that selecting super-recognizers for professional roles can improve the accuracy in real-world face identification processes (White, Kemp, et al., 2014; Bobak, Dowsett, & Bate, 2016; Noyes, Phillips, & O'Toole, 2017). Indeed, large organizations are currently changing their recruitment policies in light of this discovery. For example, the Australian Passport Office (White, Dunn, et al., 2015) and the Metropolitan Police in London (Robertson, Noyes, Dowsett, Jenkins, & Burton, 2016; Davis, Lander, Evans, & Jansari, 2016) have both established groups of individuals with superior accuracy in face identification tasks by using standardized tests of face identification ability developed by the scientific community.

At present, there is limited evidence regarding how these "super-recognizers" perform relative to forensic facial examiners. In the one study that has tested this, Phillips and colleagues (2018) found that a group of 57 forensic facial examiners were more accurate, on average, compared to a group of 13 super-recognizers that had been selected on the basis of their superior ability. Super-recognizers were selected for this study if they had performed 1 or more standard deviations above average performance on the GFMT. Notably, the 1 standard deviation criteria applied in this study was less stringent than the typical 2 standard deviation rule for classification as a super-recognizer in the scientific literature. Despite this, some super-recognizers performed remarkably well on the test, with 3 of 12 super-recognizers achieving perfect accuracy (7 of 59 forensic examiners achieved this score).

Given the impressive abilities of super-recognizers in the emerging literature on this topic (for a review, see Noyes et al., 2017), it is important to ask whether these individuals should be allowed to provide expert testimony in court. Currently, courts rely on proof of training and experience when accrediting forensic image analysts as expert witnesses (Edmond et al., 2009) but do not require performance data showing that these accredited witnesses have superior face identification abilities. Instead of defining expertise in terms of experience and training–which appear to have limited effect on face-matching accuracy—perhaps courts should instead demand proven accuracy on these tasks. This could be achieved, for example, by requiring face identification specialists to complete a standardized, empirically validated proficiency test in order to qualify as an expert witness. If this were to become the sole basis of claims to expertise, then super-recognizers would presumably qualify as expert witnesses.

This emerging literature has led some experts in evidence law to make the radical suggestion that groups of super-recognizers, established independently of police services, could in fact replace current face identification experts (Edmond & Wortley, 2016). This proposal requires careful consideration and will entail careful comparison of the relative merits of these types of testimony. For example, forensic facial examiners provide detailed court reports comparing individual facial features and explaining the basis for their identification judgment. This is a qualitatively different type of cognitive processing to the more holistic processing that appears to underpin super-recognizers' ability (White, Phillips, et al., 2015; c.f. Russell et al., 2009; Bobak, Bennetts, Parris, Jansari, & Bate, 2016). Importantly, the analytic methods used by forensic examiners are compatible with cross-examination because they can be verbalized. At the moment, it is not clear how super-recognizer testimony would achieve a similar level of transparency, as the basis of their superior abilities appears to rely on a more holistic and intuitive process.

GENERATING IMAGES OF SUSPECTS

In the final section of this chapter, we turn our attention to existing and developing approaches that allow investigators to construct a likeness of a person. This technology is used in cases in which investigators do not have a suspect.

Reconstructing Faces from Memory

One of the first questions that police might ask eyewitnesses is, "Can you describe the person you saw?" Simple verbal descriptions of an offender may be useful, but sometimes police will ask the witness to produce an image of the culprit. Historically, these likenesses were produced by a witness working alongside a police artist who would draw the culprit's face as the witness described it, but this has mostly been superseded by the introduction of facial composite systems.

Initially, composite systems consisted of a catalogue of drawings or photographs of possible features. For example, the Photofit system developed by Jacques Penry included multiple photographs of each facial feature. The witness would sort through the options for each feature to select the closest match to his or her memory and arrange the selected features on a face outline. Subsequently, these mechanical systems were replaced by computerized systems, but these retained the same feature-based approach. Early research on the quality of the likenesses produced was damning. Ellis, Davies, and Shepherd (1978) found that even when participants were able to study a photograph of the target while creating the composite, the resulting composite image bore little resemblance to the target. Further, a study by Christie and Ellis (1981) showed that drawings made by untrained mock witnesses were identified just as accurately as the composites they were able to produce.

This led to the development of a new generation of systems that were designed to build on psychological knowledge of face perception. As we discussed in the previous section, recognition memory for faces is known to operate by a holistic process that matches encountered faces to gestalt memory representations. As a result, the most recent composite systems have moved away from the feature-based Photofit approach. In "evolutionary" composite systems, such as EFIT-V and EvoFIT, witness descriptions are used to generate a small number of possible likenesses. The witness selects the best of these likenesses, which is then used to generate, or "breed," a new set of likenesses. These systems enable witnesses to search a large mathematically defined space of possible faces by manipulating facial appearance holistically and refining the overall face template until it approximates their memory (see Frowd, Hancock, & Carson, 2004; Hancock, 2000; Solomon, Gibson, & Maylin, 2009).

There is some evidence that these developments have resulted in systems that can produce more accurate likenesses. A meta-analysis of 23 published studies of the likenesses produced using feature-based and evolutionary systems found that evolutionary systems produced faces that were over four times more likely to be identified (Frowd et al., 2015). In a body of work spanning a decade, participants correctly named the individual pictured in the EvoFIT-generated likeness in around 50% of cases. Indeed, one study (Frowd et al., 2013), found that when combined with an enhanced interview and a number of other techniques, the EvoFIT system helped participant-witnesses produce likenesses that were correctly identified in 74% of cases. However, this study and the majority of other evaluations employed a relatively short retention interval of just 24 hours. Unsurprisingly, shorter retention intervals are associated with better quality composites (Frowd et al., 2015), and so these lab-based estimates may overestimate operational accuracy.

Is there anything we can do to further enhance the quality of the likenesses produced by witnesses? One interesting possibility is to "fuse" multiple likenesses. In some cases, a culprit may be seen by several independent witnesses, either in the commission of a single offense or multiple offenses. In these cases, the police may end up with several different likenesses. How can we best use these multiple images? Brace, Pike, Kemp, Turner, and Bennett (2006) investigated whether police should publish more than one of these images, or whether differences in appearance would confuse viewers. In their study, two groups of witnesses watched a mock crime and then worked with trained police composite operators to produce a likeness, resulting in eight likenesses of each of two culprits. These images were then shown in sets of one, four, or eight composites to participants who were familiar with the culprits. Showing more than one image was found to increase identification rates. Interestingly, if only one composite could be published, then the authors found that the one that looked, on average, most like the others in the set was the image that would give rise to the best identification rates.

An alternative, but conceptually similar, approach is to combine composites produced by different witnesses by digital morphing. Using this approach, Bruce, Ness, Hancock, Newman, and Rarity (2002) found that the resulting average was rated as a better likeness than single composites, on average, and as good as the best composite. A similar pattern of results emerged when participants used the composite to try to select the culprit's photograph from an array. Taken together, the results of these two studies suggest that it may be possible to leverage some additional value from the composites by aggregating likenesses produced by independent witnesses. These findings are also in line with studies of unfamiliar face matching showing that aggregating identification judgments made by independent viewers (White, Burton, Kemp, & Jenkins, 2013; White, Phillips, et al., 2015) and presenting multiple images of the target (White, Burton, et al., 2014) enhances matching accuracy.

Composites Without Witnesses

Perhaps in the future it may even be possible to construct facial composites without the involvement of witnesses. Facial appearance is largely determined by our DNA. We see evidence of this every time we look into the faces of members of our family; we look like our close relatives, with identical twins providing the clearest demonstration of this fact. As a result, geneticists are currently working on methods to construct a likeness of a person from a sample of his or her DNA, raising the possibility that this could be used to generate images of suspects in police investigation.

Until recently the idea of "genetic photofitting"—or, more formally "forensic DNA phenotyping"—sounded like science fiction, but it is now a rapidly advancing field of research. For some time geneticists have been able to identify genes controlling certain basic facial characteristics, such as eye and hair color (Kayser, 2015). Callaway (2009) describes how forensic scientists investigating the 2004 Madrid train bombing analyzed DNA samples recovered from a toothbrush found at an apartment used by the bombers. The DNA recovered from the toothbrush did not match any known suspects, but analysts were able to determine that the sample was likely to belong to a person originating from North Africa rather than Europe, a finding that helped investigators identify the likely terrorists.

More recently, researchers have begun to identify genes that control the structural appearance of the face. Liu et al. (2012) examined three-dimensional shape data from MRI scans and photographs of almost 10,000 people of European origin. Using these data, they selected nine facial "landmarks," including the locations of the left and right eyes and the bridge and tip of the nose. The authors were then able to identify five genes that were associated with the locations of these landmarks in a predictable way. For example, variation in gene PRDM16 was associated with changes to the nose width and length, while variants of gene TP63 were associated with changes in the distance between the eyes. This work was advanced further by a team of researchers who collected DNA and 3-D face scans of 592 individuals of European and African ancestry and identified 20 genes associated with changes in face shape (Claes et al. 2014; Claes, Hill, & Shriver, 2014). Exploring the forensic implications of this work, Claes, Hill, and Shriver (2014) used this database to generate facial composites from DNA. This work remains exploratory, and the resemblance between likenesses generated by DNA modeling and the individuals' actual appearance were not compelling. It appears that much of the variation in appearance, for this population at least, could be predicted from ancestry and sex information alone.

Nevertheless, genetics research is expanding at a rapid rate, and progress in this area is accelerating in tandem with available computing power. This may lead to "genetic photofitting" becoming a viable technology in the future, with investigators estimating appearance of a suspect based on a DNA sample found at the crime scene. This leads to some important psychological and legal questions. How will the investigators use this information? For example, will they publish these images in the hope that someone will note a similarity to someone they know, or will it be possible to use the composite as a template to search databases of images sourced from government identity documents or CCTV?

Imagine that such a search returns your face. Who will decide whether you match the genetic photofit, and how will they make this determination? Will this similarity in appearance be sufficient evidence to require you to provide a DNA sample for testing? Another intriguing possibility is that the genetic photofit may be combined with other sources of information. For example, it may be possible to fuse the DNA and eyewitness-derived likeness—either by averaging these images (Bruce et al., 2002) or perhaps by using the DNA photofit as a prompt for the eyewitness or as a starting point for the latest generation of composite systems such as EvoFIT. These suggestions will, of course, require careful empirical testing, but for now they are a further illustration of how current and future technologies change but do not eliminate human involvement in the process of identifying unfamiliar faces.

CONCLUSIONS AND FUTURE DIRECTIONS

In this chapter, we have outlined how face identification from images affects multiple stages of the legal system. This task plays an important role in protecting against identity fraud and in identifying people in day-to-day life, but the accuracy of photo identification is less reliable than one would hope or expect. This limitation of human perception causes vulnerabilities at many stages in the legal system: Is this person who he or she claims to be? Does the suspect match the culprit on CCTV? Is the person depicted on this police "Wanted" poster someone I know? These are all critical decisions in legal processes that rely on people's ability to identify faces from images. As we have seen, errors in these tasks are prevalent in both novices and experts.

The nature of human involvement in face identification systems is changing at a rapid rate. Deployment of face recognition technology, combined with increased use of digital imagery in casework, is producing qualitative changes in the operation of legal identity verification. All too often, policy plays catchup with technological change, and face recognition is no exception. Evidence suggests that these new tools in fighting crime may also pose an increased risk of false identification evidence being presented in court. In this context, it is critical that modern systems are designed in a way that balances computer and human processing to optimize the accuracy of these systems (Towler, Kemp, & White, 2017) and to ensure that they are not biased toward incriminating minority groups. Human decision making is a critical component of this new identification paradigm, and successful implementation of these systems demands a thorough understanding of human performance on these tasks.

Responsibility therefore falls on psychologists and vision scientists to develop a theoretical understanding of the mechanisms driving high levels of performance. This can help, for example, to ensure that face recognition software is adjudicated by human users who are selected on the basis of their ability to perform the task accurately. In light of evidence showing stable individual differences in novice and expert populations and genetic studies showing that this ability is largely hereditary, it appears likely that this solution can help minimize false identifications. However, current definitions that are used by courts to decide whether to admit expert testimony will need to be revised before super-recognizer testimony can be utilized effectively (Edmond & Wortley, 2016). Proper treatment of these legal issues will require a better theoretical understanding of superior face identification abilities than what we currently have.

AUTHOR NOTE

The answer to the face-matching array in Figure 10.1 is "target absent."

REFERENCES

Attwood, A. S., Penton-Voak, I. S., Burton, A. M., & Munafò, M. R. (2013). Acute anxiety impairs accuracy in identifying photographed faces. *Psychological Science, 24*, 1591–1594.

Beattie, L., Walsh, D., McLaren, J., Biello, S. M., & White, D. (2016). Perceptual impairment in face identification with poor sleep. *Royal Society Open Science, 3*, 160321.

Bertillon, A. (1889). *Instructions for taking descriptions for the identification of criminals and others by the means of anthropometric indications.* Chicago: American Bertillon Prison Bureau.

Bobak, A. K., Bennetts, R. J., Parris, B. A., Jansari, A., & Bate, S. (2016). An in-depth cognitive examination of individuals with superior face recognition skills. *Cortex, 82,* 48–62.

Bobak, A. K., Dowsett, A. J., & Bate, S. (2016). Solving the border control problem: Evidence of enhanced face matching in individuals with extraordinary face recognition skills. *PLOS ONE, 11,* e0148148.

Brace, N., Pike, G., Kemp, R., Turner, J., & Bennett, P. (2006). Does the presentation of multiple facial composites improve suspect identification? *Applied Cognitive Psychology, 20,* 213–226.

Breen, N. (2009, March 22). Pauline Hanson: We're sorry, the nude photos weren't you. *Daily Telegraph.* Retrieved from *www.dailytelegraph.com.au/news/national/pauline-were-sorry-they-werent-you/news-story/ff13b1b8d6a519d80dba03c42c7dff99.*

British Security Industry Associations. (2015). *The picture is not clear: How many CCTV surveillance cameras in the UK?* Retrieved August 8, 2017, from *www.bsia.co.uk/publications/publications-search-results/195-the-picture-is-not-clear-how-many-cctv-surveillance-cameras-in-the-uk.aspx.*

Bruce, V., Henderson, Z., Greenwood, K., Hancock, P. J. B., Burton, A. M., & Miller, P. (1999). Verification of face identities from images captured on video. *Journal of Experimental Psychology: Applied, 5,* 339–360.

Bruce, V., Ness, H., Hancock, P. J., Newman, C., & Rarity, J. (2002). Four heads are better than one: Combining face composites yields improvements in face likeness. *Journal of Applied Psychology, 87,* 894–902.

Burton, A. M., Schweinberger, S. R., Jenkins, R., & Kaufmann, J. M. (2015). Arguments against a configural processing account of familiar face recognition. *Perspectives on Psychological Science, 10,* 482–496.

Burton, A. M., White, D., & McNeill, A. (2010). The Glasgow Face Matching Test. *Behavior Research Methods, 42,* 286–291.

Burton, A. M., Wilson, S., Cowan, M., & Bruce, V. (1999). Face recognition in poor-quality video: Evidence from security surveillance. *Psychological Science, 10,* 243–248.

Callaway, E. (2009, August 18). "DNA mugshots" narrow search for Madrid bombers. *New Scientist.* Retrieved from *www.newscientist.com/article/dn17630-dna-mugshots-narrow-search-for-madrid-bombers.*

Campbell-Tiech, A. (2005). "Stockwell" revisited: The unhappy state of facial mapping. *Archbold News, 6,* 4–6.

Carey, S., De Schonen, S., & Ellis, H. D. (1992). Becoming a face expert. *Philosophical Transactions of the Royal Society B: Biological Sciences, 335,* 95–103.

Christie, D. F., & Ellis, H. D. (1981). Photofit constructions versus verbal descriptions of faces. *Journal of Applied Psychology, 66,* 358–363.

Claes, P., Hill, H., & Shriver, M. D. (2014). Toward DNA-based facial composites: Preliminary results and validation. *Forensic Science International: Genetics, 13,* 208–216.

Claes, P., Liberton, D. K., Daniels, K., Rosana, K. M., Quillen, E. E., Pearson, L. N., et al. (2014). Modeling 3D facial shape from DNA. *PLoS Genetics, 10,* e1004224.

Davis, J. P., Lander, K., Evans, R., & Jansari, A. (2016). Investigating predictors of superior face recognition ability in police super-recognisers. *Applied Cognitive Psychology, 30*, 827–840.

Davis, J. P., & Valentine, T. (2009). CCTV on trial: Matching video images with the defendant in the dock. *Applied Cognitive Psychology, 23*, 482–505.

Edmond, G., Biber, K., Kemp, R. I., & Porter, G. (2009). Law's looking glass: Expert identification evidence derived from photographic and video images. *Current Issues in Criminal Justice, 20*, 337–377.

Edmond, G., Kemp, R., Porter, G., Hamer, D., Burton, M., Biber, K., et al. (2010). Atkins v The Emperor: The "cautious" use of unreliable "expert" opinion. *International Journal of Evidence and Proof, 14*, 146–166.

Edmond, G., & Wortley, N. (2016). Interpreting image evidence: Facial mapping, police familiars and super-recognisers in England and Australia. *Journal of International and Comparative Law, 3*, 473–522.

Ellis, H. D., Davies, G. M., & Shepherd, J. W. (1978). A critical examination of the photofit system for recalling faces. *Ergonomics, 21*, 297–307.

Facial Identification Scientific Working Group. (2012). Guidelines for facial comparison methods. Retrieved August 1, 2018, from *https://fiswg.org/FISWG_GuidelinesforFacialComparisonMethods_v1.0_2012_02_02.pdf*.

Frowd, C. D., Erickson, W. B., Lampinen, J. M., Skelton, F. C., McIntyre, A. H., & Hancock, P. J. (2015). A decade of evolving composites: Regression-and meta-analysis. *Journal of Forensic Practice, 17*, 319–334.

Frowd, C. D., Hancock, P. J., & Carson, D. (2004). EvoFIT: A holistic, evolutionary facial imaging technique for creating composites. *ACM Transactions on Applied Perception, 1*, 19–39.

Frowd, C. D., Skelton, F., Hepton, G., Holden, L., Minahil, S., Pitchford, M., et al. (2013). Whole-face procedures for recovering facial images from memory. *Science and Justice, 53*, 89–97.

Fysh, M. C., & Bindemann, M. (2017). Effects of time pressure and time passage on face-matching accuracy. *Royal Society Open Science, 4*, 170249.

Garvie, C., Bedoya, A. M., & Frankle, J. (2016). The perpetual line-up: Unregulated police face recognition in America. Washington, DC: Georgetown University Law Center on Privacy and Technology. Retrieved August 1, 2017, from *www.perpetuallineup.org*.

Grother, P., & Ngan, M. (2014). *Face Recognition Vendor Test (FRVT) performance of face identification algorithms* (NIST Interagency Report No. 8009). Gaithersburg, MD: U.S. Department of Commerce, National Institute of Standards and Technology.

Hancock, P. J. (2000). Evolving faces from principal components. *Behavior Research Methods, 32*, 327–333.

Hancock, P. J., Bruce, V., & Burton, A. M. (2000). Recognition of unfamiliar faces. *Trends in Cognitive Sciences, 4*, 330–337.

Henderson, Z., Bruce, V., & Burton, A. M. (2001). Matching the faces of robbers captured on video. *Applied Cognitive Psychology, 15*, 445–464.

Jenkins, R., & Burton, A. M. (2011). Stable face representations. *Philosophical Transactions of the Royal Society of London B: Biological Sciences, 366*, 1671–1683.

Jenkins, R., White, D., van Montfort, X., & Burton A. M. (2011). Variability in photos of the same face. *Cognition, 121*, 313–323.

Kayser, M. (2015). Forensic DNA phenotyping: Predicting human appearance from crime scene material for investigative purposes. *Forensic Science International: Genetics, 18,* 33–48.

Kemp, R. I., Towell, N., & Pike, G. (1997). When seeing should not be believing: Photographs, credit cards and fraud. *Applied Cognitive Psychology, 11,* 211–222.

Kleinberg, K. F., Vanezis, P., & Burton, A. M. (2007). Failure of anthropometry as a facial identification technique using high-quality photographs. *Journal of Forensic Sciences, 52,* 779–783.

Klontz, J. C., & Jain, A. K. (2013). *A case study on unconstrained facial recognition using the Boston Marathon bombings suspects* (Technical Report MSU-CSE-13-4). East Lansing: Michigan State University.

Lee, W. J., Wilkinson, C., Memon, A., & Houston, K. (2009). Matching unfamiliar faces from poor quality closed-circuit television (CCTV) footage. *Axis: The Online Journal of CAHId, 1,* 19–28.

Leys, N. (2009, March 22). Majority of experts say photos not Pauline Hanson. *The Australian.* Retrieved from *www.theaustralian.com.au/news/latest-news/photos-arent-of-hanson-paper-says/news-story/368cdffbe30296594df7e4d0a322cefa.*

Liu, F., Van Der Lijn, F., Schurmann, C., Zhu, G., Chakravarty, M. M., Hysi, P. G., et al. (2012). A genome-wide association study identifies five loci influencing facial morphology in Europeans. *PLOS Genetics, 8,* e1002932.

Megreya, A. M., & Burton, A. M. (2006). Unfamiliar faces are not faces: Evidence from a matching task. *Memory and Cognition, 34,* 865–876.

Megreya, A. M., & Burton, A. M. (2007). Hits and false positives in face matching: A familiarity-based dissociation. *Perception and Psychophysics, 69,* 1175–1184.

Megreya, A. M., & Burton, A. (2008). Matching faces to photographs: Poor performance in eyewitness memory (without the memory). *Journal of Experimental Psychology: Applied, 14,* 364–372.

Megreya, A. M., Sandford, A., & Burton, A. M. (2013). Matching face images taken on the same day or months apart: The limitations of photo ID. *Applied Cognitive Psychology, 27,* 700–706.

Megreya, A. M., White, D., & Burton, A. M. (2011). The other-race effect does not rely on memory: Evidence from a matching task. *Quarterly Journal of Experimental Psychology, 64,* 1473–1483.

Meissner, C. A., & Brigham, J. C. (2001). Thirty years of investigating the own-race bias in memory for faces: A meta-analytic review. *Psychology Public Policy and Law 7,* 3–35.

Montgomery, D., Horwitz, S., & Fisher, M. (2013, April 20). Police, citizens and technology factor into Boston bombing probe. *The Washington Post.* Retrieved from *www.washingtonpost.com/world/national-security/inside-the-investigation-of-the-boston-marathon-bombing/2013/04/20/19d8c322-a8ff-11e2-b029-8fb7e977ef71_story.html?utm_term=.c5712a87dacc.*

Norell, K., Läthén, K. B., Bergström, P., Rice, A., Natu, V., & O'Toole, A. (2015). The effect of image quality and forensic expertise in facial image comparisons. *Journal of Forensic Sciences, 60,* 331–340.

Noyes, E., & Jenkins, R. (2016). Deliberate disguise in facial image comparison. *Journal of Vision, 16,* 924.

Noyes, E., & Jenkins, R. (2017). Camera-to-subject distance affects face configuration and perceived identity. *Cognition, 165*, 97–104.

Noyes, E., Phillips, P. J., & O'Toole, A. J. (2017). What is a super-recognizer? In M. Bindemann & A. M. Megreya (Eds.), *Face processing: Systems, disorders and cultural difference*. Hauppauge, NY: Nova Science.

Phillips, P. J., Hill, M. Q., Swindle, J. A., & O'Toole, A. J. (2015, September). *Human and algorithm performance on the PaSC face recognition challenge*. Paper presented at the IEEE Seventh International Conference on Biometrics: Theory, Applications and Systems, Arlington, VA.

Phillips, P. J., Jiang, F., Narvekar, A., Ayyad, J., & O'Toole, A. J. (2011). Another-race effect for face recognition algorithms. *ACM Transactions on Applied Perception, 8*, 14.

Phillips, P. J., Yates, A. N., Hu, Y., Hahn, C. A., Noyes, E., Jackson, K., et al. (2018). Face recognition accuracy in forensic examiners, super-recognisers and algorithms. *Proceedings of the National Academy of Sciences of the USA, 115*(24), 6171–6177.

Ritchie, K. L., Smith, F. G., Jenkins, R., Bindemann, M., White, D., & Burton, A. M. (2015). Viewers base estimates of face matching accuracy on their own familiarity: Explaining the photo-ID paradox. *Cognition, 141*, 161–169.

Robertson, D. J., Noyes, E., Dowsett, A. J., Jenkins, R., & Burton, A. M. (2016). Face recognition by Metropolitan Police super-recognisers. *PLOS ONE, 11*, e0150036.

Russell, R., Duchaine, B., & Nakayama, K. (2009). Super-recognizers: People with extraordinary face recognition ability. *Psychonomic Bulletin and Review, 16*, 252–257.

Shakeshaft, N. G., & Plomin, R. (2015). Genetic specificity of face recognition. *Proceedings of the National Academy of Sciences of the USA, 112*, 12887–12892.

Solomon, C., Gibson, S., & Maylin, M. (2009). A new computational methodology for the construction of forensic, facial composites. In Z. J. M. H. Geradts, K. Y. Franke, & C. N. Veenman (Eds.), *Computational forensics* (pp. 67–77). Berlin: Springer.

Spiteri, V. R., Porter, G., & Kemp, R. (2015). Variation of craniofacial representation in passport photographs. *Journal of Criminological Research, Policy and Practice, 1*, 239–250.

Strathie, A., & McNeill, A. (2016). Facial wipes don't wash: Facial image comparison by video superimposition reduces the accuracy of face matching decisions. *Applied Cognitive Psychology, 30*, 504–513.

Strathie, A., McNeill, A., & White, D. (2012). In the dock: Chimeric image composites reduce identification accuracy. *Applied Cognitive Psychology, 26*, 140–148.

Towler, A. (2017). *Match me if you can: Evaluating professional training for facial image comparison*. Unpublished doctoral thesis, University of New South Wales, Sydney, Australia.

Towler, A., Kemp, R. I., & White, D. (2017). Unfamiliar face matching systems in applied settings. In M. Bindemann & A. M. Megreya (Eds.), *Face processing: Systems, disorders and cultural difference*. Hauppauge, NY: Nova Science.

Towler, A., White, D., & Kemp, R. I. (2014). Evaluating training methods for facial image comparison: The face shape strategy does not work. *Perception, 43*, 214–218.

Towler, A., White, D., & Kemp, R. I. (2017). Evaluating the feature comparison strategy for forensic face identification. *Journal of Experimental Psychology: Applied, 23*, 47–58.

White, D., Burton, A. M., Jenkins, R., & Kemp, R. I. (2014). Redesigning photo-ID to improve unfamiliar face matching. *Journal of Experimental Psychology: Applied, 20*, 166–173.

White, D., Burton, A. M., Kemp, R. I., & Jenkins, R. (2013). Crowd effects in unfamiliar face matching. *Applied Cognitive Psychology, 27*, 769–777.

White, D., Dunn, J. D., Schmid, A. C., & Kemp, R. I. (2015). Error rates in users of automatic face recognition software. *PLOS ONE, 10*, e0139827.

White, D., Kemp, R. I., Jenkins, R., Matheson, M., & Burton, A. M. (2014). Passport officers' errors in face matching. *PLOS ONE, 9*, e103510.

White, D., Norell, K., Phillips, J. P., & O'Toole, A. J. (2017). Human factors in forensic face identification. In M. Tistarelli & C. Champod (Eds.), *Springer handbook of biometrics for forensic science* (pp. 195–218). Cham, Switzerland: Springer.

White, D., Phillips, P. J., Hahn, C. A., Hill, M., & O'Toole, A. J. (2015). Perceptual expertise in forensic facial image comparison. *Proceedings of the Royal Society of London B: Biological Sciences, 282*, 1814–1822.

Wilmer, J. B., Germine, L., Chabris, C. F., Chatterjee, G., Williams, M., Loken, E., et al. (2010). Human face recognition ability is specific and highly heritable. *Proceedings of the National Academy of Sciences of the USA, 107*, 5238–5241.

Wirth, B. E., & Carbon, C. C. (2017). An easy game for frauds?: Effects of professional experience and time pressure on passport-matching performance. *Journal of Experimental Psychology: Applied, 23*, 138.

Woodhead, M. M., Baddeley, A. D., & Simmonds, D. C. V. (1979). On training people to recognize faces. *Ergonomics, 22*, 333–343.

CHAPTER 11

Plea Bargaining

Miko M. Wilford
Annabelle Shestak
Gary L. Wells

Over 97% of U.S. federal convictions and 94% of state convictions are secured via guilty pleas and are never presented at trial (Bureau of Justice Statistics, 2015). Although we cannot discern what proportion of these guilty pleas were prompted by plea negotiations, it is broadly acknowledged that plea bargaining has become common practice in the U.S. legal system (Fisher, 2000). This trend toward plea convictions is not isolated to the United States, though the practice goes by different names in different countries (e.g., abbreviated trials, cooperation agreements, crown witness programs). The nonprofit organization Fair Trials (2016) identified 46 countries that have introduced forms of plea bargaining in the last 30 years (since 1990). A number of other countries have increased their reliance on plea bargaining. China provides the most dramatic example, with a plea rate of 33% in 2010 and 83% 3 years later. Russia's plea rate has also grown considerably, with 37% of cases disposed of via "abbreviated trials" in 2008 and 64% in 2014. Clearly, pleas are on the rise, increasing the importance of further plea research.

This chapter provides a unique analysis of plea-bargaining research. We begin with a discussion of plea bargaining's complexity and the power of the situation. We also present current plea trends, particularly in the United States, and briefly define plea components, as well as types of pleas. We then highlight the social components of plea bargaining and the dilemma plea researchers face, comparing and contrasting pleas with confessions, and reviewing current plea research, as well as related issues. We conclude by reviewing current models of plea decision making and their potential strengths and weaknesses.

Plea bargaining is a documented practice in a number of countries. This chapter, however, focuses primarily on the United States. In large part, this focus is due to most of the relevant research data originating from the United States. This trend is likely the result of several U.S. plea characteristics, including the prevalence of guilty pleas, the diversity in laws governing pleas, and the various types of plea bargains accepted across U.S. jurisdictions (Fair Trials, 2016). Although a number of countries accept just one or two forms of plea bargaining, the United States accepts all four documented types, bargains that can: (1) reduce defendants' charges (charge bargaining), (2) reduce defendants' sentences (sentence bargaining), (3) alter the facts of a case (fact bargaining), and (4) involve defendants in assisting with investigations (cooperation agreements). The United States also has the highest prevalence of guilty pleas and maintains a number of public reports in which certain plea-relevant statistics are recorded (e.g., Bureau of Justice Statistics, 2015). Finally, the heterogeneity across American states and jurisdictions provides a wide foundation for research examining a vast array of plea-related variables (Zottoli et al., 2018).

THE POWER OF THE SITUATION

Plea bargaining occurs when criminal defendants are provided the option of accepting some form of leniency (e.g., sentence discounts) in exchange for forgoing their right to a trial. Although defendants can be counseled during pleas, the decision is ultimately left up to them. Consequently, plea bargaining represents a unique and dynamic social situation involving several actors and engaging an unknown number of psychological phenomena. Psychological research has long demonstrated people's propensity to make decisions and engage in behaviors that seem completely inexplicable to outside observers. Thus, the question as to why anyone, particularly innocent individuals, would accept the terms of a plea offer is well suited to psychological research and interpretation. Psychologists have already been able to create a number of situations in which the vast majority of people will act in a certain way, regardless of individual differences. For instance, studies examining how onlookers react to emergency situations showed that the number of bystanders (a situational variable) strongly predicted the likelihood that people would intervene and how long it took them to help (Darley & Latané, 1968; Latané & Darley, 1968). Yet, only one of the 16 individual-difference variables was found to have a significant correlation with reporting speed (i.e., the larger the community in which the participant grew up, the slower the response time; Darley & Latané, 1968). Thus, regardless of the reason, most acted in a predictable way, assuming that if an emergency existed, someone else would be acting accordingly. Given the rate at which current cases are resolved by plea (95% or higher), it seems the legal system has created another situation in which most people will act in a predictable way, regardless of individual differences.

The Stanford Prison Experiment

The plea process is one of many situations that have reduced the impact of individual differences on behavioral outcomes. The Stanford Prison Experiment is perhaps the most infamous example of the power that situations can exert on individuals. Twenty-one male college students chosen because of their homogeneity ("emotionally stable, physically healthy, mature, law-abiding citizens"; Haney, Banks, & Zimbardo, 1973) were assigned the roles of 10 prisoners and 11 prison guards. The prisoners vacillated among feelings of rebelliousness, despondency, and anguish; the prison guards were at times merely aggressive and at others sadistic. Although their similarities outweighed their differences, they soon accepted the roles of opposing forces. The power of a mock prison took hold. Even the principal investigator of this study, Philip Zimbardo, admits to feeling like a prison warden as the study was being conducted (Haney et al., 1973).

The scientific implications of this work are numerous, but the ethical implications are equally numerous. Obtaining the dramatic effects that Zimbardo and his colleagues (1973) were able to document required them to subject their participant-prisoners to a number of psychologically traumatic experiences. The prisoners were stripped naked upon admission to the prison, as well as on several random occasions at the whims of the guards. They were deprived of sleep, robbed of their personal identities (which were replaced with ID numbers), and at times put into solitary confinement. They were subjected to guards randomly calling them names, forcing them to sing, compelling them to do pushups, requiring them to complete meaningless and tedious tasks, and more. The ecological validity of this study is clear, but the cost of achieving this ecological validity is equally clear. Plea researchers face a similar dilemma—how can we study the power of plea situations while also respecting the ethical rights of research participants? To facilitate further discussion of these issues in plea research, we provide a brief description of current plea trends in the United States, as well as a legal background on plea bargaining.

CURRENT PLEA TRENDS

The U.S. Supreme Court has authorized prosecutors to offer sentencing discounts (*Brady v. United States*, 1970) and charge reductions (*Bordenkircher v. Hayes*, 1978) as part of plea deals. In a few decisions, the Court has likened plea bargaining to any "give-and-take" negotiations, making allegations of prosecutorial vindictiveness nearly impossible to prove (*United States v. Goodwin*, 1982). However, legal scholars have questioned the applicability of such terms as *negotiations* or *bargaining* to the plea process, emphasizing the asymmetric power of the actors involved (McCoy, 2005; Rakoff, 2014). The Court has at least recognized plea bargaining to be crucial enough to warrant the right to advice from competent counsel when deciding to accept or reject a plea offer (*Hill v. Lockhart*, 1985; *Lafler v. Cooper*, 2012; *Missouri v. Frye*, 2012). In other words, when defendants accept an unfavorable plea or reject a favorable plea deal as a result of inaccurate legal advice, they are granted an avenue for appeal.

Although the majority of convictions have been obtained by guilty plea for many years, these pleas have not always been as dominant as they are today. For decades, the plea rate hovered around 80%, but it began its continued rise in the 1980s (Oppel, 2011). This increase in guilty pleas has also corresponded with a rise in the discovery of false guilty pleas, a rise that was not recorded until 2009 (National Registry of Exonerations, 2017). The 30-year delay could be misinterpreted as evidence contradicting the relationship between the increase in plea convictions and an increase in false guilty pleas. However, it is important to consider the difficulty in documenting convictions arising from false pleas, as well as the time it takes to exonerate someone (the Innocence Project's exonerees spent an average of 14 years in prison before they were exonerated). In fact, the systematic documentation of false convictions did not begin until the 1990s, when advances in DNA testing provided groups such as the Innocence Project with the necessary evidence to exonerate the wrongfully convicted (Wells, 2014). Yet the documentation (and reversal) of false guilty pleas poses even more challenges.

People who accept pleas limit their avenues for appeal, which inevitably leads to a reduction in exonerations (Stephens, 2013). Relatedly, if defendants accept a standard plea deal (i.e., admitting guilt in exchange for some favorable outcome), the guilty plea they entered can be used as evidence against them in appeals. Guilt admissions (including those made as part of plea deals) are strong evidence against innocence (Kassin, 2012). Further, overburdened groups like the Innocence Project often rely on standard criteria for considering cases, which can bar those that involved guilty pleas. Yet the National Registry of Exonerations (2017) continues to report record-breaking numbers of exoneration cases involving false guilty pleas. This increase might also be attributed, at least in part, to improved abilities to detect these cases, despite the obstacles in place. Nonetheless, it is clear that false guilty pleas occur and that the increase in plea convictions could correspond to an increase in false plea convictions. So what specifically could have contributed to the general increase in plea convictions around the 1980s?

In the 1970s, President Richard Nixon declared the "war on drugs," and, over the next decade, Congress passed a number of laws to increase the regulation of drugs (e.g., establishment of the Drug Enforcement Agency, expansion of the Comprehensive Drug Abuse Prevention and Control

Act), and eventually ratified the Anti-Drug Abuse Act of 1986. This Act broadened the scope of mandatory minimum penalties by applying them to drug-related crimes (U.S. Sentencing Commission, 2011). Laws such as these have vastly increased prosecutorial discretion, providing prosecutors with a substantial toolbox with which to secure plea convictions. The average duration of incarceration for drug-related convictions has also greatly increased, from an average of 48 months to 139 months for those convicted under mandatory minimums in 2010.

An increase in crime rates and the resulting federal crime-reduction strategies employed in the 1980s and 1990s can also provide insight into the increase in plea dispositions. Crime rates, particularly violent crimes, rose sharply across the United States in the 1980s (Federal Bureau of Investigation, 1995). In response, the federal government, as well as many states, expanded the presence and authority of law enforcement (e.g., "stop-and-frisk" strategies) and enacted "tough-on-crime" legislation (e.g., "three-strikes" laws) that increased custodial sentences (Greenwood et al., 1994). These changes led to an increase in criminal prosecution activity, which posed added burdens on prosecutorial and court systems. Plea bargaining reduced these burdens by allowing prosecutors to limit the number of cases they actually brought to court.

Although we cannot definitively conclude that the increase in mandatory minimum sentences and tough-on-crime laws led to the increase in pleas, several legal scholars and judges have decried the prevalence of mandatory minimum sentences, stating that they shift sentencing power from judges to prosecutors, who make charging decisions (Horwitz, 2015). Prosecutors now possess an immense amount of authority in sentencing; they also determine what plea offers are made to defendants. Although mandatory minimum sentencing for drug crimes have come under repeated scrutiny since 1995 (first by the U.S. Sentencing Commission), these policies are still supported by powerful lawmakers, as well as the current U.S. Justice Department.

PLEA-BARGAINING BACKGROUND

Plea Components

Plea bargains are usually initiated by a prosecutor, who offers a sentence or charge discount in exchange for a defendant's willingness to plead guilty and forgo his or her right to a trial. These offers can be made before defendants have been granted or had the opportunity to request counsel (e.g., at arraignment). The defendant, sometimes with guidance from legal counsel, decides whether to accept or reject the prosecution's offer. Once both the defense and prosecution agree to the terms of a plea, the agreement is presented to a judge, who must confirm that the defendant is entering the plea knowingly, intelligently, and voluntarily in a ceremony known as the plea colloquy. Defendants must also formally waive their right to a trial and all the rights that right encompasses (e.g., right to confront one's accusers). At this time, the judge must also establish a factual basis of guilt. If the defendant affirms that his or her decision to enter a plea meets these three requirements and the judge agrees to the terms, the plea is recorded on public record and the defendant is convicted (*Santobello v. New York*, 1971; *Blackledge v. Allison*, 1977).

Plea Types

Notably, accepting a plea offer does not necessarily require the defendant to plead guilty (or to accept responsibility for the crime), though defendants do so in most cases. If prosecutors (and judges) permit, defendants can accept a plea deal entering a plea of *nolo contendere* (Latin for "I do not contest"). They can also accept a plea deal while maintaining their innocence via an Alford plea, also known as the West plea in California (see *People v. West*, 1970), or the Kennedy plea in West Virginia (see *Kennedy v. Frazier*, 1987). Although these types of pleas are less common than standard guilty pleas, they are permitted in most jurisdictions (Redlich & Özdoğru, 2009). Alternatively, it is also possible that defendants enter a plea of guilty with no sentencing-related promises (i.e., no plea offer) in the hope that the judge will exercise leniency because they are accepting responsibility and showing remorse or because they are not seeking any sentence reductions.

EXISTING PLEA RESEARCH

Who Pleads Guilty?

Recent studies have sought to identify the demographic and individual characteristics that distinguish defendants who are more likely to enter pleas from those who are more likely to proceed to trial. Specifically, defendants who enter guilty pleas can differ in race, culture, language, age, cognitive and mental status, criminal history, and so on, though only two of these areas, race and age, have received a notable level of research attention.

Research has indicated that race and age can have direct effects on the likelihood of plea acceptance and the relative value of the plea offer. Further, race and age can also moderate plea outcomes due to their interaction with other variables that have their own effects on pleas. For instance, both defense attorneys and prosecutors can have a direct influence on defendants' decisions to plead guilty, and the advice or offers they provide can be influenced by these characteristics (Edkins, 2011). Other case characteristics, such as whether the defendant is in pretrial detention (through denied or unattainably high bail), could also influence the decision to plead and differ by the race or age of the defendant.

Race

Several studies have concluded that black defendants were less likely to resolve criminal charges by plea (Frenzel & Ball, 2008; Kellough & Wortley, 2002). In New York, black defendants were less likely to receive plea offers with reduced charges, and both black and Latino defendants were more likely to receive offers that included a prison sentence than their white defendant counterparts (Kutateladze, Andiloro, & Johnson, 2016). Although some of these differences were related to other case differences (e.g., initial charge severity, prior convictions), black defendants were still more likely to receive offers with custodial sentences, even after controlling for these other factors. An earlier analysis in Virginia also found that minority defendants were less likely to confess or to accept a plea offer (possibly due to more mistrust of the justice system; Albonetti, 1990). Yet Redlich, Summers, and Hoover (2010) found that minority defendants (among a sample of mentally ill self-reported confessors) were more likely to falsely plead than defendants not from minority groups. Thus, current research seems to indicate that minority defendants generally receive less attractive plea offers than their non-minority counterparts and are, consequently, less likely to accept plea offers; though one study indicates that they might be more likely to plead guilty when innocent (other studies have not recorded guilt status; Redlich, 2010a).

Many moderating effects of minority status have also been documented. For instance, minority defendants are more likely to be held in pretrial detention (Albonetti, 1990), and defendants in pretrial detention are more likely to accept plea offers (Kellough & Wortley, 2002). Minorities are also less likely to retain private defense counsel (Albonetti, 1990; Kutateladze et al., 2016), and public defenders may have less time available than private counsel to educate their clients about plea decisions (Daftary-Kapur & Zottoli, 2014), as well as the collateral consequences of these decisions (Chin, 2010). This is particularly troubling in light of the possibility that non-U.S. citizens can be deported as the result of any felony-level conviction. In fact, the U.S. Supreme Court recently reversed a District Court decision to reject a defendant's claim of ineffective assistance of counsel during plea procedures (*Jae Lee v. United States,* 2017). The Court ruled that the defendant's counsel failed to accurately inform him of a *determinative issue* (whether he would be deported postconviction) when he waived his right to trial, rendering his chance of acquittal (which was decidedly low) irrelevant to his appeal.

Defense attorneys have also been found to advise African American clients to accept less favorable plea offers than Caucasian American clients, believing that they will receive worse sentences upon conviction (Edkins, 2011). Similarly, minority defendants are more likely to have a prior arrest and/or conviction history, as well as more charges against them, which could result in less favorable plea offers (Kutateladze et al., 2016). Minorities are also more likely to face longer prison sentences, making them more likely to accept a plea (Albonetti, 1990).

Age

Age has also been implicated as a significant factor in plea outcomes, as well as false guilty pleas. Juvenile defendants are often more vulnerable to suggestion, and thus more likely to follow the advice of their counsel or to make a confession based on evidence presented to them (Redlich & Goodman, 2003; Viljoen, Klaver, & Roesch, 2005). Research has also suggested that juveniles may not fully understand the plea-bargaining process and may be overly influenced by the short-term benefits of accepting a plea offer (Daftary-Kapur & Zottoli, 2014; Redlich & Shteynberg, 2016).

Several moderating effects of defendants' age have also been recorded. For instance, a variety of adverse outcomes (e.g., pretrial detention in adult correctional facilities, the potential for a criminal conviction, the possibility of a life sentence) are dependent upon the judicial decision to transfer a juvenile defendant's case from juvenile court to adult criminal court (Redding, 2003). The court in which juvenile defendants' cases are tried could have a profound impact on subsequent plea offers, as well as their decision to plead, because of differences in juvenile and adult court attitudes toward leniency, diversion, and rehabilitation. Juvenile courts have been historically more lenient in sentencing their defendants than adult courts, and several recent Supreme Court decisions (*Miller v. Alabama*, 2012; *Roper v. Simmons*, 2005) have further limited the use of the harshest sentences (e.g., capital punishment, life in prison without the possibility of parole) for juvenile defendants. Yet research has shown that youths of minority status are far more likely to be tried as adults (Males & Macallair, 2000), which exposes them to the previously discussed biases experienced by adult minority defendants. Similarly, juvenile defendants whose cases are tried in adult criminal court are much more likely to have significant mental health problems (compared with those whose cases are tried in juvenile courts), which further affects these youths' ability to make informed plea decisions (Washburn et al., 2008). Defendants with mental health problems and/or cognitive deficits are also more likely to accept a plea agreement, even if the plea requires admitting guilt to a crime they did not commit (Redlich et al., 2010). However, younger defendants are often less likely to be placed in pretrial detention (Freiburger & Hilinski, 2010), suggesting that adults may experience additional vulnerabilities in plea bargaining due to pretrial confinement.

It is important to note that minority and juvenile defendants, as well as other underprivileged groups (e.g., defendants with mental health problems), may possess other unique biases and beliefs that affect their plea decisions (e.g., the belief that the system is unfairly biased against them, as noted by Albonetti, 1990). Recent research has started to focus on cognitive processes (e.g., cognitive biases) that influence individuals' plea decision making (Covey, 2007), but this research is still in its infancy. Differences regarding the impact that certain beliefs or cognitive biases can have on plea outcomes have yet to receive adequate research attention. Other individual characteristics (e.g., personality traits and mental states) could also influence the decision to plead, but these have not been sufficiently studied.

Why Plead Guilty?

Early research investigating why defendants pled guilty was limited primarily to surveys of convicted offenders. Because many prison inmates continue to assert their innocence and challenge their cases in appeals courts throughout their custodial sentences, this research cannot definitively distinguish between true and false guilty pleas. One of the first field analyses of reasons for pleading guilty recruited a sample of convicted defendants and identified seven primary factors: prosecutorial pressure, expediency, perceived likelihood of conviction, sentence-related concerns, indirect pressures (e.g., family suffering), remorse, and acquiescence/cooperation (Bordens & Bassett, 1985). Other field studies have echoed these reasons, finding that the strength of evidence (which is strongly related to the perceived likelihood of conviction) is a strong predictor of plea acceptance among adults (Albonetti, 1990) but not adolescents (Viljoen et al., 2005). An analysis of self-reported false guilty pleaders with mental illness also produced similar reasons, with participants citing expediency, sentencing concerns, and pressure, though others claimed to have accepted a plea to protect someone else or because their situation was futile (Redlich et al., 2010).

A number of studies have relied on vignettes to systematically manipulate factors that could influence plea decisions. Factors such as guilt status, the likelihood of conviction (or evidence strength), and plea discount (or sentence severity) consistently influence the decision to plead, though the effects of the latter two are sometimes moderated by juvenile or guilt status (Bordens, 1984; Gregory, Mowen, & Linder, 1978, Experiment 1; McAllister & Bregman, 1986; Redlich & Shteynberg, 2016). A more recent study (Helm & Reyna, 2017) also found that guilty individuals are more likely to accept pleas than innocent individuals and produced similar effects of the likelihood of conviction, conviction charge, and sentence length, though the size of these effects varied by whether participants were engaged in gist or verbatim processing. Other vignette studies have examined the impact of comparative fairness (whether the plea offer was presented as relatively better or worse than offers made for comparable crimes) on willingness to accept a plea and found mixed results (Redlich & Shteynberg, 2016; Tor, Gazal-Ayal, & Garcia, 2010).

High-stakes simulations have also been employed to examine factors that influence plea-related decisions. As with vignette studies, the impact of guilt status has been clear (Dervan & Edkins, 2013; Gregory et al., 1978, Experiment 2; Wilford & Wells, 2018; Wilford, Wells, & Shestak, 2018). The impact of the plea discount or trial penalty on plea outcomes has been more mixed in these studies (Dervan & Edkins, 2013; Wilford et al., 2018). Only one of these studies has examined the impact of probability of conviction, and its authors found that a higher probability of conviction increased plea rates among the innocent, but not the guilty (Wilford et al., 2018). In sum, research examining factors that influence the decision to plead remain somewhat limited, though it has been expanding in recent years. Future research should examine how guilt status could moderate the effect of other variables (e.g., plea discount) to inform policymakers' efforts in revising plea procedure to simultaneously minimize false guilty pleas and the burdens posed by trial procedures (e.g., through preserving true guilty pleas).

THE RESEARCHER'S DILEMMA

Given the complexity of the plea situation, researchers interested in examining the plea decision face the same practical and ethical dilemmas that have plagued social scientists for decades. Do we accept the limited applicability of research that asks participants to pretend or imagine that they are in these situations? Or do we put them in simulated, ecologically valid situations in which they believe there are stakes involved? Thus far, the bulk of plea experiments have relied on the former method, providing participants with narratives (or vignettes) and asking them to respond as if they were in these described scenarios (Bordens, 1984; McAllister & Bregman, 1986; Redlich & Shteynberg, 2016). Although these paradigms have conferred valuable information, they also miss a potentially important component of plea bargaining—that is, the power plea situations could exert on individual decision making.

Some might argue that plea bargaining is not subject to situational influences; it is an extended process in which defendants are able to negotiate desirable terms with no serious time constraints (Easterbrook, 1992). In fact, the U.S. Supreme Court has repeatedly described plea bargaining as an extended give-and-take process of negotiation flowing from parties with mutual advantage (*Bordenkircher v. Hayes*, 1978; *United States v. Goodwin*, 1982). Yet several scholars have argued that the term *plea bargaining* is a misnomer and that the power structure of pleas is inherently asymmetrical (Fisher, 2000; Rakoff, 2014). After all, the items up for negotiation are qualitatively different for prosecutors and defendants and carry dramatically different consequences for each party. Prosecutors might be trying to secure a lighter caseload or a higher conviction rate, whereas defendants are negotiating their future freedoms. Further, there have been a growing number of so-called "exploding" offers, in which defendants are provided a quick deadline for accepting the plea (e.g., 24 hours; Gross, 2015; Zottoli, Daftary-Kapur, Winters, & Hogan, 2016). Thus, the current plea environment is increasingly transforming into one that more closely resembles those that have been studied by psychologists for decades—situations with powerful authorities and innumerable external and internal pressures.

More recently, research has employed high-stakes deception studies in which participants believe they are being accused of cheating in an academic research study (Dervan & Edkins, 2013; Wilford & Wells, 2018; Wilford et al., 2018). Researchers randomly assign innocence and guilt in scenarios in which participants truly believe their actions could have serious personal costs (i.e., academic sanctions). Results from these studies differ somewhat from those of vignette studies. Most notably, on average, high-stakes studies report higher false guilty plea rates (Dervan & Edkins, 2013; Wilford & Wells, 2018; Wilford et al., 2018; see Gregory et al., 1978, Experiment 2, for an exception) than vignette studies (Redlich & Shteynberg, 2016; Tor et al., 2010). If this research is truly more ecologically valid than vignette research, it is troubling that it produces false guilty plea rates that are about double those of vignette research (approximately 50% vs. 20–25%).

Although high-stakes simulation studies address many of the limitations of vignette studies, they cannot easily capture the extended time line of plea bargains. Specifically, even defendants facing exploding offers are typically allotted a few hours to make their decisions (though see Zottoli et al., 2016). More importantly, during this time, they can be provided an opportunity to consult with defense attorneys, and defense attorneys can be the conduit through which offers are made (i.e., prosecutors must approach recognized counsel with offers). These are important factors when considering the situational influences of pleas, but even if we could create such elaborate ruses, the level of deception required would raise ethical concerns. In this scenario, participants would have to be kept in a state of uncertainty for several hours—during which time they would believe that they face serious potential academic sanctions. Is it ethical to ask a participant who has consented to contributing to a study on problem solving to instead be subjected to an intricate study of human behavior in a specific, stressful legal situation?

On the other hand, if we limit ourselves to imaginary scenarios, we will further our understanding of pleas while limiting that knowledge in an important capacity. But more high-stakes deceptions will force many research participants into increasingly complex situations for which they did not provide informed consent. Clearly, future plea researchers must get creative. In addition to furthering research relying on existing paradigms, we need to invest resources into new paradigms—those that reduce the tasks participants are asked to complete (e.g., not requiring them to imagine that they are accused of a crime, facing certain types of evidence, being offered a plea) and do not significantly raise their blood pressures.

ISSUES RELATED TO PLEA RESEARCH

Several important factors have limited the inferences that could be made from research on guilty pleas. These factors can be broadly grouped into three distinct categories: (1) issues of process transparency, whereby significant information about the plea process (e.g., rejected offers, details of negotiations) is not included in data available to researchers; (2) problems of variability, which are common due to differences in state (as well as international) laws governing sentencing and plea agreements; and (3) challenges due to the complexity of the plea-bargaining process, which includes multiple actors, procedural elements, and legal steps.

Transparency

The opacity of the plea-bargaining process is a significant limitation of research on the practice, as well as of the public's ability to assess and accept the practice as fair and legitimate (Bibas, 2006). Yet many aspects of plea decisions continue to be excluded from criminal and public case records today. Such details include plea offer specifics (e.g., time-limited conditional offers), offers made but ultimately rejected by the defendant, and attorney negotiations that did not result in an accepted offer. The dearth of details related to rejected and withdrawn plea offers is particularly important to note, as this information could have important implications for assessing defendants' decision making. For example, Valdes (2005) reported that 85% of plea offers were accepted and that a number of prosecutors made time-limited offers and withdrew offers when defense motions required that witnesses be produced. Of the accepted offers, about 10% resulted in nonprosecution (e.g., due to alternative resolution or immunity in exchange for testimony against a third party). Such deals may not be documented as plea dispositions and thus may be excluded from plea research.

Variability

Another significant barrier to plea research is rooted in the American justice system's variability of laws, practices, and procedures across states and jurisdictions, as well as between state and federal courts (Frase, 1999; Zottoli et al., 2018). For example, in Minnesota, Arizona, South Dakota, Washington, and Maine, the prosecutor must inform the court of the victim's opinion (when applicable) of any plea agreement before the judge decides whether to accept the agreement. In Michigan, two state Supreme Court cases (*People v. Killebrew* and *People v. Briggs*) have resulted in the requirement that defendants be allowed to retract their guilty pleas if the judge does not accept sentencing recommendations that were made as part of the agreement. Similar cases (and resulting decisions) have been enacted in Missouri and Massachusetts, among others. In contrast, Nebraska does not allow defendants to withdraw pleas when sentencing recommendations are not followed (see *State v. Evans*). Further, even prior to sentencing, defendants' motions to withdraw a plea are subject to judicial discretion and not subject to appeal unless the defendant can show abuse of discretion (see *State v. Carr*). Even the role of judges varies among jurisdictions, with Florida and Connecticut allowing more judicial involvement in the plea-bargaining process (including moderating plea discussions and offering feedback on plea offers) than the majority of other U.S. states (Turner, 2006).

Significant variability in the plea process even exists within jurisdictions, as plea offers are affected by each jurisdiction's sentencing guidelines (Frase, 2005; Johnson, Ulmer, & Kramer, 2008). For instance, plea bargaining was banned in Alaska (by the state's district attorney) for several decades (Marenin, 1995). Messitte (2010) outlined the significant variability in rules and procedures governing plea agreements across multiple jurisdictions. As a result, outcomes from one jurisdiction are often difficult to interpret and compare with those of another jurisdiction. In addition, prosecutors in the American justice system have a notable amount of discretion, which causes additional variability in outcomes (Ball, 2006). Further, unwritten policies may influence practice, but those are difficult to assess. For instance, district attorneys might guide assistant prosecutors in their districts to offer pleas or proceed to trial under specific circumstances (or given specific charges), but this guidance is not publicly available to researchers evaluating plea-bargaining outcomes.

Complexity

Some have argued that plea bargaining is best understood as a complex negotiation process. The process includes direct action from multiple parties: prosecutors, defendants, defense attorneys, and judges (Hessick & Saujani, 2002). At times, additional parties may be involved (e.g., investigators, attorneys prosecuting related cases, victims). Other individuals and groups (e.g., news media, defendants' families, policymakers) may not be party to the plea negotiation but may, nonetheless, have an indirect influence on the outcomes of a particular plea agreement. Even if information regarding these influences was made readily available to researchers, they would still be difficult to differentiate and separate from the specific decision-making factors that are the focus of a given research project. Further, the aforementioned issues of transparency compound issues related to the complexity of any plea decision and mask the full impact complexity has on plea research.

PLEAS VERSUS CONFESSIONS

The plea situation has been regularly compared with another legal situation, which has received much more research attention—interrogations (Redlich, 2010a). Both pleas and confessions typically require that an individual make an admission of guilt to a legal authority (e.g., attorney, judge, police officer) regarding a specific crime. Indeed, there are multiple psychological similarities between the two decisions, in regard to circumstances, influences, and outcomes. For instance, an analysis of exoneration cases showed that exonerees who had falsely confessed were four times more likely to accept a plea deal than those who had not confessed. In another analysis of a separate pool of exonerees, this general pattern was replicated (Kassin, 2012). Further, the emergent high-stakes plea-bargaining simulation studies have relied on a paradigm originally developed to study false confessions. Thus, to fully appreciate plea research, it is important to acknowledge its overlap with confession research.

Similarities

Both confessors and plea-bargaining defendants often face unfamiliar and unpleasant settings (e.g., interrogation room, jail) with unpredictable prospects and substantial stress. Many pleas and confessions are motivated by the desire to escape the present situation (e.g., end an interrogation, get out of jail through a "time-served" sentence; Redlich et al., 2010). Further complicating the circumstances, the accused may or may not have an attorney to consult and may lack a full understanding of the decision and its consequences.

Both confessions and guilty pleas are often secured by similar means. Confessions made during police interrogations can be motivated by implicit offers of leniency or covert threats of criminal prosecution and collateral consequences (Kassin et al., 2010). Similar threats are present during plea negotiations, where "exploding" offers and talk of more severe penalties at trial may make plea offers more attractive. Whereas police investigators may use overt deception (Inbau, Reid, Buckley, & Jayne, 2001), prosecutors may lie by omission (Bibas, 2004) and avoid disclosing information (ranging from omitting collateral consequences to outright violations of discovery rules, which are then difficult to demonstrate in the appeal process) that may dissuade acceptance of plea offers. In fact, an analysis from the Center for Public Integrity revealed that, of 2,012 convictions overturned by appellate courts in 2003, a majority were overturned for prosecutorial misconduct stemming from failure to provide complete discovery to the defense (Weinberg, Gordon, & Williams, 2006). Defendants whose cases are resolved through plea agreements lack the opportunities to examine the case against them, often leaving such violations undiscovered. Further, in at least 10 states (including New York), defendants can be pressured to plead guilty long before prosecutors are expected to submit key evidence (Schwartzapfel, 2017).

When suspects are factually innocent, false pleas and confessions require the accused to take responsibility for a crime he or she did not commit (Redlich, 2010b). These are often motivated by similar considerations, such as protecting the guilty party or some vulnerable other, especially when there is a strong personal relationship between the accused and another party (Willard, Guyll, Madon, & Allen, 2016). Further, research shows that false confessions and pleas often co-occur for the same crime and defendant (Kassin, 2012; Redlich, 2010a, 2010b). Despite this, false pleas have received much less research attention than false confessions. In research on false confessions, coercive and improper interrogation has often been implicated (Drizin & Leo, 2004; Davis & Leo, 2014). Coercion may also play a role in false pleas (see McCoy, 2005, for an example), but this has not been made clear through research.

Another important similarity can be seen in a phenomenon whereby factually innocent defendants overestimate the obviousness of their innocence to others and perceive it as a shield from conviction (Kassin, 2005). Illusions of transparency, along with beliefs in a just world, are believed to contribute to this phenomenon, which has been referred to as "the phenomenology of innocence." In both plea and confession decisions, the phenomenology of innocence can cause innocent defendants to make admissions that could later be used against them, believing that their innocence will ultimately be revealed. Alternatively, the same phenomenon could cause innocent people to reject even highly favorable plea agreements because the phenomenology of innocence leads them to overestimate the likelihood of vindication at trial.

Differences

Despite significant similarities, several factors distinguish confessions and guilty pleas. Specifically, pleas are inherently a more prolonged process that involves explicit disclosure of consequences and benefits (Redlich, 2010a). Even in situations in which a plea offer is time limited, a defendant typically has at least several hours to consider the offer. Consequently, some researchers have argued that even in the face of factual innocence, a guilty plea can represent a rational decision (Bibas, 2004). Although an individual may spontaneously choose to confess (without having been warned of the consequences), the same individual must continue to affirm that original decision to take responsibility in the face of multiple warnings about the consequences of doing so, in order to accept and complete the process of a guilty plea. Even after defendants agree to an offer, they must continue to reaffirm acceptance of this offer throughout the course of legal proceedings before it is finalized. Though research shows that once a commitment to a position is made, one is much less likely to break it or change one's position (Cialdini, 2001), the opportunities to do so are nonetheless available in the plea process, though not in the decision to confess. In fact, a defendant's retracted confession would still be presented at trial against him or her (unless the defendant can show the confession was coerced), requiring a judge or jury to decide whether the retraction is more credible than the original confession. The alternative, excluding a confession from the evidence to be presented at trial, requires proof that the confession was elicited by brute force, through use of threats of harm, subsequent to deprivation of basic necessities (e.g., food, sleep), or through violation of constitutional rights of the defendant (Kassin, 1997).

Similarly, unlike confessions, pleas are commonly associated with explicit promises of specific outcomes. In interrogations, confessions obtained with explicit threats or promises are inadmissible, resulting in frequent use of implied rather than explicit leniency or threat. Consequently, those who confess continue to face uncertainty (in regard to conviction, sentencing, etc.), whereas those who accept a plea, by so doing, end their uncertainty. Although pretrial detention, as well as communication from prosecutors, may have a coercive influence on some defendants, this influence is distinct from that of an aggressive interrogator who demands an immediate confession. Furthermore, though many false confessors report that they believed they could leave once they told the investigators what they wanted to hear (Drizin & Leo, 2004), those who plead guilty rarely anticipate an immediate reward or relief. In this sense, the expectations of those who plead are often more realistic than the expectations of those who confess in an interrogation room (Redlich, 2010a).

One final difference between guilty pleas and confessions relates to the decision-making processes involved in each. Considering the outcomes of interrogation (which do not include any explicit guarantees), confession is a decision in which the accused decides between one set of uncertain outcomes and another set of uncertain outcomes. Defendants may face the uncertainty of trial regardless of their decision to confess. Consequently, confession decision making is not particularly conducive to the application of rational decision-making models. In contrast, the defendant's plea-bargaining decision is a choice between the uncertainty of trial (including the possibility of conviction) and the certainty of a plea agreement, which includes predictable, and possibly favorable, sentencing outcomes (as compared with sentencing upon conviction at trial). Hence, decision-making models (such as prospect theory) can be applied to the defendant's plea decision making. This is not to say that these decision-making models will ultimately prove to be a good fit to the plea decision process, but these models provide good starting points.

THE PLEA DECISION

The dominant model of plea decision making was inspired by expected utility theory, a theory that assumes that people choose between risky or uncertain prospects based on a comparison of their value, in combination with the probability of outcome occurrence (Mongin, 1997). Expected utility theory assumes that decision makers are rational actors whose main goal is to maximize the expected value of their decisions.

Plea Bargaining in the Shadow of the Trial

The "shadow-of-the-trial" model is premised on the idea that defendants make plea-bargaining decisions based on their perceived likely outcomes at trial, which is driven by the strength of evidence in the case (Bushway & Redlich, 2012). The theory suggests that, in plea-bargaining situations, the defendant faces a choice between two outcomes: the certain plea outcome and the uncertain trial outcome. The value of the plea outcome is equal to the offer (e.g., 5 years in prison), because the probability of the outcome (if the plea is accepted) is certain (i.e., 100% probability). The value of the trial outcome depends on the perceived probability of conviction at trial multiplied by the punishment if convicted at trial. For instance, if the perceived probability of conviction were 50% and the punishment if convicted were 10 years in prison, then the value of going to trial is equal to 5 years in prison. Both the value of a trial and the value of a plea interact with a defendant's natural propensities toward risk taking, whereby risk-averse defendants would be more likely to avoid uncertainty and risk-prone defendants would prefer it. If defendants are offered a plea, then their choice is between two values: the value of the plea deal and the value of the expected sentence. Thus, the shadow-of-the-trial model generally predicts that a favorable plea offer will be equal to (or less than) the sentence at trial multiplied by the probability of conviction at trial. As a result, plea discounts (the difference between the sentence faced at trial and the sentence offered as part of a plea) will be greater for weaker cases and smaller for stronger cases (Landes, 1971).

At first glance, the shadow-of-the-trial model appears to offer a promising method of predicting both prosecutor and defendant behavior. However, the model has drawn significant criticism regarding its oversimplification of the plea-decision process. Specifically, Bibas (2004) questions the assumption that criminal defendants possess complete knowledge of the evidence against them, as well as the ability to produce an accurate estimate of their conviction probability. Research bolsters Bibas's (2004) critiques. Defendants' perceptions regarding conviction probability are often biased, and the opacity of the criminal discovery process (along with prosecutorial "bluffing") can make defendants' predictions even less consistent with reality. Similarly, in their attempt to test the model, Bushway and

Redlich's (2012) predicted outcomes did not match those actually achieved by defendants. Although their data seemed to fit with the shadow-of-the-trial model in aggregate (predicting the same proportion of convictions at trial as observed in their data), individual-level observations included several findings in conflict with the shadow-of-the-trial model. Specifically, there was significant variability in individuals' predicted incarceration at trial, no significant impact of evidence on the model's projected likelihood of conviction, and, after a confession, an inexplicable reduction in the projected likelihood of conviction (for those who pled guilty) was observed. Bushway and Redlich's (2012) results suggest that the shadow-of-the-trial model may, in fact, be only partially in line with real plea-bargaining offers and agreements.

Trial Penalty Model

Alternatively, some theorists suggest that defendants accept plea agreements because they believe they will receive harsher sentences for exercising their right to trial (Abrams, 2013; McCoy, 2005; Walsh, 1990). Scholars posit that the overburdened legal system rewards defendants who are perceived as remorseful and who are willing to forgo trial. The legal system is posited to consist of a unitary workgroup who share an interest in maintaining system efficiency (Redlich, Wilford, & Bushway, 2017). Thus, the system punishes defendants who use up resources at trials (McCoy, 2005). Based on this theory, defendants should receive shorter sentences as part of plea agreements (Abrams, 2013). Indeed, some research has indicated support for a trial penalty or plea discount (Walsh, 1990). However, some studies on federal plea bargaining cast doubt on this idea, reporting trial penalties (or plea discounts) that are quite modest, around 3–15% of the average plea sentence, and others report that going to trial has no significant effect on defendants' sentences (Kim, 2014). In fact, Abrams (2011, 2013) reported a negative penalty, suggesting that defendants actually benefited from proceeding to trial. Abrams (2013) posits that this discrepancy could be driven by the exclusion of cases that did not result in a conviction at trial, as well as cases without a custodial sentence (e.g., in which the defendant is only sentenced to probation), from other researchers' comparisons of outcomes. He argues that these explorations do not adequately account for the variability that is inherent in the unpredictable decision to go to trial.

Several important limitations exist in both models. Most crucially, both models presume defendants to be rational actors who engage in calculated comparisons. Yet defendants can be impulsive (due to age or other factors) and irrational (e.g., due to mental health), resulting in decision making that is incompatible with these models. Additionally, both models presume that sentence length is a deciding factor in defendants' plea decisions. However, even the U.S. Supreme Court has, in a recent decision, acknowledged that this may not be true for all defendants (*Jae Lee v.*

United States, 2017). Instead, some defendant subgroups may have other priorities (e.g., avoiding deportation, as in Jae Lee's case) related to the collateral consequences of conviction. In such circumstances, defendant decision making will be independent of expected sentence length. Both models also neglect the potential impact of guilt status on plea outcomes. Although it is fairly safe to assume that, on average, innocent defendants will face weaker cases (and lower probabilities of conviction) than guilty defendants (Easterbrook, 1992; Gazal-Ayal, 2006), it is also important to acknowledge that many innocent defendants have faced strong cases (and many have been convicted). Further, the most robust and reliable finding in plea research is that innocent participant-defendants are less likely to accept a plea than guilty participant-defendants, regardless of the probability of conviction or sentence discount (Bordens, 1984; Gregory et al., 1978; Dervan & Edkins, 2013, Tor et al., 2010).

Prospect Theory

Prospect theory was originally introduced as an alternative to expected utility theory and other normative models of decision making (Kahneman & Tversky, 1979). The model incorporated three principles that described, rather than prescribed, human decision making: reference points, loss aversion, and diminished sensitivity. Reference points refer to the impact one's current status (or perceptions of one's current status) has on the evaluation of decision outcomes—whether an outcome would be a gain or a loss. Loss aversion refers to the finding that a perceived loss is associated with a stronger negative reaction than an equivalent gain is with a positive reaction. In other words, the absolute value of a $20 loss is not equivalent to the value of a $20 gain. Diminished sensitivity refers to the finding that, as gains or losses increase, the psychological value (or impact) of a given amount of additional gain or loss decreases. For example, winning $2 million does not feel twice as good as winning $1 million. Although prospect theory has been traditionally applied to economic decisions, it could theoretically be extended toward decision making in a plea context.

Reference Points

As already discussed, plea deals typically provide defendants with an explicit assurance of *leniency* in exchange for their acceptance of conviction without trial. Some have referred to this leniency as a plea discount, whereas others have coined it a trial penalty or trial tax (Covey, 2007). The way in which defendants perceive this leniency could have important implications for their plea outcomes. If they perceive the plea offer as providing a discount (or gain), prospect theory would posit that they will be risk averse and accept; if they perceive the plea offer as providing a penalty (or loss), they will be risk seeking and likely to reject the deal. Some have speculated that guilty individuals will be more likely to perceive plea offers as providing gains, whereas innocent individuals will be more likely to perceive any punishment as undeserved loss (Tor et al., 2010; Wilford et al., 2018). Importantly, reference points do not refer to one's actual position but to perceptions of one's position. Thus, guilty people who feel they do not deserve punishment would also be generally risk seeking. Similarly, innocent people who believe they are guilty (e.g., after being subjected to coercive interrogation techniques; Kassin et al., 2010) would be expected to avoid risk. Thus, the distinction should not be between innocent and guilty people but, rather, between those who believe they are innocent and those who believe they are guilty. The debate regarding whether plea offers confer a sentencing (plea) discount or (trial) penalty should incorporate some discussion regarding defendants' perceptions of these labels and how they could affect their decision making.

Loss Aversion

Individuals who perceive any punishment as an unjust loss (because they believe they are innocent, or because they believe an aspect of the investigative process was unfair) should be particularly motivated to avoid conviction, at plea or at trial. Thus, innocent defendants should be generally more resistant to plea offers than guilty defendants. This hypothesis is in opposition to the shadow-of-the-trial model, which does not directly account for any impact of guilt status on plea outcomes; however, it is in agreement with numerous research studies, which have consistently documented an impact of guilt status on plea outcomes (Gregory et al., 1978; Dervan & Edkins, 2013; Tor et al., 2010). This difference between innocent and guilty pleas could be explained, at least in part, by differences in the reference points of innocent versus guilty individuals, which lead them to preferences that are consistent with their aversion to loss.

Diminished Sensitivity

There has been no research that directly examines the effect of diminished sensitivity in the plea context. However, there have been studies examining the effect of the plea discount on plea outcomes. Vignette research employing these manipulations has shown a fairly consistent impact of the plea discount's magnitude such that, as the magnitude of the plea discount increases, pleas increase as well (Bordens, 1984; Gregory et al., 1978, Experiment 1; McAllister & Bregman, 1986). High-stakes simulation studies have produced more mixed results (Dervan & Edkins, 2013; Wilford et al., 2018), but these studies, at most, employed three (or only two) variations of the plea discount. Clearly, a more definitive test of the effect of diminished sensitivity on plea outcomes, employing more discount variations, is needed.

CONCLUSION

Plea dispositions have become increasingly common throughout the world, and their use is continuing to grow (Fair Trials, 2016). As such, the spotlight on pleas has become increasingly bright. In January 2017, the Innocence Project (and Innocence Network) began a new campaign to expose issues with a justice system that relies heavily on guilty pleas (*guiltypleaproblem.org*). The U.S. Supreme Court has also increased its attention to pleas, accepting five cases (although two were companion cases) concerning defendants' rights during the plea-bargaining process in the last few years (*Class v. United States*, 2017; *Jae Lee v. United States*, 2017; *Lafler v. Cooper*, 2012; *Missouri v. Frye*, 2011; *Padilla v. Kentucky*, 2010). To put this number of cases in perspective, the Supreme Court has heard just one case concerning eyewitness testimony in the same length of time, and that case was the first they had heard on that subject in 34 years (Liptak, 2011). Now is the time for scientific research to increase our understanding of the plea bargaining process so that it can inform the shaping of these procedures.

Among the most important needs for future plea research is the creation of new experimental paradigms with which to study plea decision making (Redlich, Bibas, Edkins, & Madon, 2017). In a popular social psychology treatise on research methods, Aronson and Carlsmith (1968) introduced the concepts of experimental realism versus mundane realism. Studies high in experimental realism make participants feel involved in the experiment (i.e., it makes an impact on them). In contrast, mundane realism refers to how well an experiment captures elements of the real world. Although these two constructs are not mutually exclusive, current methods of plea research seem primarily restricted to either mundane realism (vignettes) or experimental realism (high-stakes deception studies). Wilson, Aronson, and Carlsmith (2010) have since introduced another type of realism, psychological realism—the extent to which an experiment activates psychological processes that are similar to those that occur in reality.

Whereas Aronson and Carlsmith (1968) emphasized the importance of experimental realism over mundane realism, in the case of plea decision research, there are still reasons to value mundane realism. Critics have often disparaged research studies for failing to mimic real-world environments and are more skeptical of research that seems (even superficially) less realistic (Wells, 2008). It is also unclear how well current research paradigms capture psychological realism, though it seems that high-stakes deception studies would be better at capturing this type of realism than vignettes studies. Unfortunately, the fact that plea researchers adopted their paradigm from confession research increases the likelihood that any psychological differences between plea and interrogation situations are masked by the similarities in how they are studied (Wilford & Wells, 2018). This may hold true, for instance, for adaptations of the cheating paradigm (see Dervan & Edkins, 2013; Wilford & Wells, 2018; Wilford et al., 2018). Further, due to the deception involved in high-stakes simulation studies, there are a number of limitations to the manipulations that can be employed without diminishing the plausibility of the situation or increasing ethical concerns. Researchers should keep these forms of realism in mind when considering the design of future paradigms in this area (Redlich et al., 2017). We need paradigms that can capture elements of the real world (to appease policymakers), engage research participants (to appease social scientists), and activate similar psychological processes (to appease psychological science).

Ultimately, an effective plea paradigm must be able to incorporate real-world components of plea bargaining (e.g., advice from a defense attorney), involve seemingly real consequences for participants (e.g., provide participants with a situation in which they feel personally invested), and present pros and cons that mimic those in the real world (e.g., risk going to trial or accept a relatively less severe punishment). Psychologists have already created a number of unique research paradigms in which participants engaged in seemingly inexplicable behaviors. The field of psychology is therefore particularly well suited to discovering a research paradigm with which pleas can be studied systematically. Although it is currently unclear what such plea research innovation would look like, one potential avenue may be to utilize new technologies in plea research. Simulation technologies could afford the opportunity to immerse participants in highly realistic situations, without exposing them to real-life stressors and their consequences.

REFERENCES

Abrams, D. S. (2011). Is pleading really a bargain? *Journal of Empirical Legal Studies, 8*, 200–221.

Abrams, D. S. (2013). Putting the trial penalty on trial. *Duquesne Law Review, 51*, 777–833.

Albonetti, C. A. (1990). Race and the probability of pleading guilty. *Journal of Quantitative Criminology, 6*, 315–334.

Aronson, E., & Carlsmith, J. M. (1968). Experimentation in social psychology. In G. Lindzey & E. Aronson (Eds.), *The handbook of social psychology* (2nd ed., Vol. 2, pp. 1–79). Reading, MA: Addison-Wesley.

Ball, J. D. (2006). Is it a prosecutor's world?: Determinants of count bargaining decisions. *Journal of Contemporary Criminal Justice, 22*, 241–260.

Bibas, S. (2004). Plea bargaining outside the shadow of trial. *Harvard Law Review, 117*, 2463–2547.

Bibas, S. (2006). Transparency and participation in criminal procedure. *New York University Law Review, 81*, 911.

Blackledge v. Allison, 431 U.S. 63 (1977).

Bordenkircher v. Hayes, 434 U.S. 357, 370 (1978).

Bordens, K. S. (1984). The effects of likelihood of conviction, threatened punishment, and assumed role on mock plea bargaining decisions. *Basic and Applied Social Psychology, 5*, 59–74.

Bordens, K. S., & Bassett, J. (1985). The plea bargaining process from the defendant's perspective: A field investigation. *Basic and Applied Social Psychology, 6,* 93–110.

Brady v. United States, 397 U.S. 742, 743–44 (1970).

Bureau of Justice Statistics. (2015). *Federal justice statistics, 2012: Statistical tables* (NCJ Report No. 248470). Washington, DC: U.S. Department of Justice. Retrieved from *www.bjs.gov/index.cfm?ty=pbdetail&iid=5217.*

Bushway, S. D., & Redlich, A. D. (2012). Is plea bargaining in the "shadow of the trial" a mirage? *Journal of Quantitative Criminology, 28,* 437–454.

Chin, G. J. (2010). Making Padilla practical: Defense counsel and collateral consequences at guilty plea. *Howard Law Journal, 54,* 675–795.

Cialdini, R. B. (2001). *Influence: Science and practice.* New York: Harper Collins.

Class v. United States, 583 U.S. (2018)

Covey, R. (2007). Reconsidering the relationship between cognitive psychology and plea bargaining. *Marquette Law Review, 91,* 213–247.

Daftary-Kapur, T., & Zottoli, T. M. (2014). A first look at the plea deal experiences of juveniles tried in adult court. *International Journal of Forensic Mental Health, 13,* 323–336.

Darley, J. M., & Latané, B. (1968). Bystander intervention in emergencies: Diffusion of responsibility. *Journal of Personality and Social Psychology, 8,* 377–383.

Davis, D., & Leo, R. A. (2014). The problem of interrogation-induced false confession: Sources of failure in prevention and detection. In S. J. Morewitz & M. Goldstein (Eds.), *Handbook of forensic sociology and psychology* (pp. 47–75). New York: Springer.

Dervan, L. E., & Edkins, V. A. (2013). The innocent defendant's dilemma: An innovative empirical study of plea bargaining's innocence problem. *Journal of Criminal Law and Criminology, 103,* 1–48.

Drizin, S. A., & Leo, R. A. (2004). The problem of false confessions in the post-DNA world. *North Carolina Law Review, 82,* 891–1008.

Easterbrook, F. H. (1992). Plea bargaining as compromise. *Yale Law Journal, 101,* 1969–1978.

Edkins, V. A. (2011). Defense attorney plea recommendations and client race: Does zealous representation apply equally to all? *Law and Human Behavior, 35,* 413–425.

Fair Trials. (2016, October). *Hard bargain: Human rights protection in global plea bargaining.* Paper presented at the Understanding Guilty Pleas Research Coordination Network meeting, Arlington, VA.

Federal Bureau of Investigation. (1995). *Crime in the United States, 1995.* Washington, DC: U.S. Department of Justice.

Fisher, G. (2000). Plea bargaining's triumph. *Yale Law Journal, 109,* 857–1086.

Frase, R. S. (1999). Sentencing guidelines in Minnesota, other states, and the federal courts: A twenty-year retrospective. *Federal Sentencing Reporter, 12,* 69–82.

Frase, R. S. (2005). State sentencing guidelines: Diversity, consensus, and unresolved policy issues. *Columbia Law Review, 105,* 1190–1232.

Freiburger, T. L., & Hilinski, C. M. (2010). The impact of race, gender, and age on the pretrial decision. *Criminal Justice Review, 35,* 318–334.

Frenzel, E. D., & Ball, J. D. (2008). Effects of individual characteristics on plea negotiations under sentencing guidelines. *Journal of Ethnicity in Criminal Justice, 5,* 59–82.

Gazal-Ayal, O. (2006). Partial ban on plea bargains. *Cardozo Law Review, 27*(5), 2295–2351.

Greenwood, P. W., Rydell, C. P., Abrahamse, A. F., Caulkins, J. P., Chiesa, J., Model, K. E., et al. (1994). *Three strikes and you're out: Estimated benefits and costs of California's new mandatory-sentencing law.* Santa Monica, CA: RAND.

Gregory, W. L., Mowen, J. C., & Linder, D. E. (1978). Social psychology and plea bargaining: Applications, methodology, and theory. *Journal of Personality and Social Psychology, 36,* 1521–1530.

Gross, S. R. (2015, July 24). The staggering number of wrongful convictions in America. *The Washington Post.* Retrieved from *www.washingtonpost.com/opinions/the-cost-of-convicting-the-innocent/2015/07/24/260fc3a2-1aae-11e5-93b7-5eddc056ad8a_story.html.*

Haney, C., Banks, C., & Zimbardo, P. G. (1973). Interpersonal dynamics in a simulated prison. *International Journal of Criminology and Penology, 1,* 69–97.

Helm, R. K., & Reyna, V. F. (2017). Logical but incompetent plea decisions: A new approach to plea bargaining grounded in cognitive theory. *Psychology, Public Policy, and Law, 23,* 367–380.

Hessick, F. A., & Saujani, R. (2002). Plea bargaining and convicting the innocent: The role of the prosecutor, the defense counsel, and the judge. *Brigham Young University Journal of Public Law, 16,* 189–242.

Hill v. Lockhart, 474 U.S. 52 (1985).

Horwitz, S. (2015, August 15). Unlikely allies. *The Washington Post.* Retrieved from *www.washingtonpost.com/sf/national/2015/08/15/clemency-the-issue-that-obama-and-the-koch-brothers-actually-agree-on.*

Inbau, F. E., Reid, J. E., Buckley, J. P., & Jayne, B. C. (2001). *Criminal interrogation and confessions* (4th ed.). Gaithersburg, MD: Aspen.

Jae Lee v. United States, 582 U.S. (2017).

Johnson, B. D., Ulmer, J. T., & Kramer, J. H. (2008). The social context of guidelines circumvention: The case of federal district courts. *Criminology, 46,* 737–783.

Kahneman, D., & Tversky, A. (1979). Prospect theory: An analysis of decision under risk. *Econometrica: Journal of the Econometric Society, 47,* 263–291.

Kassin, S. M. (1997). The psychology of confession evidence. *American Psychologist, 52,* 221–323.

Kassin, S. M. (2005). On the psychology of confessions: Does innocence put innocents at risk? *American Psychologist, 60,* 215–228.

Kassin, S. M. (2012). Why confessions trump innocence. *American Psychologist, 67,* 431–445.

Kassin, S. M., Drizin, S. A., Grisso, T., Gudjonsson, G. H., Leo, R. A., & Redlich, A. D. (2010). Police-induced confessions: Risk factors and recommendations. *Law and Human Behavior, 34,* 3–38.

Kellough, G., & Wortley, S. (2002). Remand for plea: Bail decisions and plea bargaining as commensurate decisions. *British Journal of Criminology, 42,* 186–210.

Kennedy v. Frazier, 178 W.Va. 10, 357 S.E.2d 43 (1987).

Kim, A. C. (2014). Underestimating the trial penalty: An empirical analysis of the federal trial penalty and critique of the Abrams study. *Mississippi Law Journal, 84*, 1195–1256.

Kutateladze, B. L., Andiloro, N. R., & Johnson, B. D. (2016). Opening Pandora's box: How does defendant race influence plea bargaining? *Justice Quarterly, 33*, 398–426.

Lafler v. Cooper, 132 S. Ct. 1376, 139 (2012).

Landes, W. (1971). An economic analysis of the courts. *Journal of Law and Economics, 14*, 61–107.

Latané, B., & Darley, J. M. (1968). Group inhibition of bystander intervention in emergencies. *Journal of Personality and Social Psychology, 10*, 215–221.

Liptak, A. (2011, August 22). 34 years later, Supreme Court will revisit eyewitness IDs. *The New York Times.* Retrieved from *www.nytimes.com/2011/08/23/us/23bar.html.*

Males, M., & Macallair, D. (2000). *The color of justice: An analysis of juvenile adult court transfers in California.* Washington, DC: Center on Juvenile and Criminal Justice. Retrieved from *http://files.eric.ed.gov/fulltext/ED438379.pdf.*

Marenin, O. (1995). The state of plea bargaining in Alaska. *Journal of Crime and Justice, 18*, 167–197.

McAllister, H. A., & Bregman, N. J. (1986). Plea bargaining by defendants: A decision theory approach. *Journal of Social Psychology, 126*, 105–110.

McCoy, C. (2005). Plea bargaining as coercion: The trial penalty and plea bargaining reform. *Criminal Law Quarterly, 50*, 1–41.

Messitte, P. J. (2010). Plea bargaining in various criminal justice systems. Retrieved from *www.law.ufl.edu/_pdf/academics/centers/cgr/11th_conference/Peter_Messitte_Plea_Bargaining.pdf.*

Miller v. Alabama, 567 U.S. 460 (2012).

Missouri v. Frye, 132 S. Ct. 1399, 1409 (2012).

Mongin, P. (1997). Expected utility theory. In J. Davis, W. Hands, & U. Maki (Eds.), *Handbook of economic methodology* (pp. 342–350). London: Elgar.

National Registry of Exonerations. (2017). Exonerations in the United States Map [Interactive data display]. Ann Arbor: University of Michigan Law School. Retrieved from *www.law.umich.edu/special/exoneration/Pages/Exonerations-in-the-United-States-Map.aspx.*

Oppel, R. A. (2011). Sentencing shift gives new leverage to prosecutors. *The New York Times.* Retrieved from *www.nytimes.com/2011/09/26/us/tough-sentences-help-prosecutors-push-for-plea-bargains.html?pagewanted=all&_r=2&.*

Padilla v. Kentucky, 559 S. Ct. 356 (2010).

People v. Briggs/People v. Killebrew (Decided Jointly), 416 Mich. 189 (1982).

People v. West, 3 Cal. 3d 595 (1970).

Rakoff, J. (2014, November). Why innocent people plead guilty. *New York Review of Books.* Retrieved from *www.nybooks.com/articles/archives/2014/nov/20/why-innocent-people-plead-guilty.*

Redding, R. E. (2003). The effects of adjudicating and sentencing juveniles as adults: Research and policy implications. *Youth Violence and Juvenile Justice, 1*, 128–155.

Redlich, A. D. (2010a). False confessions, false guilty pleas: Similarities and differences. In G. D. Lassiter & C. Meissner (Eds.), *Interrogations and confessions: Current research, practice, and policy* (pp. 49–66). Washington, DC: APA Books.

Redlich, A. D. (2010b). The susceptibility of juveniles to false confessions and false guilty pleas. *Rutgers Law Review, 62,* 943–957.

Redlich, A. D., Bibas, S., Edkins, V. A., & Madon, S. (2017). The psychology of defendant plea decision making. *American Psychologist, 72,* 339–352.

Redlich, A. D., & Goodman, G. S. (2003). Taking responsibility for an act not committed: The influence of age and suggestibility. *Law and Human Behavior, 27,* 141–156.

Redlich, A. D., & Özdoğru, A. A. (2009). Alford pleas in the age of innocence. *Behavioral Sciences and the Law, 27,* 467–488.

Redlich, A. D., & Shteynberg, R. V. (2016). To plead or not to plead: A comparison of juvenile and adult true and false plea decisions. *Law and Human Behavior, 40,* 611.

Redlich, A. D., Summers, A., & Hoover, S. (2010). Self-reported false confessions and false guilty pleas among offenders with mental illness. *Law and Human Behavior, 34,* 79–90.

Redlich, A. D., Wilford, M. M., & Bushway, S. (2017). Understanding guilty pleas through the lens of social science. *Psychology, Public Policy, and Law, 23*(4), 458–471.

Roper v. Simmons, 543 U.S. 551 (2005).

Santobello v. New York, 404 U.S. 257 (1971).

Schwartzapfel, B. (2017). Defendants kept in the dark about evidence, until it's too late. *The New York Times.* Retrieved from *www.nytimes.com/2017/08/07/nyregion/defendants-kept-in-the-dark-about-evidence-until-its-too-late.html.*

State v. Carr, 181 Neb. 251 (1967).

State v. Evans, 194 Neb. 559 (1975).

Stephens, R. (2013). Disparities in postconviction remedies for those who plead guilty and those convicted at trial: A survey of state statutes and recommendations for reform. *Journal of Criminal Law and Criminology, 103,* 309–342.

Tor, A., Gazal-Ayal, O., & Garcia, S. M. (2010). Fairness and the willingness to accept plea bargain offers. *Journal of Empirical Legal Studies, 7,* 97–116.

Turner, J. I. (2006). Judicial participation in plea negotiations: A comparative view. *American Journal of Comparative Law, 54,* 199–267.

United States v. Goodwin, 457 U.S. 368 (1982).

U.S. Sentencing Commission. (2011). *Mandatory minimum penalties in the federal criminal justice system.* Retrieved from *www.ussc.gov/research/congressional-reports/2011-report-congress-mandatory-minimum-penalties-federal-criminal-justice-system.*

Valdes, S. G. (2005). Frequency and success: An empirical study of criminal law defenses, federal constitutional evidentiary claims, and plea negotiations. *University of Pennsylvania Law Review, 153,* 1709–1814.

Viljoen, J. L., Klaver, J., & Roesch, R. (2005). Legal decisions of preadolescent and adolescent defendants: Predictors of confessions, pleas, communication with attorneys, and appeals. *Law and Human Behavior, 29,* 253–277.

Walsh, A. (1990). Standing trial versus copping a plea: Is there a penalty? *Journal of Contemporary Criminal Justice, 6*, 226–236.

Washburn, J. J., Teplin, L. A., Voss, L. S., Simon, C. D., Abram, K. M., & McClelland, G. M. (2008). Psychiatric disorders among detained youths: A comparison of youths processed in juvenile court and adult criminal court. *Psychiatric Services, 59*, 965–973.

Weinberg, S., Gordon, N., & Williams, B. (2006). *Harmful error: Investigating America's local prosecutors.* Washington, DC: Center for Public Integrity.

Wells, G. L. (2008). Field experiments on eyewitness identification: Towards a better understanding of pitfalls and prospects. *Law and Human Behavior, 32*, 6–10.

Wells, G. L. (2014). Eyewitness identification: Probative value, criterion shifts, and policy regarding the sequential lineup. *Current Directions in Psychological Science, 23*, 11–16.

Wilford, M. M., & Wells, G. L. (2018). Bluffed by the dealier: Distinguishing false pleas from false confessions [Special section on Guilty Pleas]. *Psychology, Public Policy, and Law, 24*(2), 158–170.

Wilford, M. M., Wells, G. L., & Shestak, A. (2018). *Plea-bargaining law: The impact of innocence, trial penalty, and conviction probability on plea outcomes.* Unpublished manuscript.

Willard, J., Guyll, M., Madon, S., & Allen, J. E. (2016). Relationship closeness and self-reported willingness to falsely take the blame. *Behavioral Sciences and the Law, 34*, 767–783.

Wilson, T. D., Aronson, E., & Carlsmith, K. (2010). The art of laboratory experimentation. In S. T. Fiske, D. T. Gilbert, & G. Lindzey (Eds.), *The handbook of social psychology* (5th ed., Vol. 1, pp. 51–81). Hoboken, NJ: Wiley.

Zottoli, T. M., Daftary-Kapur, T., Edkins, V. A., Redlich, A. D., King, C. M., Dervan, L. E., et al. (2018). State of the states: Advancing guilty plea research through a national survey of U.S. law. In M. M. Wilford (Chair), *A system of pleas.* Symposium conducted at the annual meeting of the American Psychology-Law Society, Memphis, TN.

Zottoli, T. M., Daftary-Kapur, T., Winters, G. M., & Hogan, C. (2016). Plea discounts, time pressures, and false-guilty pleas in youth and adults who pleaded guilty to felonies in New York City. *Psychology, Public Policy, and Law, 22*, 250–259.

CHAPTER 12

Competence to Stand Trial and Criminal Responsibility

Lauren E. Kois
Preeti Chauhan
Janet I. Warren

Competence to stand trial and criminal responsibility are psycholegal concepts intended to uphold respect and fairness for defendants while maintaining the dignity of the criminal justice system. Forensic mental health evaluators serve a pivotal role in this process by assessing and forming opinions regarding defendants' competency and sanity, which are then typically considered by the courts. Both constructs require a close assessment of a defendant's mental health and the use of forensic methodology as applied to legal standards that are relatively stable across jurisdictions. Therefore, we are able to present general frameworks for evaluating competence and sanity, review relevant research findings, and offer future research directions. The majority of competence and sanity commentaries and research are conducted in the United States and Canada and provide the bulk of the chapter's content. However, we also incorporate international psycholegal practices from Australia, China, East Timor, Ghana, Hong Kong, India, New Zealand, South Africa, Taiwan, and the United Kingdom.

COMPETENCE TO STAND TRIAL

The concept of adjudicative competence dates back centuries. For example, in English Common Law, Hale (1736) stated that if a defendant "before arraignment becomes absolutely mad, he ought not to be arraigned ... but remitted to prison till he recover" (p. 34). In doing so, Hale implied the court's responsibility to uphold the right to a fair trial for defendants with mental illness, thereby offering an early conceptualization of competence to stand trial. A century later, this construct was formally defined in *Rex v. Pritchard* (1836). Per the *Pritchard* ruling, when assessing defendants' "capability to take trial," the following must be examined:

> First, whether the prisoner is mute of malice or not; secondly, whether he can plead to the indictment or not; thirdly, whether he is of sufficient intellect to comprehend the course of the proceedings in the trial so as to make a proper defence (*sic*)—to know that he might challenge any of (the jury) to whom he may object—and to comprehend the details of the evidence. (*Rex v. Pritchard,* 7 Car., & P. 303 [1836])

In sum, the court opined that defendants with mental illness with impaired abilities to comprehend their legal situation and participate in their case are *incompetent* to stand trial. Trial is halted for incompetent defendants until they are able to meet *Pritchard*'s criteria.

Like many legal concepts derived from English Common Law, the spirit of competence to stand trial was adopted in the United States. Interest in competence accelerated throughout the 20th century, evidenced by landmark Supreme Court cases, scholarly debate, and research. In 1960, a U.S. trial court found Milton Dusky, a 33-year-old man diagnosed with schizophrenia, guilty of kidnapping and raping a young woman while in the company of two adolescent males. He was sentenced to 45 years in prison. Dusky appealed his conviction, claiming his severe and persistent mental health symptoms rendered him incompetent to stand trial. Specifically, Dusky proposed that schizophrenia impaired his ability to meaningfully participate in the trial process. Initially, the United States Court of Appeals for the Eight Circuit affirmed the outcome of the state court. However, the Supreme Court then issued a writ of certiorari and, based upon the review of the case, overturned the conviction. In *Dusky v. United States* (1960), the U.S Supreme Court provided the U.S. federal minimum standard of competency to stand trial: A defendant must have "sufficient present ability to consult with his lawyer with a reasonable degree of rational understanding" and "a rational as well as factual understanding of the proceedings against him" (p. 402). The issue of competency can be raised at any time during the trial process by the defense, prosecution, or judge if it is believed that a defendant's mental state has deteriorated to such a point as to undermine active participation in the adjudicatory process. Once raised, the adjudicative process must be halted until an evaluation can be conducted and a decision concerning competency is made by the court.

Within the United States and around the world, the construct of competence to stand trial is sometimes termed *capacity* or *fitness to stand trial, capacity* or *fitness to proceed,* and *capacity* or *fitness to plead.* Competence is most studied by U.S. and Canadian researchers, and the two countries' standards are so similar that any differences are unlikely to affect research findings (Zapf & Roesch, 2009). Generally, many international jurisdictions use criteria similar to *Dusky* or the United Kingdom's *Pritchard* criteria, whereas others have more ambiguous criteria. For example, in Ghana, defendants must have "sufficient capacity to understand an issue and manage a situation as determined by a court" (Mental Health Act, Act 846, 2012).

Some countries establish criteria for competence after a case enters the international stage. East Timor, a now-sovereign Southeast Asian nation, tried militants during an International Criminal Tribunal in 2002. One defendant, charged with crimes against humanity, claimed he was incompetent to stand trial given that he had schizophrenia and did not understand the court process. The East Timorese judge hearing the case had no competence standard as precedent and drew his definition from *Dusky* and *Pritchard.* A similar practice has taken place during other international war tribunals (Freckelton & Karagiannakis, 2014).

CRIMINAL RESPONSIBILITY

Dating back to the Code of Hammurabi, it has long been recognized that a crime's blameworthiness is hinged upon its underlying intention. Some ancient Greek and Roman philosophers believed that free individuals ("agents") have the ability to choose between right and wrong. Those who act wrongfully under free agency are criminally responsible and should be held accountable. Stated differently, individuals who are *not* free and cannot discern right from wrong should not be held criminally liable. The belief that punishment for *actus reus* (criminal behavior) is justified by the presence of *mens rea* (guilty mind) continued throughout English Common Law. English legal documents dating back to the 1500s report that a "madman" or a "natural fool" who does not know right from wrong cannot face criminal responsibility.

The landmark case of Daniel M'Naghten clarified standards for the insanity defense. M'Naghten, under the delusion that the Tory party conspired against him, fatally shot a Parliamentary administrator. M'Naghten's delusions were irrational and not based in reality. He claimed insanity at the trial, stating that he lacked criminal intent at the time of the offense and therefore should not be held responsible. The *Queen v. M'Naghten* (1843) court concluded that,

> to establish a defense on the ground of insanity, it must be clearly proved that, at the time of the committing of the act, the party accused was laboring under such a defect of reason, from disease of mind, as not to know the nature and quality of the act he was doing; or, if he did know it, that he did not know he was doing what was wrong.

In sum, defendants under *M'Naghten* cannot be held criminally responsible if, due to mental disease or defect, they lacked the cognitive capacity to understand their behavior or lacked the ability to distinguish right from wrong at the time of the offense. The *M'Naghten* standard remains the United Kingdom's insanity standard today. Similarly, according to the contemporary Criminal Code of Canada (R.S. 1985, c. C-46, s. 16), defendants are not criminally responsible if they meet a variation of *M'Naghten*. Many countries colonized by England, such as Ghana, use *M'Naghten* variants (Adjorlolo, Agboli, & Chan, 2016), and slightly more than half of U.S. states and its federal system have adopted *M'Naghten* or a similar cognitive capacity standard (Packer, 2009).

Some legal scholars argued that defendants' mental illness can become so debilitating that, although they *could* distinguish right from wrong, they could not resist their impulses to act. In *Parsons v. State* (1886), a mother, Nancy Parsons, murdered her husband, Bennett, with their daughter as an accomplice. The mother–daughter dyad argued that they suffered from severe mental illness and had been under the delusional impression that Bennett held "supernatural power" by inflicting his wife with a disease that she believed would ultimately kill her. The court ruled that some defendants may be so overcome by their mental illness that they lose the ability to control their behavior. *Parsons* criteria of irresistible impulse moved beyond *M'Naghten* by including the volitional capacity or the (in)ability to conform behavior to the law and was adopted by various jurisdictions. Together, the concepts of cognitive and volitional capacity provided the foundation for modern interpretations of criminal responsibility.

The criteria for insanity were expanded even further in *Durham v. United States* (1954). Monte Durham, a man with long-standing criminal and psychiatric histories, was found guilty of breaking and entering. He claimed he was insane at the time of the offense because of his past diagnoses of psychosis and personality disorder, as well as a past suicide attempt. The court found Durham guilty. However, he appealed on grounds that the insanity criteria were too restrictive. The U.S. District of Columbia Court of Appeals agreed by stating "an accused is not criminally responsible if his unlawful act was the product of mental disease or defect." Whereas some found *M'Naghten* and the "irresistible impulse" tests too narrowly defined, many viewed the *Durham* standard as too broad. Indeed, the only insanity criterion according to *Durham* was that the behavior resulted from mental disorder. Further, the standard did not discern what constituted "product" or "mental disease." Clarification was later provided by *McDonald v. United States* (1962), which determined that "a mental disease or defect includes any abnormal condition of the mind which substantially affects mental or emotional processes and substantially impairs behavior controls." Today, only New Hampshire uses the *Durham* standard.

Eight years after *Durham*, the American Law Institute (ALI) brought forth a standard composed of both cognitive and volitional criteria in its Model Penal Code (MPC; 1962):

A person is not responsible for criminal conduct if at the time of such conduct as a result of mental disease or defect he lacks substantial capacity either to appreciate the criminality (wrongfulness) of his conduct or to conform his conduct to the requirements of the law.

The ALI standard was praised for its nuanced word choice of "substantial," rather than "result of." ALI criteria were considered less stringent compared with previous legal tests and afforded flexibility in considering the cognitive or volitional domains. Notably, "mental disease or defect" was limited in some cases, such as *State v. Hall* (1974) and *State v. Hartfield* (1990), which ruled that an insanity plea primarily founded on voluntary substance intoxication did not suffice for a successful insanity defense.

Non-Western countries, such as China, also consider both the cognitive and the volitional criteria. On the other hand, Hong Kong, which is subsumed by China but is politically autonomous, has a more loosely defined criteria for insanity, more similar to *Durham*.

ASSESSMENT OF TRIAL COMPETENCE AND SANITY

Referral Processes

Research suggests that U.S. defense attorneys have concerns about clients' trial competence in approximately 15% of cases (Hoge, Bonnie, Poythress, & Monahan, 1992), and at least 60,000 competency evaluations are performed each year (see Melton et al., 2018). Defense counsel most often requests a competency evaluation on the behalf of a defendant (although the prosecution or ruling judge may do so as well), and judges usually grant such evaluations (Melton et al., 2018). Questions regarding trial competence are usually prompted by signs of intellectual disability or psychosis, such as hallucinations, delusions, or odd speech. Some attorneys question defendants' competence based solely on history of psychiatric treatment (Aubrey, 1988). In the United States, defense counsel may seek privately retained forensic mental health evaluators to test the defendant's trial competence, with private evaluations protected by privilege. Alternatively, the defense and/or prosecution may request a court-ordered evaluation. After receiving a referral, mental health professionals evaluate defendants' psycholegal abilities and subsequently proffer an opinion—whether a defendant is competent to stand trial—to the retaining attorney and/or court.

In the states that recognize legal insanity, defense counsel refer defendants for criminal responsibility evaluations when it appears that psychiatric impairment could have affected defendants' behavior at the time of the alleged offense (e.g., attorneys have reported suicidal ideation and disorganized behavior as reasons for referrals; Pasewark & Craig, 1980). These evaluations are protected by attorney–client privilege, in that the defense reviews and considers findings before release of this information to other parties. Once the defense gives notice of its intent to plead insanity, the prosecution may request further evaluation of the defendant. In most countries, defendants are referred for a sanity evaluation after they have been formally charged with an offense. In China, the referral process can precede arraignment, and police frequently refer defendants to assess criminal responsibility prior to filing charges. Hu, Yang, Huang, Liu, and Coid (2010) found that police referred individuals more frequently (92%) than did the court or other legal entities (8%) for criminal responsibility evaluations.

Similar to the competence evaluation process, forensic mental health professionals in the United States evaluate defendants and provide their opinion on sanity to the retaining attorney, who then determines with the defendant whether they will proceed with raising an insanity defense at trial. Despite their similarities in the referral process, it must be underscored that competency and sanity are two separate psycholegal constructs. Competence applies only to defendants' abilities during the adjudicative process, whereas a plea of insanity is an affirmative defense that pieces together motives and behavior at the time of the crime.

In the United States and Canada, evaluators most often conduct evaluations on an individual basis, although evaluations may also be conducted in teams. A commonality among evaluation protocols is that psychiatrists are almost always able to conduct competency and sanity assessments, and in many U.S. jurisdictions, clinical psychologists conduct them as well (Pirelli, Gottdiener, & Zapf, 2011; Warren, Murrie, Chauhan, Dietz, & Morris, 2004). In the United Kingdom and Hong Kong, the courts require at least two psychiatrists to evaluate each defendant for competency and sanity cases. According to Hu et al. (2010), in China, at least three psychiatrists must jointly undertake competency and sanity evaluations and together issue a report for the court's consideration. In South Africa, psychiatrists, not clinical psychologists, are typically appointed to conduct the evaluations for most severe, violent cases (e.g., murder). Pillay (2016) identified the underutilization of clinical psychologists in South African evaluations as a contributor to lengthy "forensic wait lists" of defendants awaiting evaluation.

Preparing and Conducting the Clinical Interview

As a first step, it is critical to specify the referral question (Packer, 2009; Zapf & Roesch, 2009). For example, evaluators should discern the general psycholegal issue (e.g., sanity) and specific psycholegal criteria (e.g., M'Naghten vs. ALI standard). Next, evaluators can systematically approach the psycholegal inquiry. Evaluators should request and, if received, review collateral records, including educational, occupational, medical, psychological, sociocultural, and criminal histories, preferably prior to the assessment. This allows the evaluator to gain a general sense of the defendant's background and to tailor the clinical interview as appropriate. Neal and Grisso (2014) found that, among their sample of forensic evaluators practicing in the United States, Canada, Australia, and New Zealand, over

90% reviewed mental health and medical records, and over 91% reviewed criminal records. Given the retrospective nature of sanity evaluations, it is important to obtain records, especially witness statements.

Per the "Specialty Guidelines for Forensic Psychology" (2013), at the evaluation's onset, evaluators must inform defendants of the evaluation's purpose and that the information provided will not be kept confidential, given the legal, rather than therapeutic, nature of the evaluator–evaluatee relationship. Further, defendants should be notified that the findings will be reported to the retaining party (e.g., defense, prosecution, or the court). In most court-ordered evaluations, defendants may refuse to participate, but evaluators may still submit an opinion informed by collateral information only.

For both competency and sanity, many jurisdictions require a mental disease or defect as the source of defendants' psycholegal impairment. For example, in the U.S. federal system, defendants are found incompetent "if there is reasonable cause to believe that the defendant may presently be suffering from a mental disease or defect rendering him mentally incompetent to the extent that he is unable to understand the nature and consequences of the proceedings against him or to assist properly in his defense" ("Determination of mental competency to stand trial to undergo postrelease proceedings," 18 U.S.C. § 4241[a]). Similarly, *M'Naghten,* ALI, and their variants all necessitate a finding of mental disease or defect. This is a common international practice, as well. Therefore, in most cases, determining whether a mental disorder exists is a top priority of the clinical interview.

With respect to trial competency, evaluators focus on defendants' present ability to meaningfully participate in their cases—that is, whether defendants have a rational and factual understanding of the charges against them and whether they can assist their defense. For example, do defendants understand the purpose of the interview? Can defendants accurately explain the allegations? Do they understand the nature of the adversarial process? Are they able to identify key players (e.g., judge, defense counsel, prosecution, and jury) and their respective roles in the courtroom? What is their relationship with their attorneys? Do they understand the evidence, the strength of the case, and potential outcomes? Can they reasonably decide among various plea-bargaining scenarios? A semistructured clinical interview can help to assess the defendant's trial competence abilities, and the evaluator can pursue questioning outside of the interview format if relevant to the psycholegal question.

Somewhat differently, sanity evaluations require a retrospective inquiry into defendants' mental state at the time of the alleged crime. Appropriate interview questions incorporate the defendants' physical, psychological, and cognitive experiences leading up to and during the instant offense, as well as their current symptomatology. Evaluators should attempt to account for discrepancies in a defendant's personal account of the crime versus how the defendant was perceived by others at that time. For example, a defendant may claim to have experienced paranoid delusions and assaulted another individual out of self-defense and may argue that this sequence of events meets *M'Naghten* criteria. Contradictory to this defendant's self-report, witnesses who were present at the time may describe the defendant as being provocative toward the victim, thereby calling into question the self-defense motive. It is the evaluator's task to reconcile inconsistent accounts of the offense. Depending on the jurisdictional standard, evaluators focus on cognitive and/or volitional prongs, in addition to assessing for a mental disorder.

Psychological Assessment

To supplement clinical interviews, evaluators may utilize psychological instruments to provide diagnostic clarification to subsequently inform their competency and sanity opinions. As with clinical interviewing, test selection should be systematic and appropriate for the referral question. According to Borum and Grisso's (1995) survey of board-certified forensic evaluators, approximately 56% of psychologists and 31% of psychiatrists reported frequently or almost always using testing during competency evaluations. Regarding sanity, 57% of psychologists and 42% of psychiatrists surveyed reported test use frequently or almost always when conducting criminal responsibility evaluations. As such, it appears evaluators as a whole place slightly greater importance on testing during sanity relative to competency evaluations, and psychologists place more emphasis on testing relative to psychiatrists.

Psychodiagnostic tools are often used to assess the defendants' clinical presentations. In Lally's (2003) survey, the majority of board-certified forensic evaluators reported that multiscale inventories, intelligence scales, and neuropsychological batteries are appropriate for use in both trial competence and criminal responsibility evaluations. In McLaughlin and Kan's (2014) survey, forensic evaluators reported using multiscale inventories in about 27% of competency evaluations, compared with 38% of sanity evaluations. Slightly more evaluators reported using cognitive and/or neuropsychological instruments in competency (26%) relative to sanity (21%) evaluations. Among their 434 international evaluators, Neal and Grisso (2014) found that evaluators reported using multiscale inventories more often during sanity (22%) relative to competency (12%) evaluations, but administered intelligence testing (specifically, the Wechsler Adult Intelligence Scale) in approximately 13% of both competency and sanity evaluations. These results, in conjunction with those of Borum and Grisso (1995), suggest that testing does not occur in all evaluations and use is variable across evaluators, both in the United States and internationally. Indeed, Melton et al. (2018) noted that an extensive psychological testing battery is not always warranted. Psychiatric disorders are routinely diagnosed without the use of time-consuming and expensive testing protocols. Overdependence on psychological testing can dilute rigorous use of the forensic method, which combines skilled interviewing with third-party contacts and a thorough review of all relevant collateral information.

Forensic Assessment Instruments

Although the aforementioned psychodiagnostic tools help to determine the presence of a mental disorder and ascertain defendants' general cognitive abilities, they do not provide information explicitly tied to the psycholegal questions at hand. To address these directly, researchers developed forensic assessment instruments (Heilbrun, Grisso, & Goldstein, 2009), some with the specific purpose of determining trial competency and sanity.

Borum and Grisso (1995) found that among evaluators who administered testing during competency evaluations, at least two-thirds had administered an instrument specific to competency. Given that trial competency is the most common psycholegal question, it is not surprising that there are a multitude of competency assessment instruments. Melton et al. (2018) refer to three types of instruments: trial competence screening instruments, nonstandardized semistructured interviews, and second-generation tools. Brief, cost-effective competency screening devices include the Georgia Court Competency Test (GCCT; Wildman et al., 1979). Some researchers have had variable success identifying a three-factor *Dusky* model with the GCCT (Rogers, Ustad, Sewell, & Reinhardt, 1996), although a revised version of the GCCT (Mississippi State Hospital Revision; GCCT-MSH) has demonstrated strong internal consistency for at least one general factor, *Legal Knowledge* (Ustad, Rogers, Sewell, & Guarnaccia, 1996). More in-depth measures, such as the Competency Assessment Instrument—Revised (CAI; Laboratory of Community Psychology, Harvard Medical School, 1973), are semistructured interviews that afford more flexibility and allow for fine-grained assessment of case-specific details during the evaluation.

Second-generation assessments target key *Dusky* components with a standardized approach. These include the MacArthur Competence Assessment Tool—Criminal Adjudication (MacCAT-CA; Otto et al., 1998) and Evaluation of Competency to Stand Trial—Revised (ECST-R; Rogers, Tillbrook, & Sewell, 2004). Researchers (Otto et al., 1998) found moderate to high interrater reliability and adequate support for the MacCAT-CA's three-factor solution (i.e., Understanding, Reasoning, Appreciation) that are analogous to *Dusky* criteria. Furthermore, Otto et al. (1998) identified good convergent validity between the MacCAT-CA and various measures of psychiatric symptomatology, and both research groups found the Mac-CAT-CA had moderate concurrent validity with forensic evaluators' competence opinions. The ECST-R has presented a good model fit for its *Dusky* three-factor solution and high interrater reliability for each *Dusky* subscale (Rogers, Jackson, Sewell, Tillbrook, & Martin, 2003). Instruments for special populations, such as juveniles and defendants suspected of intellectual disability, are available as well. These include the Juvenile Adjudicative

Competence Interview (JACI; Grisso, 2005) and Competence Assessment for Standing Trial for Defendants with Mental Retardation (CAST-MR; Everington, 1990).

Lally (2003) found that the majority of his sample recommended the MacCAT-CA when evaluating trial competency abilities and that the CAI was also deemed acceptable. In Archer, Buffington-Vollum, Stredny, and Handel's (2006) survey of forensic evaluators, the MacCAT-CA was the most widely used competency assessment instrument. Similarly, Neal and Grisso (2014), with an international sample, found that the ECST-R, Mac-CAT-CA, and JACI were among the "top 10" most frequently used forensic assessments in competency evaluations.

The aforementioned competency assessments were conceived by U.S. and Canadian researchers and developed with U.S. and Canadian samples. Relatively few forensic assessments have been validated with cross-cultural samples, a problem that is gaining increasing attention from researchers (Weiss & Rosenfeld, 2012). Akinkunmi (2002), using the *Pritchard* criteria, found that the MacCAT-CA showed promise in distinguishing incompetent from competent English and Welsh defendants, albeit with a small sample. Nonetheless, Rogers, Blackwood, Farnham, Pickup, and Watts (2009) later reported that no standardized measures are used with regularity in the United Kingdom. Although competency criteria tend to be based on *Dusky* and *Pritchard,* this pattern does not always hold internationally. Adjorlolo et al. (2016) noted that Ghananese competency criteria are vague, and it is unclear whether U.S. or Canadian competency tools would be helpful in that country's legal context.

Although Borum and Grisso (1995) found that evaluators believed that it was more important to conduct psychological testing in sanity, compared to competency, evaluations, the authors also found that many evaluators never use a forensic assessment instrument specific to sanity. This finding may reflect a lack of testing options. The Rogers Criminal Responsibility Assessment Scales (R-CRAS; Rogers, 1984) is the only standardized forensic assessment instrument specifically for assessing sanity. Rogers (1984) theorized that use of such a measure would strengthen the sanity construct, help to refine evaluators' decision-making process, and improve evaluator agreement. The R-CRAS requires a thorough record review and clinical interview that explore the defendant's biopsychosocial history, criminal history, and experience (e.g., thought process and emotional experience) at the time of the offense. R-CRAS interrater reliability has been excellent (Rogers, Seman, & Wasyliw, 1983). Although the R-CRAS was originally developed with the ALI standard in mind, it has also been validated for use with *M'Naghten* criteria and showed good discriminant validity (Rogers, Seman, & Clark, 1986). Archer et al. (2006) found that 29 (about 34%) of the 86 evaluators they surveyed reported using the R-CRAS. International samples of evaluators have not endorsed common use of the R-CRAS (Neal & Grisso, 2014).

Performance and Symptom Validity

Although evaluators may use testing, findings are not fully informative when results are invalid due to defendants' poor effort, attentional deficits, negative response style, or malingering. Although it is not a diagnosis, malingering, the "false or grossly exaggerated physical or psychological symptoms motivated by external incentives" (American Psychiatric Association, 2013, p. 726), is an important clinical consideration that warrants special attention in forensic settings. Defendants may feign psychiatric and/or psycholegal impairment in hopes of receiving dismissed or reduced charges, less severe punishment (mental illness can serve as a mitigating factor in courtroom proceedings), or transfer to a different facility (e.g., from prison to a forensic psychiatric hospital, where rules may be less stringent). Vitacco, Rogers, Gabel, and Munizza (2007) found a 21% rate of suspected malingering in their sample of competence to stand trial evaluatees.

For these reasons, it is critical for evaluators to assess defendants' performance validity, such as test effort, and symptom validity, meaning the genuineness of defendants' clinical symptom presentation. Psychometrically sound tools such as the Test of Memory Malingering (TOMM; Tombaugh, 1996), Validity Indicator Profile (VIP; Frederick, 1997), Structured Inventory of Malingered Symptomatology (SIMS; Widows & Smith, 2005), and Structured Interview of Reported Symptoms—Second Edition (SIRS-2; Rogers, Sewell, & Gillard, 2010) can be used for these purposes. Several forensic assessment instruments have internal validity scales intended for the purpose of assessing feigned psycholegal impairment. The ECST-R has a strong ability to discriminate between real and feigned incompetency (Norton & Ryba, 2010; Vitacco, Rogers, & Gabel, 2009). The Inventory of Legal Knowledge (ILK; Otto, Musick, & Sherrod, 2010) is an assessment instrument specifically designed to detect competency evaluation response style. It shares strong convergence with performance validity measures such as the TOMM and does well at classifying honest evaluatees from those feigning poor legal comprehension (Otto, Musick, & Sherrod, 2011), although there is some debate over appropriate cutoff scores to best distinguish incompetent from feigning groups (Gottfried, Hudson, Vitacco, & Carbonell, 2017).

As previously noted, there is a new focus on better understanding cross-cultural forensic issues. Nijdam-Jones and Rosenfeld (2017) found significant variability in the classification accuracy of 34 independent international measures that assess performance validity. Thus, although predictive power may be strong for select measures, it may be more limited in the context of cross-cultural validity testing. Encouragingly, 87 of the 100 forensic evaluators in Kois and Chauhan's (2016) practice survey reported that they usually or always had familiarity with psychometric properties of instruments when administered specifically to racially, ethnically, and/or culturally diverse populations. It should be noted, however, that this general finding is based on self-report data and may not represent evaluators' actual practice.

Case Formulation and Report Writing

Skilled interviewing of defendants and reviews of collateral information are the bedrock of these two forensic assessments. These methods can be combined with thoughtful use of psychological assessment to inform competency or sanity opinions (Packer, 2009; Zapf & Roesch, 2009). Further, Zapf and Roesch (2009) noted that case complexity should be taken into account when forming an opinion regarding trial competency. Defendants should demonstrate more nuanced *Dusky* abilities with complicated cases.

Relevant to both competence and sanity, Packer (2009) cautions evaluators of the illusory correlation, the assumption that, because a mental disorder is present while a psycholegal ability is in question, the former is the cause of the latter. Because mental disorder does not equate to incompetence or insanity, a fine-grained analysis is needed. A defendant's symptom presentation is more relevant than a blanket diagnosis. For example, delusional thought content is a departure from reality and reason and more likely to provide support for an insanity opinion as compared with a general schizophrenia diagnosis, which could be in remission (i.e., without active symptoms present). As such, evaluators should consider how specific symptom patterns can exert influence on cognitive and/or volitional insanity criteria before drawing final conclusions and provide as much data as possible in their reports to substantiate their opinions. Finally, it is important to recall that competency and sanity are separate constructs and that one does not equal the other; not all incompetent defendants would meet criteria for an insanity acquittal, and vice versa.

Jurisdictional standards, reviewed at the beginning of the chapter, are also key considerations during competency and sanity case formulations. Research has identified minimal differences in competency criteria across jurisdictions (Zapf & Roesch, 2009), and it is unlikely that jurisdictional differences have a significant impact on evaluators' opinions of trial competence. Jurisdictional standards play a greater role in insanity opinions, given that several states do not recognize insanity, and among those that do, case law and statutory standards differentiate between the various cognitive and volitional legal tests. Nevertheless, Daniel, Beck, Herath, Schmitz, and Menninger (1984) found that impairments in cognitive ability (specifically, understanding the act) and volitional control accounted for 79% of the variance in their discriminant function analysis of insanity acquittals, even after accounting for demographic, clinical, and legal variables. The authors proposed that there is no real need to discern between cognitive and volitional criteria, given that the two were so strongly correlated in their analyses. Warren et al. (2004) found that the cognitive criteria were solely considered in approximately 43% of opinions, whereas volitional control was solely considered in 9% of opinions. Evaluators considered both the volitional and cognitive criteria in 48% of opinions.

Although the literature on how to conduct competency and sanity evaluations is robust, there is little work on how evaluators should communicate their findings. Research demonstrates that evaluators are more comprehensive in competency reports relative to sanity. In their survey of Florida state competence evaluations, Heilbrun and Collins (1995) found that in inpatient settings, evaluators almost always (at least 95% of the time) explained inpatient defendants' specific competency impairments according to state statute. However, in outpatient evaluations, evaluators commented on defendants' specific competency impairments 61–81% of the time. Only inpatient report data were available for sanity evaluations in their study. Among these reports, only about 27% of community-based evaluators addressed the issue of understanding consequences of the act; 29%, understanding the wrongfulness of the act; and 41%, understanding of the act. The authors noted that this lack of comprehensiveness is concerning, as evaluators should provide clear reasoning for their opinion in their reports by directly tying mental health symptoms to psycholegal abilities or impairments. Further, forensic assessment research often uses forensic evaluators' reports as prime data sources. Therefore, the nature and quality of these reports is not only a practical consideration but is also relevant for research data collection.

Field Reliability

Researchers are increasingly attending to the field reliability of forensic evaluations. In Virginia, Murrie and Warren (2005) found significant variation in evaluators' opinions of insanity. On average, evaluators who conducted more evaluations were more likely to opine defendants sane. This suggests that more experienced evaluators may be more conservative in applying insanity standards relative to their less experienced counterparts. However, within the subset of less experienced evaluators, six evaluators never opined a defendant insane. This small group had conducted very few evaluations each ($M = 12$) relative to the study's average evaluator ($M = 96$). Plausibly, these evaluators may not have encountered defendants who would be opined insane by other evaluators. Murrie and Warren (2005) recommended that evaluators monitor the proportion of defendants they opine sane versus insane as means to assess opinion bias. In their study, the majority of evaluators opined 5–25% of defendants in their evaluations insane. Thus evaluators who opine fewer than 5% or more than 25% of their referrals insane should consider how their referral stream, evaluation approach, and/or application of insanity standards might lead to an atypical insanity opinion rate. Somewhat similarly, Murrie, Boccaccini, Zapf, Warren, and Henderson (2008) found significantly different trial incompetence opinions across Virginia state evaluator disciplines. Among their sample, psychiatrists were most likely to opine defendants incompetent, followed by psychologists and social workers.

In the United States, Guarnera and Murrie (2017) meta-analyzed competency and sanity field reliability research. They found that kappa statistics, a measure of interrater agreement, were poor, with an average of .41 for sanity and .49 for competency. Discrepancies may be partially explained by diagnostic differences or how evaluators apply legal standards in their evaluations. Alternatively, poor interrater agreement among evaluators may be a function of referral source. Research indicates that forensic evaluators sometimes demonstrate adversarial allegiance, meaning a tendency to opine in favor of their retaining party (Murrie, Boccaccini, Guarnera, & Rufino, 2013). Thus evaluators retained by opposing parties are less likely to agree on competency and sanity opinions, which further reduces interrater agreement.

In Hawaii, differences in diagnostic opinion were related to agreement in evaluators' competency and sanity opinions (Gowensmith, Murrie, & Boccaccini, 2012, 2013). Specifically, when evaluators agreed that defendants were psychotic, they were more likely to agree that defendants were incompetent or insane. When evaluators agreed that defendants were not psychotic, they more often agreed that defendants were competent or sane. Research shows that competency and sanity interevaluator agreement fares best (from approximately 65–90% agreement) when diagnosing discrete psychotic, mood, substance, or cognitive disorders (Gowensmith, Sessarego, et al., 2017). However, once clinical presentations grow more complex, such as diagnostic combinations of psychosis and substance abuse, interevaluator agreement declines (approximately 47%).

Compared to interevaluator agreement, research suggests that the competency opinion consensus among individual evaluators and the courts is high. Zapf, Hubbard, Cooper, Wheeles, and Ronan (2004) found a 99.7% concordance rate among evaluators and judges and speculated that judges may relinquish their ultimate opinion by deferring to clinicians. Similarly, when evaluators in Gowensmith et al.'s (2012, 2013) studies disagreed, judges typically made decisions consistent with the evaluators' majority opinion. When judges departed from the evaluators' majority, they more often opined defendants incompetent or sane. Research from different states and different time periods has found that the insanity defense was successful only one out of four times it was raised by a state court (for a review, see Melton et al., 2018).

Taken together, research suggests that, although evaluators may have low agreement on competency and sanity opinions, the courts more often agree with evaluators on competency, but not insanity, opinions. These low rates of agreement may be due to valid differences in opinion, a lack of standardization in the process of evaluating sanity, or other unknown factors. Little research concerning competency and sanity opinions' field reliability has been conducted internationally, although some data are available. Yang, Yu, and Pan (2017) found strong concordance among Taiwanese sanity evaluators and the courts. Evaluators and judges came to the same sanity opinion in approximately 92% of cases in their inpatient evaluation sample.

OUTCOMES OF DEFENDANTS OPINED INCOMPETENT OR INSANE

Competence Restoration of Incompetent Defendants

Meta-analytic results indicate that approximately 28% of U.S. and Canadian defendants evaluated for competency are opined incompetent by evaluators or the courts (Pirelli et al., 2011). Incompetent defendants whose charges are not dismissed are referred for competency restoration, which is essentially nontherapeutic "treatment" for trial incompetence. Defendants may be admitted on an inpatient or, less commonly, outpatient basis to undergo attempts at competence restoration. For defendants with severe and persistent mental disorders, psychotropic medications are typically the first line of treatment for restoration. In the United States, incompetent defendants have the right to refuse medication while awaiting competence restoration as long as they are not a danger to themselves or others. However, in cases in which other treatment methods have been ineffective, all less invasive attempts have failed, and the government's interest outweighs medication side effects and defendants' right to refuse, defendants may be involuntarily medicated if medications will increase the likelihood of restoration (*Sell v. U.S.*, 2003). *Sell* research conducted at the U.S. Federal Bureau of Prisons found that among 132 defendants who were involuntarily medicated for the purpose of competence restoration, 79% were restored to competence and later met *Dusky* criteria (Cochrane, Herbel, Reardon, & Lloyd, 2013).

Alternative restoration methods may be adopted in conjunction with medication or when medication is ineffective (as in refractory psychosis), inappropriate (medication cannot "treat" intellectual disability), or when medications are refused by defendants and *Sell* procedures are not pursued. Nonpharmacological restoration techniques vary, with competence instruction as the most common. Some methods have garnered stronger empirical support than others. Defendants who participated in a criminal justice system board game ("Fitness Game") intervention were no more likely to be opined competent postintervention than defendants who received general health education instruction (Mueller & Wylie, 2007). Bertman et al. (2003) found no differences between competence restoration groups who received individualized deficit-focused training (aimed at informing defendants of their charges and potential consequences, for example) versus legal processes and rights education. Importantly, however, both groups fared better on competence reevaluation than a group of incompetent defendants who received treatment as usual (standard hospital care). Cognitive remediation is a promising direction for competency restoration. Schwalbe and Medalia (2007) proposed that given the neuropsychological deficits common among individuals with severe and persistent mental illness, general cognitive remediation (without a legal focus) could be an important first step in the process of competence restoration.

For most of the 20th century in the United States, incompetent defendants facing serious charges could be indefinitely confined to a forensic hospital for competence restoration, despite the tenet of "innocent until proven guilty." Hence, these defendants were essentially punished for a crime without due process. This issue received attention in *Jackson v. Indiana* (1972). Jackson, a man who could not hear, speak, or read, was charged with petty theft and opined incompetent to stand trial based on his intellectual deficits and inability to communicate with counsel. Those who evaluated Jackson's competence opined it was unlikely he would be restored to competence given his disabilities, reading deficits, and inability to learn sign language. Jackson was ordered to a psychiatric hospital, where clinicians attempted to develop his trial competence.

Defense counsel moved that committing Jackson despite the poor competence restoration prognosis constituted cruel and unusual punishment and appealed the restoration order. The appellate court agreed, stating that defendants opined unrestorable should be subject to civil, rather than criminal, proceedings, or charges should be dismissed altogether. In addition, defendants should be reevaluated after a "reasonable" amount of time and not be held for more than a "reasonable" period for competence restoration. Finally, duration of competence restoration attempts should not exceed the length of a guilty sentence. Although the *Jackson* court ruled that evaluators should assess defendants' competence in "reasonable" intervals, we do not know of a federal mandate on how often reviews occur, and the time between reevaluations differs across jurisdictions (Kaufman, Way, & Suardi, 2012). In India, the Supreme Court faced a case similar to *Jackson* in its own jurisdiction in 2007, in that incompetent defendants were held for indeterminate lengths of time, sometimes upward of 34 years. The court made similar conclusions as those in *Jackson* (Freckelton, 2014).

Those unlikely to be restored are often individuals with significant intellectual disability or traumatic brain injuries, and in some instances cognitive immaturity associated with young age, as in incompetent juveniles who have not yet fully developed abstraction and reasoning skills. Morris and Parker (2009) considered the circumstances of more mature defendants and/or those who were diagnosed with dementia. Restoration in these cases is a particular challenge, given that age cannot be manipulated and dementia is a progressive illness.

Civil Commitment of Insanity Acquittees

As stated earlier, of all defendants who plead insanity at trial, approximately 25% are acquitted not guilty by reason of insanity. Postacquittal, these defendants are subject to civil commitment proceedings and can be hospitalized for a period exceeding that of a guilty sentence (*Jones v. United States*, 1983). Acquittees have the potential to be released from commitment, also known as conditional release, when the court opines the individual can be safely managed in the community. The first step is for forensic evaluators to assess the acquittee's likelihood of successful conditional release, with "success" indicating that the acquittee will refrain from violent behavior and will not psychiatrically decompensate and necessitate rehospitalization.

In Virginia, psychologists and psychiatrists recommended conditional release more often for inpatient acquittees without a history of suicidal or self-injurious behavior, who have adequate community support, and who were not transferred to the hospital directly from jail (Stredny, Parker, & Dibble, 2012). With respect to interrater agreement, Gowensmith, Murrie, Boccaccini, and McNichols (2017) assessed concordance regarding conditional release opinions among sets of three forensic evaluators in Hawaii. The authors found that in only half of cases did all three evaluators come to the same forensic opinion.

How well do acquittees' postrelease outcomes reflect evaluators' risk assessment custody recommendations? Gowensmith, Murrie, et al. (2017) found that when Hawaiian evaluators anticipated that acquittees would be successful on conditional release, they were correct in two-thirds of cases. Evaluators may fare better in their predictions of successful conditional release once they are presented with more empirically based research that explores methods that can improve acquittees' likelihood of success. At present, research indicates that whereas some acquittee risk factors are static (e.g., criminal history), others are dynamic (e.g., substance use) and have the potential for management in the community. Findings from violence risk assessment can shine light on acquittees' conditional release vulnerabilities (Vitacco, Tabernick, Zavodny, Bailey, & Waggoner, 2016), and forensic evaluators and treatment providers may consider approaching acquittee release treatment planning in a similar framework as that of violence risk management.

MOVING FORWARD WITH COMPETENCY AND SANITY RESEARCH

Forensic Wait Lists and Outpatient Competence Restoration

There is a growing consensus among U.S. mental health practitioners and policymakers that community outpatient restoration is a reasonable and possibly more just intervention for incompetent defendants. This option, which emerged around 1997, was met with some ambivalence. Whereas some practitioners embraced the idea, others viewed it as a financial maneuver designed to shortchange incompetent defendants in need of costly psychiatric care. At the time, few community or jail outpatient restoration programs were funded or implemented, and the issue largely remained a policy debate. However, psychiatric admission backlogs were common across jurisdictions, with some dire stories emerging of defendants sitting in local jails for months, awaiting admission to a forensic unit where they could then undergo competency restoration. It also became increasingly clear that forensic populations were inundating state psychiatric hospitals and absorbing vital resources (e.g., hospital beds, case management) at the cost of shortchanging civil patients in need of inpatient psychiatric care.

With the passing of juvenile competency laws across the country, the need to provide programming for youth ages 8–17 years became a challenge that was increasingly required by state statute. When viewing this new requirement, it was clear that most incompetent juveniles did not suffer from psychotic disorders and that their young age and presumed innocence made their separation from family unfair and distressing. Further, inpatient psychiatric hospitals were scarce, and residential programs were costly.

These factors prompted the emergence of youth-centered restoration programs that were community based and individually oriented. These programs used a system-of-care approach to case management designed to address the various factors contributing to the incompetency of a specific youth. In Virginia, this type of programming proved to be highly effective with 72–80% of youth being restored to competency over a 3- to 6-month period (Warren et al., 2009; personal communication, Director, Virginia Juvenile Competency Program). These outcomes were found to be comparable to those of adult defendants, with research indicating that approximately 72% of incompetent defendants admitted to state psychiatric facilities are restored within 6 months and 84% within 1 year (Morris & Parker, 2008).

Further, the effectiveness of individualized restoration for youth called into question the group restoration format used in adult inpatient facilities. The group programs are often generic in nature, offered to large groups of defendants with varied and severe forms of mental illness, and presented by staff with limited knowledge of the adjudicative process. Explicit concerns were articulated regarding their appropriateness and effectiveness for individuals suffering only from an intellectual disability, traumatic brain injury, or dementia. These types of conversations prompted a revisiting of *Jackson v. Indiana* (1972) and the Supreme Court's ruling that this type of detainment could constitute cruel and unusual punishment.

The confluence of these factors prompted a development of U.S. outpatient restoration programs that are designed to complement and support the inpatient restoration required by some adult defendants. These community-based programs provide a high standard of psychiatric consultation, support medication compliance, and provide individualized restoration sessions to defendants multiple times each week. Case management is used to address any other factors that may influence the competence-related abilities of a defendant. At least 16 states have programs in operation. Anecdotal information suggests they are highly effective and that inpatient commitment is largely due to defendants' psychotropic medication refusal (personal communication, Forensic Assistant Director, Virginia Department of Behavioral Health and Disability Services). Emerging descriptive research suggests that inpatient and outpatient restoration rates are similar, that outpatient programs are less costly, and that resources (e.g., inpatient psychiatric hospital beds) are freed when incompetent defendants undergo restoration in the community (Gowensmith, Frost, Speelman, & Therson, 2016).

In contrast to the development of outpatient restoration programs, Finkle, Kurth, Cadle, and Mullan (2009) have proposed that competency examinations and restoration efforts should be assimilated into the realm of mental health courts. Mental health courts are less punitive than traditional courts, with a focus on treatment of mental illness rather than adversarial procedures (Boothroyd, Poythress, McGaha, & Petrila, 2003). Typically, a single judge oversees all trials, and psychiatric treatment plans are tailored to each defendant. Judges may dismiss charges for defendants who agree to seek treatment and make significant advances through the therapeutic process. However, Stafford and Wygant's (2005) research suggests that it is problematic to divert incompetent defendants to mental health courts, as these defendants lack the ability to choose this route of diversion from the criminal justice system, just as they are incompetent to stand trial. Perhaps even more importantly, it is unlikely that defendants charged with serious and possibly repetitive violent crime would be viewed as appropriate for this type of setting.

FORENSIC DATABASES

The development of forensic databases has been surprisingly slow given the significant human costs associated with mental illness and criminal justice involvement. These range from pretrial evaluations through remediation or restoration services and placement following a finding of not guilty by reason of insanity. The relative absence of any systematic way of tracking these individuals or assessing the outcome of services reflects the difficulty of integrating data collection across mental health services and the court system. These interagency issues are compounded by the confidentiality and privilege that accrue with mental health involvement in the court process, causing only a small segment of forensic work to be visible or accessible to the courts, to researchers, and to the community. These challenges have particular impact on the sanity literature. Given the low base rate of defendants evaluated for sanity and even lower rates of defendants who plea insanity at trial, data on sanity is scant when compared with other forensic evaluations. Indeed, much of the sanity literature was produced in the 1980s, and more current research is warranted. Consolidated data are needed to further this study area.

Two forensic databases have emerged through a long-standing collaboration between the Institute of Law, Psychiatry and Public Policy at the University of Virginia and the Virginia Department of Mental Health and Disability Services. The first of these, which began in 1985, tracked competency and sanity evaluations conducted by both community-based and inpatient forensic evaluators. The system used a two-page forensic evaluation form that queries defendants' demographic, clinical, and legal information. Evaluators complete these forms after conducting their evaluations and submit the forms with their reimbursement requests to the Virginia Supreme Court. The Virginia Supreme Court arranges for payment of the evaluator while transmitting the forensic evaluation forms to the University of Virginia for data analysis.

A second forensic database has been developed more recently by the Custom Application Consulting Service at the University of Virginia for use in managing data collection related to the processing of youth determined incompetent by the juvenile courts. The electronic case management software is streamlined in that it facilitates program management with easy access in a paperless format. Varied and appropriate levels of access are afforded to restoration counselors, restoration supervisors, and the program administrator according to their contact and involvement with the youth. Moreover, the system provides process and outcome data used for the establishment of an evidence-based standard for juvenile attainment services and to further collaborative research. Currently under revision, the system is moving toward wireless smartphone data entry and ongoing development of modules using SalesForce online applications (*http://juvenilecompetency.virginia.edu/case-management-applications*). The goal is to provide flexibility across different jurisdictions. We hope these databases can serve as models for the development of other forensic databases among other states and countries. They are imperative to better understanding of all aspects of forensic evaluations and service delivery.

CONCLUSION

Although competency to stand trial and sanity are concepts that have endured for centuries, the vast majority of competency and sanity research is conducted in the United States. Still, researchers and forensic practitioners elsewhere—from Australia to India, from Ghana to England and Wales—also value these psycholegal constructs intended to uphold respect, dignity, and fairness of the adjudicative process. As demonstrated in this chapter, both concepts have rich histories and promising directions for future research. We hope discussion of competency and sanity among the international community of researchers and evaluators will stimulate advances in theory, empirical work, and clinical practice.

REFERENCES

Adjorlolo, S., Agboli, J. M., & Chan, H. (2016). Criminal responsibility and the insanity defence in Ghana: The examination of legal standards and assessment issues. *Psychiatry, Psychology and Law, 23*, 684–695.

Akinkunmi, A. A. (2002). The MacArthur Competence Assessment Tool—Fitness to plead: A preliminary evaluation of a research instrument for assessing fitness to plead in England and Wales. *Journal of the American Academy of Psychiatry and the Law, 30*, 476–482.

American Law Institute. (1962). *Model Penal Code*. Philadelphia: Author.

American Psychiatric Association. (2013). *Diagnostic and statistical manual of mental disorders* (5th ed.). Arlington, VA: Author.

Archer, R. P., Buffington-Vollum, J. K., Stredny, R. V., & Handel, R. W. (2006). A survey of psychological test use patterns among forensic psychologists. *Journal of Personality Assessment, 87*, 84–94.

Aubrey, M. (1988). Characteristics of competency referral defendants and non-referred criminal defendants. *Journal of Psychiatry and Law, 16*, 233–245.

Bertman, L. J., Thompson, J. J., Waters, W. F., Estupinan-Kane, L., Martin, J. A., & Russell, L. (2003). Effect of an individualized treatment protocol on restoration of competency in pretrial forensic inpatients. *Journal of the American Academy of Psychiatry and the Law, 31*, 27–35.

Boothroyd, R. A., Poythress, N. G., McGaha, A., & Petrila, J. (2003). The Broward Mental Health Court: Process, outcomes, and service utilization. *International Journal of Law and Psychiatry, 26*, 55–71.

Borum, R., & Grisso, T. (1995). Psychological test use in criminal forensic evaluations. *Professional Psychology: Research and Practice, 26*, 465–473.

Cochrane, R. E., Herbel, B. L., Reardon, M. L., & Lloyd, K. P. (2013). The Sell effect: Involuntary medication treatment is a "clear and convincing" success. *Law and Human Behavior, 37*, 107–116.

Criminal Code of Canada (R.S. 1985, c. C-46, s. 16).

Daniel, A. E., Beck, N. C., Herath, A., Schmitz, M., & Menninger, K. (1984). Factors correlated with psychiatric recommendations of incompetency and insanity. *Journal of Psychiatry and Law, 12*, 527–544.

Determination of Mental Competency to Stand Trial to Undergo Postrelease Proceedings 1, 18 U.S.C. § 4241[a].

Durham v. U.S., 214 F.2d 862 (1954).

Dusky v. United States, 362 U.S. No. 402 (1960).

Everington, C. T. (1990). The Competence Assessment for Standing Trial for Defendants with Mental Retardation (CAST–MR): A validation study. *Criminal Justice and Behavior, 17*, 147–168.

Finkle, M. J., Kurth, R., Cadle, C., & Mullan, J. (2009). Competency courts: A creative solution for restoring competency to the competency process. *Behavioral Sciences and the Law, 27*, 767–786.

Freckelton, I. (2014). Fitness to stand trial in India: The legacy of Machal Lalung. *Psychiatry, Psychology and Law, 21*, 315–320.

Freckelton, I., & Karagiannakis, M. (2014). Fitness to stand trial under international criminal law: The ramifications of a landmark East Timor decision: Case commentary. *Psychiatry, Psychology and Law, 21*, 321–332.

Frederick, R. I. (1997). *Validity Indicator Profile manual*. Minnetonka, MN: NCS Assessments.

Gottfried, E. D., Hudson, B. L., Vitacco, M. J., & Carbonell, J. L. (2017). Improving the detection of feigned knowledge deficits in defendants adjudicated incompetent to stand trial. *Assessment, 24*, 232–243.

Gowensmith, W. N., Frost, L. E., Speelman, D. W., & Therson, D. E. (2016). Lookin' for beds in all the wrong places: Outpatient competency restoration as a promising approach to modern challenges. *Psychology, Public Policy, and Law, 22*, 293–305.

Gowensmith, W. N., Murrie, D. C., & Boccaccini, M. T. (2012). Field reliability of competence to stand trial opinions: How often do evaluators agree, and what do judges decide when evaluators disagree? *Law and Human Behavior, 36*, 130–139.

Gowensmith, W. N., Murrie, D. C., & Boccaccini, M. T. (2013). How reliable are forensic evaluations of legal sanity? *Law and Human Behavior, 37*(2), 98–106.

Gowensmith, W. N., Murrie, D. C., Boccaccini, M. T., & McNichols, B. J. (2017). Field reliability influences field validity: Risk assessments of individuals found not guilty by reason of insanity. *Psychological Assessment, 29*, 786–794.

Gowensmith, W. N., Sessarego, S. N., McKee, M. K., Horkott, S., MacLean, N., & McCallum, K. E. (2017). Diagnostic field reliability in forensic mental health evaluations. *Psychological Assessment, 29*, 692–700.

Grisso, T. (2005). *Evaluating juveniles' adjudicative competence: A guide for clinical practice*. Sarasota, FL: Professional Resource Press.

Guarnera, L. A., & Murrie, D. C. (2017). Field reliability of competency and sanity opinions: A systematic review and meta-analysis. *Psychological Assessment, 29*, 795–818.

Hale, M. (1736). *The history of the pleas of the crown*. London: In the Savoy, printed by E. and R. Nutt, and R. Gosling for F. Gyles.

Heilbrun, K., & Collins, S. (1995). Evaluations of trial competency and mental state at time of offense: Report characteristics. *Professional Psychology: Research and Practice, 26*, 61–67.

Heilbrun, K., Grisso, T., & Goldstein, A. M. (2009). *Foundations of forensic mental health assessment*. New York: Oxford University Press.

Hoge, S. K., Bonnie, R. J., Poythress, N., & Monahan, J. (1992). Attorney-client decision-making in criminal cases: Client competence and participation as perceived by their attorneys. *Behavioral Sciences and the Law, 10*, 385–394.

Hu, J., Yang, M., Huang, X., Liu, X., & Coid, J. (2010). Forensic psychiatry assessments in Sichuan Province, People's Republic of China, 1997–2006. *Journal of Forensic Psychiatry and Psychology, 21*(4), 604–619.

Jackson v. Indiana, 406 U.S. 715 (1972).

Jones v. United States, 463 U.S. 354 (1983).

Kaufman, A. R., Way, B. B., & Suardi, E. (2012). Forty years after Jackson v.

Indiana: States' compliance with "reasonable period of time" ruling. *Journal of the American Academy of Psychiatry and the Law, 40*, 261–265.

Kois, L., & Chauhan, P. (2016). Forensic evaluators' self-reported engagement in culturally competent practices. *International Journal of Forensic Mental Health, 15*, 312–322.

Laboratory of Community Psychiatry, Harvard Medical School. (1973). *Competency to stand trial and mental illness final report, September 1, 1966–June 30, 1972*. Rockville, MD: National Institute of Mental Health, Center for Studies of Crime and Delinquency.

Lally, S. J. (2003). What tests are acceptable for use in forensic evaluations?: A survey of experts. *Professional Psychology: Research and Practice, 34*, 491–498.

McDonald v. United States, 312 F.2d 347 (1962).

McLaughlin, J. L., & Kan, L. Y. (2014). Test usage in four common types of forensic mental health assessment. *Professional Psychology: Research and Practice, 45*, 128–135.

Melton, G. B., Petrila, J., Poythress, N. G., Slobogin, C., Otto, R. K., Mossman, D., & Condie, L. O. (2018). *Psychological evaluations for the courts: A handbook for mental health professionals and lawyers* (4th ed.). New York: Guilford Press.

Mental Health Act, 864 Ghana (2012).

Morris, D. R., & Parker, G. F. (2008). Jackson's Indiana: State hospital competence restoration in Indiana. *Journal of the American Academy of Psychiatry and Law, 36*, 522–534.

Morris, D. R., & Parker, G. F. (2009). Effects of advanced age and dementia on restoration of competence to stand trial. *International Journal of Law and Psychiatry, 32*, 156–160.

Mueller, C., & Wylie, A. M. (2007). Examining the effectiveness of an intervention designed for the restoration of competency to stand trial. *Behavioral Sciences and the Law, 25*, 891–900.

Murrie, D. C., Boccaccini, M. T., Guarnera, L. A., & Rufino, K. A. (2013). Are forensic experts biased by the side that retained them? *Psychological Science, 24*, 1889–1897.

Murrie, D. C., Boccaccini, M. T., Zapf, P. A., Warren, J. I., & Henderson, C. E. (2008). Clinician variation in findings of competence to stand trial. *Psychology, Public Policy, and Law, 14*, 177–193.

Murrie, D. C., & Warren, J. I. (2005). Clinician variation in rates of legal sanity opinions: Implications for self-monitoring. *Professional Psychology: Research and Practice, 36*, 519–524.

Neal, T. S., & Grisso, T. (2014). Assessment practices and expert judgment methods in forensic psychology and psychiatry: An international snapshot. *Criminal Justice and Behavior, 41*, 1406–1421.

Nijdam-Jones, A., & Rosenfeld, B. (2017). Cross-cultural feigning aseesment: A systematic review of feigning instruments used with linguistically, ethnically, and culturally diverse samples. *Psychological Assessment, 29*, 1321–1336.

Norton, K. A., & Ryba, N. L. (2010). An investigation of the ECST-R as a measure of competence and feigning. *Journal of Forensic Psychology Practice, 10*, 91–106.

Otto, R., Musick, J., & Sherrod, C. (2010). *Inventory of Legal Knowledge: Professional manual*. Lutz, FL: Psychological Assessment Resources

Otto, R. K., Musick, J. E., & Sherrod, C. (2011). Convergent validity of a screening measure designed to identify defendants feigning knowledge deficits related to competence to stand trial. *Assessment, 18*, 60–62.

Otto, R. K., Poythress, N. G., Nicholson, R. A., Edens, J. F., Monahan, J., Bonnie, R. J., et al. (1998). Psychometric properties of the MacArthur Competence Assessment Tool–Criminal Adjudication. *Psychological Assessment, 10*, 435–443.

Packer, I. K. (2009). *Evaluation of criminal responsibility.* New York: Oxford University Press.

Parsons v. State, 2 So. 854 (1886).

Pasewark, R., & Craig, P. (1980). Insanity plea: Defense attorneys' views. *Journal of Psychiatry and Law, 8*, 413–442.

Pillay, A. L. (2016). Changing legislation and legislating for change: Fitness to stand trial and criminal responsibility evaluations. *South African Journal of Psychology, 46*, 432–435.

Pirelli, G., Gottdiener, W. H., & Zapf, P. A. (2011). A meta-analytic review of competency to stand trial research. *Psychology, Public Policy, and Law, 17*, 1–53.

Queen v. M'Naghten, 10 Clark & F.200, 2 Eng. Rep. 718 (H. K. 1843).

Rex v. Pritchard, 7 Car., & P. 303 (1836).

Rogers, R. (1984). *Rogers Criminal Responsibility Assessment Scales (R-CRAS) and test manual.* Odessa, FL: Psychological Assessment Resources.

Rogers, R., Jackson, R. L., Sewell, K. W., Tillbrook, C. E., & Martin, M. A. (2003). Assessing dimensions of competency to stand trial: Construct validation of the ECST-R. *Assessment, 10*, 344–351.

Rogers, R., Seman, W., & Clark, C. C. (1986). Assessment of criminal responsibility: Initial validation of the R-CRAS with the *M'Naghten* and GBMI standards. *International Journal of Law and Psychiatry, 9*, 67–75.

Rogers, R., Seman, W., & Wasyliw, O. E. (1983). The RCRAS and legal insanity: A cross-validation study. *Journal of Clinical Psychology, 39*, 554–559.

Rogers, R., Sewell, K. W., & Gillard, N. D. (2010). *SIRS-2: Structured Interview of Reported Symptoms: Professional manual.* Odessa, FL: Psychological Assessment Resources.

Rogers, R., Tillbrook, C. B., & Sewell, K. W. (2004). *ECST–R: Evaluation of Competency to Stand Trial–Revised professional manual.* Lutz, FL: Professional Assessment Resources.

Rogers, R., Ustad, K. L., Sewell, K. W., & Reinhardt, V. (1996). Dimensions of incompetency: A factor analytic study of the Georgia court competency test. *Behavioral Sciences and the Law, 14*, 323–330.

Rogers, T. P., Blackwood, N., Farnham, F., Pickup, G., & Watts, M. (2009). Reformulating fitness to plead: A qualitative study. *Journal of Forensic Psychiatry and Psychology, 20*, 815–834.

Schwalbe, E., & Medalia, A. (2007). Cognitive dysfunction and competency restoration: Using cognitive remediation to help restore the unrestorable. *Journal of the American Academy of Psychiatry and the Law, 35*, 518–525.

Sell v. United States, 123 S. Ct. 2174 (2003).

Specialty guidelines for forensic psychology. (2013). *American Psychologist, 68*, 7–19.

Stafford, K. P., & Wygant, D. B. (2005). The role of competency to stand trial in mental health courts. *Behavioral Sciences and the Law, 23*, 245–258.

State v. Hall, 214 N.W.2d 205 (1974).

State v. Hartfield, 388 S.E.2d 802 (1990).

Stredny, R. V., Parker, A. S., & Dibble, A. E. (2012). Evaluator agreement in placement recommendations for insanity acquittees. *Behavioral Sciences and the Law, 30,* 297–307.

Tombaugh, T. N. (1996). *Test of memory malingering: TOMM.* North Tonawanda, NY: Multi-Health Systems.

Ustad, K. L., Rogers, R., Sewell, K. W., & Guarnaccia, C. A. (1996). Restoration of competency to stand trial: Assessment with the Georgia court competency test and the competency screening test. *Law and Human Behavior, 20,* 131–146.

Vitacco, M. J., Rogers, R., & Gabel, J. (2009). An investigation of the ECST-R in male pretrial patients: Evaluating the effects of feigning on competency evaluations. *Assessment, 16*(3), 249–257.

Vitacco, M. J., Rogers, R., Gabel, J., & Munizza, J. (2007). An evaluation of malingering screens with competency to stand trial patients: A known-groups comparison. *Law and Human Behavior, 31,* 249–260.

Vitacco, M. J., Tabernik, H. E., Zavodny, D., Bailey, K., & Waggoner, C. (2016). Projecting risk: The importance of the HCR-20 risk management scale in predicting outcomes with forensic patients. *Behavioral Sciences and the Law, 34,* 308–320.

Warren, J. I., DuVal, J., Komarovskaya, I., Chauhan, P., Buffington-Vollum, J., & Ryan, E. (2009). Developing a forensic service delivery system for juveniles adjudicated incompetent to stand trial. *International Journal of Forensic Mental Health, 8,* 245–262.

Warren, J. I., Murrie, D. C., Chauhan, P., Dietz, P. E., & Morris, J. (2004). Opinion formation in evaluating sanity at the time of the offense: An examination of 5175 pre-trial evaluations. *Behavioral Sciences and the Law, 22,* 171–186.

Weiss, R. A., & Rosenfeld, B. (2012). Navigating cross-cultural issues in forensic assessment: Recommendations for practice. *Professional Psychology: Research and Practice, 43,* 234–240.

Widows, M. R., & Smith, G. P. (2005). *Structured Inventory of Malingered Symptomatology professional manual.* Odessa, FL: Psychological Assessment Resources.

Wildman, R. W., II, Batchelor, E. S., Thompson, L., Nelson, F. R., Moore, J. T., Patterson, M. E., et al. (1979). *The Georgia Court Competency Test.* Unpublished manuscript, Forensic Services Division, Central State Hospital, Milledgeville, GA.

Yang, T., Yu, J., & Pan, C. (2017). Analysis of concordance between conclusions of forensic psychiatric evaluation and court decisions after 2005 criminal code amendment in a Taiwan psychiatric hospital. *International Journal of Law and Psychiatry, 54,* 148–154.

Zapf, P. A., Hubbard, K. L., Cooper, V. G., Wheeles, M. C., & Ronan, K. A. (2004). Have the courts abdicated their responsibility for determination of competency to stand trial to clinicians? *Journal of Forensic Psychology Practice, 4,* 27–44.

Zapf, P. A., & Roesch, R. (2009). *Evaluation of competence to stand trial.* New York: Oxford University Press.

CHAPTER 13

Expert Testimony

Stephanie Marion
Jeffrey Kaplan
Brian Cutler

Decades of psychological research on peoples' perceptions, thought processes, emotions, and behaviors has revealed numerous insights that can inform lawyers, judges, and juries in resolving disputes and adjudicating civil and criminal matters. One of the more common ways in which psychological knowledge is sought and applied to the field of law is through expert psychological testimony. Psychologists offer testimony on a wide range of topics in both civil and criminal matters. In this chapter, we first review the content of expert testimony and then review several streams of empirical research on expert testimony. We include both the research on the process that takes place before an expert testifies at a hearing or trial (what we have termed the "anticipatory process" of expert testimony) and the research on what happens when an expert provides the courts with a sworn statement (what we have termed the "expert testimony event"). We discuss the reliability and validity of the research upon which psychological experts rely when preparing their reports. For example, as members of a scientific and professional discipline, we should aspire to offer expert testimony that is objective, and we therefore address the factors that can influence experts' objectivity in their research reports and opinions relating to the case at hand. Next, we discuss the research that relates to expert testimony events, such as the abilities of judges to serve their gatekeeping function of letting valid science into the courtroom and keeping unreliable science and pseudoscience out of the courtroom. We also review research on several questions pertaining to the helpfulness of expert psychological testimony: Is expert psychological testimony informative—in other words, does it tell lawyers, judges, and juries something they don't already know? And what impact does expert testimony have on judicial outcomes in depositions, pretrial hearings, and trial contexts?

Before reviewing the content of expert testimony, we begin by explaining some important aspects about the process of expert testimony. Too often in the psychological literature, expert testimony is treated as an event in which a psychologist appears in court and answers questions under direct and cross-examination – that is, an expert testimony event. For several reasons, this characterization of expert testimony is highly distorted. First, in many—perhaps most—cases in which psychologists become involved, there is no trial, and hence no expert testimony. There is often no actual testimony given at trial because most cases are resolved without the need of a trial, such as with plea bargains in criminal matters and negotiated agreements among the parties involved in civil matters. Second, in many cases the psychological expert is consulted early on during the judicial process and performs services in anticipation of a trial, such as reviewing materials, conferring with the lawyers, conducting research or psychological assessments, writing reports or affidavits (i.e., a type of report offered under oath that can later be used as evidence), and being deposed by opposing counsel (i.e., giving an oral report under oath before a trial takes place). A psychological expert may spend 20–40 hours on a case offering these services before it resolves without a trial. In such cases, there has been a great deal of expert psychological work performed, with or without expert testimony events (in the form of pretrial hearings or depositions), but no trial. Even when the psychologist's work culminates in an expert testimony event, the testimony is typically the concise summarization of many hours of psychological work that was performed in anticipation of the court appearance.

We explained the distinction between the anticipatory process of expert work and actual expert testimony events in order to draw attention in advance to the dearth of research on the anticipatory process of expert work. Much that is written about expert psychological testimony pertains to the testimony events, and primarily the trial testimony event, but not to the anticipatory process of expert testimony, as just discussed. Of course, most of what *is* known about the anticipatory process of expert testimony is about the foundational research and techniques upon which experts rely in doing their work, such as, for example, the research on false confessions on which an expert would rely in a case involving an alleged false confession. Nevertheless, when we scan the literature, we find many gaps in our knowledge of this anticipatory process and, for those developing research agendas, many productive avenues for future research. For example, with respect to psychological services provided prior to, or in anticipation of, expert testimony events, what do we know about *how* psychological experts review and synthesize foundational psychological research for use in their reports and testimony? What do we know about how psychological experts communicate their findings to the lawyers who retain them? What do we know about how the opinions of psychological experts are received by the lawyers who hire them?

In contrast, more research has been published on expert testimony events, but gaps in our knowledge still exist with respect to many pertinent questions. For example, what do we know about the extent to which expert testimony is needed—in other words, whether the testimony informs fact finders beyond what they already know from their life experiences? What do we know about the effectiveness of quality control mechanisms for expert testimony in court? What do we know about the effectiveness of expert testimony? In the remainder of this chapter, we review the research addressing these questions and identify gaps in the literature. We begin, however, with an overview of the content of expert psychological testimony.

CONTENT OF EXPERT TESTIMONY

Psychology is a diverse discipline. Historically, psychology encompasses six distinct approaches: biological, clinical, cognitive, developmental, personality/individual differences, and social. Modern psychology, however, contains many more perspectives. The American Psychological Association now has 54 separate divisions, each representing a unique area of research and/or practice. Psychologists from each of the six historical approaches and many of the newer divisions (e.g., psychology of trauma, school psychology) offer expert psychological testimony. Psychologists may offer the results of psychological assessments of individuals, may testify in general about the results of psychological research on a topic relevant to a case, or may offer opinions about the appropriateness of procedures used in the course of the investigation that led to the court case. Of utmost importance, and regardless of the content of their testimony, the information experts provide should be accessible to lay people; information that is not effectively communicated is unlikely to affect judicial decisions. This means that psychological experts should avoid jargon and instead use plain language that will be understood by lawyers, judges, and jurors and keep their testimony clear and concise while remaining objective and sharing all of the necessary information.

Expert Testimony Based on Psychological Assessments

Clinical psychologists are likely the most commonly appointed experts. They offer testimony on individuals' current and past mental states. In criminal cases, for example, they can provide testimony on a defendant's level of competence, such as his or her competence to stand trial or to waive his or her rights. In cases in which an insanity defense is raised, clinical psychologists will testify as to the defendant's mental state at the time he or she committed the crime and provide an opinion as to whether the defendant understood the nature and quality of his or her actions and that they were wrong. Clinical psychological experts also conduct risk assessments and advise the courts regarding the potential dangerousness of individuals to themselves and to others. In civil and family cases, clinical psychologists can testify about an individual's competence to serve as a parent, to provide consent, or to manage his or her financial affairs. As yet another example, in workplace injury cases, clinical psychologists may be hired to assess the risk of malingering—that is, the likelihood that a claimant is feigning his or her injuries or the physical or psychological damage caused by an injury. Clinical psychologists are unique among experts in that they provide specific opinions about specific individuals (e.g., suspects, victims, or witnesses) that are based on formal assessments made using psychological tests of various kinds. In contrast, psychologists with training in other subdisciplines generally do not do assessments of individuals, as such assessments require clinical training. The content of their testimony is instead based more generally on psychological concepts and research.

Expert Testimony Based on Psychological Science

Psychological scientists who are not clinically trained are also hired as expert witnesses. Instead of testifying about individuals' mental states, however, they educate lawyers, judges, and jurors on psychological topics about which they are experts and that are relevant to the case at hand. The content of their testimony is more general than that of clinical psychologists in that they normally do not offer an opinion about the facts of the case and in fact are often not allowed to do so. Instead, they offer broader information on psychological principles intended to assist the triers of fact in their decision making. For example, cognitive psychologists may testify about factors affecting the reliability of eyewitness memory in cases in which an eyewitness has identified the defendant as the perpetrator or, in contract dispute cases, about how people process the language in contracts. Sometimes, the defense or the prosecution may question the reliability of a child witness. In such cases, a developmental psychologist may be called to testify about factors that affect the reliability and suggestiveness of children's memories and about children's abilities to distinguish truth from fantasy. Social psychologists may testify about social influence processes that affect the reliability of eyewitness memory; for example, if several eyewitnesses discussed the details of the witnessed event before providing the police their individual reports. When a defendant claims to be innocent despite having confessed, social psychological experts can also testify about how coercive interrogation methods can influence the risk of false confessions. An industrial/organizational psychologist may testify about conditions of employment that lead to a hostile work environment and how hostile work environments affect employees' quality of life at work and at home. In other civil lawsuits, psychopharmacologists may testify about the impact of pharmaceuticals or illegal drugs on cognition and behavior. These examples by no means represent an exhaustive list of all of the potential types of psychological experts who may be retained by an attorney or the court, as the possibilities for psychological topics relevant to legal matters are likely endless.

As mentioned earlier, the content of nonclinical expert testimony often involves summarizing conclusions from research that are relevant to a case without providing an opinion about ultimate issues in the case, such as the accuracy of an eyewitness identification or the veracity of a confession. For example, a social psychologist testifying in a case in which a defendant claims that he falsely confessed may testify that research shows that the presentation of false evidence during the interrogation of a suspect increases the risk of a false confession. In such cases, he or she would not provide an opinion as to the veracity of this specific defendant's confession; the scientific research typically does not yet support such assessments, and courts typically reserve those assessments for judges and juries. Instead, the expert would more broadly discuss a factor that is known to affect the veracity of confessions in general. Similarly, a cognitive psychologist testifying in a case involving eyewitness identification might testify regarding research showing that short exposure times, extreme duress, and the visual presence of a weapon interfere with forming a memory trace for the perpetrator and increase the risk of mistaken eyewitness identification. Again, this expert would not offer his or her opinion as to whether a specific witness has made an erroneous identification.

Expert Testimony Regarding Investigative Procedures

In addition to testifying about psychological knowledge that is relevant to the details of a case, nonclinical psychological experts occasionally offer opinions about the procedures used in criminal investigations. Specifically, psychologists are sometimes called upon to testify about how certain aspects of an investigation (e.g., an interviewer's behavior, the timing of witness interviews) can yield information that is more or less reliable. For example, a social psychologist may testify that the interrogation of a witness was highly coercive and could have led to false information. Again, in this instance, the social psychologist would not normally testify that a specific witness's statement was false. Similarly, a developmental psychologist might testify that the procedures used by an investigator to interview a child in a sexual abuse investigation were suggestive and did not meet modern best practices (but would not opine about the veracity of the child's testimony). In other instances, a cognitive psychologist may testify that a fingerprint examiner's knowledge of the case details creates bias in favor of a match (but would not state that the match was erroneous), or that the instructions given to a witness during the administration of a lineup were suggestive (but would not testify that the witness misidentified the suspect).

Regardless of the content of the testimony prepared by a psychological expert, much work is involved before it is given, a process that could potentially have an impact on the testimony itself and/or its overall effect on the case outcome, topics we turn to next.

RESEARCH ON THE ANTICIPATORY PROCESS OF EXPERT TESTIMONY

As we previously mentioned, there has been little research published on the anticipatory process of expert testimony, despite the fact that much of the work performed on a case by an expert happens before he or she testifies in court. Several aspects of this process are appropriate for empirical inquiry and are of interest to the psychological and legal communities. For example, what do we know about how psychological experts review and synthesize foundational psychological research for use in reports and testimony? When clinical psychological experts conduct assessments in forensic contexts, are there aspects of the forensic context that influence their assessments and findings? What do we know about how psychological experts communicate their findings to lawyers who retain them? What do we know about how the opinions of psychological experts are received by the lawyers who hire them? Although many of these questions remain unanswered, there are two existing areas of research that speak to the processes that occur before the trial testimony event, and we discuss these in the remainder of this section. The first area of research relates to the consensus among experts on the psychological knowledge that makes up the content of the expert testimony. The question of consensus is important because this may affect whether the expert will be allowed to testify in court. The second area of research relates to the adversarial nature of court systems and how it can affect the objectivity of experts and their testimony.

Foundational Knowledge and Expert Consensus

In the 1970s some psychologists began to offer expert testimony on the psychology of eyewitness memory, and the number of cases in which such expert testimony was proffered increased. The admissibility of this form of expert testimony, however, was often challenged for several reasons. Two of the reasons for these challenges were foundational: the lack of a scientific basis and the lack of expert consensus in the field about the content of the testimony. Both issues are now enshrined in admissibility criteria in U.S. courts, as well as in many other Western jurisdictions. To be admissible, an expert's testimony must be based on sound, empirical research and must be accepted as true and reliable by the vast majority of experts in the respective field (e.g., *Daubert v. Merrell Dow Pharmaceuticals Inc.*, 1993; *Frye v. United States*, 1923; *R v. Mohan*, 1994). Although the challenges and related research are relevant to expert testimony events (as they were meant to address admissibility decisions by judges), they are also relevant to the anticipatory process of developing expert testimony because they speak to the development of psychology's foundational knowledge and thus of the review and synthesis process of psychological research.

Kassin, Ellsworth, and Smith (1989) were the first researchers that we know of who empirically examined expert consensus on eyewitness research findings. They surveyed 63 scholars, most of whom had published research and/or testified as experts on the topic of eyewitness testimony. They found high degrees of consensus (80% or more of their respondents) about the reliability of certain findings (e.g., that the wording of a question can influence an eyewitness's testimony, that postevent information can bias eyewitnesses, that an eyewitness's identification accuracy is unrelated to his or her confidence, and that the lineup instructions given to an eyewitness can affect the likelihood and accuracy of an identification). Other findings were met with lower levels of consensus. For example, only 57% of respondents believed that the empirical evidence supporting the weapon focus effect—that an eyewitness's ability to identify a perpetrator is impaired by the presence of a weapon—was reliable enough to be admissible in court, and only 36% believed that the evidence that violent events are more difficult to remember than nonviolent events was reliable enough to present in court. About 12 years later, Kassin, Tubb, Hosch, and Memon (2001) conducted a new survey of 64 experts. They found that those eyewitness testimony research findings that were rated as reliable by at least 80% of respondents in 1989 again had high rates of consensus in 2001. They also found higher rates of consensus on some findings among the 2001 respondents as compared with the 1989 sample. Specifically, there was now greater consensus among potential experts that the weapon focus effect was reliable (87%) and that hypnosis increases eyewitnesses' suggestibility (91% in 2001 vs. 69% in 1989). Daftary-Kapur and Penrod (2017) conducted additional followup surveys in 2007 and 2012 and found levels of consensus that were as high as or higher than those reported by Kassin et al. (2001). For example, there was a 94% consensus among experts that showing a suspect's mug shot to an eyewitness increases the chances that he or she will later identify that suspect from a lineup, and a 92% consensus that eyewitnesses are more accurate when identifying individuals of their own race than individuals of other races.

The increase in consensus among experts on certain eyewitness topics likely reflects an increase in published literature on these topics during the interim decades. The results of the later surveys also identified new areas within eyewitness research that were consistently rated as reliable by potential experts. For example, 95% of Kassin et al.'s (2001) respondents endorsed the notion that an eyewitness's level of confidence is malleable, and 87% of Daftary-Kapur and Penrod's (2017) respondents believed reliable the notion that alcohol intoxication reduced an eyewitness's recall ability. Despite significant limitations associated with these studies that may have led to overestimates of the amount of actual agreement between psychological experts (e.g., Hosch, Jolly, Schmersal, & Smith, 2009), the expert consensus research represents a unique approach to empirically addressing the question of whether there is scientific consensus underlying the content of expert testimony. No other expert testimony disciplines that we know of conduct empirical research on expert consensus. In addition, the research tells us where experts agree that findings are reliable, where they agree that findings are not reliable, and where there is expert disagreement. A similar literature on psychological topics relating to false confession is also emerging (Kassin et al., 2017), with preliminary findings suggesting a high level of expert consensus on the reliability of several research findings. Finally, this research can also help judges determine whether an expert's testimony is admissible at trial, a topic we discuss later in this chapter.

Adversarial Allegiance in Expert Opinions

The issue of expert consensus is most relevant to expert testimony based on psychological science and when, as described earlier, such experts educate the triers of fact on a certain psychological issue relevant to the case. Related to the issue of the reliability of expert psychological testimony, a growing body of research also examines whether there are aspects of the forensic context that influence *clinical* psychological experts' forensic assessments and ensuing conclusions. In adversarial justice systems, the most common way that expert testimony is introduced in court is by one party. Occasionally, both parties introduce experts, and, not surprisingly, experts do not always agree with one another. Expert witnesses, however, are expected to be objective and to faithfully represent their disciplines and professions; they are not meant to be advocates for either party.

To what extent are expert witnesses objective? A series of studies has examined this question empirically through unique research methods comparing expert opinions. Murrie, Boccaccini, Johnson, and Janke (2008) assessed expert agreement in Hare Psychopathy Checklist—Revised (PCL-R) scores. Their sample consisted of 23 pairs of forensic psychologists who evaluated the same individuals in sexual-offender civil commitment cases. For each case, however, one forensic psychologist was retained by the defense and the other by the prosecutor. Murrie et al. (2008) demonstrated in this archival analysis that the experts' evaluations differed in the direction associated with the parties that retained them and to a greater degree than one would expect given the instrument's margin of error. Moreover, the level of agreement in PCL-R scores among the psychologists working in an adversarial forensic context was found to be much lower than the agreement generally found among clinical psychologists working in a neutral research context. Their results raise questions about the objectivity of the experts and suggest a level of adversarial allegiance among expert witnesses.

Concerns about adversarial allegiance have been raised in subsequent research as well. Researchers have found evidence of adversarial allegiance with several forensic psychological assessments in civil commitment hearings under sexually violent predator laws (Murrie et al., 2009), assessments of psychopathy (Boccaccini, Turner, Murrie, & Rufino, 2012; Rufino, Boccaccini, Hawes, & Murrie, 2012), assessments of sanity at the time of offense (Gowensmith, Murrie, & Boccaccini, 2012), and other risk assessment instruments (Chevalier, Boccaccini, Murrie, & Varela, 2015). In a survey of a large sample of clinical psychologists who had served as expert witnesses, Neal and Grisso (2014) found that three-quarters of their respondents had used psychometric tools in their most recent assessments. Despite the fact that many of these tools have been established as reliable and valid in a research context, when they are applied and their results are interpreted by an expert retained in an adversarial context, there is a potential for bias. Neal and Grisso (2014) also found that, in addition to psychometric assessment tools, the vast majority of clinical forensic psychologists used clinical interviews and reviewed case file information to formulate their reports, methods that also have the potential to lead to biased assessments (Gutheil & Simon, 2004; Rosen, 1995).

This is not to suggest that expert witnesses are completely susceptible to the expectations of the side that retained them. For example, McAuliff and Arter (2016) found evidence of adversarial allegiance among child witness suggestibility experts only when the police interview of the alleged victim was low in suggestibility (i.e., adhered to proper investigative interviewing practices). When it was evident that the child's testimony was unreliable due to a highly suggestible interview, no evidence of adversarial allegiance was detected in the experts' reports. Also on a more positive note, evidence of adversarial allegiance is not universally obtained (e.g., Blais & Forth, 2014). Boccaccini, Murrie, Rufino, and Gardner (2014) found that the degree of adversarial allegiance was less prominent among expert witnesses who had received formal training in the administration of a forensic instrument. As well, the more highly structured the instrument used is, the lower the degree of adversarial allegiance that emerges tends to be (Murrie & Boccaccini, 2015). The research on adversarial allegiance is still relatively novel, and further study is needed to determine its full effect on the anticipatory process and how to minimize its impact on expert testimony events.

RESEARCH ON THE EXPERT TESTIMONY EVENT

The anticipatory process of expert testimony involves some combination of reviewing background materials (e.g., police reports, affidavits, hearing transcripts, medical and education records of individuals), forensic psychological assessment, conferences with lawyers, and report writing. The next logical stage is expert testimony in depositions, hearings, and/or trials. We refer to these stages as "expert testimony events." For the purpose of this chapter, we define an expert testimony event as any instance in which an expert witness gives sworn testimony. Many cases resolve through plea bargaining or settlement by agreement before there is any expert testimony.

Others may proceed through depositions and hearings but resolve before a judge or jury trial. Only a small percentage of cases actually proceed to trials. The following questions pertain to expert testimony events: (1) What do we know about the processes and outcomes of expert testimony in depositions? (2) In what types of hearings do experts testify, and what is the effectiveness of their testimony? (3) How effective are experts when they testify in trials?

Expert Testimony in Depositions

What research is there on expert testimony events? We know of no research on expert testimony in depositions. Depositions are very interesting processes and different in many ways from in-court testimony. For example, depositions typically take place in a less formal setting than a courtroom. The location is typically a conference room, with no judge or jury. Instead, there is typically a court reporter and a recording device. Lawyers are permitted wide scope in the questions they ask, and the deposition can go on for a full day; hence, expert fatigue can become a factor. Courtroom testimony can also last one or more days but typically takes only a couple of hours. In depositions, experts are encouraged to give full explanations, whereas in court, experts on cross-examination may be constrained to yes/no answers. In depositions, lawyers may object for the record, but almost all questions are nevertheless answered (as there is no judge to rule on the objection). The topic is ripe for investigation. With respect to hearings, a body of research addresses questions surrounding admissibility challenges to expert psychological testimony on eyewitness memory.

Expert Testimony in Pretrial Hearings

Experts testify in a variety of pretrial hearings. In some of the pretrial hearings, the expert offers substantive opinions about key issues in the case, such as whether an individual is fit to stand trial, whether a police lineup was overly suggestive, or whether a confession was coerced. Other pretrial hearings involve determining the admissibility of the expert psychological testimony proffered by one of the parties. In these hearings, the expert might preview the planned testimony for the judge, and the judge then determines whether the testimony will be admissible.

With respect to substantive expert opinions, much of the research on adversarial allegiance described herein is relevant to expert testimony in pretrial hearings. With respect to admissibility of expert testimony, two lines of research that have emerged are discussed: (1) the quality of expert testimony and gatekeeping function of judges, and (2) the informativeness of expert testimony to juries.

Expert psychological testimony is sometimes controversial in courts. Indeed, nearly 100 years ago in a U.S. case involving the introduction of a lie detection technique, the U.S. courts developed the "*Frye* test" for determining the admissibility of a scientific technique (*Frye v. United States,* 1923). Although clinical assessments are regularly accepted in courts, other topics of expert psychological testimony (e.g., expert testimony about eyewitness memory and false confessions) are often challenged on the basis of the quality of research. Some have gone so far as to refer to psychological research as "junk science." It is certainly likely that at times psychologists have offered expert testimony that had not met scientific standards and would qualify as junk science, just as scientists in other disciplines may offer expert testimony about research that has not met standards in its respective disciplines. Indeed, the whole field of forensic science has recently been the subject of scrutiny for its scientific rigor.

Given the potential for poor-quality science to be introduced by expert witnesses, judges play a critical gatekeeping role. They have the responsibility of ensuring that good science is admitted when appropriate and that bad science is not admitted. While in theory this seems like a reasonable safeguard, in practice the safeguard has significant limitations. There is some evidence, at least in a European context, that judges possess knowledge of the psychological principles pertinent to these decisions at a level comparable to nonforensic psychologists (Magnussen & Melinder, 2012); however, most research has not been as affirmative of judges' capabilities of acting as gatekeepers. A survey of judges revealed that they lacked the training necessary to distinguish valid from invalid science, and, when tested, 5% or fewer had clear understandings of scientific terms such as *falsifiability* and *error rate* (Gatowski et al., 2001). Another series of experiments examined judges' abilities to identify methodological flaws in scientific research. In one such experiment, Kovera and McAuliff (2000) asked judges to give admissibility decisions in a hypothetical case in which one party wished to offer expert psychological testimony about hostile work environments. In particular, the expert proposed to discuss the results of a relevant psychological experiment. Kovera and McAuliff (2000) manipulated the quality of the experiment to be discussed by including or excluding a control group, a significant confound, and the potential for experimenter bias (due to a confederate not being blind to the experimental condition). The judges who served as participants were insensitive to each of the three methodological shortcomings; their decision to admit the expert testimony or not was not dependent on the quality of the experiment. These findings raise questions about judges' abilities to fulfill their roles as gatekeepers and keep bad science out of the courtroom. This is especially true because, in many cases, the expert does not propose to discuss one single study but, rather, the findings from many studies or meta-analyses. It cannot be reasonably expected of a judge to review a large body of research in preparation for a case, even if he or she did possess the ability to critically review the research. This is of particular concern given that jurors, if exposed to junk or pseudoscience should it be admitted into evidence, also perform quite poorly at distinguishing it from valid science.

McAuliff and Duckworth (2010) found that jury-eligible participants recognize that not having a control group was a threat to validity. However, confounding variables, experimenter bias, and whether or not a study had been peer reviewed did not affect participants' ratings of a study's validity. Koehler, Schweitzer, Saks, and McQuiston (2016) conducted a study similar to that of Kovera and McAuliff (2000). They manipulated the quality of expert testimony, and mock jurors rated the strength of the testimony evidence. Koehler et al. (2016) found that the expert's perceived level of experience significantly influenced jurors' perceived strength of the expert testimony, but the actual quality of the science behind the testimony was not significantly related to jurors' perceptions of the strength of the testimony evidence.

Expert testimony is helpful insofar as it provides triers of fact with information that they did not already possess. In some domains, the informational value of expert psychological testimony is obvious and not normally questioned. For example, a judge or jury could not have already known how a defendant performed on a formal assessment of his or her competence to waive rights, stand trial, or make informed medical or financial decisions. In other domains, however, expert psychological testimony has been challenged and ruled inadmissible on the basis that it does not go beyond common sense. Expert testimony on the psychology of eyewitness memory, in particular, has been highly susceptible to this challenge. Upon hearing an expert's proposed testimony, many courts have concluded that juries are already well equipped to evaluate eyewitness memory and that the principles and findings offered by the expert are within the realm of jurors' common knowledge.

A substantial body of psychological research, however, has assessed whether eyewitness research findings are a matter of common sense. This research has used a variety of methodologies, including surveys and general knowledge tests given to lay people, studies in which lay people are asked to predict the results of psychological experiments, and trial simulation experiments in which participants evaluate eyewitness memory under various conditions and in which their sensitivity to factors that affect the reliability of eyewitness testimony is assessed. A review of this research (Read & Desmarais, 2009) indicated mixed findings. Surveys and general knowledge tests showed that lay people's opinions are often consistent with experts' opinions (though there are some exceptions). More indirect methods of general knowledge assessment, such as trial simulation methods, however, tend to show that jurors are insensitive to many factors that influence eyewitness identification. For example, Cutler, Penrod, and Dexter (1990) created a realistic videotaped criminal trial in which eyewitness identification played a central role. They systematically manipulated 10 factors associated with viewing conditions and the manner in which the lineups were conducted, then showed the videotaped trials to 321 students and 129 eligible and experienced jurors in Wisconsin. They found that mock jurors' evaluations of the eyewitness identifications were not significantly influenced by factors that are known in the research to influence the accuracy of eyewitness identifications, such as a disguise worn by the perpetrator, the presence of a weapon, the presence of violence, the passage of time between the crime and the identification, the suitability of selected fillers, and the instructions given to the eyewitness. The results of Cutler et al.'s (1990) experiment and related research raise questions about jurors' ability to evaluate eyewitness identification.

Several other sources of evidence further challenge the notion that eyewitness research findings are a matter of common sense. First, about 85 years of research on wrongful convictions has consistently revealed eyewitness misidentification to be one of the most common precursors to miscarriages of justice (Smith & Cutler, 2013a). In those cases, judges or juries erroneously concluded that mistaken eyewitness identifications were accurate, or at least proven beyond a reasonable doubt. It is likely that if the fact finders better understood eyewitness memory and its fallacies, the number of wrongful-conviction cases would be far fewer. Second, the knowledge that mistaken eyewitness identification has been a main contributor to wrongful convictions has led to a wave of reforms in eyewitness identification procedures (Smith & Cutler, 2013b). These reforms were guided by and conformed to eyewitness research findings from the 1980s onward. Likewise, states such as Oregon, Massachusetts, and New Jersey have modified legal procedures in light of the eyewitness research findings. If these research findings were merely a matter of common sense, they would have been implemented much earlier.

Another topic of expert testimony, false confessions, has also been challenged on the basis that lay people, when left to their own devices, understand that people are susceptible to coercive influence. Some such challenges have been successful and have led judges to decline to admit expert testimony on false confessions. Psychological research using opinion surveys reveals substantial gaps in knowledge about interrogations and confessions. For example, Chojnacki, Cicchini, and White (2008) surveyed 502 jury-eligible citizens from 38 states about their understanding of interrogations, confessions, and related topics. They found that substantial numbers of respondents did not understand the role of constitutional rights, thought that police officers were better than the average person at detecting deception, and underestimated the prevalence of false confessions and the role of coercion in producing them. The authors concluded that laypeople lack the knowledge possessed by experts and may harbor serious misconceptions that may interfere with defendants' rights to fair trials. Indeed, most respondents endorsed the view that an expert witness would be helpful in a trial, a view also endorsed by prospective jurors in a study by Costanzo, Shaked-Schroer, and Vinson (2010). In another study, Leo and Liu (2009) assessed public opinions in a sample of 264 jury-eligible students in southern California. They found that respondents recognized the coerciveness of outright violence and physical threats but overestimated the typical interrogation duration needed to obtain a confession from a suspect and failed to appreciate the impact of other coercive techniques on the risk of false confessions. A follow-up study by Blandón-Gitlin, Sperry, and Leo (2011) involving 126 jurors from Orange County, California, found that Leo and Liu's (2009) results were not idiosyncratic to student samples but were also found for actual jurors.

Trial simulation experiments likewise revealed gaps in jurors' abilities to evaluate confessions. These experiments reveal, for example, that mock jurors underappreciate the influence of promises of leniency on confessions and rely on coerced confessions despite judicial warnings (Kassin & Wrightsman, 1980). Research by Kassin, Meissner, and Norwick (2005) found that students and professional investigators from Florida and Texas operated at nearly chance levels when attempting to distinguish true from false confessions by prison inmates. As with the eyewitness research, the frequency of false confessions in known cases of wrongful conviction further raises questions about jurors' abilities to evaluate confessions in actual trials.

In conclusion, research on lay knowledge and decision making allows for evidence-based assessments of the need for expert psychological testimony. Rather than relying on instincts about whether psychological knowledge is a matter of common sense, the use of surveys and trial simulation methods provide data upon which judges, as gatekeepers, can make informed admissibility decisions.

Expert Testimony in Trials

To the extent that the expert witness provides insights that are beyond the ken of the ordinary layperson, we would expect that expert testimony would improve the jury's understanding of case-relevant information and lead to more informed judgments. In an attempt to bring data to bear on this notion, some researchers have examined the impact of expert psychological testimony in trial simulation research. In this section we review the research on the effects of expert testimony in several different domains, including eyewitness identification, false confessions, intimate partner violence, and risk assessment. Within and across these domains, the effects of expert testimony are rather mixed.

With respect to expert testimony on eyewitness identification, Cutler, Penrod, and Dexter (1989) explained several distinct effects that expert testimony could have on jury decision making. One potential effect is that expert testimony makes jurors more skeptical of eyewitness identification. After hearing expert testimony, jurors might be less likely to believe an eyewitness identification to be accurate, regardless of the strength of the evidence (a "skepticism effect"). A second potential effect is that expert testimony sensitizes jurors to factors that influence accuracy. After hearing expert testimony, jurors might be more likely to believe an eyewitness identification if the conditions surrounding the crime and the identification facilitate accuracy and less likely if the conditions increase the risk of errors (a "sensitization effect"). A third potential effect is that, after hearing expert testimony, jurors choose not to rely on the expert testimony, and thus it has no effect on their decisions. Trial simulation research by Cutler and colleagues (1989) tended to support the sensitization effect. A comprehensive review of the available research, however, better supports the skepticism effect (Leippe & Eisenstadt, 2009).

Two studies have examined the impact of expert testimony about interrogation and false confession. Blandón-Gitlin et al. (2011) asked 147 students to read a transcript of a representative case involving a coerced confession and related expert testimony. They found that expert testimony led to a decrease in the percentage of mock jurors who convicted the defendant and an increase in the ratings of coerciveness of some of the interrogation tactics. Blandón-Gitlin and colleagues' (2011) findings suggest that expert testimony has its intended effect on juror decision making, at least in the domain of confession evidence. In contrast, Jones and Penrod (2016) found that expert testimony on the coercive effect of minimization, maximization, false evidence, and bluff tactics did not significantly influence mock jurors' perceptions of the voluntariness of the defendant's confession or their verdicts.

Focusing on intimate partner violence, Schuller and Hastings (1996) examined the impact of various forms of expert testimony about battered women in a case in which a woman killed her husband. Jurors who heard testimony on battered women from an expert called by the defense gave more lenient verdicts and more defense-favorable evaluations than did jurors who did not hear expert testimony.

Other research has examined the impact of expert testimony in the domain of risk assessment. Krauss and Scurich (2014) presented mock jurors in sexually violent predator commitment hearings with an expert psychological witness testifying based on actuarial and clinical assessment and found that those who were told that the defendant was at moderate risk to reoffend were more than three times as likely to recommend committing the defendant as those told he was at low risk to reoffend. In contrast, Boccaccini, Turner, Murrie, Henderson, and Chevalier (2013) surveyed jurors from actual sexually violent predator hearings in which the defendants' risk of reoffense was assessed using the PCL-R, the Minnesota Sex Offender Screening Tool—Revised (MnSOST–R), and Static-99R. Instrument scores from these measures presented by the prosecutor's expert witness were not significantly related to jurors' perceptions of the risk of recidivism and self-reported difficulty in reaching disposition decisions. When an expert was called by the defense, however, jurors were more optimistic regarding the offender's risk of recidivism and more skeptical of the prosecutor's expert witness testimony evidence.

In sum, the nature of expert testimony effects varies considerably within and across expert testimony domains. The four domains reviewed above are representative of the research on expert testimony but are not exhaustive, for there is also research on the effects of expert testimony in cases involving child sexual abuse (Kovera, Gresham, Borgida, Gray, & Regan, 1997), death penalty cases (Krauss & Sales, 2001), and cases involving forensic science (McQuiston-Surrett & Saks, 2009).

The differential effects of expert testimony are not well understood and are deserving of further research attention. One potential moderating factor is the form of expert testimony. For example, some research has focused on the actuarial versus clinical testimony. In this research, jurors were more influenced by clinical (i.e., interview-based) as compared with actuarial testimony (Cox, DeMatteo, & Foster, 2010; Krauss, McCabe, & Lieberman, 2012; McCabe, Krauss, & Lieberman, 2010) and by qualitative as compared with quantitative testimony (Cox et al., 2010; Varela, Boccaccini, Cuervo, Murrie, & Clark, 2014). Boccaccini et al. (2013) found that expert testimony based on actuarial assessment had a modest but significant adverse effect on perceptions of the risk of recidivism when proffered by the defense but not when proffered by the prosecution. The preference among jurors for clinical and qualitative testimony over actuarial and quantitative testimony presents some challenges. On the one hand, quantitative measures are often more precise than qualitative ones, and actuarial instruments are usually more accurate in risk assessment than clinical judgment (Grove, Zald, Lebow, Snitz, & Nelson, 2000). Clinical judgments may also be subject to a greater degree of adversarial bias, as some research has found that the degree of adversarial allegiance increases with the subjectiveness of the measure (Murrie, Boccaccini, Guarnera, & Rufino, 2013). On the other hand, if quantitative information (i.e., from actuarial measures) does not influence fact finders' judicial decisions, it is of little use to the criminal court system.

In addition to the format of expert testimony, the demeanor of the expert may also moderate the effect of expert testimony. Cramer, DeCoster, Harris, Fletcher, and Brodsky (2011) conducted a mock-juror experiment in which they manipulated the confidence level of an expert who testified that the defendant was at a high risk of recidivism in the context of the sentencing portion of a homicide trial. The level of confidence exuded by the expert witness and the expert's perceived credibility were both positively correlated with death sentence decisions. Perceived credibility of the expert is influenced by perceived likeability, trustworthiness, and confidence of the expert (Brodsky, Griffin, & Cramer, 2010.

In sum, the mixed effects of expert psychological testimony on juror decision making may be attributable to the form of expert testimony and the demeanor of the expert. One significant limitation to the research on the effects of expert testimony is that the research is narrowly constrained to the effects on trial outcomes. Expert testimony, however, can have broader impact. Indeed, most cases do not end up in trials before juries. It is important to understand that expert testimony at trial is the culmination of a consulting process in which the expert learns the case details and confers with the lawyer who retained the expert regarding opinions reached in the course of review. In some cases, the expert might also submit an affidavit or report and may participate in a lengthy deposition in which he or she is questioned by opposing counsel. Thus the expert has considerable opportunity to influence the case outcome at various stages of the adjudication process. The expert's opinion may inform the lawyer about the strength of his or her case and may affect the nature of the plea bargain or settlement reached. The expert's opinion may influence how a lawyer positions a case to the court. Regardless of the practical effect an expert may have on a given trial outcome, the expert may educate lawyers, judges, and jurors about psychology and affect their future actions and decisions. We know of no empirical research on these broader impacts of expert testimony.

In conclusion, expert psychological testimony provides a natural bridge between scientific psychological research, professional psychology practice, and social justice in a wide variety of legal arenas. Expert testimony has been the subject of a growing body of psychological research and provides fertile ground for additional research, particularly in the understudied areas identified above. The distinction between the anticipatory process and the expert testimony event, we hope, provides some additional conceptual foundation for guiding future research and practice regarding expert testimony.

REFERENCES

Blais, J., & Forth, A. E. (2014). Prosecution-retained versus court-appointed experts: Comparing and contrasting risk assessment reports in preventative detention hearings. *Law and Human Behavior, 38,* 531–577.

Blandón-Gitlin, I., Sperry, K., & Leo, R. (2011). Jurors believe interrogation tactics are not likely to elicit false confessions: Will expert witness testimony inform them otherwise? *Psychology, Crime and Law, 17,* 239–260.

Boccaccini, M. T., Murrie, D. C., Rufino, K. A., & Gardner, B. O. (2014). Evaluator differences in Psychopathy Checklist—Revised factor and facet scores. *Law and Human Behavior, 38,* 337–345.

Boccaccini, M. T., Turner, D. B., Murrie, D. C., Henderson, C. E., & Chevalier, C. (2013). Do scores from risk measures matter to jurors? *Psychology, Public Policy, and Law, 19,* 259–269.

Boccaccini, M. T., Turner, D. B., Murrie, D. C., & Rufino, K. A. (2012). Do PCL-R scores from state or defense experts best predict future misconduct among civilly committed sex offenders? *Law and Human Behavior, 36,* 159–172.

Brodsky, S. L., Griffin, M. P., & Cramer, R. J. (2010). The Witness Credibility Scale: An outcome measure for expert witness research. *Behavioral Sciences and the Law, 28,* 892–907.

Chevalier, C. S., Boccaccini, M. T., Murrie, D. C., & Varela, J. G. (2015). Static-99R reporting practices in sexually violent predator cases: Does norm selection reflect adversarial allegiance? *Law and Human Behavior, 39*, 209–219.

Chojnacki, D., Cicchini, M., & White, L. (2008). An empirical basis for the admission of expert testimony on false confessions. *Arizona State Law Journal, 40*, 1–45.

Costanzo, M., Shaked-Schroer, N., & Vinson, K. (2010). Juror beliefs about police interrogations, false confessions, and expert testimony. *Journal of Empirical Legal Studies, 7*, 231–247.

Cox, J., DeMatteo, D. S., & Foster, E. E. (2010). The effect of the Psychopathy Checklist—Revised in capital cases: Mock jurors' responses to the label of psychopathy. *Behavioral Sciences and the Law, 28*, 878–891.

Cramer, R. J., DeCoster, J., Harris, P. B., Fletcher, L. M., & Brodsky, S. L. (2011). A confidence-credibility model of expert witness persuasion: Mediating effects and implications for trial consultation. *Consulting Psychology Journal: Practice and Research, 63*, 129–137.

Cutler, B. L., Penrod, S. D., & Dexter, H. R. (1989). The eyewitness, the expert psychologist, and the jury. *Law and Human Behavior, 13*, 311–332.

Cutler, B. L., Penrod, S. D., & Dexter, H. R. (1990). Juror sensitivity to eyewitness identification evidence. *Law and Human Behavior, 14*, 185–191.

Daftary-Kapur, T., & Penrod, S. (2017). *General acceptance among experts of eyewitness research findings.* Manuscript in preparation.

Daubert v. Merrell Dow Pharmaceuticals Inc., 113 S.Ct. 2786 (1993).

Frye v. United States, 54 App. D.C. 46, 293 F. 1013 (1923).

Gatowski, S. I., Dobbin, S. A., Richardson, J. T., Ginsburg, G. P., Merlino, M. L., & Dahir, V. (2001). Asking the gatekeepers: A national survey of judges on judging expert evidence in a post-Daubert world. *Law and Human Behavior, 25*, 433–458.

Gowensmith, W. N., Murrie, D. C., & Boccaccini, M. T. (2012). Field reliability of competence to stand trial opinions: How often do evaluators agree, and what do judges decide when evaluators disagree? *Law and Human Behavior, 36*, 130–139.

Grove, W. M., Zald, D. H., Lebow, B. S., Snitz, B. E., & Nelson, C. (2000). Clinical versus mechanical prediction: A meta-analysis. *Psychological Assessment, 12*, 19–30.

Gutheil, T. G., & Simon, R. I. (2004). Avoiding bias in expert testimony. *Psychiatric Annals, 34*, 260–270.

Hosch, H. M., Jolly, K. W., Schmersal, L. A., & Smith, B. A. (2009). Expert psychology testimony on eyewitness identification: Consensus among experts? In B. L. Cutler (Ed.), *Expert testimony on the psychology of eyewitness identification* (pp. 143–164). Oxford, UK: Oxford University Press.

Jones, A. M., & Penrod, S. (2016). Can expert testimony sensitize jurors to coercive interrogation tactics? *Journal of Forensic Psychology Practice, 16*, 393–409.

Kassin, S. M., Alceste, F., Luke, T. J., Cheiffetz, R., Crozier, W., Strange, D., et al. (2017, March). *Police interrogations and confessions: Problems and remedies.* Paper presented at the American Psychology-Law Society Annual Conference, Seattle, WA.

Kassin, S. M., Ellsworth, P. C., & Smith, V. L. (1989). The "general acceptance" of psychological research on eyewitness testimony: A survey of the experts. *American Psychologist, 44,* 1089–1098.

Kassin, S. M., Meissner, C. A., & Norwick, R. J. (2005). I'd know a false confession if I saw one: A comparative study of college students and police investigators. *Law and Human Behavior, 29,* 211–227.

Kassin, S. M., Tubb, V. A., Hosch, H. M., & Memon, A. (2001). On the "general acceptance" of eyewitness testimony research: A new survey of the experts. *American Psychologist, 56,* 405–416.

Kassin, S. M., & Wrightsman, L. S. (1980). Prior confessions and mock juror verdicts. *Journal of Applied Social Psychology, 10,* 133–146.

Koehler, J. J., Schweitzer, N. J., Saks, M. J., & McQuiston, D. E. (2016). Science, technology, or the expert witness: What influences jurors' judgments about forensic science testimony? *Psychology, Public Policy, and Law, 22,* 401–413.

Kovera, M. B., Gresham, A. W., Borgida, E., Gray, E., & Regan, P. C. (1997). Does expert psychological testimony inform or influence juror decision making?: A social cognitive analysis. *Journal of Applied Psychology, 82,* 178–191.

Kovera, M. B., & McAuliff, B. D. (2000). The effects of peer review and evidence quality on judge evaluations of psychological science: Are judges effective gatekeepers? *Journal of Applied Psychology, 85,* 574–586.

Krauss, D. A., McCabe, J. G., & Lieberman, J. D. (2012). Dangerously misunderstood: Representative jurors' reactions to expert testimony on future dangerousness in a sexually violent predator trial. *Psychology, Public Policy, and Law, 18,* 18–49.

Krauss, D. A., & Sales, B. D. (2001). The effects of clinical and scientific expert testimony on juror decision making in capital sentencing. *Psychology, Public Policy, and Law, 7,* 267–310.

Krauss, D., & Scurich, N. (2014). The impact of case factors on jurors' decisions in a sexual violent predator hearing. *Psychology, Public Policy, and Law, 20,* 135–145.

Leippe, M. R., & Eisenstadt, D. (2009). The influence of eyewitness expert testimony on jurors' beliefs and judgments. In B. L. Cutler (Ed.), *Expert testimony on the psychology of eyewitness identification* (pp. 169–199). New York: Oxford University Press.

Leo, R. A., & Liu, B. (2009). What do potential jurors know about police interrogation techniques and false confessions? *Behavioral Sciences and the Law, 27,* 381–399.

Magnussen, S., & Melinder, A. (2012). What psychologists know and believe about memory: A survey of practitioners. *Applied Cognitive Psychology, 26,* 54–60.

McAuliff, B. D., & Arter, J. L. (2016). Adversarial allegiance: The devil is in the evidence details, not just on the witness stand. *Law and Human Behavior, 40,* 524–535.

McAuliff, B. D., & Duckworth, T. D. (2010). I spy with my little eye: Jurors' detection of internal validity threats in expert evidence. *Law and Human Behavior, 34,* 489–500.

McCabe, J. G., Krauss, D. A., & Lieberman, J. D. (2010). Reality check: A comparison of college students and a community sample of mock jurors in a simulated sexual violent predator civil commitment. *Behavioral Sciences and the Law, 28,* 730–750.

McQuiston-Surrett, D., & Saks, M. J. (2009). The testimony of forensic identification science: What expert witnesses say and what factfinders hear. *Law and Human Behavior, 33*, 436–453.

Murrie, D. C., & Boccaccini, M. T. (2015). Adversarial allegiance among expert witnesses. *Annual Review of Law and Social Science, 11*, 37–55.

Murrie, D. C., Boccaccini, M. T., Guarnera, L. A., & Rufino, K. A. (2013). Are forensic experts biased by the side that retained them? *Psychological Science, 24*, 1889–1897.

Murrie, D. C., Boccaccini, M. T., Johnson, J. T., & Janke, C. (2008). Does interrater (dis)agreement on Psychopathy Checklist scores in sexually violent predator trials suggest partisan allegiance in forensic evaluations? *Law and Human Behavior, 32*, 352–362.

Murrie, D. C., Boccaccini, M. T., Turner, D. B., Meeks, M., Woods, C., & Tussey, C. (2009). Rater (dis)agreement on risk assessment measures in sexually violent predator proceedings: Evidence of adversarial allegiance in forensic evaluation? *Psychology, Public Policy, and Law, 15*, 19–53.

Neal, T. M., & Grisso, T. (2014). Assessment practices and expert judgment methods in forensic psychology and psychiatry: An international snapshot. *Criminal Justice and Behavior, 41*, 1406–1421.

R v. Mohan, 2 SCR 9 (1994).

Read, J. D., & Desmarais, S. L. (2009). Lay knowledge of eyewitness issues: A Canadian evaluation. *Applied Cognitive Psychology, 23*, 301–326.

Rosen, G. M. (1995). The *Aleutian Enterprise* sinking and posttraumatic stress disorder: Misdiagnosis in clinical and forensic settings. *Professional Psychology: Research and Practice, 26*, 82–87.

Rufino, K. A., Boccaccini, M. T., Hawes, S. W., & Murrie, D. C. (2012). When experts disagreed, who was correct?: A comparison of PCL-R scores from independent raters and opposing forensic experts. *Law and Human Behavior, 36*, 527–537.

Schuller, R. A., & Hastings, P. A. (1996). Trials of battered women who kill: The impact of alternative forms of expert evidence. *Law and Human Behavior, 20*, 167–187.

Smith, A. M., & Cutler, B. L. (2013a). Identification procedures and conviction of the innocent. In B. L. Cutler (Ed.), *Reform of eyewitness identification procedures* (pp. 3–21). Washington, DC: American Psychological Association.

Smith, A. M., & Cutler, B. L. (2013b). Identification test reforms. In B. L. Cutler (Ed.), *Reform of eyewitness identification procedures* (pp. 203–219). Washington, DC: American Psychological Association.

Varela, J. G., Boccaccini, M. T., Cuervo, V. A., Murrie, D. C., & Clark, J. W. (2014). Same score, different message: Perceptions of offender risk depend on Static-99R risk communication format. *Law and Human Behavior, 38*, 418–427.

CHAPTER 14

Jury Decision Making

Liana C. Peter-Hagene
Jessica M. Salerno
Hannah Phalen

A juror's job is incredibly challenging. Jurors' official task is to make accurate factual judgments of guilt or liability based on weighing case facts against legal definitions and categories. To do so, jurors take time out of their lives to listen to often tedious and technical testimony for days, weeks, or even months. They do so with little and sometimes confusing guidance, such as complex and highly technical jury instructions packed with legalese. They are expected to live up to an unrealistic ideal of purely rational decisions—free from emotion, cognitive bias, prejudice, and social pressures. Finally, they must engage in a difficult group deliberation process with strangers who hold diverse opinions and backgrounds. In high-profile trials, jurors carry the weight of their community's (even their country's) need for justice—and bear the brunt of public outrage if they do not deliver the expected outcome.

A juror's job is also incredibly important—even though the vast majority of legal cases are not decided in jury trials, but rather in dispute resolution and plea bargaining. For example, in 2016, in the United States, only 1% of 226,168 civil court actions reached trial at the federal court level and only 2% of 76,891 criminal cases ended in trials—further, only a subset of trials were decided by juries (United States Courts, 2016). But the importance of juries extends beyond the frequency of jury trials. Juries are one of the rare instances of direct democracy enacted by citizens (rather than filtered through elected officials), and they are literally responsible for life-and-death decisions. High-profile jury cases reveal the beliefs and values of the communities they serve (Bornstein & Greene, 2017)—via the verdict itself, or via society's reaction to it.

Thus it is important to understand jury decision processes that help juries realize their full potential in delivering these ideals. Jury researchers face many challenges. Given the confidentiality afforded to juries, research-ers must innovate ways to capture their decision-making processes, while balancing the internal validity necessary to make scientific causal claims with external and ecological validity necessary for generalizing to actual juries. There are many thoughtful reviews of methodological issues in jury research (e.g., Diamond, 1997; Bornstein, 2017). We, instead, summarize empirical findings about juries, focusing on relatively recent advances.

JURIES VERSUS JUDGES

Why entrust such an important job to and burden laypeople? Critics of the jury claim that judges would reach more competent, less biased, and overall fairer adjudication than juries, because their formal training in the law and experience on the bench would help them avoid the pitfalls of sym-pathy, prejudice, and misunderstanding. Supporters of the jury value it as the voice of the community and welcome the safeguards inherent in deci-sions made by groups rather than individuals (Ellsworth, 1989). Although it is difficult to evaluate the fairness and accuracy of legal decisions—we simply do not know, in most cases, which verdict or what amount of dam-ages is "correct"—we can compare decisions made by juries to decisions judges would have made and evaluate them in this way. In the seminal Chicago Jury Project (Kalven & Zeisel, 1966), trial judges in the United States selected jury trials over which they had presided and reported their own hypothetical verdicts and the verdicts reached by jurors. In criminal trials, judges agreed with the jury verdict in 75% of the cases; most discrep-ancies reflected jurors' reaching more lenient verdicts. In civil trials, judges agreed with juries in 78% of cases with little systematic difference between the two. More recent studies support these conclusions, albeit with some contradictory results (e. g., Eisenberg et al., 2005).

Overall, jurors appear to be more lenient toward criminal defendants. Judges surveyed by Kalven and Zeisel (1966) attributed this to "jury senti-ments," or extralegal factors such as empathy; yet recent research dem-onstrates that judges can also be influenced by extralegal factors such as defendant race or even time of day (e.g., Danziger, Levav, & Avnaim-Pesso, 2011). Jurors' apparent leniency could also stem from the deliberation pro-cess: Unlike trial judges, whose decisions are individual affairs, jurors' deci-sions involve a group deliberation process, which has been found to favor acquittal.

JURY DELIBERATION PROCESSES

One of the most valued safeguards against unfair legal decisions is the jury deliberation process. Deliberation is believed to improve the quality and fairness of jurors' decisions because it allows jurors to correct each other's factual errors, it improves understanding of the evidence and jury instructions, and it reduces the impact of individual biases on the final verdict. Yet the value of deliberation is not beyond dispute. As part of the first large-scale effort to understand jurors' decisions, Kalven and Zeisel (1966) collected retrospective reports from jurors about the number of guilty votes recorded during their group's first voting ballot. In 90% of cases, the initial distribution of verdict options predicted the final group verdict. Thus, the authors concluded, the deliberation process simply reflects these initial preferences, much like developing exposed film: "It brings out the picture, but the outcome is predetermined" (p. 489).

This view of deliberation has been—and continues to be—debated (Kovera, 2017). Although jurors do form opinions about the case before deliberation begins, these views are often tentative and subject to change during deliberation. Even jurors' votes during those initial ballots are already subject to the influence of other jurors' opinions, given that jurors rarely take a vote before discussing the case at all (Diamond, Vidmar, Rose, & Ellis, 2003). Further, the voting process itself is commonly interrupted by questions and discussions (Diamond & Casper, 1992), and jurors who vote first can influence those who vote later via classic conformity mechanisms. Still, it is undeniable that the initial distribution of votes can, under certain conditions, determine the final group verdict, and researchers have tried to develop ways to quantify this relationship. The social decision scheme framework (Davis, 1973), for example, provides a probabilistic approach to deriving final group verdicts from the distribution of individual jurors' verdict preferences. In general, research using the social decision scheme confirms a majority effect—when this majority is large enough, at least. For example, Davis and colleagues (Davis, Kerr, Atkin, Holt, & Meek, 1975) measured mock jurors' verdict preferences before deliberation and found that, as long as two-thirds of the jurors favored a verdict at the onset of deliberation, the group reached that final verdict after deliberation.

This pattern is complicated, however, by the fact that jurors might be more easily swayed toward acquittal than toward conviction. Jurors are instructed to convict only if legal guilt is established "beyond a reasonable doubt." This standard offers a strategic advantage to jurors who favor acquittal, because it is easier to raise one single reasonable doubt in the minds of jurors who favor conviction than it is to assuage all reasonable doubts of acquittal-prone jurors (MacCoun, 2012). As a result, proacquittal factions are more likely to sway the group than are proconviction factions of the same size. This *leniency asymmetry effect* or *leniency bias* (i.e., group verdicts tend to be more lenient than individual or predeliberation verdicts; e.g., Kerr & MacCoun, 2012) is also reflected in findings that a large majority (i.e., 10 out of 12 jurors) is required to ensure a guilty verdict, whereas a large minority (i.e., 5 jurors) can be enough to sway the group toward acquittal in mock jury studies (Devine, Clayton, Dunford,

Seying, & Pryce, 2001). Devine and colleagues questioned whether this effect generalized to real trials based on surveys of actual jurors' retrospective accounts in criminal trials (Devine et al., 2004). Kerr and MacCoun (2012) argued, however, that the absence of leniency effects in the original studies could be attributed to coding undecided and missing votes during the first ballot as *not guilty* votes—an assumption that is not necessarily correct. In fact, reanalyses excluding or dividing these cases 50:50 between guilty and not guilty revealed the leniency asymmetry effect.

Normative and Informational Influence

How do jurors reach consensus during deliberation? Kaplan and Miller (1987) distinguish between informational and normative influence in group decision making. Informational influence corresponds to jurors actively considering others' statements and deciding they are correct. In contrast, jurors who express an opinion first can exert normative influence on others' opinions simply because people are inclined to agree with the group and endorse emergent group norms, with or without outright pressure to conform. Experimental research suggests that informational influence is stronger than normative influence, as jurors respond to the number of arguments discussed (e.g., Kaplan & Miller, 1977) more than they respond to the number of group members who endorse an opinion (Kaplan, 1977). This is good news: Jurors engage in thoughtful deliberation and are swayed more by arguments than by social pressure, confirming that they take their task seriously and try to reach informed decisions (Ellsworth, 1989).

Yet this pattern depends on the type of decision. In a civil trial, mock juries who had to make factual decisions (e.g., the amount of compensatory damages, which can be derived with some precision from information such as medical costs and salary loss) relied on informational influence; but mock juries who had to make judgmental decisions (e.g., the amount of punitive damages, which is related to jurors' subjective perceptions of moral blame and harm) relied on normative influence (Kaplan & Miller, 1987). The authors concluded that, in judgmental decisions, jurors have fewer hard facts and informational arguments on which they can rely, so they appeal to fairness and group values to persuade their fellow group members.

The Influence of Minority Opinions

Although majority opinions are likely to prevail, jurors holding the minority opinion can influence the quality and the outcome of jury deliberation. Nemeth's (1986) model of minority influence highlights many ways in which majority and minority group members exert influence. The majority can persuade minority group members through informational influence when their opinion is supported by the strongest evidence or arguments, but also through normative influence by exerting direct pressure on minority members to conform. Further, the majority opinion can be automatically perceived as correct because it is endorsed by most group members (Moscovici, 1980). Yet the opinion minority can stimulate divergent thinking and encourage both sides to develop novel arguments as they try to persuade each other, and the minority can persuade the majority when their opinion is consistent and expressed with confidence. The potential for minority jurors to persuade increases as the opinion minority demonstrates consistency and competence over time, which in turn signals to majority members that the opinion is valuable (Nemeth, 2012).

For groups to benefit from divergent opinions, minority group members must have some leverage—they need to be operating under a *unanimous* decision rule. Although the U.S. Supreme Court deemed nonunanimous majority decisions constitutional (e.g., *Johnson v. Louisiana*, 1972), ample research demonstrates that unanimous decision rules have definitive advantages for deliberation quality and jurors' satisfaction with the group verdict (Davis et al., 1975; Diamond, Rose, & Murphy, 2005). In 2005 the American Bar Association recommended unanimous verdicts. The Arizona Jury Project, unique because researchers were allowed to videotape several civil trials and corresponding jury deliberations, enabled an investigation of minority influence under majority decision rules used by Arizona civil juries (Diamond et al., 2005). This and other studies show that, under majority rules, deliberations tend to end once the necessary majority is reached (Diamond et al., 2005), which means majority rules significantly reduce the group's motivation to consider all aspects of the case and to generate counterarguments (Rijnbout & McKimmie, 2014). In a mock civil case in which jurors had to decide the amount of punitive and compensatory damages, outliers whose preferences were either very low or very high compared with the rest of the group influenced the final group award only when the decision was unanimous (Ohtsubo, Miller, Hayashi, & Masuchi, 2004).

Juries operating under majority rules also tend to take votes earlier and more often (Hastie, Penrod, & Pennington, 1983). Such verdict-driven (vs. evidence-driven) juries review evidence less thoroughly because they are focused on monitoring their progress toward a sufficient majority, rather than discussing the case evidence until everybody is satisfied. These empirical findings are in direct opposition to the Supreme Court's theory that the majority would not outvote a minority until all rational "reasoned discussion" is exhausted (*Johnson v. Louisiana*, 1972).

Does Jury Size Matter?

The 2013 trial of George Zimmerman for the fatal shooting of Trayvon Martin sparked intensive media coverage, and his acquittal by the six-person, all-female jury after 3 weeks of deliberation was met with public outrage. Of course, issues related to race rightfully took center stage in trial coverage; but Diamond (2013) identified another problematic aspect of the trial: the six-person jury size. In response to concerns about the frequency of hung juries, courts began to reduce jury sizes to reduce the chance of holdouts on each jury (Bornstein & Greene, 2017). The U.S. Supreme Court has decided to allow smaller jury sizes, reasoning that six-person juries are functionally equivalent to 12-person juries (e.g., *Williams v. Florida*, 1970). Are they?

Empirical research largely contradicts the Supreme Court's conclusion that jury size does not matter. Smaller juries are less diverse in terms of demographics and opinion (Diamond, 2013)— and thus less representative. Smaller (vs. larger) juries (1) are less likely to include a variety of talents, skills, and knowledge (e.g., scientific background) that increase the quality of arguments and the accuracy of verdicts (Diamond, 2013), (2) more often reach unpredictable conclusions because outlier opinions carry increased weight in smaller groups (Saks, 1996), and (3) exhibit less accurate recall of case facts because there are fewer chances for others to correct mistakes (Saks & Marti, 1997). One advantage to small juries is that all jurors are likely to contribute to the deliberation (Horowitz & Bordens, 2002), perhaps due to less social loafing.

Of note, neither 12- nor 6-person options were empirically determined; both stem from tradition, intuition, and common law. The optimal number might be somewhere in the middle. King and Nesbit (2009) developed an economic cost-minimization model considering three potential costs in civil trials: finding an innocent defendant liable, failing to find a responsible defendant liable, and the time and cost of jury deliberation. Data from the Civil Justice Survey of U.S. State Courts revealed that total costs were minimized when juries had nine members and used a unanimous decision rule; yet only one state, North Dakota (North Dakota Century Code Civil Justice Procedure, 2017), employs nine-person juries.

Does Deliberation Facilitate Information Processing?

A competent jury must first remember trial information accurately. From a cognitive psychology perspective, the jury's task is encumbered by certain trial procedures. For example, evidence is not presented to facilitate accurate recall (i.e., as a coherent story). Instead, each testimony is focused on a specific aspect of the case, and order does not follow the causal chain of events. In addition, some courts are reluctant to allow mnemonic devices such as note taking (Bornstein & Greene, 2017), and jurors are rarely allowed access to trial transcripts or recordings during deliberation (Hirst & Stone, 2017). Thus jurors need all the help they can get to remember case facts. One of the assumed advantages of deliberation is that it produces more accurate recall of case facts because jurors pool their factual recollections and correct each other's errors as they deliberate (e.g., *U.S. v. Montgomery*, 1998). Is this assumption warranted?

Although research on jurors' collective recall is limited, research on group versus individual recall reveals that groups perform better than individuals but worse than nominal groups (i.e., groups in which individuals perform the task separately but are pooled at the end) in memory tasks such as word lists and story recollection (Weldon & Bellinger, 1997). Group discussion can also induce greater susceptibility to the influence of false memories (Reysen, 2007). Deliberating groups might also underperform compared with nominal groups due to *collaborative inhibition* (Weldon & Bellinger, 1997). That is, information shared by group members who talk first interferes with the recollection efforts of other group members, which makes some group members perform worse than they would have if left to their own devices.

Research specific to *juries'* recall performance permits a more optimistic view of deliberation effects on memory. Pritchard and Keenan (2002), for example, found modest improvements in evidence recall due to deliberation. They compared mock jurors' answers on a memory test before and after deliberation. Factual errors that had been discussed by mock jurors during deliberation were more likely to be corrected from pre- to postdeliberation than factual errors that were not brought up during deliberation. Another in-depth analysis of the deliberation process confirmed that certain aspects of the evidence were discussed in depth, whereas others were mentioned and forgotten, and individual jurors were more likely to remember evidence that was in line with their initial verdict (Ellsworth, 1989). The content analysis revealed that "the important facts and issues would come up again and again, while trivial issues would be dropped" (p. 216) and that "none of the juries maintained an erroneous perception of an important fact after the hour of deliberation" (p. 217). Thus collaborative inhibition phenomena might be less problematic in the jury context than group performance research suggests, especially if forgetting primarily involves less important facts.

Deliberation Can Both Reduce and Exacerbate Jurors' Biases

Another advantage of the deliberation process is that, at least in theory, it reduces the risk of individuals' beliefs, attitudes, and stereotypes biasing verdicts, because jurors come into the trial situation with a variety of personal differences and must reconcile them to reach unanimous decisions. For example, Meissner, Brigham, and Pfeifer (2003) found that jurors' attitudes toward euthanasia (i.e., morally acceptable or not) strongly influenced their predeliberation verdict preferences in a euthanasia trial. Those attitudes, however, no longer influenced postdeliberation individual verdicts because jurors had to set aside their personal beliefs and try to reach agreement with other people. In contrast, others have found that deliberation can exacerbate individual biases due in part to *group polarization,* a shift in individual responses toward greater extremes following deliberation (Kaplan & Miller, 1978). For example, deliberation seems to increase racial bias against black defendants in death penalty sentencing trials (Lynch & Haney, 2009). Some studies suggest that deliberation is more likely to exacerbate biases *shared* by jurors within a jury. Haegerich, Salerno, and Bottoms (2013) found that the impact of jurors' preexisting negative stereotypes of juvenile offenders on their verdicts was reduced by deliberation, but the impact of experimentally induced biases (i.e., all jurors in a group read attorneys' descriptions of juvenile offenders as super-predators or as wayward youths) was exacerbated by deliberation. Similarly, deliberation can exacerbate biases due to pretrial publicity when jurors within a jury were exposed to the same publicity, but not when jurors on the same jury were exposed to conflicting pretrial publicity (Ruva & Guenther, 2017). Overall, it is likely that, when multiple jurors hold similar opinions, these opinions are strengthened by deliberation, as jurors realize they are in agreement with each other; yet when jurors hold opposing opinions, verdicts reflect efforts to reach a common middle ground.

Jury Diversity and the Deliberation Process

Over the past 40 years, legislative reforms to jury selection processes aimed to ensure representation of women and ethnic minorities on American juries. White jurors still constitute the majority on most U.S. juries, because jury selection relies primarily on voter registration lists, where minorities are underrepresented (Sweeney & Dizikes, 2013). Although the Supreme Court banned attorneys' use of peremptory challenges to exclude jurors based on race (*Batson v. Kentucky*, 1986) and gender (*J. E. B. v. Alabama ex rel. T. B.*, 1994), ethnic minorities are often eliminated through peremptory challenges because judges tend to accept attorneys' ostensibly race-neutral justifications for exclusion (Sommers & Norton, 2007).

Diverse juries are desirable for several reasons. They draw on diverse experiences and viewpoints (Sommers, 2006), such as racial minorities' increased perceptions of police officers as racially biased (Weitzer & Tuch, 2005), which could lead minority jurors to be more skeptical of police. For example, black jurors in O. J. Simpson's murder trial were convinced by the defense's claim that the racist detective planted evidence to incriminate Simpson. Female (vs. male) jurors are also more sympathetic to victims and harsher on defendants in cases involving child sexual assault and domestic violence (e.g., Bottoms et al., 2014). This diversity of perspectives can affect deliberation outcomes. A recent archival analysis of real juries demonstrated that the more race–gender subgroups are present on a jury (i.e., black males, black females, Latinos, Latinas), the less likely the jury was to convict (Devine, Krouse, Cavanaugh, & Basora, 2016), although the effect of such diversity on sentencing was found not significant in actual capital jury decisions (Devine & Kelly, 2015).

Diversity of perspectives can improve the deliberation process itself by prompting white jurors to control their biases against minority defendants and to work harder at reaching a fair verdict. Sommers (2006) asked white and black mock jurors to deliberate about a rape case involving a black defendant in either racially homogeneous (six white jurors) or diverse (4 white and 2 black jurors) juries. During deliberations on diverse (vs. same-race) juries, white jurors were more lenient toward the black defendant, remembered and discussed more information, and made fewer errors. Sommers (2006) reasoned that the presence of black jurors motivated white jurors to overcome biases and process the case carefully to reach a just verdict.

Yet racial diversity can also place a strain on jurors' cognitive and emotional resources due to increased anxiety, efforts to control one's behavior to avoid appearing racist, or heightened vigilance against prejudiced reactions toward them from one's interlocutor (e.g., Richeson & Trawalter, 2005). Renaud (2010) described several race-based altercations from actual jury deliberations: the only black juror slamming his hand on the table and accusing the others of "wanting to hang the black man," or a white juror accusing a black juror of flashing gang signs at her during an argument—a statement uncorroborated by other jurors.

Thus several factors might block the benefits of diversity for jury decisions. First, historically underrepresented jurors might have unequal opportunity to express their opinions. A meta-analysis of group decision-making studies revealed that men talk more than women, and that the effect size is larger among mixed-gender than same-gender groups (Leaper & Ayres, 2007)—perhaps because men interrupt women five times as frequently as women interrupt men, but they interrupt other men less than half as often as they interrupt women (McMillan, Clifton, McGrath, & Gale, 1977). On real juries, jurors talk less when they are female versus male (Diamond et al., 2005), minority versus white (Rose & Diamond, 2008), and of lower versus higher socioeconomic status (SES) (Cornwell & Hans, 2011).

Second, even when jurors from historically underrepresented groups (e.g., women and African Americans) do contribute, there is recent evidence that their contributions are not as influential as those of white men (Salerno & Peter-Hagene, 2015; Salerno, Peter-Hagene, & Jay, 2017). Mock jurors who thought they were deliberating online with five other participants were in fact reading prescribed deliberation comments. This script included one holdout juror who disagreed with the participant and the other four jurors; the holdout's gender and race were manipulated by user-name cues. Despite all holdouts expressing the exact same arguments, mock jurors discounted the dissenting opinions of women and black jurors—either in general or when these opinions were expressed with anger. In contrast, white men gained social influence (i.e., made mock jurors less certain of their initial opinions) when they expressed anger (vs. no anger). Thus anger, a powerful tool commonly used in persuasive speech, creates a gender and racial gap in social influence during jury deliberation because it helps white men gain influence but hinders women and black men from exerting influence.

PSYCHOLOGICAL MODELS OF INDIVIDUAL JUROR DECISION MAKING

Although jurors reach their verdicts through group deliberation, many implicit and explicit psychological processes can best be studied at an individual level, in carefully controlled conditions without the additional complexity brought by group deliberation processes. Given that individual jurors' initial verdicts strongly predict group verdicts, factors that influence individual jurors' decisions greatly shape the jury's final, postdeliberation verdict.

Computational Models

Several models rely on cognitive psychology to explain and predict the process by which individual jurors decide on a verdict. Bayesian models describe how jurors adjust the probability that the defendant committed the crime along a "mental meter" with each new unit of information (i.e., evidence presented at trial). After all evidence is presented, jurors mentally compare the level of probability in their minds with the standard of proof required for conviction; if the probability of guilt is above the standard, they vote to convict. In other models, jurors assign weights to different pieces of evidence, such that some evidence moves the "mental meter" quite a lot, whereas other evidence has little or no impact (Pennington & Hastie, 1986). Bayesian models have received recent attention in work investigating jurors' thresholds for reasonable doubt and processing of expert evidence (e.g., Thompson & Newman, 2015).

The Story Model

A criminal (or civil) trial is inherently about a set of events that resulted in the involvement of legal authorities: a home was vandalized, someone died, a woman suffered third-degree burns from spilled coffee. What chain of events preceded them, what was the cause-and-effect relationship between them, and what was the defendant's role in this causal chain? Pennington and Hastie (1986) observed that jurors try to make sense of the information presented at trial by trying to build just such causal-chain narratives of the events.

The story model stipulates that jurors rely on the evidence presented at trial, their own experiences and knowledge, and implicit knowledge about narrative structures (e.g., causal and temporal relationships) to construct a story (Pennington & Hastie, 1986). Although formal presentation of trial information violates narrative rules (i.e., the information is not presented in chronological order, causal relationships are not always explicit, and witnesses do not narrate but rather answer questions), mock jurors recall case evidence in a story format. Jurors also appear better able to choose verdicts supported by the preponderance of the evidence (i.e., three out of four witnesses supporting either a *guilty* or a *not guilty* verdict) when information is presented in sequential, story-like formats, instead of organized by topic (Pennington & Hastie, 1992).

When multiple case narratives are presented, the "winning" story is the one that accounts for most of the evidence, has few internal contradictions, and has unique explanatory power of the evidence (Pennington & Hastie, 1986). Thus, because the defense in criminal trials does not have to offer an account of what happened, defense attorneys might be better served by offering no alternative account if their evidence is weak. In support, McKenzie, Lee, and Chen (2002) found that weak cases actually increase the perceived plausibility of the other side's case.

Inasmuch as story construction is an automatic process, jurors are likely to begin constructing a story as soon as enough narrative elements are provided but before all the evidence is presented. Jurors might give stronger consideration to subsequent evidence that fits their emerging story and to ignore disconfirming evidence, a phenomenon known as *confirmation bias*. Thus the relationship between evidence and conclusion (i.e., verdict) is *bidirectional*: Early verdict preferences influence the encoding and interpretation of subsequent evidence.

Cognitive Consistency Model

The bidirectional relationship between evidence and emerging verdict preferences is highlighted by Dan Simon's cognitive consistency model of judicial decision making (Simon, 2004). A core assumption of the model is that complex reasoning tasks that involve drawing a global conclusion from the integration of multiple pieces of evidence—such as jurors' reasoning—includes inferences from the evidence influencing the conclusion, but also the emerging conclusion influencing the evaluation and incorporation of evidence. Psychologically, the goal of reasoning tasks is to achieve coherence—a state in which the conclusion is strongly supported by evidence and no other conclusion is strongly supported. As evidence in support of a specific decision (e.g., defendant's guilt) accumulates, coherence is achieved by evidence processing biased toward maintaining and supporting the emerging decision.

Empirical support for this model comes from a series of clever experiments. Simon, Snow, and Read (2004) had participants evaluate several pieces of evidence and background beliefs (e.g., accuracy of eyewitness identifications) presented outside of a legal context. Next, participants were presented with evidence from a criminal trial (e.g., man accused of stealing money from his employer) that mirrored the nonlegal evidence they had previously evaluated. In one study, the authors manipulated whether DNA traces incriminated or exonerated the defendant, meant to push jurors toward one verdict or the other. Jurors then chose verdicts (convict or acquit) and reevaluated the same evidence they had evaluated as part of the nonlegal vignettes. This methodology revealed that mock jurors' preference for one verdict over the other (based on DNA evidence) motivated them to shift eyewitness accuracy evaluations toward coherence with their verdict (see also Charman, Douglass, & Mook, Chapter 2, this volume).

Does this mean that jurors' minds are made up before all the evidence is in? Although people seek consistency in thoughts and actions and dislike cognitive dissonance (Festinger, 1964), we are not insensitive to novel evidence. When new evidence is strong enough, it can produce the appropriate shift in opinion. In another experiment, Simon et al. (2004) asked jurors to evaluate evidence separately in a nonlegal context, then again as part of the trial, along with reporting their initial verdict preferences. But after the first two rounds of evidence evaluation and the verdict preference assessment, some jurors learned new information about the case (either proacquittal or proconviction), and a control group learned no new information. As before, jurors shifted their evaluation of the evidence to cohere with their initial verdict. But for those whose initial verdict changed as a result of the new evidence, evaluations of the rest of the evidence changed again to cohere with their newly changed verdict. Even when participants were randomly assigned to specific verdicts, this assignment resulted in similar shifts in evidence evaluation toward verdict coherence (Simon et al., 2004, Study 4).

The bidirectional relationship between emerging conclusions and evidence evaluation is in line with other psychological mechanisms involved in decision making, such as confirmation bias, cognitive dissonance, and motivated reasoning. Once an opinion or decision path begins to take shape based on incomplete information, we are naturally inclined to maintain that opinion or position, potentially because we experience cognitively dissonant beliefs as unpleasant and we enjoy the experiences of certainty and coherence. The cognitive coherence approach is also in line with the story model, yet it extends beyond legal decisions that hinge on narratives and can be applied to abstract legal reasoning (Simon, 2004).

Integrating Individual and Group Decision Models

There have been very few models that attempt to integrate individual-juror *and* jury decision making in ways that place the individual processes in group contexts and account for the interpersonal aspects of deliberations. Levett and Devine (2017) provide a rare conceptualization of a model that integrates principles of group dynamics, such as normative and informational influence, with the story model of individual-juror decision making. Specifically, Levett and Devine's multilevel theory of jury decision making stipulates that individual jurors first create narratives of case facts, which are then sampled during group deliberation to create a shared story that accounts for the evidence in a way that is compelling to most group members. Recent developments in multilevel statistical analysis of mediating mechanisms open the door for researchers to think in more innovative ways about how to simultaneously assess individual-level processes and group-level processes and, critically, their interaction (Lovis-MacMahon, 2015).

FACTORS THAT INFLUENCE JURORS' VERDICTS

Trial Evidence

Despite public perceptions of the jury as easily biased by pretrial publicity or defendant and victim characteristics, research has repeatedly shown that jurors' verdicts are most influenced by the strength of the evidence presented at trial (e.g., Devine et al., 2016). Of course, jurors are not impervious to biases, but overall they do what they are supposed to: decide the case primarily on the strength of the evidence. Ironically, the trial context itself can bias jurors' perceptions of evidence strength. Despite the legal system's insistence on the presumption of innocence, the common psychological reaction to seeing a defendant on trial is the exact opposite: suspecting that the defendant is probably guilty (Simon, 2012). Perceptions of evidence strength can be both weakened and strengthened when included in the trial context. On the one hand, the exact same alibi evidence was perceived as weaker when presented in a trial context, compared with the context of an ongoing police investigation, arguably because participants assumed the alibi evidence was weak if the prosecutor decided to bring the case to trial in spite of it (Sommers & Douglass, 2007). On the other hand, mock jurors are more persuaded by weak scientific evidence when presented in a trial (vs. nontrial) context because they assume it has been effectively vetted by a judge (Schweitzer & Saks, 2009). Next, we discuss how jurors' interpretation of specific types of evidence can also be subject to unintended, but common, psychological biases such as confirmation bias, truth bias, and the fundamental attribution error.

Confession Evidence

Defendants' confessions carry a lot of weight with jurors. Yet, under the right circumstances, innocent people confess to and provide details about crimes they did not commit (see Kassin, 2008). Confession evidence is perhaps the most persuasive evidence of guilt, although research is mixed as to whether verdicts are sensitive to the coerced nature of confessions (Woestehoff & Meissner, 2016). False confession evidence is persuasive to jurors because people are inclined to believe what others tell them (i.e., a "truth bias"; Bond & DePaulo, 2006); tend to make internal attributions about others' behavior, often failing to consider situational pressures; and know little about interrogation techniques. Bornstein and Greene (2017) suggest three approaches to reduce the impact of false confessions on jurors' judgments: video recordings of the interrogation, expert testimony about false confessions (Henderson & Levett, 2016), and jury instructions.

Eyewitness Evidence

One of the most convincing types of evidence is provided by witnesses who claim they saw the defendant commit the crime. Despite mountains of research showing memory is unreliable and can be tainted by postevent misinformation, mock jury studies demonstrate that eyewitness testimony is the evidence that has the most impact. Jurors intuitively believe memory is reliable and are not good at recognizing factors that can reduce eyewitness accuracy (Cutler, Penrod, & Dexter, 1990). Of ten manipulations, only witness confidence influenced jurors' verdicts, with more-confident witnesses being more influential. Confidence displayed in the courtroom, however, is not a reliable predictor of actual accuracy—although witness confidence during the actual identification is related to accuracy under certain conditions (Sporer, Penrod, Read, & Cutler, 1995).

Another misleading but convincing cue is the level of detail in a witness's testimony. Mock jurors inappropriately perceived eyewitnesses to be more credible when they provided more detailed accounts (Bell & Loftus, 1988). Dodson and Dobolyi (2015), however, found that providing additional detailed comments to *justify* confidence in a lineup identification (e.g., "I am very certain. I remember his hair"; p. 4) resulted in increased variability among raters about the witnesses' confidence level. Unfortunately, courts assume that the shortcomings of cognitive processes such as perception and memory are common knowledge, so they often exclude expert testimony about the problematic nature of eyewitness testimony (*State v. McClendon*, 1999). Expert testimony has been shown, however, to help jurors be more skeptical of and sensitive to unreliable eyewitness testimony (Laub, Kimbrough, & Bornstein, 2016).

Scientific Evidence and Expert Witness Testimony

Mock jurors' verdicts tend to reflect that they are convinced by expert testimony (e.g., Kovera, McAuliff, & Hebert, 1999), with some exceptions, such as expert testimony on false confessions (see above) or the dangers of paid informants (Maeder & Pica, 2014). Some research suggests that jurors are able to successfully evaluate the quality of scientific evidence (e.g., Kovera et al., 1999). Other research, however, suggests that jurors are unable to correctly distinguish between strong (reliable, valid) and weak (unreliable, invalid) scientific research and forensic science (e.g., Koehler, Schweitzer, Saks, & McQuiston, 2016). The good news is that legal safeguards can help jurors evaluate the quality of scientific evidence—although findings are somewhat mixed. For example, educating jurors about scientific methodology, either in a brief training (Schweitzer & Saks, 2012) or through cross-examination (e.g., Austin & Kovera, 2015; Salerno & McCauley, 2009), can sensitize jurors to flawed science, although other studies have found cross-examination ineffective (e.g., Kovera et al., 1999). One way in which cross-examination has been shown to help sensitize jurors to low-quality science in court is by making deliberation more helpful in this regard (Salerno, Bottoms, & Peter-Hagene, 2017). Some studies show that opposing experts can improve jurors' sensitivity to the strength of scientific evidence (Jones & Kovera, 2015), whereas others show that it can create a general skepticism of all experts, rather than sensitizing jurors to experts presenting high-quality science (Levett & Kovera, 2008).

Recent Bayesian approaches reveal that perceptions of forensic science depend on prior expectations about specific forensic techniques. For example, people give appropriate weight and are sensitive to the strength of DNA evidence but undervalue and are insensitive to the strength of shoeprint evidence (Thompson & Newman, 2015; but see Scurich & John, 2013). Jurors also seem somewhat insensitive to variations in forensic evidence strength—variations in forensic expert testimony and in information about gunshot residue did not elicit changes in verdict to the degree warranted by the differences in evidence strength (Thompson, Scurich, Dioso-Villa, & Velazquez, 2017).

Technological and theoretical advances in brain imaging (e.g., functional magnetic resonance imaging) have resulted in increased use of neuroimaging techniques in court. This raised some concern that jurors might be unduly persuaded by this type of evidence, especially given the considerable disagreement on how neuroimages should be interpreted. Schweitzer and colleagues (e.g., Schweitzer & Saks, 2011) tested the effects of expert testimony based on neuroimaging versus traditional forms of psychological evaluation on jurors' verdicts and found little cause for worry: Jurors were not more persuaded by the neuroimaging evidence compared with the other types of neuroscientific evidence in cases involving the insanity defense, and neuroscientific evidence in general (regardless of whether it includes a neuroimage) does not always carry greater influence on verdicts compared with psychological evidence. More recent evidence, however, suggests neuroimages might have a stronger impact depending on the type of disorder they document, at least in death penalty trials (Saks, Schweitzer, Aharoni, & Kiehl, 2014).

Jury Instructions

Jury instructions are an important safeguard to ensure fair and legally appropriate verdicts, although some studies found that jurors reach similar verdicts with or without instructions, often because jurors apply their own preexisting knowledge of legal categories, such as definitions of crimes and standard-of-proof thresholds (Simon, 2012). Diamond, Murphy, and Rose (2012) found that actual deliberating juries in civil trials reach adequate understanding of legal concepts during deliberation. The authors, however, identified resistance errors due to jurors' intentional failure to follow the law in favor of applying their common sense (e.g., considering attorney fees, which instructions had deemed irrelevant) as a primary source of error in jurors' processing of instructions—the other being comprehension errors due to unclear language, misunderstanding of technical jargon, or missing information.

Evidence of whether deliberation helps jurors' understanding of instructions is mixed. Ellsworth (1989) concluded that, although jurors spent about 21% of their deliberation time working very hard to understand instructions, their recall of the instructions was very poor after deliberation—despite their overall good memory for case facts. Some studies suggest that deliberation does not help improve understanding (Lynch & Haney, 2009), yet others found that deliberation can enhance the benefits of reforming jury instructions—both rewriting them in clearer terms (Severance, Greene, & Loftus, 1984) and offering them before, rather than after, the trial (Bourgeois, Horowitz, ForsterLee, & Grahe, 1995). Thus, as long as jury instructions are delivered in language that at least some jurors can understand, jurors can help each other understand the instructions through deliberation (Diamond et al., 2012).

Although simplified instructions might be a solution to comprehension errors, recent reanalysis of 75 published studies has demonstrated that the approach to simplification is important; some attempts to simplify jury instructions (e.g., reducing conceptual complexity) increased application of jury instructions to decisions, whereas others (e.g., reducing the amount of information) did not—and even had adverse effects on decisions (Baguley, McKimmie, & Masser, 2017). A helpful strategy for improving jurors' understanding of jury instructions and satisfaction is providing these not only at the end of the trial but also at the beginning, so they can guide jurors' interpretation of the evidence (Diamond et al., 2012).

A particular challenge for jurors is posed by *curative instructions*—instructions meant to correct the biasing effect of inadmissible evidence, attorney statements, or pretrial publicity (Simon, 2012). Psychological theory and research illustrate why curative instructions are often ineffective. First, attempts to suppress thoughts often result in increased salience of those thoughts (e.g., "Don't think about a white bear"; Wegner, Schneider, Carter, & White, 1987). Second, people can persist in their opinions, even when the information on which those opinions are based is retracted (e.g., Ecker, Lewandowsky, & Tang, 2010). Third, if the information jurors are asked to disregard is reliable and probative, jurors are reluctant to discount it based on legal technicalities because it would violate their sense of justice (Simon, 2012).

In civil cases, jurors receive instructions about the appropriate amounts of damage awards. Damage award information can bias jurors' award decisions through a process called *anchoring,* a heuristic bias in which a decision maker starts with a reference point (or anchor) and adjusts that reference point to arrive at a final decision (Robbennolt & Studebaker, 1999). Anchoring influences juror decisions in three ways. First, jurors given large anchors generally award more in damages than jurors given small anchors (Reyna et al., 2015), although extraordinarily high requests may result in jurors rejecting the anchor (Marti & Wissler, 2000), and the effect depends on how the request is quantified (McAuliff & Bornstein, 2010). Second, anchors are more effective if they are perceived as meaningful rather than meaningless (e.g., a number given in terms of median income rather than arbitrarily; Reyna et al., 2015). Finally, when given only one recommendation, jurors tend to award damages near that anchor, but when given damage recommendations from both the plaintiff and defense, they tend to use those recommendations as upper and lower bounds of their damage awards (Marti & Wissler, 2000).

Defendant Characteristics

A particularly concerning question is whether a defendant's fate is affected by extralegal factors outside of his or her control. A recent meta-analysis assessed the impact of defendant SES, criminal history, gender, physical attractiveness, and race on mock jurors' verdict preferences (Devine & Caughlin, 2014). Only being of low SES and having a criminal history led to more convictions, but the effects were modest. The null effects were somewhat surprising given that previous meta-analyses have found that defendant attractiveness, gender (e.g., Mazzella & Feingold, 1994) and race (e.g., Mitchell, Haw, Pfeifer, & Meissner, 2005) affect verdicts.

The null effect of race was particularly surprising given that one of the largest problems facing the criminal justice system is racial bias in arrests, prosecutions, convictions, and punishment and that this continues to be the object of empirical investigation (Mitchell et al., 2005). Some studies and meta-analyses found evidence of racial bias against black defendants in convictions and in death penalty sentencing (Baldus et al., 1997; Mitchell et al., 2005), whereas others did not (Mazzella & Feingold, 1994). Why this disparity? Mitchell et al. (2005) noted that Mazzella and Feingold's meta-analysis did not differentiate between white and black jurors and therefore failed to account for race effects driven by outgroup bias. In contrast, Mitchell and colleagues operationalized race as jurors who were judging a defendant of their own race or another race and found that this operationalization did result in significant race effects.

This difference in how the two meta-analyses operationalized race is important. A robust social psychological effect is people's tendency to favor ingroup versus outgroup members. Jury research demonstrates that white jurors are more lenient toward white versus black defendants (Lynch & Haney, 2009), whereas black jurors are more lenient toward black versus white defendants (Sommers & Ellsworth, 2000). This tendency has been reflected in high-profile cases such as the acquittals of O. J. Simpson by a predominantly black jury and of the white police officers in the Rodney King beating trial by an all-white jury. The pattern of ingroup favoritism is complicated, however, by a long history of racial inequality in the criminal justice system. Namely, Sommers and Ellsworth (2000) found that black jurors were more lenient toward a black compared with a white defendant, presumably because they see the verdict as "an opportunity to personally contribute to the elimination of racial inequality" (p. 1376). In contrast, white jurors favored a white (vs. black) defendant only when race was not highlighted as a salient issue at trial. This suggests that white jurors might also be mindful of the potential for racial bias but are motivated to avoid it only when race is made salient. This explanation is in line with modern racism theories, which broadly stipulate that modern cultural values prompt some white individuals' concerns with fairness, social justice, and racial equality, while unconscious negative prejudice toward black Americans persists (Dovidio & Gaertner, 2004). Thus people's motivation to be and/or at least appear nonprejudiced prompts efforts to inhibit bias, but only when the possibility of being or appearing biased is obvious.

Victim race can moderate how defendant race influences verdicts in criminal trials. In death penalty sentencing, white victims elicited harsher verdicts than black or Latino victims (Lynch & Haney, 2009); death penalty sentences were most frequent in cases involving black defendants and white victims and least frequent in cases involving white defendants and black victims (Baldus et al., 1997). Black and Latino (vs. white) victims are perceived as more responsible for the childhood sexual abuse they experienced (Bottoms, Davis, & Epstein, 2004). In these cases, however, mock jurors assigned higher guilt ratings when the defendant and victim were of the same race, because they perceived same-race abuse as more plausible than interracial abuse. Jurors' plausibility considerations are also apparent in race-congruency effects: Defendants are convicted more often when the crime fits a racial stereotype about their group. For example, white versus black defendants elicit harsher judgments in embezzlement cases, whereas the opposite is true in auto theft cases (Jones & Kaplan, 2003).

Recent jury research has identified extralegal bias based on novel defendant and victim characteristics, such as veteran status (Jay, Salerno, & Ross, 2018) and sexual orientation. Researchers have found that mock jurors are more likely to convict gay (vs. heterosexual) defendants in cases of rape and child sexual abuse (e.g., Wiley & Bottoms, 2009) due to persisting stereotypes of gay men as promiscuous and prone to pedophilia. Politically conservative (but not liberal) jurors rendered more lenient verdicts in a murder case when the defendant invoked the "gay panic" defense (i.e., argued that the victim had made an unwanted sexual advance which threw him into a state of panic; Salerno et al., 2014).

Emotional Evidence

Through laws, procedures, and jury instructions, the legal system takes a complicated stance on whether emotions are relevant to legal decisions. Emotion is often vilified as an enemy to rationality (e.g., in verdicts), while sometimes being considered an important part of legal decisions (e.g., in punishment; Bandes & Salerno, 2015). Many jury decisions involve emotionally upsetting situations, such as violent crimes or custody cases. The intense emotional symptoms resulting from jury service can qualify for mild posttraumatic stress disorder, may last long after a trial is over, and may require court interventions (Miller & Bornstein, 2004).

Despite encouraging jurors to keep their emotions from affecting their judgments, courts allow intense, emotionally disturbing evidence, such as gruesome photographs and emotional victim impact statements (VIS), into evidence. When trial evidence is likely to rouse emotions, judges must weigh the potential *probative* value (i.e., providing legally relevant information) against its *prejudicial* effects (e.g., biasing jurors against the defendant, demotivating them to consider all evidence carefully; *Payne v. Tennessee,* 1991). Yet the demarcation between probative and prejudicial is not as clear from a psychological perspective as the law makes it out to be. Mock juror studies indicate that emotions such as sympathy, anger, disgust, or sadness become entangled in jurors' decision-making processes (e.g., Salerno & Peter-Hagene, 2013). Emotion can bias legal judgments both directly (jurors interpret their feelings as cues to the defendant's culpability and guilt) and indirectly (jurors experiencing negative emotion engage in a biased information search favoring incriminating evidence and discounting exculpatory evidence; Feigenson & Park, 2006). For example, jurors who see gruesome photographs of a victim are more conviction prone because they elicit anger (Bright & Goodman-Delahunty, 2006) and disgust (Salerno, 2017), and jurors who view VIS are more likely to endorse the death penalty due to empathy and sympathy for the victim (Paternoster & Deise, 2011).

Emotional evidence can also affect verdicts indirectly by making jurors process incriminating evidence more and exculpatory evidence less. For example, viewing gruesome photographs led mock jurors to rate the prosecution's case as stronger overall (Bright & Goodman-Delahunty, 2006), made them less likely to take the defendant's difficult childhood (i.e., mitigating evidence) into account (Nuñez, Schweitzer, Chai, & Myers, 2015), and made their verdicts less sensitive to strong (vs. weak) defense evidence (Salerno, 2017). These results are in line with cognitive coherence models that incorporate the bidirectional effect of emotional reactions on assessment of other evidence in the case (Simon, Stenstrom, & Read, 2015).

Juror Morality and Jury Nullification

Just as the heinousness of a crime can motivate jurors to convict even when legal guilt is not beyond reasonable doubt, strong case evidence might not guarantee conviction when the law does not reflect jurors' moral values. Jurors' decisions are susceptible to influence from moral emotions and attitudes, particularly because criminal and civil cases often involve issues of morality and justice. When jurors are asked to judge a *legal* transgression, they often also judge the underlying *moral* transgression. Many recent advances in juror scholarship are due to the incorporation of psychological theory regarding moral reasoning to the juror context. For example, Miller and Borgida (2016) found that moral typecasting of perpetrators who committed the exact same crime together (i.e., assigning them moral agent and moral patient "roles" based on prior incidents) influenced people's recommended sentencing. The target that had been presented as a victim (vs. criminal) was assigned a more lenient sentence. Moral intuitionist models have revealed that mock jurors were less likely to assign custody to a morally transgressing parent, even though the transgression was unrelated to the children (e.g., adultery; Votruba, Braver, Ellman, & Fabricius, 2014). Similarly, concepts of moral outrage (e.g., Salerno & Peter-Hagene, 2013; Salerno et al., 2014) and moral character (Nadler & McDonnell, 2011) have advanced our understanding of how moral reasoning influences jurors' decisions.

When jurors find little moral guilt, or find that the law demands a punishment that is disproportionate to the moral transgression, they can acquit the defendant even if legal guilt is proven beyond reasonable doubt— a phenomenon known as jury nullification. Some legal scholars argue that nullification ensures that the legal system reflects the community's sense of justice and morality (Rubenstein, 2006), and that, when laws are perceived as unjust, jurors (as representatives of the community) should have the power to bypass them. Nadler (2005) argues that perceptions of laws as just (i.e., "moral credibility" of laws) ensure compliance not only with that specific law but also with laws in general. Thus, to maintain its moral credibility in general, the legal system must reflect public morality.

The jury's power to nullify—nullification cannot be legally overturned—is controversial. Jurors are not explicitly informed about nullification out of concern that it would encourage them to ignore the law (*United States v. Dougherty*, 1972). Empirical support for this concern is mixed. Some found that jurors who read nullification (vs. typical) instructions rely more on extralegal factors (e.g., defendant characteristics) during deliberation (e.g., Horowitz, 1988), whereas others found that nullification instructions did little to encourage reliance on defendant characteristics, beliefs about penalty severity, or attitudes (e.g., Meissner et al., 2003). In a recent study, Peter-Hagene and Bottoms (2017) found that in a euthanasia case, when the crime did not violate jurors' moral attitudes, mock jurors nullified the law. This effect was exacerbated when mock jurors received explicit instructions about nullification and when they were experimentally induced to feel unrelated anger. Rather than making all jurors more punitive (Tiedens & Linton, 2001), the anger induction led jurors to rely more on their "gut feeling" about the defendant's moral guilt (see also Salerno & Peter-Hagene, 2013)—that is, unrelated anger made pro-euthanasia jurors more likely to rely on their moral attitudes and nullify the law.

CONCLUSIONS AND RECOMMENDATIONS

This overview paints a picture of the jury as a generally competent and motivated body, operating in an imperfect justice system and subject to universal psychological limitations. Simon (2012) argues that the most problematic aspects of the criminal justice system occur before the trial, during the evidence-gathering phases, so that that the jury is often faced with inadequate or misleading evidence and given few tools to discern it from adequate evidence. Thus, knowing that curative instructions are ineffective, judges should take better care to exclude problematic evidence before jurors ever hear it, because it is unrealistic to expect jurors to suppress that knowledge once gained. Further, jury instructions should be written in plain language, while taking into account what types of simplification are effective (Baguley et al., 2017). Providing instructions both at the beginning and at the end of the trial before closing statements is also recommended (Diamond et al., 2012). Courts should also make jurors' cognitive work as easy as possible by allowing note taking, routinely providing jurors with trial transcripts during deliberation, allowing jurors to ask questions, and answering those questions when possible. Emotional evidence should be allowed thoughtfully and sparingly, maintaining the delicate balance between its probative and empirically demonstrated prejudicial effects. For example, simply showing gruesome photographs in black and white rather than color can reduce convictions driven by jurors' emotional responses (Salerno, 2017). Attorneys would be well served by shaping their opening statements into a coherent, complete narrative that accounts for as much evidence as possible and perhaps even by placing their strongest evidence at the beginning of the trial to maximize cognitive coherence effects.

Courts can also help jurors reach correct verdicts by indirectly shaping the deliberation process. By now we have ample empirical evidence that unanimity rules are better than majority rules and that larger juries yield more thoughtful, consistent verdicts. Courts should continue to take steps to increase the diversity of jury pools and to actively question race- and gender-related peremptory challenges, even when attorneys provide a nominal reason for them. One possibility that has received little scrutiny is including empirically based advice about deliberation best practices in jury instructions. For example, jurors could be instructed to begin by discussing the evidence rather than by taking initial votes and advised that each jury member has a duty and should be given the opportunity to voice his or her opinion. Normative influence could be discouraged and informational influence could be emphasized as the ideal way to persuade other jurors.

More research is needed to reconcile apparently conflicting findings, such as the effects of race on jurors' verdicts or the effect of group deliberation on cognitive performance. Such research would be ideally informed by psychological theory and would in turn attempt to advance theory even as it addresses practical questions about the legal system. For example, moving beyond the black–white binary in jury research, focusing on defendants of Arab descent would be timely—not only because the widespread prejudice against this group exposes them to unjust treatment in the criminal and civil justice systems but also because studying this newer, more overt form of prejudice could challenge, complement, and advance theories of modern racism. Efforts to develop lines of research that integrate broader models, such as testing cognitive coherence model hypotheses in group contexts, could be invaluable in moving the field forward. With increasingly sophisticated statistical techniques and software, perhaps the time has come to attempt truly integrative theories of individual and group processes. These efforts necessitate conducting more group-level research (of note, most of the research on group processes reviewed in this chapter is decades old) and rewarding the effort such research entails.

REFERENCES

Austin, J. L., & Kovera, M. B. (2015). Cross-examination educates jurors about missing control groups in scientific evidence. *Psychology, Public Policy, and Law, 21,* 252–264.

Baguley, C. M., McKimmie, B. M., & Masser, B. M. (2017). Deconstructing the simplification of jury instructions: How simplifying the features of complexity affects jurors' application of instructions. *Law and Human Behavior, 41,* 284–304.

Baldus, D. C., Woodworth, G., Zuckerman, D., & Weiner, N. A. (1997). Racial discrimination and the death penalty in the post-Furman era: An empirical and legal overview with recent findings from Philadelphia. *Cornell Law Review, 83,* 1638–1770.

Bandes, S., & Salerno, J. M. (2015). Emotion, proof and prejudice: The cognitive science of gruesome photos and victim impact statements. *Arizona State Law Journal, 46,* 1003–1056.

Batson v. Kentucky, 476 U.S. 79 (1986).

Bell, B. E., & Loftus, E. F. (1988). Degree of detail of eyewitness testimony and mock juror judgments. *Journal of Applied Social Psychology, 18,* 1171–1192.

Bond, C. F., Jr., & DePaulo, B. M. (2006). Accuracy of deception judgments. *Personality and Social Psychology Review, 10,* 214–234.

Bornstein, B. H. (2017). Jury simulation research: Pros, cons, trends, and alternative. In M. B. Kovera (Ed.), *The psychology of juries* (pp. 207–226). Washington, DC: American Psychological Association.

Bornstein, B. H., & Greene, E. (2017). *The jury under fire: Myth, controversy, and reform*. New York: Oxford University Press.

Bottoms, B. L., Davis, S. L., & Epstein, M. A. (2004). Effects of victim and defendant race on jurors' decisions in child sexual abuse cases. *Journal of Applied Social Psychology, 34*, 1–33.

Bottoms, B. L., Peter-Hagene, L. C., Stevenson, M. C., Wiley, T. R., Mitchell, T. S., & Goodman, G. S. (2014). Explaining gender differences in jurors' reactions to child sexual assault cases. *Behavioral Sciences and the Law, 32*, 789–812.

Bourgeois, M. J., Horowitz, I. A., ForsterLee, L., & Grahe, J. (1995). Nominal and interactive groups: Effects of preinstruction and deliberations on decisions and evidence recall in complex trials. *Journal of Applied Psychology, 80*, 58–67.

Bright, D. A., & Goodman-Delahunty, J. (2006). Gruesome evidence and emotion: Anger, blame, and jury decision-making. *Law and Human Behavior, 30*, 183–202.

Cornwell, E. Y., & Hans, V. P. (2011). Representation through participation: A multilevel analysis of jury deliberations. *Law and Society Review, 45*, 667–698.

Cutler, B. L., Penrod, S. D., & Dexter, H. R. (1990). Juror sensitivity to eyewitness identification evidence. *Law and Human Behavior, 14*, 185–191.

Danziger, S., Levav, J., & Avnaim-Pesso, L. (2011). Extraneous factors in judicial decisions. *Proceedings of the National Academy of Sciences of the USA, 108*, 6889–6892.

Davis, J. H. (1973). Group decision and social interaction: A theory of social decision schemes. *Psychological Review, 80*, 97–125.

Davis, J. H., Kerr, N. L., Atkin, R. S., Holt, R., & Meek, D. (1975). The decision processes of 6- and 12-person mock juries assigned unanimous and two-thirds majority rules. *Journal of Personality and Social Psychology, 32*, 1–14.

Devine, D. J., & Caughlin, D. E. (2014). Do they matter?: A meta-analytic investigation of individual characteristics and guilt judgments. *Psychology, Public Policy, and Law, 20*, 109–134.

Devine, D. J., Clayton, L. D., Dunford, B. B., Seying, R., & Pryce, J. (2001). Jury decision making: 45 years of empirical research on deliberating groups. *Psychology, Public Policy, and Law, 7*, 622–727.

Devine, D. J., Krouse, P. C., Cavanaugh, C. M., & Basora, J. C. (2016). Evidentiary, extraevidentiary, and deliberation process predictors of real jury verdicts. *Law and Human Behavior, 40*, 670–682.

Devine, D. J., Olafson, K. M., Jarvis, L. L., Bott, J. P., Clayton, L. D., & Wolfe, J. M. (2004). Explaining jury verdicts: Is leniency bias for real? *Journal of Applied Social Psychology, 34*, 2069–2098.

Diamond, S. S. (1997). Illuminations and shadows from jury simulations. *Law and Human Behavior, 21*, 561–571.

Diamond, S. S. (2013, July 15). Zimmerman trial: Time to reconsider six-member jury. *Miami Herald*.

Diamond, S. S., & Casper, J. D. (1992). Blindfolding the jury to verdict consequences: Damages, experts, and the civil jury. *Law and Society Review, 26*, 513–563.

Diamond, S. S., Murphy, B., & Rose, M. R. (2012). The kettleful of law in real jury deliberations: Successes, failures, and next steps. *Northwestern University Law Review, 106*, 1537–1608.

Diamond, S. S., Rose, M. R., & Murphy, B. (2005). Revisiting the unanimity requirement: The behavior of the non-unanimous civil jury. *Northwestern University Law Review, 100,* 201–230.

Diamond, S. S., Vidmar, N., Rose, M., & Ellis, L. (2003). Juror discussions during civil trials: Studying an Arizona innovation. *University of Arizona Law Review, 45,* 1–81.

Dodson, C. S., & Dobolyi, D. G. (2015). Misinterpreting eyewitness expressions of confidence: The featural justification effect. *Law and Human Behavior, 39,* 266–280.

Dovidio, J. F., & Gaertner, S. L. (2004). Aversive racism. *Advances in Experimental Social Psychology, 36,* 1–52.

Ecker, U. K., Lewandowsky, S., & Tang, D. T. (2010). Explicit warnings reduce but do not eliminate the continued influence of misinformation. *Memory and Cognition, 38,* 1087–1100.

Eisenberg, T., Hannaford-Agor, P. L., Hans, V. P., Waters, N. L., Munsterman, G. T., Schwab, S. J., et al. (2005). Judge–jury agreement in criminal cases: A partial replication of Kalven and Zeisel's *The American Jury. Journal of Empirical Legal Studies, 2,* 171–207.

Ellsworth, P. C. (1989). Are twelve heads better than one? *Law and Contemporary Problems, 52,* 205–224.

Feigenson, N., & Park, J. (2006). Emotions and attributions of legal responsibility and blame: A research review. *Law and Human Behavior, 30,* 143–161.

Festinger, L. (1964). *Conflict, decision, and dissonance.* Stanford, CA: Stanford University Press.

Haegerich, T. M., Salerno, J. M., & Bottoms, B. L. (2013). Are the effects of juvenile offender stereotypes maximized or minimized by jury deliberation? *Psychology, Public Policy, and Law, 19,* 81–97.

Hastie, R., Penrod, S., & Pennington, N. (1983). *Inside the jury.* Clark, NJ: Lawbook Exchange.

Henderson, K. S., & Levett, L. M. (2016). Can expert testimony sensitize jurors to variations in confession evidence? *Law and Human Behavior, 40,* 638–649.

Hirst, W., & Stone, C. B. (2017). The effects of collaborative remembering on trial verdicts. In M. B. Kovera (Ed.), *The psychology of juries* (pp. 37–57). Washington, DC: American Psychological Association.

Horowitz, I. A. (1988). Jury nullification: The impact of judicial instructions, arguments, and challenges on jury decision making. *Law and Human Behavior, 12,* 439–453.

Horowitz, I. A., & Bordens, K. S. (2002). The effects of jury size, evidence complexity, and note taking on jury process and performance in a civil trial. *Journal of Applied Psychology, 87,* 121–130.

Jay, A., Salerno, J. M., & Ross, R. (2018). When hurt heroes do harm: Collective guilt and leniency toward war-veteran transgressors. *Psychiatry, Psychology and Law, 25,* 32–58.

J. E. B. v. Alabama, 511 U.S. 127 (1994).

Johnson v. Louisiana, 406 U.S. 356 (1972).

Jones, A. M., & Kovera, M. B. (2015). A demonstrative helps opposing expert testimony sensitize jurors to the validity of scientific evidence. *Journal of Forensic Psychology Practice, 15,* 401–422.

Jones, C. S., & Kaplan, M. F. (2003). The effects of racially stereotypical crimes on juror decision-making and information-processing strategies. *Basic and Applied Social Psychology, 25,* 1–13.

Kalven, H., Jr., & Zeisel, H. (1966). *The American jury.* Chicago: University of Chicago Press.

Kaplan, M. F. (1977). Discussion polarization effects in a modified jury decision paradigm: Informational influences. *Sociometry, 40,* 262–271.

Kaplan, M. F., & Miller, C. E. (1977). Judgments and group discussion: Effect of presentation and memory factors on polarization. *Sociometry, 40,* 337–343.

Kaplan, M. F., & Miller, C. E. (1987). Group decision making and normative versus informational influence: Effects of type of issue and assigned decision rule. *Journal of Personality and Social Psychology, 53,* 306–313.

Kaplan, M. F., & Miller, L. E. (1978). Reducing the effects of juror bias. *Journal of Personality and Social Psychology, 36,* 1443–1455.

Kassin, S. M. (2008). The psychology of confessions. *Annual Review of Law and Social Science, 4,* 193–217.

Kerr, N. L., & MacCoun, R. J. (2012). Is the leniency asymmetry really dead?: Misinterpreting asymmetry effects in criminal jury deliberation. *Group Processes and Intergroup Relations, 15,* 585–602.

King, K. A., & Nesbit, T. M. (2009). The empirical estimation of the cost-minimizing jury size and voting rule in civil trials. *Journal of Economic Behavior and Organization, 71,* 463–472.

Koehler, J. J., Schweitzer, N. J., Saks, M. J., & McQuiston, D. E. (2016). Science, technology, or the expert witness: What influences jurors' judgments about forensic science testimony? *Psychology, Public Policy, and Law, 22,* 401–413.

Kovera, M. B. (Ed.). (2017). *The psychology of juries.* Washington, DC: American Psychological Association.

Kovera, M. B., McAuliff, B. D., & Hebert, K. S. (1999). Reasoning about scientific evidence: Effects of juror gender and evidence quality on juror decisions in a hostile work environment case. *Journal of Applied Psychology, 84,* 362–375.

Laub, C. E., Kimbrough, C. D., & Bornstein, B. H. (2016). Mock juror perceptions of eyewitnesses vs. earwitnesses: Do safeguards help? *American Journal of Forensic Psychology, 34,* 33–56.

Leaper, C., & Ayres, M. M. (2007). A meta-analytic review of gender variations in adults' language use: Talkativeness, affiliative speech, and assertive speech. *Personality and Social Psychology Review, 11,* 328–363.

Levett, L. M., & Devine, D. (2017). Integrating individual and group models of juror decision making. In M. B. Kovera (Ed.), *The psychology of juries* (pp. 37–57). Washington, DC: American Psychological Association.

Levett, L. M., & Kovera, M. B. (2008). The effectiveness of opposing expert witnesses for educating jurors about unreliable expert evidence. *Law and Human Behavior, 32,* 363–374.

Lovis-McMahon, D. (2015). *Multilevel potential outcome models for causal inference in jury research* (Doctoral dissertation). Available from ProQuest Dissertations and Theses database. (UMI No. 3718690)

Lynch, M., & Haney, C. (2009). Capital jury deliberation: Effects on death sentencing, comprehension, and discrimination. *Law and Human Behavior, 33,* 481–496.

MacCoun, R. J. (2012). The burden of social proof: Shared thresholds and social influence. *Psychological Review, 119,* 345–372.

Maeder, E. M., & Pica, E. (2014). Secondary confessions: The influence (or lack thereof) of incentive size and scientific expert testimony on jurors' perceptions of informant testimony. *Law and Human Behavior, 38,* 560–568.

Marti, M. W., & Wissler, R. L. (2000). Be careful what you ask for: The effect of anchors on personal injury damages awards. *Journal of Experimental Psychology: Applied, 6,* 91–103.

Mazzella, R., & Feingold, A. (1994). The effects of physical attractiveness, race, socioeconomic status, and gender of defendants and victims on judgments of mock jurors: A meta-analysis. *Journal of Applied Social Psychology, 24,* 1315–1338.

McAuliff, B. D., & Bornstein, B. H. (2010). All anchors are not created equal: The effects of per diem versus lump sum requests on pain and suffering awards. *Law and Human Behavior, 34,* 164–174.

McKenzie, C. R., Lee, S. M., & Chen, K. K. (2002). When negative evidence increases confidence: Change in belief after hearing two sides of a dispute. *Journal of Behavioral Decision Making, 15,* 1–18.

McMillan, J. R., Clifton, A. K., McGrath, D., & Gale, W. S. (1977). Women's language: Uncertainty or interpersonal sensitivity and emotionality? *Sex Roles, 3,* 545–559.

Meissner, C. A., Brigham, J. C., & Pfeifer, J. E. (2003). Jury nullification: The influence of judicial instruction on the relationship between attitudes and juridic decision-making. *Basic and Applied Social Psychology, 25,* 243–254.

Miller, A. L., & Borgida, E. (2016). Moral typecasting underlies punitive responses to crime. *Law and Human Behavior, 40,* 697–706.

Miller, M. K., & Bornstein, B. H. (2004). Juror stress: Causes and interventions. *Thurgood Marshall Law Review, 30,* 237–270.

Mitchell, T., Haw, L., Pfeifer, R., & Meissner, M. (2005). Racial bias in mock juror decision-making: A meta-analytic review of defendant treatment. *Law and Human Behavior, 29,* 621–637.

Moscovici, S. (1980). Toward a theory of conversion behavior. *Advances in Experimental Social Psychology, 13,* 209–239.

Nadler, J. (2005). Flouting the law. *Texas Law Review, 83,* 1399–1441.

Nadler, J., & McDonnell, M. H. (2011). Moral character, motive, and the psychology of blame. *Cornell Law Review, 97,* 255–304.

Nemeth, C. J. (1986). Differential contributions of majority and minority influence. *Psychological Review, 93,* 23–32.

Nemeth, C. J. (2012). Minority influence theory. In P. A. M. Van Lange, A. W. Kruglanski, & E. T. Higgins (Eds.), *Handbook of theories of social psychology, Volume 2* (pp. 362–378). Thousand Oaks, CA: SAGE.

North Dakota Century Code Civil Judicial Procedure, N.D. Cent. Code, § 28-14-03.1 (2017). Available at *https://law.justia.com/codes/north-dakota/2017/title-28/chapter-28-14.*

Nuñez, N., Schweitzer, K., Chai, C. A., & Myers, B. (2015). Negative emotions felt during trial: The effect of fear, anger, and sadness on juror decision making. *Applied Cognitive Psychology, 29,* 200–209.

Ohtsubo, Y., Miller, C. E., Hayashi, N., & Masuchi, A. (2004). Effects of group decision rules on decisions involving continuous alternatives: The unanimity rule and extreme decisions in mock civil juries. *Journal of Experimental Social Psychology, 40,* 320–331.

Paternoster, R., & Deise, J. (2011). A heavy thumb on the scale: The effect of victim impact evidence on capital decision making. *Criminology, 49,* 129–161.

Payne v. Tennessee, 501 U.S. 808 (1991).

Pennington, N., & Hastie, R. (1986). Evidence evaluation in complex decision making. *Journal of Personality and Social Psychology, 51,* 242–258.

Pennington, N., & Hastie, R. (1992). Explaining the evidence: Tests of the Story Model for juror decision making. *Journal of Personality and Social Psychology, 62,* 189–206.

Peter-Hagene, L., & Bottoms, B. (2017). Attitudes, anger, and nullification instructions influence jurors' verdicts in euthanasia cases. *Psychology, Crime and Law, 23,* 983–1009.

Pritchard, M. E., & Keenan, J. M. (2002). Does jury deliberation really improve jurors' memories? *Applied Cognitive Psychology, 16,* 589–601.

Renaud, T. (2010). The biggest bully in the room. *Jury Expert, 22,* 23–26.

Reyna, V. F., Hans, V. P., Corbin, J. C., Yeh, R., Lin, K., & Royer, C. (2015). The gist of juries: Testing a model of damage award decision making. *Psychology, Public Policy, and Law, 21,* 280–294.

Reysen, M. B. (2007). The effects of social pressure on false memories. *Memory and Cognition, 35,* 59–65.

Richeson, J. A., & Trawalter, S. (2005). Why do interracial interactions impair executive function?: A resource depletion account. *Journal of Personality and Social Psychology, 88,* 934–947.

Rijnbout, J. S., & McKimmie, B. M. (2014). Deviance in organizational decision making: Using unanimous decision rules to promote the positive effects and alleviate the negative effects of deviance. *Journal of Applied Social Psychology, 44,* 455–463.

Robbennolt, J. K., & Studebaker, C. A. (1999). Anchoring in the courtroom: The effects of caps on punitive damages. *Law and Human Behavior, 23,* 353–373.

Rose, M. R., & Diamond, S. S. (2008). Judging bias: Juror confidence and judicial rulings on challenges for cause. *Law and Society Review, 42,* 513–549.

Rubenstein, A. M. (2006). Verdicts of conscience: Nullification and the modern jury trial. *Columbia Law Review, 106,* 959–993.

Ruva, C. L., & Guenther, C. C. (2017). Keep your bias to yourself: How deliberating with differently biased others affects mock-jurors' guilt decisions, perceptions of the defendant, memories, and evidence interpretation. *Law and Human Behavior, 41,* 478–493.

Saks, M. J. (1996). The smaller the jury, the greater the unpredictability. *Judicature, 79,* 263–265.

Saks, M. J., & Marti, M. W. (1997). A meta-analysis of the effects of jury size. *Law and Human Behavior, 21,* 451–467.

Saks, M. J., Schweitzer, N. J., Aharoni, E., & Kiehl, K. A. (2014). The impact of neuroimages in the sentencing phase of capital trials. *Journal of Empirical Legal Studies, 11,* 105–131.

Salerno, J. M. (2017). Seeing red: Disgust reactions to gruesome photographs in color (but not in black and white) increase convictions. *Psychology, Public Policy, and Law, 23,* 336–350.

Salerno, J. M., Bottoms, B. L., & Peter-Hagene, L. C. (2017). Individual versus group decision making: Jurors' reliance on central and peripheral information to evaluate expert testimony. *PLOS ONE, 12*(9), e0183580. Available at *https://journals.plos.org/plosone/article?id=10.1371/journal.pone.0183580.*

Salerno, J. M., & McCauley, M. R. (2009). Mock jurors' judgments about opposing scientific experts: Do cross-examination, deliberation and need for cognition matter? *American Journal of Forensic Psychology, 27,* 37–60.

Salerno, J. M., Murphy, M. C., & Bottoms, B. L. (2014). Give the kid a break—but only if he's straight: Retributive motives drive biases against gay youth in ambiguous punishment contexts. *Psychology, Public Policy, and Law, 20,* 398–410.

Salerno, J. M., & Peter-Hagene, L. C. (2013). The interactive effect of anger and disgust on moral outrage and judgments. *Psychological Science, 24,* 2069–2078.

Salerno, J. M., Peter-Hagene, L. C. (2015). One angry woman: Anger expression increases influence for men, but decreases influence for women, during group deliberation. *Law and Human Behavior, 39,* 581–592.

Salerno, J. M., Peter-Hagene, L. C., & Jay, A. C. (2017). Women and African Americans are less influential when they express anger during group decision making. *Group Processes and Intergroup Relations.*retrieved from *www. researchgate.net/publication/317022032_Women_and_African_Americans_are_less_influential_when_they_express_anger_during_group_decision_making.*

Schweitzer, N. J., & Saks, M. J. (2009). The gatekeeper effect: The impact of judges' admissibility decisions on the persuasiveness of expert testimony. *Psychology, Public Policy, and Law, 15,* 1–18.

Schweitzer, N. J., & Saks, M. J. (2011). Neuroimage evidence and the insanity defense. *Behavioral Sciences and the Law, 29,* 592–607.

Schweitzer, N. J., & Saks, M. J. (2012). Jurors and scientific causation: What don't they know, and what can be done about it? *Jurimetrics, 52,* 433–455.

Scurich, N., & John, R. S. (2013). Mock jurors' use of error rates in DNA database trawls. *Law and Human Behavior, 37,* 424–431.

Severance, L. J., Greene, E., & Loftus, E. F. (1984). Toward criminal jury instructions that jurors can understand. *Journal of Criminal Law and Criminology, 75,* 198–233.

Simon, D. (2004). A third view of the black box: Cognitive coherence in legal decision making. *University of Chicago Law Review,71,* 511–586.

Simon, D. (2012). *In doubt: The psychology of the criminal justice process.* Cambridge, MA: Harvard University Press.

Simon, D., Snow, C. J., & Read, S. J. (2004). The redux of cognitive consistency theories: Evidence judgments by constraint satisfaction. *Journal of Personality and Social Psychology, 86,* 814–837.

Simon, D., Stenstrom, D. M., & Read, S. J. (2015). The coherence effect: Blending cold and hot cognitions. *Journal of Personality and Social Psychology, 109,* 369–394.

Sommers, S. R. (2006). On racial diversity and group decision making: Identifying multiple effects of racial composition on jury deliberations. *Journal of Personality and Social Psychology, 90,* 597–612.

Sommers, S. R., & Douglass, A. B. (2007). Context matters: Alibi strength varies according to evaluator perspective. *Legal and Criminological Psychology, 12,* 41–54.

Sommers, S. R., & Ellsworth, P. C. (2000). Race in the courtroom: Perceptions of guilt and dispositional attributions. *Personality and Social Psychology Bulletin, 26,* 1367–1379.

Sommers, S. R., & Norton, M. I. (2007). Race-based judgments, race-neutral justifications: Experimental examination of peremptory use and the Batson challenge procedure. *Law and Human Behavior, 31,* 261–273.

Sporer, S. L., Penrod, S., Read, D., & Cutler, B. (1995). Choosing, confidence, and accuracy: A meta-analysis of the confidence-accuracy relation in eyewitness identification studies. *Psychological Bulletin, 118,* 315–327.

State v. McClendon, 248 Conn. 572 (1999).

Sweeney, A., & Dizikes, C. (2013, March 27). The balancing act of jury selection. *Chicago Tribune.* Retrieved from *http://articles.chicagotribune.com/2013-03-27.*

Thompson, W. C., & Newman, E. J. (2015). Lay understanding of forensic statistics: Evaluation of random match probabilities, likelihood ratios, and verbal equivalents. *Law and Human Behavior, 39,* 332–349.

Thompson, W. C., Scurich, N., Dioso-Villa, R., & Velazquez, B. (2017). Evaluating negative forensic evidence: When do jurors treat absence of evidence as evidence of absence? *Journal of Empirical Legal Studies, 14,* 569–591.

Tiedens, L. Z., & Linton, S. (2001). Judgment under emotional certainty and uncertainty: The effects of specific emotions on information processing. *Journal of Personality and Social Psychology, 81,* 973–988.

United States Courts. (2016). U.S. District Courts—Civil cases terminated, by nature of suit and action taken, during the 12-month period ending December 31, 2016 [Table C-4]. *Statistical Tables for the Federal Judiciary.* Retrieved from *www.uscourts.gov/statistics/table/c-4/statistical-tables-federal-judiciary/2016/12/31.*

United States v. Dougherty, 473 F. 2d 1113 (1972).

United States v. Montgomery. 150 F. 3d 983 (1998).

Votruba, A. M., Braver, S. L., Ellman, I. M., & Fabricius, W. V. (2014). Moral intuitions about fault, parenting, and child custody after divorce. *Psychology, Public Policy, and Law, 20,* 251–262.

Wegner, D. M., Schneider, D. J., Carter, S. R., & White, T. L. (1987). Paradoxical effects of thought suppression. *Journal of Personality and Social Psychology, 53,* 5–13.

Weitzer, R., & Tuch, S. A. (2005). Racially biased policing: Determinants of citizen perceptions. *Social Forces, 83,* 1009–1030.

Weldon, M. S., & Bellinger, K. D. (1997). Collective memory: Collaborative and individual processes in remembering. *Journal of Experimental Psychology: Learning, Memory, and Cognition, 23,* 1160–1175.

Wiley, T. R., & Bottoms, B. L. (2009). Effects of defendant sexual orientation on jurors' perceptions of child sexual assault. *Law and Human Behavior, 33,* 46–60.

Williams v. Florida. 399 U.S. 78 (1970).

Woestehoff, S. A., & Meissner, C. A. (2016). Juror sensitivity to false confession risk factors: Dispositional vs. situational attributions for a confession. *Law and Human Behavior, 40,* 564–579.

CHAPTER 15

Aggression, Violence, and Psychopathy

Devon L. L. Polaschek

Aggression and violence are ubiquitous to humanity, albeit that, despite the keen awareness of danger cultivated by media reporting, we have never lived in a less violent time (Pinker, 2011). Violence is an intriguing problem for psychological study, both because of this ubiquity and because definitions of violence span the extremes, from terrorist mass murders, torture, and drone strikes to the actions of professional athletes on and off the field, to unpleasant verbal altercations in close relationships.

The primary focus of this chapter is on the relevance of both violence and psychopathy in the criminal justice system, which inevitably leads us to those who are of most societal concern for their violent behavior. Specifically, this chapter is mainly about *high-risk violent offenders;* this term defines a small subgroup of the community that is distinctive for its repetitive use of criminal forms of aggression and violence in the context of careers devoted to general law breaking. The chapter first considers how criminal violence fits into wider definitions of violence and aggression, before introducing the two strands of theory and research that contextualize the behavior of high-risk violent offenders: the social psychology of aggression and developmental theories of persistent criminal violence. The next sections focus on criminal perpetrators: understanding the risks they pose and approaches to ameliorating those risks to reduce the likelihood of crime and violence. Finally, because high-risk violent offenders also are typically high on psychopathy, the chapter ends by examining the relevance of psychopathy to the criminal justice system and to high-risk violent offenders in particular.

DEFINITIONS OF AGGRESSION AND VIOLENCE

Within the discipline of psychology, social psychology has led the way in defining and researching aggression. The most widely accepted definition is "any form of behavior directed toward the goal of harming or injuring another living being who is motivated to avoid such treatment" (Baron & Richardson, 1994, p. 7), where "harm" is defined as causing physical injury or hurt feelings, damaging a person's image, reputation, or social relationships, and stealing or damaging valued possessions, other people, or animals owned by the person. Therefore, the essential elements of aggressive behavior are that (1) it is understood and intended by the actor to harm or injure, regardless of whether that intent is realized, and (2) the recipient has not consented to and does not accept the imposition of the harm (Krahé, 2013). This latter portion of the definition thus rules out surgery, for instance, and consenting sadistic sexual practices.

Defining violence is more challenging. Violence is a leading cause of death, serious injury, and psychological trauma, and therefore a public health issue. The World Health Organization's definition is broad: "the intentional use of physical force or power, threatened or actual, against oneself, another person, or against a group or community, that either results in or has a high likelihood of resulting in injury, death, psychological harm, maldevelopment or deprivation" (Krug, Dahlberg, Mercy, Zwi, & Lozano,, 2002, p. 5), and provides a typology of 38 types of violence that includes suicide and self-harm, and collective forms such as social, political, and economic.

Many types of aggression are not illegal, and even fatal violence can be legal under some circumstances (e.g., war, self-defense). However, criminal violence, by definition, is illegal. Criminal violence is a subset of aggression. It includes a core of acts widely agreed to comprise violence, such as intentional killing, but also some that may be illegal in one culture or time but not in another (Tolan, 2007). In contrast to definitions of violence used in other subdomains of psychology (e.g., Anderson & Bushman, 2002; Warburton & Anderson, 2018), criminal violence is not limited to acts that reliably cause serious physical or emotional harm. The most serious types of criminal violence, such as grievous assaults or homicide, are intended to—and do—cause serious physical injury and even death. But minor assaults and offenses involving threats of harm, such as in aggravated robbery, are included as well. Depending on the jurisdiction, acts of property damage, intimidation, public fighting between men, and so on may also be included. More recently, stalking, cyberbullying, acts intended to cause psychological harm without physical injury (e.g., in families), and smacking children for disciplinary purposes are now subject to legal sanctions in some jurisdictions, thus widening the definition. Placing criminal violence in a wider context helps to identify some of the challenges of working with violent offenders: Violence and aggression are commonplace, hitting people remains an Olympic sport, and noncriminalized and minor criminal forms

of violence are widely tolerated. The legal system is charged with identifying and responding to both the tiny minority of aggressive and violent acts
that are brought to its attention and the equally small proportion of people
who are overinvolved in committing violent acts. A focus on criminal violence requires us to examine behavior that is *both* intended to harm *and*
law violating—a complexity that is not always reflected in psychological
approaches to explaining violent offending (Felson, 2014).

THEORIES OF AGGRESSION

Theories of aggression have two main phenomena to explain: why individual people vary in their propensity for aggressive behavior, and the
key determinants of a specific violent event. A widely accepted theoretical
explanation for each of these is contained in the general aggression model
(GAM; Anderson & Bushman, 2002).

Development of Propensity for Aggression

The GAM integrates several strands of social psychology theory together
to explain how individual differences in aggressiveness develop. The first
is one of the most influential theories in psychology: social learning theory (SLT; Bandura, 1973), which over time evolved into social cognitive
theory (Bandura, 1986). When (1) aggressive behavior is modeled, (2) the
model is reinforced for the behavior, and (3) observers believe that they are
capable of enacting the modeled behavior and that *they* will be reinforced
for it, they may imitate the behavior. Over time the behavior may become
entrenched, especially because of our capacity to deliver self-reinforcement,
such as positive self-talk, and to disengage morally from reprehensible acts
(Bandura, Barbaranelli, Caprara, & Pastorelli, 1996).

In the GAM, SLT is integrated with social and social-cognitive theories
to explain how individual differences in aggressiveness develop. Exposure
to aggressive and violent behavior enhances the development of various
aggression-supportive cognitive structures (Anderson & Bushman, 2002).
These structures include beliefs and attitudes (e.g., normalizing aggression), perceptual schemas (e.g., the hostile attribution bias), expectation
schemas (e.g., expecting aggression from others), behavioral scripts (tem-
plates for how to respond to insults, resolve conflicts, etc.), and desensitiza-
tion to aggression. Over time, these structures become automated, lead to
changes in personality, and take on an active role in the processing of social
situations.

Modeling Aggressive Events

The second phenomenon to explain is an individual aggressive event: the
GAM draws on both the above-mentioned personality differences and on

theories and research on situational factors for this explanation. Social-psychological research indicates that key situational factors that increase the likelihood of violence include alcohol, physical pain, heat, noxious stimuli, anonymity, provocation, recent exposure to violent media, and recent exposure to weapons. In fact, even pictures of weapons prime aggressive cognition and make aggression more likely (Anderson, Benjamin, & Bartholow, 1998).

These situational and person-based inputs feed three distinct routes—affective, cognitive, and arousal-based—to the final outcome in an event model: aggressive or nonaggressive action. These routes are referred to collectively as the person's *present internal state*. The affective route is the most familiar: reflecting increases in anger and hostility. But other forms of negative affect, such as anxiety or feeling down, can be a route to aggression, too. Less intuitive is the arousal route. Drawing on excitation transfer theory (Zillman, 1988), the GAM's event-based model recognizes that arousal caused by experiences such as physical exercise or hot weather can be misidentified as anger-based in the presence of provocation, leading to the perception that the stimulus was far more provoking than if the person had been calm at the time. All three modes—cognitive, affective, and arousal—typically interact with each other. In cognitive-behavioral treatment models, the idea that cognition guides affect and behavior is widely accepted, but research underpinning the GAM reminds lawyers, judges, correctional staff, and therapists that arousal and affect can alter cognition, too, creating complex loops of reciprocal action.

This internal state feeds a series of appraisal and decision-making processes that vary in both their speed and quality. Under time pressure, appraisals are rapid and automatic and may lead to aggression if the immediate impression is that the outcome would be satisfying. With more time, and more self-regulatory capacity, a more effortful, conscious reappraisal may occur. The person may actively look for an alternative view of the situation based on relevant memories or information from the scene about likely causes, and so on, which in turn may alter the present internal state. There can be a number of cycles of evaluating alternative inferences and discarding them. At some point, the person will reach a final appraisal and then will act; but the outcome may still be aggressive and committed in a state of high arousal.

To illustrate this event-based portion in the GAM, I have elaborated on an example popular in violent offender treatment, precisely because it captures the processes well. Dave, a person with a violent history, is bumped from behind in a crowded room at a party. He whirls around to see who it is, prepared to fight and instantaneously emotionally aroused. But before he can act he sees it's a man he knew as an acquaintance years ago. They chat briefly, he calms down and thinks no more of it. Then later he sees the man talking with a rival gang member, and at the same time, a friend comes up to Dave and says the man is boasting about having confronted

Dave, who did not respond; "he thinks you're getting soft," the friend says. Dave quickly becomes angry again, now regarding the man's behavior as a type of direct affront to his status for which a violent response is expected. But Dave is on parole, so it's important not to make a scene and get arrested. He quietly seethes and plots, waiting for the man to leave the house. When he does, Dave goes outside and assaults him. He's still angry about the insult, still thinks he needs to retaliate, but in control of himself enough now to choose thoughtfully where and when to act.

The event-based model (Anderson & Bushman, 2002) can accommodate a wide range of factors involved in aggressive and criminally violent behavior, making it useful for offender self-management strategies (see later discussion). The person-based part of the model—the development of aggressive personality—is somewhat limited in that it gives a heavy emphasis to the development of aggression-specific cognitive structures, whereas the research on high-risk violent offenders would suggest that a wider range of factors lead to between-person variations in readiness to aggress, including attitudes and beliefs derived from a general criminal lifestyle.

Hostile versus Instrumental Aggression

As I noted earlier, aggression can be classified into many different types. In psychology, especially in clinical psychology, the most highly regarded typological distinction is between *expressive* (also called *affective, reactive,* or *hostile*) aggression and instrumental or *proactive* aggression (Buss, 1961). Affective aggression has harm as its goal, is driven by anger, and is often viewed as impulsive, reactive, and retaliatory. It is a type of reflexive "lashing out" that reflects a loss of self-control capacity. Instrumental or proactive aggression is premeditated, with a goal beyond immediate victim harm, such as gaining material goods, addressing damage to one's social standing, or dispensing justice. This distinction has legal implications, because the law considers evidence of premeditation versus provocation to have probative value (Fontaine, 2008), leading violent offenders to deemphasize the premeditative aspects of their offending because premeditation makes them seem more culpable (Laurell, Belfrage, & Hellström, 2014).

But the distinction between the types quickly comes apart in practice, and social psychologists have argued that there is no need for a separate model for affective aggression, at least not for human behavior (Bushman & Anderson, 2001). Consider the Dave scenario above, for example. Dave is insulted and ruminates angrily about how to restore his social status, choosing a tried and true method that also hides him from detection. Afterward he feels relieved and satisfied. Is his behavior affective or instrumental? Goal setting is more nuanced and complex than this distinction recognizes. Behavior can be underpinned by more than one goal at a time, and it is important to distinguish between proximate, immediate goals ("to harm . . . ") and ultimate goals ("in order to achieve" . . .). In addition, the

expressive–instrumental distinction confounds types of cognitive processing with types of aggression. For example, instrumental aggression can
be driven by automated processes, especially for experienced aggressors,
drawing on scripts to rapidly enact aggressive behavior. The concept of
planned impulsivity has been used to refer to this behavior, because the
perpetrator can claim a lack of premeditation, when in fact the only spontaneous part of the behavior is the decision to carry it out *here* and *now*
(Pithers, 1990). Conversely, anger is not uniquely associated with expressive aggression. Several distinct roles for anger can be delineated in relation to aggression (Bushman & Anderson, 2001); for example, becoming
angry (1) because of a perceived transgression by the victim and seeking to
put that right through force, (2) while thwarted in the violent attainment
of other people's property, leading to a severe beating of the victim, or (3)
because the victim is not responding to physical "disciplining" with the
"right" reaction. And even reactive aggression is often carried out after
meaningful decision making on the part of the offender, not in a mindless,
or "knee-jerk" way (Felson, 2014). One implication of arguing for the integration of these types of aggression is that there is no argument for distinct
intervention approaches to different forms of violence.

THEORIES OF CRIMINAL VIOLENCE

The GAM has been applied to criminal violence, but the preferred theories
of criminal violence have been primarily developmental.

Extending the General Aggression Model

Several authors have applied or extended the GAM to explain criminal violence. First, DeWall, Anderson, and Bushman (2011) outlined four applications of the GAM: to intimate partner violence, to group or internecine
violence, to climate change, and to suicide. This application to intimate
partner violence is somewhat narrow in that the authors assume that when
sufficient time is available for thoughtful processing, the perpetrator will
choose a nonaggressive option; but, as I noted above, this is not a "given"
if the person still reaches the conclusion that aggression is useful or justified. The application to intergroup violence may have some portability to
gang warfare, a pervasive concern for criminal justice systems, though the
examples given by DeWall et al. (2011) are ethnic or nation-based. Second,
Warburton and Anderson (2018) give a much more detailed account of the
application of the GAM to intimate partner violence.

Finally, a review by Gilbert and Daffern (2010) supports the relevance
of the aggression-related knowledge structures described in the person-
based portion of the GAM. Though their review noted the limited body of
research on the psychological treatment of violent offenders, it supported

the idea that programs for violent offenders need to be more specialized (possibly even individualized) to adequately address the degree of entrenchment and the range of cognitive factors built into the GAM.

Developmental Theories of Criminal Violence

These theories of aggression are probably incomplete as explanations for violent offenders' behavior, because those who use violence the most tend also to be experienced and versatile criminals. For example, in the Dunedin Multidisciplinary Study cohort, 18-year-old men with violence convictions also had almost four times as many convictions as those with no violence convictions (Henry, Caspi, Moffitt, & Silva, 1996). Although there is some evidence for specialization in violent offending (Lynam, Piquero, & Moffitt, 2004), violence specialists and chronic versatile offenders have more in common with each other than they do with nonviolent and nonoffenders.

Furthermore, their violent behavior often emerges after the establishment of a more general criminal repertoire, suggesting that some of the relevant etiological factors come from general criminal development. For example, as Lynam et al. put it: "violence in an individual's criminal history is an important factor that marks a subgroup of offenders who begin [crime] early and are characterized by a particular set of personality traits" (2004, pp. 225–226). So, to explain the violence of this subgroup more completely, we turn to developmental and lifespan criminology and to longitudinal cohort studies.

The concept of criminal propensity assumes that offenders are generalists and that, for the most part, the biological, psychological, and social factors that predict criminal involvement are predictive of a wide range of crimes for a particular individual. An individual's *criminal propensity* refers to the psychological features people take with them from situation to situation that increase *their* risk of crime in contrast to others. In adults, high levels of criminal propensity are usually the result of an extended and somewhat distinctive developmental process, which for the most prolific and violently criminal individuals may begin at or soon after conception (Caspi, Roberts, & Shiner, 2005). The process is distinctive in the sense that it stands out in contrast to healthy development, but not in the sense that its only outcome is increased criminal risk. It culminates in a wide variety of social and health disparities (Odgers et al., 2008).

Moffitt's (1993) *life-course-persistent* antisocial syndrome is the most popular theory of this type. It weaves together adverse temperamental, neurocognitive, and social factors with learning theory into mechanisms for the development of this propensity over time. Her account of the development and functioning of life-course-persistent offenders maps closely onto what is known from research on persistent and violent criminals. According to Moffitt, life-course-persistent offenders are born already at increased risk of antisocial behavior, mediated through the neuropsychology of infants' nervous systems (Moffitt, 1993).

Consistent with Moffitt's theorizing, variations in neuropsychological functioning, defined as *lack of control*—"an inability to modulate impulsive expression, impersistence in problem solving, as well as sensitivity to stress and challenge that is expressed in affectively charged negative reactions" (Caspi, Henry, McGee, Moffitt, & Silva, 1995, p. 59)—measured as early as 3 and 5 years old predicted violence convictions at 18 years in men in the Dunedin Multidisciplinary Health and Development study. Disadvantageous family factors (e.g., birth socioeconomic status [SES], parental authoritarianism, the quality of family relationships), more conventionally regarded as causes of crime, predicted both violent and other convictions (Henry et al., 1996). These results support the idea that in life-course-persistent offenders, both temperament and social factors underpin the propensity for violence, but social factors underpin the propensity for nonviolent crime. The work of Moffitt and colleagues also draws attention to the large number of risk factors that may contribute to criminal propensity in these offenders.

Moffitt's theory provides an elegant and appealing psychological account of the development of criminal propensity in the most persistently criminal individuals and is well supported by subsequent research (Moffitt, 2003; Odgers et al., 2008; Piquero, Farrington, Nagin, & Moffitt, 2010). Still, its ability to account for behavior beyond the early years of adulthood has been questioned, with some preferring the term "early-onset stable antisocial behavior" to "life-course-persistent" (Hodgins, 2007), to reflect diverse possibilities for desistance. Later environmental events (e.g., successful employment or relationships) can and do influence (im)persistence (Sivertsson & Carlsson, 2015). Furthermore, most high-risk violent offenders show improvements in criminal and other outcomes later in life, albeit slowly (Farrington et al., 2006), and the theory does not address the important question of how desistance and other positive life outcomes occur or develop.

The Cambridge Study in Delinquent Development independently supports Moffitt's theory about common pathways to persistent crime and violence. It has shown that those adults with violence convictions tend to have started offending earlier, have most of their convictions for nonviolence (versatility), and have more convictions overall than those with no violence convictions (Farrington, 2007). Triangulating further, New Zealand research has also found that the majority of a prisoner sample identified as being at high risk of future violence and crime reported that their early development was consistent with the life-course-persistent profile (Cahill, Polaschek, & Wilson, 2012).

These well-established links between life-course versatile and persistent criminality and violent offending make Farrington's integrated cognitive antisocial potential (ICAP) theory (Farrington, 2003) another relevant framework for perpetrators of criminally violent behavior (Farrington, 2007). The ICAP was designed first and foremost to explain offending in young men of low SES. It draws together research findings with ideas from many different sociological and psychological theories. The ICAP describes the potential of an offender to commit criminal acts (i.e., criminal propensity), and this potential varies both over time and across people. Variations across people in "trait" criminal propensity are explained by factors that differ from those that explain short-term variations in antisocial potential. The two interact for those who commit violent and other criminal acts the most.

As the top portion of Figure 15.1 (p. 376) shows, childhood and adolescent development of trait dispositions and vulnerabilities feed into criminal propensity in high-risk violent offenders. The bottom portion shows the circumstantial or situational factors that can trigger a specific offense, whether violent or otherwise, given individual and stable differences in criminal propensity. Figure 15.1 shows that ICAP resembles a combination of the GAM personality and event models.

UNDERSTANDING AND EVALUATING ADULT OFFENDERS' PROPENSITIES FOR CRIME AND VIOLENCE

There are three major components to the work done by psychologists and others with violent offenders in the criminal justice system: (1) estimating the current risks to others posed by an offender, (2) understanding the psychological and social factors that underpin risks, and (3) designing and implementing interventions to reduce or manage risks. The previous sections on theories of aggression, crime, and violence provide a basis for understanding why some people have more potential for antisocial and harmful behavior than others, likely factors that contribute to that potential, and to some extent how difficult or easy to modify they may be in an active offender.

Actuarial Assessment of Risk

Tools to improve accuracy of estimation of a person's level of risk were first developed over 30 years ago and are still widely used (see Monahan & Skeem, 2014). These assessment tools use an actuarial method, predominantly based on historic and demographic information, or static factors, such as age of first conviction and current age. This information has little inherent psychological meaning; such items are markers of more meaningful processes such as those contained in the preceding theories. The underlying processes—which are much harder to measure than history and demographic factors—are themselves often slow to change without direct intervention, which helps to explain the continuity of aggressive, violent, and criminal behavior over time.

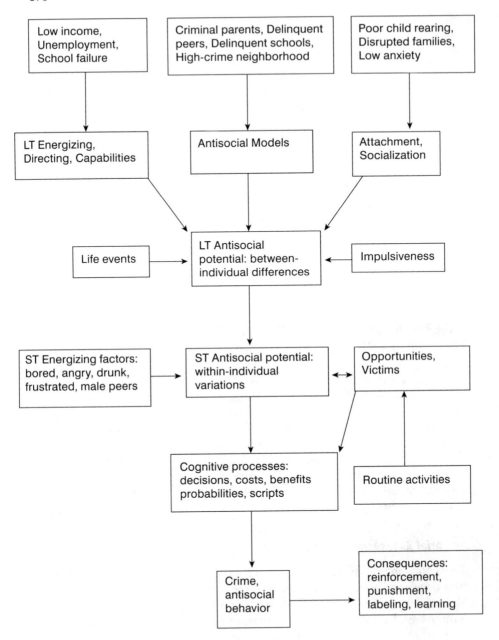

FIGURE 15.1. Farrington's integrated cognitive antisocial potential (ICAP) theory. LT, long-term; ST, short-term. From Farrington (2003). Copyright 2003 by American Society of Criminology. Reprinted by permission.

Actuarial methods for assessing risk share the ability to be scored and for the score then to be compared with those of a range of other offenders—ideally thousands of them—whose subsequent recidivism, or absence of new convictions, has already been established for some time interval after the score was calculated. Scores are often categorized into bands such as high, medium, and low risk. People with persistent and violent criminality will often be categorized as high risk for much of their criminal careers, regardless of the types of risk factors included in the scale.

Actuarial scales based on static factors are widely used, and some are scored automatically, using computer algorithms. They are helpful in making decisions quickly about large numbers of individuals: for allocating levels of resources needed to safely manage a person or whether to give parole. But they provide little guidance about what to monitor or how to reduce risk for a specific person.

There are two other classes of more changeable—dynamic—risk factors. Stable factors are somewhat durable adult psychological dispositions. They are more psychologically meaningful. They make up the "LT antisocial potential" box in the middle of the ICAP model in Figure 15.1, and examples of these factors (and ideas for reducing their strength) appear in Table 15.1. When these traits interact with certain external triggers, such as losing one's job or an encounter with antisocial peer, or with other environmental sources of risk, such as heat or sources of pain (e.g., a heavy object falling on one's foot), the interaction creates an acute risk state in which the person is temporarily at heightened risk for some type of offense. The combination of stable dynamic factors, triggering events, and acute dynamic states is essentially a model of an offender's most current level of risk of reconviction, what underpins it psychologically, and the circumstances in which it may become high or very high (Beech & Ward, 2004).

For example, Eli, a high-risk offender with temperamental negative emotionality and generally poor self-control (commonly occurring stable dynamic risk factors), is more likely to react to a setback such as unexpectedly losing his job (trigger) with strong negative affect. Instead of talking to a helpful friend or working out some logical next steps for seeking employment, Eli heads for home in a really bad mood (acute dynamic risk factor), picks a fight with his girlfriend, and goes off on a drinking spree. In this even more acutely risky state—angry, drunk, thinking hostile thoughts about his girlfriend and his employer, and possibly in a bar surrounded by like-minded people—he is much more likely to commit a variety of violent offenses than he was at the beginning of the day.

Scales with stable dynamic risk factors or a mix of stable and static factors can also be scored and used actuarially (e.g., the Level of Service/Case Management Inventory; Andrews, Bonta, & Wormith, 2004). Usually this process is more resource intensive, because stable factors require more training and oversight to score reliably. Once the score is determined,

TABLE 15.1. Common Dynamic Risk Factors for Persistent Violence and Criminality (and Strategies for Their Remediation)

- Emotional regulation difficulties (distress tolerance, mindfulness, relaxation training)
- Offense-supportive beliefs (cognitive restructuring, thought records, behavioral experiments)
- Criminal friends and associates (strategies for managing risks posed by continued association, skills for developing and enhancing prosocial supports)
- Poor self-control, lack of long-term goals, and tendency to act without thinking things through ("impulsivity"; identifying most important goals and values, cost–benefit analyses, distress tolerance, problem solving)
- Alcohol and/or drug abuse (specific alcohol and drug treatments oriented toward moderation or abstinence, emotional regulation strategies, mindfulness, self-control training, relapse prevention)
- A preference for aggressive methods of communication (positive communication skills and assertiveness training, nonaggressive conflict resolution).
- Inability to maintain a stable, prosocial intimate relationship (relationship and communication skills, problem solving, and nonviolent conflict resolution)
- Inability to maintain a positive work ethic and engagement in the workforce or in education (identifying preferred work activities, specific vocational skills training, goal setting, self-regulation, impulse control, problem solving, communication skills)
- Aimless use of leisure time (goal setting, employment, identifying valued activities, planning structured day)
- Little or no prosocial community support (assistance in developing relationships with key community agencies that can provide needed support, remediation of dysfunctional family relationships, rebuilding relationships with prosocial family members or friends, developing structured plans with them for needed support)
- Few or no plans for managing high-risk situations (developing understanding of pathways to offending, identifying and developing resources and plans for acute risk management).
- Noncompliance with sentence requirements (self-control skills, cost–benefit analyses, prosocial relationship-building skills, problem solving, commitment to prosocial lifestyle)

as for any actuarial scale, reference to established norms identifies the estimated risk level (see Wong & Gordon, 2006, for an example).

Scales that measure stable factors have immediate relevance for rehabilitation programs, which aim to reduce the strength of these factors. If stable factors change, the offender's interactions with environmental triggers will also change, making acute states less problematic and less frequent (Richards, Wilson, Robson, & Polaschek, 2017). Therefore, dynamic risk assessments help to identify treatment targets for this offender and which programs might be the best fit to those targets.

Acute factors are not worthwhile targets for longer term change because of their fleeting nature, but instead they provide the basis for crisis management plans. For example, a probation officer who detects a recent increase in acute factors (e.g., mounting financial problems, depressed mood) may in turn immediately increase active monitoring and support for that offender. One scale designed for this sort of dynamic management of offenders in the community is the Dynamic Risk Assessment for Offender Re-entry (DRAOR; Serin, 2007; Serin, Mailloux, & Wilson, 2012), which includes stable, protective, and acute risk factors. Research on the DRAOR has shown it is sensitive to changes in risk state that have implications for offenders' day-to-day management (Polaschek & Yesberg, 2018).

The empirical definition of a stable dynamic risk factor variable is both that it is changeable and that change will correspond to a change in recidivism probability (Douglas & Skeem, 2005). Some risk instruments have been constructed purposefully to detect and document change in stable dynamic risk factors. One such instrument, the Violence Risk Scale (Wong & Gordon, 2006), has been used to demonstrate that treatment gains on stable dynamic risk for violence significantly reduced the likelihood of violence reconviction in a sample of high-risk violent prisoners who were paroled after treatment (Lewis, Olver, & Wong, 2013). The Violence Risk Scale is the basis for the factors listed in Table 15.1. Change on those factors is measured against the degree of engagement in change the offender shows during or after treatment or over some other period of time.

Static, stable, and acute risk factors are usually attributed to the person, but situational or environmental factors are also theorized to exacerbate or deactivate more trait-like or stable within-person factors, leading to a temporary increase or decrease in risk. Situational factors for violence in violent offenders have been little investigated. In a recent study based on prisoner self-report, the most common triggers for violence were arguments with nonintimate victims, followed by being hit by someone else (Freestone, Ullrich, & Coid, 2017). Together these accounted for more than 50% of the events studied. Examples of some situational factors are found in the bottom half of the IPCA (Figure 15.1). Situational factors are important in understanding why violent behavior occurs at a particular time and place. Attention to situational factors is useful when designing individual reintegration plans around avoiding high-risk situations.

Situational factors have also received attention in prison settings, where it is now well recognized that some units and institutions are far more violence-prone than others (Cooke, 2019). Based on research and experience, Cooke and colleagues devised the PRISM, a rating tool to evaluate relative strengths and weaknesses with regard to violence-proneness based on physical and security features, organizational factors, staff features, and what resources the institution provides for prisoners (e.g., visits, programs). A PRISM evaluation provides a clear direction for reducing violence risk in poorly scoring environments.

But the earlier example of Eli shows one of the limitations of relying too much on an environmental approach to managing the risk of any one offender: It can be subverted by human agency. Eli, whether intentionally or relatively unreflectively, took himself off into an environment where he has been comfortable in the past, as part of a habitual method of coping with triggering events and difficult emotions. It is also a violence-prone environment. A postintervention personal safety plan structured around low-risk situations, even when the offender is otherwise committed to it, can be cast aside by a habitual response to crisis that actually enhances rather than reduces the risk posed, when the offender intentionally transports him- or herself into a violence-prone environment (for related ideas, see the later section on posttreatment reintegration approaches).

REDUCING PROPENSITY FOR VIOLENCE AND OTHER CRIME: THE GENERAL APPROACH

The history of correctional intervention is replete with commonsense ideas that, when evaluated, turn out not to reduce reconviction risk (Gendreau, Smith, & Thériault, 2009). Even prison sentences, at best, have no effect on subsequent recidivism and may even increase risk for criminality after release (Cullen, Jonson, & Nagin, 2011). But since about the 1980s (e.g., Andrews, Bonta, & Hoge, 1990; Andrews, Zinger, et al., 1990), a steadily growing body of scientific research has resulted in the development of well-supported principles for designing psychological and other intervention programs that reduce the likelihood of participants committing new offenses.

Key developments by the "Canadian school" of criminological psychologists—Don Andrews, Jim Bonta, Paul Gendreau, Steve Wormith, and others (Cullen, 2002)—led to a still-growing body of research referred to as the "what works" principles, and the risk–need–responsivity (RNR) model. Their crucial insight was that it was not an intervention's label that determined whether it reduced recidivism but what went on "inside the box": for example, at the level of interpersonal interactions between staff and offenders. Over 30 years or so, this work has had the most profound impact of any psychological research—and arguably of any research findings—on the management of offenders. It has been used to design and implement numerous programs for offenders on community and custodial sentences. The most common format is a highly proscribed and manualized psychologically based group program of between 100 and 200 hours, delivered by trained and supervised nonpsychologists (McGuire et al., 2008). This response is unlikely to be sufficient to reduce risk in high-risk persistently violent offenders, but the RNR model still provides the scaffold for programs that may do so.

Treating High-Risk, Persistently Violent Criminals

High-risk violent offenders require a more complex, intensive, and multi-stage process of intervention, provided by more skilled and highly trained therapists to achieve sufficient change to reduce risk. RNR's risk principle states that those with the most substantial histories of offending should be a high priority for treatment because altering their risk will have the most effect.

But they also are the hardest to treat. A high level of current criminal propensity indicates a relatively large number of stable dynamic risk factors, such as those in Table 15.1. In the RNR model, these factors are criminogenic needs, and the need principle (the $\underline{N}$ in RNR) holds that these factors should be prioritized for treatment over others not empirically linked to recidivism. Programs that target such factors for change are likely to reduce criminal propensity and subsequent violence (Jolliffe & Farrington, 2007). Assessments of persistent and violent criminals using tools such as the Violence Risk Scale suggest that most dynamic risk factors are high in most cases (Polaschek, Yesberg, Bell, Casey, & Dickson, 2016).

Effective treatment of high-risk violent offenders requires not only that a program be intensive and address a wide range of dynamic risk factors for violence and crime, but also that it accommodate a third class of factors. Collectively, these factors relate to the RNR model's specific responsivity principle (the second $\underline{R}$), which states that interventions need to adapt themselves so that they engage with offenders "where they are." For example, temperament and childhood experiences translate into adult personality features that make these offenders challenging to work with (Polaschek & Daly, 2013). High-risk violent adult offenders are emotionally labile and angry, easily develop feelings of victimization, can be hostile and suspicious of others' motives, antagonistic and mean, aggressive, untrustworthy, egocentric, noncompliant, and uncommitted to change (Krueger et al., 1994; Lowenkamp & Latessa, 2004; Moffitt, Caspi, Harrington, & Milne, 2002; Moffitt, 2003; Ross, Fabiano, & Ewles, 1988).

RNR-based psychological treatments center on helping these offenders to master new skills that will enable them to live more satisfying prosocial lives, but the participants make challenging "students." They give up readily when they find tasks hard, and, just as they did as children, they often lack self-reflection and self-control (Cale, 2006). Their deficient verbal abilities, neuropsychological impairments, schooling history, and negative attitudes to new learning only make matters worse (Golden, Jackson, Peterson-Rohne, & Gontkovsky, 1996; Moffitt, Lynam, & Silva, 1994). Yet despite these challenges, men attending responsive programs can form strong therapeutic alliances and make commendable changes in behavior that help them to avoid reconviction (Lewis et al., 2013; Polaschek, 2011; Polaschek, 2019; Polaschek & Ross, 2010).

Psychological treatment programs that ameliorate dynamic risk factors have their roots in cognitive and behavioral therapy traditions. They are structured toward and concentrate on changing thinking and teaching skills for new, more prosocial behavior. They work to reduce risk by building strengths in persistent and violent offenders and are usually residentially and group-based and conducted over months, with at least 300–400 hours of formal treatment sessions. Typical programs have three phases (Polaschek & Kilgour, 2013; Wong & Gordon, 2013). The initial phase socializes participants to the treatment process, teaches group skills (e.g., giving and receiving feedback), and begins to build positive relationships between group members and facilitators. The middle portion concentrates on skill building, and the final phase prepares the attendee for life after the program (reintegration and relapse prevention; see the next section). A challenge in these programs is ensuring that new skills get enough practice, are reinforced, and generalize to other situations. Finally, many of these offenders have missed out on ordinary opportunities to behave as members of a community, theorized to be an essential experience for enhancing survival after release from a program (Whitehead, 2014), so some programs also work to create a change-supportive environment that not only enhances practice and generalization of skills but also simulates opportunities to take new roles in community life as far as possible.

Posttreatment Reintegration Approaches and Supporting Desistance

Desistance from crime is both a process and an outcome: Rehabilitative interventions for people with high levels of criminal propensity usually represent just one piece of their often-zigzagging desistance pathway (Burnett, 1992). Institutional systems that provide rehabilitative interventions have given more recognition in recent years to the importance of helping graduates with postprogram support and strategies to enhance success. Weakening the influence of Moffitt's (1993) concept of *snares*—consequences of convictions for youth offenders that trap in the system those who would otherwise exit easily—may be as important as offenders' deliberate effort to desist. Although imprisonment does not appear in most cases to damage intellectual or emotional functioning (Zamble & Porporino, 1990), it can damage the ability to reconnect with the community, keeping offenders engaged with the criminal justice system despite efforts to desist (Paternoster, 2010).

High-risk violent offenders in intensive custodial treatments are often in their early 30s. In treatment programs, they commonly will say that they want to give up crime, that they are sick of it, and that it is costly in increasingly important areas of their lives, such as intimate relationships and parenting or even grandparenting. When a person who, on paper, remains at high risk of offending is subsequently reconvicted, it is easy to dismiss this "desistance talk" as having been just that: talk. But there are other possible interpretations. For example, Burnett's Oxford Recidivism Study (Burnett, 1992) followed 130 property offenders for up to 20 months after imprisonment. Eighty percent wanted to desist before release, and most thought they'd "probably" or "definitely succeed," but 75% were reconvicted (Burnett, 1992). What caused this discrepancy? Prior to release, interviewees reported that they saw a crime-free life as the "best-case scenario": desirable, but if it proved too challenging to achieve, then "Plan B" was to revert to crime. And, indeed, those who did reoffend reported more difficulties with employment, accommodation, relationships, alcohol and drugs, and other common predictors of reconviction (Burnett, 2000).

Findings for high-risk violent prisoners in New Zealand confirm and extend Burnett's (1992) results. The New Zealand Parole Project (NZPP) recently tracked 300 high-risk violent men from just prior to release from prison through their first months in the community (Polaschek et al., 2016). All were serving prison sentences of at least 2 years. By any standard, these men's histories make desistance unlikely; it is estimated that one-quarter of this risk cohort will be reimprisoned for a new offense within 3 months of release (Nadesu, 2007).

Just prior to release, most of the NZPP sample reported that they (1) had been trying to desist prior to the current sentence; (2) had been desisting for some time in prison, and (3) intended to continue desisting (Polaschek & Yesberg, 2015). We later found that those who were conviction-free at 12 months had reported higher prerelease ratings on engagement in desistance (i.e., a combination of wanting to desist, confidence, and planning for desistance, regardless of their prerelease risk as determined by an actuarial measure of dynamic risk factors; Polaschek, 2016a).

Traditionally, rehabilitation programs emphasized preparing the offender for situations in which triggers could lead to acute risk states. Relapse prevention teaches offenders to identify common patterns of pre-offending events, circumstances, and responses, so they can act to avoid triggers or seek support when exposed to precursors. For example, an offender might be encouraged not to spend time with a sibling who is a heavy drug user or to interact with his ex-partner only over child custody arrangements and when he has lined up a prosocial friend to "debrief" with afterward.

More recently, a complementary approach—reintegration, release, or resettlement planning—has been implemented more widely for persistent and violent prisoners as they approach release. Plans developed prior to release address known predictors of reconviction, such as employment, accommodation, relationships, and alcohol and drug use (Burnett, 2000; Zamble & Quinsey, 1997). Research with NZPP data fits with these findings: lower preparedness for release and poorer quality of release plans predicted recidivism. Release plan quality predicted quality of life 2 months after release, which in turn predicted (the absence of) recidivism in the first 12 months (Polaschek, 2016b). Findings such as these support

a through-care approach to rehabilitating high-risk violent offenders that
includes assistance with release plans.

PSYCHOPATHY

Defining Psychopathy and Its Relationship to Crime and Violence

Although psychopathy is widely recognized as a personality disorder, it
has yet to be included in major diagnostic systems for mental disorders;
instead, antisocial personality disorder (AsPD) has been its closest relative.
The most recognized criteria for AsPD, until recently, were, in essence, a
history of antisocial behavior from childhood into adulthood, with few
accompanying traits (e.g., deceitfulness, lack of remorse; American Psychiatric Association, 1994). Consequently, it included many people with low
psychopathy, and in the prison population was likened to "looking for hay
in a haystack" (Flint-Stevens, 1993 p. 1). People diagnosed with psychopathy are more unusual, even in criminal populations; they usually also have
AsPD, but the reverse is often not the case.

But there are no agreed-upon criteria for psychopathy. The best established method of diagnosis is based on high scores on one of the Hare
Psychopathy Scales. For example, on the Psychopathy Checklist Screening
Version, or PCL:SV (Hart, Cox, & Hare, 1995), specifically trained psychologists score the person's lifetime functioning, based on information
gathered from interviews with the person and file records. Each of 12 items
is given a score between 0 and 2; total scores range from 0 to 24, and the
higher the score, the more psychopathic the person is said to be.

Psychopathy has several components. For example, the Hare scales
have two factors (Interpersonal–Affective, Antisocial) that each break
down into two more facets: interpersonal (glib, grandiose, manipulative),
affective (shallow emotional experiences, callousness), lifestyle (boredom
prone, parasitic, impulsive), and antisocial (early antisocial behavior, versatile criminal history, parole violation, and poor self-control over behavior).
Information about previous criminal behavior is used to score a number of
the items in each facet, which contributes to the reasons that persistently
violent individuals tend to score high on this measure of psychopathy.
Largely because criminal history is also a good predictor of future crime,
scores on the longer Psychopathy Checklist—Revised (PCL-R; Hare, 2003)
predict future crime and violence about as well as risk prediction tools that
concentrate only on criminal history factors (Kroner, Mills, & Reddon,
2005). But much of this predictive power comes from the scores on Factor
2, the Antisocial and Impulsive Lifestyle components, which are not unique
to psychopathy but instead reflect a personality trait called *disinhibition*.

Disinhibition underlies a variety of forms of psychopathology, including AsPD, and substance use disorders. Disinhibition refers to a combination of poor planning and foresight, with deficiencies in self-control

over affect, urges, and behavior (Patrick & Drislane, 2015). As such, it manifests behaviorally as "irresponsibility, impatience, rapid action with negative consequences, alienation and distrust, volatile emotional displays including reactive aggression, untrustworthiness, proneness to drug and alcohol problems, and illicit and other norm-violating activities," including suicidal behavior (Skeem, Polaschek, Patrick, & Lilienfeld, 2011, p. 105). It includes high negative emotionality—a proneness to anxiety disorders and emotional distress—which is contrary to the emotionally shallow and stress-resilience features that fit with the common understanding of psychopathy (Skeem et al., 2011). But negative emotionality is often seen in people with high PCL-psychopathy scores, including persistent offenders (Blackburn, Logan, Donnelly, & Renwick, 2008; Kirkpatrick et al., 2010; Poythress et al., 2010).

The heterogeneity of clustered personality characteristics found in offenders suggests that in contrast to lay understanding, psychopathy is not *the* personality disorder that underlies criminal and violent behavior. Its value in understanding the personality styles of persistent and violent criminals, and its role in the etiology of criminal and violence propensity, may have been overstated (Poythress et al., 2010). But psychopathy, especially Factor 1 (Interpersonal–Affective) features, may be relevant in tailoring treatment to optimize offender change (Wong, Gordon, Gu, Lewis, & Olver, 2012).

Psychopathy has long been given a special clinical status with regard to violence. A meta-analysis of the ability of nine scales to predict violence—all designed as violence or crime prediction tools except the PCL-R/PCL:SV—found all to be equivalently predictive, with the exception of the PCL Factor 1, which contains the distinctive psychopathic traits (Yang, Wong, & Coid, 2010). Factor 1 did not significantly predict violence.

The PCL-R manual states that "the violence of psychopathic offenders often is also qualitatively different from that of other offenders" (Hare, 2003, p. 136). This view is supported by a small number of studies that have shown that offenders with a history of instrumental violence tended to have higher PCL-R scores. The research relies on the theoretically disputed distinction between instrumental and reactive violence discussed early in this chapter. Few offenses in these studies are purely one type or the other, and offenders' histories tend not to be specialized to one or another category. Finding that PCL-R scores are higher in violent offenders with a history of instrumentality should be no surprise. High-risk violent offenders use violence, and crime in general, to achieve a variety of goals, suggesting that criminal instrumentality should be associated with criminal risk. In fact, in a study using the PCL-R alongside a self-report measure of psychopathy, it was impulsive antisociality (from Factor 2), not psychopathic interpersonal and affective traits (Factor 1), that was associated with lifetime instrumental violence (Camp, Skeem, & Barchard, 2013). Most recently, a meta-analysis of 53 studies concluded: "the current findings do not support the conclusion that psychopathy is more related to instrumental violence as opposed to reactive violence" (Blais, Solodukhin, & Forth, 2014, p. 797). Taken together, these findings do not support the view that there is a special link between psychopathy and violence.

Psychopathy and the Treatment of High-Risk Violent Offenders

Data from samples of high-risk violent offenders in prison settings suggest that high psychopathy scores are the norm (Polaschek, 2014). For example, a New Zealand sample scored 20 out of 24 on the PCL:SV, over the cut-off for a diagnosis of psychopathy (Polaschek, 2014; see also Lewis et al., 2013). On this basis, the treatment of high-risk prisoners becomes the treatment of criminal risk in people with PCL-psychopathy, a realization that has led to reconsideration of the treatability of psychopathic offenders.

There is general pessimism about the treatability of people with psychopathy, despite tentative evidence of effectiveness, most often in case studies of psychodynamic therapies (Salekin, 2002). But a study published in the 1990s set back interest in investigating effective treatment approaches for the next two decades. Shortly after the PCL-R criteria became available, they were retrospectively applied to graduates of the 1960s Oak Ridge treatment regimen in Penetanguishene, Canada, a revolutionary cutting-edge approach to treating psychopathy at the time. It featured compulsory treatment, including drugs (e.g., LSD, scopolamine, sodium amytal) administered by one patient to another, long periods in which groups of patients were closed together into rooms, naked, fed only through tubes in the walls and left without staff input, and seclusion and other punishments for noncompliance (Polaschek, 2014).

Disturbingly for the researchers, although attendees with low psychopathy showed reductions in subsequent recidivism, those who retrospectively scored high on the PCL-R had a higher rate of subsequent violence convictions than comparison high-scoring prisoners who were only transferred to the hospital for assessment and then moved back to prison. The authors of the study (Rice, Harris, & Cormier, 1992) and some subsequent commentators (see Salekin, 2002) suggested caution in the treatment of psychopaths, because Oak Ridge provided evidence that treatment can increase the risk of violence reconviction. There is little doubt that this intervention had ingredients that were capable of causing increased risk for violence, but it does not follow that other therapeutic interventions might not be more successful.

A handful of studies since this time suggests that psychopathy levels are not related to program attendees' success in reducing their risk of future violence or crime. A recent review found positive studies with youth, community mental health patients, and prisoners (Polaschek, 2014). Two found improved violence outcomes that were unrelated to psychopathy levels prior to the program (Caldwell, Skeem, Salekin, & van Rybroek, 2006;

Skeem, Monahan, & Mulvey, 2002). Research with high-risk violent New Zealand prisoners has also found no link between levels of psychopathy and later recidivism (Polaschek & Bell, 2008) in attendees of a program that reduces recidivism (Polaschek, 2011).

Another study from the intensive program for high-risk violent offenders in Saskatchewan showed that (1) the more change was made, the less likely it was that treated prisoners would be reconvicted for violent recidivism, and (2) prisoners with high psychopathy and high levels of change had equivalent recidivism outcomes to prisoners with low psychopathy, whether the latter showed low or high levels of change (Olver, Lewis, & Wong, 2013). The subgroup with high psychopathy and low change fared significantly more poorly; their lack of response is an area worthy of further investigation. A comparison of recidivist and nonrecidivist attendees with psychopathy in these programs found that it was scores on dynamic risk factors for violence rather than psychopathy status that accounted best for violent recidivism (Wong & Burt, 2007).

But even if people with psychopathy can be treated effectively to reduce their propensity for violence by tackling change on the dynamic factors that contribute to that propensity, that still does not make them necessarily easy to work with. People with psychopathy are not attractive clients for all but the most persistent of therapists. They can be evasive, argumentative, hostile, resistant to change, uncommitted, and noncompliant. They are less likely to finish treatment, whether because they leave prematurely or because therapists terminate their treatment early (Polaschek & Daly, 2013). Naturally, therapists notice their difficult behavior, rating such clients as less motivated and less malleable (e.g., Hobson, Shine, & Roberts, 2000). The subjective experience of working with them, if it is the only source of information on progress, could easily lead to discouragement. But studies of other high-risk offenders—identified using tools unrelated to psychopathy—have revealed that many of them also behave poorly, as we noted earlier. So it appears that high-risk criminals in general behave that way. But high-risk criminals are the highest priority for treatment, so dealing with poor behavior is part of the fabric of working therapeutically with those whose progress has the most personal and societal impact, whether they have psychopathy or not.

Wong and colleagues (2012) recently proposed a two-component conceptual framework for treating people with psychopathy based on the PCL scales: Factor 1 scores indicate the magnitude of treatment-interfering (i.e., disruptive client) behavior that can be expected from the client. The treatment approach should work around this Interpersonal component, to keep the client in the program, but should not expect to change it. Factor 2 scores are proposed as static proxies for the Criminogenic (second) component, which indicates the person's potential to benefit from an intensive cognitive and skills-based intervention to weaken dynamic risk factors for violence (Wong et al., 2012). There is little evidence yet of the accuracy or clinical utility of the model, but it is an appealing heuristic.

So, although the extant research on the treatment of offenders with psychopathy suggests that they can benefit as others do from treatments for those at high risk of violence, there remains little research on the topic. For instance, does high psychopathy go hand-in-hand with proneness to treatment-interfering behavior? Does it affect how much change is made on risk factors focused on in treatment? And we have no evidence to date with offenders as to whether characteristics of psychopathy itself respond to this type of intervention: There is no accepted method yet of measuring change in psychopathy rather than in the dynamic risk correlates found in criminals with high PCL psychopathy. Finally, the reliance on the PCL-R scales with violent and other offenders means that we have a poor understanding as yet of how psychopathy and violent criminality are actually related across alternative operationalizations of the disorder (see Skeem et al., 2011).

SUMMARY AND CONCLUSIONS

Aggressive and violent behaviors are relatively common in everyday life, but they also comprise many types of acts that can be harmful in both the short and long term. This chapter considered the challenges of definitions that embrace this range before briefly introducing exemplars from the two fields that provide the best accounts of the etiology of individual differences in the propensity for aggressive and violent behavior and the occurrence of specific violent episodes: social cognition and criminal development. The focus then shifted to the key areas of psychological practice with high-risk violent offenders: assessing and understanding violence and criminal propensity and treating and managing it with intervention programs and reintegration planning. Finally, I examined the relationship between psychopathy and violence, concluding that there is little argument that psychopathy signals a risk of perpetrating violence over and above other risk factors for violence. With high-risk violent offenders, psychopathy—at least when measured using one of the PCL scales—is common and to date has been found to have little impact on the treatability or management of high-risk violent offenders, given the challenges they pose in any case. To conclude, this area of psychological research and practice is an important one, and one that needs significantly more investment in primary research. Most notably, there are very few studies of treatment outcomes for violent offenders, including robust change measurement and recidivism evaluations. There are even fewer studies testing a range of program models, given the scope for variations in design and content inherent in both the etiological models and the RNR model. And a significant information gap exists in ascertaining the relevance of psychopathy in the treatment of violent offenders.

REFERENCES

American Psychiatric Association. (1994). *Diagnostic and statistical manual of mental disorders* (4th ed.). Washington, DC: Author.

Anderson, C. A., Benjamin, A. J., & Bartholow, B. D. (1998). Does the gun pull the trigger? Automatic priming effects of weapon pictures and weapon names. *Psychological Science, 9*, 308–314.

Anderson, C. A., & Bushman, B. J. (2002). Human aggression. *Annual Review of Psychology, 53*, 27–51.

Andrews, D. A., Bonta, J., & Hoge, R. D. (1990). Classification for effective rehabilitation: Rediscovering psychology. *Criminal Justice and Behavior, 17*, 19–52.

Andrews, D. A., Bonta, J., & Wormith, J. S. (2004). *The Level of Service/Case Management Inventory (LS/CMI)*. Toronto, Ontario, Canada: Multi-Health Systems.

Andrews, D. A., Zinger, I., Hoge, R. D., Bonta, J., Gendreau, P., & Cullen, F. T. (1990). Does correctional treatment work? A clinically relevant and psychologically informed meta-analysis. *Criminology, 28*, 369–404.

Bandura, A. (1973). *Aggression: A social learning analysis*. Englewood Cliffs, NJ: Prentice-Hall.

Bandura, A. (1986). *Social foundations of thought and action: A social-cognitive theory*. Englewood Cliffs, NJ: Prentice-Hall.

Bandura, A., Barbaranelli, C., Caprara, G. V., & Pastorelli, C. (1996). Mechanisms of moral disengagement in the exercise of moral agency. *Journal of Personality and Social Psychology, 71*, 364–374.

Baron, R. A., & Richardson, D. R. (1994). *Human aggression* (2nd ed.). New York: Plenum.

Beech, A. R., & Ward, T. (2004). The integration of etiology and risk in sexual offenders: A theoretical framework. *Aggression and Violent Behavior, 10*, 31–63.

Blackburn, R., Logan, C., Donnelly, J. P., & Renwick, S. J. D. (2008). Identifying psychopathic subtypes: Combining an empirical personality classification of offenders with the Psychopathy Checklist—Revised. *Journal of Personality Disorders, 22*, 604—622.

Blais, J., Solodukhin, E., & Forth, A. E. (2014). A meta-analysis exploring the relationship between psychopathy and instrumental versus reactive violence. *Criminal Justice and Behavior, 41*, 797–821.

Burnett, R. (1992). *The dynamics of recidivism*. Oxford, UK: University of Oxford Centre for Criminological Research.

Burnett, R. (2000). Understanding criminal careers through a series of in-depth interviews. *Offender Program Report, 4*, 1–15.

Bushman, B. J., & Anderson, C. A. (2001). Is it time to pull the plug on the hostile vs. instrumental aggression dichotomy? *Psychological Review, 108*, 273–279.

Buss, A. H. (1961). *The psychology of aggression*. New York: Wiley.

Cahill, J. C., Polaschek, D. L. L., & Wilson, N. J. (2012). *Offending outcomes for childhood- and adolescent-onset offenders in a New Zealand high-risk adult prisoner sample*. Unpublished manuscript.

Caldwell, M. F., Skeem, J., Salekin, R., & van Rybroek, G. (2006). Treatment response of adolescent offenders with psychopathy features. *Criminal Justice and Behavior, 33*, 571–596.

Cale, E. M. (2006). A quantitative review of the relations between the "Big 3" higher order personality dimensions and antisocial behavior. *Journal of Research in Personality, 40*, 250–284.

Camp, J., Skeem, J. L., & Barchard, K. (2013). Psychopathic predators? Getting specific about the relation between psychopathy, antisociality and violence. *Journal of Consulting and Clinical Psychology, 81*, 467–480.

Caspi, A., Henry, B., McGee, R., Moffitt, T., & Silva, P. (1995). Temperamental origins of child and adolescent behavior problems: From age 3 to age 15. *Child Development, 66*, 55–68.

Caspi, A., Roberts, B. W., & Shiner, R. L. (2005). Personality development: Stability and change. *Annual Review of Psychology, 56*, 453–484.

Cooke, D. J. (2019). Violence and the pains of confinement: PRISM as a promising paradigm for violence prevention. In D. L. L. Polaschek, A. Day, & C. R. Hollin (Eds.), *Handbook of correctional psychology.* Chichester, UK: Wiley.

Cullen, F. T. (2002). Rehabilitation and treatment programs. In J. Q. Wilson & J. Petersilia (Eds.), *Crime: Public policies for crime control* (pp. 253–289). Oakland, CA: ICS Press.

Cullen, F. T., Jonson, C. L., & Nagin, D. S. (2011). Prisons do not reduce recidivism: The high cost of ignoring science. *Prison Journal, 91* 48S–65S.

DeWall, C. N., Anderson, C. A., & Bushman, B. J. (2011). The general aggression model: Theoretical extensions to violence. *Psychology of Violence, 1*, 245–258.

Douglas, K. S., & Skeem, J. L. (2005). Violence risk assessment: Getting specific about being dynamic. *Psychology, Public Policy, and Law, 11*, 347–383.

Farrington, D. P. (2003). Developmental and life-course criminology: Key theoretical and empirical issues—The 2002 Sutherland Award address. *Criminology, 41*, 221–255.

Farrington, D. P. (2007). Origins of violent behavior over the life span. In D. J. Flannery, A. T. Vazsonyi, & I. D. Waldman (Eds.), *The Cambridge handbook of violent behavior and aggression* (pp. 19–48). Cambridge, UK: Cambridge University Press.

Farrington, D. P., Coid, J. W., Harnett, L., Jolliffe, D., Soteriou, N., Turner, R., et al. (2006). *Criminal careers up to the age of 50 and life success up to the age of 48: New findings from the Cambridge Study in Delinquent Development.* London: Home Office.

Felson, R. B. (2014). What are violent offenders thinking? In B. LeClerc & R. Wortley (Eds.), *Cognition and crime: Offender decision making and script analyses* (pp. 12–25). Abingdon, UK: Routledge.

Flint-Stevens, G. (1993). Applying the diagnosis antisocial personality disorder to imprisoned offenders: Looking for hay in a haystack. *Journal of Offender Rehabilitation, 19*, 1–2.

Fontaine, R. G. (2008). Reactive cognition, reactive emotion: Toward a more psychologically informed understanding of reactive homicide. *Psychology, Public Policy and Law, 14*, 243–261.

Freestone, M., Ullrich, S., & Coid, J. (2017). External trigger factors for violent offending: Findings from the U.K. prisoner cohort study. *Criminal Justice and Behavior, 44*, 1389–1412.

Gendreau, P., Smith, P., & Thériault, Y. L. (2009). Chaos theory and correctional treatment: Common sense, correctional quackery, and the law of fartcatchers. *Journal of Contemporary Criminal Justice, 25*, 384–396.

Gilbert, F., & Daffern, M. (2010). Integrating contemporary aggression theory with violent offender treatment: How thoroughly do interventions target violent behavior? *Aggression and Violent Behavior, 15*, 167–180.

Golden, C. J., Jackson, M. L., Peterson-Rohne, A., & Gontkovsky, S. T. (1996). Neuropsychological correlates of violence and aggression: A review of the clinical literature. *Aggression and Violent Behavior, 1*, 3–25.

Hare, R. D. (2003). *The Hare Psychopathy Checklist—Revised technical manual* (2nd ed.). Toronto, Ontario, Canada: Multi-Health Systems.

Hart, S., Cox, D., & Hare, R. (1995). *Manual for the Psychopathy Checklist: Screening Version* (PCL:SV). Toronto, Ontario, Canada: Multi-Health Systems.

Henry, B., Caspi, A., Moffitt, T. E., & Silva, P. A. (1996). Temperamental and familial predictors of violent and nonviolent criminal convictions: Age 3 to age 18. *Developmental Psychology, 32*, 614–623.

Hobson, J., Shine, J., & Roberts, R. (2000). How do psychopaths behave in a prison therapeutic community? *Psychology, Crime & Law, 6*, 139–154.

Hodgins, S. (2007). Persistent violent offending: What do we know? *British Journal of Psychiatry, 190*(Suppl. 49), s12–s14.

Jolliffe, D., & Farrington, D. P. (2007). *A systematic review of the national and international evidence of interventions with violent offenders* (Research Series 16/07). London: Ministry of Justice.

Kirkpatrick, J. T., Draycott, S., Freestone, M., Cooper, S., Twiselton, K., Watson, N., et al. (2010). A descriptive evaluation of patients and prisoners assessed for dangerous and severe personality disorder. *Journal of Forensic Psychiatry and Psychology, 21*, 264–282.

Krahé, B. (2013). *The social psychology of aggression* (2nd ed.). London: Psychology Press.

Kroner, D. G., Mills, J. F., & Reddon, J. R. (2005). A coffee can, factor analysis, and prediction of antisocial behavior: The structure of criminal risk. *International Journal of Law and Psychiatry, 28*, 360–374.

Krueger, R. F., Schmutte, P. S., Caspi, A., Moffitt, T. E., Campbell, K., & Silva, P. A. (1994). Personality traits are linked to crime among men and women: Evidence from a birth cohort. *Journal of Abnormal Psychology, 103*, 328–338.

Krug, E. G., Dahlberg, L. L., Mercy, J. A., Zwi, A. B., & Lozano, R. (Eds.). (2002). *World report on violence and health.* Geneva: World Health Organization.

Laurell, J., Belfrage, H., & Hellström, Å. (2014). Deceptive behavior and instrumental violence among psychopathic and non-psychopathic violent forensic psychiatric patients. *Psychology, Crime and Law, 20*, 467–479.

Lewis, K., Olver, M. E., & Wong, S. C. P. (2013). The Violence Risk Scale: Predictive validity and linking treatment changes with recidivism in a sample of high risk and personality disordered offenders. *Assessment, 20*, 150–164.

Lowenkamp, C. T., & Latessa, E. J. (2004). Increasing the effectiveness of correctional programming through the risk principle: Identifying offenders for residential placement. *Criminology and Public Policy, 4*, 501–528.

Lynam, D. R., Piquero, A. R., & Moffitt, T. E. (2004). Specialization and propensity to violence: Support from self-reports but not official records. *Journal of Contemporary Criminal Justice, 20*, 215–228.

McGuire, J., Bilby, C. A. L., Hatcher, R. M., Hollin, C. R., Hounsome, J., & Palmer, E. J. (2008). Evaluation of structured cognitive-behavioral treatment programs in reducing criminal recidivism. *Journal of Experimental Criminology, 4*, 21–40.

Moffitt, T. E. (1993). Adolescence-limited and life-course-persistent antisocial behavior: A developmental taxonomy. *Psychological Review, 100*, 674–701.

Moffitt, T. E. (2003). Life-course-persistent and adolescence-limited antisocial behavior: A 10-year research review and a research agenda. In B. B. Lahey, T. E. Moffitt, & A. Caspi (Eds.), *Causes of conduct disorder and juvenile delinquency* (pp. 49–75). New York: Guilford Press.

Moffitt, T. E., Caspi, A., Harrington, H., & Milne, B. J. (2002). Males on the life-course-persistent and adolescence-limited antisocial pathways: Follow-up at age 26 years. *Development and Psychopathology, 14*, 179–207.

Moffitt, T. E., Lynam, D. R., & Silva, P. A. (1994). Neuropsychological tests predicting persistent male delinquency. *Criminology, 32*, 277–300.

Monahan, J., & Skeem, J. L. (2014). Risk redux: The resurgence of risk assessment in criminal sanctioning. *Federal Sentencing Reporter, 26*, 158–166.

Nadesu, A. (2007). *Reconviction patterns of released prisoners: A 36-months follow-up analysis.* Retrieved June 26, 2007, from *www.corrections.govt.nz/resources/research_and_statistics/reconviction-patterns-of-released-prisoners-a-36-months-follow-up-analysis.html.*

Odgers, C. A., Moffitt, T. E., Broadbent, J. M., Dickson, N., Hancox, R. J., Harrington, H., et al. (2008). Female and male antisocial trajectories: From childhood origins to adult outcomes. *Development and Psychopathology, 20*, 673–716.

Olver, M. E., Lewis, K., & Wong, S. C. P. (2013). Risk reduction treatment of high risk psychopathic offenders: The relationship of psychopathy and treatment change to violent recidivism. *Personality Disorders: Theory, Research, and Treatment, 4*, 160–167.

Paternoster, R. (2010). How much do we really know about criminal deterrence? *Journal of Criminal Law and Criminology, 100*, 765–823.

Patrick, C. J., & Drislane, L. E. (2015). Triarchic model of psychopathy: Origins, operationalizations, and observed linkages with personality and general psychopathology. *Journal of Personality, 83*, 627–643.

Pinker, S. (2011). *The better angels of our nature: Why violence has declined.* New York: Viking.

Piquero, A. R., Farrington, D. P., Nagin, D. S., & Moffitt, T. E. (2010). Trajectories of offending and their relation to life failure in late middle age: Findings from the Cambridge study in delinquent development. *Journal of Research in Crime and Delinquency, 47*, 151–173.

Pithers, W. D. (1990). Relapse prevention with sexual aggressors: A method for maintaining therapeutic gain and enhancing external supervision. In W. L. Marshall, D. R. Laws, & H. E. Barbaree (Eds.), *Handbook of sexual assault: Issues, theories, and treatment of the offender* (pp. 343–361). New York: Plenum.

Polaschek, D. L. L. (2011). High-intensity rehabilitation for violent offenders in New Zealand: Reconviction outcomes for high- and medium-risk prisoners. *Journal of Interpersonal Violence, 26*, 664–682.

Polaschek, D. L. L. (2014). Adult criminals with psychopathy: Common beliefs about treatability and change have little empirical support. *Current Directions in Psychological Science, 23*, 296–301.

Polaschek, D. L. L. (2016a). Desistance and dynamic risk factors belong together. *Psychology, Crime and Law, 22*, 171–189.

Polaschek, D. L. L. (2016b, September). *Succeeding in the short-term: Some factors that contribute to desistance in high-risk prisoners on parole.* Paper presented at the New Zealand Psychological Society Conference, Wellington, New Zealand.

Polaschek, D. L. L. (2019). Prevention of recidivism in violent and aggressive offenders. In P. Sturmey (Ed.), *The Wiley handbook of violence and aggression.* Chichester, UK: Wiley.

Polaschek, D. L. L., & Bell, R. K. (2008). *Psychopathy Checklist: Screening Version (PCL:SV) backfill project: Retrospective file scoring of PCL:SV measures for VPU evaluation sample.* Wellington, NZ: Unpublished report, Department of Corrections.

Polaschek, D. L. L., & Daly, T. (2013). Treatment and psychopathy in forensic settings. *Aggression and Violent Behavior, 18*, 592–603.

Polaschek, D. L. L., & Kilgour, T. G. (2013). New Zealand's Special Treatment Units: The development and implementation of intensive treatment for high-risk male prisoners. *Psychology, Crime and Law, 11*, 511–526.

Polaschek, D. L. L., & Ross, E. C. (2010). Do early therapeutic alliance, motivation, and change readiness predict therapy outcomes for high risk violent prisoners? *Criminal Behavior and Mental Health, 20*, 100–111.

Polaschek, D. L. L., & Yesberg, J. A. (2015). Desistance in high-risk prisoners: Pre-release self-reported desistance commitment and perceptions of change predict 12-month survival. *Practice: The New Zealand Corrections Journal, 3*(1), 24–29.

Polaschek, D. L. L., & Yesberg, J. A. (2018). High-risk violent prisoners' patterns of change on parole on the DRAOR's dynamic risk and protective factors. *Criminal Justice and Behavior,45*, 340–363.

Polaschek, D. L. L., Yesberg, J. A., Bell, R. K., Casey, A. R., & Dickson, S. R. (2016). Intensive psychological treatment of high-risk violent offenders: Outcomes and pre-release mechanisms. *Psychology, Crime and Law, 22*, 344–365.

Poythress, N. G., Edens, J. F., Skeem, J. L., Lilienfeld, S. O., Douglas, K. S., Frick, P. J., et al. (2010). Identifying subtypes among offenders with antisocial personality disorder: A cluster-analytic study. *Journal of Abnormal Psychology, 119*, 389–400.

Rice, M. E., Harris, G. T., & Cormier, C. A. (1992). An evaluation of a maximum security therapeutic community for psychopaths and other mentally disordered offenders. *Law and Human Behavior, 16*, 399–412.

Richards, C. M., Wilson, M. S., Robson, S., & Polaschek, D. L. L. (2017). *Release plan quality, the DRAOR and desistance in high-risk parolees.* Manuscript in preparation.

Ross, R. R., Fabiano, E. A., & Ewles, C. D. (1988). Reasoning and rehabilitation. *International Journal of Offender Therapy and Comparative Criminology, 32*, 29–36.

Salekin, R. T. (2002). Psychopathy and therapeutic pessimism: Clinical lore or clinical reality? *Clinical Psychology Review, 22*, 79–112.

Serin, R. C. (2007). *The dynamic risk assessment for offender re-entry (DRAOR)*. Unpublished manuscript, Carleton University.

Serin, R. C., Mailloux, D. L., & Wilson, N. J. (2012). *The dynamic risk assessment for offender re-entry (DRAOR), New Zealand adaptation*. Unpublished manuscript, Carleton University.

Sivertsson, F., & Carlsson, C. (2015). Continuity, change, and contradictions: Risk and agency in criminal careers to age 59. *Criminal Justice and Behavior, 42*, 382–411.

Skeem, J. L., Monahan, J., & Mulvey, E. (2002). Psychopathy, treatment involvement, and subsequent violence among civil psychiatric patients. *Law and Human Behavior, 26*, 577–603.

Skeem, J. L., Polaschek, D. L. L., Patrick, C. J., & Lilienfeld, S. O. (2011). Psychopathic personality: Bridging the gap between scientific evidence and public policy. *Psychological Science in the Public Interest, 12*, 95–162.

Tolan, P. H. (2007). Understanding violence. In D. J. Flannery, A. T. Vazsonyi, & I. D. Waldman (Eds.), *The Cambridge handbook of violent behavior and aggression* (pp. 5–18). Cambridge, UK: Cambridge University Press.

Warburton, W., & Anderson, C. A. (2018). On the clinical applications of the general aggression model to understanding domestic violence. In R. A. Javier & W. G. Herron (Eds.), *Understanding domestic violence: Theories, challenges, remedies* (pp. 71–107). Lanham, MD: Rowman & Littlefield.

Whitehead, P. R. (2014). Therapeutic communities: From a programme in prison to the prison as a programme. *Practice—The New Zealand Corrections Journal, 2*, 47–53.

Wong, S. C. P., & Burt, G. (2007). The heterogeneity of incarcerated psychopaths: Differences in risk, need, recidivism, and management approaches. In H. Herve & J. C. Yuille (Eds.), *The psychopath: Theory, research, and practice* (pp. 461–483). Mahwah, NJ: Erlbaum.

Wong, S. C. P., & Gordon, A. (2006). The validity and reliability of the Violence Risk Scale: A treatment-friendly violence risk assessment tool. *Psychology, Public Policy, and Law, 12*, 279–309.

Wong, S. C. P., & Gordon, A. (2013). The violence reduction program: A treatment program for violence prone forensic clients. *Psychology, Crime and Law, 11*, 461–475.

Wong, S. C. P., Gordon, A., Gu, D., Lewis, K., & Olver, M. E. (2012). The effectiveness of violence reduction treatment for psychopathic offenders: Empirical evidence and a treatment model. *International Journal of Forensic Mental Health, 11*, 336–349.

Yang, M., Wong, S. C. P., & Coid, J. W. (2010). The efficacy of violence prediction: A meta-analytic comparison of nine risk assessment tools. *Psychological Bulletin, 136*, 740–767.

Zamble, E., & Porporino, F. (1990). Coping, imprisonment and rehabilitation: Some data and their implications. *Criminal Justice and Behavior, 17*, 53–70.

Zamble, E., & Quinsey, V. L. (1997). *The criminal recidivism process*. Cambridge, UK: Cambridge University Press.

Zillman, D. (1988). Cognitive-excitation interdependencies in aggressive behavior. *Aggressive Behavior, 14*, 51–64.

CHAPTER 16

Judicial Decision Making

Gregory Mitchell

Everyone is a judge of many things, but few of us have the power of the government behind our judgments. Those who do—the judges of trial courts and appellate courts within legal systems—possess power to decide the fates of criminal defendants, interpret constitutions to determine what basic rights and obligations exist within a society, award custody of children to one parent or another, and award damages to compensate for harms and punish misdeeds. Despite the tremendous importance and power of judges within legal systems, and the much greater likelihood that judges rather than jurors will decide a legal case or influence it to settle (e.g., Kritzer, 2004; Schlanger, 2005), judges have been the subject of relatively little psychological research compared with jurors. Political scientists, economists, and legal scholars devote more empirical resources and theory building to judicial decision making, but their efforts rarely incorporate psychological theory and constructs.

One simple explanation for the greater attention paid to judicial decision making by political scientists and economists is that those researchers are more conversant with archive-based research than are psychologists, who typically utilize laboratory or field experiments, for which sitting judges can be hard to recruit. Because judges rarely participate in controlled experiments in which independent variables can be systematically manipulated and their effects compared using sensitive dependent measures tailored for the theory at hand, judicial decision-making studies often make use of rough proxies of psychological constructs of interest (e.g., the political party of the president who appoints a federal judge as a measure of that judge's own political ideology) or examine easily observed individual and situational differences across judges (e.g., race or gender of the judge or type of court on which the judge sits). Fortunately, many databases containing information about judges and their output are publicly available, at least for American courts.[1] Greater attention to these databases by psychologists would likely lead to the addition of a number of variables aimed at applying psychological theories to judicial decision making. For example, although a few studies have examined the integrative complexity of judicial opinions (i.e., the level of complexity with which a judge writes about the factual and legal issues in a case, as measured by the judge's acknowledgment of legitimate competing perspectives on an issue and the degree to which the judge integrates the competing perspectives into a coherent decision) and how that complexity varies with judicial ideology, coalitions, and case type (Gruenfeld, 1995; Tetlock, Bernzweig, & Gallant, 1985), the lack of inclusion of integrative complexity variables in judicial archives surely has impeded this line of research (for a discussion of ways to measure the integrative complexity of public statements by government officials, see Suedfeld, Guttieri, & Tetlock, 2003).

Despite the limitations of conducting research into judicial decision making, much has been learned. This chapter first provides an overview of this knowledge and then proposes a framework for the study of judicial decision making that emphasizes the judge's place within an accountability matrix provided by the legal system and the players within that system. Although some research uses participants who are not judges to study how legal judges might behave, the focus here is on research directly examining legal judges, because this research requires no assumptions about the external validity of findings based on a nonjudge sample for true judicial behavior (see Dhami & Belton, 2017, for a detailed discussion of how to make judicial research findings more compelling). The chapter closes with a discussion of the norms that one may use to analyze the quality of judicial decision making.

INDIVIDUAL DIFFERENCES

If we could hold the situation of all acts of judging constant—same law, same evidence, same parties and audience, and same consequences of the decision—would we observe the same outcomes across decisions? How reliable is the act of judging, and what are the sources of variance across judicial decisions? In an ideal world, the only sources of variance would be the law and relevant facts of a case, with irrelevant facts and nonlegal concerns having no influence on decisions. In this ideal world, like cases would be treated alike, the law would be followed scrupulously, and only relevant facts would matter.

---

[1]Perhaps the most used judicial database is the U.S. Supreme Court database begun by political scientist Harold Spaeth. This public database continues to be updated annually: *http://scdb.wustl.edu/about.php.*

Many studies examine these questions of reliability and validity, examining the impact of legal and extralegal influences on judicial decision making. Some studies focus on judge-level variables, such as a judge's age or years of experience. Other studies focus on variables located within the judging environment, such as elements of the law, evidentiary strength, characteristics of the parties, or how recently the judge took a meal break (Danziger, Levav, & Avnaim-Pesso, 2011). I first discuss research into individual-difference variables and then turn to research into situational-difference variables.

An important preliminary note on individual-difference judicial research is that, although this research sometimes portrays its results as if they reveal domain-general tendencies, most individual-difference research in fact focuses on a particular type of case under a particular set of circumstances (e.g., judges sentencing minority defendants in criminal cases or deciding whether to grant a defendant's motion to dismiss the plaintiff's claim for sexual harassment) because the judicial characteristic of interest is predicted to influence decision making in that particular context. Very few individual-difference studies sample across a wide range of cases and judicial tasks to examine whether the variable of interest has domain-specific or domain-general effects, a notable exception being studies of the impact of judicial ideology on the decision making of U.S. Supreme Court justices across a variety of cases. Thus much of the individual-differences research is best viewed as revealing interactions of individual-difference variables with domain-specific variables, such as the type of case or race of the defendant or victim.

A second preliminary note is that research examining observable differences at the individual-judge level often assumes that the observable variable is a rough proxy for a constellation of psychological differences that could not be directly measured or ascertained from the archives. Years on the bench, for instance, serves as a compendium of many different influences, including the learning and change in status that comes with greater seniority. A key role for psychologists should be to unpack these rough proxies to examine which psychological factors may in fact be at play across individuals within the different groups formed by the proxy variables.

The study of the impact of a judge's race on decision making well illustrates these two points. Most studies of the relationship of a judge's race or ethnicity to case outcomes examine judicial race in the context of discrimination cases or sentencing. The idea is that judges from minority groups are likely to bring different perspectives (and biases) to these cases than white judges, with judicial race potentially having cognitive and motivational consequences for individual decisions and social influence and information effects for panel decisions (see Fischman, 2015a; Kastellec, 2013). Yet few studies delve into the precise psychological and social mechanisms that may give rise to differences in outcomes. The best we can presently say is that the race of judges appears to have some relationship to case outcomes, at

least in cases in which the race of the parties is salient or relevant. Research
has found that federal judges from minority groups ruled more favorably
for plaintiffs in Voting Rights Act cases (Cox & Miles, 2008), affirmative
action cases (Kastellec, 2013), and race discrimination cases (e.g., Boyd,
2016; Chew & Kelley, 2009), but not sexual harassment cases (Kulik, Perry,
& Pepper, 2003) or cases in general (Ashenfelter, Eisenberg, & Schwab,
1995; see also Lim, Silveira, & Snyder, 2016), findings consistent with the
view that a judge's race interacts with case-specific variables. However, that
interaction may not always take the form one expects: In the domain of
sentencing, some studies have found that minority judges imposed harsher
sentences on minority defendants than white judges (Steffensmeier & Britt,
2001) or imposed the same sentences as white judges (Spohn, 1990; Spohn,
Gruhl, & Welch, 1981–1982; Walker & Barrow, 1985), whereas other
studies have found minority judges being more lenient on minority defendants (e.g., Johnson, 2006; Welch, Combs, & Gruhl, 1988). Furthermore,
one should not assume that all minority groups will exhibit the same patterns: Morin (2013) found that, whereas black federal judges were more
likely to rule in favor of black plaintiffs than white judges in employment
cases, Latino judges were generally less likely to rule in favor of plaintiffs
regardless of plaintiff identity.

Similar patterns have been observed with respect to the gender, age,
and religious affiliations of judges. These judge-level variables sometimes
correlate with case outcomes, at least when personal identity is relevant to
the claims in the case, and sometimes do not (e.g., Ashenfelter et al., 1995;
Bornstein & Miller, 2009; Boyd, 2016; Goldman, 1966, 1975; Johnson,
2006; Manning, Carroll, & Carp, 2004; Ramji-Nogales, Schoenholtz,
& Schrag, 2007; Segal, 2000; Stribopoulos & Yaha, 2007). For instance,
Kulik et al. (2003) failed to find an effect for sex of the judge in sexual
harassment cases but found that younger judges ruled more favorably for
plaintiffs (suggesting a possible generational effect for views on or concerns about sexual harassment; see also Walker & Barrow, 1985). As with
race, many opportunities exist for psychologists to dig more deeply into
the explanations for the observed patterns. One of the most interesting
findings that could benefit from psychological insight is the finding that
female judges sometimes give harsher sentences to female defendants than
male judges (Gruhl, Spohn, & Welch, 1981). Although this behavior could
reflect a form of paternalism or benevolent sexism on the part of male
judges, that hypothesis and alternatives (e.g., perhaps female judges are
responding more punitively to violations of prescriptive stereotypes about
how women should behave) have not been subjected to serious testing.

Some argue that the observed effects of judicial demographics justify
greater diversity on the bench, the idea being that different identities bring
different perspectives to cases and a diversity of viewpoints reduces the
risk of group bias influencing outcomes (e.g., Chew & Kelley, 2009; Stribopoulos & Yaha, 2007). But given the mixed results and many omitted

variables in the studies, it is perilous to argue that race, gender, age, or religion of a judicial candidate will be a good predictor of how that judge will behave on the bench. The diversification argument should also take into account differences in court structure that may impact the need for greater diversity. Bonneau and Rice (2009) found no effects for a judge's race on the likelihood that a criminal conviction would be overturned at a state's highest court when considering cases in the aggregate, but when they contrasted the highest courts with no intermediate appellate court with those above an intermediate appellate court, they found that black justices sitting on the former courts (i.e., courts in the which the supreme court was the only appellate court) were more likely to vote to overturn a conviction than white judges. In short, minority justices in states with a single error-checking appellate court appeared to be more open to minority appellants' claims of trial error. Where multiple error-checking courts exist, the empirics-based argument for judicial diversity would appear to be weaker.

Compared to the argument for greater demographic and religious diversity, the empirics-based argument for ideological diversity on the bench is much stronger. The most-studied individual-difference variable for judges is by far political identity or ideology, and the effects associated with political identity are stronger and more consistent than those observed for social background variables. Baum (2010, 2017) and Epstein, Landes, and Posner (2013) provide good surveys of this voluminous literature, which finds that measures of a judge's political values and policy preferences often explain considerable variance in judicial decisions, with the effects tending to be larger in civil rights and employment/labor cases, in high-visibility cases (Bartels, 2011), and among judges sitting at the top of a court system (Cross, 2007; Klein, 2002). Where ambiguity exists about the proper legal outcome (many studies of judicial ideology exclude from analysis unanimous decisions of multimember courts), conservative judges tend to favor outcomes that promote a conservative policy agenda, and liberal judges tend to favor outcomes that promote a liberal agenda (e.g., conservative justices have tended to side with opponents of greater regulation in environmental protection and endangered species cases, whereas liberal justices have tended to side with advocates of greater regulation in such cases).

For psychologists, the most interesting aspect of this research may be the largely unexplored nature of political identity and ideology. The ideology proxies used by political scientists (e.g., party of the appointing president or party of the judge before appointment) perform well in studies of judicial behavior and are easy to gather and apply across court systems. Accordingly, as Baum (2017) discusses, the meaning of ideology in the context of judicial studies is often vague and typically aligns judges along a single liberal-to-conservative continuum (see also Brace, Langer, & Hall, 2000). Yet many different motivational and cognitive processes may contribute to these ideological differences (e.g., Carmines & D'Amico, 2015; Hibbing, Smith, & Alford, 2014), and many legal cases present multiple value trade-offs and do not occupy a single location on a left–right continuum (Fischman, 2015b). Bringing the history of psychological research to studies of judicial decision making could greatly enrich our understanding of judicial ideology and when it is more and less likely to influence how judges decide cases.

Yet another individual-difference variable that has received considerable attention is the role of judicial experience and expertise. In an impressive line of research, Guthrie and colleagues have persuaded many sitting judges to participate in experiments that examine the degree to which judges fall prey to cognitive and motivational biases commonly exhibited by laypeople (e.g., Guthrie, Rachlinski, & Wistrich, 2007; Rachlinski, Guthrie & Wistrich, 2006; Rachlinski, Johnson, Wistrich, & Guthrie, 2009; Wistrich, Guthrie, & Rachlinski, 2005). These researchers have found that many judges rely on an intuitive mode of thought and fall prey to biases and heuristics in their legal judgments. For example, damages awarded by judges, just like those awarded by mock jurors, can be influenced by anchoring effects in the form of the amount of damages demanded by a plaintiff (i.e., holding evidence in the case constant, plaintiffs making a higher monetary demand on average receive a larger award than plaintiffs making a lower demand; e.g., Guthrie, Rachlinski & Wistrich, 2001). However, they have also found that judges are more resistant to some common biases and errors. For instance, they have found that judges are better than laypeople in disregarding certain forms of inadmissible evidence when deciding issues in a case (Wistrich et al., 2005; Rachlinski, Guthrie, & Wistrich, 2011) and are less susceptible to framing effects (i.e., less likely to treat equivalent outcomes differently when the outcome is framed as a potential gain—50% chance of winning $100—or a loss—50% chance of losing $100) and the representativeness heuristic (i.e., basing likelihood judgments on how representative a particular piece of evidence is of a category, such as inferring lying from how nervous a witness appears to be instead of basing that judgment on the entire body of evidence relevant to that judgment; Guthrie et al., 2001). They have found mixed evidence on the ability of judges to avoid the hindsight bias in their judgments (i.e., information obtained only after an accident, which a defendant could not have known before the accident occurred, sometimes did and sometimes did not affect judges' judgments about whether a defendant was acting reasonably when the accident occurred; Guthrie et al., 2001; Rachlinski et al., 2011; see also Oeberst & Goeckenjan, 2016). They have also found that judges' implicit racial biases did not produce racial differences in sentencing recommendations or predictions of recidivism (Rachlinski et al., 2009). Other researchers have found other positive expertise effects. For instance, Schmittat and Englich (2016) found that legal experts were less likely to exhibit confirmation bias (i.e., searching for evidence to confirm one's initial belief), and Chang, Chen, and Lin (2017) found that more experienced judges were less likely to exhibit anchoring effects. Guthrie et al. (2001) draw fairly pessimistic conclusions about the impact of legal experience and training on the rationality of judicial decision making, but they acknowledge that some aspects of judicial procedure (e.g., procedures that reduce time demands on decision making to encourage deliberation and avoid reliance on flawed intuitions) and the situation of judging (appellate courts that hold trial judges accountable and provide guidance on how decisions should be made) can promote more rational decision making.

That legal training would not insulate judges from rationality errors is not terribly surprising, because legal education rarely includes training in proper statistical and causal reasoning. Thus, when judges make decisions on the admissibility of scientific evidence, they often focus on an expert's credentials and whether an expert claims to be following a field's established methods and procedures, rather than carefully scrutinizing the rigor of the expert's methods and whether the expert's opinions are justified by the empirical data (e.g., Dahir et al., 2005; Merlino, Murray, & Richardson, 2008; Wingate & Thornton, 2004). (There is some evidence, however, that changes in evidentiary rules can prompt closer scrutiny of expert opinions; e.g., Cecil, 2005; Groscup, Penrod, Studebaker, Huss, & O'Neil, 2002; Krafka, Dunn, Johnson, Cecil, & Miletich, 2002.) That judicial experience may not translate across the board into more formally rational decision making is also not surprising, because some types of errors, such as anchoring on irrelevant information, will likely escape attention on appeal. Other errors, such as attending to irrelevant evidence or failing to follow applicable precedent, however, may be more amenable to judicial review and thus produce opportunities for learning. In short, any gains due to judicial expertise are likely to be task- and domain-specific (Shanteau & Dalgliesh, 2010).

An important goal of psychological studies of individual differences among judges should be the identification of domains in which judges tend to converge and diverge and seek to understand why. To the extent that it is possible to identify better and worse ways of judging, then the goal should be to identify ways of promoting judicial expertise through selection, training, deployment of decision aids, and legal procedure. In particular, as suggested by the work of Guthrie and colleagues, psychologists should collaborate with judges to examine whether common tools for debiasing (see Larrick, 2004), such as the use of incentives, bias-awareness training, and decision-support systems, can improve judicial decision making.

SITUATIONAL DIFFERENCES

In addition to examining variation in decisions across judges, much research examines variation in decisions across cases and courts. Many of these studies resemble mock-juror studies that examine whether potential jurors attend to irrelevant party characteristics, such as the race and attractiveness of the parties. Other studies examine unique features of the situation that judges inhabit and of the tasks that judges perform. I first provide an overview of institutional variables that appear to affect decision making before turning to features located at the level of the case. A detailed examination of this voluminous literature is beyond the scope of this chapter. The goal is to highlight some of the more important situational variables that affect judicial decision making.

Institutional Variables

One of the most notable institutional-level differences among judges is the method by which judges obtain their positions. In many legal systems, including the federal courts within the United States and federal and state courts within Australia, judges are selected by a government executive and/or government body and appointed for life or for a specified term. In other systems, including many state court systems within the United States, judges are elected for a set term by popular vote, with some elections partisan (i.e., the candidate is selected through a primary system connected to political parties and party affiliation is disclosed) and some nonpartisan (i.e., party affiliation is not disclosed on ballots).

Manner of selection and retention theoretically relates to the degree to which a judge will be independent of extralegal influences. Elected judges, the theory goes, will be subject to capture by industries facing serious legal threats and will be beholden to the political parties and donors who either directly or indirectly help get them elected. Appointed judges, on the other hand, particularly those appointed for life, should be independent of political influences and more attentive to what the law and facts of a case demand, or so the theory goes. Complicating this theory are the findings mentioned earlier that even appointed judges with life tenure exhibit ideological differences in their decisions. Notwithstanding this well-established fact of judicial life, a fair amount of research has been devoted to studying the question of whether elected judges are susceptible to capture because of the demands of elections and reelections.

On the question of whether campaign donations can be used to create a judiciary biased in the donor's favor, a number of studies find a correlation between the amounts contributed by interest groups (including lawyers) likely to appear before the judge and the favorability of opinions affecting these groups, at least where the races have been competitive, but a few do not (e.g., Cann, 2007a; Bonneau & Cann, 2009; Hazelton, Montgomery, & Nyhan, 2016; Rebe, 2016; Shepherd, 2009). Despite efforts to overcome the identification problem in these studies (see McCall, 2003; Hazelton et al., 2016), when a correlation is observed, we cannot be sure whether voters elect judges inclined to support particular viewpoints (which predictably garner donations from like-minded groups) or whether donations from particular groups lead judges to favor particular viewpoints. Nonetheless, the existing evidence provides some basis to argue that elected judges are sensitive to how their decisions will be viewed by the interest groups most likely to support them (Baum, Gray & Klein, 2017). And other research has found that, in periods leading up to reelection, judges are more likely to decide cases and write opinions in ways that will be favored by their constituencies (e.g., liberal judges become more likely to vote in favor of the death penalty and become more punitive in their sentencing in more conservative districts; e.g., Brace & Boyea, 2008; Hall, 1995; Huber & Gordon, 2004; Kritzer, 2016).

Efforts to compare directly the quality of decision making by elected versus appointed judges have yielded mixed results. Choi, Gulati, and Posner (2008) found that elected judges decided more cases than appointed judges, but the opinions of appointed judges garnered few citations on average, and they found that both types of judges exhibited similar levels of independence as measured by the likelihood of voting with judges who share the same ideology. Cann (2007b), analyzing survey data provided by judges who were selected either through a merit system, appointment, or partisan election, found that systems using partisan elections were rated lower in the quality of work performed by the courts. Because it is difficult to agree on the criteria of "good" judicial decisions where ambiguities exist about what the law and facts of a case require (Oldfather, 2014), it is hard to know how much weight to give to studies such as these, which seek to compare the quality of judicial decision making across courts. Collectively, however, the evidence suggests that elected judges are less independent than appointed judges, but this evidence does not mean that appointed judges make better or less biased opinions. Indeed, greater independence among appointed judges may simply mean a greater independence to act on personal biases. Furthermore, one should not assume that judges elected through nonpartisan systems are more independent than judges elected through partisan systems. Lim, Snyder, and Strömberg (2015) found that judges selected through nonpartisan elections were more likely to increase sentence length in a case receiving media attention than appointed judges and judges selected through partisan elections. Nor should one assume that appointed judges are immune from audience effects: Even Supreme Court justices appear to take into account how other branches of the government and the public will react to their decisions (e.g., Baum, 2006; Hall, 2014). The larger point is that the behavior of appointed versus elected judges may differ greatly depending on the accountability matrix in which they find themselves, and this reality places limits on the external validity of studies using only appointed or elected judges deciding low- versus high-profile cases.

Yet another important difference in institutional structure is whether the judge has the power to decide a case alone (as in the trial courts within the United States) or votes as a member of a panel considering a case (as in appellate courts within the United States). Research consistently finds that, among collegial or multimember courts, the composition of the panel deciding the case influences the decisions made (e.g., Cross, 2007;

Fischman, 2015a; Hettinger, Lindquist, & Martinek, 2006; Szmer, Christensen, & Kaheny, 2015). For instance, Fischman (2011) found that the
ideological makeup of the panel of appellate judges deciding asylum cases
greatly affected the outcomes of the cases (i.e., a panel composed of three
conservative justices was more likely to deny asylum than a panel containing a moderate or liberal judge, and a panel composed of three liberal
judges was more likely to grant asylum than a panel containing a moderate
or conservative judge). Although it is clear that panel composition matters, why it matters is not so clear (Devins & Federspiel, 2010; Martinek,
2010). It may be that exposure to different informational, legal, and policy
perspectives leads to different reasoning and outcomes; the results could
be due to a norm of collegiality paired with a desire to issue unanimous
opinions; or perhaps strategic effects (e.g., vote trading across cases) are at
work (see Fischman, 2015a).

Multimember courts typically serve as appellate, error-checking
courts overseeing the decisions of single-member trial courts. This difference in locations within the judicial hierarchy, and not just the group-
versus-individual decision-making nature of a court, can also have important effects on judicial decisions. Evidence indicates that both trial-level
and intermediate courts of appeal act strategically, taking into account
how their decisions will be reviewed by courts higher up in the hierarchy (Cross, 2007; Epstein et al., 2013; Klein, 2002). The likelihood that a
reviewing court may overturn a lower court's decision that runs contrary
to established precedent can affect both the nature of the decision and how
opinions explaining decisions are written. The standard of review that the
reviewing court applies may also matter: Stricter standards of appellate
review, under which little deference is given to the trial court's judgment,
should lead to decisions that are more defensible in terms of the relevant
facts and applicable law (Cross, 2007; Epstein et al. 2013; Fischman &
Schanzenbach, 2011; but see Schanzenbach, 2015).

These institutional arrangements—how judges obtain their positions,
whether judges decide cases individually or as a group, and the imposition
of oversight through appellate courts that can use stricter or looser standards of review—seek to promote efficient resolution of disputes, as well as
just and accurate decisions that honor the rule of law. Legal systems differ
in how they seek to achieve the right balance among these sometimes conflicting goals, but all systems seek to have judges decide their cases on the
basis of the applicable law and relevant facts, rather than improper considerations such as the race of the parties or victims of a crime.

Case-Level Variables

Many judicial studies seek to determine whether justice is dispensed in
accordance with law or whether decisions are influenced by improper
considerations or inadmissible evidence, such as coerced confessions (e.g.,

Wistrich et al., 2005; for evidence on jurors' ability to ignore inadmissible evidence, see Steblay, Hosch, Culhane, & McWethy, 2006). Judges' bail and sentencing decisions have provided a particularly fertile area for studying the comparative influence of legal and extralegal influences. Dhami (2003) and Dhami and Ayton (2001) found that judges' bail decisions were best predicted by a noncompensatory model of decision making that focuses on one or a small set of cues, including both legal and extralegal cues, rather than a compensatory model in which the full range of legally specified factors are weighed and combined to reach an individualized decision. Further research by Dhami (2005) found again that judges used noncompensatory strategies in making bail decisions, with those decisions driven by the judges' judgments about risk of flight and further offense in case of release, and those judgments in turn driven primarily by proper case-specific considerations, such as the nature of the offense and the defendant's ties to the community. Years of research have found that the seriousness of the offense charged is the most important determinant of bail decisions and the amount of bail required, but other factors may also be influential, such as the type of offense (Beattey, Matsuura, & Jeglic, 2014) or recommendations of the police or prosecutor (Dhami, 2003; Dhami & Ayton, 2001); prosecutors also play a significant role in judge's sentencing decisions (Kim, Spohn, & Hedberg, 2015). This range of possible influences can result in considerable disagreement among judges in the perceived risk associated with granting bail and consequently among judges' bail decisions (see Dhami, 2003, 2005, 2010). These results demonstrate the importance of observing both what considerations drive decisions and how consistent those decisions are: Even when judges act within the range of acceptable legal outcomes, greater legal structure or training may be needed to ensure greater equality of treatment across cases.

Many sentencing studies likewise find that judges attend to legally proper factors when determining punishments, such as the defendant's offense history and the nature of the offense for which the conviction occurred (Spohn, 2009). But research also finds that improper considerations appear to influence punishments (see Kapardis, 2016). For instance, female offenders are less likely to be incarcerated and, at least in some jurisdictions, are more likely receive shorter sentences when they are incarcerated, as compared with males convicted for similar offenses (e.g., Philippe, 2017; Spohn & Beichner, 2000). (There is, however, some evidence that the gender gap has narrowed a bit over the past few decades; Harmon & O'Brien, 2011). The race and age of the defendant likewise have been found in some studies to relate to sentencing outcomes, with older defendants tending to be treated less severely and minority defendants more severely (e.g., Freiburger, 2010; Hester & Hartman, 2017; Morrow, Vickovic, & Fradella, 2014; Mueller-Johnson & Dhami, 2010). Sentencing decisions also appear sometimes to be influenced by characteristics of the victim; for example, Lewis, Klettke, and Day (2014) found that credibility of child assault victims influenced sentence length, and Gillespie, Loughran, Smith, Fogel, and Bjerregaard (2014) found that the death penalty was more likely to be recommended for defendants who murdered females with whom they were acquainted or who were not participants in the defendant's illegal activities. A major impetus behind the adoption of sentencing guidelines among state and federal courts was the desire to reduce the influence of these improper considerations on judges' punishment decisions. However, the evidence is ambiguous as to whether sentencing guidelines do in fact reduce unwanted sentencing disparities (see Kim et al., 2015).

One area in which structuring judicial decision making has improved the validity and reliability of decisions is in the use of risk assessments that inform sentencing and parole decision making. One goal of sentencing is to incapacitate those who pose a future risk of harm to their communities, and therefore risk assessments have an important role to play in sentencing decisions (Monahan & Skeem, 2014a). As Dhami (2005) found in the context of bail decision making, however, judges' intuitive risk assessments can be an important and unwanted source of variation in sentencing decisions. An example of the benefits of collaboration between the courts and psychologists is found in psychologists' development of validated risk assessment instruments that are now informing the practices of many judges and parole boards, providing structure that improves the validity and reliability of risk assessments used to make sentencing and release decisions (Monahan & Skeem, 2014b, 2016).[2] Greater collaboration between psychologists and courts on other ways to structure judicial decision-making tasks, such as how to approach the admissibility of expert evidence that presents complex scientific issues (as discussed by Marion, Kaplan, & Cutler, Chapter 13, this volume), could

ACCOUNTABILITY AS A DEFINING FEATURE OF JUDICIAL DECISION MAKING

Due to the greater difficulty of recruiting judges as participants, fewer experimental studies of judicial decision making have been conducted compared with studies of jury decision making, and it is often difficult to operationalize psychological variables of interest in archival studies of judicial

---

[2]However, the use of structured risk-assessment instruments does not guarantee objective risk assessments. Boccaccini, Murrie, and their colleagues have found that party-retained evaluators may score the instruments in ways that favor the side that retained them, but formal training in the scoring of the instruments can reduce this client-side bias (e.g., Murrie, Boccaccini, Guarnera, & Rufino, 2013; Boccaccini, Murrie, Rufino, & Gardner, 2014). This evidence suggests that courts should favor risk assessments from both sides or should seek a structured assessment from an evaluator not retained by either party.

decision making. It may be tempting, therefore, to use studies of jury decision making, or studies of decision making in general, to draw inferences
about judicial decision making. However, such inferences are quite perilous
because of the unique situation that judges inhabit compared with most
other decision makers.

One of the most significant differences between judges and jurors,
from a psychological standpoint, is that judges must explain their decisions
in terms of applicable law and facts, whereas jurors are under no obligation
to do so. Indeed, American evidentiary law and procedure include rules
and doctrines specifically designed to insulate the jury's deliberations, no
matter how irrational and even lawless they may have been, from public revelation and scrutiny (see, e.g., *Tanner v. United States,* 1987). Having to explain one's judgments and decisions to an audience often affects
how and what decisions are made (Lerner & Tetlock, 1999; Tetlock, 2002;
Oldfather, 2008). Depending on the anticipated views of the audience and
the norms that exist about how a decision should be made, accountability
may encourage independence or conformity to public opinion, accuracy or
dissembling, greater search for relevant information or greater attention
to irrelevant information (e.g., Pennington & Schlenker, 1999; Quinn &
Schlenker, 2002; Tetlock & Boettger, 1989).

Judges must explain themselves not only to the parties and their attorneys (who often share membership with judges in the local bar) but also
to the public at large (particularly in high-profile cases), to their fellow
judges when sitting on multimember courts, to the superior courts likely
to review their decisions, to judicial regulatory bodies that enforce codes
of conduct, and to the electorate or selecting body if a judge is not life
tenured. In addition, many state judges are subject to judicial performance
reviews in which attorneys and parties (and sometimes expert observers) are given an opportunity to evaluate the performance of judges along
multiple dimensions (including attention to the law, respect for those in
the court, and timeliness of decisions), with the results being made public
(Paynter & Kearney, 2010). Researching how judges navigate these many
layers of accountability, which at times may push in opposing directions,
and how different types of judges make different navigation choices should
be a key task of psychological studies of judicial decision making. Tetlock's
(2002) social functionalist framework provides an excellent starting point
for investigating how judges resolve trade-offs created by sometimes competing accountability pressures, and it acknowledges that any given judge
may at times express different mind-sets depending on which pressures
seem more important or pressing.

Although experimental studies of judging sometimes acknowledge the
importance of appellate review and other forms of judicial accountability,
those studies rarely include even a mild form of accountability as an independent variable. Indeed, experimental studies of judging rarely ask the
judicial participants to offer even an oral explanation of their judgments

and decisions, and many studies allow anonymous responses from judicial participants, implicitly recognizing that an identified participant might well exhibit different judgments and decisions. Until we identify biases and errors made by judges under realistic conditions, we cannot know how effective institutional forms of accountability are at flushing these biases and errors out of the judicial system. The lack of pre- and postdecision accountability to known audiences, some of whom value accuracy and fidelity to the law and others of whom may favor particular outcomes regardless of the merits, renders the external validity of many simulations of judicial decision making suspect.

NORMS FOR JUDGING JUDGES

The primary goal of many studies of judicial decision making is descriptive: to provide an accurate picture of how judges go about making decisions. But often a secondary goal is to compare actual judicial behavior to ideal judicial behavior, as in the many studies investigating whether extralegal factors influence judicial decisions. Sometimes the ideal that serves as the comparison is easy to identify and uncontroversial. No one would argue that the appearance of the defendant or victim should not have an impact on sentencing decisions, and thus a judge influenced by the attractiveness of either would deviate from the ideal. Other times determining what ideal judicial behavior looks like can be quite difficult. Commentators from both sides of the political aisle will agree that the law rather than a judge's personal political preferences should drive the decisions of Supreme Court justices, but on abstract constitutional matters, ambiguities in how best to interpret and apply the law make finding the ideal outcome controversial. A decision that appears to favor conservative interests may also be quite defensible from a textualist interpretive perspective (e.g., the text of the U.S. Constitution's Commerce Clause seems to support deferring to states on the question of whether to permit the growing of marijuana for medical purposes), whereas a decision that appears to favor liberal interests may also be quite defensible within a purposivist interpretive perspective (e.g., the Commerce Clause's purpose of allowing the federal government to regulate state activities with important effects on interstate commerce seems to support greater federal power over medical marijuana; for this contrast in perspectives, see Gonzalez v. Raich, 2005). Difficulties defining ideal behavior may even exist at the trial level, because often there are alternative ways to interpret and apply evidentiary and procedural rules.

We see the difficulty in finding measures of judicial quality play out in debates about judicial diversity. Arguments for greater judicial diversity often reduce down, at least implicitly, to replacing one set of biases with another: By appointing more female and minority judges, perhaps the constellation of ingroup–outgroup biases present in white male judges can be offset by different constellations of biases. Because there is no objective, consensual metric for good judicial decisions (Mitchell, 2010; Wistrich, 2010), the argument is never made that one demographic group is better suited to judging per se or that members of one demographic group produce higher-quality decisions or more accurate decisions than members of another group (although some are close to making the latter argument by arguing about the different perspectives that different groups will bring to judging and, in the process, endorsing stereotypes about the different groups).

Even when defining ideal judicial behavior is easy, a useful alternative comparison is between how judges behave and how others who might perform the same task behave. Most commonly that comparison will be between elected versus appointed judges or between judges versus juries, but the comparison may also be between a single judge versus a panel of judges or between, say, a panel of white male judges and a more diverse panel of judges. These decision maker–to–decision maker comparisons provide important information from an institutional design perspective: Even if judges exhibit nonideal behavior, if they deviate less from the norm than the alternative decision makers do when performing the same task, then the judge is the better decision maker.

Take for example the Guthrie–Rachlinski–Wistrich line of research, which compares judges with laypeople on a variety of rational judgment tests and finds notable similarities and differences between the groups. One can argue from this line of work for greater attention to the training of judges on statistical reasoning, causal inference, and methods that promote rational deliberation. But given that laypeople also fall prey to biases and errors, this line of work hardly supports taking power away from judges and giving it to juries. Rather, this research supports the present arrangement at trials, where there is a separation of the fact finder, in the form of the jury, from the evidentiary gatekeeper, in the form of the judge, so that we can prevent the ultimate decision maker from being exposed to irrelevant evidence and inflammatory arguments that could bias its final decision.

Researchers undertaking judicial studies should be mindful that the results of their studies will likely be used in some policy or normative debate, whether or not the researchers themselves take a position in that debate. That awareness should inform not only how results are interpreted and limitations expressed but also how the research is designed, including choices that affect the external validity of a simulation or archival study. Studies of judicial decision making have found numerous areas in which judges fail to attend only to the applicable laws and relevant facts, but studies have also found that a number of institutional mechanisms impose accountability and structure that can reduce the influence of judges' personal preferences or faulty beliefs. Efforts should certainly be made to further structure judicial decision making and flush out improper influences, and psychological research has an important role to play in these efforts (Dhami & Belton, 2017; Vidmar, 2011). But any reform should itself be subjected to empirical testing, because often reforms present their own unanticipated problems.

REFERENCES

Ashenfelter, O., Eisenberg, T., & Schwab, S. J. (1995). Politics and the judiciary: The influence of judicial background on case outcomes. *Journal of Legal Studies, 24,* 257–281.

Bartels, B. L. (2011). Choices in context: How case-level factors influence the magnitude of ideological voting on the U.S. Supreme Court. *American Politics Research, 39,* 142–175.

Baum, L. (2006). *Judges and their audiences: A perspective on judicial behavior.* Princeton, NJ: Princeton University Press.

Baum, L. (2010). Motivation and judicial behavior: Expanding the scope of inquiry. In D. Klein & G. Mitchell (Eds.), *The psychology of judicial decision making* (pp. 3–25). Oxford, UK: Oxford University Press.

Baum, L. (2017). *Ideology in the Supreme Court.* Princeton, NJ: Princeton University Press.

Baum, L., Gray, T. R., & Klein, D. E. (2017). Measuring the impact of election outcomes on voting in state supreme courts. In C. W. Bonneau & M. G. Hall (Eds.), *Judicial elections in the 21st century* (pp. 195–216). London: Routledge.

Beattey, R. A., Jr., Matsuura, T., & Jeglic, E. L. (2014). Judicial bond-setting behavior: The perceived nature of the crime may matter more than how serious it is. *Psychology, Public Policy, and Law, 20,* 411–420.

Boccaccini, M. T., Murrie, D. C., Rufino, K. A., & Gardner, B. O. (2014). Evaluator differences in PCL-R factor and facet level scoring. *Law and Human Behavior, 38,* 337–345.

Bonneau, C. W., & Cann, D. M. (2009). The effect of campaign contributions on judicial decision making. Available at *https://papers.ssrn.com/sol3/papers.cfm?abstract_id=1337668.*

Bonneau, C. W., & Rice, H. M. (2009). Impartial judges? Race, institutional context, and U.S. state supreme courts. *State Politics and Policy Quarterly, 9,* 381–403.

Bornstein, B. H., & Miller, M. K. (2009). *God in the courtroom: Religion's role at trial.* Oxford, UK: Oxford University Press.

Boyd, C. L. (2016). Representation on the courts: The effect of race and gender. *Political Research Quarterly, 69,* 788–799.

Brace, P., & Boyea, B. D. (2008). State public opinion, the death penalty, and the practice of electing judges. *American Journal of Political Science, 52,* 360–372.

Brace, P., Langer, L., & Hall, M. G. (2000). Measuring the preferences of state supreme court judges. *Journal of Politics, 62,* 387–413.

Cann, D. M. (2007a). Justice for sale? Campaign contributions and judicial decision-making. *State Politics & Policy Quarterly, 7,* 281–297.

Cann, D. M. (2007b). Beyond accountability and independence: Judicial selection and state court performance. *Judicature, 90*, 226–232.

Carmines, E. G., & D'Amico, N. J. (2015). The new look in political ideology research. *Annual Review of Political Science, 18*, 205–216.

Cecil, J. S. (2005). Ten years of judicial gatekeeping under *Daubert. American Journal of Public Health, 95*, S74–S80.

Chang, Y., Chen, K., & Lin, C. (2017). Anchoring effect in real litigation: An empirical study, Available at *https://papers.ssrn.com/sol3/papers.cfm?abstract_id=2726903*.

Chew, P. K., & Kelley, R. E. (2009). Myth of the color-blind judge: An empirical analysis of racial harassment cases. *Washington University Law Review, 86*, 1117–1166.

Choi, S. J., Gulati, G. M., & Posner, E. A. (2008). Professionals or politicians: The uncertain empirical case for an elected rather than appointed judiciary. *Journal of Law, Economics, and Organization, 26*, 290–336.

Cox, A. B., & Miles, T. P. (2008). Judging the Voting Rights Act. *Columbia Law Review, 108*, 1–54.

Cross, F. B. (2007). *Decision making in the U.S. Courts of Appeals*. Stanford, CA: Stanford University Press.

Dahir, V. B., Richardson, J. T., Ginsburg, G. P., Gatowski, S. I., Dobbin, S. A., & Merlino, M. L. (2005). Judicial application of *Daubert* to psychological syndrome and profile evidence: A research note. *Psychology, Public Policy, and Law, 11*, 62–82.

Danziger, S., Levav, J., & Avnaim-Pesso, L. (2011). Extraneous factors in judicial decisions. *Proceedings of the National Academy of Sciences of the USA, 108*, 6889–6892.

Devins, N., & Federspiel, W. (2010). The Supreme Court, social psychology, and group formation. In D. Klein & G. Mitchell (Eds.), *The psychology of judicial decision making* (pp. 85–100). Oxford, UK: Oxford University Press.

Dhami, M. K. (2003). Psychological models of professional decision-making. *Psychological Science, 14*, 175–180.

Dhami, M. K. (2005). From discretion to disagreement: Explaining disparities in judges' pre-trial decisions. *Behavioral Sciences and the Law, 23*, 367–386.

Dhami, M. K. (2010). Lay magistrates' interpretations of "substantial grounds" for denying bail. *Howard Journal of Criminal Justice, 49*, 349–360.

Dhami, M. K., & Ayton, P. (2001). Bailing and jailing the fast and frugal way. *Journal of Behavioral Decision Making, 14*, 141–168.

Dhami, M. K., & Belton, I. K. (2017). On getting inside the judge's mind. *Translational Issues in Psychological Science, 3*, 214–226.

Epstein, L., Landes, W. M., & Posner, R. A. (2013). *The behavior of federal judges: A theoretical and empirical study of rational choice*. Cambridge, MA: Harvard University Press.

Fischman, J. (2015a). Interpreting circuit court voting patterns: A social interactions framework. *Journal of Law, Economics, and Organization, 31*, 808–842.

Fischman, J. (2015b). Do the justices vote like policy makers? Evidence from scaling the Supreme Court with interest groups. *Journal of Legal Studies, 44*, S269–S293.

Fischman, J. B. (2011). Estimating preferences of circuit judges: A model of consensus voting. *Journal of Law and Economics, 54*, 781–809.

Fischman, J. B., & Schanzenbach, M. M. (2011). Do standards of review matter? The case of federal criminal sentencing. *Journal of Legal Studies, 40*, 405–437.

Freiburger, T. L. (2010). The effects of gender, family status, and race on sentencing decisions. *Behavioral Sciences and the Law, 28*, 378–395.

Gillespie, L. K., Loughran, T. A., Smith, M. D., Fogel, S. J., & Bjerregaard, B. (2014). Exploring the role of victim sex, victim conduct, and victim-defendant relationship in capital punishment sentencing. *Homicide Studies, 18*, 175–195.

Goldman, S. (1966). Voting behavior on the United States Courts of Appeals, 1961–1964. *American Political Science Review, 60*, 374–383.

Goldman, S. (1975). Voting behavior on the United States Courts of Appeals revisited. *American Political Science Review, 69*, 491–506.

Gonzalez v. Raich, 545 U.S. 1 (2005).

Groscup, J. L., Penrod, S. D., Studebaker, C. A., Huss, M. T., & O'Neil, K. M. (2002). The effects of *Daubert* on the admissibility of expert testimony in state and federal criminal cases. *Psychology, Public Policy, and Law, 8*, 339–372.

Gruenfeld, D. H. (1995). Status, ideology, and integrative complexity on the U.S. Supreme Court: Rethinking the politics of political decision making. *Journal of Personality and Social Psychology, 68*, 5–20.

Gruhl, J., Spohn, C., & Welch, S. (1981). Women as policymakers: The case of trial judges. *American Journal of Political Science, 25*, 308–322.

Guthrie, C., Rachlinski, J. J., & Wistrich, A. J. (2001). Inside the judicial mind. *Cornell Law Review, 86*, 777–830.

Guthrie, C., Rachlinski, J. J., & Wistrich, A. J. (2007). Blinking on the bench: How judges decide cases. *Cornell Law Review, 93*, 1–43.

Hall, M. E. K. (2014). The semiconstrained court: Public opinion, separation of powers, and the U.S. Supreme Court's fear of nonimplementation. *American Journal of Political Science, 58*, 352–366.

Hall, M. G. (1995). Justices as representatives: Elections and judicial politics in the American states. *American Politics Quarterly, 23*, 485–503.

Harmon, M. G., & O'Brien, R. M. (2011). Gendered arrests or gendered sentencing: Explaining the narrowing of the gender gap in imprisonment over time: 1970–2008. *Sociological Perspectives, 54*, 641–664.

Hazelton, M. L. W., Montgomery, J. M., & Nyhan, B. (2016). Does public financing affect judicial behavior? Evidence from the North Carolina Supreme Court. *American Politics Research, 44*, 587–617.

Hester, R., & Hartman, T. K. (2017). Conditional race disparities in criminal sentencing: A test of the liberation hypothesis from a non-guidelines state. *Journal of Quantitative Criminology, 33*, 77–100.

Hettinger, V. A., Lindquist, S. A., & Martinek, W. L. (2006). *Judging on a collegial court: Influences on federal appellate decision making.* Charlottesville, VA: University of Virginia Press.

Hibbing, J. R., Smith, K. B., & Alford, J. R. (2014). Differences in negativity bias underlie variations in political ideology. *Behavioral and Brain Sciences, 37*, 297–350.

Huber, G. A., & Gordon, S. C. (2004). Accountability and coercion: Is justice blind when it runs for office? *American Journal of Political Science, 48*, 247–263.

Johnson, B. D. (2006). The multilevel context of criminal sentencing: Integrating judge- and county-level influences. *Criminology, 44*, 259–298.

Kapardis, A. (2016). Extra-legal factors that impact on sentencing decisions. In A. Kapardis & D. P. Farrington (Eds.), *The psychology of crime, policing and courts* (pp. 201–230). London: Routledge.

Kastellec, J. P. (2013). Racial diversity and judicial influence on appellate courts. *American Journal of Political Science, 57*, 167–183.

Kim, B., Spohn, C., & Hedberg, E. C. (2015). Federal sentencing as a complex collaborative process: Judges, prosecutors, judge–prosecutor dyads, and disparity in sentencing. *Criminology, 53*, 597–623.

Klein, D. E. (2002). *Making law in the United States Courts of Appeals*. Cambridge, UK: Cambridge University Press.

Krafka, C., Dunn, M. A., Johnson, M. T., Cecil, J. S., & Miletich, D. (2002). Judge and attorney experiences, practices, and concerns regarding expert testimony in federal civil trials. *Psychology, Public Policy, and Law, 8*, 309–332.

Kritzer, H. M. (2004). Disappearing trials? A comparative perspective. *Journal of Empirical Legal Studies, 1*, 735–754.

Kritzer, H. M. (2016). Impact of judicial elections on judicial decisions. *Annual Review of Law and Social Science, 12*, 353–371.

Kulik, C. T., Perry, E. L., & Pepper, M. B. (2003). Here comes the judge: The influence of judge personal characteristics on federal sexual harassment case outcomes. *Law and Human Behavior, 27*, 69–86.

Larrick, R. P. (2004). Debiasing. In D. J. Koehler & N. Harvey (Eds.), *Blackwell handbook of judgment and decision making* (pp. 316–337). Malden, MA: Blackwell.

Lerner, J. S., & Tetlock, P. E. (1999). Accounting for the effects of accountability. *Psychological Bulletin, 125*, 255–275.

Lewis, T., Klettke, B., & Day, A. (2014). Sentencing in child sexual assault cases: Factors influencing judicial decision-making. *Journal of Sexual Aggression, 20*, 281–295.

Lim, C. S. H., Silveira, B., & Snyder, J. M., Jr. (2016). Do judges' characteristics matter? Ethnicity, gender, and partisanship in Texas state trial courts. Available at *https://lim.economics.cornell.edu/texaspaper.pdf*.

Lim, C. S. H., Snyder, J. M., Jr., & Strömberg, D. (2015). The judge, the politician, and the press: Newspaper coverage and criminal sentencing across electoral systems. *American Economic Journal: Applied Economics, 7*, 103–135.

Manning, K. L., Carroll, B. A., & Carp, R. A. (2004). Does age matter? Judicial decision making in age discrimination cases. *Social Science Quarterly, 85*, 1–18.

Martinek, W. L. (2010). Judges as members of small groups. In D. Klein & G. Mitchell (Eds.), *The psychology of judicial decision making* (pp. 73–84). Oxford, UK: Oxford University Press.

McCall, M. (2003). The politics of judicial elections: The influence of campaign contributions on the voting patterns of Texas Supreme Court Justices, 1994–1997. *Politics and Policy, 31*, 314–343.

Merlino, M. L., Murray, C. I., & Richardson, J. T. (2008). Judicial gatekeeping and the social construction of the admissibility of expert testimony. *Behavioral Sciences and the Law, 26*, 187–206.

Mitchell, G. (2010). Evaluating judges. In D. Klein & G. Mitchell (Eds.), *The psychology of judicial decision making* (pp. 221–248). Oxford, UK: Oxford University Press.

Monahan, J., & Skeem, J. L. (2014a). Risk redux: The resurgence of risk assessment in criminal sanctioning. *Federal Sentencing Reporter, 26*, 158–166.

Monahan, J., & Skeem, J. L. (2014b). The evolution of violence risk assessment. *CNS Spectrums, 19*, 419–424.

Monahan, J., & Skeem, J. L. (2016). Risk assessment in criminal sentencing. *Annual Review of Clinical Psychology, 12*, 489–513.

Morin, J. L. (2013). The voting behavior of minority judges in the U.S. Courts of Appeals: Does the race of the claimant matter? *American Politics Research, 42*, 34–64.

Morrow, W. J., Vickovic, S. G., & Fradella, H. F. (2014). Examining the prevalence and correlates of a "senior citizen discount" in US federal courts. *Criminal Justice Studies, 27*, 362–386.

Mueller-Johnson, K. U., & Dhami, M. K. (2010). Effect of offenders' age and health on sentencing decisions. *Journal of Social Psychology, 150*, 77–97.

Murrie, D. C., Boccaccini, M. T., Guarnera, L. A., & Rufino, K. A. (2013). Are forensic experts biased by the side that retained them? *Psychological Science, 24*, 1889–1897.

Oeberst, A., & Goeckenjan, I. (2016). When being wise after the event results in injustice: Evidence for hindsight bias in judges' negligence assessments. *Psychology, Public Policy and Law, 22*, 271–279.

Oldfather, C. M. (2014). Against accuracy (as a measure of judicial performance). *New England Law Review, 48*, 493–502.

Paynter, S., & Kearney, R. C. (2010). Who watches the watchmen? Evaluating judicial performance in the American states. *Administration and Society, 41*, 923–953.

Pennington, J., & Schlenker, B. R. (1999). Accountability for consequential decisions: Justifying ethical judgments to audiences. *Personality and Social Psychology Bulletin, 25*, 1067–1081.

Philippe, A. (2017). Gender disparities in criminal justice. Available at *www.tse-fr.eu/sites/default/files/TSE/documents/doc/wp/2017/wp_tse_762.pdf*.

Quinn, A., & Schlenker, B. R. (2002). Can accountability produce independence? Goals as determinants of the impact of accountability on conformity. *Personality and Social Psychology Bulletin, 28*, 472–483.

Rachlinski, J. J., Guthrie, C., & Wistrich, A. J. (2006). Inside the bankruptcy judge's mind. *Boston University Law Review, 86*, 1227–1265.

Rachlinski, J. J., Guthrie, C., & Wistrich, A. J. (2011). Probability, probable cause, and the hindsight bias. *Journal of Empirical Legal Studies, 8*, 72–98.

Rachlinski, J. J., Johnson, S. L., Wistrich, A. J., & Guthrie, C. (2009). Does unconscious bias affect trial judges? *Notre Dame Law Review, 84*, 1195–1246.

Ramji-Nogales, J., Schoenholtz, A. I., & Schrag, P. G. (2007). Refugee roulette: Disparities in asylum adjudication. *Stanford Law Review, 60*, 295–411.

Rebe, R. J. (2016). Analyzing the link between dollars and decisions: A multi-state study of campaign contributions and judicial decision making. *American Review of Politics, 35*, 65–91.

Schanzenbach, M. M. (2015). Racial disparities, judge characteristics, and standards of review in sentencing. *Journal of Institutional and Theoretical Economics, 171,* 27–47.

Schlanger, M. (2006). What we know and what we should know about American trial trends. *Journal of Dispute Resolution, 2006*(1), 35–50.

Schmittat, S. M., & Englich, B. (2016). If you judge, investigate! Responsibility reduces confirmatory information processing in legal experts. *Psychology, Public Policy and Law, 22,* 386–400.

Segal, J. (2000). Representative decision making on the federal bench: Clinton's district court appointees. *Political Research Quarterly, 53,* 137–150.

Shanteau, J., & Dalgliesh, L. (2010). Expertise of court judges. In D. Klein & G. Mitchell (Eds.), *The psychology of judicial decision making* (pp. 269–278). Oxford, UK: Oxford University Press.

Shepherd, J. M. (2009). Money, politics, and impartial justice. *Duke Law Journal, 58,* 623–685.

Spohn, C. (1990). The sentencing decisions of Black and White judges: Expected and unexpected similarities. *Law and Society Review, 24,* 1197–1216.

Spohn, C. (2009). *How do judges decide? The search for fairness and justice in punishment* (2nd ed.). Thousand Oaks, CA: Sage.

Spohn, C., & Beichner, D. (2000). Is preferential treatment of female offenders a thing of the past? A multistate study of gender, race, and imprisonment. *Criminal Justice Reform, 11,* 149–184.

Spohn, C., Gruhl, J., & Welch, S. (1981–1982). The effect of race on sentencing: A re-examination of an unsettled question. *Law and Society Review, 16,* 71–88.

Steblay, N., Hosch, H. M., Culhane, S. E., & McWethy, A. (2006). The impact on juror verdicts of judicial instruction to disregard inadmissible evidence: A meta-analysis. *Law and Human Behavior, 30,* 469–492.

Steffensmeier, D., & Britt, C. L. (2001). Judges' race and judicial decision making: Do Black judges sentence differently? *Social Science Quarterly, 82,* 749–764.

Stribopoulos, J., & Yaha, M. A. (2007). Does a judge's party of appointment or gender matter to case outcomes? An empirical study of the Court of Appeal of Ontario. *Osgoode Hall Law Journal, 45,* 315–363.

Suedfeld, P., Guttieri, K., & Tetlock, P. E. (2003). Assessing integrative complexity at a distance: Archival analyses of thinking and decision-making. In J. Post (Ed.), *The psychological assessment of political leaders* (pp. 246–270). Ann Arbor: University of Michigan Press.

Szmer, J., Christensen, R. K., & Kaheny, E. B. (2015). Gender, race, and dissensus on state supreme courts. *Social Science Quarterly, 96,* 553–575.

Tanner v. United States, 483 U.S. 107 (1987).

Tetlock, P. E. (2002). Social functionalist frameworks for judgments and choice: Intuitive politicians, theologians, and prosecutors. *Psychological Review, 109,* 451–471.

Tetlock, P. E., Bernzweig, J., & Gallant, J. L. (1985). Supreme Court decision making: Cognitive style as a predictor of ideological consistency of voting. *Journal of Personality and Social Psychology, 48,* 1227–1239.

Tetlock, P. E., & Boettger, R. (1989). Accountability: A social magnifier of the dilution effect. *Journal of Personality and Social Psychology, 57,* 388–398.

Vidmar, N. (2011). The psychology of trial judging. *Current Directions in Psychological Science, 20,* 58–62.

Walker, T. G., & Barrow, D. J. (1985). The diversification of the federal bench: Policy and process ramifications. *Journal of Politics, 47,* 596–617.

Welch, S., Combs, M., & Gruhl, J. (1988). Do Black judges make a difference? *American Journal of Political Science, 32,* 126–136.

Wingate, P. H., & Thornton, G. C., III. (2004). Industrial/organizational psychology and the federal judiciary: Expert witness testimony and the *Daubert* standards. *Law and Human Behavior, 28,* 97–114.

Wistrich, A. J. (2010). Defining good judging. In D. Klein & G. Mitchell (Eds.), *The psychology of judicial decision making* (pp. 249–267). Oxford, UK: Oxford University Press.

Wistrich, A. J., Guthrie, C., & Rachlinski, J. J. (2005). Can judges ignore inadmissible information?: The difficulty of deliberately disregarding. *University of Pennsylvania Law Review, 153,* 1251–1385.

CHAPTER 17

Translating Psychological Science into Policy and Practice

Nancy K. Steblay

Psychological science has come a long way in terms of its application to legal issues. United States Supreme Court cases within memory of some scientists speak to the paucity of science-based legal knowledge just a few decades ago. At that time, social science research was absent from courtroom discussion, fragmentary, or misunderstood by the court on topics such as jury attitudes on the death penalty (*Witherspoon v. Illinois*, 1968), jury size (*Williams v. Florida*, 1970), evaluation of eyewitness memory evidence (*Manson v. Brathwaite*, 1977) and prediction of dangerousness (*Barefoot v. Estelle*, 1983). Indeed the *Barefoot* case included the infamous claim that clinical predictions were not always wrong, "only most of the time" (p. 901). As these examples illustrate, the breadth of psychological science relevant to the legal area is immense—including memory, social influence, clinical assessment, evidence evaluation, jury decision processes, and issues of punishment and deterrence, to name a few—and trajectories of psychological content into law have varied, as have levels of success in moving to policy and practice.

One avenue for broad impact of psychological science is through case-specific evidence-based forensic evaluations by mental health professionals. Clinical knowledge often goes to the heart of a legal decision rendered for an individual in a criminal case, civil proceeding, specialty court, or diversion program. Psychological expertise likewise can be applied to address nonclinical specific case facts—for example, in assessment of pretrial publicity, assistance in attorney trial preparation and jury selection, employment discrimination analysis, and testing for police lineup quality. This case-specific approach infrequently leads to policy reform. A notable exception is when the case rises to a higher court, as in the U.S. Supreme Court decision in *Miller v. Alabama* (2012) that struck down mandatory life without parole in juvenile sentencing, concordant with research regarding developmental immaturity in young offenders.

Another means to apply scientific knowledge to law is via direct attempts to influence policies such as law enforcement practice, legal standards, or courtroom procedures. The purpose of this chapter is to draw insight from the experiences of psychological scientists who have actively pursued change in legal policy and practice. The chapter begins with broad discussion of what psychological science brings to law: relevant principles, a method to test legal assumptions and innovations, and understanding of cognitive biases that impinge on individual and collective efforts to make effective decisions. The first section also posits ideas about how scientific knowledge can be effectively delivered to legal audiences and how collaborators from the legal field can enrich both content and presentation of our research. The chapter next examines specific catalysts that have helped to draw attention to science-based policy initiatives and the obstacles that have stymied efforts to implement psychological knowledge in law. The final section details the myriad avenues for moving science to policy and practice.

This chapter draws from multiple lines of research but relies most heavily on the example of eyewitness science, for two primary reasons. First, eyewitness science has been lauded as one of the most successful collaborations between psychological science and law, a narrative that has been richly documented (e.g., Doyle, 2005; Steblay & Loftus, 2013). Second, I am an eyewitness scientist with the good fortune to have played a small part over three decades in the evolving story of eyewitness science in its translation to law. My perspective is that of a scientist who has been drawn far outside of the lab and in the process has viewed the scope of efforts necessary for policy change. My experiences have included partnerships with law enforcement to revise evidence collection protocols and analyze field-test outcomes; presentations, collaborations, trainings, and consultations with police, judges, prosecutors, defense attorneys, legal scholars, policymakers, and journalists; testimony before policy and government officials; consultation on criminal and civil cases and expert testimony in court; and innumerable conversations with remarkable colleagues in science, law, and policy. From such on-the-ground experiences—mine and those of other researchers—I attempt to derive some practical ideas regarding the translation of science to law.

THE FOUNDATION FOR POLICY AND PRACTICE

The preceding 16 chapters in this volume summarize an impressive and immense body of scientific knowledge on psychological topics relevant to law. In this chapter I consider how to move this knowledge into policy and practice.

Presentation of Scientific Content: Message, Audience, and Speakers

At the core of the psychology and law interface is the exploration of fascinating psychological phenomena. Law then adds an intricacy and intensity to the research endeavor, requiring that scientists design studies and deliver research findings in anticipation of sometimes harsh scrutiny from the legal world. Hence, the first step toward policy is for researchers to consider how to faithfully and effectively present relevant science to legal audiences.

The Message: Sometimes Less Is More

One of our greatest scientific strengths—the comprehensive understanding and reporting of research—can also be our greatest weakness for translation to policy. The audience simply gets lost in the details or becomes so focused on a small weak point that the broader message is compromised. That being so, a sharply focused *white paper* is one means by which a consensus of scientific knowledge can be brought to the legal community. Constraint may be the wise strategy regarding the number of core principles advanced in a white paper and the level of detail offered as to how these principles might be operationalized. For example, the seminal report of eyewitness researchers developed by Wells et al. (1998) was a relatively conservative recommendation of just four foundational principles. Even at risk of producing an incomplete summary of intriguing research findings, the authors opted for a limited approach. In hindsight, this was a good strategy: "The general idea behind a recommendation is likely to be more important and enduring than are the specific details of how that idea is operationalized" (Wells & Quigley-McBride, 2016 p. 292).

How effective is a white paper? The progression of eyewitness lineup reform over two decades reveals the original core reforms running through United States national-level organizations such as U.S Department of Justice, The Innocence Project, The Justice Project, the International Association of Chiefs of Police, and the National Academy of Sciences. Rose (2017), in a review of court opinions, notes that the Wells et al. (1998) document has been cited in nearly all state cases involving eyewitness evidence reform. A more recent white paper on the topic of police-induced confessions (Kassin et al., 2010) has already informed an American Psychological Association (2014) resolution on the interrogations of criminal suspects. Rose (2017) laments that no such white paper exists in the jury literature, a vast research domain that has had difficulty moving to policy.

Within a white paper or elsewhere, psychologists know that a good story well told is compelling, and this is certainly true in the legal field. Audiences and juries can often better follow the narrative of a single vivid study (or case) than a string of statistics. The legal world also likes a good theory; not an excruciatingly nuanced treatise, but a relatable concept that logically connects the research dots. The notion of *relative judgment*—a witness decision made by comparing lineup members to determine which is the closest relative to the others—is easily grasped by audiences, who can then understand lineup procedural reforms that remediate negative effects of relative judgment. *Minimization* and *maximization*—the strategies that underlie how police move a suspect to confession—are similarly straight-forward and productive concepts in the explanation of false confessions. It should go without saying that the single study as example or the memorable concept must be representative of the broader research base.

The Audience: Sound Science Made Relevant and Practical

For the broader and deeper base of research findings, the field of psychol-ogy and law has embraced meta-analysis as a means to consolidate infor-mation. "Scientific framework evidence" is a phrase used by the National Academy of Sciences (2014) to denote an informed and orderly account of research findings provided to triers of fact. This notion fittingly describes a good meta-analysis: a structure for organizing research findings and illu-minating patterns across studies. Meta-analysis is uniquely positioned to highlight converging evidence across labs, samples, stimuli, and partici-pant response measures—thereby supporting external validity and replica-bility—as well as to reveal limitations in quality and scope of the research base. The value to law of meta-analysis (or of any comprehensive review) can be judged in part by how well the author has positioned the work to translate into expert scientific framework testimony, addressing issues of consensus, reliability (validity), and relevance (*Daubert v. Merrell Dow Pharmaceuticals*, 1993). A meta-analysis further provides a safeguard against the temptation to cherry-pick an unrepresentative single study to champion a position. It coaches the reader to understand that the good money is on the pattern, not the outlier.

There is benefit to simplicity even within a thorough research review. Elaborate statistical outcomes are often dry and soporific (even for research-ers), when what the reader really wants to know in straightforward terms is whether a claim holds up or not, whether it holds up under certain condi-tions and not others—in short, what difference does it make? Too often a meta-analysis leaves the reader cold; the implicit follow-up question ("Well, so what?") cannot be answered by a slick statistical package.

The challenge is to frame scientific data from a useful legal perspec-tive: What constitutes strong evidence, weak evidence, or tainted evidence? What are the compelling implications of the research for policy? Statisti-cal effect sizes can be translated into forensically relevant indices of pro-bative value ("How does this evidence make a legal proposition more or less likely?") and error reduction or increase. For example, the impact of postidentification feedback on eyewitness confidence can be discussed using a traditional statistic: "Feedback increases the certainty of mistaken eyewitnesses by one full standard deviation" (stunning to researchers; less meaningful to most others). Or, better: "The percentage of mistaken eye-witnesses who will display high certainty rises from a mere 6% (with no feedback) to 29% (with feedback), a near five-fold increase in very confident but mistaken eyewitnesses" (Steblay, Wells, & Douglass, 2014, p. 9). In short, the audience must be treated to the practical knowledge that exists in all this information (e.g., Steblay, 2016).

Consider the current burden for judges created by rapid scientific advances (Smalarz & Wells, 2012). It behooves researchers to assist the court in its charge as gatekeeper for court evidence and to make a complex literature accessible to others as well: triers of fact, legal scholars, and policymakers. To do so also requires that we present and publish our work in venues beyond research journals. A lawyer and long-time advocate for reform commented to me years ago: "You folks need to publish this stuff in places where people will actually see it." The comment is still apropos.

The Speakers (Participants): Science Is Necessary but Not Sufficient

Successful inroads to policy and practice require expertise beyond science. Attorneys, judges, law enforcement personnel, policymakers, legislators, legal scholars, and others offer insight into the substance and know-how of policy and practice, and they have the connections and power to develop and move policy along. Scientists may become myopic about a specific research-based principle, particularly when it is viewed away from the broader context of costs, benefits, and unintended consequences that must be appraised by policymakers. Nonscience partners can provide a productive counterbalance to what has been called this "single-effect problem." In an analogous manner, diverse collaborators may be able to temper a one-sided perspective that arises from the fundamental role differences of law enforcement personnel, attorneys, policymakers, and researchers. An example of truly amazing success from very diverse participants (described, perhaps charitably, by one member as "extremely unruly" and "not mixing well") is the technical working group convened by U.S. Attorney General Janet Reno that ultimately crafted a national guide for eyewitness evidence (Doyle, 2005, p. 172; National Institute of Justice, 1999).

There are benefits to casting a wide net of collaborating experts, each playing to strengths and to the relevant constituency. Some have the talent to write books for broad audience appeal or to author articles for periodicals of professional groups (judges, lawyers, law enforcement), some have the credentials for amicus curiae briefs, court decisions, law review articles, and model policies. The Innocence Project (more broadly, the Innocence Network), as an example, has been an indispensable source for expertise and resources in education, legal proceedings, and policy reform. The breadth of expertise that accompanies policy change also is revealed in the treasure trove of American Psychological Association (2018) amicus briefs on topics of psychology and law.

Nonscience collaborators can communicate with appropriate tone, perspective, and credibility augmented by their experiences, especially for audiences of their constituencies in law enforcement, law, or policy. For example, a speaking panel to a police audience on the topic of eyewitness evidence often includes a victim of wrongful conviction, a member of law enforcement, an attorney, and a scientist. In short order, the problem is brought into sharp relief through the stories of those who have lived with the error (the wrongfully convicted, the crime victim, the remorseful investigator or prosecutor) and those who have tried to correct it. And, whereas a scientist has academic gravitas, a police chief has the inside scoop from the station house. Sometimes the statement a scientist well knows to be on point is nevertheless better received when coming from a nonscientist.

An intangible element of success is the appeal to audiences of certain personal qualities in speakers: some mystery mix of expertise, credibility, sincerity, listening and questioning skills, good humor, and down-to-earth practical perspective. I have also noticed that the most successful contributors to policy change are faultlessly generous in sharing their time, knowledge, and expertise (a prerequisite for a task that may take years to get real traction). The somewhat amorphous quality of these personal characteristics makes for difficult analysis, and yet they are critically important.

Furthermore, a presentation to police, judges, legislators, jurors, or others is often a one-shot chance at a good impression. If a speaker's style is off-putting or seems to be one-sided, if content is pitched at the wrong level, if the presentation is disorganized and bumbling or too academic and esoteric, then the opportunity is lost, and, regrettably, audience members may dismiss or avoid hearing from psychological scientists in the future. Given this onus, a speaker cannot be cavalier or lazy in preparation. It is indeed satisfying to know more about a scientific topic than anyone in the room, but therein also lies the responsibility to build the audience's new appreciation and understanding of science that connects to their experience. The scientific knowledge remains the same regardless of audience, but one must prepare meticulously for each specific group. Once again, local sponsors can be enormously helpful in anticipating the level of audience members' expertise and knowledge, their inclination to ask questions and participate in posing answers, as well as the potential areas for confusion, misconception, or blatant hostility. The upshot is that speakers who wish to influence practice and policy must respect their audiences.

Knowledge about Judgment Biases, Social Influences, and Cognitive Errors as Obstacles to Good Practice and Productive Policy Change

Errors in human perception and judgment intrude in legal matters as they do elsewhere. Findley and Scott (2006) have masterfully described how cognitive shortcuts and logical fallacies—familiar to psychologists through classic works in cognitive and social psychology—can afflict police investigators and triers of fact (see also Findley, 2010). Tunnel vision and its component parts—confirmation bias, hindsight bias, belief perseverance, outcome bias—steer investigators and decision makers to focus on a single conclusion or suspect and to collect, reject, and filter information through a lens of an already established belief. The list of cognitive biases is long (see Wilford, Shestak, & Wells, Chapter 11, this volume). For example, judgment can run amuck when automatic intuition overrides informed deliberation (Kahneman, 2011). Truth bias can induce jurors to believe a false confession, and attribution errors can underestimate the power of police procedures to taint eyewitness memory (Appleby & Kassin, 2016). Anchoring effects are revealed when judges fail to disregard prejudicial information from pretrial hearings (Wistrich, Guthrie, & Rachlinski, 2005). Defendants' plea decisions sometimes employ satisficing (choosing a satisfactory short-term outcome) rather than applying the rational reasoning that would benefit their long-term situation (Redlich & Shteynberg, 2016).

Of particular consequence is a *forensic confirmation bias,* through which preexisting beliefs, expectations, motives, and context influence evidence evaluation during the course of a case (Kassin, Dror, & Kukucka, 2013). Such bias can operate when an individual piece of evidence is evaluated (e.g., a fingerprint or a confession). This developing literature also illuminates how knowledge of one piece of evidence contaminates evaluation of others (e.g., Hasel & Kassin, 2009; Charman, Kavetski, & Mueller, 2017). Psychological contamination of evidence merits greater attention and the development of safeguards. In fact, research topics that have received little policy consideration (e.g., alibi evidence) may become more salient in the context of an evidentiary snowball bias that brings multiple forms of evidence into question.

A difficulty in bringing this knowledge to law is that people are not easily convinced that they are vulnerable to biases or that their behaviors exhibit, even innocently, such irrationality (Zapf & Dror, 2017). Thus, for example, a call for double-blind administration of lineups sometimes is seen as slandering the integrity of police officers (Lappas & Loftus, 2013).

The Research Method Required to Develop and Test Policy Innovations

The nexus of psychology and law is behavioral assumptions about how people act, why they behave as they do, and how behavior can be changed or controlled. Scientific testing of hypotheses about human behavior is in "our wheelhouse," as the phrase goes. But there is more: The psychology–law interface pulls us out of the experimental laboratory to address policy questions with a variety of methods. It is perhaps trite to state that public policy will benefit when scientists are careful to discern the limits of what we can learn from laboratory and from field to counter untenable leaps of logic such as unsupported causal inferences. Yet experience tells us that this role is particularly challenging in the messy world of policy, in which correlational and quasi-experimental research designs muddy outcomes and a status quo bias can harden allegiance to an existing policy. In the often-adversarial environment of public policy, sound science must remain front and center.

The Questions Law Asks of Science . . .
and the Questions Science Asks of Law

Law asks questions of scientists that follow from the court's doctrines and rules, notably to determine admissibility of scientific evidence. In the United States, this encompasses the general acceptance of scientific knowledge in the relevant science community (*Frye v. United States,* 1923) and whether a scientific claim is reliable (valid) and helpful to the trier of fact (*Daubert v. Merrell Dow Pharmaceuticals,* 1993). For example, the 2017 U.S. Supreme Court decision in the death penalty case of *Moore v. Texas* turned on the question of whether a state's diagnosis of intellectual disability must be guided by consensus and (presumably reliable) professional standards for diagnosis, as presented in the American Association on Intellectual and Developmental Disabilities clinical manual and the *Diagnostic and Statistical Manual of Mental Disorders* (DSM-5; American Psychiatric Association, 2013). In nonclinical realms, and absent a DSM, questions of consensus require a creative strategy. Three decades ago, Kassin, Ellsworth, and Smith (1989) took a direct approach to the legal question of "general acceptance" through a survey of eyewitness experts, with a follow-up a decade later (Kassin, Tubb, Hosch, & Memon, 2001). The usefulness of expert surveys was, and still is, to provide one indicator to the courts of scientific consensus and research reliability and to shape expert testimony to reflect the opinions of the scientific community.

It should not be surprising that the interests of policymakers and practitioners often center on the *viability* rather than the scientific underpinning of policy recommendations. My initial foray into the translation of science to policy came by volunteering to collect descriptive data for a 1-year pilot project conducted by the county attorney in Hennepin County, Minnesota, who was already convinced that scientific advice was sound (for double-blind sequential lineups). The remaining questions were about practicability (Klobuchar, Steblay, & Caligiuri, 2006): Will these procedures compromise investigations? How will eyewitnesses react? What will this cost? How will these changes play out in court? Will the sky fall? (It did not.)

There are benefits to working at ground level beyond the direct objective of policy change. Those who know daily operations can navigate the personalities and bureaucracies involved. Resistance to change will manifest in all manner of ways, and onsite partners can discern the truly serious obstacles ("Our computer systems cannot access the online photo repository") from simple skepticism ("We will never get another identification"; "This cannot work in a department of this size"). A procedure that operated seamlessly in the lab can become downright clumsy in the field, but law enforcement and policymakers committed to best practices figure out how to make things work. A procedural element that is considered imperative by investigators but unpopular with scientists can be negotiated and worked into the protocol. One example involves the number of allowed witness viewings of a sequential lineup (photos one at a time): Prior to 2006 the answer given by scientists was "just one." However, police simply would not adhere to that requirement ("If the witness wants a second view, I'm going to show the lineup again"). The agreed-upon resolution for Hennepin County law enforcement was to allow a second lineup viewing only at the witness's request and to fully document what occurred during each of the two "laps" (to my knowledge, the now-common term "lap" originated from law enforcement during that field study). This procedural change also provided focus for subsequent laboratory testing.

Scientists also directly challenge legal assumptions. Survey research has documented what others *don't know* about psychological principles. This work has addressed the often-erroneous court assumption that memory principles are "not beyond the ken" of the average juror (Schmechel, O'Toole, Easterly, & Loftus, 2006). There is need for additional research that addresses juror knowledge: What do jurors believe about detection of deception, DNA, child witnesses, and other forms of evidence? How do jurors understand and react to diagnostic labels and mental state descriptions (Douglas, Nikolova, Kelley, & Edens, 2014)?

It has often occurred to me that among scientists who have secured successful policy change, there seems to be a near-freakish prescience regarding the next critical research question to address. "What do we need to know next? "How can we devise a stronger and more compelling research design to answer the question?" I have alleged that these colleagues are able to see around corners, a very useful superpower.

Method Matters in Policy Testing

Much can be learned from descriptive studies regarding how formal and informal structures of law operate and the manifest outcomes of these structures. In the 1960s and 1970s, the Chicago Jury Project's trio of archival data analysis, natural observation, and field study became the catalyst for future experimental tests (described by Devine, 2012). Ongoing examination of DNA exoneration case archives has spurred research ideas and produced in-depth knowledge about sources of error in wrongful conviction (Garrett, 2011). Surveys of police practices for identification evidence collection (Police Executive Research Forum, 2013) and for interviewing suspects (Kassin et al., 2007) illuminate commonplace procedures that can inform training, policy, and laboratory tests. Archival data from police field investigations have validated concerns about eyewitness unreliability in real eyewitnesses to crimes (Wells, 2014).

However, the problem of multicollinearity plagues archival and non-experimental field studies. For example, archival analyses of judge-versus-jury decisions may allow for an intriguing perspective from real-world cases. However, obtained differences may also reflect the different kinds of cases routed to judge versus jury (Bornstein, 2017). The intractable problems in archival analysis of lineups have led Horry, Halford, Brewer, Milne, & Bull (2014) to conclude that not much at all can be learned from them. Archival and descriptive analyses simply cannot answer questions that require an experimental approach to isolate causal factors.

Furthermore, a field study (good or bad) may have disproportionate persuasive appeal. Audiences may lock onto the phrase "field study" and place trust not only in the descriptive outcome (what happened) but in the "why"—with unwarranted causal conclusions. In essence, a single field study may eclipse carefully controlled experimental tests. Misreading the implications of a correlational, quasi-experimental, or limited sample field test can do enormous harm, and it can be difficult to dispel the allegiance to a test of "real world" (see, e.g., Schacter et al., 2008; Steblay, 2008; Wells, 2008).

Two methodological properties are essential to the clear interpretation of policy research yet sadly are often absent from field studies: *random assignment* to experimental conditions and *double-blind procedure*. As researchers well know, an experiment that lacks interval validity cannot speak effectively to issues of practical concern (external validity). Not surprisingly, field experiments are difficult to design and operationalize. Consider, for example, the *five-year* labor of Wells, Steblay, and Dysart and their many colleagues (2015) to deliver a double-blind field experiment with true random assignment to conditions.

The difficulty of interpreting comparisons of new versus old policy under conditions of nonrandom assignment and lack of double blind was apparent in the ill-fated Illinois study of lineup procedure (Mecklenburg, 2006). In this field study, new recommendations for lineup procedure (double-blind lineup administration *and* sequential lineup display of lineup members) were compared with current practice (nonblind *and* simultaneous display), thereby confounding the two factors tested *and* allowing nonblind contamination in the current-practice condition. The errors were further compounded by nonrandom assignment to the two study conditions, leading to a priori differences between conditions (in time delays between crime and lineup, and in prior familiarity between witness and offender). These problems made the results of the old-versus-new policy comparison indecipherable (Schacter et al., 2008; Steblay, 2011a, 2011b). Amendola and Wixted (2015) suffered the same criticism in their comparison of two lineup procedures using nonrandom convenience samples from a larger dataset (Wells, Dysart, & Steblay, 2015; Steblay, Dysart, & Wells, 2015).

The pernicious impact of experimenter effects under nonblind conditions necessitates safeguards in the field as in the lab, at the same time that safeguards are likely to be much tougher to achieve. In fact, risks for examiner effects may be elevated in the field, where multiple procedural steps in the same investigation are each vulnerable to bias (i.e., witness interviews, lineup construction, prelineup conversation with the witness, lineup delivery, postidentification feedback to the witness, and documentation of the lineup outcome) and where unreported outcomes and noncompliance are motivated by resistance to change. In point of fact, double-blind procedure is so critical to evidence accuracy that it is advised for multiple police evidence procedures such as lineup administration and evaluation of physical forensic evidence and to limit the potential for psychological contamination when multiple lines of evidence are evaluated in the same case (Kassin et al., 2013; Wells, Steblay, & Dysart, 2015). A related line of early research detailed the hallmarks of interviewer bias that can similarly affect evidence obtained from children (Bruck, Ceci, & Helmbrook, 1998).

These methodological safeguards may seem elementary. However, Kovera and colleagues have addressed the assumption underlying *Daubert* that judges are capable of differentiating valid science from junk science. Judges, attorneys, and jurors all demonstrate failures to identify flawed research such as missing control groups and nonblind conditions (Kovera & McAuliff, 2000; Kovera, Russano, & McAuliff, 2002; McAuliff, Kovera, & Nunez, 2009).

Clinical forensic field research can also suffer from lack of proper randomized clinical trials (RCTs). In a review of offender treatment outcomes, Rosenfeld, Howe, Pierson, and Foellmi (2015) note that ethical challenges inherent to research in forensic criminal justice settings mean that true experimental research is rare. It is common that a clinical intervention is applied to an entire group in a pre–post design or that a comparison group is evaluated from an untreated rather than a true control group. A frequent field research design is a pre–post quasi-experimental prospective study; for example, a comparison of outcomes for youth who were adjudicated prior to versus after implementation of a Structured Assessment of Violence Risk in Youth (SAVRY) in a juvenile probation context (Vincent, Guy, Gershenson, & McCabe, 2012). Yet, without randomization, "disentangling treatment effects from sample biases is often more challenging than the investigators acknowledge" (Rosenfeld et al., 2015, p. 163) and Rosenfeld et al. note the "glaring need for systematic research (e.g., RCTs)" (2015, p. 184). Of particular concern is a seemingly successful clinical intervention effect that disappears when tested with a better method (e.g., with youth diversion programs, as in Wilson & Hoge, 2013).

Resistance to Psychological Science

"Are you aware of the fact that what you are talking about isn't even science? You don't even have agreement in your own field about eyewitness testimony! Your experiments aren't like real life. Your experiments aren't like real crimes. I have been dealing with real criminals and real witnesses my whole career." These were the words of an Ohio prosecutor who loudly interrupted a presentation I gave in 2009 (Petro & Petro, 2011, p. 139).

The progress achieved by psychological science in law has not been without considerable resistance (e.g., Doyle, 2005; Lappas & Loftus, 2013; Steblay & Loftus, 2013). The task is one of not only establishing and disseminating new knowledge, but also of correcting misconceptions. Regrettably, these misconceptions encompass psychology's scientific method and basis for knowledge. Many experts have been confronted by condescending comments about their "classroom studies" and by the assertion that lab studies are not relevant to the real world. Whatever one's thoughtful and nuanced position on the role of internal and external validity in answering research questions, one nevertheless must be ready to respond concisely and convincingly to an attack on psychological science methods.

Common wisdom says that the best defense is a good offense. I have learned to begin trainings, presentations, and expert testimony with a quick primer of scientific method that includes analogy to the physical sciences that are seemingly more familiar to an audience: "Just like biology, chemistry . . . psychological science takes a complex phenomenon, brings it into the lab, disassembles it, uses controlled testing to understand how it works, and then goes back to the field to see how these scientifically derived principles play out." From that point, the convergence of evidence from lab and field makes a compelling narrative. Consider the body of work from Elizabeth Loftus on the misinformation effect, a research program that moved from demonstrations that observers will misremember simple subtle details to witness reconstruction of false memories for an entire event (Loftus, 2005, 2013). Another example is in the combination of laboratory and field experiments that can preempt the claim that "You're not subjecting people to the stress of a real crime." The meta-analysis of stress impact in the laboratory (Deffenbacher, Bornstein, Penrod, & McGorty, 2004) has been supplemented by experimental tests in real-world circumstances of military survival training camps (Morgan et al., 2004), police training (Hope, Lewinski, Dixon, Blocksidge, & Gabbert, 2012) and the London Dungeon (Valentine & Mesout, 2009).

Simply put, for some audiences the word *science* cannot be used often enough. The research done by psychological *scientists* is supported by the National *Science* Foundation. The National Academy of *Sciences* (NAS) has vetted the work. And, for the more recalcitrant resistance, unabashed name-dropping of NAS psychologists can be useful. "Not a science? This will come as a surprise to Dr. Loftus, who is a member in good standing of the NAS."

HOW CHANGE HAPPENS: CATALYSTS AND SOLUTIONS

Social psychologists tell us that a persuasive appeal is more likely to compel action if the following are true: the harm is clear, audience vulnerability to the threat is apparent, and there is a solution to avert the threat.

The Catalyst: Revealed Systemic Evidence Problems

There is a fundamental reality to the use of psychological science in law: *Evidence* is the currency of law. Evidence allows a police investigation to stall or go forward; evidence drives prosecutorial decisions about indictment and influences defense decisions about plea bargains and strategy; trial evidence is entered for or against a defendant. Sound and fair evidence underlies due process. This means that some of the research about psychological processes and behavior that fascinates scientists will not engage the legal community or court unless it is linked directly to the quality of legal evidence. Yet the legal system has recognized problems of unreliable evidence for decades: Eyewitness memory is notoriously unreliable, confessions spring from coercive police actions, jailhouse snitches fabricate testimony, experts opine without a solid foundation of science, and jurors are swayed by extralegal information. However, faith that the *system* is generally sound can thwart action, as can a persistent belief that traditional safeguards will mitigate problematic evidence and that errors that slip through are rare. How to break through this faith in the status quo? The first question to prompt science-based reform is this: Is there *systemic* error that undermines the reliability of legal evidence and that can defeat the prescribed safeguards of due process? If this question can be answered affirmatively—and the professional responsibility to address this problem is in the legal actors' sphere of influence—policy reforms can gain a purchase in the legal community. Eyewitness and confession research have gained traction in policy reform through exposure of a systemic error in evidence that dealt severe repercussions for the wrongly convicted, for crime victims, and for public trust in law enforcement and the legal system. Furthermore, this false evidence survived the prescribed safeguards of the court (cross-examination, jury instruction, jury deliberation).

Yet there can be a frustrating disconnection between an obvious macro-level problem (wrongful conviction) and micro-level practice ("I can tell a liar when I see one"; "We never put an innocent suspect in a lineup"; "I don't influence the witness"; "Let it go to weight—the jury decides"). Even more compelling in inspiring change, then, is revelation of a systemic error that hits home, sometimes driven by a civil lawsuit against law enforcement, sometimes with heartfelt regret about how a case went so wrong. It is not surprising that the early evidence reforms occurred in jurisdictions that had experienced a wrongful conviction.

Confessions and eyewitness identifications are direct and powerful evidence of guilt. A false confession or mistaken eyewitness identification presents an unambiguous instance of deficient evidence that undermined due process for the defendant. Although wrongful-conviction cases have very powerfully exposed errors linked to specific types of flawed evidence, they do not reveal clear lines back to jury process or courtroom procedure. It can be much more difficult to discern violation of due process in courtroom procedural elements, such as jurors' review of case facts or comprehension of judge's instructions (Devine, Clayton, Dunford, Seying, & Pryce, 2001). There is simply no flawed evidence to point to. How does one parse the impact on jury decisions of pretrial publicity, juror attitudes, inadmissible evidence, or any other single courtroom factor? Even the very sensible notion of simplifying the language of jury instructions is difficult to score. Will jurors err less often if instructions are changed? What can be judged to be an error or a correct decision? This echoes the essential dilemma of the "harmless error" determinations made by appellate courts: Would the outcome have been different, and justice less well served, had Factor X been different? Application of jury research may be hindered by its inability (thus far) to demonstrate direct links to faulty evidence and erroneous jury decisions.

The Solution: System Variables ("If You're So Smart, Fix the Problem")

Wells (1978) outlined an incisive two-factor framework for conceptualization of eyewitness factors that has become immensely productive as a theoretical and practical tool. (Again, notice the elegant *simplicity* of this proposition.) *Estimator* variables are factors that are not under control of the justice system because, at the time their influence is exerted, law enforcement is not yet on the scene. *System* variables, on the other hand, are potentially under the control of the justice system because these factors have impact during the time that the legal actors are directly involved in the investigation and interacting with citizens. The power of a system variable is to provide a preventative for the exposed problem. This approach looks forward to intercept errors well before they arrive at the courtroom rather than backward to assess in hindsight. Thus, law enforcement cannot repair a weak eyewitness memory, but it can intercede to reduce the likelihood of identification error that stems from weak memory. A system-variable approach can be very appealing to police and policymakers in the wake of a wrongful conviction, when the sense of professionalism is shaken and a closer look at scientific recommendations for best practices seems warranted to manage future risk. The system-variable approach initiated in 1978 itself served as a catalyst for change.

System variables are not limited to eyewitness memory issues. Research on false confessions has led to a consensus for changes in police interrogation procedures now endorsed by scientists and legal professionals. In the United States, the United Kingdom, and Australia, the central reform initiative is for full recording of the interrogation (see American Bar Association, 2004; the Justice Project, 2007; Kassin et al., 2010; Sullivan, 2010). Less successful is the attempt to address the nature of U.S. police interrogation (the ubiquitous Reid technique; Inbau, Reid, Buckley, & Jayne, 2001), which is essentially guilt-presumptive and confrontational. Other strategies exist (the PEACE model in the United Kingdom) but have been slow to gain traction in the states (The Innocence Project, 2017). A momentous change has occurred recently in that a large U.S. police consulting firm has decided to remove the Reid technique from training methods (The Marshall Project, 2017).

This conceptualization of estimator and system variables can be used in an analogous way to direct research in other areas toward systemic change that can prevent unreliability in future evidence. Kassin et al. (2013) consider ways to intercede to protect evidence quality in forensic science. Wells, Yang, and Smalarz (2015) have advanced a proposal for a reasonable suspicion criterion that rests on principles of base rates for guilty suspects (the likelihood that the procedure is conducted with a guilty suspect).

Devine et al. (2001) noted a change in jury research direction from descriptive to prescriptive. Some aspects of jury research have moved into practice of individual courts or jurisdictions (e.g., allowing jurors to take notes or submit questions). However, the impact of this research has not been as strong as one might hope. More recently, Kovera (2017) underscored the need for a targeted system-variable approach to jury research that focuses on aspects of the trial that are under control of litigants or the courts, such as judicial instructions, as opposed to estimator variables, such as defendant or witness characteristics, that are immutable. There also may be opportunities to piggyback on the recent successes of eyewitness-evidence and false-confession research programs. As the courts seriously consider measures to lessen the risk of unreliable courtroom evidence, the relevance of research on expert testimony, jury instruction, and juror teaching aids is heightened (see, e.g., Dillon, Jones, Bergold, Hui, & Penrod, 2017; Wise, Fishman, & Safer, 2009).

A much broader systems approach to error reduction in the justice system has been initiated by the Quatrone Center of University of Pennsylvania Law School (Hollway, 2014). This is a different use of the term "system." The strategy employs examination of both root and proximate causes and "near-miss" analysis to better understand error. A promising aspect of this approach is the recognition of how an entire series of checks and balances in the system may align and fail or, alternatively, may be strengthened to reduce risk. For example, a wrongful conviction based on a false confession means that error survived multiple points of contact: the detective who elicited the confession, a supervisor who approved the procedure, a prosecutor who screened the evidence prior to charging the case, a judge who allowed the evidence in court, a defense attorney who was unable to diminish the power of the confession at trial, and the jury who weighed the evidence for a verdict. This systems approach thus reveals multiple points at which the system may require adjustment.

A system-variable approach presents an interesting dilemma for psychological science. If and when law is ready to consider policy change, is the science ready? For example, the 2012 *Miller v. Alabama* decision now requires fast development of applied protocols for juvenile sentencing

(Grisso & Kavanaugh, 2016). A similar conundrum may ensue if and when death penalty jurisdictions in the United States enact laws that would prohibit the death penalty for people whose culpability is reduced by serious mental illness.

AVENUES FOR MOVING SCIENCE TO POLICY AND PRACTICE

Public policy is, by definition, a multifaceted system of regulatory measures, laws, and principles employed to change, maintain, or create conditions conducive to human welfare to shape society in desirable ways (Shafir, 2013). Policy is often informal and unwritten and thereby inferred from practices that may vary widely. Regardless of the national or international context under consideration, the challenge to realize policy reform is exacerbated by the sheer number of independent police jurisdictions, courts, and levels of authority and by intricate legal and political environments. Policy change is a messy and often unpredictable adventure of starts and stops, progress and reversals.

Not surprisingly, then, experience within the psychology and law interface over three decades informs us that there is no single avenue for policy change. Brief illustration of the myriad ways in which police lineup reform has occurred may be instructive for other science-based reform efforts (described more fully by Steblay & Loftus, 2013). A mandate from a high government level will prompt direct change for law enforcement practice ("top down"), as occurred when New Jersey became the first state to uniformly adopt lineup reform. A directive from the New Jersey State Attorney General in 2002 forced the changes for all police, with only a 180-day window for the new procedures to be implemented. However, the New Jersey Attorney General's single authority over all state law enforcement is unique in the United States, perhaps more akin to the centralized control of law enforcement in countries outside the United States. For example, identification procedures in the United Kingdom and Wales have been regulated nationally by the Police and Criminal Evidence Act of 1984 and Code of Practice in 2005 (see details in Valentine, Darling, & Memon, 2007).

In other circumstances, detectives, police chiefs, and/or county attorneys have initiated lineup reform ("bottom up"). Early reform in Northampton, Massachusetts, began at the ground level with a long-time investigator who developed and introduced training, structure, and policy to his department (Patenaude, 2006).

Of course, there are many variations on these two themes. In the state of Minnesota, two county attorneys independently began pilot programs in 2004 to assess the practicability of new lineup procedures. Law enforcement helped to develop training materials and protocols, and policy was enacted at the close of the pilot period. In Boston, eyewitness scientists, law enforcement officers, prosecutors, and defense attorneys sat on a task force that ultimately recommended changes to the county district attorney and police commissioner that were followed by reforms in lineup practice. Of course, these "bottom-up" changes are limited to a specific jurisdiction, and statewide change may not arrive for years or at all.

A multistep process is not unusual. North Carolina reform began with high-profile DNA exoneration cases. The North Carolina Actual Innocence Commission was established by the State Supreme Court as a permanent interdisciplinary study commission, independent of the judiciary, with participation of law enforcement, defense attorneys, social scientists, and judges. The Commission created a series of recommendations for state law enforcement officers that became the basis for change in individual jurisdictions and later was mandated by state legislation in an Eyewitness ID Reform Act.

Best scientific practices can be brought to jurisdictions through mandate or through guidelines (and the difference in format can spur debate). A statewide statute is a strong and effective remedy when resistance or jurisdictional inaction is likely. Of course, legislated reforms may need to be revisited as science develops stronger protocols. A more flexible option is for state statutes to simply require that jurisdictions formulate a written policy, leaving open the specific components of the policy. Such policy mandates may move the process along to garner statewide change. Wisconsin lineup reform was implemented through a best-practices approach, where the Training and Standards Bureau of the Wisconsin Department of Justice, working with the University of Wisconsin Law School, wrote model policy guidelines for law enforcement. Subsequent legislation required that each law enforcement agency adopt policies or guidelines (State of Wisconsin Office of Attorney General, 2005). The wide availability of the National Institute of Justice (NIJ) guide (1999) and subsequent model policies and training materials online makes adoption more palatable for jurisdictions that are leaning toward reform or mandated by legislation to make changes in policy and practice (see, e.g., U.S. Department of Justice, 2017, and *www.norwoodma.gov/departments/police/about_the_chief.php*).

The alternate route is to allow individual jurisdictions to change at their own pace. Local autonomy offers flexibility and local buy-in, but also may lead to inefficient progress, protracted delays, and less than ideal outcomes. The difficulty of policy change when law enforcement control exists in many independent jurisdictions can be seen in the current circumstance of lineup reform in the United States. To date, 22 of 50 U.S. states have implemented lineup reform. However, the Police Executive Research Forum in 2013 reported that a majority of U.S. law enforcement agencies still did not employ the core feature of double-blind procedure. It is sometimes startling that the very professions that should seemingly embrace evidence reforms have instead resisted them.

Law enforcement (police and prosecutors) response to reforms varies substantially. On the very supportive end of the continuum are those who emphasize updates to best practices as a standard for law enforcement professionalism and integrity and who are enthusiastic about the benefits of higher quality ("bulletproof") evidence brought to court cases and plea bargains (see Kois, Chauhan, & Warren, Chapter 12, this volume) and for the protections afforded against wrongful conviction and charges of poor policing. In other words, they have their eyes on the big picture (e.g., Gaertner & Harrington, 2009). On the other end of the continuum are those who see their professionalism impugned by reforms, as a personal insult to integrity and a restriction on pursuing cases as they see fit, as well as a disproportionate advantage for the defense (Wilford & Wells, 2013). Of course, in the middle are those who are unaware of best practices, confused, harried by other volatile issues, or caught between competing messages and political agendas. Yet adoption of system-variable changes requires police and prosecutors; if they buy into the best practices, then systemic change will occur.

The Policy Is Good . . . the Practice Is Shaky

Almost as painful as resistance is a gradual slippage backward on reforms. As I wrote this chapter, our local paper (Minneapolis) reported an exposé of lineup practice gone wrong; this is in a jurisdiction that a decade ago was a leader in lineup reform. The policy is still on the books, but the practice has strayed at times. The three recent cases portrayed in the news article included a trifecta of improper procedure: (1) a lineup for a suspect, described by the witness as a "young Hispanic man," with only two lineup members matching both race and age, emailed to the victim for the ID (yes, really); (2) an all-suspect lineup for a sex offense (DNA evidence cleared the identified suspect 2 months later); and (3) a proper double-blind sequential lineup with no ID after two laps that was followed by the case detective entering the room, spreading out the photos, and asking if any one was possible (the case went to trial with the confident eyewitness identification as centerpiece); ("When police lineups can be suspect," 2017).

Perhaps these are the only three problem lineups in hundreds delivered in this jurisdiction, and luckily they were exposed. But the situation is relevant to this discussion of practice and policy. First, the media can be an articulate and potent watchdog and educator for scientific policy and a catalyst for change. Second, adherence to a written policy cannot be taken for granted. Vigilance regarding training and education is warranted. To that point, the Innocence Project has been instrumental in working with the Peace Officers Standards and Training Board in Minnesota to work best-lineup practices into the training curricula of all police officers. At its best, training imparts not only the rules but an understanding of the underlying rationale for the practice. This is done because some odd set of circumstances inevitably will test a police investigator and, absent an understanding of *why* the policy exists, what seems like a good investigative strategy at the time can undermine evidence quality (Why *not* put all the local sex offenders in the same lineup?).

Third, there is a clear responsibility for police chiefs, prosecutors, defense attorneys, and judges to catch deviations from policy and to signal their displeasure regarding noncompliance and the increased vulnerability for corruption of evidence and undermining of due process that such errors incur. Police chiefs and prosecutors have the power to demand high standards for evidence before proceeding with an investigation or charging a case. Attorneys can seek expert opinion to help develop trial strategy, including motions to suppress or expert testimony. Judges have the ability to suppress unreliable evidence, to allow an expert witness to provide context for the jury's weighing of evidence, to issue appropriate judicial instructions, and thereby to put pressure on the system to inculcate adherence to science-based evidence standards. Finally, reinforcing action from various levels of authority is often necessary to sustain positive change. As noted by Wilford and Wells (2013), a system variable has a useful characteristic: It carries responsibility of "best practice" and blame for those who violate the protocol. One can hope that the reaction of administrators in the face of failures of protocol is to steer police back toward best practices.

The Court: A Very Slow Slog

Psychological scientists can provide expert testimony, and cases can influence and educate (one judge/jury at a time). This is not always an easy or pleasant task for a scientist (e.g., consider the "memory wars"; Patihis, Ho, Tingen, Lilienfeld, & Loftus, 2014). A change in the court's consideration of psychological science demands remarkable patience, stamina, and effort on the part of scientists and the lawyers who pursue the changes. The impact of court testimony on broader evidence policy is indirect and slow.

Newirth (2016) traces the U.S. courts' gradual (as yet quite incomplete) acceptance of research on eyewitness identification evidence. She notes that the trial courts historically ignored the science for a number of reasons, including a seeming general discomfort with social science research and an adherence to precedent. Even as clear problems with *Manson v. Brathwaite* (1977) were catalogued in scientific and legal articles (e.g., Wells & Quinlivan, 2009), courts continued to affirm the *Manson* ruling, limit expert testimony, and reject changes to jury instructions. Today all but two states permit expert court testimony on identification evidence, a dramatic change from 20 years ago. Yet attorneys who attempt to bring psychological expertise to trial continue to meet with limited success, dependent upon the judge's determination about the strength of the science represented in the proffered testimony and its match to evidentiary standards, and about the need for the jury to hear the testimony. Judges may be hesitant to address science findings unless the implications are clear for constitutional or state-specific due process protections. To this point, the Minnesota State

Supreme Court has recently issued a directive for study and recommendations regarding eyewitness evidence issues to its advisory committee on rules of evidence. More than a decade after local police implemented best practices for eyewitness-evidence collection, the court will consider how available tools of jury instruction and expert-witness testimony can assist a jury in its evaluation of evidence reliability.

Prosecutors commonly resist admission of expert testimony on scientific topics by arguing a set of core points: (1) the research literature on the topic is insufficient or irrelevant; (2) the findings are not generally (or fully) accepted in the scientific community; (3) courtroom safeguards will suffice to reduce error (cross-examination, jury instruction, jury deliberation); (4) the testimony will invade the province of the jury to determine the reliability of the evidence; (5) the research findings are simply a matter of common sense, not "beyond the ken" of the average juror; and (6) the expert testimony is more prejudicial than probative. Psychological science must anticipate and respond to such arguments. As an example, amicus briefs to state supreme courts have been entered in recent cases to clarify the reliability and relevance of scientific research on false confessions, the risks of current interrogation techniques to undermine court evidence and due process, and the inherent difficulties experienced by triers of fact when weighing confession evidence (American Psychological Association, 2011, in *Rivera v. Illinois*).

A (denied) motion to suppress evidence or to bring in expert testimony may slowly make its way into appellate rulings and beyond. State appellate court rulings may mandate police procedural changes, as was the case for videotaped suspect interrogations (*State of Minnesota v. Scales*, 1994), or pave the way for state statute or local action. Should a case arrive at a U.S. state supreme court, there is opportunity for momentous change. For example, two recent landmark state supreme court cases have rejected the *Manson* precedent, shaped new rules for the admissibility of eyewitness evidence in court (*State of New Jersey v. Henderson*, 2011), and, in Oregon, structured a new legal framework for evaluation of eyewitness evidence reliability (*State of Oregon v. Lawson*, 2012). According to Doyle (2012), "perhaps most importantly, the Oregon Supreme Court emphasized that whether or not anyone has committed misconduct, judges are required to carefully balance the probative value of eyewitness evidence against that evidence's prejudicial effect *in light of the findings of modern psychology*" (italics added).

CHALLENGES AND OBSERVATIONS

This chapter has offered a multicomponent and daunting task structure for the translation of psychological science to policy and practice. Movement from the lab to the legal arena calls for adjustment in nearly every facet of academic research activity—except the touchstone of sound science on which it depends. A brief review includes:

- Formulating questions of interest to both law and psychology
- Employing multiple methods to assess lab and field convergence
- Gauging and documenting scientific consensus
- Aggregating the science (white papers, meta-analyses, and reviews)
- Increasing relevance, readability, and accessibility of science in legal contexts
- Correcting myths and misconceptions
- Preparing foundational research to address courtroom queries
- Engaging partners and collaborators within the discipline and outside of science
- Employing a system-variable approach to prescribe change policy
- Linking policy to evidence quality
- Exploring multiple avenues for policy enactment (top down, bottom up, in between)
- Participating in legal and policy processes

This list may seem to present an insurmountable charge, a suggestion that all these pieces need to fall into place in order to proceed within the legal system. Who would ever begin such a Sisyphean task? The reality is that just as science progresses, with many contributors slowly adding pieces to an overall mosaic of knowledge, so goes policy work.

Scientists, juries, judges, and policymakers additionally share a common conundrum: Policy decisions involve risk because such decisions must be made under conditions of uncertainty, and uncertainty spurs disagreement. Some discussants will voice apprehension about policy change in the absence of complete or wholly consistent information. It is further true that any change may ripple through with unforeseen consequences, so decisions also must involve a wise and wider view of practice and policy. Yet the status quo bias looms large. Long-held practice may survive not because of comparative evidence of success but rather because of an assumed inherent superiority in habit. Shaky or slim evidence is a poor basis for policy, whether that policy is newly advised or has been in existence for decades.

Science and law can engage productively even with the expectation for inevitable policy update and modification. The interdependence of science and law, as noted by U.S. Supreme Court Justice Stephen Breyer (1998), "is not a search for scientific precision. . . . The law must seek decisions that fall within the boundaries of scientifically sound knowledge and approximately reflect the scientific state of the art" (p. 537). Scientists cannot have all the answers. However, we can and should speak with our best scientific evidence and judgment at a given point in time.

REFERENCES

Amendola, K., & Wixted, J. T. (2014). Comparing the diagnostic accuracy of suspect identification made by actual eyewitnesses from simultaneous and sequential lineups in a randomized field trial. *Journal of Experimental Criminology, 11*, 263–284.

American Bar Association. (2004). Resolution 8A: Videotaping custodial interrogations. Retrieved from *www.americanbar.org.aba.html.*

American Psychiatric Association. (2013). *Diagnostic and statistical manual of mental disorders* (5th ed.). Arlington, VA: Author.

American Psychological Association. (2011). Brief for amicus curiae in support of appellant. Rivera v. Illinois, No 2-09-1060. Retrieved from *www.apa.org/about/offices/ogc/amicus/rivera.aspx.*

American Psychological Association. (2014). Resolution on interrogations of criminal suspects. Retrieved from *www.apa.org/about/policy/interrogations.aspx*

American Psychological Association. (2018). Amicus briefs by year. Retrieved from *www.apa.org/about/offices/ogc/amicus/index-chron.aspx.*

Appleby, S. C., & Kassin, S. M. (2016). When self-report trumps science: Effects of confessions, DNA, and prosecutorial theories on perceptions of guilt. *Psychology, Public Policy, and Law, 22*, 127–140.

Barefoot v. Estelle, 463 U.S. 880 (1983).

Bornstein, B. H. (2017). Jury simulation research: Pros, cons, trends, and alternatives. In M. B. Kovera (Ed.), *The psychology of juries*. Washington, DC: American Psychological Association.

Breyer, S. (1998, April 24). The interdependence of science and law. *Science, 280*, 537–538.

Bruck, M., Ceci, S. J., & Hembrooke, H. (1998). Reliability and credibility of young children's reports: From research to policy and practice. *American Psychologist, 53*, 136–151.

Charman, S. D., Kavetski, M., & Mueller, D. H. (2017). Cognitive bias in the legal system: Police officers evaluate ambiguous evidence in a belief-consistent manner. *Journal of Applied Research in Memory and Cognition, 6*, 193–202.

Daubert v. Merrell Dow Pharmaceuticals, Inc., 509 U.S. 579 (1993).

Deffenbacher, K. A., Bornstein, B. H., Penrod, S. D., & McGorty, E. K. (2004). A meta-analytic review of the effects of high stress on eyewitness memory. *Law and Human Behavior, 28*, 687–706.

Devine, D. (2012). *Jury decision making: The state of the science*. New York: New York University Press.

Devine, D. J., Clayton, L. D., Dunford, B. B., Seying, R., & Pryce, J. (2001). 45 years of empirical research on deliberation groups. *Psychology, Public Policy, and Law, 7*, 622–727.

Dillon, M. K., Jones, A. M., Bergold, A. N., Hui, C. Y. T., & Penrod, S. D. (2017). Henderson instructions: Do they enhance evidence evaluation? *Journal of Forensic Psychology Research and Practice, 17*, 1–24.

Douglas, K. S., Nikolova, N. L., Kelley, S., & Edens, J. F. (2014). Psychopathy: A review and analysis of controversial contemporary issues. In B. Cutler & P. Zapf (Eds.), *APA handbook of forensic psychology* (pp. 257–323). Washington, DC: American Psychological Association.

Doyle, J. (2005). *True witness: Cops, courts, science and the battle against misidentification*. New York: Palgrave Macmillan.

Doyle, J. M. (2012, December 13). Oregon's eyewitness decision: Back to basics. *The Crime Report*. Retrieved from *www.thecrimereport.org/viewpoints/2012-12-oregons-eyewitness-decision-back-to-basics*.

Findley, K. A., (2010) Tunnel vision. In B. L. Cutler (Ed.), *Conviction of the innocent: Lessons from psychological research* (pp. 303–323). Washington, DC: American Psychological Association.

Findley, K. A., & Scott, M. S. (2006). The multiple dimensions of tunnel vision in criminal cases. *Wisconsin Law Review, 2006*(2), 291–397.

Frye v. United States, 293 F. 1013 (D.C. Cir. 1923).

Gaertner, S., & Harrington, J. (2009, April). Successful eyewitness identification reform: Ramsey County's blind sequential lineup protocol. *The Police Chief*.

Garrett, B. L. (2011). *Convicting the innocent: Where criminal prosecutions go wrong*. Cambridge, MA: Harvard University Press.

Grisso, R., & Kavanaugh, A. (2016). Prospects for developmental evidence in juvenile sentencing based on *Miller v. Alabama*. *Psychology, Public Policy, and Law, 22*, 235–249.

Hasel, L. E., & Kassin, S. M. (2009). On the presumption of evidentiary independence: Can confessions corrupt eyewitness identifications? *Psychological Science, 20*, 122–126.

Hollway, J. (2014). A systems approach to error reduction in criminal justice (University of Pennsylvania Law School Public Law Research Paper No. 14-6). Retrieved from *https://ssrn.com/abstract=2409234*.

Hope, L., Lewinski, W., Dixon, J., Blocksidge, D., & Gabbert, F. (2012). Witnesses in action: The effect of physical exertion on recall and recognition. *Psychological Science, 23*, 386–390.

Horry, R., Halford, P., Brewer, N., Milne, R., & Bull, R. (2014). Archival analyses of eyewitness identification test outcomes: What can they tell us about eyewitness memory? *Law and Human Behavior, 38*, 94–108.

Inbau, F. E., Reid, J. E., Buckley, J. P., & Jayne, B. C. (2001). *Criminal interrogation and confessions* (4th ed.). Gaithersburg, MD: Aspen.

Innocence Project. (2017). How the UK police interview suspects. Retrieved from *www.innocenceproject.org/how-the-uk-police-interview-suspects*.

Justice Project. (2007). *Electronic recording of custodial interrogations: A policy review*. Washington, DC: Author. Available at *http://web.williams.edu/Psychology/Faculty/Kassin/files/Justice%20Project(07).pdf*.

Kahneman, D. (2011). *Thinking, fast and slow*. New York: Farrar, Straus, & Giroux.

Kassin, S. M., Drizin, S. A., Grisso, T., Gudjonsson, G. H., Leo, R. A., & Redlich, A. D. (2010). Police-induced confessions: Risk factors and recommendations. *Law and Human Behavior, 34*, 3–38.

Kassin, S. M., Dror, I. E., & Kukucka, J. (2013). The forensic confirmation bias: Problems, perspectives, and proposed solutions. *Journal of Applied Research in Memory and Cognition, 2*, 42–52.

Kassin, S. M., Ellsworth, P. C., & Smith, V. L. (1989). The "general acceptance" of psychological research on eyewitness testimony. *American Psychologist, 44*, 1089–1098.

Kassin, S. M., Leo, R. A., Meissner, C. A., Richman, K. D., Colwell, L. H., Leach, A., et al. (2007). Police interviewing and interrogation: A self-report survey of police practices and beliefs. *Law and Human Behavior, 31*, 381–400.

Kassin, S. M., Tubb, V. A., Hosch, H. M., & Memon, A. (2001). On the "general acceptance" of eyewitness testimony research: A new survey of the experts. *American Psychologist, 56*, 405–416.

Klobuchar, A., Steblay, N., & Caligiuri, H. (2006). Improving eyewitness identifications: Hennepin County's blind sequential lineup pilot project. *Cardozo Public Law, Policy and Ethics Journal, 4*, 381–413.

Kovera, M. B. (2017). Conclusion: The future of jury research. In M. B. Kovera (Ed.), *The psychology of juries* (pp. 287–297). Washington, DC: American Psychological Association.

Kovera, M. B., & McAuliff. B. D. (2000). The effects of peer review and evidence quality on judge evaluations of psychological science: Are judges effective gatekeepers? *Journal of Applied Psychology, 85*, 574–586.

Kovera, M. B., Russano, M. B., & McAuliff, B. D. (2002). Assessment of the commonsense psychology underlying *Daubert*: Legal decision makers' abilities to evaluate expert evidence in hostile work environment cases. *Psychology, Public Policy, and Law, 8*, 180–200.

Lappas, S. T., & Loftus, E. F. (2013) The rocky road to reform: State innocence studies and the Pennsylvania story. In C. R. Huff & M. Killias (Eds.), *Wrongful convictions and miscarriages of justice* (pp. 309–327). New York: Routledge.

Loftus, E. F. (2005). Planting misinformation in the human mind: A 30-year investigation of the malleability of memory. *Learning and Memory, 12*, 361–366.

Loftus, E. F. (2013). 25 years of eyewitness science . . . finally pays off. *Perspectives on Psychological Science, 8*, 556–557.

Manson v. Brathwaite, 432 U.S. 98, 114 (1977).

Marshall Project. (2017). The seismic change in police interrogations. Retrieved from *www.themarshallproject.org/2017/03/07/the-seismic-change-in-police-interrogations#.ri5BHPqJj.*

McAuliff, B. D., Kovera, M. B., & Nunez, G. (2009). Can jurors recognize missing control groups, confounds, and experimenter bias in psychological science? *Law and Human Behavior, 33*, 247–257.

Mecklenburg, S. H. (2006). Report to the legislature of the state of Illinois: The Illinois pilot program on double-blind, sequential lineup procedures. Retrieved from *www.cga.ct.gov/jud/tfs/20130901_Eyewitness%20Identification%20Task%20Force/20110921/Illinois%20ID%20Pilot%20Program.pdf.*

Miller v. Alabama, 67 U.S. 460 (2012).

Moore v. Texas, 581 U. S. (2017). Available at *www.apa.org/about/offices/ogc/amicus/moore.aspx.*

Morgan, C. A., Hazlett, G., Doran, A., Garrett, S., Hoyt, G., Thomas, P., et al. (2004). Accuracy of eyewitness memory for persons encountered during exposure to highly intense stress. *International Journal of Law and Psychiatry, 27*, 265–279.

National Academy of Sciences of the USA. (2014). *Identifying the culprit: Assessing eyewitness identification.* Washington, DC: National Academies Press.

National Institute of Justice. (1999). *Eyewitness evidence: A guide for law enforcement*. Washington, DC: U.S. Department of Justice, Office of Justice Programs.

Newirth, K. A. (2016). An eye for the science: Evolving judicial treatment of eyewitness identification evidence. *Journal of Applied Memory and Cognition, 5*, 314–317.

Patenaude, K. (2006). Police identification procedures: A time for change. *Cardozo Public Law, Policy and Ethics Journal, 4*, 415–419.

Patihis, L., Ho, L. Y., Tingen, I. W., Lilienfeld, S. O., & Loftus, E. F. (2014). Are the "memory wars" over?: A scientist–practitioner gap in beliefs about repressed memory. *Psychological Science, 25*, 519–530.

Petro, J., & Petro, N. (2011). *False justice: Eight myths that convict the innocent*. New York: Kaplan.

Police Executive Research Forum. (2013). *A national survey of eyewitness identification procedure in law enforcement agencies*. Washington, DC: Police Executive Research Forum. Retrieved from *www.policeforum.org/free-online-documents*.

Redlich, A. D., & Shteynberg, R. V. (2016). To plead or not to plead: A comparison of juvenile and adult true and false plea decisions. *Law and Human Behavior, 40*, 611–625.

Rose, M. R. (2017). How typical is Lockhart v. McCree: Ecological validity concerns in court opinions. In M. B. Kovera (Ed.), *The psychology of juries* (pp. 227–253). Washington, DC: American Psychological Association.

Rosenfeld, B., Howe, J., Pierson, A., & Foellmi, M. (2015). Mental health treatment of criminal offenders. In B. L. Cutler & P. A. Zapf (Eds.), *APA handbook of forensic psychology: Vol. 1. Individual and situational influences in criminal and civil cases* (pp. 159–190). Washington, DC: American Psychological Association.

Schacter, D., Dawes, R., Jacoby, L., Kahneman, D., Lempert, R., Roediger, H., et al. (2008). Studying eyewitness investigations in the field. *Law and Human Behavior, 32*, 3–5.

Schmechel, R. S., O'Toole, T. P., Easterly, C. E., & Loftus, E. F. (2006, Winter). Beyond the ken?: Testing jurors' understanding of eyewitness reliability evidence. *Jurimetrics, 46*, 177–214.

Shafir, E. (2013). Introduction. In E. Shafir (Ed.), *The behavioral foundations of public policy* (pp. 1–9). Princeton, NJ: Princeton University Press & Russell Sage Foundation.

Smalarz, L., & Wells, G. L. (2012). Eyewitness identification evidence: Scientific advances and the new burden on trial judges. *Court Review, 48*, 14–21.

State of Minnesota v. Scales, 518 N.W.2d 587, 592 (Minn. 1994).

State of New Jersey v. Henderson, 27 A.3d 872 (N.J. 2011).

State of Oregon v. Lawson, 352 Or. 724 (Or. 2012).

State of Wisconsin Office of the Attorney General. (2005, April). Model policy and procedure for eyewitness identification. Retrieved from *www.doj.state.wi.us/sites/default/files/2009-news/eyewitness-public-20091105.pdf*.

Steblay, N. (2008). Commentary on "Studying eyewitness investigations in the field": A look forward. *Law and Human Behavior, 32*, 11–15.

Steblay, N. K. (2011a). What we know now: The Evanston, Illinois, lineups. *Law and Human Behavior, 35*, 1–12.

Steblay, N. K. (2011b, June). A second look at the Illinois pilot program: The Evanston data. *The Champion*, pp. 10–15.

Steblay, N. K. (2016). Meta-analysis as an aid for judicial decision-making. *Court Review*, *52*. Retrieved from *https://heinonline.org/HOL/LandingPage?handle=hein.journals/ctrev52&div=27&id=&page=*.

Steblay, N. K., Dysart, J. E., & Wells, G. L. (2015). An unrepresentative sample is unrepresentative regardless of the reason: A rejoinder to Amendola and Wixted. *Journal of Experimental Criminology*, *11*, 295–298.

Steblay, N. K., & Loftus, E. F. (2013). Eyewitness memory and the legal system. In E. Shafir (Ed.), *The behavioral foundations of public policy* (pp. 145–162). Princeton, NJ: Princeton University Press & Russell Sage Foundation.

Steblay, N. K., Wells, G. L., & Douglass, A. B. (2014). The eyewitness post-identification feedback effect 15 years later: Theoretical and policy implications. *Psychology, Public Policy, and Law*, *20*, 1–18.

Sullivan, T. P. (2010). The evolution of law enforcement attitudes to recording custodial interviews. *Journal of Psychiatry and Law*, *38*, 137–175.

U.S. Department of Justice. (2017). Eyewitness identification: Procedures for conducting photo arrays. Retrieved from *www.justice.gov/file/923201/download*.

Valentine, T., Darling, S., & Memon, A. (2007). Do strict rules and moving images increase the reliability of sequential identification procedures? *Applied Cognitive Psychology*, *21*, 933–949.

Valentine, T., & Mesout, J., (2009). Eyewitness identification and stress in the London Dungeon. *Applied Cognitive Psychology*, *23*, 151–161.

Vincent, G. M., Guy, L. S., Gershenson, B. G., & McCabe, P. (2012). Does risk-assessment make a difference?: Results of implementing the SAVRY in juvenile probation. *Behavioral Sciences and the Law*, *30*, 384–405.

Wells, G. L. (1978). Applied eyewitness testimony research: System variables and estimator variables. *Journal of Personality and Social Psychology*, *36*, 1546–1557.

Wells, G. L. (2008). Field experiments on eyewitness identification: Towards a better understanding of pitfalls and prospects. *Law and Human Behavior*, *32*, 6–10.

Wells, G. L. (2014). Eyewitness identification: Probative value, criterion shifts, and policy. *Current Directions in Psychological Science*, *23*, 11–16.

Wells, G. L., Dysart, J. E., & Steblay, N. K. (2015). The flaw in Amendola and Wixted's conclusion on simultaneous versus sequential lineups. *Journal of Experimental Criminology*, *11*, 285–289.

Wells, G. L., & Quigley-McBride, A. (2016). Applying eyewitness identification research to the legal system: A glance at where we have been and where we could go. *Journal of Applied Research in Memory and Cognition*, *5*, 290–294.

Wells, G. L., & Quinlivan, D. S. (2009). Suggestive eyewitness identification procedures and the Supreme Court's reliability test in light of eyewitness science: 30 years later. *Law and Human Behavior*, *33*, 1–24.

Wells, G. L., Small, M., Penrod, S., Malpass, R. S., Fulero, S. M., & Brimacombe, C. A. E. (1998). Eyewitness identification procedures: Recommendations for lineups and photospreads. *Law and Human Behavior*, *22*, 603–653.

Wells, G. L., Steblay, N. K., & Dysart, J. E. (2015). Double-blind photo lineups using actual eyewitnesses: An experimental test of the sequential versus simultaneous lineup procedure. *Law and Human Behavior, 39*, 1–14.

Wells, G. L., Yang, Y., & Smalarz, L. (2015). Eyewitness identification: Bayesian information gain, base rate effect equivalency curves, and reasonable suspicion. *Law and Human Behavior, 39*, 99–122.

When police lineups can be suspect. (2017, June 6). *Star Tribune.* Retrieved from *www.startribune.com/minnesota-cops-weak-on-photo-lineup-procedures-critics-say/427682743.*

Wilford, M. M., & Wells, G. L. (2013). Eyewitness system variables. In B. L. Cutler (Ed.). *Reform of eyewitness identification procedures.* Washington, DC: American Psychological Association.

Williams v. Florida, 399 U.S. 78 (1970).

Wilson, H. A., & Hoge, R. D. (2013). The effect of youth diversion programs on recidivism: A meta-analytic review. *Criminal Justice and Behavior, 40*, 497–518.

Wise, R. A., Fishman, C., & Safer, M. A. (2009). How to analyze the accuracy of eyewitness testimony in a criminal case. *Connecticut Law Review, 42*, 435–513.

Wistrich, A. J., Guthrie, C., & Rachlinski, J. J. (2005). Can judges ignore inadmissible information?: The difficulty of deliberately disregarding. *University of Pennsylvania Law Review, 53*, 1251.

Witherspoon v. Illinois, 391 U.S. 510 (1968).

Zapf, P. A., & Dror, I. E. (2017). Understanding and mitigating bias in forensic evaluation: Lessons from forensic science. *International Journal of Forensic Mental Health, 16*(3), 227–238.

Index

Note. *f* or *t* following a page number indicates a figure or a table.

Accountability, 406–408
Achieving Best Evidence (ABE), 134–135
Actuarial assessment of risk, 375, 377–380, 378*t*. *See also* Risk assessments
Adjudicative competence, 293–294. *See also* Competence to stand trial
Adversarial allegiance, 325–326
Affective aggression, 371–372. *See also* Aggression
Affective factors, 370
Age factors
  judicial decision making and, 398
  plea outcomes and, 273–274
Aggression. *See also* Psychopathy; Violence
  definitions of, 368–369
  overview, 367, 388
  propensities for, 375, 377–384, 378*t*
  theories of, 369–372
Allegations, 157, 159–162
Alt-key paradigm, 59. *See also* Police interrogation
Ambiguous evidence, 34–38. *See also* Evidence evaluation
American Law Institute (ALI), 296–297
Anchoring
  judicial decision making and, 400–401
  jury instructions and, 354
Anecdotal evidence, 23
Anger, 346–347, 357–358
Anticipatory process of expert work, 319–320, 323–325, 334. *See also* Expert testimony
Anti-Drug Abuse Act of 1986, 270
Antisocial behavior, 372–375

Antisocial personality disorder (AsPD), 384–385. *See also* Psychopathy
Appellate review, 407–408
Applied research, 224–225
Arizona Jury Project, 342
Arousal-based factors, 370
Assessing witnesses' reports, 162–175. *See also* Witnesses
Assessment. *See also* Competence to stand trial; Mental illness
  adversarial allegiance in expert opinions and, 325–326
  case formulation and report writing and, 304–305
  expert testimony and, 320–321, 332
  measures of judicial quality and, 408–410
  propensities for crime and violence and, 375, 377–380, 378*t*
  of trial competence and sanity, 297–307
Asymmetric skepticism, 31. *See also* Cognitive bias
Attempted control theory, 83
Attention studies, 110–111
Attentional narrowing, 112
Attentional processes, 197
Attorneys. *See* Defense attorneys; Prosecutors
Attributes, 19–20
Autobiographical Implicit Association Test (aIAT), 94–96
Autobiographical memory, 186–188, 194–196. *See also* Memory

B

Backloading, 217
Bail decisions, 405, 406
Barefoot v. Estelle (1983), 417
Bayesian approach
   cognitive bias and, 39–40
   coherence-based reasoning model and,
      42–43
   jury decision making and, 352
Behavior
   cognitive bias and, 35–36
   deception detection and, 81–84, 93–94
   false confessions and, 62–63
Behavioral analysis interview, 55–57. *See
   also* Police interrogation
Behavioral case analysis, 21–22. *See also*
   Criminal profiling
Behavioral coding, 93–94
Bias. *See also* Cognitive bias; Stereotypes
   age factors and, 273–274
   connection of psychology to the law and, 2
   emotional evidence and, 356–357
   in evidence evaluation, 32–33, 34–38
   evidence integration and, 38–45
   judicial decision making and, 398–400,
      408–409
   jury decision making and, 344–347, 350,
      352–357
   jury instructions and, 352–354
   lineup administration and, 215–216
   minority status of defendants and, 272–273
   overview, 30–32, 48
   possible solutions, 45–48
   psychological science and, 422–423
   research method and policy innovations
      and, 426–427
Biphasic model, 70–71
Body language
   deception detection and, 86
   eyewitness identification and, 226
   interviewing witnesses, 135
Brain imaging technology, 352
Burden of proof, 24

C

Calibration, 211–212
Cambridge Study in Delinquent
   Development, 374
Capacity to stand trial. *See* Competence to
   stand trial
Case formulation, 304–305

Case management, 311
Case-level variables
   judicial decision making and, 404–406
   policy and practice and, 417–418
"Category clustering recall" mnemonic, 149
Cheating paradigm, 59–60. *See also* Police
   interrogation
Child assault victims, 405–406
Child sexual abuse cases, 332–333. *See also*
   Sexual abuse cases
Child witnesses. *See also* Eyewitness
   identification; Witnesses
   accusations against familiar adults and,
      159–162
   assessing reports of, 162–175
   false autobiographical memories from
      childhood and, 186–188
   formal reticence and, 170–175
   language factors, 174–175
   novel approaches to evidence collection
      and, 220–221
   overview, 157–159, 175–176
   recall versus recognition, 163–165
   suggestibility and, 165–175
CI protocol of interviewing. *See also*
   Interviewing
   overview, 134, 141–143, 149
   training and retention of interviewing
      skills and, 145–146
   translational issues, 143–145
Citizenship, 272
Civil cases
   expert testimony and, 321–322
   jurors and, 338, 354
Clinical interviews. *See also* Assessment
   assessment of trial competence and
      sanity and, 298–300
   case formulation and report writing and,
      304
Closed questions. *See also* Questioning
   assessing child witnesses' reports and,
      163, 167–169, 172, 176
   investigative interviewing and, 138–139
Closed-circuit television (CCTV),
      identifying people from. *See also*
      Identifying offenders; Images,
      identifying people from
   facial identification and, 240
   forensic face identification, 244–256,
      246f, 253f
   genetic photofitting and, 259
   overview, 238, 259–260
Coercive interrogation tactics, 61–63. *See
   also* Interrogations

Cognitive approach to lie detection, 89–90. *See also* Deception detection
Cognitive bias. *See also* Bias
  connection of psychology to the law and, 2
  in evidence evaluation, 32–33, 34–38
  evidence integration and, 38–45
  overview, 30–32, 48
  possible solutions, 45–48
Cognitive consistency model, 348–349
Cognitive factors
  aggression and, 370
  assessment of trial competence and sanity and, 304–305
  expert testimony and, 321–322
  judicial decision making and, 399–400
  psychological science and, 422–423
Cognitive forensic research, 3, 4
Cognitive interventions, 387. *See also* Treatment
Cognitive Interview, 200
Cognitive load theory, 83, 84
Cognitive-behavioral perspective, 67–68
Coherence effects, 31, 39–40. *See also* Cognitive bias
Coherence-based reasoning model, 41–45
Collaborating experts, 421–422. *See also* Experts
Collaborative inhibition, 344
Collaborative recall, 114–116. *See also* Memory; Recall
Commission errors, 163–164
Communication, 133
Competence Assessment for Standing Trial for Defendants with Mental Retardation (CAST-MR), 302
Competence to stand trial. *See also* Assessment; Insanity defense; Mental illness
  assessment of, 297–307
  competence restoration, 307–308, 309–311
  criminal responsibility, 295–297
  forensic databases and, 311–312
  outcomes of, 307–309
  overview, 293–295, 312–313
  research in, 309–311
Competency Assessment Instrument—Revised (CAI), 301
Complex events, memory for. *See also* Memory
  eyewitness memory and, 111–112
  research in eyewitness memory and, 121–122

Compliance, 59
Comprehension
  assessing child witnesses' reports and, 174–175
  eyewitness memory and, 110–111
Computational models, 347–349
Confabulation, 59
Confessions. *See also* False confessions; Guilty pleas; Plea decisions
  compared to pleas, 279–281
  future directions in, 73–74
  interrogation reforms and, 71–73
  jury decision making and, 350–351
  overview, 4, 54–58
  policy innovation and change and, 429–430
  relative judgment and, 420
Confidence
  biases and, 42, 45, 47
  deception detection and, 80
  expert testimony and, 333
  eyewitness identification and, 118, 210, 211–213, 214–215, 217, 218–219, 229, 324–325, 351, 420–421
  eyewitness recall and, 117
  false memories and, 184, 192, 194, 195, 196, 201, 202
  identification from images and, 244, 250–251
Confidence–accuracy relation, 211–213
Confirmation bias, 31, 43–44. *See also* Cognitive bias
Confirmatory interviewer feedback, 196–197
Confrontational approach to questioning, 57–58
Consolidation, 106
Context reinstatement, 227
Contextual bias, 31. *See also* Cognitive bias
Contradictory information, 199
Control processes, 117–118
Conviction. *See also* Wrongful conviction
  false confessions and, 63
  identification from images and, 247–248
  interrogation tactics and, 61, 62–63, 65, 66–67
  jury decision making and, 340, 347, 357
  likelihood of and guilty pleas, 274–275
  plea bargaining and, 269, 275–276, 280, 282–285
  policy innovation and change and, 429–432
  race and, 272–273

Cooperative witnesses, 134–141. *See also* Witnesses
Counterinterrogation strategies, 88–89. *See also* Interrogations
Courts, 434–436
Credibility of sources, 199
Crime rates, 270
Crime-reduction strategies, 270
Criminal cases, 158, 338
Criminal investigative analysis, 9–10. *See also* Criminal profiling
Criminal profiling
  connection of psychology to the law and, 2
  debates regarding, 19–24
  effectiveness of, 22–24
  empirical foundations, 15–17
  overview, 7–9, 24–25
  prevalence of, 9–10
  process of, 10–11
  qualifications of a criminal profiler and, 11–12, 23–24
  theoretical foundations of, 13–15
  types of, 12–13
  validating, 17–19
Criminal propensity, 373
Criminal responsibility, 295–307. *See also* Competence to stand trial
Criminal violence. *See also* Violence
  overview, 368–369, 388
  propensities for, 375, 377–380, 378*t*
  psychopathy and, 386–388
  reducing the propensity for, 380–384
  theories of, 372–375, 376*f*
  treatment and, 381–384, 386–388
Cross-cultural factors. *See also* Bias; Diversity
  assessment of trial competence and sanity and, 303–304
  investigative interviewing and, 144–145
Cued invitations, 165
Cued recall, 163, 169. *See also* Closed questions
Cues to deception. *See also* Deception detection; Lies
  actual cues, 82–84
  perceived cues, 81–82
  research in, 85–88
  seeking multiple cues, 92–93
  strategic use of evidence (SUE) technique and, 90
Culprit likelihood ratings, 218–219
Culprit-absent lineups, 228–229. *See also* Lineups

Culprit-present lineups, 228–229. *See also* Lineups
Cultural factors. *See also* Bias; Diversity
  assessment of trial competence and sanity and, 303–304
  investigative interviewing and, 144–145
Curative instructions for juries, 353

D

Death penalty cases
  expert testimony and, 333
  judicial decision making and, 405–406
Deception detection. *See also* Guilt; Lies
  accuracy of, 56, 80
  advances in, 85
  behavioral coding and, 93–94
  connection of psychology to the law and, 2
  cues to deception, 81–84
  indirect deception detection, 96–98
  interrogation tactics and, 57, 71–72
  overview, 79–80, 98–99
  plea decisions and, 276
  psychological science and, 2
  research in, 85–88
  seeking multiple cues to deception, 92–93
  strategic interviewing styles and, 88–92
Decision model of interrogation, 69
Decision making in legal settings. *See* Legal decision making
Decision-making models of confessions, 68–70, 281–282. *See also* Confessions
Deductive profiling, 12. *See also* Criminal profiling
Deese–Roediger–McDermott word lists (DRM paradigm), 114
Defendants. *See also* Competence to stand trial; Plea bargaining
  characteristics of, 271–274, 354–356, 397–399, 405–406
  criminal responsibility and, 295–297
  identification from images and surveillance video and, 248–251
  jury decision making and, 339–347, 354–356, 357–358
  juvenile defendants, 273–274
  outcomes when deemed incompetent or insane, 307–309
  plea process and, 267–268, 270–271, 275–277, 279–281, 423
  restoration of competency, 309–311
  trial penalty model and, 283–284

Defense attorneys
    cognitive bias and, 40, 272–274
    jury decision making and, 348
    minority status of defendants and,
        272–273
    plea process and, 272–274, 276–277,
        278–279
    policy and practice and, 432–433
Deliberation process, 339–347, 358–359,
    423. *See also* Jury decision making
Dependency court cases, 158
Deportation, 272
Depositions, 327
Desistance, 382–384
Detecting deception. *See* Deception
    detection
Developmental theories, 373–375, 376*f*
Diagnostic evaluations, 300–304. *See also*
    Assessment
Disclosures, 161–175
Disinhibition, 384–385
Disorganized crime, 12–13
Disposition, 13–14
Diversity. *See also* Bias; Cultural factors
    judicial decision making and, 398–399
    jury decision making and, 345–347
Divided attention studies, 110–111
Divorce proceedings, 158–159. *See also*
    Family court cases
DNA evidence
    cognitive bias and, 37
    generating images of suspects and,
        258–259
    overview, 1–2
Domestic violence cases. *See also* Violence
    accusations against familiar adults and,
        160–162
    child witnesses and, 158
Double-blind testing for lineups, 215–216.
    See also Lineups
Drug use, 386
Dual-process theories of recognition, 108,
    109
Due process, 429–432, 435–436
Durham v. United States (1954), 296–297
Dusky v. United States (1960), 294
Dynamic Risk Assessment for Offender
    Re-entry (DRAOR), 379

E

Ecologically valid research, 85–88
Emotion, 111–112

Emotional evidence, 356
Encoding. *See also* Memory
    eyewitness memory and, 110–111, 121
    investigative interviewing and, 133, 144
    overview, 105–106
Encoding specificity, 106, 140
Environmental factors, 374
Evaluation of Competency to Stand Trial—
    Revised (ECST-R), 301, 302, 303
Evidence collection
    eyewitness identification and, 218–220
    novel approaches to, 218–220
Evidence evaluation
    biases of, 31
    cognitive bias and, 34–38, 40–41, 46–47
    cognitive bias in, 32–33
    jury decision making and, 348, 350–352
    policy innovation and change and,
        429–432
    psychological science and, 420–421
Evidence integration, 31, 38–45, 47
Evidence line-ups, 46
EvoFIT-generated likeness
    generating images of suspects and, 257
    genetic research and, 259
Expectancy effects, 31. *See also* Cognitive
    bias
Expectations, 134, 136–137
Experimental realism, 286–287
Expert testimony. *See also* Anticipatory
    process of expert work; Experts
    content of, 320–323
    jury decision making and, 351–352
    overview, 4, 318–320, 334
    policy innovation and change and,
        434–436
    research in, 323–334
Experts. *See also* Expert testimony
    adversarial allegiance in, 325–326
    consensus and, 323–325
    policy innovation and change and,
        434–436
    psychological science and, 421–422
    surveillance images and, 249–251
Explanatory functions, 197–198
Exposure duration, 228
Eye contact, 90
Eyewitness identification. *See also* Child
    witnesses; Eyewitness memory;
    Identifying offenders; Lineups
    accuracy of, 210–215
    confidence in, 211–213
    expert testimony and, 331–332
    genetic photofitting and, 259

Eyewitness identification *(cont.)*
    interactions between factors that
        influence, 228–229
    jury decision making and, 351
    overview, 208–210, 229
    policy innovation and change and,
        429–432
    psychological science and, 420–421
Eyewitness memory. *See also* Child
        witnesses; Eyewitness identification;
        False memories; Memory; Witnesses
    cognitive bias and, 37
    connection of psychology to the law
        and, 2
    forms of retrieval, 113–116
    investigative interviewing and, 131–133
    metacognition and, 117–118
    overview, 104–105, 122, 182, 201–202
    perceiving, comprehending, and
        encoding, 110–111
    policy and practice and, 429–430,
        432–433
    remembering and changes in memory
        and, 116–117
    research in, 118–122
    stress, emotion, and complex events and,
        111–112
    suggestive interviews and, 183–185

F

Face recognition software, 247. *See also*
        Facial identification; Forensic face
        identification
Facial composites, 256–259
Facial expressions, 226
Facial identification. *See also* Identifying
        offenders; Photo identification
    accuracy of, 239–244, 240*f*, 241*f*, 243*f*
    forensic face identification, 244–256,
        246*f*, 253*f*
    genetic research and, 258–259
    overview, 259–260
    super-recognizers, 254–256
Facial mapping, 250. *See also* Facial
        identification
Facial thermal imaging, 93–94
False allegations, 161–162
False beliefs, 184
False confessions. *See also* Confessions
    expert testimony and, 330–331
    interrogation reforms and, 71–73
    jury decision making and, 350–351

overview, 4, 61–67
    relative judgment and, 420
    theoretical models of, 67–71
False guilty pleas, 274–275. *See also*
        False confessions; Guilty pleas; Plea
        bargaining
False memories. *See also* Eyewitness
        memory; Memory; Witnesses
    Alt-key paradigm and, 59
    assessing child witnesses' reports and,
        166–167
    autobiographical memories from
        childhood, 186–188
    collaborative recall and, 114–115
    eliciting from witnesses, 188–192
    empirical evidence for, 183–192
    factors in the creation of, 194–198
    forced fabrication and, 188–192
    mechanisms of, 192–194
    mitigating, 198–201
    overview, 182–183, 201–202
    research in, 120–121
False-event questions, 188–192
Familiarity processes, 108–109. *See also*
        Memory
Family court cases
    accusations against familiar adults and,
        159–162
    child witnesses and, 158
Family factors
    child witnesses and, 159–162
    criminal violence and, 374
Fear, 160
Federal Bureau of Investigation (FBI), 8–9
Feedback, 420–421
Field reliability
    assessment of trial competence and
        sanity and, 305–307
    policy innovation and change and,
        426–427
Fillers in a lineup, 221–225. *See also*
        Lineups
Fitness to stand trial. *See* Competence to
        stand trial
Five-factor model of confessions, 68. *See
        also* Confessions
Forced fabrication
    eliciting false memories from witnesses
        with, 188–192
    false-memory creation and, 196–197
Forced-choice questions
    assessing child witnesses' reports and,
        163, 170, 172
    Reid technique of interrogation and, 58

Forensic assessment instruments, 301–302. *See also* Assessment
Forensic confirmation bias, 423
Forensic databases, 311–312
Forensic evaluations, 417–418. *See also* Assessment
Forensic face identification, 244–259, 246*f*, 253*f*
Forensic investigative interviewing. *See* Investigative interviewing
Forensic science cases
  expert testimony and, 333
  jury decision making and, 351–352
Forensic wait lists, 309–311
Formal reticence, 170–175, 176
Foundational knowledge, 323–325
Free recall
  assessing child witnesses' reports and, 163, 165
  investigative interviewing and, 137–138
  overview, 106–107
Frye test, 327–328

G

Gender factors, 398
General aggression model (GAM), 369–375. *See also* Aggression
General invitations, 165
Genetic photofitting, 258–259
Genetic research, 258–259. *See also* DNA evidence
Georgia Court Competency Test (GCCT), 301
Glasgow Face Matching Test (GFMT)
  accuracy and, 252
  overview, 243, 243*f*
  super-recognizers and, 255
  surveillance images and, 251
Graded recollection, 120. *See also* Memory
Grooming, 160
Group bias, 398–399. *See also* Bias
Group decision models, 348–350
Group polarization, 344–345
Guilt. *See also* Confessions; Deception detection; Guilty pleas
  cognitive bias and beliefs regarding, 31–43, 47
  deception detection and, 89
  eyewitness identification and, 211, 214–215, 219–220
  interrogation process and the assumption of, 55, 57–59, 65–67, 71–72, 74

jury decision making and, 338, 340–341, 347, 350–351, 356, 357–358
lineup administration and, 220
policy innovation and change and, 429–430
Guilty pleas. *See also* Confessions; Guilt; Plea decisions
  compared to confessions, 279–281
  plea bargaining and, 269, 273, 274–275, 279, 284–285
  reasons for, 274–275

H

Hare Psychopathy Checklist—Revised (PCL-R). *See* Psychopathy Checklist—Revised (PCL-R)
Heuristic bias, 354. *See also* Bias
Homology assumption, 14–15
Hostile aggression, 371–372. *See also* Aggression

I

Identifying offenders. *See also* Criminal profiling; Eyewitness identification; Images, identifying people from; Lineups
  accuracy of, 210–215
  memorial cues in, 227
  nonmemorial cues in eyewitness identification, 225–226
  overview, 10, 209–210, 229, 259–260
I-I-Eye aid, 121
Imagery, 194–195
Images, identifying people from. *See also* Identifying offenders; Photo identification
  forensic face identification, 244–256, 246*f*, 253*f*
  generating images of suspects, 256–259
  overview, 238, 259–260
  surveillance images and, 245–256, 246*f*, 253*f*
Imagination, 194–195
Implicit Association Test (IAT), 94–96
Individual decision models, 348–350
Individual differences, 396–401
Inductive profiling, 12. *See also* Criminal profiling
Informed deliberation, 423. *See also* Deliberation process

Innocence
    cognitive bias and beliefs regarding,
        31–32, 34–35, 37–38, 40, 43
    deception detection and, 89
    false confessions and, 63–64
    interrogation process and, 58–59, 65–66,
        71–72
    juvenile defendants and, 310–311
    phenomenology of, 63–64, 280
    plea bargaining and, 269, 274, 280–281
Innocence Project
    plea bargaining and, 269, 286
    policy innovation and change and,
        430–431, 433–434
    white paper and, 419
Innocent pleas, 274. *See also* Plea decisions
Insanity defense. *See also* Competence to
        stand trial; Mental illness
    adversarial allegiance in expert opinions
        and, 325–326
    competence to stand trial and, 295–296,
        297–307
    expert testimony and, 320–321
    outcomes of, 307–309
Institutional variables, 402–404
Instructions for juries, 352–354, 358. *See
        also* Jury decision making
Instrumental aggression, 371–372. *See also*
        Aggression
Integrated cognitive antisocial potential
        (ICAP) theory
    actuarial assessment of risk and,
        377–379, 378*t*
    criminal violence and, 374–375, 376*f*
Interaction-process model of confessions,
        68. *See also* Confessions
Internalization, 59
International Association of Chiefs of
        Police, 419
International Criminal Investigative
        Analysis Fellowship, 11
Interrogation decision-making model,
        69–70. *See also* Confessions
Interrogation-related acute situational
        suggestibility model, 70–71
Interrogations. *See also* Interviews; Police
        interrogation
    criminal profiling and, 10–11
    cues to deception and, 81–84
    false confessions and, 61–71
    future directions in, 73–74
    overview, 4, 54
    pleas versus confessions and, 279–281
    policy innovation and change and, 430–431

reforms in, 71–73
relative judgment and, 420
strategic interviewing styles and, 88–92
Interviewing. *See also* Questioning;
        Victims; Witnesses
    assessing child witnesses' reports and,
        162–175
    CI and NICHD protocols of, 141–143
    confirmatory interviewer feedback and,
        196–197
    eliciting false memories from witnesses
        with, 188–192
    false memories and, 201–202
    investigative interviewing, 131–141
    overview, 130–131, 150
    training and retention of skills in,
        145–147
    translational issues, 143–145
Interviews, 106–107. *See also*
        Interrogations; Investigations
Intimate partner violence, 332
Intoxicated witnesses, 132. *See also*
        Witnesses
Intuition, 423
Inventory of Legal Knowledge (ILK), 303
Investigations
    cognitive bias and, 2
    criminal profiling and, 10, 21–22,
        24–25
    expert testimony and, 322–323
    investigative interviewing, 131–141
    qualifications of a criminal profiler and,
        11
Investigative interviewing. *See also*
        Interviewing
    CI and NICHD protocols of, 141–143
    new developments in, 148–150
    overview, 131–141, 150
    training and retention of skills in,
        145–147
    translational issues, 143–145

J

Jackson v. Indiana (1972), 308, 310
Judges. *See also* Judicial decision making
    accountability and, 406–408
    expert testimony and, 328–329
    measures of judicial quality and,
        408–410
    power of, 403–404
    process of becoming a judge, 402–403
    psychological science and, 421

Judgments of Memory Characteristics
    Questionnaire (JMCQ), 121
Judicial decision making. *See also* Judges
    accountability and, 406–408
    case-level variables in, 404–406
    individual differences in, 396–401
    institutional variables in, 402–404
    measures of judicial quality and, 408–410
    overview, 4, 395–396
    psychological science and, 421
    situational differences in, 401–406
Jurors. *See also* Jury decision making
    expert testimony and, 328–329, 331–332
    factors that influence the verdicts of,
        350–358
    versus judges, 339
    jury instructions and, 352–354, 358
    overview, 338–339
    surveillance images and, 248–249
Jury decision making. *See also* Jurors
    deliberation processes, 339–347
    factors that influence, 350–358
    jury size and, 342–343
    overview, 338–339, 358–359
    psychological models of, 347–350
Jury instructions, 352–354, 358. *See also*
    Jury decision making
Justice Project, 419
Juvenile Adjudicative Competence
    Interview (JACI), 301–302
Juvenile defendants. *See also* Defendants
    biases and, 273–274
    competence to stand trial and, 310–311,
        312
    forensic assessment instruments for,
        301–302
    jury decision making and, 345
    psychological science and, 418, 427,
        431–432
    sentencing and, 418

K

Knowledge, 117–118, 185

L

Language factors
    assessing child witnesses' reports and,
        174–175
    deception detection and, 86, 93
    expert testimony and, 320, 321–322

guilty pleas and, 271
    interviewing witnesses, 133, 135, 144
    jury decision making and, 353, 358, 430
Latency, response. *See* Response latency
Law. *See also* Policy
    evidence problems and, 429–430
    policy innovation and change and,
        424–425
    psychological science and, 418
Law enforcement, 1–2, 433–434
Leading questions. *See also* Questioning
    assessing child witnesses' reports and,
        162–163
    false memories and, 201–202
Legal decision making. *See also* Cognitive
    bias
    coherence-based reasoning model and,
        42
    eyewitness identification and, 211–213,
        214
    overview, 30–31
Leniency
    confessions and, 62–63, 279
    interrogation process and, 69–70
    jury decision making and, 331, 339,
        340–341
    juvenile defendants and, 273
    plea bargaining and, 267
    plea process and, 271, 281, 284–285
Leniency asymmetry effect, 340–341
Lie detection. *See* Deception detection
Lies. *See also* Deception detection
    cues to deception, 81–84
    overview, 79–80
    research in, 85–88
    types of, 84
Life-course-persistent antisocial syndrome,
    373–374
Likenesses, 257–258
Lineups. *See also* Eyewitness identification;
    Identifying offenders
    applied settings, 224–225
    child witnesses and, 220–221
    composition of, 221–225
    culprit-present or -absent lineups,
        228–229
    interactions between factors that
        influence, 228–229
    memorial cues and, 227
    nonmemorial cues and, 225–226
    novel approaches and, 219–220
    overview, 229
    policy and practice and, 432–433
    presentation of, 215–218

Linguistic Inquiry and Word Count
     (LIWC), 93
Loss aversion, 285

M

MacArthur Competence Assessment Tool—
     Criminal Adjudication (MacCAT-CA),
     301, 302
Majority effect, 340
Manson v. Brathwaite (1977), 434–435
Maximization interrogation tactics, 61–63,
     420. *See also* Interrogations
Memory. *See also* Eyewitness memory;
     False memories
  assessing child witnesses' reports and,
     163–165, 175
  changes in, 116–117
  connection of psychology to the law
     and, 2
  as construction, 107
  forced fabrication and, 188–192
  forms of retrieval, 113–116
  generating images of suspects and,
     256–258
  investigative interviewing and, 131–133
  memorial cues in eyewitness
     identification, 227
  memory processes, 105–107
  metacognition and, 117–118
  nonmemorial cues in eyewitness
     identification, 225–226
  overview, 122
  policy innovation and change and, 429
  theoretical models of, 107–109
Memory Characteristics Questionnaire
     (MCQ), 120
Memory implantation method, 186–187
Memory trace, 105–106
Mental illness. *See also* Assessment;
     Competence to stand trial; Insanity
     defense; Psychopathy
  adversarial allegiance in expert opinions
     and, 325–326
  assessment of trial competence and
     sanity and, 297–307
  case formulation and report writing and,
     304–305
  competence to stand trial and, 294,
     295–296
  outcomes of, 307–309
Metacognition, 117–118
Miller v. Alabama (2012), 418, 431–432

Minimization interrogation tactics, 61–63,
     420. *See also* Interrogations
Minnesota Sex Offender Screening Tool—
     Revised (MnSOST-R), 332
Minority status
  judicial decision making and, 398
  jury decision making and, 345–347,
     354–356
  plea outcomes and, 272–273
Miranda rights
  deception detection and, 89
  false confessions and, 64
Miranda v. Arizona (1966), 64
Misattribution, 109
Misinformation effect, 109, 183–185, 199
M'Naghten, Daniel, 295–296
Mock-crime paradigm, 58–59. *See also*
     Police interrogation
Modality, 140–141
Monitoring processes, 117–118
Morality, 357–358
Motivation
  assessing child witnesses' reports and,
     176
  deception detection and, 84
  judicial decision making and, 399–400
  rapport during interviewing and, 135
Mundane realism, 286–287

N

National Academy of Sciences
  overview, 428
  psychological science and, 420
  white paper and, 419
National Center for the Analysis of Violent
     Crime (NCAVC), 11
National Institute of Justice (NIJ) guide,
     433
National Science Foundation, 428
Negative emotionality, 385
Negotiation, 278–279
Nervousness
  cues to deception and, 82–83
  eyewitness identification and, 226
Neuropsychological functioning, 374
New Zealand Parole Project (NZPP),
     383–384
NICHD protocol of interviewing. *See also*
     Interviewing
  assessing child witnesses' reports and,
     163
  child witnesses and, 161

overview, 134, 141–143
training and retention of interviewing
    skills and, 147
translational issues, 143–145
Nondisclosure, 160
Nonmemorial cues, 225–226
Nonverbal communication, 135. *See also*
    Body language
North Carolina Actual Innocence
    Commission, 433
Nullification, 357–358

O

Observer effects, 31. *See also* Cognitive bias
Offender consistency, 14
Offender identification. *See* Identifying
    offenders
Omissions, 163–164
Open-ended questions, 134. *See also*
    Questioning
Operational definition debate, 21–22
Opinion-eliciting answers, 91–92
Option-posing questions, 163
Organized crime, 12–13
Organized–disorganized typology model
    of criminal profiling, 12–13. *See also*
    Criminal profiling
Outpatient restoration programs, 309–311.
    See also Competence to stand trial;
    Restoration of competence
Overconfidence, 212
Oxford Recidivism Study, 383

P

Parsons v. State (1886), 296
PEACE interview framework, 146,
    430–431. *See also* Investigative
    interviewing
Perception, 107, 110–111
Personality disorders, 384. *See also*
    Psychopathy
Personality factors
    aggression and, 369–371, 375, 381, 384,
        385
    characteristics of the suspect, 68
    criminal profiling and, 8–9, 13–14
    expert testimony and, 320
    interrogation process and, 73
    plea bargaining and, 274
    psychopathology and, 385

Person-based inputs, 369–370
Perspective, 173–174
Phenomenology of innocence, 63–64
Photo identification. *See also* Images,
    identifying people from
    false-memory creation and, 195–196
    overview, 239–244, 240f, 241f, 243f
Photofit system, 256–257
Physical abuse cases
    accusations against familiar adults and,
        159–162
    child witnesses and, 158
Plausibility, 168, 198, 287, 348, 355
Plea bargaining. *See also* Plea decisions;
    Sentencing
    background of, 270–271
    compared to confessions, 279–281
    current trends in, 268–270
    overview, 266–268, 286–287
    prospect theory and, 284–285
    research in, 271–279
    shadow-of-the-trial model and,
        282–283
    trial penalty model and, 283–284
Plea decisions. *See also* Confessions; Guilty
    pleas; Innocent pleas; Plea bargaining
    compared to confessions, 279–281
    connection of psychology to the law
        and, 2
    overview, 282–285, 286–287
    plea types, 271
    research in, 271–279
Police interrogation. *See also* Interrogations
    future directions in, 73–74
    laboratory analogues of, 58–61
    overview, 54–58
    reforms in, 71–73
Police procedures, 1–2, 433–434. *See also*
    Police interrogation
Policy
    catalysts and solutions, 428–432
    evidence problems and, 429–432
    foundation for, 418–428
    policy decisions, 437
    policy innovation and change and,
        422–432, 437
    psychological science and, 417–418,
        432–436, 437
Postidentification feedback, 420–421
Practice
    foundation for, 418–428
    psychological science and, 417–418,
        432–436, 437
Predicting behaviors, 14, 19–21

Prejudicial effects of emotional evidence, 356. *See also* Emotional evidence
Preparation, 84
Pretrial factors and decisions
    age factors and, 273–274
    anchoring effects and, 423
    competence to stand trial and, 2
    expert testimony and, 319, 327–331
    forensic databases and, 311
    guilty pleas and, 271
    jury decision making and, 430
    juvenile defendants and, 273
    minority status of defendants and, 272
    plea process and, 271, 272, 273, 281
    publicity and, 4, 32, 345, 350, 353, 417, 430
Prior knowledge, 107
PRISM evaluation, 379
Proactive aggression, 371–372. *See also* Aggression
Probable cause, 73
Probative value of emotional evidence, 356. *See also* Emotional evidence
Profiling, criminal. *See* Criminal profiling
Proof, burden of, 24
Prosecutors
    child witnesses and, 158, 163
    expert testimony and, 436
    plea process and, 33, 268–270, 271, 275–276, 278, 279–280
    psychological science and, 435
    sentencing and, 270, 405
Prospect theory, 281–282, 284–285
Pseudoscience, 328–329
Psychological assessment. *See also* Assessment
    adversarial allegiance in expert opinions and, 325–326
    assessment of trial competence and sanity and, 300–304
    expert testimony and, 320–321
Psychological factors, 63–67, 347–350. *See also* Mental illness; Psychopathy
Psychological research, 4–5
Psychological science
    court processes and, 434–436
    evidence problems and, 429–432
    expert testimony and, 321–322
    overview, 417–418, 436–437
    policy and practice and, 422–427, 432–436
    presentation of scientific content, 419–423
    research method and policy innovations and, 423–427
    resistance to, 427–428

Psychopathy, 367, 381–388. *See also* Mental illness
Psychopathy Checklist—Revised (PCL-R), 325, 332, 384–388
Public policy. *See* Policy
Punishment, 63, 65–66

Q

Queen v. M'Naghten (1843), 295–296
Questioning. *See also* Interrogations; Interviewing; Police interrogation
    assessing child witnesses' reports and, 162–175
    child witnesses and, 157
    confrontational approach to, 57–58
    false memories and, 188–192, 201–202
    investigative interviewing and, 133–134, 137–139
    training and retention of skills in, 145–147

R

Race discrimination cases, 398
Race factors
    judicial decision making and, 398–399
    jury decision making and, 345–347, 354–356
    plea outcomes and, 272–273
Rapport, 133, 134–135
Reaction times (RTs), 94–96
Reactive aggression, 371–372. *See also* Aggression
Recall. *See also* Memory
    assessing child witnesses' reports and, 163–165
    child witnesses and, 157
    collaborative recall, 114–116
    context reinstatement and, 227
    investigative interviewing and, 137–138
    overview, 113–114
Recall questions, 166–167, 172–173, 176. *See also* Questioning
Recall tests, 106–107
Receiver operating characteristics (ROC) analyses, 217
Recidivism risk
    actuarial assessment of risk and, 377
    expert testimony and, 333
    treatment and, 382–384

Recognition, 163–165
Recognition memory, 257–258
Recognition questions, 169–170, 171–173, 176
Recollective processes, 109. *See also* Memory
Referential ambiguity, 171–172
Referral process, 297–298
Reflective elaboration, 194–195
Rehabilitative interventions, 382–384. *See also* Treatment
Reid technique of interrogation. *See also* Police interrogation
    cues to deception and, 81–82
    deception detection and, 88
    overview, 4, 55, 57–58
    policy innovation and change and, 431
Reintegration approaches, 382–384
Relative judgment, 419–420
Religious factors, 398
Remembering. *See also* Memory
    changes in memory and, 116–117
    compared to knowing, 185
Repetitive-question paradigm, 60–61, 65. *See also* Police interrogation
Report writing, 304–305
Representations, 105–106
Resistance, 14
Response latency, 213–215
Response patterns, 216–217
Responsivity principle, 380–384
Restoration of competence, 307–308, 309–311. *See also* Competence to stand trial
Reticence, formal. *See* Formal reticence
Retrieval support techniques, 134, 137–138, 140–141
Rex v. Pritchard (1836), 294, 295
Risk assessments. *See also* Assessment; Risk factors
    expert testimony and, 321, 332
    judicial decision making and, 406
    propensities for crime and violence and, 375, 377–380, 378t
Risk factors. *See also* Risk assessments
    propensities for crime and violence and, 377–379, 378t
    treatment and, 382
Risk–need–responsivity (RNR) model, 380–384, 388
Rogers Criminal Responsibility Assessment Scales (R-CRAS), 302
Rules, setting, 136–137

S

Scientific evidence, 351–352. *See also* Expert testimony
Self-Administered Interview (SAI), 148–149
Self-blame, 160
Self-control, 384–385
Self-fulfilling prophecy, 35–36
Self-generated cues
    assessing child witnesses' reports and, 164
    investigative interviewing and, 141
Self-incrimination
    false confessions and, 61
    interrogation reforms and, 71–73
    interrogations and, 70–71
    phenomenology of innocence and, 63–64
    Reid technique of interrogation and, 57
Self-presentation, 89
Self-regulation perspectives, 70–71
Self-regulatory decline, 66–67
Sensitization effect, 332
Sentencing. *See also* Plea bargaining
    biases and, 345, 354, 355, 405–406
    confessions and, 281
    guilty pleas and, 274, 277–278, 281
    judicial decision making and, 397–398, 400, 403, 405–406, 408
    jury decision making and, 345, 354, 355, 357
    juvenile defendants and, 418, 431–432
    plea decisions and, 283–284
    plea process and, 268–269, 270, 271, 273, 277, 281, 285
    videotaping and, 72
Sequential lineup presentations, 216–218. *See also* Lineups
Serious lies, 79. *See also* Lies
Sexual abuse cases
    accusations against familiar adults and, 159–162
    child witnesses and, 158
    jury decision making and, 355–356
    overview, 332–333
Sexual harassment cases, 398
Sexual orientation, 355–356
Shadow-of-the-trial model
    loss aversion and, 285
    plea decisions and, 282–283
Short-sighted thinking, 65–66
Signal detection theory (SDT), 107–109
Signal-detection analyses, 217

Simultaneous lineup presentations, 216–218. *See also* Lineups

Single-blind testing for lineups, 215–216. *See also* Lineups

Single-suspect lineups, 215. *See also* Lineups

Situational factors
  aggression and, 369–370
  judicial decision making and, 401–406
  propensities for crime and violence and, 379

Size of lineups, 222. *See also* Lineups

Skepticism effect, 332

Skills-based interventions, 387. *See also* Treatment

Social decision scheme framework, 340

Social factors
  criminal violence and, 374
  investigative interviewing and, 136
  psychological science and, 422–423

Social forensic research, 3, 4

Social learning theory (SLT), 369

Social lies, 79. *See also* Lies

Social metacognition, 117. *See also* Metacognition

Social psychology, 368

Source-misattribution errors, 192–194

Source-monitoring framework (SMF), 108, 109, 192–194
  assessing child witnesses' reports and, 166
  false memories and, 200–201

Source-monitoring test, 184–185

Specific questions. *See* Closed questions

Stability bias, 83

Standard-of-proof thresholds, 353

Stanford Prison Experiment, 268

Statement–evidence inconsistency, 89

Stereotypes. *See also* Bias
  eyewitness identification and, 226
  memory processes and, 110–111
  plea outcomes and, 272–273

Story model, 347–348

Storytelling, 116–117

Strategic use of evidence (SUE) technique, 88–92

Stress, 111–112

Structured Assessment of Violence Risk in Youth (SAVRY), 427

Structured Inventory of Malingered Symptomatology—Second Edition (SIRS-2), 303

Substance use disorder, 384–385

Suggestibility
  assessing child witnesses' reports and, 165–175
  child witnesses and, 158
  mitigating false memories and, 198–201

Suggestive questions. *See also* Questioning
  assessing child witnesses' reports and, 162–163, 165–175
  eliciting false memories from witnesses with, 188–192
  false memories resulting from, 183–185

Super-recognizers, 254–256. *See also* Facial identification

Suppression of evidence, 436

Surveillance images, 245–256, 246*f*, 253*f*. *See also* Images, identifying people from

Suspects, 256–259

T

TED (Tell/Explain/Describe) questions, 138

Temporal discounting, 65

Testimonial evidence, 23

Tests of Memory Malingering (TOMM), 303

Time limits of interrogations, 72. *See also* Interrogations

Tipping framework of lie detection, 98. *See also* Deception detection

Training
  CI protocol of interviewing and, 143–144
  cues to deception and, 81–82
  facial identification and, 252–254, 253*f*
  interrogation reforms and, 71–72
  investigative interviewing and, 145–147
  judicial decision making and, 400–401
  policy innovation and change and, 431

Traits, 13–14

Translational issues, 143–145

Transparency, 277

Treatment
  high-risk violent offenders and, 381–384, 386–388
  policy innovation and change and, 427
  risk–need–responsivity (RNR) model and, 380–384

Trial competence. *See* Competence to stand trial

Trial penalty model, 283–284

Trials, 331–334
Truth/lie understanding tasks, 174–175
Two-factor framework, 430

U

Unconscious transference, 227

V

Validity Indicator Profile (VIP), 303
Variability of laws, 277–278
Veracity, 97
Verdicts
    biases and, 43, 45
    emotional evidence and, 356–357
    expert testimony and, 332
    factors that influence, 350–358
    interrogation process and, 143
    jury decision making and, 340–341, 342,
        343, 344–345, 347–349, 350–358,
        359
    overview, 358–359
Veteran status, 355–356
Victims. *See also* Interviewing; Witnesses
    judicial decision making and, 405–406
    jury decision making and, 355–356
Videotaping of interrogations. *See also*
        Interrogations
    cues to deception and, 81–82
    interrogation reforms and, 72
Violence. *See also* Aggression; Psychopathy
    definitions of, 368–369
    domestic violence cases, 158, 160–162
    overview, 367, 388
    propensities for, 375, 377–380, 378*t*
    reducing the propensity for, 380–384
    theories of, 372–375, 376*f*
    treatment and, 381–384, 386–388
Violence Risk Scale, 378*t*, 379
Vocabulary, 174–175

Volitional control, 305
Vulnerabilities, psychological. *See*
        Psychological vulnerabilities
Vulnerable populations, 73

W

WH (Who–What–Where–When–How)
        questions. *See also* Questioning
    assessing child witnesses' reports and,
        165, 168
    investigative interviewing and, 138
White paper, 419–420
Withholding evidence, 89
Within-statement inconsistency, 89
Witnesses. *See also* Child witnesses;
        Eyewitness memory; False memories;
        Interviewing; Victims
    attentional narrowing and, 112
    lineup administration and, 215–218
    memorial cues in, 227
    nonmemorial cues in eyewitness
        identification, 225–226
    research in eyewitness memory and, 120
Wrongful conviction. *See also* Conviction
    cognitive bias and, 30
    eyewitness identification and, 104, 208,
        330–331
    false confessions and, 54
    identification from images and, 247
    investigative interviewing and, 133
    investigator overconfidence and, 80
    overview, 1–2, 4
    phenomenology of innocence and,
        63–64
    psychological science and, 425, 429–430

Y

Yes-bias, 167–169
Yes/no questions. *See* Closed questions